Prasannapadā madhyamakavṛtti
A Commentary on the Madhyamaka[-śāstra] In Clear Words

Pratyayaparīkṣā nāma prathamaṃ prakaraṇam
Chapter One: Examination of Conditions

A Note on the Title

The Sanskrit titles for Candrakīrti's MMK commentary and its chapters occur only at the end of each chapter in the respective manuscript colophons. The text of the PsP in Tibetan translation as found in the four Tanjur xylograph editions and in the Golden Tanjur manuscript is preceded, in accord with the general convention for translated texts, by a Sanskrit title transcribed in Tibetan characters followed by a Tibetan translation of the title. The Peking and Narthang editions of the PsP as well as the Golden Tanjur manuscript give the Sanskrit title as "*mulamādhyamikavṛtti prasannapada*" ([sic] Derge and Cone attest *mūlamādhyāmika*°).[1] It is well known that the oldest Tibetan translations, i.e., those from Dunhuang and the works mentioned in the lDan dkar ma catalogue, lacked Sanskrit titles and

[1] Title (P, N, G): *rgya gar skad du | mu la mā dhya mi ka vṛtti pra sanna pa da nā ma | bod skad du | dbu ma rtsa ba'i 'grel pa tshig gsal ba zhes bya ba |*. Cp. this title to that at the beginning of the stand-alone MMK as found in the Peking Tanjur: *prajñā nāma mūlamādhyamakakārikā*; Derge reads °*madhyāmakakārika*. It is unlikely that Nāgārjuna applied this or a similar title to his work; see Vetter 1982: 100f.; Seyfort Ruegg 1981: 1, n. 3.

that later Tibetan redactors re-sanskritized many of the titles.[2] Whereas the individual PsP Tib chapter-colophons refer to Candrakīrti's work only as "*tshig gsal ba*," the final colophon characterizes it as "*bstan bcos dbu ma rtsa ba'i 'grel pa tshig gsal ba*." De La Vallée Poussin places the Peking/Narthang version of the Sanskrit title (omitting *mula*) at the beginning of his Sanskrit edition of the PsP, but in the first note in his "Additions et Corrections," he corrects the title from *Mādhyamikavṛtti* to *Madhyamakavṛtti*.[3]

Stcherbatsky, obviously alluding to the difficulties he experienced when translating the first chapter of the PsP, states that Candrakīrti has titled his commentary "The Clear-worded" "probably not without some dose of irony, since, as Prof. Wassilieff attests, its extreme dialectical subtlety, especially in the first chapter, is equalled by no other work in the whole domain of northern Buddhist literature."[4] Hopkins asserts, "It strikes me that Chandrakīrti gave his commentary on Nāgārjuna's *Treatise on the Middle Way* (*Madhyamakashāstra*) this title in contrast to Bhāvaviveka's commentary, *Lamp for* (*Nāgārjuna's*) '*Wisdom*' (*Prajñāpradīpa*) which, due to its brevity and lack of elaboration, is often difficult to fathom and thus unclear."[5] His brief comment on his own translation choice, viz., "*Prasannapadā* is translated as *Clear Words* though it would be just as suitable as *The Lucidly Worded*, or *The Clear Worded* as Stcherbatsky does in his *The Conception of Buddhist Nirvana* ... or *Lucid Exposition of the Middle Way* as Mervyn Sprung does in his condensation of the text"[6] may (excepting Sprung's title) hold as far as the Tibetan translation of the title is concerned, but the Sanskrit chapter-colophons of all the PsP manuscripts consistently understand "*prasannapadā*," i.e., a *bahuvrīhi*, and not a *karmadhāraya* as Hopkins' preferred translation would assume. For example, the first-chapter colophon in the palmleaf manuscripts reads *ācāryacandrakīrtipādoparacitāyāṃ prasanna-*

---

[2] Cf., e.g., Erb 1990: xliv; 106, n. 2.

[3] Cf. PsP_L 1, n. 1 and PsP_L 595.

[4] Stcherbatsky 1927: 67, n. 1.

[5] Hopkins 1983: 845, n. 496.

[6] Ibid., 845, n. 496.

ANNE MACDONALD

IN CLEAR WORDS
THE *PRASANNAPADĀ*, CHAPTER ONE

ÖSTERREICHISCHE AKADEMIE DER WISSENSCHAFTEN
PHILOSOPHISCH-HISTORISCHE KLASSE
SITZUNGSBERICHTE, 863. BAND

BEITRÄGE ZUR KULTUR- UND GEISTESGESCHICHTE ASIENS
NR. 86

ÖSTERREICHISCHE AKADEMIE DER WISSENSCHAFTEN
PHILOSOPHISCH-HISTORISCHE KLASSE
SITZUNGSBERICHTE, 863. BAND

In Clear Words

The *Prasannapadā*, Chapter One

Vol. II

Annotated Translation, Tibetan Text

Anne MacDonald

Verlag der
Österreichischen Akademie
der Wissenschaften

ÖAW

Wien 2015

Vorgelegt von w. M. Ernst Steinkellner
in der Sitzung vom 24. Oktober 2014

Diese Publikation wurde einem anonymen, internationalen
Peer-Review-Verfahren unterzogen.

This publication has undergone the process of anonymous, international peer review.

Die verwendete Papiersorte ist aus chlorfrei gebleichtem Zellstoff hergestellt,
frei von säurebildenden Bestandteilen und alterungsbeständig.

ISBN 978-3-7001-7673-2

Druck und Bindung: Ferdinand Berger & Söhne Ges.m.b.H., 3580 Horn
Printed and bound in the EU
http://hw.oeaw.ac.at/7673-2
http://verlag.oeaw.ac.at

Contents

padāyāṃ madhyamakavṛttau pratyayaparīkṣā nāma prathamaṃ prakaraṇaṃ samāptam.[7] David Seyfort Ruegg therefore renders the title as the "Clear-Worded Commentary on the Madhyamaka-[kārikās],"[8] while Jacques May paraphrases it as "Commentaire (*vṛtti*) au Traité du milieu, rédigé en termes (*pada*) clairs ou limpides (*prasanna*)."[9] My own rendering of Candrakīrti's title *prasannapadā* as "In Clear Words" attempts to improve upon the more clumsy "The Clear(ly) Worded" while still retaining the sense of the *bahuvrīhi*; that is, the reference is to a commentary which has been composed in clear words.

All of the Sanskrit manuscripts, with the exception of ms P whose first folio has been lost, commence with a short statement of homage. The object of homage for manuscripts A through M is the Buddha and that for manuscript N Vajrasattva and the Three Jewels. Ms Q's damage has left only *ddhāya* intact, suggesting that its object of homage was also the Buddha. De La Vallée Poussin has added in square brackets after his edition's Sanskrit chapter title the salutation *āryamañjuśriye kumārabhūtāya namaḥ*, taken over from the Tibetan translation, which immediately following the work's main title presents the words *'phags pa 'jam dpal gzhon nur gyur pa la phyag 'tshal lo*, "Homage to noble Mañjuśrī-Kumārabhūta." An identical statement of homage is found antecedent to the main Tibetan text of, for example, the MA, the MABh and the YṢ, works also translated by Pa tshab nyi ma grags, and occurs as part of the homage at the beginning of, for example, MMK_T and the Tibetan translations of BP and PP. The less frequently occurring homage to Jñānasattva-Mañjuśrī ('Jam dpal ye shes sems dpa') occurs in two related texts that were translated by Ye shes sde, namely, Candrakīrti's YṢV and the ŚSV attributed to Nāgārjuna.[10] Erb notes that in forty of the approximately two hundred and forty-seven works Ye shes sde was involved with in his function as a translator, Mañjuśrī is honoured, as here at the

[7] I have corrected ms P's and Q's minor scribal errors.

[8] Seyfort Ruegg 2002: 3.

[9] May 1959: 5.

[10] On YṢV's title, see Scherrer-Schaub 1991: 101, n. 1.

commencement of PsP Tib, as Kumārabhūta, and that only the two works just mentioned, the YṢV and the ŚSV, contain an homage directed toward Mañjuśrī in his aspect of Jñānasattva.[11] Seyfort Ruegg, referring to the invocation of Mañjuśrī-Kumārabhūta that appears at the beginning of the Dharmadhātustava, writes that according to Tsong kha pa and Gung thang dkon mchog bstan pa'i sgron me, homage to Mañjuśrī-Kumārabhūta serves to indicate a work's belonging to the category of *śāstra* connected with the Abhidharma in a broad sense, that is, to the treatises related to *prajñā*, of which Mañjusrī is the master.[12]

[11] Erb 1990: 106f., n. 3.

[12] Seyfort Ruegg 1971: 464, quoted in Scherrer-Schaub 1991: 101, n. 1. See also Erb 1990: 106, n. 3. De La Vallée Poussin (La Vallée Poussin 1907: 251, n. 1) notes in his MABh translation that the ninth *bhūmi* is that of the *kumārabhūta*, the "royal prince," and the tenth that of the (*bodhisattva*) princes associated with royal power ("*yuvarāja*"), but in his Hastings article "Bodhisattva" (La Vallée Poussin 1909: 747f.) he connects the eighth *bhūmi* with the *kumārabhūta* and the ninth with the "*yauvarāja*." In RĀ V.55ab the *kumārabhūta* is assigned to the eighth *bhūmi*. On Mañjuśrī-Kumārabhūta, see also Lamotte 1960: 2, 14, n. 38 and Hirakawa 1990: 291-293, 304. Dayal (1978: 46-47) refers briefly to this form of Mañjuśrī.

Translation

§1. After paying obeisance to Nāgārjuna,[13] to the one

whose abode (*vāsa*) is free of the odour (*āvāsa*)[14] of the pair of extremes (*antadvaya*),[15]

---

[13] *LṬ's author commences his text by explaining the name 'Nāgārjuna' as a *karmadhāraya*: *nāgaś cāsau śuklatvād arjunaś ceti nāgārjunaḥ śeṣo nāgaḥ sa iva nāgārjuno* [']*pi* |. "This [one] is a *nāga* and, because of being white/bright, also *arjuna*; thus, 'Nāgārjuna,' i.e., the *nāga* [called] Śeṣa. Nāgārjuna for his part is like this [*nāga*]." (Ādi)Śeṣa (also known as Ananta), often praised as the sovereign of the *nāga*s, is said in the Rāmāyaṇa to be "white like the moon" (cf. Vogel 1926: 198). Vogel (ibid.) writes, "The poets of the classical period ... refer in particular to the white colour of his body and to the amazing splendour of the jewels shining in his thousand heads." These jewels adorning Śeṣa's heads illumine the nether realms; on Śeṣa, see, e.g., Vogel 1926: 25, 57, 192-198. Shortly after this explication of the name Nāgārjuna in the *LṬ, an alternative *karmadhāraya* explanation is presented: *atha vā arjunaḥ pāṇḍavaḥ* | *nāgaḥ śreṣṭhaḥ* | *arjunāt śreṣṭho Nāgārjunaḥ* | (cf. Yonezawa 2004: 120, 128 [fol. 1b1-2]). "Or, *arjuna* is [the] Pāṇḍava [brother]. *nāga* is the best. [The one who is] superior to *arjuna* is Nāgārjuna" (thus, Nāgārjuna means the "superior Arjuna"). See also the explanation of the name Nāgārjuna that is based directly on the introductory verses in the PsP as recorded by Bu ston in Obermiller 1932: II, 128.

[14] De La Vallée Poussin (PsP_L 1, n. 4) points out that *āvāsa* appears in place of *vāsa* due to the exigencies of the metre. The Tibetan, on the other hand, translates *āvāsa* as *gnas* (cf. also PsP_L 595 for Page 1, ligne 4). The Tibetan thus presents *mtha' gnyis gnas la gnas bsal* for *antadvayāvāsavidhūtavāsaḥ*, and apparently in reliance on this translation Stcherbatsky (1927: 81) translates, "who has done away with all recourse to the abode of Duality."

[15] The *LṬ explains *antadvaya* of these initial verses as referring to the extremes of eternity and annihilation: *antadvayaṃ śāśvatocchedau* (cf. Yonezawa 2004: 120, 128 [fol. 1b1]; as Yonezawa indicates, the *LṬ incorrectly attests ... *śāśvatecchedai* |; see also PsP_L 1, n. 2 and PsP_L 595 for Page 1, note 4; La Vallée Poussin 1933: 30-33). The YṢV homage verse refers to the YṢ as that in/by which the pair of extremes is refuted (Skt in $YṢV_{ed}$ 19, n. 4: *nirākṛtāntadvayayuktiṣaṣṭikām*; YṢV Tib: *mtha' gnyis sel ba'i rigs pa drug cu pa*). In Candrakīrti's commentary following the YṢV homage verse, he refers to the extremes of arising and perishing, and of existence and non-existence (*skye ba dang 'jig pa dang yod pa dang med pa'i mthar* [$YṢV_{ed}$ 20.11-12]); see also $YṢV_{tr}$ 102, n. 3. At PsP_L 135.10 and 270.11-12 he cites *astīti nāstīti ubhe 'pi antā śuddhī aśuddhīti ime 'pi antā* from the Samādhirājasūtra (verse 9.27ab), and at PsP_L 270.7-9 he cites *astīti kāśyapa ayam eko 'nto nāstīti kāśyapa ayam eko 'ntaḥ* from the KP (see Staël-Holstein 1977: 90). At PsP_L 393.9-12 he rejects the *antadvaya* which consists in existence and non-existence (*sattvāsattva*) (PsP_L 495.3-8 *āstitā* and

who attained birth in the ocean of mind (*dhī*) of the completely awakened one(s) (*sambuddha*),[16]

who imparted, out of compassion, the depths of the water[17] of the true Dharma exactly as [he] had understood it,[18]
whose flames of the [correct] view (*darśana*)[19] consume even today the kindling of opponents' doctrines (*mata*) and the mental darkness of the world,[20]

whose host of arrows, [his] words of unparalleled wisdom, destroy the entire army of the enemy, existence (*bhava*),[21] [and]

---

nāstitā; PsP$_L$ 508.13 *bhāvābhāva*). Candrakīrti does not refer back to the words of the initial verses in the commentary which follows.

16 *LṬ's author glosses *sambuddhadhī* with *bodhicitta* (cf. Yonezawa 2004: 120, 128 [fol. 1b1]).

17 All of the Sanskrit manuscripts attest *toyasya*. Stcherbatsky (1927: 81 and n. 3), following PsP Tib (*dam chos* mdzod *kyi zab mo nyid*), emends *toyasya* to *kośasya*; he translates, "Who mercifully has explained the deeper meaning of the treasury of the religion, according to his own conceptions of it." Thurman (1991: 22) and Loizzo (2007: 41 and 42, n. 49) both present the Sanskrit as reading *toyasya* but translate Tibetan *mdzod* "treasury." The Tibetan translators probably read *koṣasya*. The reading *koṣasya* does not fit as well as *toyasya* in a verse focussed on water imagery (in verse 2 fire metaphors are used, and in verse 3, battle imagery). It is also somewhat unusual to speak of the *depth* of a treasury or of a treasure. De La Vallée Poussin (PsP$_L$ 595) points to Aṣṭa 229.22-26 for its reference to *dharmakoṣa*; there the word *akṣaya* qualifies *dharmakoṣa*.

18 The metre for this initial verse is *upajāti*, a mixture of *indravajrā* and *upendravajrā*. The first three quarters are in *indravajrā* and the last in *upendravajrā*.

19 *LṬ's author glosses *darśana* with *śūnyatādṛṣṭi* (cf. Yonezawa 2004: 120, 128 [fol. 1b1]). Both *darśana* and *dṛṣṭi* are more commonly used in a Madhyamaka context to refer to soteriologically harmful theories/views/speculation; note, however, that Candrakīrti does refer to his own system/view as *madhyamakadarśana* (*tad evaṃ madhyamakadarśana evāstitvanāstitvadvayadarśanasyāprasaṅgo na vijñānavādiṣv iti vijñeyam* [PsP$_L$ 275.4-5]). On *darśana*, see Halbfass 1988: 263-273.

20 The second verse is composed in (*pathyā*) *anuṣṭubh*.

21 Stcherbatsky (1927: 81) freely translates *nighnanti niḥśeṣabhavārisenām* as "completely destroy the army of our foes (and deliver us from the bonds of phenomenal) existence," a translation that obfuscates the metaphor (*rūpaka*) "*bhavāri*." *LṬ's author explains: *bhavaḥ saṃsāraḥ sa evāris tasya senā mārādayaḥ* (cf. Yonezawa 2004: 120, 128 [fol. 1b2]). See also de La Vallée Poussin's comments at PsP$_L$ 2, n. 1.

assume sovereign majesty (*rājyaśrī*)[22] in the kingdom of the three realms[23] for persons to be educated (*vineya*) and the gods,[24]

I shall compose a commentary for his *kārikā*s which is laced with sentences apparent [in their meaning] (*uttāna*)[25] and well-fashioned (*satprakriya*),[26] [one] undisturbed by the winds[27] of reasoning (*tarka*), calm and clear (*prasanna*).[28]

---

[22] *LṬ's author comments on *rājyaśrī*: ... *arisenārjunena nirjitā* | *rājyaśrī* (ms: *rākṣaśrī*) *buddhatvaṃ nṛpatvañ ca* (cf. Yonezawa 2004: 120, 128 [fol. 1b2]).

[23] The reference is to the desire realm (*kāmadhātu*), the realm of [subtle] corporeality (*rūpadhātu*) and the realm of incorporeality (*ārūpyadhātu*). Cf. YṢV$_{tr}$ 134, n. 88; 205, n. 350.

[24] These first three verses are translated freely and somewhat imprecisely in Thurman 1991: 22 and Loizzo 2007: 41f. The metre for the third verse is *upajāti*; the first two quarters are in *indravajrā* and the last two in *upendravajrā*.

[25] Cf. BHSD s.v. *uttāna*: "(of doctrines ...) obvious, simple, easily comprehensible." See also PsP$_L$ 2, n. 3 and "Additions et Corrections" for PsP$_L$ 2, n. 3 (PsP$_L$ 595). PsP Tib: *sla ba*.

[26] Yonezawa (2004: 120, 128 [fol. 1b2]) reads the *LṬ here as: *satī prakriyā kleśakṣayo pāpam āṅgī* (?) *yasmin vākye tena grathitām*. Perhaps one should read *kleśakṣayopāyamārgo* instead of *kleśakṣayo pāpam āṅgī*.

[27] Stcherbatsky (1927: 82) either misreads or interprets de La Vallée Poussin's *anila* as *anala* and translates "fires." All three of de La Vallée Poussin's manuscripts read *anila*, and all but four of the manuscripts used for the present study attest *anila*; the four exceptions attest *atila*, the result of the frequently occurring confusion of *n* and *t* in Nepalese manuscripts. PsP Tib presents *rlung*. Stcherbatsky's error leads him to assume a connection between the compound *tarkānila* and the title of a work attributed to Bhāviveka, namely, the Tarkajvālā, even though it is not the work of Bhāviveka's which is critiqued in the first chapter of the PsP and is not, to my knowledge, ever referred to by Candrakīrti in the PsP. He (ibid., 82, n. 1) writes, "This is a jeer at Bhāvaviveka who is called a champion of logic (*tārkika*). It does not mean that dialectical subtleties will be avoided, but that all arguments will be indirect. The word *tarkānila* evidently alludes to *Tarkajvāla* (sic) the title of Bhāvaviveka's work." Stcherbatsky translates *tarkānilāvyākulitā* as "unobscured by the fires of dialectics," but *avyākulita* means "not agitated, undisturbed"; fire would in any case tend to destroy rather than "obscure." My translation "reasoning" for *tarka* is not ideal, for the first chapter deals extensively with logical methods and reasons, but it is difficult to find a suitable translation; it would seem that excessive, unnecessary analysis and speculation, including unacceptable logical methods, are intended (Candrakīrti will refer to Bhāviveka as a *tārkika*). A wind-water metaphor is intended with the penultimate compound and the final word of the verse: water (=

§2. In this regard, the treatise (*śāstra*) about to be explained is the one which commences "Not from self, nor from other, nor from both"[29] [namely, Nāgārjuna's Madhyamakaśāstra].[30] With regard to the question "What is its [i.e., this treatise's] connection (*sambandha*), subject matter (*abhidheya*) and purpose (*prayojana*)?",[31] this, first, is

---

Candrakīrti's commentary) that is undisturbed by the wind (= reasoning) remains calm and transparent/clear (*prasanna*).

[28] This final verse is in *indravajrā* metre.

[29] MMK I.1: *na svato nāpi parato na dvābhyāṃ nāpy ahetutaḥ | utpannā jātu vidyante bhāvāḥ kvacana kecana ||*.

[30] Candrakīrti refers to Nāgārjuna's main work as the Madhyamakaśāstra; see, e.g., PsP_M §71 (PsP_L 40.7), and $MABh_{ed}$ 231.7 where he makes reference to the *dbu ma'i bstan bcos* (*Madhyamakaśāstra). The Madhyamakaśāstrastuti—accepted by de Jong as composed by Candrakīrti—which appears (only) in ms D after the final colophon of the PsP (the last folio of ms P and ms Q is missing), refers to Nāgārjuna's work in a similar way (verse 4: *madhyamake śāstre*); it also refers to the *kārikās* constituting it (verse 10: *śāstragaditās tāḥ kārikā[ḥ]*) (see de Jong 1979: 543f.; 549).

[31] The discussion of the *sambandha*, *abhidheya* and *prayojana* of the treatise commented upon is a methodological feature of many commentaries, both Buddhist and non-Buddhist (the three appear to be anticipated already in Patañjali's Mahābhāṣya), and primarily serves to confirm the treatise's meaningfulness, which is discerned with the aid of these three (or more) criteria. According to Edwin Gerow (2008: ix-x), the (later) four traditional *anubandhas* include these three plus the *adhikārin*, the qualified reader. Ms Q reads *saṃbandhābhidheyaprayojanaprayojana* (unfortunately, the initial folio for ms P is missing) and PsP Tib also presents the third and final member as *dgos pa'i dgos pa* (**prayojanaprayojana*); nine of the PsP paper manuscripts attest a similar compound consisting, however, of four members, namely, *saṃbandhābhidheyaprayojanatatprayojana*. The "purpose of the purpose" was, as de Jong (1978: 28) states, probably introduced only by later authors (in the frequent cases where the *prayojana* was considered to be comprehension of the subject matter, the benefit of this knowledge was indicated with the *prayojana-prayojana*). Neither a *prayojanaprayojana*, in place of *prayojana*, nor a *tatprayojana* as an additional fourth item is mentioned in either the Sanskrit or the Tibetan text of the PsP in the explanation of the individual members of the compound that immediately follows this listing, and both must have been added by later hands, though *prayojanaprayojana* early enough for the scholars involved with the PsP Tib translation to have found it in at least one of the two manuscripts they relied on. Ms Q's attestation of the reading is presumably due to the appropriation by a scribe earlier in Q's line of this and other readings from a manuscript in the γ line (according to the Stemma, ms η's scribe would have borrowed it from ms δ). I presume that the paper manuscripts' reading also derives from ms δ, and that their *tat*

the connection (*sambandha*)[32] for the treatise: Having started with,[33] according to the manner enjoined in the Madhyamakāvatāra,[34] the first generation of the resolve [to strive for awakening] (*cittotpāda*)[35]

---

represents an additional clarificatory interpolation (it is also possible that *tat* was omitted from Q). Buddhapālita refers to and explains only the *prayojana* of the MMK; Bhāviveka mentions and explains only the *sambandha*. On the *abhidheya*, the *prayojanaprayojana* and other terms as used in tantric texts, see Broido 1983. For further remarks on *sambandha*, *abhidheya* and *prayojana*, see below, Appendix I.

[32] The connection (*sambandha*) as presented by many commentators is the connection or relation existing between two of the other introductory terms, usually that occurring between the subject matter (*abhidheya*) and discourse/text (*abhidhāna*) or *prakaraṇa/śāstra*, or between the purpose and the subject matter, both often described as in an *upeya-upāya* or *sādhya-sādhana* relationship. The *sambandha* described here, however, appears to be similar to one of the types of connection discussed by Kumārila, namely, the category of *sambandha* expressed as the relation between two actions, the former action ultimately being the cause of, or leading directly to, the composing of a *sūtra/śāstra*. According to Candrakīrti, the "action" of accomplishing the first *cittotpāda* inspired Nāgārjuna, who was intent on rescuing beings from *saṃsāra*, to undertake in service of this goal the "action" of composing his work. For details, see below, Appendix I.

[33] For examples involving the construction *ādiṃ kṛtvā*, see BHSD, s.v. *ādi*. *LṬ's author comments on the word *yāvat* as follows: *yāvad ity uktāṃ* (ms: *uktai*) *prajñāpāramitānītiṃ jñātvā śāstraṃ kṛtam ity arthaḥ* (cf. Yonezawa 2004: 120, 128 [fol. 1b3]).

[34] Candrakīrti is referring to his description in chapter one of the MA (given its reference here and elsewhere in the PsP presumably composed prior to the PsP) of the first *bhūmi*, the "Joyful" (*pramuditā*), and of the resolve to attain full awakening, i.e., Buddhahood, for the sake of other beings that informs this *bhūmi*. MA I.1 lists the three factors held to be the cause of bodhisattvahood, namely, (a mind of) compassion (*kāruṇyacetas*; *snying rje'i sems*), non-dual knowledge (*advayadhī*; *gnyis su med blo*) and the intent/resolve to fully awaken (*sambodhicitta*; *byang chub sems*): MA I.1: *munīndrajāḥ śrāvakamadhyabuddhāḥ sambodhisattvaprabhavāś ca buddhāḥ | kāruṇyaceto 'dvayadhīś ca hetuḥ sambodhicittaṃ ca jinātmajānām* ||; MA Tib: *nyan thos sangs rgyas 'bring rnams thub dbang skyes || sangs rgyas byang chub sems dpa' las 'khrungs shing || snying rje'i sems dang gnyis su med blo dang || byang chub sems ni rgyal sras rnams kyi rgyu* || (cf. MHK I.6, which includes *mahāmaitrī* as a cause of Buddhahood). For further details, see Appendix II and the following notes.

[35] The technical term *cittotpāda*, with its modifier *prathama*, may have been employed instead of *bodhicitta* to distinguish it from the more general *bodhicitta* and to specify that Nāgārjuna's generation of (*sam*)*bodhicitta* corresponds to that of the first *bodhisattva* level. In the introduction to MA I.4cd-5ab a tenfold differentiation of *bodhicitta* is announced and in 5ab the first is called the *prathamaṃ cetas*; MA

which is adorned with non-dual gnosis (*advayajñāna*)[36] [and]

I.4cd-5ab: *kṛpāsvatantraṃ jagatāṃ vimuktaye samantabhadrapraṇidhipraṇāmitam* ‖ *yad asya ceto muditāpratiṣṭhitaṃ jinātmajasya prathamaṃ tad ucyate* |; MA Tib: *rgyal ba'i sras po 'di yi sems gang 'gro ba rnams* ‖ *rnam par grol bar bya phyir snying rje'i dbang gyur cing* ‖ *kun tu bzang po'i smon pas rab bsngos dga' ba la* ‖ *rab tu gnas pa de ni dang po zhes bya'o* ‖ "The mind of this son of the Conqueror that, for the sake of liberating beings, is under the sway of compassion [and] dedicated [to full awakening] by the vow of Samantabhadra, [and] that abides in joy, is called the first [*bhūmi*]." He clarifies in his commentary that it is *anāsravajñāna* imbued with *karuṇā* and *bodhicitta* which is distinguished into "parts" and attains the denotation *bhūmi*. On the terms *cittotpāda*, *bodhicitta* and *bodhicittotpāda* and their historical backgrounds, see Wangchuk 2007: 144ff.; on the indispensability of and benefits of *bodhicitta*, see ibid., 154ff.

Candrakīrti quotes the Laṅkāvatārasūtra's prediction of Nāgārjuna's attainment of the [first] *bhūmi* called Pramuditā in his commentary on MA VI.3; see MABh_{ed} 76.13-16. The *bodhisattva* who has attained the first *bhūmi* is, according to MA I.6 and commentary, free from the three fetters (*saṃyojana*) of 1) the (false) view that the *skandha*s are the Self (*satkāyadṛṣṭi*), 2) doubt (*vicikitsā*) and 3) overestimation of one's moral conduct and vows (*śīlavrataparāmarśa*), and is able to shake a hundred worlds (*lokadhātu*). According to MA I.5cd and commentary, it is only upon accomplishment of the first *cittotpāda*, i.e., upon attaining the first *bhūmi*, that one may be designated a *bodhisattva*; Candrakīrti justifies his assertion by citing the Ardhatṛtīyasāhasrī, which states that only one who has realized the non-existence of *dharma*s is deserving of the appellation "*bodhisattva*." Compare, e.g., the Bodhisattvabhūmi in which it is stated that it is with the very first *cittotpāda*, i.e., right at the moment of the ordinary person's initial resolve to attain awakening, that an individual enters the Mahāyāna and can be called a *bodhisattva*: *tasya ca cittasya sahotpādād avatīrṇo bhavati bodhisattvo 'nuttare bodhimahāyāne* | *bodhisattva iti ca saṃkhyāṃ gacchati yad uta saṃketavyavahāranayena* | *tasmāt sa cittotpādaḥ avatārasaṃgṛhītaḥ* | (cf. Wangchuk 2007: 368). On the attempt in Tibet to reconcile these two opposing views, see ibid., 40, n. 83.

[36] Candrakīrti explains the *advayadhī* (*gnyis su med blo*) of MA I.1 in the pertinent section of the MABh as *dngos po dang dngos po med pa la sogs pa mtha' gnyis dang bral ba'i shes rab* "the insight free from the two extremes of existence and non-existence, etc." (MABh_{ed} 6.11-13). He refers to it at the end of the section as *gnyis su med pa'i shes rab* (MABh_{ed} 7.8) and quotes RĀ II.74 (cf. MABh_{ed} 7.10-13) in which the quasi-synonym *gnyis la mi brten ye shes* appears. Cf. MMK XV.5 where Nāgārjuna explains that worldly people speak of non-existence only in relation to something that has existed, i.e., something whose existence has "become otherwise," but when existence is logically impossible, then non-existence is totally impossible: *bhāvasya ced aprasiddhir abhāvo naiva sidhyati* | *bhāvasya hy anyathābhāvam abhāvaṃ bruvate janāḥ* ‖; see also his rhetorical question at MMK V.6ab: *avidyamāne bhāve ca kasyābhāvo bhaviṣyati* |. At MABh_{ed} 7.14-16ff., the root of non-dual gnosis (**advayajñāna*, *gnyis su med pa'i ye shes*) is said to be *karuṇā*; at MABh_{ed} 8.10-12 it

preceded by the means of great compassion (*mahākaruṇā*),[37] [the resolve that acts] as a cause for the arising of the gnosis of the Tathāgata, the Master Nāgārjuna, who had finally understood the correct method (*nīti*)[38] of the perfection of insight (*prajñāpāramitā*),[39]

---

is asserted that the individual who has vowed to bring others to the state of Buddhahood cannot do this without *advayajñāna*.

[37] The *karuṇā* that arises in the *bodhisattva* owing to the *bodhisattva*'s awareness of the suffering that ordinary beings experience and that inspires the resolve to awaken, is praised and discussed in MA I.2-4ab and in the commentary thereon. See the previous three notes and Appendix II. On *karuṇā* as the root cause of *bodhicitta*, see Wangchuk 2007: 285-289. *karuṇā* is divided into *sattvālambanā*, *dharmālambanā* and *anālambanā karuṇā* (cf. $MABh_{tr}$ 1907: 258, n. 1); see Schmithausen 2000c: 446-448; a Tibetan presentation is found in Hopkins 1980: 116-125. On *karuṇā* in early Buddhism, see Maithrimurthi 1999, chapters 3 and 6; see also Schmithausen 2000b. On the general tension in Mahāyāna between *śūnyatā* and *karuṇā* and attempts to reconcile the two, see Schmithausen 2000c.

[38] On *prajñāpāramitānīti*, see below Appendix III.

[39] The word *pāramitā* is derived from *parama* which means "highest," "most excellent," "best" (see Hirakawa 1990: 299; BHS and PTSD entries for *pārami*, °*mī* and for *pāramitā*; see also Dayal 1978: 165f.). Candrakīrti, however, like Avalokitavrata and a number of other Buddhist authors, understands *pāramitā* to be a compound with the meaning "gone to the other side" (this is also the way it has been understood by Kumārajīva, one of the early Chinese translators of Prajñāpāramitā texts; see Hirakawa 1990: 299f.). In his commentary on MA I.16ab, Candrakīrti substantiates this interpretation by referring to Pā 6.3.1 *alug uttarapade* "elision does not take place before the following member of the compound" (slightly revised translation of Vasu 1980: 1209), presenting *pāramitā* as an *aluk tatpuruṣa* compound (thus *pāramita* instead of *pāreta*). He additionally refers to Pā 6.3.109 as an alternative rule for the formation of *pāramitā*: *pṛṣodarādīni yathopadiṣṭam* "The elision, augmentation and mutation of letters seen in *pṛṣodara*, etc., though not found in treatises of grammar, are, to the extent they are taught by the sages, valid" (slightly revised translation of Vasu 1980: 1241; Böthlingk 2001: 347: "Mit *pṛṣodara* u.s.w. verhält es sich, wie gelehrt wird"). Candrakīrti asserts: *de la pha rol zhes bya ba ni gang 'khor ba'i rgya mtsho'i phar 'gram dang ngogs te* | *nyon mongs pa dang shes bya'i sgrib pa ma lus pa spangs pa'i rang bzhin mnga' ba'i sangs rgyas nyid do* || *pha rol tu son pa ni pha rol tu phyin pa'o zhes bya ste* | *tshig phyi ma yod na mi mngon par mi bya'o zhes bya ba'i mtshan nyid 'di* ($MABh_{UN}$: *'dis*) *las kyi rnam par dbye ba mi mngon par ma byas pas gzugs su 'gyur ba'am* | *pṛ ṣo da ra la sogs pa yin pa'i phyir phyi ma'i mtha' can nyid du bzhag go* || ($MABh_{ed}$ 30.11-17; see $MABh_{tr}$ 1907: 277-279 and n. 2). De La Vallée Poussin translates the *pṛṣodara* passage "ou bien, appartenant au groupe du type *pṛṣodara*, il présente la fin du second [terme]," but adds that his interpretation is conjectural, "pour ne pas dire hasardée." His

out of compassion composed the treatise (*śāstra*), for the sake of the understanding of others.

> That which subdues (√*śās*) all the enemy defilements and completely (*sam*) protects (√*trai*) from bad rebirths (*durgati*), [indeed] from becoming (*bhava*) [i.e., rebirth in general], is, in virtue of [this] subduing and the quality of protecting, a treatise (*śāstra*). This pair, however, is not [to be found] in the doctrines of others.[40]

---

interpretation assumes that "le mot *pāramitā* ne presente que la finale du second terme," i.e., that *pāramitā* is a formation from *pāra‹gā›mitā*. If I understand de La Vallée Poussin correctly, he is suggesting that Candrakīrti implies that the latter constituent, i.e., *mitā* of the compound *pāramitā*, "possesses (only) the end" of the word *gāmitā* inasmuch as its former part, i.e., *gā*, has been elided. This is an interesting but probably overly complicated solution: the Sanskrit reads merely … *pṛṣodarāditvād vā māntatvanipātanam* "or, owing to [instances like] *pṛṣodara* and so forth there is the irregularity that it (= *pāra*) has a final *m*." MABh Tib's *phyi ma'i mtha' can* would seem to mean that *pāra* "has an extreme final," i.e., the added *m*. One wonders if *phyi* is an interpolated error; removed, *ma'i mtha' can* would translate *māntatva*, and Skt and Tib would unproblematically correspond.

[40] This verse does not appear in PsP Tib, which appears to indicate that it was not in either of the manuscripts relied on to produce the Tibetan translation. It thus may be an accretion. I have retained it in the critical edition only because it occurs in all of the extant Sanskrit manuscripts of the PsP. If it is an accretion, it may have entered them via ms β since ms δ (descended from ms γ) passed on its readings to PsP Tib (see Manuscript Description: Stemma).
De La Vallée Poussin (cf. PsP_L 3, n. 3), finding *va* as the third word of the first quarter in his manuscripts, acknowledges that his conjectured reading *va*[*ḥ*] "est douteuse" and proposes *vai* or *ca* as the correct reading. De Jong (1978: 28) corrects *va*[*ḥ*] to *ca* on the basis of the verse as found at MAVṬ 3.9. The MAVṬ just previous to the verse expands it in prose; *pāda* d is elaborated with: *etac ca dvayam api sarvasmin mahāyāne sarvasmiṃś ca tadvyākhyāne vidyate nānyatreti* (3.6-8). MAVṬ Tib for the verse reads: *nyon mongs dgra rnams ma lus 'chos pa dang* ‖ *ngan 'gro srid las skyob pa gang yin pa* ‖ [']*chos skyob yon tan phyir na bstan bcos te* ‖ *gnyis po 'di dag gzhan gyi lugs la med* ‖ (P 20b8-21a1). Two sentences containing references to *durgatito bhavāt* appear in MAVṬ Tib antecedent to the verse (the MAVṬ Sanskrit is damaged for the relevant part of the sentences): the first connects the words *ngan song rnams* and *srid pa* with *dang*, i.e., understands them as a pair (for Sanskrit reconstruction, cf. Yamaguchi 1934: 3 and Stanley 1988: 4, n. 12) but the second, immediately before the verse and thus possibly intended as a gloss of the verse, uses the words *ngan 'gro'i srid pa*, i.e., unexpectedly assumes a *tatpuruṣa* (cp. Yamaguchi 1934: 3.6). Stcherbatsky (1992: 06, n. 48) notes that the etymology found here in the PsP is the same as that presented in the Vyākhyāyukti (see D 123a2-4; P

§3. And the Master [Nāgārjuna] himself presents [in his *maṅgala* verses] the subject matter (*abhidheyārtha*) along with the purpose (*prayojana*) of the entire treatise that he is about to declare. Having brought out [in these verses the Tathāgata's] greatness (*māhātmya*) as someone who without error illuminates it (i.e., this subject matter),[41]

143a4-6). Gokhale (1937: 283, n. 1) remarks that Guṇaprabha, in the introduction to his commentary on the Pañcaskandhaka, ascribes the verse to Āryadeva. The same etymology is alluded to in the TJ on MHK II.7b (*śāstralokajñatāpaṭuḥ*): *bstan bcos 'jig rten shes la mkhas* (D: ||) *zhes bya ba ni ngan song ba'i 'jigs pa las skyob pa dang | nyon mongs pa'i dgra 'dul nus pa'i bstan bcos shes pa la mkhas pa dang* | (D 52a2; P 55a7-8; Heitmann 2004: 72); Bhāviveka refers to the etymology of √*śās* as presented in the verse etymologizing *śāstra* in his explanation of the word *śāsana* in chapter 18 of the PP (see Eckel 1980: 231). The etymology for the word *śāstra* as set forth by the verse is again found in Avalokitavrata's *ṭīkā* on Bhāviveka's PP: *nyon mongs pa'i dgra rnams 'chos pa'i phyir dang | ngan song pa'i 'jigs pa las* (P: *la*) *skyob pa'i phyir bstan bcos zhes* (P: *shes*) *bya'o* || (PPṬ D 8b1; P 9b8); Avalokitavrata provides alternative explanations of *śāstra* based on both √*śās* in its meaning "subdue" and *tra* = *tri* "three," and √*śās* in its meaning "teach" and *tra* = *tri* "three": *yang na bstan bcos zhes bya ba ni rnam par rtog pa'i dgra 'chos pa'i phyir dang | bsam gyis mi khyab cing rmad du byung ba'i sku gsum thob par byed pa'i phyir bstan bcos so || yang na bstan bcos zhes bya ba ni chos zhi ba nye bar ston pa'i phyir dang | lhag pa'i tshul khrims dang | lhag pa'i sems dang | lhag pa'i shes rab kyi bslab pa gsum nye bar ston pa'i phyir dang | de bzhin gshegs pa shā kya thub pas bstan pa rnam par thar pa gsum ston pa'i phyir bstan bcos so* || (PPṬ D 8b1-3; P 9b8-10a3). Another etymology for *śāstra* appears in ŚSV$_{ed}$ 225.14-23; Erb (1997: 55) translates the section: "... so spricht man von Lehrwerk (**śāstra*), weil es [als] nicht verkehrter Weg die Befleckungen (*kleśa*) vernichtet (**śāsti*). [Die Wurzel] *śās* (*'jig pa*) [bedeutet auch] 'vernichten' (*'gog pa*). Denn [auch] im gewöhnlichen Leben sagt man ja, wenn einer hingerichtet wird, dass man ihn mit der 'grossen Strafe' vernichtet (= bestraft)." Erb notes that Candrakīrti presumably derives the meaning "correct way, method" from *tra*, the suffix indicating the means for the accomplishment of the verbal action; he suggests the reconstruction **śāsaty anena aviparītena mārgeṇa kleśān iti śāstram.* Candrakīrti, commenting at the beginning of the CŚṬ on the individual words of the compound *catuḥśatakaśāstra*, states briefly: ... *'dzin pa rnam pa sna tshogs pa 'chos pa'i phyir na de nyid bstan bcos* (see CŚṬ D 32a7-32b1; P 34b6-7).

[41] De La Vallée Poussin has overlooked that his manuscripts present *tadaviparīta-saṃprakāśa<u>ka</u>tvena* (L without °*saṃ*°) and presents the compound *tadaviparīta-saṃprakāśatvena*; he does understand the compound to be referring to the Tathāgata (see PsP$_L$ 3, n. 4). Stcherbatsky (1927: 84 and n. 1) understands the compound as referring the *śāstra*, and paraphrases: "He tries to impress upon us that it will be a grand and fundamental treatise, because it will present this idea in a thorough and unflinching manner."

[Nāgārjuna,] desiring to pay homage to the Tathāgata,[42] to the supreme teacher (*paramaguru*) who exists undifferentiated from the nature of that[43] [subject matter]—[a homage] inspired by [his] composition of the treatise—[thus] states [the two verses] which commence

> [He] who, [fully awakened, taught] dependent-arising [which is]
>
> Without cessation, without arising, without annihilation, not eternal,
> Without one thing, without separate things,[44] without coming, without going.[45]

---

[42] For references to and etymologies of the word Tathāgata, see PsP_L 31, n. 1; May 1959: 122, n. 317; $YŚV_{tr}$ 105, n. 10; Erb 1997: 110, n. 59. Candrakīrti writes in CŚṬ to CŚ IX.1cd ($CŚṬ_{ed}$ 164.13-15): *sa evānityaśūnyatopadeśena yathā bhāvānāṃ svabhāvas tathā gato buddhas tathāgata ity ucyate* | and cites the (unidentified) etymology (*yathā coktam*) *atītā tathatā yadvat pratyutpannāpy anāgatā* | *sarvadharmās tathā dṛṣṭās tenoktaḥ sa tathāgataḥ* || ($CŚṬ_{ed}$ 164.17-18), as well as the etymology found in the Vajracchedikā Prajñāpāramitā: *tathāgata iti subhūte ucyate na kvacid gato na kutaścid āgataḥ* | *tenocyate tathāgato 'rhan samyaksambuddha iti* (ed. E. Conze, Serie Orientale XIII, Rome: Istituto Italiano per il Medio ed Estremo Oriente, 1957, p. 59.5-7; Tib at $CŚṬ_{ed}$ 167.1-5; CŚṬ Skt not preserved). See also Avalokitavrata's PPṬ for a list of etymologies (D 19b2-21b1; P 23b3-25b5).

[43] *LṬ: *tat*(ms: *tata*)*svabhāveti pratītyasamutpādasvabhāvaḥ* (cf. Yonezawa 2004: 120, 128 [fol. 1b3]).

[44] In PsP Tib, *anekārtham* and *anānārtham* are interpreted as *karmadhāraya* compounds, not as *bahuvrīhis*: *tha dad don min don gcig min* ("not different things, not one thing"). See n. 102. Pa tshab has not translated the two verses but has rather inserted Klu'i rgyal mtshan and Jñānagarbha's translation of them; cf. the Tibetan in, e.g., ABh_{ed} 237f. and BP_{ed} 1.

[45] MMK verses of homage I-IIa. The Sanskrit manuscripts at this point present only the first verse and the first quarter of the second, thus do not include the terms that indicate the *prayojana*, i.e., *nirvāṇa*. The Tibetan continues on with the second quarter of the second verse, thereby adding *prapañcopaśamaṃ śivam* (*spros pa nyer zhi zhi*). The translators may have supplied the second quarter in order to provide for explicit mention of the words indicating the purpose. The citation in the Sanskrit possibly ends with the compound *pratītyasamutpāda* because it will be the main topic in the paragraphs that follow.
Note that the order of *anekārtham anānārtham* and *anāgamam anirgamam* is reversed in PsP Tib so that the verse-half reads *'ong ba med pa 'gro med pa* || *tha dad don min don gcig min* ||. When the individual words of this verse-half are explained in prose, PsP Tib follows the order in PsP Tib's verse.

Thus here, (i.e., according to these verses) dependent-arising (*pratītyasamutpāda*) qualified by the eight qualifiers "without cessation" (*anirodha*), etc., is the subject matter of the treatise.

nirvāṇa [of homage verse IIb], characterized as the calming of all manifoldness (*prapañcopaśama*) and [ultimate] welfare (*śiva*), is indicated as the purpose of the treatise.

With this [quarter, i.e., homage verse IId],

> To him, the best of expounders, I pay homage

the [actual] homage [is indicated].[46]

§4. Thus (*iti*) this, to start, is the meaning of the pair of verses as a whole (*samudāyārtha*).

§5. [Now,] on the other hand, the meaning of the [individual] elements (*avayavārtha*) (i.e., the words) is analyzed. Among them,[47] cessation (*nirodha*) [means] stopping (*niruddhi*); [that is,] momentary destruction (*kṣaṇabhaṅga*) is called cessation.[48] Arising (*utpāda*) [means] originating (*utpādana*),[49] [that is,] the coming forth of individual existence (*ātmabhāvonmajjana*). Annihilation (*uccheda*) [means] termination (*ucchitti*); the meaning is: the cutting off of the continuum (*prabandhavicchitti*). Eternal (*śāśvata*) [means] permanent (*nitya*); the meaning is: abiding for all time (*sarvakālasthāsnu*). One thing (*ekārtha*), [a *karmadhāraya* compound dissolved as] "this is one and a thing as well," [is used in the sense of] a thing not different

---

[46] PsP Tib adds the verb *bstan* (*nirdiṣṭa*), apparently to clarify the *anuvṛtti* of the previous nominal predicate.

[47] The explanation of the individual words of the introductory verses does not occur in PsP Tib after its equivalent for *tatra*, and rather appears only after the discussion of the compound *pratītyasamutpāda* (see Tibetan edition §15). For the reasons for this and further comments, see below Appendix IV.

[48] Cf. Candrakīrti's refutation of the Sautrāntika tenet of the uncaused perishing of things at PsP_L 173.8-12 (cp. $AKBh_{ed}$ 193.7-8) in the context of the rejection of the *saṃskṛtalakṣaṇa nirodha* where *nirodha*, *vināśa*, *nāśa* and *kṣaṇabhaṅga* are used as quasi-synonyms.

[49] PsP Tib *skye ba* for *utpādana*, which is normally attested in its causal sense.

(*abhinnārtha*) [from another thing]; the meaning is: not distinct (*na pṛthak*). Separate thing (*nānārtha*) [is used in the sense of a] thing different (*bhinnārtha*) [from another]; the meaning is: distinct (*pṛthak*). Coming (*āgama*) [means] coming toward/approaching (*āgati*), [that is,] the coming to a proximate place of those situated in a distant place. Going (*nirgama*) [means] going away/departing (*nirgati*), [that is,] the going to a distant place of those situated in a proximate place.[50]

§6. [The verbal root] *i* (*eti*)[51] has the meaning "going" (*gati*), [the prefix] *prati* has the meaning "attaining" (*prāpti*). Owing to the

---

[50] Candrakīrti's explanation of the elements to be negated for *pratītyasamutpāda* of the homage verses is merely a more elaborate version of Bhāviveka's, which reads: *'gag pa zhes bya ba ni 'jig pa'o* ‖ *skye zhes bya ba ni 'byung ba'o* ‖ *chad pa zhes bya ba ni rgyun chad pa'o* ‖ *rtag* (P: *rtags*) *pa zhes bya ba ni dus thams cad du gnas pa'o* ‖ *'ong ba zhes bya ba ni tshur 'ong ba'o* ‖ *'gro zhes bya ba ni phar 'gro ba'o* ‖ *tha dad don* (D without *don*) *ces bya ba ni don tha dad pa'o* ‖ *don gcig ches bya ba ni don tha mi dad pa* (PP D 47a4-5; P 55b5-6; see Kajiyama 1963: 44, Ames 1993: 217). Avalokitavrata comments on Bhāviveka's gloss of *nirodha*: *'jig pa dang med pa dang nyams pa gang yin pa de ni 'gag pa zhes bya'o* (cp. PsP_L 170.3: *nirodho hi nāmābhāvaḥ*); on *utpāda*: *'byung ba dang srid pa dang 'phel pa gang yin pa de ni skye zhes bya'o* ‖. To Bhāviveka's gloss on *śāśvata* he adds that that which has a nature that abides for all time is *śāśvata*; that is to say, that which does not change, being characterized also later by its previous aspect, is *śāśvata* (*gang la dus thams cad du gnas pa'i ngang tshul yod pa ste* | *rnam pa gang gis* (P: *gi*) *sngon nye bar mtshon par gyur pa'i rnam pa de nyid kyis phyis kyang nye bar mtshon par 'gyur zhing mi 'gyur ba de ni rtag pa zhes bya'o* ‖). His comments on *āgama* and *nirgama* are, interestingly, the same as Candrakīrti's (e.g., for *āgama*: *yul thag ring po nas yul thag nye bar tshur 'ong ba ni 'ong ba zhes ba'o* ‖). He explicates Bhāviveka's gloss **bhinnārtha* for *nānārtha* as: *kha dog dang sgra skad dang* | *rnam pa dang yon tan dag gis don tha dad pa ste*, providing as an example fire with regard to water (*chu la me lta bu de ni don tha dad pa zhes bya'o* ‖) and then explains **abhinnārtha* in the opposite way, giving the example "not like fire with regard to water" (*chu la me lta bu ma yin pa de ni don gcig ces bya'o* ‖). See PPṬ D 41b6-42a4; P 48a8-48b6.

[51] Candrakīrti follows the grammatical tradition's convention of referring to √*i* with the nominalized finite form *eti*. The different basic meanings of √i are classified in Pāṇini's Dhātupāṭha as different roots by way of the meta-words *iṇ*, *iṅ* and *ik*: Dhātupāṭha 2.36 glosses *iṇ* with *gatau*, thus √*i* occurring in the meaning of "going"; 2.37 glosses *iṅ* with (*nityam adhipūrvaḥ*) *adhyayane*, thus √*i*, always preceded by the prefix *adhi*, occurs in the meaning of "studying"; 2.38 glosses *ik* with (*nityam adhipūrvaḥ*) *smaraṇe*, thus √*i*, always preceded by the prefix *adhi*, occurs in the

transformation of the meaning of the [verbal] root through the influence of the prefix—

> The meaning of the [verbal] root is forcibly led elsewhere by the prefix,[52]
> As the sweetness of the water of the Ganges by ocean water[53]

---

meaning of "remembering." PsP Tib has *iti* for *eti*; see Verhagen 1985: 27, point (6), where the Tibetan scholar Blo gros brtan pa (probably thirteenth/fourteenth c.) asserts that Tibetan grammarians mistakenly use *iti* instead of *eti* (see also ibid., 31). PsP Tib presents the explanation of *prati* first.

[52] I have followed de La Vallée Poussin's lead and removed from the body of the verse the *hi* that in all the manuscripts but Q (Q is damaged) follows *upasargeṇa* because it adds a metrically disturbing ninth syllable to the *pathyā anuṣṭubh śloka*. The manuscripts' inclusion of *hi* may point to early scribal interference: an introductory enclitic *hi* may have been added by a scribe who did not realize that he was tampering with a verse; I am not aware of other instances of Candrakīrti citing a verse in which he inserts an introductory enclitic *hi*. That the verse includes *hi* may even point to the verse itself being an early intrusion. It is possible that the well-known verse (with or without *hi*) was originally a marginal gloss explaining the text's *upasargavaśena dhātvarthavipariṇamāt* that was later, yet before the Tibetan translation of the PsP was undertaken, inserted into the text by a scribe. The PsP translators may have recognized that the verse was unmetrical but translated it as a metrically correct Tibetan verse. Even though the verse gives the impression that it is an interpolation, and may not belong to the original text, there is not enough evidence to justify dispensing with it.

[53] Candrakīrti explains the change in the meaning of the root √*i* from "going" to "attaining" as due to the effect of the prefix, substantiating (if the *śloka* is original) the meaning he derives from the conjoining of *prati* and √*i* with this verse from the grammatical tradition. There is disagreement within the grammatical tradition as to the correct reading of the *śloka*, disagreement which to a large extent has its source in the discussion of whether *upasarga*s possess their own independent meanings or whether they as "illuminators" (*dyotaka*) merely "throw light" on verbal roots. Cf. SiKau ad Pā 8.4.18 and Appendix V.
A version of the *śloka* quoted here in the PsP appears at MAVṬ 3.19-20 subsequent to the citation of the *śloka* etymologizing *śāstra*, previously quoted in the PsP. Yamaguchi (1934: 3.19) emends to *anyatra nipate* but gives *anyaḥ pratīyate* as the manuscript reading. The Tibetan for the same MAVṬ verse-half, on the other hand, reads *skad dbyings don gyi stobs ldan yang* ‖ *nye bar bsgyur bas zil non 'gyur* ‖ (P 21a3-4); Bhattacharya and Tucci (1932: note 31) reconstruct *balavān api dhātvartha upasargeṇa bādhyate*; the original Sanskrit may have been closer to the version they would prefer, i.e., *upasargeṇa dhātvartho balavān abhibhūyate*. Dimitrov (2007: 9) finds the verse at the end of his manuscript of the Prādivṛtti; there *pāda* d reads *sāmudreṇāmbhasā yathā* instead of *sāgareṇa yathāmbhasā*.

—the word *pratītya* here, ending in the *lyap*[54] suffix, [that is, the gerund suffix *ya*,] is used in the sense of "attaining" (*prāpti*), [i.e.] "relying" (*apekṣā*). Because [the verbal root] *pad*[55] preceded by [the prefixes] *sam* and *ut* has the meaning "emerging" (*prādurbhāva*), the word *samutpāda* has the sense of "emerging." And therefore, the meaning of [the compound] *pratītyasamutpāda* is "the arising (*utpāda*) of things in reliance on causes and conditions."[56]

PsP Tib translates: "The meaning of the verbal root is transformed by the strength of the prefix, like the water of the Ganges, though sweet, by the ocean water." The verse and Candrakīrti's subsequent etymology are translated in Verhagen 1985: 42, n. 115.

[54] Pā 7.1.37: *samāse 'nañpūrve ktvo lyap* "In the case of a compound other than one in which the prior constituent is a term negation, the suffix *ktvā* is replaced by the suffix *lyap*."

[55] Tib: *pā ta*, obviously the transcription for *pāda*.

[56] Candrakīrti's explanation of the compound *pratītyasamutpāda* is similar to the first of two set forth in the AKBh: *atha pratītyasamutpāda iti kaḥ padārthaḥ | pratiḥ prāptyartha eti* (read: *etir*) *gatyarthaḥ | upasargavaśena dhātvarthapariṇāmāt prāpyeti yo 'rthaḥ so 'rthaḥ pratītyeti | padiḥ sattārthaḥ samutpūrvaḥ prādurbhāvārthaḥ* ($AKBh_{ed}$ 138.1-3; see $AKBh_{tr}$ III.78, La Vallée Poussin 1913a: 48-49; Verhagen 1985: 43, n. 115). Yaśomitra clarifies: *pratiḥ prāptyartha iti. prāptidyotaka ity arthaḥ. itir gatāv iti. dhātvarthaḥ. pariṇāmād iti.* (Tib reflects Skt. Read, perhaps, *itir gatāv iti dhātvarthapariṇāmād iti* ["Because the meaning of the root—viz., √i in the sense of going—is transformed"]): (with Śāstri:) *anekārthā hi dhātavaḥ. pratiś copasargaḥ prāptidyotaka ity ayam itir gatyartham ujjhitvā prāptyartham āpadyate. padiḥ sattārtha iti. padiḥ* (Śāstri *pada*; Tib: *ba da*) *sattāyām iti.* (AKVy 294.21-24; Tib: P 327b1-3). According to the Pāṇinian *dhātupāṭha* and Candragomin's *dhātupāṭha*, the verb *pad* is used in the meaning of going (*pada gatau*). The verb *vid*, two verbs after *pad* in each list, is given as used in the meaning of existing (*vida sattāyām*).
See Verhagen's comments (1985: 23-25) on the sGra sbyor bam po gnyis pa's analysis of the compound *pratītyasamutpāda*. See also Hopkins' translation (1983: 662-666) of the section on the etymology of *pratītyasamutpāda* in 'Jam dbyang bzhad pa's Grub mtha'i rnam bshad. On Pāli compounds (like *paṭiccasamuppāda*) with gerunds as the first member having originally developed from combinations of gerund and verb-form, cf. Norman 1992: 157, n. 72.
This explanation of *pratītya* as a gerund is criticized in AKBh immediately following the explanation of the compound *pratītyasamutpāda*. The opponent, identified by Yaśomitra as a Vaiyākaraṇa, states that a gerund suffix is employed in regard to an action which occurs prior to another action, and that these two actions are performed by the same agent (Pā 3.4.21: *samānakartṛkayoḥ pūrvakāle*; on this rule and the

---

discussion surrounding it see Tikkanen 1987: 37-39); for example, it is added to the verb "bathed" in the sentence "having bathed, he eats"; however, in the case of *pratītyasamutpāda*, the grammarian argues, there is nothing existing before the act of arising that, having previously depended, afterwards arises, and it is impossible that an action can exist without an agent (*ekasya hi kartur dvayoḥ kriyayoḥ pūrvakālāyāṃ kriyāyāṃ ktvāvidhir bhavati | tadyathā snātvā bhuṅkta iti | na cāsau pūrvam utpādāt kaścid asti yaḥ pūrvaṃ pratītyottarakālam utpadyate | na cāpy akartṛkāsti kriyeti* [AKBh$_{ed}$ 138.4-7]). Vasubandhu states that the criticisms do not apply, and asserts the Sautrāntika view regarding the state of the arising *dharma*, namely, that it arises as something "whose face is turned toward arising" (*utpādābhimukha*; Yaśomitra glosses with *utpitsuḥ*), that is, as something future (*anāgata*), i.e., as something ready to arise, on the verge of arising, and that it depends in this same state: *ato yadavastha utpadyate tadavastha eva pratyeti | kimavasthaś cotpadyate | utpādābhimukho 'nāgataḥ | tadavastha eva pratyayaṃ pratyetīty ucyate* (AKBh$_{ed}$ 138.13-15). He rejects the grammarian's claim that the correct use of the gerund suffix demands that one action must of necessity temporally precede another, citing examples where the gerund is used in cases of simultaneous actions: *sahakāle 'pi ca ktvāsti dīpaṃ prāpya tamo gatam | āsyaṃ vyādāya śete ca paścāc cet kiṃ na saṃvṛte ||* (see Pāsādika 1989: 60); the second is similar to the example given in Kāś to Pā 3.4.21 (*āsyaṃ vyādāya svapiti* "he sleeps with his mouth open"); on similar exceptions to the rule, see Tikkanen 1987: 39 (on temporal neutralization of the past gerund 119-127). Zakharyin (2000: 257) writes, "Thus, for Pāṇini's times, at least, NamUL= formations might be used for expressing the meaning of not only the 'priority,' but of the 'simultaneousness' of the background action as well. Only much later, at the epoch of classical Sanskrit, some (partial only!) kind of complementary distribution on the plane of contence (= contents? –A.M.) got established between Ktvā= and NamUL=, and still later NamUL= came out of use, having passed on its functions (and, namely, the ability to express 'simultaneousness') to Ktvā=." More recently, Mattia Salvini has provided valuable references for *pratītya* of *pratītyasamutpāda* understood as a gerund, introducing a pertinent comment on *ktvā* made by the Buddhist grammarian Candragomin in his Cāndravyākaraṇa. Salvini (2011: 233) notes that Candragomin does not provide the usual explanation of *ktvā* extended to temporal simultaneity but does extend its meaning to "cases of *dependence upon something else* (*parāpekṣā*)."

Vasubandhu also criticizes the grammarian's determination of agent and action, asserting, "and in this case we do not see an action 'becoming' (*bhūti*) which is something different from the thing that is the agent of becoming. Therefore, there is no blame in such linguistic usage"; *na cātra bhavitur arthād bhūtim anyāṃ kriyāṃ paśyāmaḥ | tasmād acchalaṃ vyavahāreṣu* (AKBh$_{ed}$ 138.16-17). See AKBh$_{tr}$ III.78-80; Stalker 1987: 188-191. This discussion in the AKBh is commented on in Zakharyin's article on the functions of the Sanskrit gerund (cf. Zakharyin 2000).

Candrakīrti, perhaps because he considers *pratītya* explained in the meaning *prāpti* to be sufficient clarification, does not deal with the grammarian's complaint, but in the PP Bhāviveka presents and addresses the critique regarding the lack of something

§7. However, others say that *iti*[57] [i.e., the action referred to by the root √*i*, means] going (*gati*), [that is,] departing (*gamana*), [that is,] perishing (*vināśa*). [The noun] *ityāḥ*[58] [thus] means "things that are fit for going [i.e., perishing]."[59] *prati* is [used] in the meaning of distribution (*vīpsārtha*).[60] Having thus etymologically explained the word *itya* as ending in a secondary suffix (*taddhita*) [i.e., in the suffix *ya*, not in the primary suffix *lyap*] they describe [the compound] *pratītyasamutpāda* as [meaning] the respective (*prati prati*) arising (*samutpāda*) of things that are fit for going, that is, characterized by

---

existing prior to arising that could depend and the lack of an agent: *'dir kha cig na re | gal te 'byung ba'i snga rol du 'bras bu rkyen dang phrad nas phyis 'byung na ni de'i rten cing 'brel par 'byung ba zhes bya bar 'gyur ba zhig na | 'byung ba'i snga rol du 'bras bu rkyen dang mi 'phrad* (P: *phrad*) *de med pa'i phyir ro || de lta bas na rten cing 'brel par 'byung ba'i sgra mi 'grub po || gal te rten cing 'brel par zhes bya ba dang | 'byung zhes bya ba gnyis dus gcig tu khas len bas nyes pa med do* (P: ||) *zhe* (P: *ce*) *na yang rten cing 'brel par 'byung ba'i sgra la bya ba gnyis dus gcig na med de | par zhes brjod ba'i phyir dper na khru byas te bza' zhes bya ba bzhin no || byed pa po med par yang gzhi med pa'i bya ba mi rung ste | med pa'i phyir mo gsham gyi bu 'gro ba bzhin no | zhes zer ro ||* (D 46b4-7; P 55a2-6; translated in Kajiyama 1963: 42-43; Ames 1993: 215). Avalokitavrata identifies the criticism as that of opponents who base themselves on considerations of the grammarians: *kha cig na re zhes bya ba ni de dag nyid 'dir skabs med bzhin du brda sprod pa'i tham lag gi rjes su zhugs nas dgras rgol bar byed pa kha cig na re'o ||*. Ames (1993: 237, n. 40) notes, "According to Avalokitavrata, the Buddhist may try to avoid the difficulty presented by the first syllogism by admitting that the result pre-exists potentially (*nus pa'i tshul gyis*). The grammarian then puts forward the second syllogism." Bhāviveka, like Vasubandhu in the AKBh, argues that the gerund may be applied when two actions are simultaneous, and presents *kha gdangs te nyal* (*āsyaṃ vyādāya śete/svapiti*) and *lam khyab par byas te 'gro* ("it moves along filling the roadway") as examples (see D 46b7-47a2; P 55a6-55b1). See PPṬ for further comments on Bhāviveka's refutation of the criticism that an agent of action is required (D 33b6-34a7; P 39b5-40a8).

[57] Verhagen (1985: 45, n. 130) considers the appearance of *iti* here to be an error for *eti*, which is also possible, and would have to be ascribed to scribal error.

[58] *ityāḥ* appears in the masculine gender and in the plural for reasons of coherence, i.e., because it is intended to refer to things (*bhāva*; *dharma*).

[59] Pā 4.4.98: *tatra sādhuḥ* "good in respect to this." Kāś: *tatreti saptamīsamarthāt sādhur ity etasminn arthe yatpratyayo bhavati ... sādhur iha pravīṇo yogyo vā gṛhyate, nopakārakaḥ*.

[60] PsP Tib begins the alternative explanation of *pratītyasamutpāda* with the sentence explaining *prati*: *gzhan dag ni pra ti ni zlos pa'i don to ||*.

perishing.[61] For them, in the case [of statements] like "O monks, I am about to teach you *pratītyasamutpāda*,"[62] [or] "Who sees *pratītya-samutpāda* sees the Dharma,"[63] [this] etymology would be fine

---

[61] At $AKBh_{ed}$ 138.24-27 a second explanation of the compound *pratītyasamutpāda* is set forth which avoids the grammarian's criticism in that it does not assume that the compound contains a gerund. It is somewhat more explicit than Candrakīrti's presentation: *anye punar asya codyasya parihārārtham anyathā parikalpayanti* | *pratir vīpsārthaḥ* | *itau sādhava ityā anavasthāyinaḥ* | *utpūrvaḥ padiḥ prādur-bhāvārthaḥ* | *tāṃ tāṃ kāraṇasāmagrīṃ pratītyānāṃ samavāyenotpādaḥ pratītya-samutpāda iti* ($AKBh_{ed}$ 138.24-27; see $AKBh_{tr}$ III.80, La Vallée Poussin 1913a: 49; Stalker 1987: 192). Yaśomitra identifies the proponent of this explanation of the compound as Śrīlāta. He specifies that the prefix *sam* is used in the meaning of conjunction (*samavāya*) and, as stated in the AKBh, that it is (only) the root *pad* preceded by the prefix *ut* that means emerging (*prādurbhāva*). Thus, the word *pratītyasamutpāda* means the arising, in conjunction, of things fit for going, that is, of things fit for perishing, with respect to this and that causal complex (*tāṃ tāṃ sāmagrīṃ pratīti. prater vīpsārthatāṃ darśayati. ityānāṃ vinaśvarāṇāṃ samavā-yenotpādaḥ pratītyasamutpādaḥ*. Further elucidating the meaning of the prefix *sam*, he adds: *na kaścid dharma eka utpadyate sahotpādaniyamāt. rūpādīnāṃ "kāme 'ṣṭa-dravyako 'śabdaḥ paramāṇuḥ*" (AK II.23ab) *yāvac "citta-caittāḥ sahāvaśyam*" (AK II.24a) *iti niyamāt* (see AKVy 296.22-33; quoted in PsP_L5, n. 10).
Cp. with these two etymologies presented by Candrakīrti the two very different ones set forth in VM, the second of which is metaphorically applied to the conditions (*dvedhā tato pavatte dhammasamūhe yato idaṃ vacanaṃ, tappaccayo tato yaṃ phalopacārena iti vutto*); see VM 520f., VM_{tr} 606f.
See also the comments by Schmithausen on the misinformed rendering of *pratītyasamutpāda* as "*inter*dependence" and the often misleading but "ubiquitous rendering of *samutpāda* as '*co*-origination'" (in a meaning different than Śrīlāta's) in secondary literature in Schmithausen 1997: 12-14, 52-59 and n. 65, 67, 73 and 76, and 2000a: 63-65 (see also 2000d: 44, n. 12).

[62] Cf. SN II.1.5-6: *paṭiccasamuppādam vo bhikkhave desissāmi*; SN II.2.13-14: *paṭiccasamuppādam vo bhikkhave desissāmi vibhajissāmi*; SN II.25.11-12: *paṭicca-samuppādañca vo bhikkhave desissāmi paṭiccasamuppanne ca dhamme* = $AKBh_{ed}$ 136.2: *pratītyasamutpādaṃ vo bhikṣavo deśayiṣyāmi pratītyasamutpannāṃś ca dharmān*; AKVy 298.26-27: *pratītyasamutpādaṃ vo bhikṣavo deśayiṣyāmi*. See Pāsādika 1989: 58. The *paṭiccasamuppāda* taught at these references in the SN is that characterized by twelve links. On the varying chains of conditions to be discerned in the Canon, see Schmithausen 2000d.

[63] Candrakīrti refers here to a sentence from the Śālistambasūtra: *yo bhikṣavaḥ pratītyasamutpādaṃ paśyati sa dharmaṃ paśyati, yo dharmaṃ paśyati sa buddhaṃ paśyati* (Skt attested in AKVy 293.20-22; see Schoening 1995: 701). This version of the citation appears at PsP_L 160.5-7 (the vocative *bhikṣavaḥ* is not attested there either), shorter ones at VV_{ed} 74.12-14 (*uktaṃ hi bhagavatā yo hi bhikṣavaḥ pratītya-*

because the meaning of distribution is possible and because there is a compound [in which the case-ending of the noun *pratītya* would be elided].[64] But when a specific object is directly referred to in a case like this [viz., the statement] "Depending on the visual faculty[65] and

---

samutpādaṃ paśyati sa dharmaṃ paśyati) and YṢV$_{ed}$ 48.6-9 (*mdo sde las kyang sus rten cing 'brel par 'byung ba mthong ba des chos mthong ngo* ||). A citation similar to the one in the Bodhisattvapiṭakasūtra which attests *de bzhin gshegs pa* instead of *sangs rgyas* (see Schoening 1995: 4, n. 3) is quoted at ŚSV$_{ed}$ 245.4-7 by an opponent who argues that if the Mādhyamika holds that causes (*rgyu*) do not really exist, then he ruins dependent-arising: ... *de la gnod pa yang rung ba ma yin te* | *de mthong bas chos mthong bar bcom ldan 'das kyis gsungs te* | *gang rten cing brel par 'byung ba mthong ba des chos mthong la* | *gang gis chos mthong ba des de bzhin gshegs pa mthong ngo zhes mdo las gsungs pa'i phyir ro* ||. The quotation is translated by Erb (cf. ŚSV$_{tr}$ 83) as "Wer das Entstehen in Abhängigkeit sieht, der sieht die [wahre] Gesetzmäßigkeit [aller Daseinsfaktoren], und wer die [wahre] Gesetzmäßigkeit [aller Daseinsfaktoren] sieht, der sieht den Tathāgata." The Śālistamba passage is based on Canonical statements: MN I.190.37-191.2: *yo paṭiccasamuppādaṃ passati so dhammaṃ passati, yo dhammaṃ passati so paṭiccasamupādaṃ passati*; SN III.120.28-29: *yo kho Vakkali dhammaṃ passati so maṃ passati; yo maṃ passati so dhammaṃ passati*; Iti 91: *Dhammaṃ hi so bhikkhave bhikkhu passati, dhammaṃ passanto maṃ passatīti*. See Scherrer-Schaub 1991: 173, n. 231; La Vallée Poussin 1913a: 70, n. 2; PsP$_L$ 596 ad PsP$_L$ 6, n. 2 for further references. The PsP attests extended quotations from the *sūtra* at PsP$_L$ 560.3-570.2 and 593.3-594.6; for Sanskrit quotations of the *sūtra* in other texts, see Schoening 1995: Appendix 1.

[64] In both of the scriptural statements cited, the word *pratītya* taken as a noun satisfies the requirement that it possess the distributive meaning indicated by the element *prati* because arising can in each case be understood as applying to a multiplicity of things characterized by perishing. Further, although according to the etymology under discussion the compound *pratītyasamutpāda* would be dissolved as *pratītyānāṃ samutpādaḥ*, the noun *pratītya* as a member of the compound would not require a case ending. The first statement, according to this second etymology, could be rephrased, "O monks, I am about to teach you the respective arising of things that are fit for going, that is, of things characterized by perishing."

[65] Although the fleshy eye-ball (*māṃsapiṇḍa*) is made of primary matter (*bhūta*), the visual faculty (*cakṣurindriya*), like the other sense faculties, is made of subtle secondary matter (*bhautika*, *rūpaprasāda*; cf. AK I.9cd: *tadvijñānāśrayā rūpaprasādāś cakṣurādayaḥ* and AKBh$_{ed}$ 6.2-3 (AKBh$_{Ej}$ 7.23-26): *yathoktaṃ bhagavatā cakṣur bhikṣo ādhyātmikam āyatanaṃ catvāri mahābhūtāny upādāya rūpaprasāda iti vistaraḥ*; see also AK I.35ab and commentary). According to one opinion (AKBh$_{ed}$ 33.17-19; AKBh$_{Ej}$ 53.2-4), the atoms of the visual faculty are said to be arranged on the pupil in the form of a cumin flower, and are covered with a translucent membrane which keeps them in place; according to another, they are arranged on top of one another, as in a ball, but do not obscure each other because they are transparent,

visibles,[66] visual consciousness arises,"[67] considering that it is maintained that the arising of a single visual consciousness is, for its part, caused by a single visual faculty, how could there be the meaning of distribution in the word *pratītya* of [the phrase] *cakṣuḥ pratītya*[68]?[69] The meaning "attaining" (*prāpti*), however, is possible in

---

like crystal. See, among others, May 1959: 91, n. 198, 199; PsP_L 126, n. 1; Tillemans 1990: 251, n. 236; 255, n. 264; Stcherbatsky 1979: 12-13. Further references in Preisendanz 1994: 444, n. 151.

[66] PsP Tib attests *gzugs* (*rūpam*) for *rūpāṇi*. Candrakīrti focusses his argumentation on one individual visual consciousness and one individual visual faculty. The translators may have found the fact that visual form appeared in the plural in the Sanskrit to be distracting to the argumentation, since the idea of distribution could possibly be argued to exist in regard to *rūpāṇi*, and so restricted the number of visual forms as well. Alternatively, they may have appropriated the sentence from a pre-existing translation that contained the singular form.

[67] This often cited statement appears numerous times in the Canon: SN II.72.17-18, etc.: *cakkhuṃ ca paṭicca rūpe ca uppajjati cakkhuviññāṇam*; MN I.111.35-36: *cakkhuñ c'āvuso paṭicca rūpe ca uppajjati cakkhuviññāṇam*. The statement appears at PsP_L 250.4-5 as it does here; PsP_L 567.7-8: *cakṣuḥ pratītya rūpaṃ cālokaṃ cākāśaṃ [ca] tajjamanasikāraṃ ca pratītyotpadyate cakṣurvijñānam* |.

[68] Candrakīrti is problematizing the fact that a single *cakṣurvijñāna* relies on a single *cakṣurindriya*; multiplicity is precluded in such a case. PsP Tib reads *mig dang gzugs la brten nas* (= *cakṣuḥ pratītya rūpaṃ ca*) for *cakṣuḥ pratītya*, which is unnecessary and distracting, in fact misleading. *dang gzugs* may have been added by the translators because it appears before *brten nas* in the Tibetan translation of the cited sentence, and not after it as in the Sanskrit.

[69] Candrakīrti calls into question the credibility of the second etymology, using the argument already set forth in the AKBh. Immediately following the second explanation of *pratītyasamutpāda*, Vasubandhu states that this etymology is suitable only in certain cases, and then works the Canonical statement regarding the arising of visual consciousness into a rhetorical question: *eṣā tu kalpanātraiva kalpyate* (read: *kalpate*: AKVy: *yujyate*; AKBh Tib: *rtog pa 'di ni 'di kho na la rab tu brtag tu rung*). *iha kathaṃ bhaviṣyati cakṣuḥ pratītya rūpāṇi cotpadyate cakṣurvijñānam iti* ($AKBh_{ed}$ 138.27-28). Yaśomitra explains the critique by demonstrating that in the case of this specific Canonical statement neither the idea of distribution nor a compound—at least a sensible one—is possible: should one attempt to rescue *pratītya* as a noun by placing it in a compound with *cakṣus* (of necessity *cakṣūṃṣi* to take into account the multiplicity, demanded by *prati*, of the perishing things), thus "hiding" its lack of a case ending, the resulting compound "the visual faculties of the respective things which perish" (*pratītyacakṣūṃṣi*) will not be acceptable due to its meaninglessness in the present context: *pratir vīpsārtha ity evamādikā kalpanā 'traiva Pratītyasamutpādasūtre yujyate. iha kathaṃ bhaviṣyati cakṣuḥ pratītya rūpāṇi cotpadyate*

regard to the word *pratītya* [understood as a gerund] not only when a specific object is not referred to, namely, "arising in dependence" (*pratītya samutpāda*), that is, "coming into existence upon attaining," (*prāpya sambhava*), but also when a specific object is referred to, owing to the explanation "depending on the visual faculty," [i.e.,] "attaining the visual faculty," [that is,] "relying on the visual faculty." But in the case of the word *itya* as a secondary formation, given that [one would expect to hear] a case-ending here in [the statement] *cakṣuḥ pratītya rūpāṇi cotpadyate cakṣurvijñānam* due to the fact that 1) the word *pratītya* would not be an indeclinable and 2) it is not [part of] a compound, there should be the reading *cakṣuḥ pratītyaṃ vijñānaṃ rūpāṇi ca* ("consciousness fit for perishing on account of the visual faculty and visibles [...]").[70] But this is not so [that is, one does not encounter the word *pratītya* in this statement in a declined form]. Therefore, the etymological explanation of it being in fact an indeclinable ending in *lyap* should be accepted.

§8. [We] have, however, to start, the impression that there is sheer ineptitude (*akauśala*) in the reiteration of others' positions [regarding

---

cakṣurvijñānam iti. na hi pratītyānāṃ cakṣūṃṣi pratītyacakṣūṃṣīti samāsaḥ saṃbhavaty arthāyogāt. cakṣur hi pratītya rūpāṇi prāpya cotpadyate cakṣurvijñānam ity ayam artho gamyate (AKVy 296.33-297.4). See also Hopkins 1983: 667f.
Bhāviveka views this same Canonical statement as ground for rejecting both etymologies of the compound *pratītyasamutpāda* (Candrakīrti will claim he presents both incorrectly; see PsP_M §8): *de yang mi rung ste | mig dang gzugs rnams la brten nas mig gi rnam par shes pa 'byung ngo zhes gsungs pa 'di la don gnyi ga med pa'i phyir ro* || (PP D 46b3-4; P 54b8-55a1). Avalokitavrata clarifies that *don gnyi ga* refers to the two etymologies and explains why neither is suitable as regards this Canonical statement concerned with the arising of visual consciousness; see PPṬ D 29a7-29b6; P 34b5-35a6.

[70] Given that the word *pratītya* is not explained as a gerund in the second etymology, and since it stands alone in this third cited statement—not as a member of a compound as in the first two Canonical statements (where it does not require declination and is able to retain both its grammatical status as a secondary formation and its meaning "things fit for perishing")—it will need to be declined. It will be possible for *itya* of *pratītyam* to be interpreted according to the second etymology, but since a distributive meaning for *prati* is precluded due to the explicit determination of visual consciousness as the specific referent (*vijñānam* has been moved forward in the sentence because it is now modified by *pratītyam*), *prati* will have to be understood in its sense of "on account of."

the etymology of *pratītyasamutpāda*] on the part of [Bhāviveka,] who expresses criticism after repeating others' interpretations [as follows]:

> Some claim that because the prefix *prati* is [used] in the meaning of distribution (*vīpsā*), because [the verbal root] *i* has the meaning "attaining" (*prāpti*), and because the word *samutpāda* has the meaning "coming into existence" (*sambhava*), "arising in dependence on these and those conditions," [that is,] "coming into existence upon attaining [these and those conditions]" [is the meaning of *pratītyasamutpāda*]. [But] others assert that *pratītyasamutpāda* [means] "the respective arising of things characterized by perishing (*vināśin*)."[71]

---

[71] As can be observed time and again in the Tibetan translation of the first chapter of the PsP, such quotations have been appropriated by the translators from existing Tibetan translations of the texts cited. In the present case, Bhāviveka's restatement of the two etymologies has been copied directly from Klu'i rgyal mtshan and Jñānagarbha's Tibetan translation of the PP. Some of the citations inserted into the Tibetan text of the PsP were slightly modified for the sake of updating terminology, improving the expression or in order to bring the citations into line with the wording of the respective Sanskrit citation in the PsP. I hypothesize that much of the insertion work was done in Kashmir and that Pa tshab had access there to an assemblage of proto-Kanjur and proto-Tanjur translated works, which may have been kept in a section of the Ratnagupta monastery library in Śrīnagar. For more information, see MacDonald 2015.

Pa tshab has until the direct quotation of Bhāviveka's words taken care to transliterate the members of the compound *pratītyasamutpāda*, but when he copies in (or has an apprentice copy in) the pre-translated passage from PP Tib, he introduces Klu'i rgyal mtshan and Jñānagarbha's style of presenting the individual members of the compound. The relevant section of the PP reads: *rten cing 'brel par 'byung zhes bya ba la | kha cig na re rten cing zhes bya ba'i tshig gi phrad*[1] *ni zlos pa'i don yin pa'i phyir dang | 'brel par*[2] *zhes bya ba ni phrad pa'i don yin pa'i phyir dang | 'byung ba zhes bya ba'i sgra ni skye ba'i don yin pa'i phyir rten cing 'brel par 'byung ba ste*[3] *| de dang de la rten cing phrad nas 'byung ba'o zhe'o*[4] *| gzhan dag na re so so*[5] *'jig pa dang ldan pa rnams kyi 'byung ba ni rten cing 'brel par 'byung ba'o zhe'o | gzhan ma yin pa ni de yang mi rung ste* (D 46b2-3; P 54b6-8). PsP Tib: [1]*nye bar bsgyur ba* for *tshig gi phrad*; [2]*pa* for *par*; [3]omits *rten cing 'brel par 'byung ba ste*; [4]*rkyen de dang de la brten nas 'byung ba ste phrad nas 'byung ba'o zhe'o* for *de dang de la rten cing phrad nas 'byung ba'o zhe'o*; [5]*so so so sor* for *so so*. Translated in Kajiyama 1963: 42; Ames 1993: 215; Hopkins 1983: 669. Avalokitavrata identifies the persons asserting the first etymology as "certain proponents of Madhyamaka tenets" (*dbu ma pa'i grub pa'i mtha' smra ba kha cig na re* [PPṬ D 28b5; P 34a2]) and those asserting the second as "other proponents of Madhyamaka tenets" (*dbu ma pa'i grub*

Why? Because this [first party] who explains the word *pratītya* as meaning "attaining" does not explain *prati* as denoting distribution, nor [does he explain the verbal root] *i* as having the meaning "attaining." Rather, he describes *prati* as having the meaning "attaining," and [the verbal root] *i* as meaning "going," and the compounded (i.e., complete) word *pratītya* as [meaning] simply "attaining."[72] Now then, if reference to all possible things is intended by the word *pratītyasamutpāda* etymologically explained in this way [i.e., according to the correct version of this first etymology],[73]

---

pa'i mtha' smra ba gzhan dag na re [PPṬ D 29a3; P 34a8]). He glosses Bhāviveka's reference to the second etymology (*so sor 'jig pa dang ldan pa rnams kyi 'byung ba*) with *rgyu dang rkyen so sor nges pa skad cig so so re re la 'jig pa dang ldan pa'i 'bras bu rnams kyi tshogs shing 'byung ba* (PPṬ D 29a4; P 34b1). The anonymous author of the *LṬ identifies the person asserting the first etymology as Buddhapālita; Hopkins (1983: 668ff.), presumably in reliance on the dGe lugs pa tradition, also assumes that the specific proponent of the first is Buddhapālita. I am not aware of any passage in BP in which *pratītyasamutpāda* is etymologized. *LṬ's author identifies the person asserting the second as "a certain commentator" (*kaścit ṭīkākāraḥ*); cf. Yonezawa 2004: 121, 129 [fol. 1b3]. On the Tibetan translation of the word *pratītyasamutpāda* (*prati* = *rten cing*; *itya* = *'brel par*; *samutpāda* = *'byung ba*) see Hopkins 1983: 884, n. 703.

[72] To recapitulate:
First etymology (maintained by Candrakīrti, rejected—in its improperly restated form—by Bhāviveka): *prati* = attaining; √*i* = going; thus *pratītya* = attaining, relying; *samutpāda* = emerging; thus *pratītyasamutpāda* = the arising of things in reliance on causes and conditions.
Second etymology (rejected by Candrakīrti, rejected by Bhāviveka): *prati* = distribution; √*i* = going; *itya* = fit for going, i.e., characterized by perishing; *samutpāda* (although not specifically explained) = emerging; *pratītyasamutpāda* = the respective arising of things that are fit for going, that is, of things characterized by perishing.
Bhāviveka's presentation of the first etymology: *prati* = distribution; √*i* = attaining; *samutpāda* = coming into existence; *pratītyasamutpāda* = the coming into existence [of things] in dependence on these and those (= various) conditions.

[73] Candrakīrti refers to the etymology according to which the coalescence of the prefix *prati* in the meaning of attaining with the verbal root √*i* results in the root taking on the meaning of attaining, i.e., the version he accepts and that Bhāviveka has attempted to repeat but presented in an erroneous way. This is also the version that can be applied to statements dealing with the arising of an individual consciousness from a single entity (such as the non-plural visual faculty). He acknowledges that if the word *pratītyasamutpāda* is intended in a general way, then due to the multiplicity

namely, "arising in dependence" [means] "coming into existence attaining," a relation with distribution is effected [by the resulting implication,] viz., "arising in dependence" [means] "coming into existence attaining this and that complex of causes and conditions (*hetupratyayasamāgrī*)." But if there is reference to something specific, then there is not a relation with distribution, as [evident] in [formulations of Canonical statements such as] "attaining[74] the visual faculty and visibles." Thus, to begin, the Ācārya's reiteration is inept.

§9. The criticism stated [by Bhāviveka as regards the two etymologies, viz.],

> But this is not correct,[75] because an association with either of the meanings is not possible[76] in respect to this [Canonical

---

of things referred to distribution (which Bhāviveka presents as referred to by *prati* according to the first etymology) would indeed be implied, but he points out that the distribution associated with such general applications cannot be referred to by the prefix *prati* because distribution is not involved in cases of the arising of a specific thing. Thus Bhāviveka's restatement of the first etymology, even if one makes allowance for his lack of precision, cannot be accepted. Candrakīrti does not address the possibility that Bhāviveka may have rejected this etymology because of his erroneous presentation of it, that is, because according to his restatement of the etymology, a relation with distribution cannot be made when specific instances of arising are brought into the picture, such as in the example he brings forth and Candrakīrti borrows, namely, the arising of visual consciousness in dependence on the visual faculty and visibles.

[74] PsP Tib reads *brten nas* (*pratītya*) instead of *prāpya*, which must have been attested in one of the Sanskrit manuscripts available to the translators or was considered to be preferable given that the discussion centres on the meaning of *pratītya*, especially with respect to its meaning in specific Canonical statements.

[75] De La Vallée Poussin presents the Sanskrit text of Bhāviveka's critique of the two etymologies for *pratītyasamutpāda* as commencing with *etad vā* [*a*]*yuktaṃ kiṃ ca ayuktaṃ etat*, and punctuates it with a half-*daṇḍa* after [*a*]*yuktam*. The correct reading, attested only by ms Q (ms P has a lacuna), is simply *etac cāyuktaṃ*. All of the paper manuscripts attest variants of *etad vāyuktaṃ* | *kiṃ ca ayuktaṃ etat* for *etac cāyuktaṃ* (the *akṣara dvā* in *etad vā°* of ms J closely resembles the *akṣara ccā*). The *LṬ cites exactly the PsP text passage under discussion, revealing that its author relied on a manuscript that read as ms Q does: *anūdya bhāviveko dūṣaṇam āha* | *etac cāyuktam iti* (see Yonezawa 2004: 121, 129 [fol. 1b4]). PsP Tib's *de yang mi rung ste* has been copied in from PP Tib. For details, see below Appendix VI.

> statement], "Depending on the visual faculty and visibles, visual consciousness arises"[77]

is also not appropriate. For what reason? [It is inappropriate] because in not employing a [logical] argument (*yukti*) [to answer the question] "Why is it not possible?"[78] [his critique is just] a mere thesis (*pratijñāmātra*).[79]

---

[76] I have emended the text for the compound *atrārthadvayāsambhavāt* of PsP_L to *atrobhayārthābhisambandhāsambhavāt* on the basis of ms P (ms Q reads *atrobhayathābhisambandhāsambhavād*). PsP Tib attests *'di la don gnyi ga med pa'i phyir ro.* The lack of an equivalent for *abhisambandha* in PsP Tib could point to it having been absent in at least one of the manuscripts used by the translators; its presumed absence might be explained as the result of an early eyeskip from *rthā* to *dhā.* Its presence in the manuscripts available to this study could be considered as due to a later scribal insertion or even the result of an "improved" dittography (the *akṣara va* in certain old north Indian and Nepali scripts is easily confused with *dha*, *n* of *ndha* is often written as *anusvāra* and may have been added later; an initial dittography could have produced *atrobhayārthāsambhavāsambhavād*). It would seem more likely, however, that *abhisambandha* did indeed stand in both the manuscripts used for the PsP Tib translation, and that the translators intentionally overlooked it because, following their usual procedure for cited material, they inserted the present citation directly from the Tibetan translation of the PP which, like the transmitted PsP Tib, reads *'di la don gnyi ga med pa'i phyir ro* (**atrobhayārthābhavāt*). The author of the *LṬ appears to have read *sambandha* in the manuscript of the PsP at his disposal: *ubhayor api pakṣayo*[*r*] *vīpsoktety anūdya tayo*[*r*] *vīpsayor atrāpi sambandhābhāvaḥ* (cf. Yonezawa 2004: 121, 130 [fol. 1b4]); his employment of *sambandhābhāvaḥ* as the gloss for PsP's °*abhisambandhāsambhavāt* could indicate that he knew PP's reading °*abhāvāt* and combined this with PsP's °*sambandha*. Candrakīrti may have considered his °*abhisambandhāsambhavāt* as providing a more precise meaning, or he may have been using a manuscript of the PP which actually contained this reading. De Jong (1978: 29) suggested in his Textcritical Notes, on the basis of ms D and against Tib, that *abhisambandha* be included and that the compound be emended to *atra dvayārthābhisaṃbandhāsaṃbhavād.*

[77] Candrakīrti cites from the PP (see previous note). PP Tib reads: *de yang mi rung ste | mig dang gzugs rnams la brten nas mig gi rnam par shes pa 'byung ngo zhes gsungs pa 'di la don gnyi ga med pa'i phyir ro* || (D 46b3-4; P 54b8-55a1).

[78] De La Vallée Poussin (cf. PsP_L 9, n. 1), conjecturing the reading *katham an*[*enai*]*va tatprāpte*[*ḥ*] *saṃbhava* for the text now changed to *katham asambhavaḥ*, notes that the reading in his manuscripts is "plus que douteuse." The paper manuscripts attest *katham anava tetprāpte saṃbhava* and connected variants. Ms Q attests the correct reading *katham asambhava.* PsP Tib for the entire sentence reads: *ji ltar med ces bya ba'i rigs pa ma bkod pas | dam bca' ba tsam yin pa'i phyir ro.* Ms P is unreadable

owing to damage from (and including) *yad uktam* up to (but not including) *iti yuktyanupādānena*. The damaged area would allow for 26-27 *akṣaras*, but not the 29 expected on the basis of the evidence in the paper manuscripts or the 30 expected by de La Vallée Poussin.
The words *ji ltar med* (*ce na*) appear twice in the PPṬ in the context of Avalokitavrata's introduction to his presentation of the respective reasons for the impossibility of the application of the two etymologies to the Canonical statement: *de dang de la rten cing phrad nas 'byung ba'o zhes bya ba dang | so sor 'jig pa dang ldan pa rnams kyi 'byung ba zhes bya ba'i don de gnyi ga med pa'i phyir te | de dang de la rten cing phrad nas 'byung ba zhes bya ba'i don de ji ltar med ce na ... so sor 'jig pa dang ldan pa rnams kyi 'byung ba zhes bya ba'i don de ji ltar med ce na ...* (D 29b1; P 34b7 and D 29b5; P 35a4).
Stcherbatsky (1927: 88, n. 2) emends de La Vallée Poussin's *katham an*[*enaï*]*va tatprāpte*[*ḥ*] to *katham anava(ga)te 'prāpte sambhavaḥ* and translates, "Because 'how is it that (one thing) will arise when (the other) is not attained, not reached'?" It is difficult to explain the paper manuscripts' *anava tatprāpte*, but the interpolated words (presumably originally in a meaningful form) may have been inserted by a scribe or scholar who was influenced by the ideas presented in the next sentence (*vijñānasya cakṣuṣā prāptir nāsti rūpiṇām eva tatprāptidarśanāt*).

79 The question "Why is it not possible?" (*katham asambhavaḥ*; *ji ltar med*) is addressed by Avalokitavrata who takes pains to present reasons for Bhāviveka's judgement of the two etymologies as unsuitable with respect to the Canonical statement (see PPṬ D 29b1-6; P 34a6-35a6). He argues against the first etymology by taking recourse to an authoritative verse: *de dang de la rten cing phrad nas 'byung ba zhes bya ba'i don de ji ltar med ce na | de'i phyir lung las | de ni mig dang gzugs la med || de gnyis bar na'ang yod ma yin || gang du de ni gnas 'gyur ba || de yod ma yin de med min ||*. He explains that visual consciousness, not existing [already] in the visual faculty, in what is visible, or somewhere between the two, does not exist, and therefore cannot depend on its causes and conditions (Hopkins [1983: 166] interprets this to mean: "According to Avalokitavrata, Bhāvaviveka's objection is based on the principle that phenomena which meet must be simultaneously existent, ..."); or if visual consciousness does exist, there is no point in it arising again. Against the second etymology (*so sor 'jig pa dang ldan pa rnams kyi 'byung ba zhes bya ba'i don de ji ltar med ce na*), he argues that since causes and conditions cannot form a causal complex or produce an effect because they are perishing every single moment and would already be inexistent at the time of the arising [of an alleged effect], the arising of an effect cannot exist; neither can one say of effects which perish each moment that they have an arising because they perish each moment at the time of arising: *'di ltar rgyu dang rkyen so sor nges pa skad cig so so re re la 'jig pa gang dag yin pa de dag ni 'byung ba'i tshe yongs su ma grub pa'i gnas skabs kho nar skad cig re re la 'gag cing med par 'gyur bas tshogs shing 'bras bu bskyed par 'gyur ba* (P: *bas*) *med pas 'bras bu 'byung ba yang med de | 'bras bu yang 'byung ba'i tshe nyid na skad cig re re la 'jig par 'gyur ba'i phyir* (D: without *phyir*) *so sor 'jig pa dang ldan pa rnams kyi 'byung ba zhes bya ba de yang med do ||*.

§10. But if this would be the intention [of Bhāviveka's criticism]: On account of the immateriality (*arūpitva*) of consciousness, there is no attaining (*prāpti*) [of, that is, no direct contact] with the visual faculty because it is observed that only material things attain [that is, can have contact with] it[80]—this too is not correct, because attaining is

---

The fact that Avalokitavrata does not, as far as I am aware, address any of Candrakīrti's scathing criticisms of Bhāviveka's views in his PPṬ but does exert himself to provide answers to this question suggests that the question may have been raised by another Buddhist of the sixth or early seventh century who was familiar with the PP, possibly by another MMK commentator. As Kajiyama (1968) has shown, Avalokitavrata defends Bhāviveka on other occasions against both Dharmapāla and Sthiramati (Dr. Junjie Chu informs me that the question does not appear in the first chapter of Sthiramati's commentary on the MMK). Van der Kuijp places Avalokitavrata's *floruit* at the beginning of the mid-seventh c. (see van der Kuijp 2006: 182; see also 174-182).
Candrakīrti's critique that Bhāviveka has presented only a "mere thesis" turns one of Bhāviveka's chief weapons for discrediting the statements of his opponents—i.e., his recurring charge that his opponents argue with mere theses which lack reasons and examples—back against him.

[80] Candrakīrti has in the previous sentence criticized Bhāviveka for not properly explaining why he deems both etymologies inapplicable as regards the Canonical statement describing the arising of visual consciousness. He now focusses on a possible reason for Bhāviveka's rejection of the first etymology—indeed the one Candrakīrti accepts—by supposing that Bhāviveka considers *prāpti* in a very literal, i.e., physical, sense as an actual meeting, touching. (Thus while Candrakīrti introduced the Canonical statement "Depending on the visual faculty and visibles, visual consciousness arises" solely for the sake of arguing against the second etymology's interpretation of *prati* as "distribution," he interprets Bhāviveka's reference to it to be for the sake of showing especially/additionally the inapplicability of the first etymology's interpretation of *pratītya* as *prāpti*.)
Stcherbatsky (1927: 88) understands *cakṣuṣā* as the agent of the action implied by *prāpti* and translates, "Consciousness being mental (and the sense of vision physical), the first cannot be reached by the second. Experience teaches that only material things can be reached by the sense of vision," an interpretation that switches the focus from consciousness attaining the visual faculty—the sense of the Canonical statement quoted by Bhāviveka—to the visual faculty attaining consciousness (PsP Tib's *mig dang phrad pa* supports my interpretation). His decision to translate as he does may have been influenced by the well-known discussion on whether the senses "attain" their objects. Alternatively, he may have decided to translate thus because it is certainly not observed in daily life that material things touch the visual *faculty*, the clear, subtle matter on the pupil of the eye arranged in the shape of a cumin flower. This differentiation of the sense faculty per se and the fleshy, visible eye (*golaka*)

also accepted [in contexts such as that presented in the statement], "This monk is one who has attained the fruit (*prāptaphala*)."[81]

§11. And because the word "attaining" (*prāpya*) is synonymous with the word "relying" (*apekṣya*). [That is,] others [i.e., the present scholar and his circle[82] maintain that Bhāviveka's] criticism is also not appropriate on account of the fact that the Master Nāgārjuna accepts the word "depending" (*pratītya*) as having precisely the meaning of "attaining" (*prāpya*),[83] [as demonstrated in the Yukti-ṣaṣṭikā verse-half:]

---

would seem to have been set to the side in this argument, although it could also be argued that material things are indeed capable of touching the subtle matter of the visual faculty itself.

[81] It is unclear whether Candrakīrti is citing from *āgama* here (the sentence does not occur in the Pāli Canon) or merely taking as his example a common expression. The compound *prāptaphala* occurs, e.g., at AKBh_{ed} 108.23. Cp. the compound *phalapatto* in MN-aṭṭha IV.39: *Idha bhikkhu attano vasanaṭṭhānaṃ pavisitvā nisinno mūlakammaṭṭhānaṃ manasikaroti. Tassa taṃ manasikaroto obhāso uppajjati, ayaṃ paṭhamamaggo nāma, so dutiyaṃ obhāsañāṇaṃ nibbatteti dutiyamaggo adhigato hoti, evaṃ tatiyaṃ catutthañ ca; ettāvatā maggappatto c' eva phalapatto ca hotī ti*; and in VM 634 (VM_{tr} 758) in the context of the *vipassanūpakkilesa*: *Tattha obhāso ti vipassanobhāso. Tasmiṃ uppanne yogāvacaro: na vata me ito pubbe evarūpo obhāso uppannapubbo! Addhā maggappatto 'smi! Phalapatto 'smī ti amaggam eva maggo ti aphalam eva ca phalan ti gaṇhāti* (cf. also VM 637). Cp. also MN-aṭṭha III.269-270 (ad MN II.27-28; see MN_{tr} 1283, n. 774, 776, etc.), in the context of the cessation of the unwholesome habits and intentions; e.g. III.269: *akusalānaṃ sīlānaṃ nirodhāya paṭipanno ti ettha yāva sotāpattimaggā nirodhāya paṭipanno nāma hoti, phalapattena* (variant: *phalapatte*) *pana te nirodhitā nāma honti.*

[82] *LṬ's author comments: *apara ity anenātmānaṃ nirdiśati candrakīrtiḥ* (cf. Yonezawa 2004: 121, 130 [fol. 1b4]). Bhāviveka commenced his criticism of the two etymologies by referring to himself as *apara* (*gẓhan ma yin pa ni de yang mi rung*). Avalokitavrata identifies *apara* as Bhāviveka (see Ames 1993: 237, n. 33). De La Vallée Poussin (PsP_{L} 8, n. 7), commenting on the appellation in the PP, notes, "... *gẓhan ma yin pa ni*; c'est-à-dire, littéralement, *a-paraḥ*: ce terme désignant Bhāvaviveka, l'auteur lui-même, par opposition aux *eke* et aux *anye*." Candrakīrti, who tends to "recycle" Bhāviveka's words and phrases to add stylistic punch to his criticism of him, here appropriates the appellation, possibly setting it in the plural to emphasize that not only he considers Bhāviveka's critique to be ungrounded.

[83] Ms Q's reading *prāptyarthasya caiva* at first seems preferable to ms P's and the paper manuscripts' reading *prāpyārthasyaiva* (cf. PsP_{M} for the latter's variants). Following Q, the sentence would read: "And since the word "attaining" (*prāpya*) is

synonymous with the word "relying" (*apekṣya*), and due to the fact that the Master Nāgārjuna accepts the word "depending" (*pratītya*) as having precisely the meaning of "attaining" (*prāpti*), [as demonstrated in the YṢ verse-half …, according to others [i.e., the present scholar and his circle], [Bhāviveka's] criticism is also not appropriate." I accept, however, P's reading because the sentence in Q appears to have been tampered with, leading one to suspect that its *ca* is also the result of determined change. Ms P's and the paper manuscripts' *prāpya* (of *prāpyārthasyaiva*) appears to have been changed in ms Q to *prāpti* (*prāptyarthasya*), possibly due to the influence of the earlier instances of *prāpti* conjoined with *artha*. Note that PsP Tib supports the reading *prāpya* with *phrad nas* (*prāptyartha* was earlier translated as *phrad pa'i don*). Ms P's unemended presentation of the text passage is, however, problematic, for as it stands, the sentence beginning with *prāpyaśabdasya cāpekṣyaśabdaparyāyatvāt* carries on, i.e., is part of, the previous paragraph's sentence refuting Bhāviveka's (hypothetical) argument that immaterial consciousness cannot "attain," i.e., directly contact, the visual faculty (the initial reason Candrakīrti gives is: "because attaining is also accepted [in contexts such as that presented in the statement], 'This monk is one who has attained the fruit [*prāptaphala*]'"); there is no *daṇḍa* in P after *prāptaphalo 'yaṃ bhikṣur ity api prāptyabhyupagamāt*. Ms P would thus present a new reason, supported by a subordinate reason, against the objection that something immaterial cannot contact the visual faculty. In unemended P, this reason is: "and because, since the word "attaining" (*prāpya*) is synonymous with the word "relying" (*apekṣya*), the Master Nāgārjuna accepts the word "depending" (*pratītya*) as having precisely the meaning of "attaining" (*prāpya*), [as demonstrated in the YṢ verse-half:] … ." Ms P places a *daṇḍa* after this second reason, thus setting off the following *dūṣaṇam api nopapadyata ity apare* as an independent sentence. Bhāviveka's objection in regard to consciousness not being able to physically contact the visual faculty has, I would argue, been taken care of with Candrakīrti's reference to the well-known statement regarding attainment of the fruit, and further arguments are not really necessary. Even though the new argument could been seen as clarifying how *prāpya* in the context of passages focussed on immaterial things should be understood, the inclusion of Nāgārjuna's YṢ verse would seem to point to the new reason being independent of the objection concerning immaterial things contacting only material ones, and as having as its aim a more fundamental refutation of Bhāviveka's (cited) PP critique, specifically with respect to presumed doubt about or even rejection of the word *pratītya* as equivalent to *prāpya*. If a *daṇḍa* is set after *prāptaphalo 'yaṃ bhikṣur ity api prāptyabhyupagamāt* in ms P, then P's *prāpyaśabdasya cāpekṣyaśabdaparyāyatvāt* introduces the new rebuttal. When a further *daṇḍa* is placed after *prāpyaśabdasya cāpekṣyaśabdaparyāyatvāt*, P's reading *prāpyārthasyaiva* makes perfect sense. Interestingly, Q does attest a *daṇḍa* after *etad api na yuktaṃ prāptaphalo 'yaṃ bhikṣur ity api prāptyabhyupagamāt* as well as after *prāpyaśabdasya cāpekṣyaśabdaparyāyatvāt*; both seem to belong to the PsP's text. Of course, like P's *daṇḍa*-emended text, Q's text with *prāptyarthasya caiva* can also be understood as introducing a new idea not associated with the immateriality argument—in this case two new reasons—based on an assumption of Bhāviveka's

That which has arisen attaining this and that [cause] has not arisen by own nature.[84]

---

resistance to the equating of *pratītya* and *prāpya*. But as stated, given that an interfering hand appears to have changed an original *prāpya* in Q to *prāpti*, and given that Q's *ca* smooths a lectio difficilior, I accept P's reading without *ca*.
In contrast to my understanding of the section, the translators of PsP Tib appear to see Candrakīrti presenting not one, but three consecutive reasons for his assertion that Bhāviveka's critique is inapplicable if it is motivated by the idea that immaterial things cannot come into contact with material ones. As my investigation of the manuscripts has shown, PsP Tib was influenced by interpolated readings in one of the two Skt manuscripts its translators relied on, many of which also appear in Q; PsP Tib may have adopted the same *ca* that Q attests. PsP Tib reads: *de yang mi rigs te | dge slong 'di ni 'bras bu thob pa yin no zhes bya ba 'dir phrad pa khas blangs pa'i phyir dang | phrad nas zhes bya ba'i sgra yang* (= *ca*) *ltos nas zhes bya ba'i sgra'i rnam grangs yin pa'i phyir dang | rten cing 'brel par zhes bya ba'i sgra ni |* ... (YṢ 19ab) *zhes slob dpon klu sgrub kyis kyang phrad nas zhes bya ba'i don nyid du zhal gyis bzhes pa'i phyir ro || des na skyon yang mi 'thad do zhes gzhan dag zer ro ||* (translated in Hopkins 1983: 671; Hopkins structures his translation as follows: "This is not admissible because ... [scriptural citation]. Also, the term 'having met' ... is a synonym of the term 'having relied' ... . Also, the master Nāgārjuna ... . Therefore, others [Chandrakīrti himself] say that even [Bhāvaviveka's] refutation is not admissible." The PsP Tib translators have considered it necessary to begin their final sentence with a non-Sanskrit-attested *des na* (this inspired de La Vallée Poussin to introduce a conjectured *tataḥ* into his edition); their translation gives the impression that they too were confronted with a *daṇḍa* before *dūṣaṇam api nopapadyate ity apare*. Note that Candrakīrti's refutation of Bhāviveka's (hypothetical) argument that contact (*prāpti*) of immaterial things with material ones is impossible already contains the phrase *etad api na yuktam*; when the reasons preceding *dūṣaṇam api nopapadyate ity apare* are understood as belonging to this specific refutation, one has little choice but to construe *dūṣaṇam api nopapadyate ity apare* as an independent sentence.

[84] YṢ 19ab: *tat tat prāpya yad utpannaṃ notpannaṃ tat svabhāvataḥ |* (for Sanskrit citations of the *kārikā*, see YṢV$_{tr}$ 188, n. 290). YṢ 19ab Tib (Pa tshab YṢ translation): *de dang de brten gang 'byung de || rang gi dngos por skyes ma yin ||*; YṢ 19ab as translated in YṢV Tib (Ye shes sde, etc., YṢV translation): *de dang de brten gang byung ba || rang bzhin du ni de ma skyes ||*. In his commentary on the YṢ half-verse, Candrakīrti glosses *tat tat prāpya* with *tat tad apekṣya*: *de dang de brten zhes bya ba ni de dang de la bltos zhes bya ba'i tha tshig go ||*. He explicates the words "*tat tat*" as referring to the respective causes of the members of the twelve-linked chain of dependent-arising, i.e., the causes responsible for the rebirth of the individual, and to the respective causes of the factors involved in the arising of the external cosmos: *de dang de zhes bya ba spyir bsnyag pa thams cad bsdu ba'i phyir tshig 'dis nang gi ma rig pa la sogs pa dang phyi'i rlung gi dkyil 'khor la sogs pa ma lus pa dag 'du byed la sogs pa dang chu'i dkyil 'khor la sogs pa skye ba la rgyu'i dngos por gnas par gyur*

§12. And that too established as [his] (= Bhāviveka's) own opinion [regarding the meaning of *pratītyasamutpāda*, as it was set forth by him with]

> What then [is the correct interpretation of *pratītyasamutpāda*]? The meaning of "conditionality" (*idampratyayatā*)[85] as expressed in the statement "When this is present, that comes to be, from the

---

te. Scherrer-Schaub translates (cf. YṢV_{tr} 189, see also n. 292), "Par l'expression 'ceci et cela', du fait qu'elle a valeur distributive (*spyir bsnyag pa*) et qu'elle englobe toutes choses (*thams cad bsdu ba*), toutes les catégories sans exception, nescience et [autres catégories] internes, disque du vent (*rlung gi dkyil 'khor*) et [autre catégories] externes, sont établies en tant que causes de la production des *saṃskāra*, du disque de l'eau et [ainsi de suite]."
The entire *kārikā* is cited at MABh_{ed} 228.12-15. De La Vallée Poussin, citing the Skt for the *kārikā* from the Subhāṣitasaṃgraha, considers the reading for the third quarter as doubtful; 19cd: *svabhāve na yad utpannam utpannaṃ nāma tat katham* (see MABh_{tr} 1911: 278, n. 2). Lindtner, "in accordance with Tib. and a quotation occurring in Advayavajrasaṃgraha (ed. Śāstrī), p. 25," emends the otherwise metrical third quarter to read *svabhāvena yan notpannam* (see 1982b: 108 and 109, n. 19). His emendation, however, renders the quarter unmetrical, such that it agrees neither with the *pathyā anuṣṭubh* of the other three quarters nor with any *vipulās*.
See YṢV_{tr} 188, n. 290 for further references to the *kārikā* and comparable verses.

[85] *idampratyayatā*, literally, "being something whose condition is this," "the fact of having this as condition." Cf. SN II.25.31-33: *uppādā vā Tathāgatānam anuppādā vā Tathāgatānaṃ* || *ṭhitā va sā dhātu dhammaṭṭhitatā dhammaniyāmatā idappaccayatā* || "Whether there is an arising of Tathāgatas or no arising of Tathāgatas, that [1]element still persists, the stableness of the Dhamma, the fixed course of the Dhamma, specific conditionality" (translation Bodhi 2000: 551, see also his n. 51); [1]Bodhi's "element" should rather be translated as "law" or "[true] nature [of things]" – see Schmithausen 1969: 146f. Cf. also SN I.298-299 where conditionality and dependent-arising are presented side-by-side as synonyms. Cf. the Buddhist opponent's equating of the two as characteristics of ultimate truth at PsP_L 159.6; Candrakīrti, defining the teaching of dependent-arising as referring to conditionality at YṢV_{ed} 22.3, declares this teaching to be the cause for the seeing of the two truths (see also YṢV_{tr} 109, n. 21). The Madhyamaka reinterpretation of dependent-arising from a principle expressing the way in which real effects arise from real causes to the signifier of the conditionedness of all things, a fact that entails and proves their lack of real existence, becomes a powerful means for refuting views and arguments that maintain a *svabhāva* of things (cf. MABh_{ed} 228.5-11). It is nevertheless the conditionality of worldly things that allows for the assertion of them and—seen from the (ultimately erroneous) point of view of the world—allows for their "establishment" on the level of the surface truth; cf. PsP_L 189.1-3, PsP_L 234.6 and YṢV_{ed} 84.3-5. Further references at PsP_L 9, n. 8 and May 1959: 122, n. 319.

arising of this, that arises,"[86] is the meaning of *pratītya-samutpāda*,[87]

is not appropriate because a specific meaning for each of the words *pratītya* and *samutpāda* has not been stated and because an analysis (*vyutpāda*) of it [i.e., of the compound *pratītyasamutpāda*] was intended.

§13. Even if [Bhāviveka,] having accepted the word *pratītyasamutpāda* as a word that is employed in a conventional sense (*rūḍhiśabda*), like "sesame in the forest," etc., (*araṇyetilakādi*) [the

---

[86] Sanskrit: *asmin satīdaṃ bhavaty asyotpādād idam utpadyate*; Pāli: *imasmiṃ sati idaṃ hoti imass' uppādā idaṃ uppajjati* (e.g., MN I.262-263, II.32, III.63; SN II.28.7, II.65.5-6; further references at Pāsādika 1989: 60; PsP_L 9, n. 7; La Vallée Poussin 1913a: 50, n. 1). De La Vallée Poussin (1913a: 49) asserts that the statement is "[l]a plus archaïque des formules de causation." On preformulaic expressions of the idea, see Nakamura 1980. The formula as found in the Canonical texts is usually followed by or occurs in close proximity to its negated form: *imasmiṃ asati idaṃ na hoti imassa nirodhā idaṃ nirujjhati*. Nakamura points out that although the formula is usually set forth in connection with the twelve-linked dependent-arising, it is also referred to independently, as at MN II.32 in a conversation about past and future lives. In the AKBh, Vasubandhu presents a number of views that explain the apparent repetition of meaning in the sentences *asmin satīdaṃ bhavati* and *asyotpādād idam utpadyate*, views worked out, at least in part, to defend the Buddhist citing the formula in debate from the opponent's charge of *paunaruktya* (repetition), a point of defeat (*nigrahasthāna*); see $AKBh_{ed}$ 138.28-139.24; $AKBh_{tr}$ III.81-83; Stalker 1987: 193-198; La Vallée Poussin 1913a 50-51. See also the formula as cited from the Paramārthaśūnyatāsūtra at $MABh_{ed}$ 226.16-18.
Cf. also the Buddhist opponent's presentation of the formula at PsP_L 159.7-10. For Nāgārjuna and Candrakīrti, the formula belongs exclusively to the level of the surface truth (*saṃvṛtisatya*), inapplicable to the ultimate (*paramārtha*) level because nothing exists there; cf. MMK I.10: *bhāvānāṃ niḥsvabhāvānāṃ na sattā vidyate yataḥ | satīdam asmin bhavatīty etan naivopapadyate ||*. Although not relevant to the formula as used in the PsP, see also the unusual interpretation of the formula set forth by Prajñākaragupta in Franco 2007.

[87] Candrakīrti is citing from Bhāviveka's PP. PP Tib: *'o na gang yin zhe na | 'di yod na* (PsP: *'di yod pas*) *'di 'byung la 'di skyes pa'i phyir 'di skye ba ste zhes bya ba rkyen 'di dang ldan pa nyid kyi don ni | rten cing 'brel par 'byung ba'i don to* (P: ||) *zhes zer ro* || (PP D 46b4; P 55a1-2). Cf. $AKBh_{ed}$ 138.17-18: *eṣa tu vākyārthaḥ | asmin saty asya bhāvaḥ, asyotpādād idam utpadyata iti yo 'rthaḥ so 'rthaḥ pratītyasa-mutpāda iti |*.

meaning of which does not correspond to its individual parts],[88] states [the meaning] in this way [i.e., as above, "when this is present, that comes to be, from the arising of this, that arises," etc.], that too is not suitable, because the Ācārya [Nāgārjuna] accepts that the [compound] word *pratītyasamutpāda* precisely corresponds to the meaning of its members, [as evident in the YṢ verse-half:]

> That which has arisen attaining this and that [cause] has not arisen by own nature.[89]

§14. But with [*pratītyasamutpāda*] being explained [as]

> When this is present, that comes to be, as when there's short, there's long,"[90]

---

[88] Cf. the entry for *rūḍha/rūḍhi* in Renou 1957: 259: "*rūḍhi* 'sens traditionnel (conventionnel)' d'un mot, opp. à *yoga* ... [u]n mot de r° est caractérisé par le fait que la dérivation n'y est pas sujette à règle (*vyutpatter aniyamaḥ*)." "Sesame in the forest" (*araṇyetilaka*) is given as an example in Kāś to Pā 2.1.44's "*saṃjñāyām*," according to which a word ending in the seventh case marker is compounded with a word ending in a case marker and becomes a *tatpuruṣa* compound [i.e., the seventh case marker is not elided] when this compound is an appellative. Wild sesame does not yield oil and is thus used as a designation for anything that does not answer to one's expectations; the meaning of *araṇyetilaka* therefore is not derived directly from the meaning of its component parts. *LṬ comments: *avyutpanna evāyam araṇyetilakaśabdaḥ* (ms: °*kāśabdaḥ*) (cf. Yonezawa 2004: 121, 130 [fol. 1b4]). Other such compounds mentioned in Kāś are *vanekiṃśuka* (a blossoming *Butea frondosa* tree in a forest), *vanebilvaka* (a wood-apple tree in a forest), and *kūpepiśācaka* (a demon in a well), all used as designations for things found unexpectedly.

[89] Candrakīrti again cites YṢ 19ab. See n. 84.

[90] Cp. RĀ I.48: *asmin satīdaṃ bhavati dīrghe hrasvaṃ yathā sati* | *asyotpādād udetīdaṃ dīpotpādād yathā prabhā* ||. RĀ I.48 is cited at MABh_{ed} 227.1-4 as: *'di yod pas na 'di 'byung dper* || *ring po yod na thung ngu bzhin* || *'di skyes pas na 'di skye dper* || *mar me 'byung bas 'od bzhin no* || (RĀ Tib as MABh Tib but with the variant *ring po yod pas thung ngu bzhin*). The citation here in the PsP presents the order *hrasve dīrgham* (PsP Tib translates accordingly) instead of *dīrghe hrasvam* as in the RĀ and the corresponding Tib of the MABh. Hahn (1982: 20, n. 48b) records that both RĀ Tib and RĀ Chinese support the text of RĀ I.48b. If Candrakīrti is actually citing from the RĀ, it is possible, given that the metre is not affected by the reading found in PsP, that he simply reversed the order of long and short, possibly influenced by the fact that RĀ I.49 commences with *hrasve* in the initial position: *hrasve 'sati punar dīrghaṃ*. He may alternatively have had a RĀ manuscript, or been familiar with an RĀ tradition, that presented I.48 as he cites it.

isn't it the case that exactly that [which we maintain] ends up being accepted, [namely,] depending on [something] short, [i.e.,] attaining [something] short, relying on [something] short, [something else] comes to be [that which is] long?[91] And thus [Bhāviveka] accepts exactly what he criticizes — this is not reasonable. Enough of this digression.

§15. Therefore, [the positions] that things arise without a cause (*ahetu*), from a single cause (*ekahetu*), or from a non-corresponding cause (*viṣamahetu*),[92] and [the positions] that they are created from

---

Cp. MABh$_{ed}$ 150.9-10: *dper na ring po yod na thung ngur 'gyur la thung ngu yod na ring por 'gyur zhing* | *pha rol yod na tshu rol du 'gyur la tshu rol yod na pha rol tu 'gyur ba ltar btags par 'gyur gyi de dag la grub pa rang bzhin pa med do* ||; ŚSV$_{ed}$ 250.35-36: *pha rol dang tshu rol bzhin nam ring po dang thung ngu bzhin rgyu dang 'bras bu dang phan tshun ltos pa dang bcas pa'i phyir ngo bo nyid kyis grub pa med do* ||; also PsP$_L$ 458.14-15 (*pārāvaravat ... hrasvadīrghavat*); 459.5 and 459.9; 101.14 (*pārāvaravat*); YṢV$_{ed}$ 71.18-19 (*ring po dang* | *thung du* (read: *ngu*) *bzhin du 'am* | *mar me'i 'od bzhin*); RĀ I.95 (*ring dang thung*).

[91] The Naiyāyikas Vātsyāyana and Uddyotakara present and critique the Madhyamaka short–long example for dependent existence in their commentaries on NS IV.1.39 (*na svabhāvasiddhir āpekṣikatvāt*) and IV.1.40. Vātsyāyana presents the *pūrvapakṣa* thus: *apekṣākṛtam āpekṣikam* | *hrasvāpekṣākṛtaṃ dīrghaṃ dīrghāpekṣākṛtaṃ ca hrasvaṃ na svenātmanāvasthitaṃ kiñcit* | *kasmāt? apekṣāsāmarthyāt* | *tasmān na svabhāvasiddhir bhāvānām* || (NBh 238.5-7). Vātsyāyana asks if a long thing is "made" in reliance on a short one, and the short one is without reliance [in this special relationship], in reliance on what other thing then will the short one be grasped as short? Thus when one of two things that are mutually reliant does not exist, since the other cannot exist without it, neither can exist. Thus, the establishment of reliance as presented by the Mādhyamika is not appropriate: *yadi hrasvāpekṣākṛtaṃ dīrgham, hrasvam anāpekṣikam* | *kim idānīm apekṣya hrasvam iti gṛhyate? atha dīrghāpekṣākṛtaṃ hrasvam, dīrgham anāpekṣikam, kim idānīm apekṣya dīrgham iti gṛhyate? evam itaretarāśrayayor ekābhāve 'nyatarābhāvād ubhayābhāva ity apekṣāvyavasthānupapannā* | (NBh 238.10-13; cp. NV 453.10-12). Among other reasonings, Uddyotakara argues that reliance between things is possible only when an own-being of things is established: *svabhāvasiddhau cāsatyām apekṣā na prāpnoti* | (NV 454.1).

[92] The same triad is found in Candrakīrti's commentary on CŚ VIII.8 (CŚṬ$_{ed}$ 128.3-5): *yatra saṃsārapravṛttikramo 'vidyāsaṃskārādinā krameṇāhetvekahetuviṣamahetuvināśārthaṃ svasāmānyalakṣaṇasatyatvakalpanayā deśyate* | *jñātavyaṃ viduṣā pravṛttis tatra varṇyata iti* |. Although one finds *ahetu* and *visamahetu* discussed together in certain Pāli texts, the string *ahetvekahetuvisamahetu* does not seem to occur in the Pāli texts; Candrakīrti may have known it from the works of other

self, other, or both [self and other], end up refuted through the Exalted One illuminating in this way the arising of things in reliance on causes and conditions. And because they are refuted, the surface (*sāṃvṛta*) own nature of surface things, just as it is, becomes revealed.[93] Now because just that surface [level] dependent-arising (*pratītyasamutpāda*) has not arisen by own nature it is, with respect to the gnosis of the Nobles, qualified by the eight qualifiers beginning with "without cessation"—in the sense that cessation (*nirodha*), up to and including going (*nirgama*),[94] are not found in it.[95] And the way in which cessation and so forth do not exist for dependent-arising will be explained by the entire treatise. Even though infinite qualifiers are possible for dependent-arising, there is the employment of just these

---

schools. *LṬ exemplifies single cause (*ekahetu*) with *īśvara* and non-corresponding cause (*viṣamahetu*) with *nityānityahetutvam* (cf. Yonezawa 2004: 121, 130 [fol. 1b4]). Cp. Mūlapaṇṇāsa-ṭīkā: "*Natthi hetu natthi paccayo sattānaṃ saṃkilesāyā*" *ti ādinayappavattā ahetukadiṭṭhi.* "*Issarapurisapajāpatipakati-aṇukālādhīhi loko pavattati nivattati cā*" *ti pavattā visamahetudiṭṭhi* (Chaṭṭha Saṅgāyana CD s.v. *visamahetudiṭṭhi*; the same explanation appears in Khandhavagga-ṭīkā). See also AS where the exposition of *pratītyasamutpāda* is said to be for the sake of abandoning attachment to *ātman* and the wrong ideas that *dharma*s originate from non-causes and non-corresponding causes: *ahetuviṣamahetukātmābhiniveśatyājanārtham* (cf. Gokhale 1947: 26); Kritzer (1999: 23 and n. 34) draws attention to the fact that the ASBh on the AS statement exemplifies *viṣamahetu* with *īśvara*.

93 The 12-limbed formula of dependent-arising elucidating the causes of rebirth and of suffering (and thereby indicating the factors that must be eradicated for their elimination) and external dependent-arising considered as explaining the unfolding of the cosmos, both described in the Canon, and dependent-arising extended to all factors of existence (which in the Abhidharma schools becomes accepted as a general principle underlying all causal interaction [cf., e.g., Cox 1993]), are all accepted by the Mādhyamikas—on the surface level. However, nothing real arises by way of dependent-arising, for that which arises in dependence is bereft of own-being. The surface things (*sāṃvṛtāḥ padārthāḥ*) are fictions, recognized as such by the Nobles who consider dependently arisen things to be similar to the objects created by a magician. ŚSV on ŚS *kārikā* 1 distinguishes *sāṃvṛta* and *pāramārthika*; see Erb 1997: 212.23ff. and 37ff.

94 In order that the qualifier given accords with the final one of the translated Tibetan verse, PsP Tib must refer to *don gcig* instead of *'gro ba*.

95 Paraphrased in Seyfort Ruegg 1977: 4. PsP Tib's explanation of the individual words of the introductory verses is inserted here.

eight because they are predominantly the limbs (i.e., major topics) of debate (*vivādāṅga*).[96]

§16. And since manifoldness (*prapañca*), characterized as name (*abhidhāna*) and what is named (*abhidheya*), etc.,[97] stops in all

---

[96] Buddhapālita responds in detail to the questioner in BP who asks why all eight qualifiers are refuted and who suggests that the refutation of just the first four is sufficient, namely, of *nirodha*, *utpāda*, *uccheda* and *śāśvata*: *'dir smras pa | ci'i phyir 'gag pa la sogs pa brgyad po de dag 'gog par byed | 'gag pa med pa skye med pa || chad pa med pa rtag med pa || zhes bya ba de tsam zhig byas pas mi chog gam* (see BP_{ed} 4.23-5.2). He answers that proponents of an own-being of things generally teach that things are existent by way of these eight, and that whoever reflects on reality or starts a debate does so in reliance on ideas of cessation and so forth. As support for his assertion, Buddhapālita cites persons who declare that "All things, [in that they] are subject to arising and ceasing, are momentary and occur in continuous sequence (**prabandhena pravartante*)" (*re zhig kha cig na re dngos po thams cad ni skye ba dang 'gag pa'i chos can skad cig ma ste rgyun gyis rgyun du 'byung ngo || zhes zer ro*) and then lists various opponents who argue for the eternity, identity, difference and movement of specific substances and/or qualities posited by their respective systems (Saito identifies the former group as Vaibhāṣikas; all identifications in the following rely on Saito 1984; see BP_{tr} 5). The eternalist views presented are those of the Sāṅkhyas, who maintain that primordial matter (*prakṛti*) and spirit (*puruṣa*) are eternal, of the Vaiśeṣikas, who hold that the ten substances such as earth (*pṛthivi*), etc., are eternal, and of the Jainas, whom Buddhapālita describes as maintaining that the six substances, viz., principle of movement (*dharma*), principle of rest (*adharma*), space (*ākāśa*), time (*kāla*), matter (*pudgala*) and soul (*jīva*) are eternal. These schools are additionally said to dispute in regard to whether the soul and body, fire and fuel, cause and effect, quality and qualificand, and part and whole are identical or different. As examples of schools that propound movement, the Sāṅkhyas are presented as maintaining that the [three] constituents of primordial matter (*guṇa*) possess activity and that the subtle body (*liṅga*) transmigrates (*kha cig na re yon tan bya ba dang ldan pa rnams dang rtags 'khor ro zhes zer ro* [BP_{ed} 5.19]), the Vaiśeṣikas(?) as claiming that atoms and mind (*manas*) move (BP_{ed} 5.20 attests *gzhan dag na re rdul dang yid gnyis ni mi 'gro'o zhes zer ro*; the negation appears to be an error), and again the Jainas as maintaining that both soul and matter have/possess movement (*'gro ba dang ldan*) and that the soul ascends upon attaining perfection (on this last point—an example for *nirgama*—see Frauwallner 1984: 207f.)

[97] PsP Tib: *brjod bya dang rjod byed dang | mtshan nyid dang mtshon bya la sogs pa* (**abhidheyābhidhānalakṣaṇalakṣyādi*) for *abhidhānābhidheyādilakṣaṇa*. Supportive of the Sanskrit is the fact that Candrakīrti defines *prapañca* elsewhere as having the characteristic (*lakṣaṇa*) of speech (see the following note). One would further expect the order *mtshon bya dang mtshan nyid* (similar to the order *brjod bya dang rjod byed*) were PsP Tib to reflect the original reading. *mtshon bya* thus appears to be a

respects for the Nobles when they see dependent-arising as it really is, that very dependent-arising is called "the calming of manifoldness" (*prapañcopaśama*)[98]—in the sense that there is the

---

later determined addition, which additionally required the movement of *ādi* to the end of the compound. Tib's *ādi*, though relocated, supports ms P's reading over that of ms Q, which lacks it.

[98] On *prapañca* (and the adjectives *niṣprapañca* and *aprapañca*), see especially Schmithausen 1969: 137-142 [= n. 101] where the various aspects of *prapañca* in its dual form of subjective mental acts and the objective products, or correlates thereof, viz., the world of manifold appearances, as documented specifically, but not only, in the Yogācāra school, are discussed. As Schmithausen (ibid., 140f.) explains, *prapañca* as mental activity denotes a subjective act which is characterized by the fact that the subject does not remain calmly in the direct vision of reality but rather elevates above it or expands over it by reflecting and naming; depending on the context, some passages set the content-oriented aspect of proliferation or transference of manifold or false qualifications in the foreground, others the formal aspect of mental activity or restlessness (on *prapañca* see also May 1959: 175-6, n. 562; Lugli 2011). In the sentence here in the PsP, Candrakīrti describes *prapañca* as both name (*abhidhāna*) and the objects named (*abhidheya*) (on speech also as a mental act, cf. Schmithausen 1969: 139.2.a). In his commentary on MMK XVIII.9, Candrakīrti takes as his focus the subjective side of *prapañca* by defining it as speech, explaining that it diversifies the objects perceived: *prapañco hi vāk, prapañcayaty arthān iti kṛtvā* (PsP_L 373.9-10; cf. Schmithausen 1969: 137f. A.1.a.). Schmithausen (ibid., note a) writes that speech as a mental act is often equated with *prapañca* but that speech is also often considered the means of expression of the mental *prapañca*. In his commentary on MMK XVIII.5 Candrakīrti describes *prapañca* as having the characteristic of *jñānajñeyavācyavācakakartṛkarmakaraṇakriyāghaṭapaṭamukuṭa-ratharūpavedanāstrīpuruṣalābhālābhasukhaduḥkhayaśo'yaśonindāpraśaṃsādi*, thus all possible conceptualizing diversification connected with speech, which provides the basis for and gives rise to inappropriate conceptuality (*ayoniśo vikalpa*). As stated in MMK XVIII.5, all *prapañca* stops in emptiness, i.e., with the realization that nothing exists; see Candrakīrti's continued commentary in which the ceasing of *prapañca* and *vikalpa*, etc., in the absence of an object to be perceived is likened to the non-descent of the "net" of *prapañca* for lustful persons in the absence of a beautiful young woman.

Both the author of the ABh and Bhāviveka similarly define *prapañca* as naming (**abhilāpa*) in their commentaries on MMK XVIII.9: *mngon par brjod pa'i mtshan nyid kyi spros pa* (ABh_{ed} 438.13-14; PP P 237b3). Commenting on MMK XVIII.5, the author of the ABh states that *prapañca* is characterized by attachment to the truth of linguistic and conceptual practice (*tha snyad kyi bden pa la mngon par zhen pa'i mtshan nyid kyi spros pa* [ABh_{ed} 431.16-17]; Schmithausen [1969: 138] reconstructs **vyavahārasatyābhiniveśalakṣaṇaḥ prapañcaḥ*); that is, one becomes attached to the content of the *prapañca* in the mistaken assumption that it is reality. Bhāviveka

calming of instances of manifoldness in it. And because [it] is entirely without the misfortunes of birth, old age, death[99] and so forth owing to the ceasing of [any] dealing with [the dichotomies] cognition (*jñāna*) and cognizables (*jñeya*) in view [of the fact] that mind and mental factors (*cittacaitta*) do not arise in it, it is "[ultimate] welfare" (*śiva*).[100] Dependent-arising, qualified as stated, is indicated as the [grammatical direct] object (*karman*) [for the verses] because it is what is primarily aimed at (*īpsitatamatvāt*) by [the Exalted One's] activity of teaching.[101]

---

glosses *prapañca* of *prapañcopaśama* of the homage verse as *brjod pa'i bdag nyid* (PP P 56a2-3; D 47a7-48a1: *brjod pa'i bdag nyid* [*la*] *mngon par zhen pa zhi ba'i phyir*; *la* is attested in all citations of the sentence in PPṬ). Avalokitavrata explains *brjod pa* as *brjod par bya ba'i dngos po rnams mngon sum du byas te tshig gi sgrar brjod pa* "designation/expression in the sound of words once one has directly perceived the things to be named" (PPṬ D 44a3-4; P 50b8). It might be noted that Prajñākaramati's BCAP citation of the Āryasatyadvayāvatārasūtra includes a description of *paramārthasatya* as *abhidheyābhidhānajñeyajñānavigata* (BCAP 366.14).

99 PsP Tib adds the often associated further member "illness": *skye ba dang rga ba dang na ba dang 'chi ba la sogs pa.*

100 The word *śiva* of the homage verses has been interpreted and translated in various ways by modern scholars, in some cases by way of the nouns "bliss," "happiness," "beatitude," and the adjective "blissful." Such translations are problematic because they suggest, in the face of explicit Madhyamaka statements that it is the stopping of consciousness (*vijñāna*) and thus the discontinuance of all conceptualizing and of all (invariably temporary) positive and negative affects associated with and based on conceptuality that makes way for the experience of *nirvāṇa*, that the attainment of *nirvāṇa* may be equated with or entails the experience of a positive affect. Other translators, primarily those translating from the Tibetan, where *śiva* is rendered as *zhi ba*, have elected to represent the word with adjectives such as "peaceful," "tranquil," or "still." *śiva* of the homage verses has also been inappropriately translated as "auspicious."
It is important to give due accord to Candrakīrti's own clarification of the word *śiva*. With his explanation that *pratītyasamutpāda* is *śiva* because it is free of the misfortunes of birth, old age, death, etc. (*jātijarāmaraṇādiniravaśeṣopadravarahita*), he stresses *śiva*'s historically prominent aspect of safety and freedom from harm. Note that he uses the word *upadrava* to characterize that which is not *śiva* (cf. PW s.v. *upadrava*: widerwärtiger Zufall, Unfall ... Unheil). I therefore translate *śiva* as "[ultimate] welfare."

101 The reference here is to the definition of the grammatical object at Pā 1.4.49: *kartur īpsitatamaṃ karma* "the object is that which the agent most wishes to reach

§17. [Homage verses I-IIa-d_1:]

[He] who fully awakened taught dependent-arising [which is]

Without cessation, without arising, without annihilation, not eternal,
Without one thing, without separate things, without coming, without going,[102]

[through its action]," on which the Kāś comments: *kartuḥ kriyayā yad āptum iṣṭatamaṃ tat kārakaṃ karmasaṃjñaṃ bhavati.* Candrakīrti wishes to say that the words of the homage verses have been purposely arranged to allow for *pratītya-samutpāda* to be declined in the accusative case because *pratītyasamutpāda* is indeed that which the agent (*kartṛ*), i.e., the Buddha, with his action (*kriyā*) of teaching, is most intent upon.
This "pirouette" on the Pāṇinian *sūtra* appears to have been borrowed from Bhāviveka's PP. Bhāviveka includes this citation of Pā 1.4.49 when he defends all eight qualifiers of dependent-arising being negated in ultimate reality: *mdzad pa pos bstan pa nyid kyis bzhed pa mchog yin pa'i phyir* (PP D 47a7; P 56a2; see also PPṬ D 43b6-44a2; P 50b2-6). The *sūtra* is referred to again at PsP_L 180.14, 324.10, and 465.2. For a non-traditional interpretation of Pā 1.4.49, see Oetke 2001b: 62ff.

[102] Although the dependent-arising expounded in the homage verses as coterminous with *nirvāṇa* pertains to the ultimate nature of dependently arisen things, i.e., to the fact that dependently arisen things have in reality never arisen, the last six qualifiers also appear in traditional expositions of dependent-arising. In the PP, Bhāviveka is in fact confronted by a Buddhist opponent who argues that all eight qualifiers of dependent-arising are accepted by *śrāvaka*s and thus the composition of the MMK is unnecessary. According to this opponent, dependent-arising is without arising in the sense that a result different from, i.e., incongruous with, its conditions does not arise (PP D 48a5; P 57b5: *skye ba med pa ni de las gzhan skye ba med pa'i phyir*; for the previous and an alternative explanation, see PPṬ D 54b5-55a3; P 63a1-7); that which arises would not be "without arising" in this sense in the case of arising from *īśvara* (*dper na dbang phyug las dngos po rnams mi skye'o zhes gsungs pa las na | dbang phyug ma yin pa las dngos po rnams skye bar shes* [PPṬ D 55a3-4; P 63a7]). This same opponent considers dependent-arising to be without cessation because it is without the ceasing imagined by the non-Buddhists (*tīrthika*s) such as that considered as occurring when one says "without self" (for these and the other qualifiers, see PP D 48a5-7; P 57a5-57b1; Kajiyama 1963: 46f.; Ames 1993: 219f.; La Vallée Poussin 1933: 11f.). Bhāviveka replies that his own view of dependent-arising greatly differs, for the Madhyamaka teaches that arising has the nature of non-arising. Reference to things not having arisen or ceased in this sense, i.e., as intended in the PsP homage verses, is found throughout Prajñāpāramitā literature; cf. e.g., Aṣṭa 6.17; 135.11-15.
Traditional dependent-arising posited as involving the arising of real things from real causes is praised by Conservative Buddhism as avoiding the extremes of eternalism and nihilism. Cf. the Śālistambasūtra's statement regarding the arising of a sprout

from a seed: *pratītyasamutpādaḥ ... kathaṃ na śāśvatata iti? yasmād anyo 'ṅkuro 'nyad bījam, na ca yad eva bījaṃ sa evāṅkuraḥ | atha vā punaḥ bījaṃ nirudhyate, aṅkuraś cotpadyate | ato na śāśvatataḥ | kathaṃ nocchedataḥ? na ca pūrvaniruddhād bījād aṅkuro niṣpadyate, nāpy aniruddhād bījāt, api ca, bījaṃ ca nirudhyate, tasminn eva samaye 'ṅkura utpadyate, tulādaṇḍonnāmāvanāmavat | ato nocchedataḥ* (cf. Schoening 1995: 285, 706; on internal (*ādhyātmika*) dependent-arising being without eternity and annihilation see the Śālistambasūtra passage quoted in PsP at PsP_L 569.1-9; cp. Schoening 1995: 324, 731f.). Cf. also Candrakīrti's citation of the Lalitavistara at PsP_M §41. The Ābhidharmika's defence of traditional dependent-arising as free of the faults of eternity and annihilation at PsP_L 422.5-14 is rejected by Candrakīrti; for Mādhyamikas, the positing of the arising of real things entails both extremes (cf. also, e.g., MMK XV.10-11 and corresponding PsP; $MABh_{ed}$ 229.8-12; YṢV on YṢ 43 and 44).

On interpretations of *anekārtha* and *anānārtha* found in Western scholarship, see Tachikawa 1981. Tachikawa points to MMK XVIII.11 (*anekārtham anānārtham anucchedam aśāśvatam | etat tal lokanāthānāṃ buddhānāṃ śāsanāmṛtam ||*) and XVIII.9 (*aparapratyayaṃ śāntaṃ prapañcair aprapañcitam | nirvikalpam anānārtham etat tattvasya lakṣaṇam ||*) as substantiation for *anekārtha* and *anānārtha* of the homage verses being intended by Nāgārjuna as *bahuvrīhi* compounds, and provides an explanation for the Tibetan and Chinese translations of *anekārtha* and *anānārtha* as *karmadhāraya* compounds. Tachikawa, taking into consideration Candrakīrti's commentary on MMK XVIII.9 and 11 according to which *ekārtha* may be taken to mean *ekārthatva* ("being one object") and *nānārtha anyārthatva* ("being different objects"), concludes that Candrakīrti's identification of one factor (*ekārtha*) with the relation between two factors (*ekārthatva*) is also intended by Nāgārjuna in the homage verse. Certainly, the refutation of two things standing in a relation of dependence as being one thing or different/separate things is an important argument of Nāgārjuna's that he utilizes on a number of occasions in the MMK (whether Nāgārjuna would agree in each case with Candrakīrti's interpretation of the relevant *kārikā*s is another question); see, e.g., MMK II.18-20, where the unacceptable consequences of *gamana* and *gantā* posited as (numerically) one or other are set forth (cf. Oetke's comments in Oetke 2001a: 78-79), and Nāgārjuna's conclusion couched in a rhetorical question at MMK II.21: *ekībhāvena vā siddhir nānābhāvena vā yayoḥ | na vidyate tayoḥ siddhiḥ kathaṃ nu khalu vidyate ||*; MMK VI.4 and 5 where the simultaneous arising of desire and the desirer, be the two one thing or two different things, is shown to be impossible (cf. Oetke 2001a: 92-94); and MMK XXI.10 where *sambhava* and *vibhāva* are asserted to be not logically possible as (numerically) one or different. Canonical forerunners of such one/other arguments may be found at, e.g., SN II.61.75-76. Note also Prajñākaramati's apparent reliance at BCAP 421.5-7 on concepts presented in the homage verses: ... *ekānekasvabhāvaviviktam anutpannāniruddham anucchedam aśāśvataṃ sarvaprapañcavinirmuktam ākāśapratisamaṃ dharmakāyākhyaṃ paramārthatattvam ucyate.*

The seeing of twelve-linked dependent-arising is stated in the Canon to free the disciple of questions such as where he has come from and where he will go after

The calming of manifoldness, [ultimate] welfare,
To him I pay homage.

And the Master [Nāgārjuna], seeing that just the Tathāgata alone, owing to [his] understanding of dependent-arising as it has been described, expounds the correct meaning, and having deemed the discourse (*pravāda*) of all others to resemble the prattle (*pralāpa*) of children, completely filled with faith, further qualifies the Exalted One [as]:

[Homage verse $2d_2$:]

the best of expounders (*vadatāṃ varam*).[103]

---

death (*ahaṃ nu kho satto kuto āgato so kuhiṃgāmī bhavissatī ti*; cf. SN II.26-27; MN I.8 [*ayaṃ* for *ahaṃ*]). Cp. the Śālistambasūtra on twelve-linked dependent-arising as explaining rebirth quoted in PsP: *pratyutpannaṃ vā punar na pratisarati ... ayaṃ sattvaḥ kuta āgataḥ | sa itaś cyutaḥ kutra gamiṣyatīti* (cited PsP_L 593.11-594.1; cf. Schoening 1995: 328, 735; cp. SN II.27) and *tatra na kaścid dharmo 'smāl lokāt paralokaṃ saṃkrāmate* (cited PsP_L 568.4; cf. Schoening 1995: 321, 729). The Udānavarga's famous verse of its twenty-sixth chapter (*nirvāṇavarga*), viz., *abhijānāmy ahaṃ sthānaṃ yatra bhūtaṃ na vidyate | nākāśaṃ na ca vijñānaṃ na sūryaś candramā na ca ||* (26.24), is followed by the verse *naivāgatir na ca gatir nopapattiś cyutir na ca | apratiṣṭham anālambaṃ duḥkhāntaḥ sa nirucyate ||* (26.25); see Bernhard 1965: 329. Reference to *dharma*s neither coming nor going occurs in Prajñāpāramitā literature, but here the reason given is not, as it is in Conservative Buddhism, that the dependent-arising of real factors explains the lack of an enduring being or factors that would come or go, rather that things do not come or go because they have not arisen, that is, do not exist; see, e.g., Aṣṭa 235.14-15: *sarvadharmā nāgacchanti na gacchanty ajānānā ajātā atyantājātita iti prajñāpāramitā anugantavyā*. The beginning of Aṣṭa chapter 31 teaches that the Tathāgatas neither come nor go (e.g., *tadyathāpi nāma kulaputra māyākāranirmitasya hastikāyasya vā aśvakāyasya vā rathakāyasya vā pattikāyasya vā nāsty āgamanaṃ vā gamanaṃ vā, evam eva kulaputra nāsti tathāgatānām āgamanaṃ vā gamanaṃ vā* [Aṣṭa 253.26-28]). In BCAP it is argued that real *dharma*s would be unchanging; there do not exist *dharma*s with a real, that is, enduring, own-being that come from somewhere and then, "ceasing," go to a "*dharma* reservoir": *nāpi sa utpadyamānaḥ satsvarūpeṇa kutaścid āgacchati nirudhyamāno vā kvacit saṃnicayaṃ gacchati* (354.13-15). Note too Candrakīrti's reference to *anāgamānirgamapratītyasamutpāda* in his introduction to the second chapter of MMK/PsP at PsP_L 92.3-5. See additionally the explanations of the eight qualifiers in ABh (ABh_{ed} 242.9ff.; ABh_{tr} 2ff.)

[103] Bhāviveka delineates "expounders" (*smra rnams*) as *śrāvaka*s, *pratyekabuddha*s and *bodhisattva*s, for they, inasmuch as they teach dependent-arising correctly, teach

§18. And here the negation of cessation is first in order to show that a determination of priority and posteriority is not established for arising and cessation.[104] For he (= Nāgārjuna) will say:

> If birth were earlier, old age and death later,
> Birth would be without old age and death, and one who has not died would be born.[105]

---

the path that facilitates attainment of the higher realms and liberation (cf. PP D 47b2; P 56a4-5); he additionally includes comments on the words *sambuddha*, *deśayāmāsa* and *vara* (see Kajiyama 1963: 44; Ames 1993: 217f.). At Buddhacarita 6.42, Prince Siddhārtha, explaining his leave-taking to the grief-stricken Chandaka, is also called *vadatāṃ varaḥ*. This formulaic phrase is of course not limited to Buddhist literature; Brockington has noted that the third most frequent phrase involving the words *varaḥ* or *śreṣṭhaḥ* in the Mahābhārata is *vadatāṃ varaḥ* (63 occurrences; 12 occurrences of *vadatāṃ śreṣṭhaḥ*), and that after *rāmo dharmabṛtāṃ varaḥ* it is the second most frequent one in the Rāmāyaṇa (9 occurrences; cf. Brockington 1998: 114 and 369f.)

[104] Compare the statement here in the PsP with BP_{ed} 9.11-12: *de gnyis la snga phyi'i rnam par bzhag pa med pa de nyid rab tu bstan pa'i phyir*. Justification for the order of *anirodha* and *anutpāda* in the first homage verse is also found in the commentaries by Buddhapālita and Bhāviveka. Buddhapālita devotes a long section to refuting the opponent's objection that *anutpāda* should appear before *anirodha* in the verse, citing, as Candrakīrti also does presumably in reliance on his commentary, MMK XI.3; see BP_{ed} 6.2-9.13, BP_{tr} 6-9. Bhāviveka responds to the PP opponent who likewise argues that *anutpāda* should appear first with one of the arguments used already by Buddhapālita: since *saṃsāra* has no beginning, cessation also precedes arising (for his full response see PP D 48a1-2; P 56b6-8 and Kajiyama 1963: 45f., Ames 1993: 218-219). See also the various reasons given for the order of the two words by the author of the ABh (ABh_{ed} 240.8-242.9.; ABh_{tr} 2f.). *LṬ glosses *siddhyabhāvam* "non-existence of establishment" with *kadācid utpādānantaraṃ nirodho nirodhāntaram* (read: *nirodhānantaram*?) *vā vināśaḥ*; *vināśa* must be an error (cf. Yonezawa 2004: 121, 131 [fol. 1b5]).

[105] Candrakīrti cites MMK XI.3: *pūrvaṃ jātir yadi bhavej jarāmaraṇam uttaram* | *nirjarāmaraṇā jātir bhavej jāyeta cāmṛtaḥ* ||. In his commentary on MMK XI.3, Candrakīrti argues, as Buddhapālita does in his comments on the order of *anirodha* and *anutpāda* in the homage verses, first, that in *saṃsāra* the death of a being precedes its birth; second, that trees (which the opponent argues are not preceded by [their own] cessation) arise when there is the perishing of their respective seeds; and third, that seed and tree are not different from each other, just as cause and effect are not established as being different from each other (cp. BP_{ed} 6.17-9.3). *LṬ: *amṛta eva sann utpadyeta pūrvaṃ maraṇādyabhāvāt* (cf. Yonezawa 2004: 121, 131 [fol. 1b5]).

Therefore, there is not this restriction (*niyama*) that arising should be earlier, cessation later.[106]

§19. Now, the Master [Nāgārjuna], wanting to explain dependent-arising qualified by "without cessation," etc., [and] considering that with the refutation of arising, the refutation of cessation and so forth would be easy, right away undertakes the refutation of arising. Having ascertained that the arising postulated by the opponents would of course[107] (*hi*) be postulated as from self (*svataḥ*), from other (*parataḥ*), from both (*ubhayataḥ*), or would be postulated as without a cause (*ahetutaḥ*)[108]—but is [in fact] in no way logically possible, he says:

[MMK I.1:]

> Not arisen from self, nor from other, nor from both or without a cause
> Do any things ever exist anywhere.[109]

---

[106] De La Vallée Poussin notes that PsP Tib has translated the equivalent of *janma pūrvaṃ bhavati, jarāmaraṇaṃ paścāt* for *pūrvam utpādena bhavitavyaṃ paścān nirodhena* (PsP_L 12, n. 4; Tib: *skye ba ni snga bar gyur la | rga shi ni phyis so*). It is possible, given that both *utpāda* and *jāti* are translated as *skye ba*, that *rga shi* represents an associative error. Slightly unusual is *gyur* for *bhavitavyam*, otherwise translated here in PsP Tib accompanied by *dgos* (PsP Tib consistently translates sentences containing the conjunction *yat* using relative–co-relative clauses).

[107] This is the only translation possible for *hi* when it is construed with the *iti* sentence. One wonders if it should instead be connected with the framing *niścityāha* ("For (*hi*), having ascertained that … he says: …"); for comments on *hi* construed in a similar way, see Schmithausen 2014, n. 1763. PsP Tib with *skye ba yang* does not reflect *utpādo hi* but rather *utpādo 'pi*, the *api* presumably understood as indicating a subject change.

[108] Compare the similar statement preceding MMK I.1 in PP: *slob dpon gyis* (P: *gyi*) ... *skye ba med pa bstan nas 'gag pa med pa la sogs pa khyad par bstan sla bar dgongs pa na skye ba med pa dang por bstan par bzhed nas | gzhan gyis yongs su brtag pa'i skye ba rnam par rtog pa mngon sum du mdzad de* (D: *da*) | *'di ltar skye bar smra ba dag las kha cig ni dngos po rnams bdag las skye'o zhes zer | gzhan dag ni gzhan las so zhes zer | kha cig ni gnyis las so zhes zer | gzhan dag ni rgyu med pa las so zhes zer* ... (D 48b1-3; P 57b3-6).

[109] MMK I.1: *na svato nāpi parato na dvābhyāṃ nāpy ahetutaḥ | utpannā jātu vidyante bhāvāḥ kvacana kecana* ||. Vetter considers the *kārikā* to be a sort of citation

§20. In this context, "ever" (*jātu*) means "at any time" (*kadācit*). The word "anywhere" (*kvacana*), referring to the location (*ādhāra*), is a synonym for the word "any place" (*kvacit*). The word "any" (*kecana*), referring to that which is located, is a synonym for "some" (*kecit*). And therefore the [syntactical] connection is thus: "Definitely not

---

from the Naḷakalāpīsutta (SN II.112-115)—a *sutta* in which the (ten) limbs of dependent-arising are negated as having arisen from self, other, both self and other or without a cause—that has been extended to all things (cf. also La Vallée Poussin 1933: 11). Vetter (1982: 99) states, "Wer aber erwartet, dass Nāgārjuna nun auch wie Sāriputta sagt: 'und doch ist *y* durch *x* bedingt,' wird enttäuscht. Nicht nur dass eine solche Bemerkung fehlt, es wird auch deutlich das Gegenteil gesagt und alles Bedingtsein und Bedingungsein geleugnet, wie z.B. im Schlussvers des ersten Kapitels." De La Vallée Poussin points to the four alternatives of DN III.137 applied to the self and the world (cf. La Vallée Poussin 1910: 279, n. 1). Translations of the *kārikā* into European languages are numerous and of unequal quality. Equally plausible are those by Oetke (2001a: 36), who, in criticizing the Weber-Brosamer and Back translation of the *kārikā*, suggests the two possibilities, "Weder aus sich selbst noch aus anderem noch aus beidem (d.h. sowohl aus sich als auch aus anderem) und auch nicht ohne Ursache entstandene irgendwelche Dinge finden sich jemals (*jātu*) irgendwo" and "Nirgendwo finden sich jemals (*jātu*) irgendwelche Dinge, seien sie aus sich selbst oder aus anderem oder aus beidem (d.h. sowohl aus sich als auch aus anderem) oder ohne [irgend]eine Ursache entstanden" and that by Vetter (1982: 99), who translates, "Es gibt niemals [und] nirgendwo irgendwelche Dinge, die aus sich selbst entstanden sind oder aus anderem oder aus beiden oder ohne Ursache," as well as that by Seyfort Ruegg (2002: 17): "Never anywhere do any entities (*bhāva* = *dṅos po*) exist (*vidyante* = *yod pa*) originated from self [i.e. themselves], nor from an other, nor from the two, nor from no cause." Less precise, for example, is that by Streng (1967: 183), who translates, "Never are any existing things found to originate from ...", thereby omitting an equivalent for *kvacana* and adding the non-mirrored qualifier "existing" which suggests that "existing things" originate in some fifth way. Siderits and Katsura (2013: 18) translate *kvacana* as "in any way." Garfield (1995: 105) appears to translate *nam yang* (*jātu*) as "whatever": "... Does anything whatever, anywhere arise" (the same translation for *nam yang* appears in Samten and Garfield 2006: 61). Garfield's (1995: 105-107) view of the intention of the *kārikā* as expressed in his own commentary is, in the light of Madhyamaka thought, problematic. I translate as I do in order to accommodate Candrakīrti's comments.

Candrakīrti cites the *kārikā* in his commentary on MA VI.7 ($MABh_{ed}$ 81.7-8; $MABh_{tr}$ 1910: 279); cf. also Lamotte 1966: 326 and 1970: 1638; PsP_L 12, n. 6. Cp. MMK XXI.13: *na svato jāyate bhāvaḥ parato naiva jāyate | na svataḥ parataś caiva jāyate jāyate kutaḥ ||*.

(*naiva*)[110] arisen from self do any things ever exist anywhere."[111] The [remaining] triad of propositions (*pratijñā*) ["from other," "from both" and "without a cause"] is to be connected in that same manner.

§21. [Objection:] But when the restrictive determination "definitely not arisen from self" (*naiva svata utpannāḥ*) is made, doesn't the undesired [implication] "arisen from other" (*parata utpannāḥ*) obtain? [Response: No,] it does not obtain since a non-presuppositional negation (*prasajyapratiṣedha*) is intended [not a presuppos-

[110] PsP Tib lacks an equivalent for *eva* here, but the restrictive particle is mirrored in the following *nanu ca* sentence (*gal te bdag las skye ba ma yin pa nyid do zhes bya ba* ...).

[111] The same words of MMK I.1 are glossed in MABh on MA VI.7, where *kvacana* (*gang na yang*) and *kecana* (*gang dag*) have been explained somewhat more extensively: the scope of *kvacana* is extended to place, time and tenet systems, while *kecana* is said to refer to internal and external things: *nam yang zhes bya ba ni gzhar yang zhes bya ba'i don to* ‖ *gang na yang zhes bya ba'i sgra 'gar yang gi sgra'i rnam grangs rten gyi tshig gis ni yul dang dus dang grub pa'i mtha' bshad do* ‖ *gang dag gi sgra rten* ($MABh_{UN}$: *brten*) *pa'i tshig ni phyi dang nang gi dngos po brjod pa'o* ‖ *des na phyi* ($MABh_{UN}$: *phyi dang*) *nang gi dngos po rnams ni yul dang dus dang grub pa'i mtha' 'gar yang bdag las skye ba srid pa ma yin no zhes 'di ltar sbyar bar bya'o* ‖ ($MABh_{ed}$ 81.9-15). Candrakīrti, in his commentary on MMK XXV.5cd (*nāsaṃskṛto vidyate hi bhāvaḥ kvacana kaścana* ‖), glosses: *kvacanety adhikaraṇe deśe kāle siddhānte vā* | *kaścanety ādheya ādhyātmiko bāhyo vety arthaḥ* (PsP_L 526.6-7: ... *kaścanety ādheye ādhyātmiko bāhyātmiko vety arthaḥ*; ms P, like ms D [see de Jong 1978: 245] attests *bāhyo*, not *bāhyātmiko* as found in de La Vallée Poussin's edition and in PsP Tib [ms P: ... *ādheye* | *ādhyātmiko* ...]). Bhāviveka had already in his PP explained *kvacana* as referring to tenet systems; he specifies *kecana* as defiled and pure things: *gang dag ces bya ba ni kun nas nyon mongs pa dang* | *rnam par byang ba'i dngos po dag go* | *gang na yang zhes bya ba* (P: *bas*) *ni rang gi mdzad pa'i mtha' dang* | *so so'i rgyud grub pa dag na yang ngo* | *nam yang zhes bya ba ni lan 'ga' yang ngo* ‖ (D 53a7-53b1; P 64a8-64b1; cf. Kajiyama 1963: 62; Ames 1993: 234). The author of the ABh does not mention tenet systems in his gloss of *kvacana*, but like Candrakīrti in the MABh and PsP chapter 25, specifies it as referring to time and place; *kecana* is glossed as "any things" (*dngos po 'ga' yang*), and *bhāva* (*dngos po*) as *dharmas*; he notes that one should connect the word *bhāva* with "common to all the non-Buddhists" (*dngos po zhes bya ba ni* | *chos rnams te dngos po zhes bya ba'i sgra ni 'di mu stegs can thams cad dang thun mong ngo zhes bya bar sbyar*; he glosses all the words and phrases of the *kārikā*; see ABh_{ed} 251.10-22; ABh_{tr} 9).

itional negation (*paryudāsa*)],[112] because arising from other is going to be refuted as well.[113] And the reasoning by which arising from self

---

[112] PsP Tib presents two separate reasons conjoined with *dang*: ... *brjod par 'dod pa'i phyir dang | gzhan las skye ba yang 'gog par 'gyur ba'i phyir ro* ||.

[113] On *prasajyapratiṣedha* and *paryudāsa*, see, e.g., Kajiyama 1973 (for references, see p. 162, n. 1) and Kajiyama 1998: 38, n. 62; Seyfort Ruegg 1981: 37-38, 65 and n. 94, Seyfort Ruegg 2000: 255f., and Seyfort Ruegg 2002: 19-24 (n. 6). Candrakīrti denies that the negation applied to *svata utpannā* (*bhāvā vidyante*) implies that there exist things that have arisen in some other way, i.e., from other; the negation does not suggest another proposition, in the way, for example, that the presuppositional negation "Fat Devadatta does not eat during the day" implies his eating by night. Bhāviveka appears to have been the first to have introduced reference to the two types of negation into the Madhyamaka discussion, specifically with regard to the statement *na svata utpannā* (*bhāvā vidyante*) (see D 48b6-49a2, D lacks *gzhan las skye'o zhes bya bar nges par 'gyur ba dang | de bzhin du bdag kho na las skye ba med de 'o na ci zhe na*; P 58a3-58b1; Kajiyama 1963: 48 and 1973: 168-9; Ames 1993: 221). As Kajiyama (1973: 170-172) has pointed out, while later Buddhist scholars (in league with the Grammarians, etc.) assert that a negation construed with a nominal expresses a presuppositional negation, and one construed with a verb a non-presuppositional negation, Bhāviveka asserts that the statement *na svata utpannā bhāvā vidyante* can be made explicit as a non-presuppositional negation through restriction by way of the particle *eva*. To achieve the meaning he considers is intended, namely, "It is not the case that things arisen from self exist," he construes the restrictive particle *eva* (and the negation *na*) with the verb/predicate: *'dir dngos po rnams bdag las skye ba med pa kho na'o zhes nges par bzung bar bya'o* || (D 49a1; P 58a7); Kajiyama (1973: 169) reconstructs **bhāvāḥ svata utpannā naiva vidyante*. *eva* placed elsewhere in the sentence, as, e.g., in *naiva svata utpannā bhāvā vidyante*, would cause the sentence to yield the meaning "Things arisen from *self* do not exist," and to thereby imply that things arisen from others exist. Further, when *eva* restricts only *svata*, the sentence *svata eva utpannā bhāvā na vidyante*, "Things arisen from self alone do not exist," would imply that things arisen from self and other exist (cf. Kajiyama 1973: 168f.). Although he does not mention types of negation by name, in the MABh Candrakīrti states (one assumes also with the intent to defend Nāgārjuna's placement of the negative particle) that the negation ought to be construed with *svata utpannāḥ* and not with the verb *vidyante* because it will be evident that total non-existence is meant: *'dir ma yin zhes bya ba 'di yod pa nyid kyi sgrub byed rang las skye ba dang sbrel gyi yod pa dang ni ma yin te | de dgag pa don gyis grub pa'i phyir ro* || ($MABh_{ed}$ 81.15-17): "Here [in the first *kārikā*] this negation (*ma yin*; **nañ*, **na*) is to be construed with 'arisen from self' (*svata utpannāḥ*), (i.e., self as) the establisher of existence (*yod pa nyid kyi sgrub byed*) [– would there be any real existence –] but not with [the verb] 'exist' (*vidyante*), because the negation of that [existence] is established as a matter of course (**arthāt*)." De La Valleé Poussin ($MABh_{tr}$ 1910: 279) translates more freely, in accord with the sense given in the PsP:

is impossible[114] should be determined by way of [statements] such as,[115]

> For there is not any advantage in the coming into existence of something from itself,
> and the origination once again of what has [already] originated is simply not reasonable.[116]

"Quant à la négation (*na vidyante*), il est faux que, [ne] portant [que] sur la naissance de soi, elle ait une valeur affirmative [c'est-à-dire comporte le corollaire: "Les êtres naissent d'autrui"], car elle est acquise dans un sens purement négatif."

[114] *LṬ's author determines that the correlative pronoun *sā* in the construction *yayā copapattyā svata utpādo na sambhavati sā* relates to *upapatti*. He then adds: *parato* [']*py utpāde avaseyety* (ms: *avasety*) *abhisaṃbandhaḥ*. He appears to think that what is meant by Candrakīrti is either that the reasoning proving that arising from self is impossible extends to prove that arising from other is impossible, or, and much more loosely, that a reasoning which proves that arising from other is impossible also needs to be determined. Cp. Yonezawa 2004: 121 [fol. 1b5]: *parato py utpāde ava ety* ...; ibid., 131: *parato 'py utpāde tāvat sā ity abhisaṃbandhaḥ*.

[115] Ms Q refers to the Madhyamakāvatāra as the source text, as do all of the paper manuscripts and PsP Tib. The MA reference in ms Q, however, appears only in its lower margin, (*madhyakāvatārādidvāreṇā* [*sic*]), marked to be inserted within the main text between the *akṣaras* *nā* of *ityādinā* and *va* of *avaseyā*. Ms P, the only manuscript not affected by readings from the γ line (see Stemma), lacks the MA reference; its absence from P is difficult to explain on paleographical grounds and points to its not having been in ms β. Its presence in Q and the paper manuscripts must be the result of contamination from the γ line (note Q's further interpolated references to the MA at the end of both PsP_M §61 and §104). That ms Q's reference is in its margin suggests that its source is ms θ. Candrakīrti would have presumed his readers' familiarity with his MA; the reference was probably originally added as marginalia intended for readers/students unfamiliar with the citation. The conclusion that the reference found in Q and the paper manuscripts is an accretion is supported by the fact that *LṬ's author deems it necessary to explain *ityādinā* with *madhyamakāvatāragranthena* (cf. Yonezawa 2004: 121, 131 [fol. 1b5]). PsP Tib's *la sogs pas dbu ma la 'jug pa la sogs pa'i sgo nas nges par bya'o* merely indicates that the reference had already been incorporated into the text of at least one of the manuscripts used by the translators. For further remarks regarding this and other accretions in ms Q, see infra Manuscript Relationships. A preliminary evaluation of this reference appeared in MacDonald 2008: 25ff.

[116] MA VI.8cd: *tasmād dhi tasya bhavane na guṇo 'sti kaścij jātasya janma punar eva ca naiva yuktam* ||. MA VI.8d is cited again at PsP_L 79.11 (see PsP_M §129). MA VI.8c Tib reads *de ni de las 'byung na yon tan 'ga' yang yod ma yin* ||, while PsP Tib reads <u>*de las de ni*</u> *'byung na yon tan 'ga' yang yod ma yin* ||. The MABh, as would be

§22. The Master Buddhapālita, for his part (*tu*), states,

> Things do not arise from self because their arising would be pointless (*tadutpādavaiyarthyāt*) and because there would be the fault of over-extension (*atiprasaṅgadoṣāt*).[117] For there is no

---

expected, reflects the structure of MA VI.8c: *de ni zhes bya ba ni* .... ($MABh_{ed}$ 82.8). Candrakīrti exemplifies in the MABh the meaning of *tasmād dhi tasya bhavane* with *myu gu'i rang gi bdag nyid de nyid las myu gu'i bdag nyid de nyid 'byung ba*. The *LṬ glosses *tasmāt* with *svabhāvāt tasya* (ms: *asya*) *svabhāvasya* (ms: *svabhāvamya*) *na* (ms: *ra*) *guṇa iti vidyamānatvāt* (cp. Yonezawa 2004: 121, 131 [fol. 1b5]) "from this, [i.e.,] from own-being; of this [i.e.,] of own-being; 'there is no advantage' because [the own-being already] exists."

117 The second fault stated by Buddhapālita is presented in BP as *skye ba thug pa med par 'gyur ba'i phyir* (BP_{ed} 10.13-14; de La Vallée Poussin reconstructs as *janmānavasthānāt* [PsP_L 14, n. 1]) "because there would be a succession without end of arising." PsP Skt, in contrast, reads *atiprasaṅgadoṣāt*. The PsP Tib translators inserted the BP Tib quotation—which they have taken from either BP Tib or PP Tib (the citation is identical in both)—after making minor alterations to it, one of them being the change from *skye ba thug pa med par 'gyur ba'i phyir* to *shin tu thal bar 'gyur ba'i phyir*, a change that permits PsP Tib to better reflect PsP Skt's *atiprasaṅgadoṣāt* (*doṣa* has not been translated). Note that Candrakīrti makes reference to *anavasthā* in his defence of this statement of Buddhapālita's against Bhāviveka's critique. He also makes reference to *aniṣṭhā*, which could alternatively suggest that the reading in BP was **janmāniṣṭhāyāḥ*, or perhaps more probable, **janmāniṣṭhāpatteḥ*. Whatever the original reading was, it appears that Candrakīrti, as in the other cases noted for the first chapter, is responsible for the change in wording. Of course, it not impossible that Jñānagarbha and Klu'i rgyal mtshan, the translators of BP and PP, also read *atiprasaṅgadoṣāt* and decided to spell out the fault; Buddhapālita's explanation *atha sann api jāyeta na kadācin na jāyeta*, however, would seem to nicely explain **janmānavasthānāt/janmāniṣṭhāpatteḥ*. One might want to consider the possibility that BP attested **aniṣṭhāprasaṅgadoṣāt* and that the BP manuscript(s) Candrakīrti had access to contained the corrupt reading *atiprasaṅgadoṣāt*, but it is difficult to imagine why the BP translators would have rendered **aniṣṭhāprasaṅgadoṣāt* as *skye ba thug pa med par 'gyur ba'i phyir*. Compare the instance later on in the first chapter of PsP (PsP_M §95 end) where PsP Skt's "fault of a succession without end" (*aniṣṭhādoṣa*) is translated with *thug pa med pa'i skyon* (de La Vallée Poussin has wrongly emended to *anavasthādoṣa* [PsP_L 61.8-9]). See also PsP_L 210.16 where PsP Tib translates *aniṣṭhādoṣaprasaṅgāt* as *thug pa med par thal ba'i phyir* (de La Vallée Poussin reads *aniṣṭadoṣaprasaṅgāt*; mss P and D read *aniṣṭhādoṣaprasaṅgāt*) and $CŚṬ_{ed}$ 228.16 (CŚṬ Tib 229.25-26) where *aniṣṭhāprasaṅgāt* is translated as *thug pa med par thal ba'i phyir* (see 228, n. 13 where the text's reading *aniṣṭaprasaṅgāt* is corrected to *aniṣṭhāprasaṅgāt*).
The "over-extension" referred to by the technical term *atiprasaṅga* consists, as explained in the text, in the fact that the existing thing will never stop arising. The

purpose in the re-arising of things [already] existing by [their] own nature; but if [a thing], though [already] existing, would arise [again], it would never not arise.[118]

§23. In regard to this [statement of Buddhapālita's], some[119] [i.e., Bhāviveka] criticize:

That [mode of argumentation] is not suitable, because a reason (*hetu*) and an example (*dṛṣṭānta*) have not been stated[120] and[121]

---

translation of *atiprasaṅga* as "absurd" is defended in Franco 1984: 137, n. 33. Seyfort Ruegg (2002: 25) overlooks that *api* in the sentence explaining the *atiprasaṅga* is intended in a concessive sense and thus translates it as "also": "But (ii) if (*atha* = *ci ste*) the existent also were [once] to be [re]born, never would it not be [re]born."

Cp. the PsP citation to ŚS *kārikā* 6 (ŚSV$_{ed}$ 240; refutation of a cause): *yang na de'i rgyus dgos pa yod do zhe na | de lta na yang de ni yod pa ma yin te | skyes pa slar yang mi skye bas thug pa med pa'i skyon dang | skye ba don med pa'i phyir ro.*; ŚSV$_{ed}$ 234 (refutation of *svabhāva*): *skye ba don med pa dang | thug pa med pa'i skyon ...*; CŚṬ D 58b4-5; 175a2-3. See also PsP$_L$ 14, n. 3; Yotsuya 1999: 75.

[118] Candrakīrti is citing from BP, which reads in translation: *de la re zhig dngos po rnams bdag gi bdag nyid las skye ba med de | de dag gi skye ba don med pa nyid du 'gyur ba'i phyir dang | skye ba thug pa med par 'gyur ba'i phyir ro || 'di ltar dngos po bdag gi bdag nyid du yod pa rnams la yang skye ba dgos pa med do || gal te yod kyang yang skye na nam yang mi skye bar mi 'gyur bas de yang mi 'dod de | de'i phyir re zhig dngos po rnams bdag las skye ba med do ||* (BP$_{ed}$ 10.11-17).

PP: *'di las gzhan ni dngos po rnams bdag gi bdag nyid las skye ba med de | de dag gi skye ba don med pa nyid du 'gyur ba'i phyir dang | skye ba thug pa med par 'gyur ba'i phyir ro |* (D *without* |) *zhes rnam par bshad pa byed do ||* (D 49a5-7; P 59a7-8). Avalokitavrata states that *'di las gzhan* ("the [MMK commentator] different from this [MMK commentator Bhāviveka]") is one of the group of MMK commentators. He lists as MMK commentators Nāgārjuna, Buddhapālita, Candrakīrti, Devaśarman, Guṇaśrī, Guṇamati, Sthiramati and Bhāviveka; he identifies the author of the citation as Buddhapālita (cf. PPṬ D 73a4-6; P 85a7-85b1).

[119] LVP: "eke = Bhāvaviveka-ādayaḥ" (PsP$_L$ 14, n. 4). *LṬ's author identifies *eke* as Bhāviveka: *atraika iti Bhāvivekaḥ* (cf. Yonezawa 2004: 121, 131 [fol. 1b5-6]).

[120] Yotsuya (1999: 76, n. 10) states, "In pointing out that entities do not originate from self, Buddhapālita presents the grounds: pointlessness (*don med pa*, *vaiyarthya*) and infinite regress (*thug pa med pa*, *anavasthā*) ... . These are, however, not considered to be logical reasons, since they are not properties of the subject, i.e. entities. In other words, '*pakṣadharmatā*', which is one of the characteristics of a correct logical reason ... is not established" (more precisely, the grounds of the consequence are "pointlessness of arising" and "a succession without end of arising"). Cf. PS

because the faults pronounced by the [Sāṅkhya] opponents have not been refuted.[122] And because it is a statement of [unwanted] consequence (*prasaṅgavākya*),[123] [it follows,] in view of [the fact

---

III.17, where Dignāga states that the reason in a consequence is not a property of the subject. The PS III.17 reconstruction published in Katsura 2009: 158 (prasaṅgo *'pakṣadharmatvāt pūrvatropagame sati* | *hetupratijñayos* teṣāṃ *doṣoktyā dūṣaṇaṃ* gatam || [the words in Roman have been reconstructed from the Tibetan]) has been revised by the team working on PSṬ III to: prasaṅgo *'pakṣadharmatvād anyo hetu-pratijñayoḥ* | *doṣoktyā dūṣaṇaṃ* jñataṃ *pūrvatropagame sati* ||. I am grateful to Prof. Katsura for providing me with the revised reconstruction. De La Vallée Poussin (cf. PsP_L 23, n. 2) cites the Nyāyavārttikatātparyāṭīkā: *prasaṅgo hi na sādhanam, hetor abhāvāt.*

[121] None of the PsP manuscripts attest a *ca* at this point, but PsP Tib, PP (moreso PP Peking than Derge), and PPṬ appear to confirm that one was included in the original Skt of PP and PsP. For details, see Appendix VII.

[122] Seyfort Ruegg (2002: 26) interprets the first reason as the ground for the second, but does not provide an explanation for his interpretation. He translates, "That [argument of Buddhapālita's] is unfounded. This is so (i) because, on the one hand, no inferential reason (*gtan tshigs*) and no instance (*dpe*) having been provided, no rebuttal has been provided (*aparihāra* = *ma bsal ba*) [by Buddhapālita] of the faults (*doṣa* = *ñes pa*) alleged by the opponent [viz. the Sāṃkhya]."

[123] William Ames (1993: 244, n. 102) states that the appearance of *glags yod pa'i tshig* (**sāvakāśavacana*) in the PP instead of *thal bar 'gyur ba'i tshig* (*prasaṅga-vākya*) "does not necessarily mean that the translators had a different Sanskrit text. They may have translated *prasaṅga-vākya* in this way because of the context and because of Avalokitavrata's subcommentary. Avalokitavrata glosses *glags yod pa'i tshig* as *rgol ba gzhan gyi klan ka'i glags yod pa'i tshig*, 'a statement affording an opportunity for censure by an opponent (Ava P 86a-8, D 74a-2).'" I am inclined, against this, to think that the PP translators did read *sāvakāśavacana* in their manuscript(s) and thus translated literally, and that it was Candrakīrti who re-worded *sāvakāśavacana* here and on other occasions as *prasaṅgavākya*. His usage of *sāvakā-śavacana* in the later question *kuto nu khalv ... ācāryabuddhapālitasya sāvakāśa-vacanābhidhāyitvam* (see PsP_M §35; PsP_L 24.1-2) is otherwise unexpected and unusual, especially because it is precisely with this sentence that he directly refers to the third fault mentioned by Bhāviveka. Note that when Candrakīrti finishes his argumentation against specific faults and then refers back to them, he tends to formulate his rejection of the fault as a question, e.g., *tat kim ucyate tad ayuktaṃ hetudṛṣṭāntānabhidhānād iti*; *kutaḥ siddhasādhanapakṣadoṣāśaṅkā kuto vā hetor vi-ruddhārthatāśaṅketi*; *kuto nu khalu ... ācāryabuddhapālitasya sāvakāśavacanābhi-dhāyitvam*; the aberrant translation *de'i phyir kho bo cag la grub pa'i mtha' dang 'gal ba ga la yod* for *tataś ca siddhāntavirodhāsambhavaḥ* in the reasoning concluded by *kuto nu khalu ...* can possibly be explained as the result of the PsP translators having noticed this tendency and having decided to present this conclusion as well as a

that] through the reversal of the meaning [of the statement] under discussion the opposite of the probandum (*sādhya*) and of its properties (*taddharma*) [i.e., the probans] are expressed, that there would be contradiction with [your own] accepted tenets (*kṛtāntavirodha*), [because the resulting inference states that] "Things have arisen from other, because arising is purposeful and because arising stops [upon completion of the process of arising]."[124]

---

question. I think it more likely that with *kuto nu khalu ... ācāryabuddhapālitasya sāvakāśavacanābhidhāyitvam* Candrakīrti intentionally foregoes his earlier rewording and employs exactly Bhāviveka's terminology for the sake of having used it at least once and for the stylistic punch it delivers.

[124] Candrakīrti is citing from Bhāviveka's PP which reads in its Tibetan translation: *de ni rigs pa ma yin te | gtan tshigs dang dpe ma brjod pa'i phyir dang | gzhan gyis smras pa'i nyes pa ma bsal ba'i phyir ro ||* (D: *phyir dang |*) *glags yod pa'i tshig*[1] *yin pa'i phyir te |*[2] *skabs kyi don las bzlog pas bsgrub* (P: *sgrub*) *par bya ba dang | de'i chos bzlog pa'i don mngon pas dngos po rnams gzhan las skye bar 'gyur ba dang | skye ba 'bras bu dang bcas pa nyid du 'gyur ba dang | skye ba thug pa yod par 'gyur ba'i phyir mdzad pa'i mtha'*[3] *dang 'gal bar 'gyur ro ||* (D 49a6-49b1; P 58b8-59a2). PsP Tib: [1]*thal bar 'gyur ba'i tshig* for *glags yod pa'i tshig*; [2]without *te |*; [3]*grub pa'i mtha'* for *mdzad pa'i mtha'* (translated in Ames 1993: 222f., Kajiyama 1963: 50, Yotsuya 1999: 76). On de La Vallée Poussin's remark that *janmanirodhāt* does not correspond to PsP's (and PP's) *skye ba thug pa ...* (PsP$_{L}$ 14, n. 4), see Hopkins 1983: 817, n. 363.
The third point of criticism has received attention from both modern and Tibetan scholars; see, e.g., Hopkins 1983: 491; Seyfort Ruegg 1991: 290-292, Seyfort Ruegg 2000: 252-257 (= the 1991 section with minor changes) and Tillemans 1992. The reversal (*viparyaya*) that Bhāviveka refers to results in the probandum of the *prasaṅga* "[things] do not arise from self" changing to the inference's "[things] have arisen from other" and the first probans "because their arising would be pointless" changing to "because their arising is purposeful" and the second probans "because there would be a succession without end of arising" (or, as Candrakīrti presents it: "because there would be the fault of over-extension") changing to "because arising stops." The logical mechanism behind the process of reversal has been under dispute. According to Seyfort Ruegg (1991: n. 35; 2000: 255, n. 35), a contraposition of terms in the Dharmakīrtian sense of *prasaṅgaviparyaya* is not intended and was "to be raised in connexion with Bhavya's and Candrakīrti's passage dealing with *prakṛtārthaviparyaya* and *prasaṅgaviparītārtha* only in later discussions of the logical question it poses ..."; he (2000: 253; see also 1991: 291) writes, "As for Bhavya's objection to Buddhapālita's *prasaṅga*-statement, it apparently involves the idea not of contraposition but of implicative reversal, namely that a negation of production

from self would imply the affirmation of production from an other." See Tillemans 1992 for a presentation of dGe lugs pa interpretations of the *prasaṅgaviparyaya*.

It seems, however, that a form of technical *prasaṅgaviparyaya* is intended. Probably the most promising attempt to date to shed light on Bhāviveka's understanding of both the *prasaṅga* and its *viparyaya* is that by Toshikazu Watanabe (cf. Watanabe 2013), who examines Dignāga's explanation, criticism and (re)interpretation of Sāṅkhya *vīta* and *āvīta* reasoning, and considers its influence on Bhāviveka in the context of Bhāviveka's criticism of Buddhapālita's *prasaṅga* against the possibility of arising from other, as presented in the PsP (see PsP$_M$ §63; Watanabe's explanation is applicable also in the present case of the criticism of Buddhapālita's *prasaṅga* against arising from self). When employed by the Sāṅkhyas, *vīta* and *āvīta* are always used in conjunction with each other, with the *vīta* argument directly proving an object / state of affairs and the *āvīta* argument, always formulated as a *prasaṅga* that is introduced after the main *vīta* reasoning, included as support for the conclusion drawn by the *vīta*. As Watanabe explains, Dignāga argues in PS III.16 that *āvīta* reasoning is actually not different from its corresponding *vīta* reasoning (which he endows with a reason that meets the three requirements of a proper logical reason), because both have the same pervasion (*vyāpti*); that is, their pervasions are logically equivalent. *āvīta*, according to Dignāga, can thus be reformulated into *vīta* to form a proper logical proof (*sādhana*). Watanabe (ibid., 1232f.) adverts to the fact that the structure of Dharmakīrti's *prasaṅga* and *prasaṅgaviparyaya* corresponds to that of the *āvīta* and *vīta* accepted by Dignāga, noting that Jinendrabuddhi "explains the reformulation of *āvīta* reasoning into *vīta* reasoning in the PS(V) by using the term '*prasaṅgaviparyaya*.'" Working under the assumption that Bhāviveka is relying on Dignāga's interpretation of *āvīta* reasoning when he criticizes Buddhapālita's *prasaṅga* statements, Watanabe demonstrates that Bhāviveka's reversal of the *prasaṅga* closely resembles Dignāga's transformation of *āvīta* reasoning into *vīta*. In reliance on Watanabe's conclusions for the case of Bhāviveka's reversal of the *prasaṅga* against arising from other, we can propose that in the present case, following the structure of Dignāga's *āvīta* (cf. <Āvīta-D 1> and <Āvīta-D 2> in ibid., 1230f.), that the *prasaṅga*—leaving aside for now Buddhapālita's second reason and focussing only on *utpādavaiyarthya*—can be seen as having the structure "*bhāvāḥ* (*svata utpadyate* → *utpādavaiyarthya*). Thus *svata utpadyate* → *utpādavaiyarthya* represents the contraposition, i.e., the negative concomitance (*vyatirekavyāpti*), of the positive concomitance (*anvayavyāpti*) of the inference "Things have arisen from other because arising is purposeful," this latter *vyāpti* being *janmasāphalya* → *parata utpadyate*.

On *prasaṅga* and *prasaṅgaviparyaya* in the Dharmakīrtian tradition, see, e.g., Iwata 1993; Kajiyama 1998: 114ff.; see also discussions regarding Tsong kha pa's interpretation of the reversal in Seyfort Ruegg 1991: 292ff., Seyfort Ruegg 2000: 257ff., Hopkins 1983: 490-492; Tillemans 1992: 318ff.

PsP Tib mirrors PP Tib in separating out and listing the reversed *sādhya* and *sādhana*s that, according to Bhāviveka, are implied in Buddhapālita's original statement instead of, as PsP Skt does, merely presenting the unitary positive

§24. We[125] regard this entire critique as totally inappropriate. Why? That which is alleged first in it, namely, "because a reason and an example have not been stated," is inapplicable. For what reason? Because [with Buddhapālita's statement] the [Sāṅkhya] opponent maintaining arising from self is questioned as to the purpose of the

---

counterpart to Buddhapālita's statement interpreted as a *paryudāsa*: *parasmād utpannā bhāvā janmasāphalyāj janmanirodhāc ceti* (PsP Tib:) ... *dngos po rnams gzhan las skye bar 'gyur ba dang | skye ba 'bras bu dang bcas pa nyid du 'gyur ba dang | skye ba thug pa yod par 'gyur ba'i phyir*. In two other passages in which Bhāviveka criticizes Buddhapālita's *prasaṅga*s in a similar way, namely, his criticisms of Buddhapālita's *prasaṅga* refuting arising from other and that refuting arising from no cause, PsP Tib and PP Tib likewise only provide a serial layout of the reversed limbs of the *prasaṅga*s without construing them as a unified statement: for the former *prasaṅga*, the reversal is presented in PsP Skt (PsP$_{M}$ §63) as *svata ubhayato 'hetuto votpadyante bhāvāḥ kutaścit kasyacid utpatteḥ*, but appears in PsP Tib as: *des na de la thal bar 'gyur ba'i ngag yin pa'i phyir bsgrub par bya ba dang sgrub par byed pa bzlog par byas na | dngos po rnams bdag gam gnyis sam rgyu med pa las skye bar 'gyur ba dang | 'ga' zhig las 'ga' zhig skye bar 'gyur ba'i phyir* ... (cf. PP D 50a6; P 60a6-8); for the latter *prasaṅga*, PsP Skt (PsP$_{M}$ §67) presents the reversal as *hetuta utpadyante bhāvāḥ kadācit kutaścid utpatteḥ ārambhasāphalyāc ca*, but PsP Tib reads: *gal te bsgrub par bya ba dang sgrub par byed pa bzlog pa gsal ba ngag gi don du mngon par 'dod na | de'i tshe 'di skad du | dngos po rnams rgyu las skye bar 'gyur ba dang | lan 'ga' kha cig las kha cig skye bar 'gyur ba dang | rtsom pa 'bras bu dang bcas pa nyid du 'gyur ba'i phyir ro* || (cp. PP D 53a5-6; P 64a5-7; cp. also Bhāviveka's reversals in his critique of another *prasaṅga* statement of Buddhapālita's in his commentary on MMK I.9cd [PP D 60b5; P 72b7-8]). The same mode of presentation is found in the corresponding sections of the PPṬ (like the PP, translated by Jñānagarbha and Klu'i rgyal mtshan). Such passages show quite clearly that the PsP translators had at their disposal a translation of the PP to which they referred and from which they appropriated passages cited in PsP Skt. The translation *bdag gi bdag nyid* for *svātmanā* in the PsP citation from Buddhapālita's commentary—instead of PsP Tib's more usual *rang gi bdag nyid*—suggests that they also had a translation of BP at hand. That they must have had access to a substantial number of translated works becomes apparent from the fact that the majority of the other quotations in PsP Tib have been copied in from their respective source-text Tibetan translations. On Pa tshab and his method for dealing with citations, see MacDonald 2015.

125 *LṬ: *vayam iti Candrakīrtiḥ*. *LṬ's author states immediately before this clarification that Bhāviveka is a proponent of independent proofs: *bhāvivekaḥ kila svatantrasā[dha]navādī* (cf. Yonezawa 2004: 121, 131 [fol. 1b6]).

re-arising of something [already] existing:[126] [When you say] "from self" (*svataḥ*), you assert something [already] existing to be the cause (*hetutvena*) and [consider that] it is exactly that which arises; but we do not see [any] purpose in the arising again of something [already] existing, and we see[127] [in this claim of the arising of things already existing] an infinite succession (*anavasthā*).[128] And you do not assent to the arising again of what has arisen, or to a succession without end (*aniṣṭhā*). Therefore, your assertion [that things arise from self] is simply illogical (*nirupapattika*), and is contradicted by what [you your]self [otherwise] maintain (*svābhyupagamaviruddha*).

§25. [Is it reasonable to assume,] when [he has been] censured to such an extent (*iyati codite*),[129] that the [sensible] opponent does not accept

---

[126] PsP Tib lacks an equivalent for *vidyamānasya punarutpāde prayojanam*. It may have been dropped by the translators because *pha rol po bdag las skye bar 'dod pa la 'dri bar byed pa yin* (= *paraḥ svata utpattim abhyupagacchan pṛcchyate*) has for the sake of the Tibetan syntax been placed not before the argumentation beginning with *svata iti vidyamānaṃ hetutvena bravīṣi*, but after the final conclusion *tasmān nirupapattika eva tava vādaḥ svābhyupagamaviruddhaś ca*. They may have considered that this placement of *pha rol po bdag las skye bar 'dod pa la 'dri bar byed pa yin* made *vidyamānasya punarutpāde prayojanam* irrelevant, or misleading, since a lack of purpose relates only to the first part of the argumentation in the Sanskrit, and represents only one of the consequences of arising from self, the second having been stated in the Tibetan before *pha rol po bdag las skye bar 'dod pa la 'dri bar byed pa yin* appears. The restructuring of the passage is not completely satisfactory, though, because it presents the opponent as being directly asked the argumentation (... *zhes pha rol po ... 'dri bar byed pa yin*), whereas in the Sanskrit the opponent is "questioned" *in regard to* the purpose of re-arising, that is, is challenged with its consequences.

[127] Hopkins (1983: 474) translates "and we also see ...", taking into consideration PsP Tib's added *yang* (... *dgos pa ma mthong zhing thug pa med par yang mthong* ...).

[128] Cp. Candrakīrti on CŚ XI.10: *yadi hi tasyāstitvaṃ syāt tadā sato vidyamānasya punar api janma syāt* [|] *na ca sataḥ punar api janma nyāyyaṃ niḥprayojanatvāt* [|] *aniṣṭhāprasaṅgād ā saṃsāram ekasyaivārthasya punar utpādenāparisamāptodayasya satas tatpadārthāntarāpravṛtter hetuphalabhāvavyāghātaḥ syāt* [|] (CŚṬ$_{ed}$ 228.14-18; see also CŚṬ$_{ed}$ 228, n. 13).

[129] Yotsuya's conjecture *iyati* (1999: 57) is now confirmed by *iyati* of mss P and Q. Although the subject of the locative absolute *iyati codite* is actually *iyat*, for the sake of the English I translate as above. De La Vallée Poussin (PsP$_L$ 15, n. 8) based his conjecture *tanmātreṇa* on PsP Tib's *'di dag tsam zhig gis*. PsP Tib's *'di dag* appears

(i.e., that he rejects) [our criticism], so that the employment of a reason and example might [then in fact] be useful (*sāphalya*)?[130] [No,

to be the translators' specification of exactly what "to such an extent" (*iyat*) refers back to, namely, either the two consequences *utpādavaiyarthyāt* and **janmāniṣṭhāpatteḥ* stated by Buddhapālita, or the *nirupapattika*(*tva*) and *svābhyupagamaviruddha*(*tva*) implied by the consequences. The fact that *svābhyupagamavirodha* is referred to in the following sentence may indicate that the translators meant the latter pair.

[130] I understand *kim*'s scope to be the entire sentence, and the question as a rhetorical one. Yotsuya (1999: 56) has also understood the sentence this way, but his translation is not unambiguous. He translates, "When [the opponent (= the Sāṃkhya)] is censured to such an extent, why [should] the opponent not accept [our censure], so that the resorting (*upādāna*) to a logical reason and a logical example would be purposeful (*sāphalyaṃ*)?" Hopkins (1983: 474), too, understands the sentence as a rhetorical question implying that the opponent will accept the censure, but PsP Tib's structure has caused some confusion. He translates, "When [Buddhapālita] debates through just these [consequences] which have the effects [derived] from stating a reason and example, would the opponent not accept it?" The Tibetan reads: *gang las gtan tshigs dang dpe bkod pa 'bras bu dang bcas par 'gyur ba 'di dag tsam zhig gis brtsad pa na ci pha rol po khas len par mi byed dam* |. Earlier interpretations of the sentence by Stcherbatsky, Seyfort Ruegg and Oetke and my critiques of them appear in MacDonald 2003: 156-159. Yotsuya (1999: 56, n. 27) provides other previous translations of the sentence, none of which interpret *yataḥ* as having a consecutive function.

The sentence implies that the opponent will indeed accept the Mādhyamika's pointing out that his theory of arising from self is in contradiction with his own tenets, and will as a result abandon his stance and therefore not require further elucidation via inference. The consecutive clause of the sentence indicates what might be considered to be of value, i.e., a full-fledged inference equipped with a reason and an example, should the opponent *not* accept the criticism. Note that the following sentence rejects this possibility by stating that there is in fact no point in trying to convince such foolish opponents by way of inferences. Thus, with the first alternative, it is communicated that any reasonable Sāṅkhya opponent will promptly renounce the position of arising from self when confronted with the consequences of this position, without needing to be served up a formal inference, and with the second, it is declared that the Sāṅkhya opponent who refuses to abandon the position of arising from self even when faced with its unacceptable consequences is such a dullard that he will also not be swayed by full-fledged inferences. In neither case is an independent inference of any benefit. These two sentences constitute Candrakīrti's first argument in defense of Buddhapālita's reliance on statements of [unwanted] consequence (*prasaṅgavākya*) and against Bhāviveka's claim that these are unacceptable and need to be replaced by, or at least supplemented with, independent inferences.

he accepts it, of course!] But if the opponent does not withdraw even with the censure (*codanā*) that there is contradiction with what [he him]self maintains, then given [his] extreme shamelessness (*atinirlajjatā*) he would certainly not withdraw even with [our resorting to] a reason and example. And we do not debate with a madman (*unmattaka*). Thus, the Master [Bhāviveka],[131] introducing an inference even when it is inopportune (*asthāna*), reveals nothing but his liking—at all costs (*sarvathā*)[132]—for inference. But because he does not maintain any other position (*pakṣa*), it is not right for the Mādhyamika himself to formulate an autonomous inference (*svatantram anumānam*).[133]

§26. And accordingly, Āryadeva has said [in the Catuḥśataka],

> Criticism (*upālambha*) cannot, even with time, be levelled against one who does not hold the position that [some thing is] existent (*sat*), non-existent (*asat*), or [both] existent and non-existent (*sadasat*).[134]

---

[131] *LṬ's author identifies the "Master" as Bhāviveka: *ācārya iti bhāvivekaḥ* (cf. Yonezawa 2004: 121, 132 [fol. 1b6]).

[132] Even though de La Vallée Poussin's manuscripts read *sarvathā*, he emended to *tasmāt* under the influence of PsP Tib's *de'i phyir*. PsP Tib appears to have translated the *iti* preceding *sarvathā* as *de'i phyir*; *sarvathā* may have been unreadable, overlooked or purposely not translated. Yotsuya (1999: 57 and n. 34) also emends to *sarvathā* on the basis of his manuscript material and Tanji 1988.

[133] I understand *pakṣāntara* ("another / [any] other position") to refer to positions other than that of self-arising, such as arising from other, which might be advocated by the Mādhyamika himself and as such would need to be proved in reliance on an inference composed of a proposition, reason and example; for a detailed explanation, see Yotsuya 1999: 58-61.

[134] Candrakīrti is citing CŚ XVI.25: *sad asat sadasac ceti yasya pakṣo na vidyate | upālambhaś cireṇāpi tasya vaktuṃ na śakyate ||* (Lang 1986: 150-151). The same verse is cited by Candrakīrti at MABh_{ed} 297.9-12 where the second quarter, as in CŚ Tib, appears as *gang la phyogs ni yod min pa* (PsP Tib: *phyogs ni gang la'ang yod min pa*); translated by, among others, Tauscher (1981: 60): "Wer keinerlei Behauptung vertritt, sei es Sein, Nichtsein, oder Sein und Nichtsein zugleich, den zu widerlegen ist auch in nochsolanger Zeit nicht möglich" and Seyfort Ruegg (2000: 122): "It is not even remotely possible to level a charge against somebody who has no proposition/position [positing some entity] as existent, non-existent and both

And it has been stated in the Vigrahavyāvartanī,

> Were there some thesis (*pratijñā*) for me, this fault (*doṣa*) would as a result[135] become mine;
> But for me there is no thesis; therefore [this] fault is indeed not mine.[136]

---

existent and non-existent" (cf. also ibid., n. 21; 2002: 28; Hopkins 1983: 585; Lang 1986: 151; Yotsuya 1999: 58).

[135] Oetke (1989: 22, n. 5) addresses the problem of the meaning of *tataḥ*, i.e., as to whether it should be taken as a co-relative to *yadi* or if it carries more semantic weight in the sense of "on account of this" ("'aufgrund dessen', d.h. aufgrund des im *yadi*-Satz ausgedrückten Sachverhaltes ..."); he takes both possibilities into account in his translation "dann bestünde für mich (aufgrund dessen) dieser Fehler." I follow Yotsuya (1999: 59) and Seyfort Ruegg (2000: 115; 2002: 29) in interpreting the word as intending a reason; Westerhoff (2010: 63) understands *tataḥ* as a simple co-relative.

[136] Candrakīrti is citing VV 29: *yadi kācana pratijñā syān me tata eṣa me bhaved doṣaḥ* | *nāsti ca mama pratijñā tasmān naivāsti me doṣaḥ* ‖ (cf. Bhattacharya et al. 1986: 61; Lindtner 1982b: 80). The reason for the inclusion of the previous verse from the CŚ and this and the following verse from the VV has been explained already by Yotsuya (1999: 60) as Candrakīrti's desire to show that the Mādhyamika "does not embrace any proposition (*pratijñā*, *dam bca'*) or position (*pakṣa*, *phyogs*) of his own which would posit that something is ultimately existent or non-existent or which would be based upon something being ultimately apprehended by direct perception, etc. In the context of the negation of origination from self which we are examining now, this means that the Mādhyamika engages only in denying the theory of origination from self. In other words, the Mādhyamika does not entertain any other position, such as origination from another which would have to be demonstrated by an inferential statement fully equipped with a proposition, a logical reason and a logical example."
VV 29 represents the VV author's reply to an opponent who has argued that the Mādhyamika cannot dismiss his refutation (*pratiṣedha*) of the Madhyamaka statement (*vacana*, *pratijñā*) "*śūnyāḥ sarvabhāvāḥ*" ("all things are empty") as an impotent one by declaring that the opponent's refutation as a sentence / speech act is included in all (empty) things because only the Mādhyamika asserts that all things are empty, not the opponent. The Mādhyamika, he continues, is the one setting forth this assertion that has "attained the characteristic of a thesis" (*pratijñālakṣaṇaprāpta*) and that is therefore subject to fault (see VV 4). According to the opponent, there is an incompatibility between the Madhyamaka statement as a sentence / speech act and its content, the emptiness of all things: if it exists as a sentence / speech act it contradicts its content. In his reply to the opponent, the VV author focusses on the opponent's description of the Mādhyamika's assertion as one that has "attained the characteristic of a thesis," that is, one that is a real (*sasvabhāva*) thing, and denies the

If I perceived something by way of things like direct perception (*pratyakṣa*) [and the other means of valid cognition], I might affirm (*pravartayeyam*) or negate (*nivartayeyam*) [it];
[But] because that [object of perception] does not exist, I am without reproach.[137]

---

existence of such a thing, i.e., of the sentence / speech act, for, when all things are as the content of the statement claims them to be, that is, "when all things are empty, completely pacified, isolated by nature, how [could there be] a thesis? How [could there be] the attainment of the characteristic of a thesis? How [could there be] a fault brought about through the attainment of the characteristic of a thesis?" (see VV_{ed} 61.18-20). The focus in VV 29 and its commentary is then on the ontological status of the thesis *śūnyāḥ sarvabhāvāḥ* itself and not, as Candrakīrti would have it here in the PsP, on the rejection of all theses based on existent (or non-existent) entities. The step to reinterpreting the denial of a really existing thesis on the ground that nothing exists to the denial of the possibility of all theses on the ground that nothing exists on which to base them is, however, a small and inviting one, and one I would hesitate to deny Candrakīrti awareness of.
For a more detailed discussion of VV 29 and a critique of the interpretations that take it as evidence for the Mādhyamika's utter lack of a philosophical position, see Oetke 1988 and 1989. Oetke (1996: 70), concurring with Wood's interpretation of certain VV passages, criticizes his translation of VV 29's *nāsti ca mama pratijñā* as "but I have no proposition" (see Wood 1994: 106, 111, 313), preferring "but there is no assertion of mine," since "Nāgārjuna does not want to say that his statement does not have any propositional content or that he does not intend to state anything with a propositional content but that his act of assertion as well as the words apparently occurring as constituents of the sentence uttered are non-existent on the final level of analysis ... ." I use the translation "thesis" because it is a more faithful rendering of *pratijñā* and because Candrakīrti intends it as such. On the thesis in Madhyamaka, see Ruegg 1977: 49-50; 1981: 78; 1983 and 1986; see also his response to and critique of Oetke in Seyfort Ruegg 2000: 213-219 (= note 164).
Cp. also MA VI.173: *sun 'byin pas sun dbyung bya ma phrad sun ni 'byin byed dam* || *'on te phrad nas yin zhes smras zin nyes pa 'dir gang la* || *nges par phyogs yod de la 'gyur gyi bdag la phyogs 'di ni* || *yod pa min pas thal bar 'gyur ba 'di ni srid ma yin* ||; YṢ 50: *rtsod med che ba'i bdag nyid can* || *de dag la ni phyogs med do* || *gang rnams la ni phyogs med pa* || *de la gzhan phyogs ga la yod* || ($YṢV_{ed}$ 89) and YṢV to 50cd: *gang gi tshe de ltar dngos po med pas bdag dang gzhan gyi phyogs med pa de'i tshe de ltar mthong ba rnams kyi nyon mongs pa rnams nges par 'gag par 'gyur ro* || ($YṢV_{ed}$ 90.1-3; $YṢV_{tr}$ 294 and n. 640).

[137] Candrakīrti cites Vigrahavyāvartanī 30: *yadi kiñcid upalabheyaṃ pravartayeyaṃ nivartayeyaṃ vā* | *pratyakṣādibhir arthais tadabhāvān me 'nupālambhaḥ* || (cf. Bhattacharya et al. 1986: 62; Lindtner 1982b: 80). The VV commentary makes it clear that *pāda* c has to be construed with *pāda* a, not with b as the syntax might suggest. Translations of the verse vary as to the interpretation of the referent of the

pronoun *tat* of *tadabhāvāt*. Seyfort Ruegg does not specify the referent ("[but] because of their absence" [2000: 115; 2002: 29, 55]), but Westerhoff (2010: 68), translating "But because that does not exist," clarifies his understanding of *tat* with the statement "'That' here refers to the presupposition of substantially existent epistemic instruments." Yotsuya (1999: 59) in one instance of translation understands the referent of *tat* to be the *pramāṇa*s: "[but] since there is no such [direct perception, etc., on my part]," but in another (ibid., 103) takes the referent to be both the object perceived and the *pramāṇa*s: "[but] since there is no such [thing or direct perception, etc., on my part]." Bhattacharya, on the other hand, understands the referent of *tat* to be solely *kiñcit*; he translates: "[But] since that thing does not exist" (see Bhattacharya et al. 1986: 114); similarly Tillemans (1992: 316, n. 5): "But as such a thing is inexistent" and Wood (1994: 112): "But there is no such thing." These latter three translations are more to the point given the opponent's supposition, expressed in VV 5 and 6, that the Mādhyamika would only be able to negate the things of the world if he had first apprehended them by way of a means of valid cognition. The VV author here in his response points out that there are simply no things to be apprehended. In this way he elegantly refutes the idea that he first apprehends the things he denies existence to and neatly pulls the rug out from under the opponent's arguments, namely (see the commentary on VV 5), that the Mādhyamika cannot apprehend things because direct perception (*pratyakṣa*) is empty, because the individual perceiving the objects of perception is empty, and because any other means or objects of valid cognition presumed to be necessary for the Mādhyamika's denial of them are empty (see the commentary on VV 6). I further think it is precipitous, given the context, to interpret the negation as intended of the *pramāṇa*s since the long section refuting the *pramāṇa*s actually only commences with VV 31; VV 30 is, in one sense, a verse introducing the *pramāṇa*s as "things" (*artha*)—the term under which they will be discussed in the following section—and serves as a lead-in to VV 31 where the opponent's argument that (perceptible) things are established by the *pramāṇa*s allows the discussion refuting the establishment of the *pramāṇa*s to get underway. Note too that VV 30's commentary focusses attention on the verse's *kiñcit* with its gloss of it as "thing" (*artham*): *yato*[1] *'rtham evāhaṃ kaṃcin nopalabhe tasmān na pravartayāmi na nivartayāmi* | *tatraivaṃ sati* … (cf. VV$_{ed}$ 15). [1]The first two words of the sentence at VV$_{ed}$ 62.13 (= Johnston and Kunst's edition) are given as *yathārtham*, but this has been silently emended by Bhattacharya to *yato 'rtham* (VV$_{ed}$ 15; Bhattacharya's translation is however based on *yathā*, which he understands as having the sense of a causal particle: "[but] since I do not even apprehend an object of any kind" [VV$_{ed}$ 114]). *yathā*, originally conjectured by Sāṅkṛtyāyana and then adopted by Johnston and Kunst, does not appear in the VV manuscript (cf. VV$_{ed}$ 62, n. 7 and Yonezawa 2008: 270, n. 6) and was possibly influenced by VV Tib's *ji ltar*. This *ji ltar*, however, is construed with a following *yang*; the VV Tib translators may have read *kathaṃcit* instead of *kaṃcit/kiṃcit* (VV Tib: *ngas don ji ltar yang ma dmigs pas* [D 129a1; P 147a1; Yonezawa 2008: 271]). The VV manuscript has neuter *kiñcit* (VV ms: *kiñcin*) in place of VV$_{ed}$ commentary's *kaṃcit*.

§27. And when in this way the Mādhyamika does not state an independent inference (*svatantrānumāna*), how [could there possibly be] an independent thesis (*svatantrā pratijñā*) [like Bhāviveka's, viz.,] "The inner bases (*āyatanāni*) have not arisen from self,"[138] in regard to which the Sāṅkhyas could object,

> What is the meaning here of the thesis? Do [you deny that a thing that already] has the nature of an effect (*kāryātmaka*) [arises]

---

*LṬ's author limits his comments to: *pratyakṣādipratītair arthaiḥ karaṇabhūtaiḥ kiñcit* (ms: *kiñcita*) *pravartayeyaṃ* (ms: *pravartte*) *nivartayeyaṃ* (ms: *nirvartteyaṃ*) *vā* (cf. Yonezawa 2004: 121, 132 [fol. 1b6-7]). He may have had difficulty with the construction of the verse, i.e., with its placement of part of the protasis after the apodosis, and therefore considered it necessary to note the intended meaning.

[138] "The inner bases have not arisen from self" is the proposition of the independent inference constructed by Bhāviveka to prove non-arising from self. Immediately following his citation of MMK I.1, Bhāviveka comments that the *kārikā* sets forth [only] the general thesis (*'di ni dam bcas pa'i spyi bkod pa yin*), adding that a mere thesis (*pratijñāmātra*; *dam bcas pa tsam*) does not establish the meaning of the intended statement and thus he utilizes a property of the subject (*pakṣadharma*; *phyogs kyi chos*), namely, "existing" [as the probans]. This reason can be drawn out of "from self" of the *kārikā* because "from self" is stated in regard to own-being, which [already] exists. An example, he states, can be found by virtue of the property to be proved (*sādhya*; *bsgrub par bya ba*) and the property that proves (*sādhanadharma*; *sgrub pa'i chos*), because it is an example of a property possessor that possesses the property to be proved and the property that proves, [both of] which are generally acknowledged: *dam bcas pa tsam gyis bsams* (P: *bsam*) *pa'i tshig gi don mi 'grub pa | 'dir phyogs kyi chos ni yod pa nyid yin par gzung ste | 'di ltar bdag las zhes bya ba ni bdag nyid yod pa la snyad gdags pa'i phyir ro || dpe ni bsgrub* (P: *sgrub*) *par bya ba dang | sgrub pa'i chos kyi dbang gis te bsgrub* (P: *sgrub*) *par bya ba dang | sgrub pa'i chos grags pa dang ldan pa'i chos can gyi dpe yin pa'i phyir* (PP D 48b5-6; P 58a1-2; cf. Kajiyama 1963: 48; Ames 1993: 221).
The inference in PP is set forth as: *don dam par nang gi skye mched rnams bdag las skye ba med par nges te | yod pa'i phyir dper na shes pa yod pa nyid bzhin no ||* (D 49a2-3; P 58b1-2. Ames (1993: 222) translates: [Thesis:] In ultimate reality, it is certain that the inner *āyatana*s do not originate from themselves, [Reason:] because they exist [already], [Example:] like consciousness (*caitanya*)." Candrakīrti cites the inference at PsP_M §39 (PsP_L 25.9-26.1) with the words *na paramārthata ādhyātmikāny āyatanāni svata utpannāni vidyamānatvāc caitanyavat*. The PsP Tib translators cite directly from PP; they do not modify the text to make it accord with PsP Skt, which does not attest an equivalent for *nges*.

from self[139] (i.e., reproduces itself) or [do you deny that a thing that still] has the nature of a cause (*kāraṇātmaka*) [arises from self] (i.e., reproduces itself)?[140] And what [follows] from this? If [you deny that a thing that] has the nature of an effect [reproduces itself], there is the proving [by you the Mādhyamika] of what is [already] established (*siddhasādhana*) [for us Sāṅkhyas]. If [you deny that a thing that] has the nature of a cause [reproduces itself], [then your reason] is contradictory (*viruddhārthatā*),[141] because all that arises (*utpattimat*) arises only as something existing with the nature of a cause.[142]

---

[139] Note that PP Tib and PsP Tib attest a *zhes bya ba* after *bdag las* for which no equivalent *iti* is found in PsP Skt (*ci bdag las zhes bya ba 'bras bu'i bdag nyid las sam | 'on te rgyu'i bdag nyid las yin grang*). It is difficult to know if *zhes bya ba* is reflecting an *iti* that actually stood in PP Skt or if it represents an addition or the PP Tib translators' interpretation. A translation for the final *iti*, on the other hand, is not attested.

[140] I have already discussed ms P's readings *kāryātmakaḥ* and *kāraṇātmakaḥ* vs. PsP_L's *kāryātmakāt* and *kāraṇātmakāt* in an earlier article (cf. MacDonald 2003: 162-167); ms Q's readings *kāryātmanaḥ* and *kāraṇātmanaḥ* are discussed and rejected in MacDonald 2008: 30-33. PsP Tib's *bras bu'i bdag nyid las* (for PsP Skt's *kāryātmakaḥ*) and *rgyu'i bdag nyid las* (for PsP Skt's *kāraṇātmakaḥ*) cannot be taken as support for ms Q's ablative readings because it has been copied in from PP Tib and does not reflect PsP Skt. Candrakīrti has purposely revised what were probably ablatives in PP Skt to nominatives in order to place emphasis on things as *causes* as the subject of arising (as opposed to things as *effects* as the subject of arising). Readers unfamiliar with the earlier articles are referred to Appendix VIII for my arguments for the superiority of ms P's readings.

[141] Here in the PsP citation the Sāṅkhyas state that if the Mādhyamika intends to argue that something already existing with the nature of an effect does not reproduce itself, then the inference refuting arising from self would prove what is already established for the Sāṅkhya (*siddhasādhana*), because the Sāṅkhya rejects that things already existing as effects reproduce themselves, e.g., that a pot that has already manifested reproduces itself. In the second case, given that it is a fundamental Sāṅkhya presupposition that things exist with the nature of a cause and then arise, i.e., manifest, if the Mādhyamika intends to argue that things existing with the nature of a cause do not reproduce themselves, the thesis ends up being contradicted, because only things that exist in a non-manifest state, that is, exist with the nature of a cause, arise.

[142] The objection appears in PP Tib as follows: *'dir grangs can dag las kha cig phyir zlog par byed de | dam bcas pa 'di'i don*[1] *gang yin | ci bdag las zhes bya ba 'bras bu'i bdag nyid las sam | 'on te rgyu'i bdag nyid las des cir 'gyur*[2] *| gal te 'bras bu'i bdag*

How could there be for us (the Mādhyamikas) the reason (*hetu*) "because [they] are [already] existing" (*vidyamānatvāt*), which [the Sāṅkhyas claim] would have the [fault of] proving what is [already] established (*siddhasādhana*) or [the fault of] being contradictory (*viruddhārthatā*),[143] so that we would have to endeavour to refute this

---

nyid las[3] *na ni grub pa la sgrub bo*[4] (D: *grub pa bsgrub bo*) | *'on te*[5] *rgyu'i bdag nyid las*[6] *na ni don 'gal ba nyid de*[7] | *skye ba can*[8] *thams cad ni rgyu'i bdag nyid du yod pa kho na las*[9] *skye ba'i phyir ro zhe na* (D 49a3-5; P 58b3-5; cf. Kajiyama 1963: 49; Ames 1993: 222); PsP Tib: [1]*dam bca' ba'i don 'di* for *dam bcas pa 'di'i don*; [2]*yin grang* | *de las cir 'gyur* | for *des cir 'gyur* |; [3]adds following *yin*; [4]*grub pa la sgrub pa yin la* for *grub pa la sgrub bo*; [5]omits *'on te*; [6]adds following *yin*; [7]*'gal ba'i don nyid du 'gyur te* for *don 'gal ba nyid de*; [8]*skye ba dang ldan pa* for *skye ba can*; [9]without *las*. This section as found in the PsP is reproduced, translated and commented on in Yotsuya 1999: 61-64. Bhāviveka deals with the objection in the PP by declaring it inapplicable, since he negates mere (*tsam*) arising from self (see PP D 49a5; P 58b5-6).

On the Sāṅkhya theory of the manifestation of all entities from the "Ur-matter" *prakṛti*, see, e.g., Frauwallner 1984: 275ff., 303-307; Chakravarti 1975: 215-221; Larson and Bhattacharya 1987: 100-101, 246-249. That the Sāṅkhyas hold that an effect is not substantially different from its cause is declared, e.g., at YD 109.13-14: *na hi naḥ kāraṇād arthāntarabhūtaṃ kāryam utpadyata ity abhyupagamaḥ*. An effect is merely the differentiated manifestation of the subtle undifferentiated cause: *idānīṃ sattvaṃ rajas tamaḥ puruṣa iti padārthacatuṣṭayaṃ pratijñāyate* | *tatrāpi puruṣa-kartṛtvaṃ pratyākhyāyate* | *tasmin pratyākhyāte guṇānām evāvasthāntarāpekṣaḥ kāryakāraṇabhāvaḥ* | *sūkṣmāṇāṃ mūrtilābhaḥ kāryam* | *nivṛttaviśeṣāṇām avibhā-gātmanāvasthānaṃ kāraṇam ity ayaṃ siddhāntaḥ* | (YD 62.8-12). See YD 109-125 for its defense and explication of the five reasons set forth in Sāṅkhyakārikā 9 for the pre-existence of the effect in the cause.

[143] *viruddhārthatā* refers to the fact that the reason proves a thing or a state of affairs opposite to what the probandum aims to establish. For example, the reason "because it is created" for the probandum "sound is permanent" does not prove that sound is permanent, and instead proves that it is impermanent. The contradictory reason (*viruddho hetuḥ*) is thus classified as a fallacious reason (*hetvābhāsa*). Cf. NM 4 (Tucci 1930: 23f.) and NM 9 (= PS III.27: *dharmadharmisvarūpasya tadviśeṣasya caiva saḥ* | *viparītopakāritvād viruddho 'sati bādhane* || (cf. Katsura 2009: 159); Tib: *chos dang chos can rang ngo bo* | *yang na de yi khyad par rnams* || *phyin ci log tu sgrub pa'i phyir* | *gnod med pa la 'gal ba yin* "It is, when there is no sublation [of the proposition], a contradictory [reason] because it serves for (= proves) the opposite of the essential characteristic (*svarūpa*) of the subject (*dharmin*) or of its attribute (*dharma*) [or of both the *dharmin* and *dharma*] or of their particular characteristics (*viśeṣa*)"; cf. Tucci 1930: 35; Katsura 1979a: 78f.; also Tucci 1929: 481). I do not translate *artha* of *viruddhārthatā* ("being [something] having a contradictory

proving of what is [already] established and [this] being contradictory?[144] Therefore, simply because the faults adduced by the [Sāṅkhya] opponent are not entailed, the Master Buddhapālita does not need to describe their refutation (*tatparihāra*).

§28. Even if it were [argued]: [It] may [indeed] be,[145] since Mādhyamikas do not state independent inferences (*svatantrānumāna*) owing to the fact that propositions (*pakṣa*),[146] reasons (*hetu*) and examples (*dṛṣṭānta*) are not established [for them], that there is neither proof (*sādhana*) of the content (*artha*) of the thesis (*pratijñā*) negating arising from self nor refutation (*nirākaraṇa*) of the opponent's thesis by way of an inference established for both [parties

---

meaning/content") for the sake of simplicity. Steinkellner's (1988: 1429) translation "object" for *artha* of *viparītārtha[hetu]* ("(reasons) that have a contradictory object") presumably refers to the *sādhya* proved by this reason, i.e., this *sādhya* is opposite to the *sādhya* sought to be proved.

[144] Seyfort Ruegg (2002: 30) translates the last part of the sentence, which has a consecutive sense, as a separate sentence, and thereby brings in a meaning unintended by Candrakīrti. He translates the sentence as "How, for us [Mādhyamikas], could there be the inferential reason ... for which there might exist [the fault of either] *siddhasādhana* or *viruddhārthatā*? We will [indeed] seek to avoid any [argument] incurring [the faults in debate of either] establishment of the [already] established or a sense that is contradictory."

[145] *mā bhūt*, here in relationship with *tu*, has a concessive sense; see, e.g., the same construction at PsP_L 273.12-13: *nanu ca bhāvānāṃ svabhāvo nāstīty abhyupagacchato mā bhūd bhāvadarśanābhāvāc chāśvatadarśanam ucchedadarśanaṃ tu niyataṃ prasajyate*. The translators of PsP Tib have also understood *mā bhūt* in connection with *tu* as intended in a concessive sense (*ma gyur mod*); note that Hopkins (1983: 140) brings in the concessive sense by translating: "[Bhāvaviveka] might think, '[I might allow that] ... autonomous inferences are not to be expressed ... . Still, ...'" Seyfort Ruegg (2002: 30) translates *mā bhūt* prohibitively and his translation for *tu* is, probably merely due to an oversight, marked as a translation for *mā bhūt*: "Because Mādhyamikas do not formulate an autonomous inference ... there should exist neither the establishment of a thesis-sense ... nor the rejection of the opponent's thesis ... . Yet (*mā bhūt* : *mod*) ... ." *LṬ's author also interprets *mā bhūt* in a prohibitive sense (on his reading and interpretation of the passage, see n. 151).

[146] It is possible that *pakṣa* includes reference to both the subject of the inference and the proposition.

of the debate] (*ubhayasiddha*);[147] nevertheless, there must be criticism (*codanayā*)[148] of the opponent's thesis for being in contradiction with

[147] That the reason and subject must be established for both parties in a debate has been declared by Dignāga in PS III.11 (Skt in Katsura 2009: 157; cf. also PVBh 647.9): *dvayoḥ siddhena dharmeṇa vyavahārād viparyaye* | *dvayor ekasya sandehe* (PVBh: *cāsiddhau* for *sandehe*) *dharmyasiddhau ca neṣyate* ||: "Because one works [in a debate] with a property [of the subject] that is established for the two [parties in the debate], when [this property = the reason] is [assumed to be] the opposite for both or [even] one [of the parties], when [it is in] doubt [for both or for one] and when the property possessor (= subject) is not established [for both or for one], [it is] not accepted." At PsP_{M} §59 (PsP_{L} 35.5-6) Candrakīrti will cite Dignāga's regulation regarding the reason (*hetu*) as found in the NM and inform Dignāga and his followers of the allowance that must be made for the Madhyamaka situation. See also Dignāga's commentary ad NM *kārikā* 2 where he states that the reason must be accepted by both disputants (cf. Tucci 1930: 13; Katsura 1977: 122, where the equivalence to the words *pakṣadharmo vādiprativādiniścito gṛhyate* in Vibhūticandra's commentary ad PV 3.17 is noted). See Yotsuya 1999: 63, n. 61 for the three types of inference distinguished by Candrakīrti.

[148] My arguments for the reading *codanayā* attested by ms P, as against ms Q's and *LṬ's *codanāyām*, have been presented in an earlier article (see MacDonald 2000: 172, n. 23). In brief, the reading *codanāyām* cannot be accepted because it disturbs the obviously intended symmetry between the components of the two parts of the sentence, namely, between proof and refutation by way of a reasoning whose subject, etc., is established for both parties (*ubhayasiddhena*) being conceded as inappropriate (*mā bhūt*), on the one hand, and, on the other, criticism of contradiction with a reasoning accepted by the opponent alone by way of a *pakṣa,* etc., from the opponent's point of view alone (*svata eva*), being demanded (*bhavitavyam*) in their place. The ms Q and *LṬ reading *codanāyām* becomes definitively disqualified when the line of argumentation is taken into consideration, for *codanāyām* brings with it the implication that the Mādhyamika addressed by Candrakīrti's Bhāviveka does indeed, of his own accord, criticize the opponent's *pratijñā* by way of a *svata evānumāna* and needs merely to be reminded that this *anumāna* must have a faultless *pakṣa*, etc., an implication in no way supported by the text preceding the sentence; the *svata evānumāna* that will be drawn out of Buddhapālita's *prasaṅga* in the section following the sentence under discussion represents merely Candrakīrti's concession to the *demand* for a *svata evānumāna*. See further comments below in Appendix IX. For my criticism of Oetke's 2003 translation of the passage, see MacDonald 2003: 168ff. (Oetke's construal of the sentence in Oetke 2006: 63 is also problematic). Seyfort Ruegg (2002: 30f.) takes PsP Tib into consideration for his translation of *codanayā*: "in view of <the need for> an explicit ruling (*codanā* : *brjod par ni bya dgos pas*)" and construes *bhavitavyam* with *pakṣādibhiḥ*. Yonezawa's (2004: 132, n. 2) suggestion to accept *codanāyām* and construe *bhavitavyam* with

an inference just from [his] own (= the opponent's) [point of view] (*svata evānumāna*)[149] by way of a proposition and so forth that are free of the faults (*apakṣāla*)[150] of the proposition (*pakṣa*), reason (*hetu*) and example (*dṛṣṭānta*), [each of which is established] only from [his] (= the opponent's) own [point of view].[151] And therefore, because those [namely, a proposition together with a reason and example] have not been stated and because their faults [as

---

°*pratijñārthasādhanam* and *parapratijñānirākaraṇam* of the concessive clause would result in a serious misrepresentation of Candrakīrti's intent.

[149] As stated below in Appendix IX, Tillemans has drawn attention to Stcherbatsky's wrong understanding of *svata eva* and corrected it. Nevertheless, both Oetke (2003: 116; 2006: 55ff.) and Matsumoto (2011: 277ff.) argue for *svata eva* as referring to the Mādhyamika. See my comments on the passage in MacDonald 2003: 168ff. Hopkins (1983: 480) translates PsP Tib's *rang gi* of *rang gi rjes su dpag pas* as "one's own" and does not translate *rang nyid la* of *rang nyid la phyogs la sogs pa*, but he quite clearly understands that an inference acknowledged by the opponent (i.e., an other-acknowledged inference) is being called for; he translates *rang gi rjes su dpag pas* as "through one's own [other-approved] inference."

[150] On the emendation *apakṣāla*, see MacDonald 2000: 174, n. 24. The *LṬ precludes de La Vallée Poussin's conjecture *doṣa* in that it employs *doṣa* as the word with which *apakṣāla* is glossed; it presents, however, the corruption *apakṣātmā* for *apakṣāla* (*tm* undoubtedly a simple misreading of *l*) in the explanatory phrase *kimbhūtaiḥ pakṣādīnām apakṣālā doṣas tena rahitaiḥ* | (cf. Yonezawa 2004: 121, 133 [fol. 1b7]).

[151] An inference admitted only by the opponent (*svata evānumāna*) does not require or imply any ontological commitment on the part of the Mādhyamika. This sort of inference consists of a subject, a reason and an example taken from the opponent's own stockpile of approved and propounded entities, concepts and tenets, and is constructed in such a way that the opponent must accept its thesis; but its thesis will be in contradiction with another thesis of the opponent's, in the present case with the Sāṅkhya thesis of arising from self. The contradiction made evident by the other-acknowledged inference will force the Sāṅkhya to relinquish the thesis of arising from self. On Candrakīrti's use of this type of inference, see Yoshimizu forthcoming. *LṬ's author misunderstands the passage, taking the scope of *mā bhūt* to be limited to the preceding *svata utpattipratiṣedhapratijñārthasādhanam* and the phrases that follow *mā bhūt* as indicating the recommended, admonished mode of procedure for the Mādhyamika side of the debate: *parapratijñānirākaraṇan tu mādhyamikasya yujyate* | *ubhayasiddhānumānena* | *anumānena virodhacodanāyāṃ tasyānumānasya pakṣādibhir bhāvyam* | (cf. Yonezawa 2004: 121, 133 [fol. 1b7]).

pronounced earlier by the Sāṅkhya opponent] have not been refuted, that very fault [remains].[152]

[We would] reply: No, this is not the case. [For] what reason? Because [it is] of course (*hi*) [that disputant] who proposes a [certain] matter (*artha*) who should, with the desire to bring about certainty (*niścaya*) in others analogous to [his] own certainty,[153] teach the other [party] exactly the reasoning (*upapatti*) by means of which [he] has come to understand this matter. Therefore this, first, is the regular procedure (*nyāya*): Only the opponent (*pareṇa*) has to employ a proof

[152] Yotsuya (1999: 64) interprets *tadanabhidhānāt* as a *tatpuruṣa*-compound, understanding its *tat* to refer to criticism by way of a *pakṣa*, etc. ("Therefore, because that [censure by means of such a proposition, etc.,] is not presented"). He interprets *taddoṣāparihārāt* as a *tatpuruṣa*-compound with a *karmadhāraya*-compound as the first member: "because these faults [which are raised by the opponent]." I interpret *taddoṣāparihārāt* as a *tatpuruṣa*-compound with another *tatpuruṣa*-compound as its first member and thus take *tat* of both compounds to refer to the elements wanted by the criticism, namely, the *pakṣa*, the *hetu* and the *dṛṣṭānta*; with this, the original criticism (cf. PsP_M §23) is better reflected in the first compound, and the *tat* of the second does not require a new referent. *LṬ's author also appears to wish to indicate that both anaphoric pronouns refer to *pakṣa*, *hetu* and *dṛṣṭānta*: *tadanabhidhānāt pakṣādyanabhidhānāt* | *taddoṣaḥ pakṣādidoṣaḥ* (cf. Yonezawa 2004: 121, 133 [fol. 1b7-2a1]).

[153] Candrakīrti quotes NM 13ab = PS IV.6ab: *svaniścayavad anyeṣāṃ niścayotpādanecchayā* |. (PS IV.6cd: *pakṣadharmatvasambandhasādhyokter anyavarjanam* ||; Skt for the verse and sources attesting it in Muni Jambuvijayaji 1966: 134; cf. also Tucci 1930: 44 and n. 79; Katsura 1979a: 73f.). Tillemans (1992: 317) has also recognized that this *pāda* is embedded in Candrakīrti's text. The construction of the rest of the sentence in PsP Tib differs slightly from the Skt: ... *don 'di'i 'thad pa gang gi sgo nas khong du chud pa'i 'thad pa de nyid gzhan la bsnyad par bya dgos so* || (PsP Skt: *yayopapattyāsāv artho 'dhigataḥ saivopapattiḥ parasmāy upadeṣṭavyā*). Candrakīrti cites this famous half-verse of Dignāga's as part of his refutational strategy and not because he consistently, at least for debates dealing with the ultimate level, took as his standard Dignāgean logic. The view put forth in the part of the verse he cites, namely, that one should strive to engender in the opponent the same certainty already attained for oneself, is in fact not specific to Dignāgean logic but is applicable to the context of debate no matter what one's own position on logic and argumentation is. Candrakīrti does seem to have accepted Dignāga's regulations for debate within the context of debates dealing with aspects of superficial reality. He may secondarily cite Dignāga as an authority here in order to catch the attention of Bhāviveka's followers and have them take his response seriously.

of the matter proposed [on the basis of that] which [he him]self maintains.[154] But the [opponent] (*sa*)[155] here (*ayam*) [in the present

---

[154] *LṬ: *tasmāt pareṇaiva svapratijñātārthasādhanaṃ hetudṛṣṭāntādibhir upādeyaṃ nāsmābhiḥ* | (cf. Yonezawa 2004: 121f., 133 [fol. 2a1]). PsP Tib is translated in the usual relative-co-relative style employed for Sanskrit constructions with *yat* used as a conjunction: *de'i phyir rang gis khas blangs pa'i dam bcas pa'i don gyi sgrub par byed pa ni pha rol po kho nas nye bar dgod par bya ba gang yin pa de ni re zhig lugs yin no* ||.

[155] The relevant text for the passage as it appears in de La Vallée Poussin's edition reads: *tasmād eṣa tāvan nyāyo* | *yat pareṇaiva svābhyupagatapratijñātārthasādhanam upādeyam* | ***na cāyaṃ paraṃ prati* [*hetuḥ*]** | ***hetudṛṣṭāntāsaṃbhavāt*** *pratijñānusāratayaiva kevalaṃ svapratijñātārthasādhanam upādatta iti nirupapattikapakṣābhyupagamāt svātmānam evāyaṃ kevalaṃ visaṃvādayan na śaknoti pareṣāṃ niścayam ādhātum iti* (PsP_L 19.3-6). All of the Skt manuscripts attest the negative particle *na* in place of *sa* (*na cāyam*) at the beginning of the second sentence (ms Q's *akṣara* is poorly formed but appears to be a *na*); the PsP Tib of the four editions and the Golden manuscript unanimously support *na* with *ma yin*. De La Vallée Poussin suggests the conjecture *hetuḥ* (*na cāyaṃ paraṃ prati* [*hetuḥ*] | *hetudṛṣṭāntāsaṃbhavāt*) on the basis of PsP Tib which reads *'di ni gzhan la gtan tshigs kyang ma yin no* ||. The sentence as such, whether de La Vallée Poussin's conjecture is accepted or not, is problematic, as attested by the various modern translations of the passage (see MacDonald 2000: 174-177). The Sanskrit manuscripts, however, do not attest a *daṇḍa* after *na cāyaṃ paraṃ prati*, and thereby inform that *na cāyaṃ paraṃ prati* was understood by the tradition as the first few words of a much longer sentence. The sentence read with the manuscripts' *na* cannot be made to yield a contextually meaningful and satisfying sense and I have therefore emended *na* to *sa* (cf. ibid., 177f.). The corruption of *sa* to *na* is immediately explainable given that in various north Indian scripts *sa* can easily be mistaken for *na* if its upper left stroke has incurred damage or if the *akṣara* is faded. That this must have been an early corruption is demonstrated by PsP Tib. I assume that Pa tshab and his Indian collaborators, finding *na cāyaṃ paraṃ prati hetudṛṣṭāntāsambhavāt*, etc., in their manuscripts and struggling with the problems it presents, attempted to solve the problem by decapitating the sentence and by adding *gtan tshigs* to the severed part to set it off as an independent sentence. It is also possible that they were confronted with a dittography in one of their manuscripts, i.e., *hetuhetudṛṣṭāntāsambhavāt* and were on its account inspired to construe the extra word with their independent sentence.

The *LṬ attests the sentence in question as commencing with *tac cāyam* instead of *na cāyam*, a variant which, like *na* of the PsP manuscripts, has to be rejected (see MacDonald 2000: 178, n. 32 for reasons for the rejection and paleographical remarks on the variant). It would seem, however, that *LṬ's author was in fact relying on a manuscript of the PsP that read *sa cāyam* and that the *LṬ's copied *sa cāyam* degenerated independently to *tac cāyam* due to scribal error and interference (the

debate], (i.e., the Sāṅkhya), on account of—in the view of [his] opponent (= the Mādhyamika)[156]—the impossibility of [valid] reasons and examples, employs (*upādatte*) a proof[157] of the matter he has proposed only (*kevalam*) in such a way that [its sound] core (*sāra*) is nothing but his (*sva*) mere thesis (*pratijñāmātra*)![158] Thus, since he

---

other scribal errors in the extant *LṬ show that it is a copied manuscript). The *LṬ two sentences previous to *tac cāyam* reads: *tasmāt pareṇaiva svapratijñātārtha-sādhanaṃ hetudṛṣṭāntādibhir upādeyaṃ nāsmābhiḥ* | (cf. Yonezawa 2004: 121f., 133 [fol. 2a1]). The next sentence, which introduces the "citation" *tac cāyam*, reads: *atha so pi paro* (Yonezawa 1999 and 2004: *pare*; *LṬ manuscript and Matsumoto 2005: *paro*) *vinā hetvādibhiḥ paraṃ pratipādayiṣyatīty āha* | *tac cāyam ityādi* ||. The statement *so pi paro vinā hetvādibhiḥ paraṃ pratipādayiṣyati* clearly represents the *LṬ author's paraphrase of PsP's *sa* (according to the *LṬ manuscript's citation: *tac*) *cāyaṃ paraṃ prati hetudṛṣṭāntāsaṃbhavāt ... svapratijñātārthasādhanam upādatte*. *LṬ's *paro* is undoubtedly intended as a gloss of the *sa* of the same paraphrase. The *LṬ author's citation and gloss of *sa* confirms that he read *sa* in the PsP manuscript available to him and that the PsP_M *sa* can be definitely be accepted as the original reading. This "hidden jewel" of the *LṬ *paraphrase* (but not of the *LṬ manuscript's actual "citation" of the text, i.e., *tac cāyam*, the *sa* of which has degenerated to *tac*!) bespeaks the testimonial importance of such commentaries.

[156] Cf. MW s.v. *prati*: *māṃ prati* "according to me, in my opinion, ... to me."

[157] Ms P and the paper manuscripts attest °*mātram* in place of °*sādhanam*; ms Q's reading has been lost due to breakage. I follow de La Vallée Poussin in emending the text (cf. PsP_L 19.4 and n. 6). PsP Tib attests *rang gi dam bca' ba'i don gyi sgrub par byed pa (= svapratijñārthasādhanam)*. The change of °*sādhanam* to °*mātram* may have occurred when the scribe's eye, attracted by *svapratijñā* in the previous compound, skipped back to this compound as he was about to write *sādhanam* (the *akṣaras mā* and *sā* are easily confused in the older north Indian scripts).

[158] Candrakīrti commences the sentence beginning with *sa cāyam* by declaring that the Sāṅkhya tries to prove his position with reasons and examples that are, from the point of view of the Mādhyamika, just bogus supports for the thesis he aims to prove. Since the reasons and examples in his proof are faulty, the Sāṅkhya ends up proving his proposition by way of an argument that has nothing but (*eva*) his mere (*mātra*) claim, i.e., nothing but his own thesis (*svapratijñā*), as its "[sound] core" (*sāra*), as the sound element in it that cannot be invalidated, as the argument's solid, sturdy heartwood. Obviously Candrakīrti is using the word *sāra* ironically. Without a reason and example to support it, the thesis is not at all sturdy; it is actually extremely shaky, indeed on the verge of a total collapse. The accumulation of the elements *mātra*, *eva* and *kevalam* in the Sanskrit sentence indicates strong emphasis: *mātra* sets the limit, *eva* underscores this limit as definite ("nothing but"), and *kevalam* may be adding a nuance of the deficiency and pitifulness of such an argument.

maintains a proposition (*pakṣa*) lacking justification (*nirupapatti*), he, fooling (*visaṃvādayan*) only himself [with respect to the soundness of his inference],[159] is not able to instill certainty (*niścaya*) in [his] opponents. Just this is the [Mādhyamika's] very clear criticism of him, namely, [he] is incapable of proving the matter he has proposed;[160] under these circumstances (*atra*), what is the point of

---

The sentence is also interesting because it is an example of one of Candrakīrti's trademark methods for neutralizing an opponent's critique. The more usual version of this method involves Candrakīrti criticizing the opponent for having exactly the fault he has accused Candrakīrti of; he turns the critique back on the critiquer, sometimes with an even more devastating element added to it. Here the situation is indirect: he turns Bhāviveka's critique of Buddhapālita's *prasaṅga* statement, i.e., that it lacks a reason and example, on the opponent Sāṅkhya; he thus indirectly turns it on Bhāviveka by turning it on the Sāṅkhya. Candrakīrti here charges the opponent, as Bhāviveka does Buddhapālita and other opponents in the PP, with arguing for his position with a "mere thesis" (*pratijñāmātra*). He also takes Bhāviveka's criticism of Buddhapālita one step further: the Sāṅkhya, unlike Buddhapālita who, according to Bhāviveka, has not utilized a reason and example and must merely add them, utilizes reasons and examples that fall apart under the Mādhyamika's critical eye; logically sound reasons and examples, given the Sāṅkhya's indefensible position of arising from self, are *impossible* for the Sāṅkhya.
PsP Tib reads *khas 'ches pa'i rjes su 'brangs pa 'ba' zhig* ("solely following the thesis") for *svapratijñāmātrasāratayaiva kevalam.* De La Vallée Poussin, influenced by PsP Tib's *khas 'ches pa'i rjes su 'brangs pa*, emends to *pratijñānusāratayaiva.* Ms P and all of the paper manuscripts attest *svapratijñāmātrasāratayaiva kevalam*; Ms Q has been corrupted to *svapratijñānaṅga*(?)*ye*(?)*prāptayaiva. pratijñānusāratayaiva*, if actually responsible for PsP Tib's reading, may simply have been the result of an eyeskip from °*jñā*°'s *ā* stroke to the *ā* stroke concluding °*mā*°, which was followed by a misreading of the *akṣara tra* as the *akṣara nu.*

[159] Hopkins (1983: 481) has correctly interpreted PsP Tib's *bdag nyid kho na la slu bar byed pa*(*s*) as "deceives just himself," but has wrongly taken the agent of the act of deception to be the argument itself, which of course the masculine *ayam* as PsP Skt's agent of the action prohibits (*idam* would be required for a reference to *sādhanam*). Seyfort Ruegg (2002: 32) does not explain why he interprets *svātmānam evāyaṃ kevalaṃ visaṃvādayan* to mean "and being in conflict in respect to [the term] *svātman* '[from] itself.'"

[160] One might even be justified in reading the full passage as an interpretation of Buddhapālita's intention: His statement of unwanted consequence was merely intended to show, or at least allude to, the inability of the Sāṅkhya's argument to prove (*sādhanāsamarthya*) his own thesis.

bringing out the sublation [of his thesis] by means of an inference (*anumānabādhā*)[161]?[162]

§29. Even if [Bhāviveka insists:] The fault of contradiction with an inference from [the Sāṅkhya's] own [point of view] (*svato 'numānavirodhadoṣa*) must definitely be brought out [by way of the Mādhyamika's employment of such an inference, i.e., one acknowledged only by the Sāṅkhya].[163]

---

[161] A proposition (*pakṣa*) that is susceptible to sublation by an inference (*anumāna-bādhā*) is the fifth of the five *pakṣābhāsa*s enumerated in NM; cf. Tucci 1930: 7f.; Katsura 1977: 113; Preisendanz 1994: 319-323 (= n. 88). That sublation can be also accomplished by an other-acknowledged inference, and that the inference's reason is responsible for the sublation is confirmed and explained at PsP_M §57 (PsP_L 34.13ff.).

[162] My interpretation of the paragraph differs from that presented in Oetke 2003; a detailed critique can be found in MacDonald 2003: 168ff. Oetke's response to my critique appears in Oetke 2006. I remain unconvinced by his arguments and thus do not respond to them here. Oetke considers *sa* of *sa cāyam* to refer not to the Sāṅkhya, but to "a Mādhyamika." Matsumoto (2011: 289ff.) considers *sa* of *sa cāyam* to refer to Bhāviveka. I am also unconvinced by his arguments, and hope to respond to them in a separate article.
Pa tshab appears to be summing up this passage in his (or his student's?) Tshig gsal ba'i dka' ba bshad pa / bla ma tshong dpon pan di ta'i gdam ngag (bKa' gdams gsung 'bum, vol. 11, 149.i.7-8) when he states that the Sāṅkhya has to state a reasoning to the Mādhyamika: *de'i don ni grangs can gyis rang la[s] skye ba bsgrub pa'i phyir | dbu ma pa la rang las skye ba'i grub pa'i 'thad brjod pa bya ba yin pa la | de ma brjod pa nyid kyis rang gi khas blangs pa la rang nyid kyis gnod pa sgrub byed ma brjod pa nyid kyis bkag pa yin no* | "The meaning of this [passage in the Prasanna-padā] is: Since the Sāṅkhya [wishes to] establish arising from self, a reasoning for the establishment of arising from self is to be stated to the Mādhyamika. By the very non-stating of that, his own [= the Sāṅkhya's] assertions are invalidated by himself; by the very non-stating of a proof, [the Sāṅkhya's assertions] are negated." My thanks to Kevin Vose for bringing the comment to my attention and for providing me with the text passage.

[163] Seyfort Ruegg's (2002: 33, n. 23) understanding of the objection is not immediate-ly clear to me. He translates, "But still (*athâpi* = *ci ste yang*) the fault (*doṣa*; not in Tib.) of contradiction within the [Sāṃkhya opponent's] inference on his own account (*svatas*: *rang gi rjes su dpag pa*) has necessarily to be pointed out (*udbhāvanīya* = *brjod par bya ba*) [by Buddhapālita]," adding in a note that "the translation 'within his inference [consisting in postulating origination] "from self"' would seem to be less pertinent." The contradiction to be brought out is of course not within the inference presented by the Mādhyamika, but in regard to another thesis the Sāṅkhya holds, i.e., the thesis of arising from self.

[We reply:] That [fault of the Sāṅkhya's thesis being contradicted by an inference] has also definitely been brought out by the Master Buddhapālita,[164] [and this] by virtue of [his] statement "Things do not arise from self because their arising would be pointless" (*na svata utpadyante bhāvās tadutpādavaiyarthyāt*). For in this [statement], with [the use of] this [word] "their" (*tat*) there is reference to something [already] existing by [its] own nature. To explain,[165] this is

---

[164] PsP Tib adds *ji ltar zhe na*, which is followed by *gang gi phyir des ni 'di skad du bshad pa yin te*. De La Vallée Poussin (PsP_L 20.1) conjectures *katham iti cet* for *ji ltar zhe na* and adds this, within brackets, to his edition; he does not include a Sanskrit equivalent for *gang gi phyir des ni 'di skad du bshad pa yin te*. The question and answer phrases do not appear in ms P or in the other paper manuscripts (*iti vacanāt* is translated with *zhes bshad pa'i phyir*) but Sanskrit equivalents for both are attested in ms Q, which reads *kathaṃ kṛtvā yasmād evaṃ tenoktaṃ*. However, these phrases appear only in Q's lower margin and are marked as needing to be inserted (the point of insertion is marked with an "x" before *na svata*). It is unlikely that the text is original, primarily because *yasmād evaṃ tenoktam* combined with *na svata utpadyante bhāvās tadutpādavaiyarthyād iti vacanāt* is awkward, and creates a certain redundancy in the text (I expect it is for this reason that de La Vallée Poussin refrained from reconstructing an equivalent for *yasmād evaṃ tenoktam*). It is more likely that Q's *kathaṃ kṛtvā yasmād evaṃ tenoktaṃ* represents an accretion. In order for this question and answer to appear in the Tibetan translation, it must have been added to a manuscript in the γ line prior to the translation (see Stemma; I posit the source as ms δ). Its location in Q's margin would indicate that it was not appropriated by ms η when η's scribe took over some of δ's readings—since if it had been, one would expect it to appear in Q's main text—and was instead, in a second wave of contamination, passed directly to Q by ms θ. The question and answer were probably originally written as a marginal note, added in the course of teaching or reading to clarify Candrakīrti's concisely formed sentence. This marginal note would have been brought into the main text of a later manuscript and must have appeared in one or both of manuscripts used for the Tibetan translation. In being appropriated from the text of ms θ for insertion into Q, the question and answer once again appear as marginal; enclosed between "x"s and followed by the line number to which they belong, they give the misleading impression that they are merely words that were dropped by Q's scribe but later caught by him or his proofreader.

[165] PsP Tib adds a preceding *ci'i phyir zhe na*, an equivalent of which is not attested in ms P or in the paper manuscripts; de La Vallée Poussin (PsP_L 20.3) adds to his text, in brackets, the conjecture *kasmād iti cet*. A Sanskrit equivalent does appear in ms Q, namely, *kiṃ kāraṇam*. However, as in the case described in the preceding note, the words *kiṃ kāraṇaṃ*, followed by the *akṣara ta*, have been written in the lower margin and are marked for insertion; the "x" after *parāmarśaḥ* marking the point of

the explanatory statement (*vivaraṇavākya*) [subsequently given by Buddhapālita] for that concise statement (*grahaṇakavākya*): "For there is no purpose in the re-arising of things [already] existing by [their] own nature."[166] And with this [explanatory] statement [of Buddhapālita's], there is the appropriation of an example based on similarity of properties (*sādharmyadṛṣṭānta*) that is acknowledged by the opponent [alone] (*paraprasiddha*), [i.e., an example] with the property to be proved (*sādhyadharma*) and the proving property (*sādhanadharma*). There [in the concise statement under consideration], through [the implied use of] this [phrase pointed out as meant by *tat* and appearing in the plural in the explanatory statement just adduced, i.e.,] "of something [already] existing by [its] own nature" (*svātmanā vidyamānasya*), there is reference to the reason (*hetu*); [and] through [the use of] this [phrase, namely,] "because

insertion appears to have been written over an erased *akṣara* whose remaining vague outline could be considered that of a *sta*. It is difficult to explain the loss of *kiṃ kāraṇaṃ* from P and the paper manuscripts on paleographical grounds, and the question *kiṃ kāraṇam* seems unnecessary, given that the next sentence begins with *tathā hi*. As in the previous instance, it can be concluded that we are dealing with an accretion, probably originally a marginal teaching/reading aid, which entered the γ line (see Stemma) and was passed on to the Tibetan translation, and later to Q via ms θ.

[166] The explanatory statement is found at BP_{ed} 10.14-15: *'di ltar dngos po bdag gi bdag nyid du yod pa rnams la yang skye ba dgos pa med*. PsP Skt here, in contrast to the Skt for the same statement at PsP_M §22 (PsP_L 14.2), does not attest the words *padārthānām* and *asti*.
Stcherbatsky (1927: 99, n. 2) corrects de La Vallée Poussin's conjecture [*saṃ*]*graheṇ*[*okta*]*vākya*° to *grahaṇakavākya*°, explaining, "What a *grahaṇakavākyam* is appears clearly from Tātparyaṭīkā, p. 145.16 and an overwhelming multitude of similar phrasing in all Nyāya literature. The argument is first stated laconically (*grahaṇaka*) and then developed (*vivaraṇa*)." More precisely, a *grahaṇakavākya* is a short, concise statement in nominal style and the *vivaraṇavākya* (*vi√vṛ*: "uncovering, spreading out, unfolding") is the prose explanation of the statement in verbal style, with pronouns explained and compounds analyzed. Here in the PsP, *tadutpāda-vaiyarthyāt* is dissolved as a compound; the ablative is represented with *hi*, *vaiyarthya* is explained with *na prayojanam*, *utpāda* is placed in the locative case and its meaning clarified with *punar*, and *tat* is explained with *svātmanā vidyamānānām*.

arising would be pointless" (*utpādavaiyarthyāt*), there is reference to the property to be proved (*sādhya*).[167]

In this context, just as [in the stock five-membered inference, viz.,]

[thesis (*pratijñā*):] Sound is impermanent

[reason (*hetu*):] because it is produced[168]

[example (*dṛṣṭānta*):] whatever is produced is observed to be impermanent, like a pot

[application (*upanaya*):] and similarly, sound is produced

[conclusion (*nigamana*):] therefore, because [it] is produced, [sound] is impermanent,

"produced" (*kṛtakatva*) is here the reason (*hetu*) that is made evident [as a property of the subject "sound"] by means of the application (*upanaya*),[169]

---

[167] Candrakīrti demonstrates that when Buddhapālita states his explicit *prasaṅga* statement, it should be understood that a complete and logically correct inference is implicitly expressed; the elements of this inference claimed by Bhāviveka not to have been stated, i.e., the reason and example, are, according to Candrakīrti, contained within the *prasaṅga*'s reason *tadutpādavaiyarthyāt*. Cp. Bhāviveka's description of the extraction of a reason and example for MMK I.1 (see n. 138). Note that whereas the example referred to by Candrakīrti is *paraprasiddha*, generally established for the opponent, i.e., acknowledged by the opponent alone, the one Bhāviveka elicits for the inferential formulation of MMK I.1 is *prasiddha*, i.e., generally established for both parties in the debate, common knowledge for both parties in the debate, i.e., generally acknowledged by both parties in the debate (see PPṬ's detailed explanation of the example for Bhāviveka's inference at D 62b7-63b4; P 72b4-73a5).

[168] PsP Tib reads *byas pa mi rtag pa'i phyir ro*, for which de La Vallée Poussin (PsP_L 20, n. 6) reconstructs *kṛtakānityatvāt*, but he does not include this in the text of his edition. Ms Q presents *kṛtakatvānityatvāt*, a reading that has to be rejected because *kṛtakatvāt* is considered as the reason in the rest of the inference (ms Q attests *kṛtakam, kṛtakaḥ, kṛtakatvāt* and *kṛtakatvam* in what follows in PsP_M §29 [PsP_L 20.7-8]). Ms P has a lacuna at this point but the main paper manuscripts all give the reason as *kṛtakatvāt*. Ms Q's reading has entered from the γ line (see Stemma), probably received over ms η from ms δ.

[169] PsP Tib construes the sentence *kṛtakatvam atropanayābhivyakto hetuḥ* as *'dir nye bar sbyar bas gsal bar byas pa'i byas pa gtan tshigs yin pa*: "Here 'produced,' which is made evident by the application, is the reason" (cf. de La Vallée Poussin's

—so in the present case too (*ihāpi*), [i.e., in the inference implicit in Buddhapālita's slightly expanded concise statement]: "Things do not arise from self because the re-arising of things [already] existing by [their] own nature is pointless," [the reason is shown by the application].[170]

Here, [the inference implied by Buddhapālita's statement is:] [A thing] such as a pot that is [already] existing by own nature, which is situated in front [of one], is observed not to require re-arising. And similarly (*tathā ca*),[171] if you think that [things such as] a pot, etc., are

---

observation at PsP_L 20, n. 7: "D'aprés Tib. °*vyaktaṃ*"). PsP Skt, with *atra* separating the subject and predicate, is correct, for it is not *kṛtakatva* as such that is made evident by the application, but *kṛtakatva* as the reason (*hetu*), i.e., the reason is brought out by the application, and in this case the reason brought out is *kṛtakatva*. The application (*upanaya*) confirms the connection of the reason with the specific subject of the inference, i.e., it confirms the reason's being a property of the subject, and thus, with the conclusion (*nigamana*), its proving of the thesis. See, e.g., Junankar 1978: 258f. Candrakīrti wishes to emphasize that the reason he extracts from Buddhapālita's *prasaṅga* statement, like other reasons of correct five-membered inferences, is specifically confirmed as a property of the subject with the application step. Cp. NM *kārikā* 4d = PS III.15d: *hetus tūpanayān mataḥ* (cf. Tucci 1930: 21; Katsura 1978: 119; Katsura 2009: 158).

[170] Before presenting the inference he claims is already present in Buddhapālita's concise statement, i.e., in his *prasaṅga* statement, Candrakīrti makes explicit the elements "arising" (*utpāda*), and "their" (*tat*) with the help of the explanatory statement: "arising" is expanded to "re-arising" (*punarutpāda*), and "their" is expanded to "of things [already] existing by [their] own nature" (*svātmanā vidyamānānām*); from the latter he derives the reason "because [they already] exist" (*vidyamānatvāt*) and the example for the inference. Hopkins (1983: 484) translates this statement as part of the inference (similarly Seyfort Ruegg 2002: 34), although in his discussion of the parts of the inference (cf. Hopkins: 481-483) he does not appear to understand it as such.

[171] Stcherbatsky (1927: 100, n. 2) states that *na tu* would be preferable to *tathā ca*, "but '*tathā ca*' is also possible, since a *vaidharmyadṛṣṭānta* is also sometimes introduced in this way." However, things such as a non-manifest pot and so forth do not qualify as a *vaidharmyadṛṣṭānta* but are rather the subject for Buddhapālita's alleged inference. Stcherbatsky (ibid., 100) has misunderstood the structure of the Sanskrit sentence and therefore breaks it into two contrasting sentences (in the note in which he comments on *tathā ca*, he also asserts that a *daṇḍa* has to be inserted after °*avasthāyām*): "The jar in its (potential) condition in a clump of clay is an example (by contrast), (since it needs to be really produced). But if you mean the jar which already exists by itself, such a jar is not produced (once more)." In doing so he

also [already] existing by own nature at the stage of a lump of clay, etc.,[172] in this case as well those [pots, etc., inasmuch as they already] exist by own nature, do not arise.[173]

---

harms the expression of both the *upanaya* and the *nigamana* of the proof that Candrakīrti is showing to be implicit in Buddhapālita's *prasaṅga* statement.

[172] *ādi* ("etc.") of *mṛtpiṇḍādi* refers to all other pre-arising states of things, i.e., to the various individual causes in which the Sāṅkhya asserts the pre-existence of the effect.

[173] After demonstrating how he derives the elements of the other-acknowledged inference from Buddhapālita's statement and after repeating Buddhapālita's partially expanded concise statement, Candrakīrti sets forth the proof, i.e., the other-acknowledged inference. "[A thing] such as a pot that is [already] existing by own nature, which is situated in front" (*svātmanā vidyamānaṃ puro 'vasthitaṃ ghaṭādikam*) is the example based on similarity of properties (*sādharmyadṛṣṭānta*), which is acknowledged solely by the opponent; this example "[a thing] such as a pot that is [already] existing by own nature, which is situated in front" possesses the property to be proved, i.e., the probandum (*sādhya*) "not requiring re-arising" (*punarutpādānapekṣa*), a re-phrasing of *utpādavaiyarthya*, the probandum extracted from the reason in Buddhapālita's *prasaṅga* statement, and possesses the proving property, i.e., the probans (*hetu*), "[already] existing by own nature" (*svātmanā vidyamānam*), likewise extracted from the reason in Buddhapālita's *prasaṅga* statement. The five-limbed proof, expressed formally, therefore would be (the reference to the subject as "things disposed to arise" [*utpitsupadārtha*] is taken from Candrakīrti's comments on the subject at PsP_M §31 [PsP_L 22.1-2]):
[thesis:] [Things disposed to arise (*utpitsupadārtha*) such as] a pot, etc., at the stage of a lump of clay, etc., do not require re-arising,
[reason:] because they [already] exist by own nature (*vidyamānatvāt*);
[example:] that which [already] exists by [its] own nature is observed not to require re-arising (*punarutpādānapekṣa*), like [a thing] such as a pot situated in front, which is [already] existing;
[application:] and similarly, [things disposed to arise such as] a pot, etc., at the stage of a lump of clay, etc., [already] exist by own nature;
[conclusion:] therefore, because they [already] exist by own nature, [things disposed to arise, such as] a pot, etc., at the stage of a lump of clay, etc., do not require re-arising.
Candrakīrti expresses the *upanaya* and the *nigamana* in the form of a prose sentence in which the reason, here specifically applied to a pot, etc., at the stage of a lump of clay, etc., is explicitly shown to be accepted by the Sāṅkhya (*mṛtpiṇḍādyavasthāyām api yadi svātmanā vidyamānaṃ ... iti manyase*); this reason is intentionally repeated in the concluding part of the sentence to underscore its being, from the point of view of the opponent, a property of the logical subject. See also della Santina's (1986: 144f.) résumé of the passage.
The thesis of the other-acknowledged inference conflicts with another thesis the Sāṅkhya propounds, namely, that things arise from self. The Sāṅkhya will have to

Thus, the bringing out for the Sāṅkhya of the [fact that his thesis is in] contradiction with an inference (*anumānavirodha*) that is [accepted] just from [his] own [point of view] has definitely been effected by "[already] existing by own nature," the reason (*hetu*) shown by the application, which does not deviate (*avyabhicārin*) from [the probandum, i.e.,] the negation of re-arising. Why, then, has [Bhāviveka] voiced [this critique:] "That [mode of argumentation of Buddhapālita's] is not suitable, because a reason and an example have not been stated"?

§30. And not only is there not [the defect of] not stating a reason and an example, there is also not [the other defect Bhāviveka accuses Buddhapālita of, namely, that] the faults pronounced by the opponent have not been refuted. Why [not]? For the Sāṅkhyas certainly do not claim that there is the re-manifestation (*punarabhivyakti*) of a pot that has a manifest form, [i.e., one] situated in front; and [thus] this very [pot in front] is employed here [in the inference] as the example because [it] has an established form (*siddharūpa*) [and as such it is accepted by the Sāṅkhyas as something that does not require further arising].[174] And because something that has a non-manifest form, that has assumed a potential form (*śaktirūpa*), is to be proved as qualified by the negation of arising, how can there be [any] suspicion of the fault that the proposition is proving that which is [already] established (*siddhasādhana*) [for the opponent], or how can it be suspected that

accept this inference that proves that things do not arise from self because he certainly does not hold that things such as the clay water pots he sees before his eyes come into being once more; in order to avoid self-contradiction he will be forced to relinquish his thesis of self-arising. For a breakdown of the structure of the larger section, see MacDonald 2003: 173f.

[174] PsP Tib lacks an equivalent for *upādāna*: ... *de nyid 'dir dpe nyid du grub pa'i ngo bo yin pa'i phyir la*, "... because here just that [manifest pot] is something whose form is established as the example." When the sentence is construed in this way, the forms *siddharūpa* and *anabhivyaktarūpa* do not form a contrasting pair, as they do in Sanskrit; in PsP Tib the first would be used in an epistemological sense, the second in an ontological sense. I am unable to explain how *upādānam* came to be dropped. Hopkins (1983: 485), overlooking the first *nyid* and interpreting *ngo bo* as "entity" (*bhāva*), translates, "... and [thus] here it is an entity established as an example [of something which already exists in its own entity and is not produced again]."

the reason is contradictory (*viruddhārthatā*)?[175] Therefore, even when [we accede to Bhāviveka's demand and] there is criticism (*codanā*) that there is sublation [of the Sāṅkhya thesis] by way of an inference (*anumānabādhā*) from [the Sāṅkhya's] own point of view,[176] since the

[175] In the PP, Bhāviveka, upon employing his inference proving the non-arising of the inner bases from self, is accused by the Sāṅkhya, first, of proving what is already established for the Sāṅkhya if he assumes "from self" to mean "from something having the nature of an effect," and second, of having a contradictory reason, that is, of proving the opposite of what he intends to prove, if he assumes "from self" to mean "from something having the nature of a cause" (cf. PP D 49a4; P 58b4-5). Bhāviveka responds to the critique by saying that he simply negates arising as such, i.e., arising without any specification (*bdag las skye ba tsam dgag pa'i phyir* [PP D 49a5; P 58b5; for PPṬ references, see Ames 1993: 243, n. 97]), and that even if arising from self is considered to mean arising from something having the nature of a cause, his inference remains without fault, for he rejects arising from a cause that is the same as or different from its effect (*rgyu'i bdag nyid las na yang bdag dang gzhan du gyur pa las kyang skye ba sel ba'i phyir* [PP D 49a5; P 58b5-6]). Bhāviveka, in faulting Buddhapālita's employment of a *prasaṅga* statement, re-directs this very same Sāṅkhya critique toward his fellow Mādhyamika, saying that Buddhapālita has not articulated his own response to this expected Sāṅkhya rebuke. Candrakīrti, defending Buddhapālita, has earlier (see PsP_M §25 and §27 [PsP_L 16.2, 16.11]), declared that the (true) Mādhyamika does not state an independent inference (*svatantrānumāna*); thus for the Mādhyamika who is not encumbered by an independent proposition like Bhāviveka's *paramārthato nādhyātmikāny āyatanāni svata utpannāni* or a reason like his *vidyamānatvāt*, there exists no basis for the Sāṅkhya's charges of *siddhasādhana* and *viruddhārthatā*. In his extended defense of Buddhapālita in which he claims that an inference is couched in the *prasaṅga* statement, Candrakīrti has now set forth an inference replete with all its members that indeed, even though it is an inference whose members are accepted as established only by the Sāṅkhya, could be open to a similar Sāṅkhya attack. Candrakīrti thus presents his defense against the Sāṅkhya critique: First, there is not the proving of what is already established for the Sāṅkhya, namely, that manifest things do not arise again, because manifest effects only qualify as the example, and not the subject; the subject comprises the things the Sāṅkhya maintains only exist in a potential form, and which he claims require arising. Second, there is not the proving of the opposite of that which the Mādhyamika intends to prove, that is, there is not the proving that things that are claimed to exist as their causes *do* require re-arising, because the reason, as a property of the locus (*pakṣa*) and of the example, proves the proposition, i.e., that things in a non-manifest but existing form do *not* require re-arising.

[176] Seyfort Ruegg (2002: 35) translates *svato 'numānabādhācodanāyām api* as "also in [Buddhapālita's restrictive] specification relating to the invalidation of the inference on [the Sāṃkhya's] own account." It is of course the Sāṅkhya's original thesis

faults as described do not exist [for this inference drawn out of Buddhapālita's consequence (*prasaṅga*)], there is definitely not [the defect that] the faults pronounced by the opponent have not been refuted; it should thus be known that this critique (*dūṣaṇa*)[177] [as stated by Bhāviveka] is absolutely incoherent.[178]

§31. And because with the word "etc." (*ādi*) in [the subject] "a pot, etc." (*ghaṭādika*) the inclusion of all things that are disposed to arise (*utpitsupadārtha*) is intended, there is also definitely not inconclusiveness (*anaikāntikatā*) [of the reason] by way of [cases of] cloth, etc.[179]

---

of arising from self that is sublated by the other-acknowledged inference inherent in Buddhapālita's statement (see n. 173).

[177] PsP Tib, with *sun 'byin pa 'di dag* for *etad dūṣanam*, appears to understand *dūṣaṇa* as relating back either to the first two faults stated by Bhāviveka or to the two-fold Sāṅkhya critique. The Sanskrit would appear to refer only to the second fault stated by Bhāviveka.

[178] Candrakīrti's dismissal of this objection of Bhāviveka's as "incoherent" (*asambaddha*) may in part be meant as a jab in kind at Bhāviveka's criticism of Buddhapālita's reason in his *prasaṅga* refuting arising from other as "incoherent" (cf. PP D 50a7; P 60b1).

[179] Since the subject includes without exception all things that are inclined to arise, a counter-example such as a hypothetical case of cloth that exists in potential form and yet requires re-arising cannot be found, and thus cannot be used by the opponent to show that the reason does not exclusively prove that things do not require re-arising. Hopkins (1983: 486), relying on 'Jam dbyangs bzhad pa's interpretation of the section, also understands *ghaṭādika* of this passage to refer to the subject (see also ibid., n. 398). Della Santina (1986: 146f.), on the other hand, presenting bSod nams Sen ge's interpretation of the passage, takes *ghaṭādika* to refer to the example: "This objection, however, is without foundation because when the example was presented, it was said, 'a jar and the like.' The phrase, 'and the like', indicates the inclusion of all entities without exception which may be thought to originate." Candrakīrti has not without reason included the desiderative *utpitsu*(*padārtha*) in the phrase *niravaśeṣotpitsupadārthasaṅgrahasya vivakṣitatvāt*. He purposely employs it to indicate that he is referring to the subject, the things that the Sāṅkhya maintains exist in a potential state and which are spoken about as such because they are inclined to, ready to, keen to, arise, i.e., they are things that will arise and in their manifest forms constitute the things of the world. Candrakīrti wants to preempt the Sāṅkhya objection that according to them another group of things, i.e., things other than pots, do require re-arising. With all things declared as embraced by the subject, it is precluded that cloth, etc., in non-manifest form can constitute counter-examples where the reason is

§32. Alternatively, this is another way of formulating (*prayogamārga*) [an other-acknowledged inference]:[180] "For the [Sāṅkhya] who claims arising from self (*svata utpattivādin*), things different from Puruṣa—just on account of that (*tata eva*) [claim of self-arising]—do not arise from self, because [they already] exist by own nature, like Puruṣa." This is to be adduced as the example [in this case].[181]

---

present, and that cloth, etc., can have the property opposite to the one to be proved (= *anaikāntikatā* of the reason). *LṬ's author mistakenly takes *ghaṭādika* to be referring to the example: *ghaṭo dṛṣṭāntīkṛto* (cf. Yonezawa 2004: 122 [fol. 2a1]). Yonezawa's (ibid., 134) emendation of PsP_L's *paṭādibhir* to *ghaṭādibhir* on the basis of *LṬ's reading *ghaṭādir* is not acceptable.
In the PP, an opponent states that the reason *vidyamānatvāt* adduced by Bhāviveka for MMK I.1 has not been shown to be absent from dissimilar cases, and thus is inadmissible as a reason; Bhāviveka replies that because there is not a dissimilar case, i.e., some thing that already exists and then arises from self, there is no fault in either this or any other such inference (cf. PP D 49a3; P 58b2-3; see also Lindtner 1986: 63). Candrakīrti does not include such an objection but he may, through his use of the comprehensive subject *ghaṭādika*, also be intending to show, in a slightly more sophisticated way, that no dissimilar cases exist—and in this way avoid a charge like that made by the PP opponent.

[180] PsP Tib has a different emphasis: *yang na sbyor ba 'di ni tshul gzhan yin te* "Alternatively, this application/inference is a different sort" (Skt: *atha vāyam anyaḥ prayogamārgaḥ*).

[181] This second other-acknowledged inference is in the Dignāgean style of thesis, reason and example. De La Vallée Poussin expresses hesitancy to retain *tata eva* (PsP_L 22, n. 4), especially because these two words are lacking in PsP Tib. They are, however, attested in ms P and ms Q (ms Q's *tata* erroneously reads *tatra*) as well as in the paper manuscripts, and sense can definitely be derived from them, viz., things cannot be held to arise precisely because of the doctrinal point that they arise from themselves (according to the Buddhist critique of the theory: from already existent selves). See the translation of the same passage in Tillemans 1992: 317. Seyfort Ruegg (2002: 37) translates following PsP Tib. *LṬ's author glosses *puruṣa* with *ātmā* and paraphrases *tata eva* with *svarūpād eva*; he specifies *anya* of the introductory phrase as follows: *anya iti | pūrvaprayogāt buddhapālitasyaivāpara ity arthaḥ* (cf. Yonezawa 2004: 122, 134 [fol. 2a2]).
The example in this second inference is similar to that given by Bhāviveka in his inference for MMK I.1. Bhāviveka, however, employs *caitanya*, the own nature of *puruṣa* (instead of *puruṣa*) as the example because, according to Avalokitavrata, this example is acknowledged by both the Sāṅkhya and the Mādhyamika, for the Mādhyamika acknowledges the surface-level existence of consciousness (*skabs 'dir ni dper na chos can shes pa yod pa nyid ces bya ba de rgol ba'i phyogs la ni shes pa*

§33. And even if the proponent of manifestation (*abhivyaktivādin*) [i.e., the Sāṅkhya] does not [consider our] negation of arising (*utpādapratiṣedha*) to sublate [his thesis of arising from self], still, [due to the fact that we] employ[182] the word "arising" in the sense of manifestation—given that precisely manifestation is expressed with the word "arising" inasmuch as there is similarity in properties [in the case of the arising of a thing and that of the manifestation of a thing] with respect to [the thing's] prior non-perception and later perception—this negation [of ours] does not fail to sublate.[183]

---

yod pa nyid ces bya ba yod pa nyid du grags la | phyir rgol ba'i phyogs la ni kun rdzob tu rnam par shes pa nyid ces bya bar yod pa nyid du grags pa de la bsgrub bar bya ba chos bdag las skye ba med pa zhes bya ba rgol ba dang phyir rgol ba gnyi ga [P: *gnyis ka*] *la grags pa* ... [PPṬ D 68a4-5; P 79a4-5]).

[182] *LṬ's author glosses *nipātya* with *niyojya* (cf. Yonezawa 2004: 122, 134 [fol. 2a2]).

[183] I follow Seyfort Ruegg (2002: 37) in translating *nābādhakaḥ* (lit.: "is not a non-sublater") as "does not fail to sublate." According to Candrakīrti, the Sāṅkhya may object that the word "arising," which implies the coming into being of something new and different from its cause, cannot be equated with the manifestation he propounds, namely, the manifestation of effects that represent merely a modification of the subtle causal matter *prakṛti*, and may therefore reject that the Madhyamaka negation of arising has any bearing on his theory. Although Candrakīrti argues that arising and manifestation have similar properties, it has to be admitted that the Mādhyamikas ignore the complexities of the theory of manifestation for the sake of refuting it. A more forceful objection from the Sāṅkhya side is presented in the PP immediately following Bhāviveka's critique of Buddhapālita's *prasaṅga* statement: the Sāṅkhya rejects the Buddhist refutation of his view on the ground that the portrayal of the Sāṅkhya doctrine of manifestation from potentiality as a doctrine positing "things arising from themselves" grossly misrepresents the doctrine (*gzhan dag na re dngos po rnams bdag las skye ba med pa zhes bya ba de rigs pa ma yin te | phyogs snga ma rang dgar sbyar ba la sel ba'i phyir* | [P: *phyir ro* ||] *ri bong gi rwa las 'jig rten gsum skye ba sel ba bzhin no zhes zer ro* || [PP D 49b1, P 59a2-3; see also PPṬ D 75b4-7, P 88b2-6; Kajiyama 1963: 50; Ames 1993: 223]). Bhāviveka responds by saying that potentiality (*śakti*) and the manifest (*vyakta*) do not have different natures, and thus arising from potentiality is equivalent to "arising from self" (PP D 49b1-2; P 59a3-4). He adds that even if the position (*phyogs*) [of "arising from self"] has been made up, there is no fault because it has been included for the sake of showing that arising is not logically justifiable (PP D 49b2; P 59a4-5; D reads *phyogs rnams*). Ames (1993: 244, n. 107) explains, "Even if no one holds that entities originate from themselves, it is legitimate to refute that position in order to negate every conceivable way in which things might originate" (Ames refers to PPṬ P 90a1-

§34. If [it is asked]: But how is this meaning as you have expressed it obtained without [Buddhapālita] at all articulating such reflections (*vicāra*)?, then [we] reply: These [sentences of Buddhapālita's] are of course statements of meaning (*arthavākyāni*) [which,] possessing great import,[184] have the [entire] meaning as stated [by myself, Candrakīrti] included [within them]. And these [same statements,] being explained, yield the essential meaning (*arthātmānam*) just as [I have] asserted [it]. Therefore, nothing is postulated here that was not [already] assumed [by Buddhapālita].

§35. And connection with a meaning that is the reverse of the consequence (*prasaṅgaviparīta*) [results] only for the [Sāṅkhya] opponent, not for us, because there is no thesis [from our] own [side] (*svapratijñā*); and on account of this, contradiction with [our own]

6, D 76b7-77a3). See also Bhāviveka's reply to the Sāṅkhya who concedes that things do not arise but argues that they nevertheless manifest (... *de ma skyes pa ni bden mod kyi* | *'on kyang gsal bar byed do* || [PP D 52b7; P 63b6]); see D 52b7-53a5; P 63b6-64a4; Kajiyama 1963: 61f.; Ames 1993: 233f.

[184] De La Vallée Poussin (PsP_L 23, n. 1) reconstructs Tib's *don gyi ngag 'di dag ni don chen po can yin pas* as ... *tāni mahārtha<u>tvād</u> yathoditam* ..., but I do not think that an ablative or other causal construction has to be assumed for the Sanskrit exemplars used for the translation, for it is not uncommon for nominal attributes to bear or to be understood as bearing causal meaning and to be translated with that meaning made explicit.
The *arthavākya*s are Buddhapālita's statements, viz., his *prasaṅga* statement and its expanded version in verbal style, that he uses to argue for MMK I.1's declaration that things do not arise from self. These weighty statements of Buddhapālita's are deemed by Candrakīrti to be pregnant with meaning: the full inference exists in a condensed manner within them, and is easily delivered upon proper identification of its reason, etc. *LṬ's author states that the person asking the question how Candrakīrti obtains the inferences when they have not been explicitly stated does so because he is confused (*saṃkīrṇatvād* [ms: *saṃkīrttatvād*] *ity āha*); cf. Yonezawa 2004: 122, 135 [fol. 2a2]. Seyfort Ruegg (2002: 37f.) assumes that the preceding discussion regarding arising vs. manifestation is still relevant ("How has such an investigation (*vicāra* = *rnam par dpyod pa*) been achieved (*labhyate* = *rñed*) without the aforementioned sense [of manifestation rather than that of origination] being expressed ... [by the Mādhyamika]?") but this was concluded in the preceding paragraph.
Kevin Vose informs me that Pa tshab, in his Tshig gsal ba'i dka' ba bshad pa / bla ma tshong dpon pan di ta'i gdam ngag (bKa' gdams gsung 'bum, vol. 11, 150.i.8), notes that the reading "in a certain Kashmiri manuscript" is *'phags pa'i ngag*, that is, *āryavākyāni*, but prefers and subsequently explains the reading *arthavākyāni*.

tenets (*siddhāntavirodha*) is not possible.[185] But we do indeed welcome the fact that many faults befall the opponent through incurring the reverse of the consequence. How [could] the Master Buddhapālita, who follows the doctrine of the Master Nāgārjuna in a non-mistaken way,[186] possibly assert a statement that affords an opportunity (*sāvakāśavacana*) [for criticism][187] so that his opponent obtains an opportunity [to point out faults]? And when the proponent of [the doctrine that] things [are] without own-being (*niḥsvabhāvabhāvavādin*) adduces a consequence[188] for the proponent of [the doctrine that] things have own-being (*sasvabhāvabhāvavādin*), how [could] a meaning that is the reverse of [this] consequence entail [for the one merely pointing out the consequence]? For words do not deprive the speaker of [his] independence the way those armed with

---

185 Candrakīrti argues that the Sāṅkhya will be forced to relinquish his position of arising from self and will, as a consequence, in order to defend the arising of real things, end up with the position of arising from other (Candrakīrti has earlier stated the reverse of the consequence as *parasmād utpannā bhāvā janmasāphalyāt janmanirodhāc ca*; see also n. 124). See also della Santina 1986: 150; Hopkins' sources have understood the reverse of the consequence somewhat differently; on this latter dGe lugs pa interpretation see also Tillemans 1992, especially 323.
PsP Tib presents the last part of the sentence as a rhetorical question: "Therefore, how does there exist for us contradiction with [our] tenets?": *de'i phyir kho bo cag la grub pa'i mtha' dang 'gal ba ga la yod*; the paragraph in PsP Tib thus appears to reflect three questions, instead of two, all introduced with *kutaḥ*. One of the translators' Sanskrit manuscripts of the PsP may have attested a third rhetorical question, or the translators may have been confronted with a scribal error such as *tataś ca siddhāntavirodhasambhavaḥ* and added *kho ba cag la* and *ga la* to correct it. Alternatively, they may have met with the reading attested in our manuscripts but chose to follow Candrakīrti's earlier interrogative style in order to draw attention to the fact that another of Bhāviveka's accusations is being addressed (cp. PsP_M §29, end [PsP_L 21.7]: *tat kim ucyate tad ayuktaṃ hetudṛṣṭāntānabhidhānād iti*; PsP_M §30 [PsP_L 21.11f.]: *kutaḥ siddhasādhanapakṣadoṣāśaṅkā kuto vā hetor viruddhārthatāśaṅketi*). See also the translations of the sentence in Seyfort Ruegg 2002: 38f., Yotsuya 1999: 44, n. 56 and Tillemans 1992: 319.

186 I understand *aviparīta* as intended adverbially. PsP Tib takes it as modifying *mata* ("the unmistaken doctrine"): *slob dpon klu sgrub kyi lugs phyin ci ma log pa'i rjes su 'brang ba slob dpon sangs rgyas bskyangs.*

187 Note that Candrakīrti employs the PP's **sāvakāśavacana* at this point. See n. 123.

188 *prasaṅga āpādyamāne* lit. "when a consequence is being caused to be incurred."

sticks and rope (*dāṇḍapāśika*)[189] do. On the contrary, when they possess [semantic] capacity (*śakti*) they conform to the intention of the speaker. And therefore, because the adducing of the [undesired] consequence has as [its] result the mere negation (*pratiṣedhamātra*) of the opponent's thesis, [the Mādhyamika] does not incur the reverse of the consequence.[190]

§36. And in the same way, [in the Madhyamakaśāstra] the Master [Nāgārjuna] as a general rule (*bhūyasā*) refuted the proposition of the opponent (*parapakṣa*) exclusively by way of [the opponent's] incurring of consequences [with statements such as]:

> There is not any space (*ākāśa*) prior to the characteristic (*lakṣaṇa*) of space.
> It would follow that it would be without characteristic (*alakṣaṇa*) if it existed prior to [its] characteristic.[191]

---

[189] The dictionaries give a variety of meanings for *dāṇḍapāśika/daṇḍapāśaka*: PW: "der die Schlinge der Strafe führt, Richter, Polizeimeister"; Apte: "1) a head police officer 2) a hangman, an executioner"; MW: "a policeman"; de La Vallée Poussin (PsP_L 24, n. 3) translates: "Veilleur de nuit." Cf. Wackernagel and Debrunner 1954: 523, for the suffix *ka* in the special meaning "armed with" (and for the analogous compound *daṇḍājinika*, also derived from a *dvandva*). This would fit with the Tibetan translation *dbyug pa dang zhags pa can*. See also Tibetan interpretations of *dāṇḍapāśika*s in Hopkins 1983: 493 and della Santina 1986: 151.

[190] Cf. the translations in Seyfort Ruegg 1981: 78f. and 2002: 39f. and also Seyfort Ruegg 2000: 252-257.

[191] Candrakrīti cites MMK V.1: *nākāśaṃ vidyate kiṃcit pūrvam ākāśalakṣaṇāt* | *alakṣaṇam prasajyeta syāt pūrvaṃ yadi lakṣaṇāt* ‖. Translated in, e.g., Schayer 1931: 2; cf. Seyfort Ruegg 2002: 42; Stcherbatsky 1927: 104; Ames 1999: 75-77. The Sarvāstivādins distinguish two types of *ākāśa*, the first, unconditioned (*asaṃskṛta*) and immaterial space which has the own nature of not hindering, that is, the empty space within which material objects can exist and move ($AKBh_{ed}$ 3.23: *anāvaraṇasvabhāvam ākāśaṃ yatra rūpasya gatiḥ*; the Vātsīputrīyas and Sammatīyas, schools with which Nāgārjuna may have had early connections, deny *ākāśa* the status of an *asaṃskṛtadharma*); the second, the conditioned (*saṃskṛta*) and material *dhātu ākāśa* as the free space between material objects that is dark or light and is exemplified by the empty space of a door, of a window, or of the mouth or the nostrils (AK I.28ab: *chidram ākāśadhātvākhyam ālokatamasī kila*; $AKBh_{ed}$ 18.11-17: *tat kim ākāśam evākāśadhātur veditavyaḥ ... nety āha* | *kiṃ tarhi* | *dvāravātāyanamukhanāsikādiṣu* [AK I.28a:] *chidram ākāśadhātvākhyam* ... [AK I.28b:] *ālokatamasī kila* | ... *tasmāt kilākāśadhātur ālokatamaḥsvabhāvo rātriṃdivasvabhāvo veditavyaḥ* |) and that as

> If matter (*rūpa*) is separate from the cause of matter, it follows that matter is without a cause (*hetu*),
> But there does not exist any thing anywhere without a cause.[192]

Similarly,

> *nirvāṇa*, to start, is not a thing (*bhāva*); [if it were a thing] it would follow that it would be characterized by old age and death,
> For there is no thing without old age and death.[193]

§37. If, because they are statements of meaning (*arthavākya*), the Master [Nāgārjuna]'s statements are considered [by Bhāviveka]—

---

such belongs to the *rūpaskandha* as a type of visible matter. According to the Sarvāstivādins, both types of space exist; for arguments for *ākāśa* as an existent thing, see Dhammajoti 2009: 491-496. According to the Sautrāntikas, *ākāśa* as a *dhātu* (and as an *asaṃskṛtadharma* [AKBh_{ed} 92.5-6]) is not a real thing (*vastu; dravya*) but is simply the absence of material resistance (AKVy 57.13-14: *svamataṃ tu sapratighadravyābhāvamātram ākāśam iti abhiprāyo lakṣyate*). It is clear that the *ākāśa* which Nāgārjuna takes up in the fifth chapter of the MMK as representative of the *dhātu*s was claimed to be a real thing, and one expects that he was refuting *ākāśa* as conceived materialistically in the Sarvāstivādin or another related school. Buddhapālita, Bhāviveka and Candrakīrti must have been aware of the materialistic determination of *ākāśa*, yet nevertheless present as its characteristic the AKBh-attested *lakṣaṇa* for *asaṃskṛtākāśa*, namely, *anāvaraṇa*. However, Saṃghabhadra does state that both the *asaṃskṛtākāśa* and the *dhātu ākāśa* are non-obstructive; their difference in this respect lies in the fact that the *dhātu ākāśa* is capable of being obstructed whereas *asaṃskṛtākāśa* is not obstructed by other things (see Dhammajoti 2009: 496). The *Abhidharmamahāvibhāṣaśāstra states that the *dhātu ākāśa* is *sapratigha* (ibid., 491). On *ākāśa* see also Schayer 1931: 3, n. 3; Conze 1967: 163-166.

[192] Candrakrīti cites MMK IV.2: *rūpakāraṇanirmukte rūpe rūpaṃ prasajyate* | *ahetukaṃ na cāsty arthaḥ kaścid āhetukaḥ kvacit* || On the reading *ahetukaṃ*, see the corresponding note in PsP_{M}. Translated in, e.g., May 1959: 89: "Si la matière est dégagée de la cause de matière, il suit par conséquence nécessaire qu'elle est dépourvue de cause. Or, aucune chose n'existe nulle part sans cause"; Ames 1999: 54f.; Seyfort Ruegg 2002: 42.

[193] Candrakrīti cites MMK XXV.4: *bhāvas tāvan na nirvāṇaṃ jarāmaraṇalakṣaṇam* | *prasajyetāsti bhāvo hi na jarāmaraṇaṃ vinā* ||. Translated in, e.g., Seyfort Ruegg: 2002: 42; Stcherbatsky 1927: 104; Wood 1994: 301; Bugault 1992: 91. The three cited *kārikā*s are discussed in Hopkins 1983: 494-497; della Santina 1986: 151-153.

given that they are of great import[194]—as the cause of numerous inferences, why aren't also the statements of the Master Buddhapālita considered to be just the same?

---

[194] The sentence up to *parikalpyeta*, i.e., the protasis of the conditional sentence, is based on Bhāviveka's PP commentary on MMK XVIII.1: the opponent objects that since Nāgārjuna did not set forth the individual members of an inference his proof has the fault of incompleteness (*gal te bstan bcos mdzad pas | dam bcas pa la sogs pa'i yan lag ma brjod pa'i phyir sgrub pa ma tshang ba'i skyon yod do zhe na*), to which Bhāviveka replies: *don gyi tshig yin pa'i phyir skyon med de | 'di ltar slob dpon gyi tshig dag ni don gyi tshig dag yin te | yi ge mdor bsdus pa dang | don rgya che ba dag yin pas don gyi dbang gis sbyor ba'i tshig du ma dag gi gzhi yin par bzhed pa'i phyir ro ||* (see D 180a1-2; P 223b7-224a2). Translated in Ames 1986: 63, "Because [Nāgārjuna's verse] is a succinct statement (*don gyi tshig*, *artha-vākya*), there is no fault. For the statements of the *ācārya* are succinct statements (*artha-vākya*), because by virtue of [their] meaning (*artha*), they are held to be the basis of many syllogisms (*prayoga-vākya*), since [their] words [literally, "syllables"] are brief but [their] meaning is great" (the passage is referred to in Lindtner 1986: 79, n. 26; see also the translation in Eckel 1980: 197-8 and 242, n. 13). Bhāviveka goes on to say that not stating all the parts of an inference is a fault, but he adds that even this may not be a fault if the parts are already known to the listeners: *sbyor ba'i tshig la ni de skyon du yang 'gyur || yang na de la yang mi 'gyur te | rab tu byed pa 'am | lung las la la la yan lag 'ga' zhig grags pa yin na'o ||*.
De La Vallée Poussin emends his manuscripts' *parikalpet* to *parikalpyate* and assumes Candrakīrti to be indicated as the logical subject of this verb: "Par l'auteur de la présente Vṛtti" (PsP_L 25, n. 2); he understands the entire sentence to be uttered by Bhāviveka. Stcherbatsky (1927: 105) correctly understands the sentence up to de La Vallée Poussin's *parikalpyate* to be Bhāviveka's: "(Bhāvaviveka). But these are aphorisms. The sentences of our Master contain profound intentions. They can be variously tackled and give rise to a variety of syllogistic formulation" (the word "tackled" is noted as the translation for "*parikalpyaṉte*."). Hopkins (1983: 497 and n. 413) follows the dGe lugs pa interpretation, here specifically that of sGom sde Nam mka' rgyal mtshan, which takes the entire sentence as one formulated by Candrakīrti in a general sense and posed of a hypothetical Bhāviveka.
Bhāviveka sees in and extracts from Nāgārjuna's *kārikā*s numerous inferences; the section immediately following MMK I.1 in the PP has been referred to earlier (see n. 138). MMK V.1 just quoted by Candrakīrti as an example of a Nāgārjunian consequence is developed by Bhāviveka into various inferences. Bhāviveka explains that from V.1ab one may extract the thesis that space as a real substance does not exist, that "without arising" is a property of the subject space—and thus the reason—that is acknowledged by both sides of the debate, and that a rabbit's horn is the example established on the basis of the probandum and probans; he presents the inference, "Ultimately, space does not exist as a real substance, because it is without arising, like a rabbit's horn" (*rdzas su gyur pa'o zhes dam bca' ba nye bar bzhag pa*

§38. But if [Bhāviveka considers that] the [following] is a rule (*nyāya*) for commentators, [namely,] that there has to be a detailed stating of inferential statements (*prayogavākya*),[195]

[we reply that] this too is not [correct], because even when the Master Nāgārjuna composed the commentary on the Vigrahavyāvartanī he did not make inferential statements.

§39. Moreover, this logician's (*tārkika*) [i.e., Bhāviveka's][196] asserting—despite [his] acceptance of the Madhyamaka view (*madhyamakadarśana*)[197]—of independent inferential statements

---

yin no ‖ *de skye ba med par phyogs gnyi ga la grags pa ni chos yin no* ‖ *dpe ni de'i dbang gis te* | *ri bong gi rwa la sogs pa dag yin no* ‖ *'dir rjes su dpag pa ni* | *don dam par nam mkha' rdzas su yod pa ma yin te* | *skye ba med pa'i phyir dper na ri bong gi rwa bzhin no* ‖ [PP_{ed} 476.1-6; see PP_{tr} 212; Ames 1999: 75f.]). His attention shifting to MMK V.1d (= Tib V.1c: *gal te mtshan las snga gyur na*), Bhāviveka states that this *pāda* indicates another property of the subject space, namely, "being at a different time" (*dus tha dad pa nyid*; the reason for the new inference is "because of existing at an earlier time than that [characteristic]") on the basis of which the example "something other than space" (*de las gzhan pa*) is attained; and he presents still another inference, whose reason "because [the characteristic] is different [from space]" he considers to be additionally indicated by MMK V.1d (cf. PP_{ed} 477.6-11; 18-23; PP_{tr} 214f.; Ames 1999: 77f.).

[195] Cp. PPṬ (on PP's statement *sbyor ba'i tshig la ni de skyon du yang 'gyur* [= commentary on MMK XVIII.1]): *sbyor ba tshig la ni de skyon du 'gyur ro zhes bya ba ni 'grel pa byed pa sbyor ba'i tshig rtsom pa dag la ni sgrub pa ma tshang ba de skyon du yang 'gyur ba bden no zhes khas blangs pa'i tshig yin no* ‖ (P 63b6-7).
PsP Tib as usual presents a relative/co-relative construction where PsP Skt has a construction with the conjunction *yat*, with however loss of the sense of obligation conveyed by the Skt optative participle *kartavyam* when it is replaced with the nominalized form *rjod par byed pa*: *'on te sbyor ba'i ngag rgyas par rjod par byed pa gang yin pa 'di ni 'grel pa mkhan po rnams kyi lugs yin no zhe na*. The optative participle suggests that *nyāya* ("usual manner," "general procedure") should be translated in its extended meaning of "rule"; PsP Tib has translated, perhaps precisely because it does not take the optative sense into account, *nyāya* with *lugs*. PsP Tib further translates *vṛttikāra* with the less standard and non-literal *'grel pa mkhan po*. We are left with the overall impression that the translators took minor liberties with the sentence.

[196] *LṬ's author identifies the *tārkika* as Bhāviveka (cf. Yonezawa 2004: 122, 135 [fol. 2a4]).

[197] PsP Tib has *dbu ma pa'i lta ba* (*mādhyamikadarśana*).

(*svatantraprayogavākya*) out of a desire to communicate [therewith] no more than his extreme skill (*atikauśala*) in the science of reasoning (*tarkaśāstra*) is observed to be, to a more extreme degree (*atitarām*), the basis for an assemblage of many faults.[198] Why? To begin, here in that which was stated [by him as follows],

> The [formal] inference, for its part, turns out to be this: "Ultimately (*paramārthataḥ*), the internal bases (*adhyātmikāny āyatanāni*) have not arisen from self, because [they] are [already] existing, like consciousness (*caitanya*)"[199]

---

[198] Translated in Yotsuya 1999: 78; Hopkins 1983: 500; Seyfort Ruegg 2002: 43. The latter interprets the sentence as if it would be conditional: "Moreover, if he [viz. Bhavya] ... has formulated an autonomous (*svatantra*) formal probative argument (*prayogavākya*) out of a desire to reveal ... just his own high expertise in the science of eristics ..., this is considered ... ." Stcherbatsky (1927: 105, n. 5) translates *upalakṣyate* in the meaning "indirect indication," but Candrakīrti is pointing out that the faults are clearly observed.

[199] PP: *'dir sbyor ba'i tshig tu 'gyur ba ni don dam par nang gi skye mched rnams bdag las skye ba med par nges te | yod pa'i phyir dper na shes pa yod pa nyid bzhin no* || (D 49a2-3; P 58b1-2; cf. Kajiyama 1963: 49; Ames 1993: 221f.; Yotsuya 1999: 79; Seyfort Ruegg 2002: 44). PsP Skt lacks equivalents for *'dir* (**atra*) and *nges* (**niścitam*) and includes *etat*, which is not attested in PsP Tib or PP Tib (the translators of PsP Tib cite directly from PP Tib). Candrakīrti may have been writing from memory, or intentionally more freely, and thus the deviation.
Consciousness (*caitanya*) is the nature of *puruṣa*. It exists in *puruṣa* even before the causal process involving *prakṛti* occurs but is evident only in dependence on *prakṛti*, in the way that the burning of fire or the cutting of an axe is evident only if there is something to be burned or cut (YD 184.28-30: *prāg api kāryakaraṇasambandhāt puruṣe caitanyam avasthitam <...> tadyathā agner dahanaṃ paraśoś chedanaṃ <ca>? asati dāhye chedye ca na vyajyate*); see also, e.g., Chakravarti 1975: 231f.; 315ff.; Frauwallner 1984: 275; Larson and Bhattacharya 1987: 73-83. Pure consciousness representative of *puruṣa* is, like *prakṛti*, not an evolute of something else (cf. YD 66.18-20: *ihācetanā guṇā ity etat pratipādayiṣyāmaḥ | yac ca yenārabhyate tanmayaṃ tad bhavati | yadi guṇaiḥ puruṣāṇām ārambhaḥ syāt teṣām apy acetanatvaṃ syāt | cetanās tu te | tasmān na guṇair ārabhyanta iti siddham etat*). Consciousness has been adduced as the example for Bhāviveka's independent inference because, given that the Mādhyamikas accept consciousness, viz., *vijñāna*, on the surface level of reality, this example, which is accepted by the Sāṅkhya and the Mādhyamika in a general way, i.e., irrespective of the way in which the school of each debater specifically interprets consciousness, fulfills the requirement of being acknowledged by both parties; see Avalokitavrata's comments on this example at n. 181.

—for what purpose is the qualification (*viśeṣaṇa*) "ultimately" (*paramārthataḥ*) employed?[200]

§40. If [Bhāviveka says it is employed] because the arising accepted[201] from the point of view of the worldly surface [level] is not being negated and because if [this arising thus accepted] were denied, there would result [the logical fault of] sublation [of the thesis] by

---

[200] From this point on (up to PsP$_M$ §48 [= PsP$_L$ 28.3]), Candrakīrti considers and rejects possible responses to the question of the purpose of the qualification relative to its domain of application. Yotsuya's (1999: 80) elucidation of the structure of the text is worthy of reiteration; he presents the three hypothetical applications of the qualification thus: "On this point there are three *conceivable* alternatives: 1. The qualification "ultimately" is attached to the whole of the proposition, implying that entities such as the inner sense-fields do not originate from self. 2. The qualification 'ultimately' is attached to the whole of the proposition except the word '*svataḥ*', implying that entities such as the inner sense-fields do not originate. 3. The qualification 'ultimately' is attached only to the probandum, i.e. non-origination" (I omit Yotsuya's section and sub-section numerals). Candrakīrti considers the first alternative for the qualification, that is, *paramārthataḥ* applied to the entire proposition, which covers the section PsP$_M$ §40–end of §44 (PsP$_L$ 26.3-27.6), from both the point of view of philosophers (PsP$_M$ §40–end of §42 [PsP$_L$ 26.3-27.2]) and the point of view of ordinary persons (PsP$_M$ §42–end of §44 [PsP$_L$ 27.2-6]); the philosophers addressed are Buddhists (PsP$_M$ §40–end of §41 [PsP$_L$ 26.3-12]) and Sāṅkhyas (PsP$_M$ §41–end of §42 [PsP$_L$ 26.12-27.2]). Yotsuya (ibid., 81) states, "a) Bhāvaviveka cannot conventionally tolerate an origination from self as maintained by philosophically minded people. b) Bhāvaviveka cannot conventionally tolerate an origination from self as maintained conventionally by non-philosophically minded people ... a-i) Bhāvaviveka himself, as a Buddhist, especially as a follower of Nāgārjuna, will not be able conventionally to maintain an origination from self. a-ii) Bhāvaviveka cannot conventionally tolerate origination from self as maintained by his Sāṃkhya opponent." The second alternative for the domain of the qualification, indeed the alternative actually intended by Bhāviveka which implies that ultimately, arising (instead of arising from self) is negated, is discussed (and rejected on the grounds of subject failure) in the section PsP$_M$ §45–end of §46 (PsP$_L$ 27.7-10); the third alternative, which according to Candrakīrti would have to be reformulated as *sāṃvṛtānāṃ cakṣurādīnāṃ paramārthato nāsty utpattiḥ* but would even in this form not escape the fault of subject failure, is discussed in PsP$_M$ §47 (PsP$_L$ 27.10-28.3).

[201] Yotsuya (1999: 81) retains, against de Jong's ms R and his ms T2 (= mss D and J) and on the basis of his mss T1 and T3 (= mss H and I), de La Vallée Poussin's emendation *lokasaṃvṛtyābhyupagatasyotpādasyā°*; mss P and B (Q has a lacuna at this point) now confirm de Jong's emendation *lokasaṃvṛtyābhyupetasyotpādasyā°*. See PsP$_M$ §40.

what is accepted [by the Mādhyamika] (*abhyupetabādhā*),[202] [we reply that] this is not correct, because [a Mādhyamika] does not even from the [point of view] of the surface [level of reality] accept arising from self.[203]

---

[202] Stcherbatsky (1927: 106, n. 2) understands *abhyupeta* in de La Vallée Poussin's *cābhyupetabādhāprasaṅgāt* as an adjective to *bādhā* and must supply in brackets the object he judges repudiated: "And if denied, the admitted repudiation *(bādha)* (of the phenomenal by the absolute) would not be entailed (read *prasangāt*)" (Stcherbatsky's textual emendation appears to be based on an erroneous interpretation of *ā* of °*bādhā̠prasaṅgāt* as implying an alpha privative). Yotsuya (1999: 81) interprets the compound to mean, "it would follow that what is [generally] accepted (*abhyupeta*) [by the Mādhyamikas] would be denied." Hopkins (1983: 502) attempts to take the instrumental in PsP Tib's *khas blangs pas̲ gnod par thal bar 'gyur ba'i phyir* into consideration in his translation, "it would follow that one would be damaged by [one's own] assertion [of conventionally existent production]," but Candrakīrti intends the technical meaning of *abhyupetabādhā*, specifically, that the thesis of the inference would be sublated by what the Mādhyamika's own system accepts: the unqualified proposition that the inner bases have not arisen from self is contradicted, is sublated—has, so to speak, the rug pulled out from under it—by the fact that the Mādhyamika does accept the arising of things on the surface level; without the qualification, (hypothetical) Bhāviveka argues, the opponent would attack the proposition as being spurious (*pakṣābhāsa*). Lindtner (1986: 80, n. 29) points out that Bhāviveka recognizes, like Dignāga in NM and PS, five types of sublation (*bādhā*) with regard to the subject (*pakṣa*): the *pakṣa* is liable to contradiction/sublation (*virodha*, *bādhā*) with/by one's own statement (*svavacana*), authoritative testimony (*āgama*), what is generally acknowledged (*prasiddha*), direct perception (*pratyakṣa*), and inference (*anumāna*) (cf. Tucci 1930: 7; Katsura 1977: 113). Lindtner further notes that Bhāviveka distinguishes between what is generally acknowledged in the world and what is generally acknowledged in one's own *śāstra*s (see PP to MMK II.17cd, where Bhāviveka responds to the opponent who argues that Bhāviveka's position regarding the non-existence of a goer or of going is unacceptable because it is contradicted by what is acknowledged: *'dir gtan tshig gyi don gang yin | ci 'jig rten la grags pa sel bar byed pa'i phyir ram | 'on te bstan bcos la grags pa sel bar byed pa'i phyir ... gal te rang gi bstan bcos la grags pa* (*ba*) *sel bar byed pa'i phyir de grags pa'i gnod par 'gyur ro* (P: ||) *zhe na ni* | (P: without |) *khas blangs pa la gnod par 'gyur ro* (P: ||) *zhes brjod par bya ba'i rigs* (D 70a1-3; P 84b4-7); translated in Ames 1995: 321f. It would appear that Candrakīrti here in the PsP intends sublation by what is generally accepted in one's own *śāstra*s. On the historical development of *pakṣābhāsa*, see Preisendanz 1994: 319, n. 88, especially 319-323.

[203] As succinctly explained by Yotsuya (1999: 84), Candrakīrti rejects Bhāviveka's qualification "ultimately" as superfluous because the Mādhyamika does not accept arising from self even on the surface level; such a distinguishing of one level of reality from the other via the qualification would be necessary only if non-ultimate

§41. As has been stated in the [Śālistamba-]sūtra,

> And this very sprout that is arising, which has a seed for [its] cause, is not produced from itself, not produced from another, not produced from both [itself and another], nor has it arisen without a cause; it has not been brought about by the Lord (*īśvara*), time (*kāla*), atoms (*aṇu*), primordial matter (*prakṛti*), or the nature [of things] (*svabhāva*).[204]

---

arising from self was indeed accepted by the Mādhyamika. Thus its employment by Bhāviveka, if intended as applying to the whole of the proposition, carries with it the implication that he does accept arising from self on the surface level. The subsequent *sūtra* and *śāstra* quotations are brought forward to demonstrate the general, non-qualified rejection of arising from self for arising in dependence (cf. Hopkins 1983: 501-503; della Santina 1986: 157f.). Candrakīrti does not yet speak to the fact that Bhāviveka actually employs the qualification to avoid negating the dependent-arising of surface-level things that is accepted by Mādhyamikas (cf. §45-§47).

[204] Candrakīrti's Śālistambasūtra citation differs from the Skt for the Śālistambasūtra passage found in the BCAP and the Madhyamakaśālistamba: *sa cāyam aṅkuro na svayaṃkṛto na parakṛto nobhayakṛto neśvaranirmito na kālapariṇāmito na prakṛtisaṃbhūto na caikakāraṇādhīno nāpy ahetusamutpannaḥ* (references and variants in Schoening 1995: 705). The Dunhuang manuscript reading (as well as the readings in other Tibetan editions) is close to the Skt attested in the BCAP and the Madhyamakaśālistamba: *myu gu de yang bdag gis ma byas | gzhan gyis ma byas | gnyis kas ma byas | dbang phyug gis ma byas | dus gyis ma bsgyur | rang bzhin las ma byung | rgyu myed pa las kyang ma skyes te*; text and variants in Schoening 1995: 403f. PsP Tib differs in a number of respects from Candrakīrti's citation and shows similarities with the text as found in the Dunhuang manuscript, etc. The citation of a parallel passage from the Śālistambasūtra at PsP_L 567.2-4 generally (for variants see Schoening 725f.; see also La Vallée Poussin 1913a: 75) corresponds with other Sanskrit fragments for the passage and with the non-PsP Śālistambasūtra Skt for the earlier citation: *sa ca nāmarūpāṅkuro na svayaṃkṛto na parakṛto nobhayakṛto neśvarakṛto na kālapariṇāmito na prakṛtisaṃbhūto na caikakāraṇādhino nāpy ahetusamutpannaḥ*.

Bhāviveka, in his discussion regarding the non-arising of things without a cause, offers the alternative meaning of "bad cause" (*rgyu ngan pa*) for *ahetu* of MMK I.1's *ahetutaḥ* and lists as examples of bad causes the nature of things (*svabhāva*), the Lord (*īśvara*), spirit (or "Cosmic Man") (*puruṣa*), primordial matter (*prakṛti*), time (*kāla*), the god Nārāyaṇa, etc. (*rgyu ngan pa gang zhe na | ngo ba nyid dang | dbang phyug dang | skyes bu dang | gtso bo dang | dus dang | sred med kyi bu la sogs pa* [D 50b7-51a1; P 61a4-5]; the bad causes alluded to by *la sogs pa* are listed at PPṬ D 114a5; P 132a8; see Ames 1993: 247, n. 146). Bhāviveka explicitly addresses and refutes *svabhāva*, *īśvara* and *puruṣa* as causes for the arising of things, and *prakṛti* as the cause of the principles (*tattva*), and states that the general refutation of *prakṛti*,

In the same manner [in the Lalitavistara],

> In the way that there is a sprout when a seed exists, but the sprout is not the seed: it is neither other than that [seed] nor is it just that [seed]—so is the actual nature (*dharmatā*) [of all elements of existence]: [there is] neither annihilation (*anuccheda*) nor permanence (*aśāśvata*).[205]

---

kāla and Nārāyaṇa as causes should be considered as like that of *īśvara* (cf. D 52b6; P 63b4). The Vaiśeṣika doctrine of the arising of things from atoms (*aṇu*) is refuted when Bhāviveka argues for non-arising from a cause that is other. The group *svabhāva, īśvara, prakṛti, puruṣa, kāla* and Nārāyaṇa appears in Candrakīrti's commentary on the YṢ verse of homage, where he states that there is no chance at all for the proponents of these as causes to proceed to the city of *nirvāṇa* (cf. $YṢV_{ed}$ 21.21-22.2; $YṢV_{tr}$ 108 and n. 18 for references). Cp. the grouping found at PsP_L 159.7: *iha bhagavatā tathāgatena prakṛtīśvarasvabhāvakālāṇunārāyaṇajaiminikaṇādakapilāditīrthakarakartṛvādanirāsena sarvabhāvānāṃ tattvam ādarśitam.* References for these causes in May 1959: 122, n. 320; on *svabhāva*, cf. also Silburn 1989: 132ff. and Bhattacharya 2012; on time, Silburn 1989: 137ff. See additionally the description of the *svabhāva* doctrine at Buddhacarita 9.58-62.

205 Lalitavistara 176.11-12 (ed. Lefmann). Lefmann's version of the verse runs: *bījasya sato yathāṅkuro na ca yo bīja sa caiva aṅkuro | na ca tato na caiva tat* (= *tat* with *virāma*) *evam anuccheda aśāśvata dharmatā* ||. The citations of the verse in the PsP (PsP_L 108.8-9, 377.1-2, 428.2-5, 551.1-4; see May 1959: 74 and note 106; cited also at $MABh_{ed}$ 115.12-13) attest the word *anyu* (MABh: *gzhan*) in the third quarter. The Tibetan translation of the Lalitavistara (in both D and P) attests the verse-half as it is attested in PsP Tib, i.e., with an equivalent for *anyu*. One has to admit that *tataḥ* without *anyu* is, if not misleading, at least laconic. One also expects the fourth quarter to commence with *evam*, i.e., for the *caesura* to occur after the third quarter and not, as Lefmann's reading would have it, within the third quarter. The evidence thus would indicate that Lefmann's third quarter is faulty and that Candrakīrti's *anyu* needs to be incorporated into it. The quarter read as *na ca anyu tato na caiva tat* conforms to the requirements of the verse's Vaitālīya metre (with *anyu* in this position, the fourth syllabic instant is also correct; Lefmann's *na ca tato* breaks the Vaitālīya rule that the fourth syllabic instant not be conjoined with the fifth). This leaves the fourth quarter, however, with extra and disturbing syllabic instants. De La Vallée Poussin (cf. PsP_L 26, n. 4) seeks to partially solve the metrical problem of the fourth quarter of Candrakīrti's version of the verse by suggesting the reading *aśāśvadharmatā*, although he admits that this solution "ne va pas sans difficulté." He further emends *anuccheda* to *anucheda*, but even with this additional change metrical problems remain (see "Additions et Corrections" PsP_L 597; read "Page 26, ligne 9" for "Page 26, note 9"). It is possible that *evam* was originally Buddhist Hybrid Sanskrit *ev'* or *em* (cf. BHSD s.v. *em*), and given that metrical requirements in Buddhist Hybrid Sanskrit verse were occasionally fulfilled through oral pronun-

Also here [in the Madhyamakaśāstra, Nāgārjuna] will say,

> That which comes to be in dependence on something else, first, is of course not just that [on which it depends].
> Nor is it other than that [on which it depends]. [Thus,] it (= that which is depended on) is not annihilated, nor [is it] permanent.[206]

---

ciation, that *e* of *ev'* or *em* was pronounced as a light vowel. This would leave *aśāśvata* as the only irregularity: one short syllabic instant is expected where it has two, i.e., °*śvata*. De La Vallée Poussin's solution *aśāśvadharmatā*, which assumes a dropping of *ta*, would then provide for a metrical *pāda*, but whether this was the original reading remains uncertain.

My translation is closer to de La Vallée Poussin's translation, viz., "De même qu'il y a pousse quand il y a graine; mais la pousse n'est pas ce qu'est la graine; elle n'est ni autre ni la même chose: de la sorte, la nature des choses n'est ni permanente ni anéantie" ($MABh_{tr}$ 1910: 310) than to that of either May or de Jong, who translate the verse with emphasis on the seed as the subject being considered. May (1959: 74) translates: "Il y a une pousse s'il existe un germe. Ce germe n'est pas identique à la pousse. Il n'est ni différent d'elle, ni non plus identique à elle. De même, la nature des dharma est ni anéantissement ni éternité"; de Jong (1949: 33) translates "Il y a une pousse s'il existe une semence. Cette semence n'est pas identique à la pousse. Elle n'est ni différente de la pousse et ni non plus identique à elle. Donc la nature des chose est non-anéantie et non-éternelle." PsP Tib for the verse takes the sprout as the primary object of consideration (*sa bon gang yin myu gu de nyid min*), as does Candrakīrti in his MA commentary when he employs this quarter as the response to the claim that it is not correct if the sprout is different from the seed (*sa bon gyi rgyu can myu gu yang 'byung ba na sa bon las gzhan nyid du mi rung ngo zhe na | gsungs pa | sa bon gang yin myu gu de nyid min |* ($MABh_{ed}$ 115.17-19). It is, of course, the sprout that deserves the focus, for it is contingent on it that the permanence or annihilation of the seed might be posited. I have avoided using the words "different" or "identical" in my translation to make clear that the difference/otherness and identity/oneness being negated here is a numeric one, and not a qualitative one.

[206] MMK XVIII.10: *pratītya yad yad bhavati na hi tāvat tad eva tat | na cānyad api tat tasmān nocchinnaṃ nāpi śāśvatam ||*. The verse is again cited by Candrakīrti at PsP_L 230.1 and PsP_L 423.7, and is quoted by him at $MABh_{ed}$ 116.18-117.2 (references to translations and comparable verses in May 1959: 174, n. 555). The variant reading *nocchedo* which de La Vallée Poussin finds in his manuscripts for the citation at PsP_L 222.6-7 and mentions at PsP_L 26, n. 5 and PsP_L 375, n. 6 is not attested in ms P (he corrects his PsP_L 26, n. 5 reference to the verse as 18.7 on p. 597, and on p. 605, he corrects his PsP_L 375, n. 6 reference regarding the citation of the verse to PsP_L 222.6).

PsP Tib P, N and G for second verse-half attest *de las gzhan pa'ang ma yin phyir || de phyir chad min rtag ma yin ||* (Skt: *na cānyad api tat tasmān nocchinnaṃ nāpi śāśvatam ||*). PsP Tib D and C replace *phyir* of the third quarter with *te*. ABh_{ed}, BP_{ed}

§42. If [it is argued that] the qualification ["ultimately" has been added not in consideration of our own views, but] with reference to the [Sāṅkhya] opponent's doctrine (*paramata*), that [justification] is incorrect, because [the Mādhyamika] does not accept their (= the Sāṅkhya's) establishment (*vyavasthā*) even from the point of view of the surface [level of reality]. For [only] insofar as the non-Buddhists (*tīrthika*), who are wholly deprived of the correct view of the two truths, are refuted in both ways [i.e., on the ultimate and on the surface levels], can it (= the refutation) be considered to be truly of advantage (*guṇa*).[207] Thus, even [if it is employed] with reference to the opponent's doctrine, the stating of the qualification is not tenable.

---

and PP D and P read *de las gzhan pa'ang ma yin phyir*. MMK_T (P) reads: *de las gzhan pa'ang ma yin pa* (D: *phyir*) || *de phyir chad min rtag ma yin* ||. See also Ye 2011a: 306.
Erb presumes the verse to be attested in the ŚSV but to be veiled by the poor Tibetan translation: *brten nas byung ba gang dang gang* || *re zhig de nyid des mi bskyed* || *gzhan las kyang min de yi phyir* || *rtag min chad pa yang ma yin* || ($ŚSV_{ed}$ 252.34-37); his German translation follows MMK XVIII.10's Sanskrit ($ŚSV_{tr}$ 93); see his note 912. Seyfort Ruegg (2002: 46) translates the PsP's citation as "That which comes into existence in dependence [on a conditioning factor] is, then, not that [factor itself], nor is it other either. Hence it is neither destroyed not eternal" (read the final "not" as "nor"), but note that Candrakīrti does not understand *tasmāt* in the sense of "hence" but rather as "from that"; cf. PsP_L 376.7 and 376.10-11 and the translation in Yotsuya 1999: 82. Garfield's (1995: 252) translation of *nocchinnam* (*chad min*) and his assumption that that which depends is the subject in the final quarter ("Therefore it is neither nonexistent in time nor permanent") obfuscates the verse's meaning.

[207] Bhāviveka might argue that the qualification is added to avoid forcing the opponent into over-negation, that is, in order that the surface level of reality be preserved for the Sāṅkhya. However the Sāṅkhya, not including within his doctrinal edifice a theory of two levels of truth, will not be able to appreciate the distinction being made. Moreover, his view of surface level reality, were he to have one, would admit arising from self, and this the Mādhyamika cannot consent to, even with regard to the surface level of things. Although not explicitly referred to by Candrakīrti, the qualified inference could imply—were the Sāṅkhya to understand the two truth theory—that the Mādhyamika accepts arising from self on the surface level and is therefore indirectly utilizing the inference to establish arising from self on this level. Yotsuya (1999: 85-86) writes: "Candrakīrti thus concludes that it is better to refute the non-Buddhist such as the Sāṃkhya without drawing a line between the ultimate and conventional, but by offering arguments that are effective on both levels." Cf. Stcherbatsky 1927: 107, n. 3; della Santina 1986: 158; Seyfort Ruegg 2002: 46;

§43. Nor it is the case that the world (*loka*) (= non-philosophers) assumes arising from self, so that the qualification would be purposeful (*sāphalya*) at least with reference to it; for the world, not having launched an investigation (*vicāra*) [into whether things arise] from self [or] other, etc., presumes [merely] this much: an effect arises from a cause.[208]

§44. The Master [Nāgārjuna] has also determined [it] thus [i.e., that arising from self is negated without qualification]. It is therefore ascertained that the qualification is useless (*vaiphalya*) in every regard.[209]

Hopkins 1983: 503. Bhāviveka does in fact set forth an inference refuting arising from self on the surface level in MHK III.139: *tatra tāvat svato janma saṃvṛtyāpi na yujyate | sātmakatvād yathā dadhnaḥ svato janma na vidyate ||* (cf. Watanabe 1998: 139; Lindtner 2001: 23; Heitmann 2009: 67).

[208] Candrakīrti argues that the qualification "ultimately" is useless even if it is claimed to be employed in consideration of the world's, i.e., ordinary people's, understanding of the way things arise, since ordinary people simply assume that an effect arises from a cause without pursuing the matter further. Given that speculation as to whether things arise from themselves or not is the domain of philosophers and is foreign to the general populace, the inference as a whole is inapplicable to worldly ideas of arising.
Cp. MA VI.12, which occurs in the context of the rejection of arising from self via the rejection of the identity of cause and effect: *loko 'pi caikyam anayor iti nābhyupaiti naṣṭe 'pi paśyati yataḥ phalam eṣa hetau | tasmān na tattvata idaṃ na tu lokataś ca yuktaṃ svato bhavati bhāva iti prakalpam ||* (Li 2012: 4; Skt cited at MABh_{tr} 1910: 283, n. 7 [*prakalpyam* for *prakalpam*]; cf. MABh_{ed} 86.1-2, 9-10). See further MA VI.31 where Candrakīrti denies that the world can be an authority (*tshad ma*) at the time of discussion of final reality and thus a sublater, for sublation by what is acknowledged in the world (*'jig rten kyis gnod*) is valid only in cases where worldly things have been negated (MABh_{ed} 113; MABh_{tr} 1910: 308).

[209] I concur with Yotsuya that the *ācārya* referred to in this sentence is Nāgārjuna, not Bhāviveka as de La Vallée Poussin (PsP_{L} 27, n. 2) suggests, and that what Nāgārjuna has determined (*vyavasthāpayāmāsa*) is that the negation of arising from self is a general, unqualified negation (see Yotsuya: 1999: 87, n. 56). The commentary on MA VI.12cd (see previous note) contains the following references to Nāgārjuna's non-employment of a qualification and to Bhāviveka's inference: *de nyid kyi phyir slob dpon gyis khyad par du ma mdzad par | bdag las ma yin zhes spyir skye ba bkag pa yin no || gang zhig dngos po rnams ni don dam par bdag las skye ba ma yin te | yod pa'i phyir sems pa* (MABh_{UN}: without *pa*) *can bzhin no || zhes khyad par du byed pa de'i don dam par zhes bya ba'i khyad par don med do zhes bya bar* (MABh_{UN}:

§45. Moreover, if this qualification is employed by [Bhāviveka because] he wants to rule out (*nirācikīrṣu*) a negation[210] of arising (*utpattipratiṣedha*) on the surface [level], then there would be the

---

without *bya bar*) *bsam par bya'o* ‖ (MABh$_{ed}$ 86.11-15; MABh$_{tr}$ 1910: 284). The passage is cited and translated by Yotsuya (1999: 87, n. 56) as follows: "Therefore, the master (= Nāgārjuna) has negated origination generally, without attaching any qualification, in the following way: '[Entities] do not originate from self.' With respect to him (= Bhāvaviveka) who qualifies [the inference as follows:] 'Ultimately entities do not originate from self, because they are [already] existing, like the spirit,' it should be emphasized that the qualification 'ultimately' has no purpose." Other translators (some are mentioned by Yotsuya in his note; see in addition Hopkins 1983: 502-503 and della Santina 1986: 158, both in reliance on Tibetan exegesis, and also Seyfort Ruegg 2002: 47) have assumed that the PsP sentence refers to Nāgārjuna's establishment of cause and effect as in accord with that of the world, but if taken in this way, the sentence would be, if not a *non sequitur*, at least superfluous to the discussion. The presentation of the view of ordinary people is a last-ditch attempt on the part of hypothetical Bhāviveka to rescue and justify the addition of the qualification, and whether Nāgārjuna accepts this view or not adds no support to the argument against the meaningfulness of the qualification and in fact abruptly places the discussion in a new arena. It should be noted that unlike in de La Vallée Poussin's edition, where a half *daṇḍa* appears after *pratipannaḥ* and another half *daṇḍa* is placed after *vyavasthāpayāmāsa* (PsP$_L$ 27.5), mss P and Q and mss B, D, and K attest a single *daṇḍa* (double *daṇḍa*s appear rarely in the older manuscripts) after *pratipannaḥ*, while A, C, E, G-J, L, M, and N all attest a double *daṇḍa*, thus indicating that the manuscript tradition understood a full stop after *pratipannaḥ* and that a new thought begins with *evam* (Q also places a *daṇḍa* after *vyavasthāpayāmāseti*; ms P is damaged). The double *shad* after *rtogs pa yin no* in PsP Tib corroborates the manuscript evidence.

[210] PsP Tib lacks an equivalent for *pratiṣedha*; that is, whereas the Skt sentence begins *api ca yadi saṃvṛtyotpattipratiṣedhanirācikīrṣuṇā* ..., Tib begins *gzhan yang gal te kun rdzob tu skye ba dgag par 'dod nas* ... . Hopkins' brief introduction to his translation from the Tibetan may represent the way certain dGe lugs pa scholars have dealt with the faulty text. He appears to understand Bhāviveka to be arguing for employment of the qualification because he wants to refute the arising of truly existent inner bases such as the visual faculty both ultimately and on the surface level. Hopkins (1983: 503) states: "Bhāvaviveka might, however, say that 'ultimate' should be affixed to the subject because the production of an eye sense, which the Sāṃkhyas accept as ultimate, is refuted even conventionally: An ultimate eye sense is not produced from self because of existing, as in the case, for example, of an existent consciousness." According to Yotsuya's (1999: 80, 87) analysis, with this paragraph the second of the three alternatives for the scope of the qualification "ultimately" is taken up, namely, the qualification is attached to the whole of the proposition with the exception of the word "*svataḥ*."

fault of the proposition (*pakṣadoṣa*), [namely, that the proposition is] unestablished with respect to [its] locus (*asiddhādhāra*) from [his] own [point of view] (*svataḥ*),[211] or the fault of the reason (*hetudoṣa*), [namely, that the reason is] unestablished as regards [its] basis (*āśrayāsiddha*) [from his own point of view],[212] because the bases

---

[211] Candrakīrti rejects Bhāviveka's justification for employment of the qualification on the ground that Bhāviveka, in order to address in argumentative form the Sāṅkhya belief in the arising of ultimately existent inner bases, has declared that the (ultimately) existent inner bases are the subject of the inference even though he does not maintain that they really exist: the proposition (*pakṣa*) will be one whose basis (*ādhāra*) (= subject [*dharmin*]) is not established (*asiddha*) for Bhāviveka. Given that the subject must be established for both opponents for the proposition to be valid, the proposition incurs the fault that its basis is not established for both of the debaters. On this point, see also Yotsuya 1999: 88.
Dignāga defines the proposition (*pakṣa*) in PS III.2 as follows: *svarūpeṇaiva nirdeśyaḥ svayam iṣṭo 'nirākṛtaḥ | pratyakṣārthānumānāptaprasiddhena svadharmiṇi* ||; Tillemans (1994: 298, see also n. 10) translates: "[A valid thesis] is one which is intended (*iṣṭa*) by [the proponent] himself (*svayam*) as something to be stated (*nirdeśya*) in its [proper] form alone (*svarūpeṇaiva*) [i.e. as a *sādhya*]; [and] with regard to [the proponent's] own subject (*svadharmin*), it is not opposed (*anirākṛta*) by perceptible objects (*pratyakṣārtha*), by inference (*anumāna*), by authorities (*āpta*) or by what is commonly recognized (*prasiddha*)." Tillemans (1998: 112; see also 2000: 194f.) states, "By saying that the thesis or 'what is being proven' (*sādhya*) should not be opposed (*anirākṛta*) 'with regard to [the proponent's] own [intended] subject (*svadharmiṇi*),' Dignāga supposedly recognized that not only the property to be proved (*sādhyadharma*) should be unopposed by any means of valid cognition (*pramāṇa*), but also that the proponent's subject must be existent, for if the subject were not existent it could not have the property, and hence the thesis would be invalidated."

[212] In referring to *āśrayāsiddha*, Candrakīrti indicates the alternative fault, a fault of the reason, that Bhāviveka's inference incurs: inasmuch as its basis, i.e., the subject "the internal bases—the visual faculty, etc.," is not established for Bhāviveka, the reason "because they are [already] existing" will be invalid, for lacking an established subject it cannot meet the first requirement of a valid reason, namely, being existent in what is to be inferred (PS II.5cd: *anumeye sadbhāvaḥ*). Not being an attribute of the subject (*pakṣadharma*), it is an unestablished reason (*asiddhahetu*); see Tillemans 2000: 195, n. 160; Yotsuya 1999: 88. In the NM, Dignāga names *āśrayāsiddha* as one of four sub-types of the unestablished reason; it is exemplified by way of a non-Buddhist's inference in which *ātman* is presented as the subject for the non-Buddhist and his opponent, a Buddhist who considers *ātman* a fiction (cf. Tucci 1930: 14 and n. 26; Katsura 1977: 125); the example is presented again in PSV (P 128a1-2 (K): *chos can ma grub pa ni dper na bdag khyab pa yin | bde ba la sogs pa thams cad na yod pa'i phyir ro zhes bya ba lta bu'o* ||). According to Preisendanz

(*āyatana*)—the faculty of vision, etc.—are not ultimately accepted from [Bhāviveka's] own [side].

§46. If [Bhāviveka replies that] there is no fault because the visual faculty, etc., exist on the surface [level], [we pose the question:] This [word] "ultimately," then, [serves as] a qualification for what?[213]

§47. If [Bhāviveka argues that] because the arising of the surface [level] visual faculty, etc. (*sāṃvṛtānāṃ cakṣurādīnām*) is negated from the ultimate point of view (*paramārthataḥ*), "ultimately" is used

---

1994: 176f., Uddyotakara, influenced by Dignāga's logic and appropriating the rubric *asiddha* for the unproved (*sādhyasama*) reason, names the *āśrayāsiddha* reason as the second of three *asiddha* reasons.

Of interest in the context of Candrakīrti's reference to these faults of the proposition and reason is a short section in the NM which, according to Katsura (1992: 230f.), seems to represent an earlier standpoint of Dignāga's as regards the permissibility of subjects accepted as existent by the opponent but refused as such by oneself: in this section the use of the subject *pradhāna* in a Buddhist inference that aims to prove that *pradhāna* does not exist because it is not perceived (*anupalabdheḥ*) is allowed, even though the subject is a real thing for the opponent Sāṅkhya and a mere conceptual construction (*kalpita*) from the Buddhist point of view. Imperceptibility is considered an attribute of the subject by both debaters, thereby securing *pakṣa-dharmatva*. In the PS, however, conceptual subjects are only allowed as the subjects of consequences (*prasaṅga*), in large part because the Buddhist does not need to accept the *pakṣadharmatva* of the reason (cf. PSV on PS III.16 and 17; my thanks to Toshikazu Watanabe for providing me with a copy of his unpublished paper "How can the existence of the Sāṅkhya's *pradhāna* be negated (*dūṣaṇa*)? Dignāga's view of refutation," read at the 2011 Congress of the International Association of Buddhist Studies). See also Tucci 1930: 16f.; Katsura 1978: 110f.; Tillemans 1998: 115-117 and 2000: 197f.; Seyfort Ruegg 2002: 48, n. 51. Dignāga thus revised his earlier views and rejected the legitimacy of inferences positing unreal or conceptual subjects. On Dharmakīrti's appropriation of the NM argument and later interpretations of his position, see Tillemans 1998; Tillemans and Lopez 1998; see also Funayama 1991; on the Nyāya-Buddhist controvery, see, e.g., Matilal 1970.

[213] In order to refute the charge of having a non-established subject from his own side, Bhāviveka could retort that his subject exists from the point of view of the surface reality. Yotsuya (1999: 90) explains: "This [adopting of a conventional subject], however, would imply that the debate in which he engages is held on the conventional level. And if he intends to pursue the discussion on the conventional level, it is meaningless to adopt the qualification 'ultimately', which has the function of determining that the discussion is held on the ultimate level." See also Hopkins 1983: 504.

as a qualification for the negation of arising,[214] [we respond:] Then [this being] the case, it has to be stated exactly thus, viz., "Ultimately, there is not the arising of the surface [level] visual faculty, etc."; but [your inference] is not stated in this way. Even if it were formulated [in this way], owing to the fact that the opponent maintains that the visual faculty, etc., indeed exist substantially (*dravyasat*) and does not accept that [these bases merely] exist by designation (*prajñaptisat*), there would be, from the opponent's side (*parataḥ*), the fault of the proposition (*pakṣadoṣa*) [namely, that the proposition is] unestablished with respect to its locus (*asiddhādhāra*).[215] Thus, this [justification for the qualification] is not reasonable.

---

[214] Bhāviveka attempts to rescue his qualification "ultimately" by reducing its scope to only non-arising (the third of the three alternatives for the qualification distinguished by Yotsuya [1999: 80]). That is, hypothetical Bhāviveka, who first reduced the qualification's scope from the entire proposition to the proposition minus *svataḥ*, now argues that the qualification also does not apply to the subject *ādhyamikāny āyatanāni*; it rather applies exclusively to non-arising. His intended subject is thus the surface level *ādhyamikāny āyatanāni*, and his inference proves that there is no ultimate arising for these things that do exist, albeit only by designation, on the surface level. As Yotsuya (1999: 90) has stated, "This solution allows him to accept the subject conventionally on the one hand and to negate its origination ultimately. He thus seems able to escape both the fault of the proposition (*pakṣadoṣa*) and the fault of the logical reason (*hetudoṣa*)." See the following note.

[215] In order to avoid the faults of *asiddhādhāra* and *āśrayāsiddha*, Candrakīrti's Bhāviveka claims that the surface-level, i.e., merely designated, faculty of vision, etc., are defined by him as the subject. In his view he is shielded from critique by this surface-level subject: he could not be charged with setting forth a subject unestablished from his own side, and his intent could be realized since via the negation of the ultimate arising of the surface-level subject the real arising of the faculty of vision, etc., as maintained by the Sāṅkhya would be proven untenable. Candrakīrti initially appears to provisionally accept Bhāviveka's defense, but chastises him for not formulating his inference more precisely so that it conforms with his intended meaning. He then deals a death blow to the provisionally accepted proposal by declaring that the Sāṅkhya under no circumstance accepts the inner bases as existing merely by conventional designation, for he maintains their real existence, and thus could not consent to Bhāviveka's surface-level subject; the proposition would suffer from having a locus which is not established for the Sāṅkhya. The fact the subject is unestablished from the Sāṅkhya side would further imply the fault of the reason, *āśrayāsiddha*. See also Yotsuya 1999: 91.

§48. [Bhāviveka] might [argue]: [It is] just as [with the proposition] "Sound is impermanent," [where] only the general (*sāmānya*) [nature], not the particular (*viśeṣa*) [nature], of the property possessor (*dharmin*) and the property (*dharma*) is taken [as the subject and predicate]; for if the particular [nature] were taken [into account], there could not be conventional practice (*vyavahāra*) involving inference (*anumāna*) and the object of inference (*anumeya*).[216] To

---

[216] As will be made clear by the examples provided by hypothetical Bhāviveka, two parties whose specific views regarding their subject differ radically are able to debate on the basis of a common subject when they accept as shared the general nature of the subject unencumbered by particular doctrinal specifications. That the unqualified form of the subject, etc., is legitimately used even in a proof demonstrating the ultimate nature of things appears to have been the position actually held by the historical Bhāviveka. According to this view, the subject of his inference, e.g., the internal bases such as the faculty of vision, etc., could stand as a general subject, free of the doctrinal specifications of surface-level or ultimate existence that would attract the charges of *asiddhādhāra* or *āśrayāsiddha*. The subject from Bhāviveka's side would still be the surface-level internal bases, and for the Sāṅkhya the ultimately existing internal bases, but for the purpose of debate it would not be specified in either way.

Bhāviveka refers to general subjects, reasons and examples in other contexts in the PP. He explicitly defends the reason in some of his inferences in the first chapter of PP as being a general one (see, e.g., the discussion at PP D 49b7-50a1; P 59b5-6). Note too his explicit reference to a generally established example at PP D 52b3-4; P 63b1: *shes pa spyir grub pa kho na las dpe nyid blangs pas dpe med pa yang ma yin no* || (see Ames 1993: 232).

A defense of the logical subject defined as the internal bases is seen later in the first chapter of the PP when Bhāviveka is attacked by opponents (identified by Avalokitavrata as Naiyāyikas) who accuse his inference proving that the inner bases do not arise from other (*don dam par nang gi skye mched rnams de dag gi rkyen gzhan dag las skye ba med de* | *gzhan yin pa'i phyir* | *dper na bum pa bzhin* [D 49b4; P 59a7-8]) of having an empty subject term and thus a reason unestablished as regards its basis: *gzhan dag na re* | *don dam par phyi dang nang gi skye mched rnams khas ma blangs pa'i phyir chos can ma grub pas gzhi ma grub pa'i phyir khyod kyi don ma grub pa nyid kyi skyon du 'gyur ro zhes zer* (PP D 50a4-5; P 60a3-4). He retorts that he conventionally accepts the basis, i.e., a pot or the visual faculty, etc., as well as the reason, i.e., being different [from the causal conditions], and therefore the opponent's critique is inappropriate: *tha snyad du de'i gzhi bum pa dang mig la sogs pa skye mched rnams dang* | *gzhan nyid khas blangs pa'i phyir ji skad smras pa'i skyon mi 'thad pas de ni rigs pa ma yin no* || (PP D 50a5; P 60a4-5; translated in Kajiyama 1963: 53; Ames 1993: 225).

Yotsuya (1999: 93, n. 72) notes that Ejima points to a passage in the PP on MMK XVIII.1 where Bhāviveka employs *ātman* as the subject of inferences and defends his use of it as a subject used in a general sense. The situation differs from that being discussed in the PsP in that Bhāviveka argues for the legitimacy of the subject from his side in this instance on the ground that Buddhists apply the term "*ātman*" to consciousness. His argumentation is nevertheless worth citing: one of the inferences discussed is *don dam par bdag ni za pa po ma yin te | the tshom can gyi shes pa la sogs pa'i rgyu yin pa'i phyir | dper na sdong dum dang* (P: |) *bum pa bzhin* ("Ultimately, the self is not the experiencer, because it is a cause of doubtful knowledge, etc., like a tree stump and a pot"); the passage continues: *ci ste yang la la 'di snyam du dbu ma pas bdag* (P: *bdag gi*) *tshig gi don nyid du khas ma blangs pa'i phyir de'i khyad par bstan pa mi rigs te | dper na mo gsham gyi bu'i sngo bsangs dang | dkar sham nyid la sogs pa* (P: *dag ston pa* for *la sogs pa*) *bzhin no snyam du sems na | de ni bzang po ma yin te | yang* (P: *yang na*) *'byung ba'i srid pa len pa'i phyir bdag ces bya ste | rnam par shes pa'i yul la bdag tu tha snyad gdags pa'i phyir rnam par shes pa la bdag tu brjod de | de ltar yang bcom ldan 'das kyis | sems dul ba ni dge ba ste || dul ba'i sems kyis bde ba 'thob ||*[1] *ces gsungs nas* (P: *nas yang*) *mdo sde gzhan las | bdag gi mgon ni bdag nyid yin || gzhan ni mgon du su zhig 'gyur || mkhas pa bdag nyid legs dul bas || mtho ris dag kyang 'thob par 'gyur ||*[2] *zhes gsungs pas | de'i phyir tha snad du bdag spyir khas blangs pa'i khyad par ma grags pa sel ba'i phyir skyon med do ||* (PP D 180b2-5; P 224b4-8); "Even if some would think this: Because the self is not accepted as a thing (**padārtha*) by Mādhyamikas, it is not correct to point out its particular [features], even as [it is not correct to point out] the blackness or blondness [of the hair] of the son of a barren woman, [we respond:] This is not correct. It is called 'self' because it appropriates the rebirth existence; because the sphere of consciousness is designated as 'self,' consciousness is stated to be 'self.' In this way, too, the Bhagavān, having said, 'Taming the mind is good, a tamed mind is one that brings happiness,' [then] stated in another *sūtra*, 'The master of the self is just the self, who else could be the master? The wise person who has tamed the self well even/also attains heaven.' Therefore, because the unacknowledged particular [features] of the conventional self which is [nevertheless] accepted in a general way are omitted/excluded, the fault does not exist."

[1] Udānavarga 31.1cd: *cittasya damanaṃ sādhu cittaṃ dāntaṃ sukhāvaham ||*. Dhammapada 35cd. Cited BCAP 98.7, 484.3.

[2] Udānavarga 23.17: *ātmā tv ihātmano nāthaḥ ko nu nāthaḥ paro bhavet | ātmanā hi sudāntena svargaṃ labhati paṇḍitaḥ ||*. Dhammapada 160. Cited at PsP_L 354.5-6 (see also BCAP 483.16-17): *ātmā hi ātmano nāthaḥ ko nu nāthaḥ paro bhavet | ātmanā hi sudāntena svargaṃ prāpnoti paṇḍitaḥ ||*. Cited by Candrakīrti at $MABh_{ed}$ 245.4, 257.2, 257.7; $ŚSV_{ed}$ 218.3-6 (where *ko nu nāthaḥ* has been translated into Tib as if *ko 'nunāthaḥ* stood in the Skt); for further references see Erb 1997: 136, n. 344. Cf. $AKBh_{ed}$ 27.6-12 (corrected following $AKBh_{Ej}$ 42.19-43.1): *ātmany asati katham ādhyātmikaṃ bāhyaṃ vā | ahaṃkārasaṃniśrayatvāc cittam atmety upacaryate | ātmanā hi sudāntena svargaṃ prāpnoti paṇḍitaḥ || ity uktam | cittasya cānyatra damanam uktaṃ bhagavatā | cittasya damanaṃ sādhu cittaṃ dāntaṃ sukhāvaham || iti | ata*

explain: If sound dependent on the four primary elements (*cāturmahābhautika*) is taken [by the Buddhist as the subject in the above proposition],[217] that [sound] is not established for the opponent [Mīmāṃsaka].[218] But if [sound as] the quality of space (*ākāśaguṇa*) is taken [as the subject by the Mīmāṃsaka],[219] it is not established for the Buddhist himself. Similarly also for the Vaiśeṣika proposing the impermanence of sound: If sound is taken as a product (*kārya*), it is

---

ātmabhūtasya cittasyāśrayabhāvena pratyāsannabhāvāc cakṣurādīnām ādhyātmikatvaṃ rūpādīnāṃ viṣayabhāvād bāhyatvam |.
Seyfort Ruegg's comment (2002: 51, n. 52) on hypothetical Bhāviveka's assertion that only the general nature of the property, i.e., subject, and of the property possessor, i.e., predicate, is taken into account, viz., "The *anumānānumeyavyavahāra* would not be possible were it the particular rather than the general intended here because, according to the Pramāṇavāda, *anumāna* has to do with the *sāmānyalakṣaṇa*" should be ignored, because Candrakīrti is not intending any reference to Dignāga's *svasāmānyalakṣaṇa* distinction and its related theories but is rather pointing out that Bhāviveka holds that logical subjects and predicates that are common to both parties, i.e., free from doctrinal specifications that would otherwise render debate impossible, should be relied upon.

[217] See AK II.22 and corresponding AKBh, AKVy 123.20-28; Frauwallner 1958: 97-98.

[218] Seyfort Ruegg (2002: 51) identifies the opponent in the initial example, i.e., the opponent for whom sound dependent on the four primary elements is not established and who holds that sound is a quality of space, as the Naiyāyika and Vaiśeṣika; Stcherbatsky (1927: 109) refers to the opponent as a Vaiśeṣika. A debate, however, between the Buddhist and these philosophers would be unnecessary since the Vaiśeṣikas and Naiyāyikas maintain that sound, even though posited by them as a quality of ether, is impermanent. Hopkins (1983: 506f.), following Tsong kha pa, also assumes this opponent to be a Vaiśeṣika, and understands the second debate example to be presenting the discordant particular views of a Vaiśeṣika and a Jaina (see also the remarks in Yotsuya 1999: 93, n. 73); the Jainas, however, do not assert permanent sound which merely manifests.

[219] See Frauwallner 1956: 59; 1984 II: 36. Although the Grammarian's theories of *padasphoṭa* and *varṇasphoṭa* served as the model for the Mīmāṃsā doctrine of the eternality of sound, the Mīmāṃsakas did not use the Grammarians' theory of *varṇasphoṭa* being manifested through sounds consisting of sound atoms, and instead appropriated the Vaiśeṣika system's theory of sound as a quality of ether, rejecting, however, that sound is produced by the contact of breath and the vocal organs and is thus impermanent; see Frauwallner 1960: 241-242 (1982: 281-282) and 1961: 114-118 (1982: 312-316).

not established from the side of the [Mīmāṃsaka] opponent.[220] But if [the subject sound is considered as] something to be manifested (*abhivyaṅgya*), it is not established from the side of [the Vaiśeṣika him]self.[221] It is like this, according to the situation.[222] Also [in the case of the property (*sādhyadharma*)] cessation (*vināśa* = *anitya*): If [cessation is considered to be] something that has a cause (*sahetuka*), it is not established for the Buddhist himself. But if [cessation is taken to be] causeless (*nirhetuka*), it is not established from the side of the [Mīmāṃsaka] opponent.[223] Therefore, just as here [in the cases

---

220 According to the Vaiśeṣika, sound is a quality of ether; non-repeatable sound particulars arise in dependence on various acoustical events (*dhvani*) and then perish (see, e.g., Vaiśeṣikasūtra II.25-32; Frauwallner 1956: 51f.; 1984: II, 30f.; Halbfass 1992: 127). According to the Mīmāṃsaka, sound is eternal (see MS I.1.6-23); on the reasons for and origins of this doctrine, see Frauwallner 1961 (1982: 311-322); on certain advantages this theory had over the Vaiśeṣika doctrine, see Frauwallner 1956: 59-61; 1984: II, 36-38. Cf. also Houben 1995: 46-47.

221 According to the Mīmāṃsaka, sound, eternal and abiding in a potential form in *ākāśa*, is merely brought to manifestation (*abhivyaṅga*). Through the effort of speaking, internal air is propelled out of the mouth and into contact with the surrounding external air in which it, spreading out via contact and disjunction (*saṃyogavibhāgau*), reaches the ear of the hearer. Here it comes into contact with the auditory faculty, the *ākāśa* in the cochlea, and imparting to it a potency (*śakti*), produces modifications (*saṃskāra*) in this *ākāśa* that allow it to perceive the distinct, though in actuality eternal, now temporarily manifested words intended by the speaker (see Bhatt 1989: 180; Jha 1964: 117-118; Frauwallner 1956: 59f.; 1984: II, 36f.). The Vaiśeṣika posits sound as a quality of *ākāśa*, but considers sound to be impermanent, produced in *ākāśa* through breath touching the vocal organs during the effort of speaking. Sound moves toward the auditory faculty, the particular *ākāśa* in the ear of the hearer, by reproducing itself as it comes into conjunction with succeeding parts of external air, and is heard when it reaches the auditory faculty. On *ākāśa* as the auditory faculty, see, e.g, Frauwallner 1956: 51f., 58f.; 1984: II, 31, 35f.; on its determination as such by a process of exclusion, cf. Junankar 1978: 63 and Preisendanz 1994: 680, n. 239.

222 I understand, contrary to PsP Tib and previous translators, *evaṃ yathāsambhavam* as a separate sentence.

223 According to the Buddhist debater, cessation occurs spontaneously, without cause. Cf. AKBh$_{ed}$ 193.5-10: *saṃskṛtasyāvaśyaṃ* ***vyayāt*** (AK II.2d) | *ākasmiko hi bhāvānāṃ vināśaḥ* | *kiṃ kāraṇam* | *kāryasya hi kāraṇaṃ bhavati* | *vināśaś cābhāvaḥ* | *yaś cābhāvas tasya kiṃ kartavyam* | *so 'sāv ākasmiko vināśo yadi bhāvasyotpannamātrasya na syāt paścād api na syād bhāvasya tulyatvāt* | *athānyathībhūtaḥ* | *na yuktaṃ tasyaivānyathātvam* | *na hi sa eva tasmād vilakṣaṇo yujyate* |. Translated in von

presented, one takes] merely the general [nature] of the property possessor (*dharmin*) and the property (*dharma*), in this present case too the mere property possessor [i.e., the internal bases such as the visual faculty, etc.], whose particular [nature, i.e., the inner bases determined as existing from the point of view of the surface level or the ultimate] is waived [for the sake of debate], will be taken [as the subject].[224]

Rospatt 1995: 180-181, n. 397: "[The momentariness of everything is established] **because** the conditioned entity necessarily **perishes**. For the destruction of things is spontaneous. For which reason? For [only] an effect has a cause, but destruction is non-existence, and what should be effected with respect to non-existence? If this spontaneous destruction of the thing did not occur as soon as it had originated, it would also not occur later because the thing would [then] be [just] the same [as it was earlier] (i.e. it would also then have the nature to persist and not to perish). [Nor could it perish later] after having become different [in the meantime]. [For] it is not possible that one and the same thing becomes different, because one and the same [thing] cannot differ in character from itself." Cf. also the Yogācāra proofs for momentariness based on the non-existence of causes of cessation in ibid., 1995: 178f. and 180 n. 396. The Mīmāṃsakas, on the other hand, posit cessation as effected by causes and reject this Buddhist idea. Cf. ŚV VI.24-30 (*śabdanityatādhikaraṇa*) (24ab: *āhuḥ svabhāvasiddhaṃ hi te vināśam ahetukam* |) and Bhatt 1989: 366ff. Within the Buddhist fold but not taken into consideration by Candrakīrti in the above are the Sarvāstivādins and Vātsīputrīya-Sammatīyas, who in assuming the doctrine of the four *saṃskṛtalakṣaṇa*s maintain that an internal factor, namely, the fourth *saṃskṛtalakṣaṇa anityatā* is responsible for the cessation of an entity (see, e.g., Cox 1995: 146-151, 349-353); whereas the Sarvāstivādins deny that an entity is dependent on causes external to itself for its cessation, the Vātsīputrīya-Sammatīyas claim that external causes actualize the latent efficiency of the *lakṣaṇa anityatā* (cf. von Rospatt 1995: 53f.). Candrakīrti himself critiques the view of uncaused perishing; see PsP_L 173.8-174.4; $YṢV_{ed}$ 58.13-25; $YṢV_{tr}$ 194-196 and n. 324.

224 Bhāviveka, in applying this general debate procedure to his inference, considers the subject, the inner bases, to be free from being determined as either surface-level or ultimate, and believes that this relieves the proposition and reason of being liable to the faults of, respectively, *asiddhādhāra* and *āśrayāsiddha* (see n. 211 and n. 212). His inference in this regard (presuming that Candrakīrti still assumes the qualification in Bhāviveka's reasoning to be connected with non-arising; cf. his reformulation *sāṃvṛtānāṃ cakṣurādīnāṃ paramārthato nāsty utpatti* [see PsP_M §47; PsP_L 27.10-28.1]), may be stated as: "The inner bases, unspecified as conventional or ultimate, ultimately do not arise from self."

The author of the TJ also considers the qualification as attached to the predicate of the proposition (in this case the reasoning being discussed is MHK III.26: *tatra bhūtasvabhāvaṃ hi norvyādi paramārthataḥ* | *kṛtakatvād yathā jñānaṃ hetumattvādito 'pi vā* ||; TJ: *'dir sa la sogs pa dag ces bya ba ni chos can yin la* | *don dam*

[We reply:] But this is not the same, because this very [one, namely, Bhāviveka] himself has accepted that precisely when[225] the negation of arising (*utpādapratiṣedha*) is intended here as the property to be proved (*sādhyadharma*), there is the loss (*pracyuti*) of the property possessor (*dharmin*), the locus of that [property] (*tadādhāra*), whose [ascribed] existence (*ātmabhāva*) has been procured through sheer

---

par (D: *par na*) *'byung ba'i ngo bo nyid ma yin zhes bya ba ni de'i chos yin no* || *chos can dang chos bsdus pa ni phyogs yin te* | [ed. Iida 1980: 84f.; Heitmann 2004: 124; that the qualification is attached to the predicate has been noted also by Seyfort Ruegg 1981: 65]). Yotsuya (1999: 97, n. 86) notes that the final sentence of the defence of the qualification further on in the commentary on MHK III.26 (*'dir de dam bcas pa'i khyad par nyid bzung bas nyes pa med do*) appears to indicate that *don dam par* qualifies the whole proposition; one might presume that the TJ's author, having specified earlier that the qualification is applied to the predicate of the thesis, is here using the word *pratijñā* in a more general sense. He defends the usage of the qualification "ultimately" (and indirectly the unspecified subject; see Candrakīrti's critique beginning with the next sentence) by arguing that the qualification should be understood as intending the *paramārtha* associated with conceptuality: *don dam pa ni rnam gnyis te* | *de la gcig ni mngon par 'du byed pa med par 'jug pa 'jig rten las 'das pa zag pa med pa spros pa med pa'o* || *gnyis pa ni mngon par 'du byed pa dang bcas par 'jug pa bsod nams dang ye shes kyi tshogs kyi rjes su mthun pa dag pa 'jig rten pa'i ye shes zhes bya ba spros pa dang bcas pa ste* | *'dir de dam bcas pa'i khyad par nyid bzung bas nyes pa med do* || (TJ D 60b4-5; P 64a7-64b1; quoted in Yotsuya 1999: 97, n. 86; Tibetan text and translation in Iida 1980: 86, 87; Heitmann 2004: 130ff.). Yotsuya (ibid., n. 86) states, "As the passages ... cited from the TJ show, something which is found through cognition conformable with the ultimate, and which can be a subject that is unspecified either as 'conventional' or as 'ultimate,' is what Bhāvaviveka is assumed to maintain in this context in the PMV," and translates: "There are two kinds of *paramārthas*: one is [cognition] which arises without [conceptualizing] effort, and which is beyond the world, undefiled and without diversification; the other is [cognition] which arises possessing conceptualization and conforms with the assemblage of wisdom and virtue; it is called 'pure worldly gnosis' and possesses diversification. In this connection, since it (= the second kind of *paramārtha*) is held to be the qualification of the proposition, a fault is not incurred [by me (= Bhāvaviveka)]." The argumentation for the general subject as presented here in the PsP is also translated in Cabezon 1992: 279 but the rendering is problematic.

[225] For the sake of the English, I have not translated the corresponding *tadaiva*. P, N and G Tib correctly attest *de'i tshe kho nar* for *tadaiva*; D and C Tib, however, attest *de'i tshe de kho nar*, a reading accepted and elaborated on by Tsong kha pa. See Yotsuya 1999: 99, n. 93, and 128, n. 43; Hopkins 1983: 825, n. 424; 1989: 19f.; Seyfort Ruegg 2002: 53, n. 57.

error.[226] For error (*viparyāsa*) and non-error (*aviparyāsa*) are [utterly]

---

[226] Cp. MABh$_{ed}$ 102.18-103.1 where, in the context of describing the *saṃvṛti* aspect of things, *bdag gi yod pa* (**ātmabhāva*) is said to be found through the force of false vision: *gzhan* (= *saṃvṛti*) *ni so so'i skye bo* (MABh$_{UN}$: *bo'i*) *ma rig pa'i rab rib kyi ming* (MABh$_{UN}$: *ling*) *tog gis blo'i mig ma lus par khebs pa rnams kyi mthong ba rdzun* (MABh$_{UN}$: *brdzun*) *pa'i stobs las bdag gi yod pa rnyed pa yin te* |.
The section from PsP$_M$ §48 (response) to end of the first sentence of §50 (PsP$_L$ 29.7 to 30.16) rejects the possibility of a common subject for the proponent and the opponent and, to borrow Yotsuya's terminology, presents the "Crucial Point" in Candrakīrti's critique of *svatantra* reasoning. Its structure and argumentation are laid out in detail in Yotsuya 1999: 97-107. I agree with Yotsuya that the proponent here is Bhāviveka as a Mādhyamika, and not Bhāviveka as a Svātantrika-Mādhyamika; he states (ibid., 98, n. 87): "It seems to me, however, that Candrakīrti points out that it is inappropriate not for the Svātantrika-Mādhyamika but for a true Mādhyamika to employ svatantra-reasoning." Candrakīrti argues in this first sentence of the section (= Yotsuya's '*Passage A I*,' p. 99) that Bhāviveka's general subject, i.e., the inner bases unspecified as surface-level or ultimate—according to Candrakīrti, however, a subject necessarily surface for Bhāviveka—is ruined for Bhāviveka when non-arising is accepted as the *sādhyadharma*. The next sentence provides the reason for this. Yotsuya (ibid., 100) explains: "In Candrakīrti's interpretations of ultimate truth (*paramārtha*) we cannot find an entity of intermediate ontological status between the conventional and the ultimate such as Bhāvaviveka accepts ... . For Candrakīrti, the conventional and the ultimate are utterly distinct. This implies that the conventional entity cannot be possibly established on the ultimate level, and further that, on the ultimate level, the subject (which for him is a conventional entity) is not established in a form unspecified as conventional or ultimate" (see his translation of the present paragraph at ibid., 99-101).
Stcherbatsky (1927: 110f.) wrongly interprets the entire passage as focussed on what he considers the dual reality posited by the Madhyamaka school, viz., the universe as whole as ultimate Reality and the separate, related parts that make up the whole as phenomenal reality; see, however, his literal translation (ibid., 111, n. 4) which retains more of the sense of the passage. Cabezon's (1992: 281) translation of the section from the Tibetan where it is cited in the sTong thun chen mo would have benefited from a comparison with the Sanskrit or a perusal of Hopkins' translation from the Tibetan (Hopkins has checked at least part of the Sanskrit; see Hopkins 1983: 825, n. 424). Hopkins (ibid., 510), however, misled by PsP Tib's placement of *gang gis na de'i tshe na kun rdzob tu 'gyur ba* (*yena tadānīṃ saṃvṛtiḥ*), translates the final sentence, "Like the falling hairs and so forth of one without cataracts, when a non-erroneous [consciousness of meditative equipoise on emptiness] does not superimpose the unreal [i.e., objects established by way of their own character], how could it observe the merest portion of a conventionality that does not exist [by way of its own character]?" Thurman's (1991: 335, n. 138) literal translation from the Sanskrit has a number of problems; the first sentence, e.g., is translated as "[That is not so;] because, when as here the negation of production is accepted as probandum,

distinct (*bhinna*).[227] Thus, when through error what is inexistent (*asat*) is taken to be existent, like the hairs and so forth [seen] by a person with [the visual disorder called] *timira*,[228] how [could there be] the

---

[Bhavaviveka] himself postulates that it would be a grievous error for its basis, the subject [of the syllogism], to have an intrinsic nature established merely by erroneous [cognition]." Tillemans' (1990: 47, n. 107) translation of the section from the Sanskrit is much more accurate; *ātmabhāva* refers, however, to the [ascribed] existence (of the *dharmin*), and not, as Tillemans has it, to "the self's possessions [such as the eye, etc.]." See also the translation by Seyfort Ruegg (2002: 53f.).
I have not managed to locate the passage Candrakīrti refers to in which Bhāviveka addresses the loss of the *dharmin*. Yotsuya (1999: 100, n. 95) cites 'Jam dbyangs bzhad pa's referral to a statement by Bhāviveka in the MHK in his dBu ma la 'jug pa'i mtha' dpyod lung rigs gter mdzod zab don kun gsal skal bzang 'jug ngogs. See also Hopkins 1989: 24.
The *LṬ glosses *viparyāsa* with *bhrānti*. The *LṬ's author appears to mistakenly understand the *dharmin* to be the subject Candrakīrti has posited for Buddhapālita's inference, i.e., a pot, etc.: *viparyāso bhrāntis tanmātreṇāsāditātmabhāvasya ghaṭāde*[*r*] *dharmiṇa utpattir nāstīty ukte tasya pracyutir abhāvo 'ṅgīkṛtā* (cf. Yonezawa 2004: 122, 136 [fol. 2a4]). He may, however, have understood pot, etc., as a hypothetical general subject, in the sense proposed by Bhāviveka, that would be accepted by the Mādhyamika and his opponent.

[227] *viparyāsa* and *aviparyāsa* refer to the subjective, active side of error and have thus been translated as "mistaken [cognition] / non-mistaken [cognition]" by Yotsuya (1999: 100). Hopkins (1983: 508f.) translates *phyin ci log tsam gyis* of the previous sentence as "by a mere erroneous [consciousness]," but translates *phyin ci log dang phyin ci ma log pa dag* of the relevant sentence as "The erroneous and the non-erroneous," which he explains as the erroneous objects and non-erroneous objects found by their respective mistaken and non-mistaken consciousnesses; see his discussion of Tsong kha pa's two interpretations of the sentence in Hopkins 1989. Stcherbatsky (1927: 110f.) similarly relates (*a*)*viparyāsa* to the objective side of error, i.e., to "illusion" and "reality." Hopkins (1983: 512f.), possibly misled by Tib's use of *phyin ci* (*ma*) *log* (*pa*) for (*a*)*viparyāsa* and of *phyin ci log* for *viparīta*, goes on to translate (*a*)*viparyāsa* and *viparīta* in the first sentence of the commentary following the VV quotation in an objective sense. Candrakīrti is, however, being consistent in his usage of (*a*)*viparyāsa* as a subjective state throughout this section (he employs the word only in a subjective sense in the PsP); he resorts to *viparīta* to refer to the objective side of error.

[228] Persons with the *timira* condition are usually said to imagine that they see hairs floating in the air or lying on their food or in eating utensils; the hairs are sometimes described as a "net" of hair: cf. CŚṬ XIII where the individual with the *timira* condition is said to see only a mesh of hairs and not each hair individually (Tib in CŚṬ_{Ted} 64-65; see also CŚṬ_{tr} 275, n. 370). The condition may also cause the *taimirika*s to imagine that they see small flies or mosquitoes (cf. PsP_{L} 373.2: *yathā hi*

perception of even a trace (*leśa*) of a real thing (*sadbhūtapadārtha*)? And when something unreal (*abhūta*) is not superimposed because there is no error, just as hairs and so forth [are not superimposed] by a person without [the visual disorder] *timira*, how [could there] then [be] the perception of even a trace of an unreal thing, whereby the surface (*saṃvṛti*) could exist at that time?

Just on account of this the Master [Nāgārjuna] has said:

> If I perceived something by way of things like direct perception (*pratyakṣa*) [and the other means of valid cognition], I might affirm (*pravartayeyam*) or negate (*nivartayeyam*) [it];
> [But] because that [object of perception] does not exist, I am without reproach.[229]

And because in this way error and non-error are [utterly] distinct, then, since what is mistaken (*viparīta*) cannot exist in the state of non-error of the wise, how [could there be] a surface-level visual faculty (*sāṃvṛtaṃ cakṣuḥ*) which might be the subject (*dharmin*)? Thus, neither the fault of the proposition [namely, that the proposition is] unestablished with respect to [its] locus (*asiddhādhāra*), nor the fault of the reason [namely, that the reason is] unestablished as regards

---

taimirikā vitathaṃ keśamaśakamakṣikādirūpaṃ paśyantaḥ ...). The common translation "ophthalmia," i.e., conjunctivitis, the inflammation of the mucous membrane (conjunctiva) lining the inner eyelids and the forepart of the eyeball, has been corrected by May (1959: 226, n. 779), who cites the Indologist and ophthamologist Filliozat: "*Timira* ne peut se traduire valablement par 'ophtalmie'. Ce dernier terme désigne des conjonctivites qui ne donnent pas les symptômes de *timira*. *Timira* = 'obscurité' ou plus généralement 'trouble visuel' dû à des opacités et altérations de réfringence à l'intérieur des milieux transparents de l'œil." The opacities, as he indicates, occur in the vitreous humour, the clear gel-like substance filling the eye. See also, e.g., May 1959: 187, n. 610; La Vallée Poussin 1933: 30-31; MABh_{ed} 109.6-110.11, 216.16-18. In the context of Madhyamaka discussions the reference is usually to what is commonly known as "floaters." See also Kobayashi 2013 where the reference in certain Indian medical texts appears to be to cataracts.

[229] VV 30. Quoted earlier at PsP_{M} §26 (PsP_{L} 16.9-10).

[its] basis (*āśrayāsiddha*), is eliminated.[230] So this is definitely not a refutation [of the logical faults].[231]

§49. Nor is there similarity of the example (*nidarśana*) [that is, of the exemplifying inference proving the impermanence of sound adduced by Bhāviveka to demonstrate that a general nature of property possessor and property is accepted by both parties]. For in that [example], the general [nature] of sound (*śabdasāmānya*), and the general [nature] of impermanence (*anityatvasāmānya*), without [any] particular [nature] being intended, are agreed upon (*saṃvidyate*) by the two [debaters].[232] But it is not the case that, like this, [both] the proponent of emptiness (*śūnyatā*[*vādin*]) and the proponent of non-emptiness (*aśūnyatāvādin*) accept a visual faculty in general, either from a surface [point of view] (*saṃvṛtyā*) or ultimately. Thus, the example is not similar.[233]

§50. And precisely this method (*vidhi*) [that was employed] for bringing out (*udbhāvana*) the fault of the proposition (*pakṣadoṣa*) [namely, that the proposition is] unestablished with respect to [its] locus (*asiddhādhāra*),[234] should be employed for bringing out the fact that this reason, "because [they] are [already] existing" (*sattvāt*),[235] is

---

[230] Hopkins (1983: 513) translates: "Therefore, due to the irreversibility of having a fallacious position [thesis] in which the base [subject] is not established (*asiddhadhāra, gzhi ma grub pa*) ... ."

[231] This concludes, according to Yotsuya (1999: 98), the first aspect ("Point 1") of the Crucial Point, viz., that the "subject which is unspecified either only as 'conventional' or only as 'ultimate' is not established for the proponent." Candrakīrti now proceeds to "Point 2," viz., that "the subject is not established in common for both the proponent and the opponent either conventionally or ultimately."

[232] Seyfort Ruegg (2002: 56) is of the opinion that the two debaters referred to would be a Vaiśeṣika and a Buddhist ("... are available to both [parties to the debate, viz., the Vaiśeṣika and a Buddhist]"), but see my comments on §48.

[233] *LṬ: *ato na dṛṣṭāntena sahāsya sadṛśatā* (ms: *'śadṛśatā*) | *yato viparyāsāviparyāsāv anyonyavyavacchedasthitau* (see Yonezawa 2004: 122, 136 [fol. 2a4-5]).

[234] See PsP_M §45 to end of §47 (PsP_L 27.7-28.3).

[235] The logical reason for Bhāviveka's inference is first presented in PsP as *vidyamānatvāt* (cited PsP_M §39 [PsP_L 26.1]), and then as *sattvāt* (first sentence of PsP_M §50 [PsP_L 30.15]; see also §54 [PsP_L 33.4]), the former presented together with

unestablished (*hetor asiddhārthatā*). And this is so because this logician (*tārkika*) himself [i.e., Bhāviveka] has also accepted this matter (*artha*) as stated. How? [He states that Buddhist opponents from the Conservative school have objected:]

> [The causal conditions,] the cause (*hetu*) and so forth, which produce the inner bases do indeed exist, because the Tathāgata has instructed thus. For that which has been taught by the Tathāgata [as being] a [certain] way [truly] is thus; for example, [the Tathāgata taught that] *nirvāṇa* is peaceful (*śānta*) [and it truly is thus].[236]

[In regard to] this proof (*sādhana*) put forth by the opponent, this [logician Bhāviveka] has expressed the [following] criticism:

> What meaning of the reason do you intend here then? [Do you mean] "because the Tathāgata has instructed thus from the surface [point of view]" (*saṃvṛtyā*) or ["because the Tathāgata has instructed thus] from the ultimate [standpoint]" (*paramārthataḥ*)? If [you claim he has done so] from the surface [point of view], the reason is unestablished from [your] own

---

the rest of the inference, the latter on its own (i.e., the present instance) and later as part of the reworked inference. Cp. PsP_M §32 (PsP_L 22.4) where the *svata evānumāna* Candrakīrti presents in response to Bhāviveka's criticism contains the reason *vidyamānatvāt* (see also the penultimate sentence of the first paragraph of PsP_M §29 [PsP_L 20.5-6] where the reason indicated will have to be construed as such).
*LṬ's author specifies that *sattvāt* refers to Bhāviveka's reason: *sat[t]vād iti sāṃkhyaṃ prati bhāvivekenoktaṃ* (cf. Yonezawa 2004: 122, 136 [fol. 2a5]).

[236] The passage appears in Bhāviveka's commentary on MMK I.7. PP: *nang gi skye mched rnams skyed par byed pa rgyu la sogs pa ni yod pa kho na yin te | de ltar de bzhin gshegs pas gsungs pa'i phyir |* (D: *phyir dang*; PsP: *phyir ro |*) *gang de bzhin shegs pas ji skad gsungs pa de ni de bzhin te | dper na mya ngan las 'das pa ni zhi ba'o zhes bya ba bzhin no ||* (D 58b3-4; P 70a7-70b1; translated in Kajiyama 1964: 115; Ames 1994: 109). The fellow Buddhists voicing the objection (*rang gi sde pa dag yang phyir zlogs par byed de*) are identified by Avalokitavrata as Vaibhāṣikas and Sautrāntikas (PPṬ: *rang gi sde pa dag ces bya ba ni mdo sde pa dang bye brag tu smra ba dag* [D 191b5-6; P 223a2]).
Cf. $AKBh_{ed}$ 80.22-23; 108.25: *tadyathā sarvasaṃskārā anityāḥ sarvadharmā anātmānaḥ śāntaṃ nirvānam iti*. More references in Seyfort Ruegg 2002: 58, n. 64.

[point of view].[237] If [you claim he has done so] from the ultimate [standpoint, let us remind you that the Madhyamakaśāstra states:]

---

[237] According to Dignāga, not only the subject (*dharmin*), but also the reason (*hetu*) in an inference must be acknowledged by each of the parties in the debate; see PS III.11, as cited and translated in n. 147; PS III.12bc: *prasiddhas tu dvayor api | sādhanam* (Katsura 2009: 158; see also Steinkellner 1988: 1429 and n. 8); NM: *pakṣadharmo vādiprativādiniścito gṛhyate* (Katsura 1977: 122). A reason that is not acknowledged by one of the parties is classified amongst the four types of unestablished and therefore pseudo reasons (*asiddhahetvābhāsā*) as an *anyatarāsiddhahetvābhāsa* (cf. Tucci 1930: 14 and n. 24; Katsura 1977: 124). Cp. the example of the reason "because it is made / a product" used by the Buddhists to prove the impermanence of sound which would not be accepted by a Mīmāṃsā opponent propounding the eternality of sound as set forth by Dignāga in PSV ad PS III.11 *gcig la yang bzlog pa ni mngon par gsal bar smra ba la byas pa nyid lta bu'o* (PSV_K P 27b8; PSV_{Kit} 481). See also n. 272. If, as regards the inference set forth in the PP and cited here in the PsP, the Buddhist arguing for the existence of the causal conditions should respond to Bhāviveka's question by stating that the meaning of the reason is "because the Tathāgata has instructed thus from the surface [point of view]," the reason is not established for himself because he asserts that the Tathāgata taught thus from an ultimate point of view. Avalokitavrata also explains that when the reason is asserted from the surface point of view, it will not be established for the fellow Buddhist: *'di ltar khyed kyi sgrub pa ni de bzhin shegs pas don dam par rkyen bzhi po dag yod par gsungs pa'i phyir | don dam par de dag las dngos po rnams skye bar 'dod pa yin la | 'dir gtan tshigs kyi don ni de bzhin gshegs pas kun rdzob tu de skad gsungs pa'i phyir zhes zer na | de ni kho bo'i* (D: *bo*) *'dod pa yin pas khyed rang la ma grub pa'i don nyid yin no* || (D 192b1-2; P 224b6-7).
Seyfort Ruegg (2002: 59) understands the passage differently than I do, possibly because he has overlooked that *tathā tathāgatena nirdeśāt* of the first sentence of Bhāviveka's response merely repeats the reason just set forth by the Conservative Buddhist. He translates: "In what sense do you understand the sense of the inferential reason: on the surface-level, since the Tathāgata has taught this thus, or in ultimate reality?" His translation of the next sentence reveals that he does not take the reason (*hetu*) referred to there to be *tathā tathāgatena nirdeśāt*, i.e., that of the Conservative Buddhist, but rather to be *sattvāt*, the reason in Bhāviveka's own inference: "If you think it to be on the surface-level, then the sense of the [above-mentioned] inferential reason ['*sattvāt*, because of existing'] is unestablished for oneself (*svatas*)." A similar interpretation appears in Seyfort Ruegg 1981: 77f., where there additionally seems to be some confusion regarding the referent of the word *svataḥ*. *svataḥ* of *saṃvṛtyā cet svato hetor asiddhārthatā* here in Bhāviveka's response to the Conservative Buddhist arguing for causal conditions refers to this opponent himself, since he only accepts the real, i.e., ultimate, existence of these conditions.

> When neither an existent, nor an inexistent, nor a [both] existent and inexistent factor (*dharma*) comes forth (*nirvartate*),[238]

then because its (= the alleged cause's) being the condition (*pratyaya*) of an existent, inexistent or both [existent and inexistent] effect (*kārya*) has [thus] been refuted,

> How is the cause [condition] (*hetu*) that which brings forth (*nirvartaka*)? It being thus, [a cause condition] is not [logically] feasible.[239]

[This] statement [by Nāgārjuna] means that that [alleged] cause is definitely not [something which] brings forth [and hence in reality not a cause]. And therefore, because that to be brought forth and that which brings forth (*nirvartyanirvartaka*) are not ultimately established, the reason (*hetu*) ["because the Tathāgata has instructed thus" turns out to be either] unestablished (*asiddhārthatā*) or is contradictory [in that it proves the opposite of the probandum it aims to prove] (*viruddhārthatā*)[240].[241]

---

*LṬ's author wrongly interprets *svataḥ* ("from [your] own [point of view]") of *saṃvṛtyā cet svato hetor asiddhārthatā* to refer to a Sāṅkhya opponent: *svata iti sāṃkhyasya* (cf. Yonezawa 2004: 123, 137 [fol. 2a5]). He seems to have confused the Conservative Buddhist's reason with Bhāviveka's own reason *vidyamānatvāt/sattvāt*; if this is the case, he is at least correct in understanding that when the *saṃvṛtyā* alternative is applied to *vidyamānatvāt/sattvāt*, it is the opponent, i.e., the Sāṅkhya who only accepts existence from the ultimate standpoint, for whom this reason would be unestablished.

[238] MMK I.7ab: *na san nāsan na sadasan dharmo nirvartate yadā* |.

[239] MMK I.7cd: *kathaṃ nirvartako hetur evaṃ sati na yujyate* || (PsP_L, Ye 2011a: ... *evaṃ sati hi yujyate* ||). For the discussion regarding the emendation to I.7d, see n. 592. My translation of the *kārikā* reflects Candrakīrti's interpretation of it as found in his commentary on MMK I.7.

[240] If the Buddhist opponent answers that the reason means "because the Tathāgata has instructed thus from the ultimate standpoint," the reason will be unestablished because Nāgārjuna, communicating—according to the Mādhyamika—the Tathāgata's true intent, has shown in MMK I.7 that a cause condition does not ultimately exist. The opponent has accepted that the reason is intended from an ultimate point of view but the Mādhyamika only accepts that the Tathāgata taught causal conditions from a surface-level point of view. Just how the reason understood by the opponent as meaning "because the Tathātaga has instructed thus from the ultimate standpoint"

could, alternatively, be viewed as a contradictory reason, i.e., as one proving the opposite of the *sādhya*, is less evident: if the reason "because the Tathātaga has instructed thus from the ultimate standpoint" is taken to mean that the Tathāgata taught that causal conditions truly exist, then there is no contradiction, for the opponent wishes to prove the ultimate existence of causal conditions. It seems that Bhāviveka, in order to be able to present a contradiction between the reason and probandum, intended that the opponent's reason, in being claimed to be from the ultimate point of view, would mean "because the Tathāgata has instructed thus from the ultimate standpoint, i.e., he taught that causal conditions do not truly exist, for he taught from the ultimate point of view which denies the existence of all things." This interpretation would deliver a contradiction inasmuch as the *hetu* communicating that the teaching of causal conditions was given from the ultimate standpoint of no real existence would contradict the *sādhya* claiming the real existence of causal conditions. This alternative interpretation demands, however, an unexpected change in the meaning of *paramārthataḥ* construed with the reason from "because the Tathāgata taught them as existing in an ultimate sense" (as assumed for the unestablished reason) to "because the Tathāgata talked about them from the ultimate standpoint of no real existence." The understanding of the contradiction gleaned by Hopkins (1983: 518) from his dGe lugs pa sources and/or informants is different; he translates: "Or it is just contradictory [if the referent is to ultimate existence due to being very contradictory with a predicate of the probandum which should be a conventionality]." This interpretation assumes the reason "because the Tathāgata taught them as existing in an ultimate sense" but factors in the Madhyamaka viewpoint, according to which the causal conditions of the *sādhya* are strictly surface level. The reason would thus be unestablished from the Mādhyamika's point of view and contradictory from the Mādhyamika's point of view.
Avalokitavrata states that should the Buddhist opponent assert that the reason meant is "because the Tathāgata instructed thus from the ultimate standpoint," the reason would be unestablished because, as demonstrated by Nāgārjuna in his *kārikā*, a cause that brings forth is not possible. In explaining the contradiction, he states that even if the opponent maintains that the Tathāgata taught the meaning of the reason to be that the conditions exist from the standpoint of the surface level, the resultant establishment of own nature as existing on the surface level would imply that he agrees with the Mādhyamika view that it does not exist ultimately, and this surface-level establishment would thus conflict with his actual position that own nature exists ultimately. It is not clear to me if this represents the alternative interpretation of "ultimately" suggested above (i.e., "because the Tathāgata has instructed thus from the ultimate standpoint" taken to mean "because the Tathāgata talked about them from the ultimate standpoint of no real existence") or if Avalokitavrata considers the contradictory reason as applicable solely in the context of the reason asserted from the surface point of view, i.e., understood as "because the Tathāgata has instructed thus from the surface point of view." The outcome is of course in each case the same, i.e., the opponent's reason proves something other than the probandum it aims to prove. PPṬ: *'on te don dam par na ni zhes bya ba ni 'on te rang la ma grub pa'i don*

And because in this way this very [one] himself (= Bhāviveka), by virtue of this procedure (*nyāya*), has accepted the non-establishment (*asiddhi*) of the reason, as a result, since indeed in all inferences with reasons adduced as properties of real things (*vastudharmopanyasta-*

---

nyid mi 'dod pas | gtan tshigs kyi don de de bzhin gshegs pas don dam par de skad gsungs pa'i phyir ro zhes zer na ni'o || de ltar na | gang tshe chos ni yod pa dang || (P: |) *med dang yod med mi bsgrub* (P: *sgrub*) *pa || zhes bya ba brjod do ||* (P: *de* |) ... *gtan tshigs kyi don de ltar de bzhin gshegs pas gsungs pa'i phyir zhes bya ba de ma grub pa nyid do ||* (P: *nyid* for *nyid do* ||) *gtan tshigs kyi don 'gal ba nyid do zhes bya ba ni ci ste de bzhin gshegs pas kun rdzob tu rkyen rnams yod par gsungs pa de nus pa'i ngo bo nyid kyi* (D: *kyis*) *med na mi 'byung ba'i tshul gyis gtan tshigs su 'dod na 'di la yang khyed kun rdzob tu ngo bo nyid yod par sgrub* (P: *bsgrub*) *pa ni don dam par ngo bo nyid med par sgrub pa yin pas | de ltar na khyod don dam par ngo bo nyid yod par 'dod pa dang 'gal ba'i don nyid yin no ||* (D 192b2-7; P 224b7-225a7). Ames (1994: 129, n. 104) appears to understand Avalokitavrata's explanation of the contradictory reason to be referring to the reason as asserted from the surface-level point of view (*saṃvṛtyā*): "If it is asserted of superficial reality, it is contradictory to try to prove a thesis about ultimate reality using a reason which holds only in superficial reality."

241 Bhāviveka's response in the PP to the Buddhist opponent follows upon the opponent's presentation of the application and conclusion (omitted in the following) for his inference. PP: *'dir khyod kyi gtan tshigs kyi don du 'dod pa gang yin | de bzhin gshegs pas kun rdzob tu de skad gsungs pa'i phyir ram | 'on te don dam par gsungs pa'i phyir | gal te kun rdzob tu na ni* (P without *na ni*) *rang la* (P without *la*) *gtan tshigs kyi* (P without *gtan tshigs kyi*) *don ma grub pa nyid do || 'on te don dam par na ni |* (D: ||) *gang tshe chos ni yod pa dang || med dang yod med mi bsgrub*[1] *pa || de'i tshe 'bras bu yod pa dang med pa dang | gnyi ga'i bdag nyid kyi rkyen bsal* (D: *bstsal*) *ba'i phyir | ji ltar sgrub byed rgyu zhes bya || de lta yin na mi rigs so || de ni sgrub par byed pa'i rgyu ma yin pa kho na'o* (P: *na'o* ||) *zhes bya ba'i tshig*[2] *gi don to || de'i phyir don dam par bsgrub* (P: *grub*) *par bya ba dang | sgrub bar byed ba nyid ma grub pa'i phyir gtan tshigs kyi don ma grub pa nyid*[3] *dang | don 'gal ba nyid*[4] *do ||* (D 58b6-59a1; P 70b3-6). PsP: [1]*'grub* (ABh, BP and MMK_T also attest *'grub*); [2]*zhes bya ba ni ngag* for *zhes bya ba'i tshig*; [3]*gtan tshigs ma grub pa'i don nyid* for *gtan tshigs kyi don ma grub pa nyid*; [4]*don 'gal ba'i don nyid* for *don 'gal ba nyid*. Translated in Kajiyama 1964: 116; Ames 1994: 109-110; both Kajiyama and Ames translate *khyod kyi* of the first sentence as a possessive genitive qualifying *gtan tshigs* "eures Grundes; your reason," but *khyod kyi* is the literal translation for *bhavatām* used in the meaning of "on your part."

hetuka) the reason and so forth are not established right from [his] own [point of view], truly all proofs (*sādhana*) are ruined.[242]

§51. For example, here [in Bhāviveka's inferences against arising from other which he has stated as follows],

> It is not the case, ultimately, that the inner bases arise from their conditions (*tatpratyaya*), which are other [than the inner bases], because [they] are other [than their conditions] (*paratvāt*), just as a pot [does not arise from the conditions for the inner bases which are other than the pot].[243]

Or,

> It is not the case, ultimately, that the others (*pare*), the alleged (*vivakṣita*) [conditions] that bring forth inner bases such as the visual faculty, are admitted/recognized (*pratīyante*) as conditions, because [they] are other [than the inner bases] (*paratvāt*), like threads, etc. [which, other than the inner bases, are not conditions for the inner bases],[244]

---

242 *ādi* of *hetvādīnām* refers to the other parts of an inference, such as the example. *LṬ's author wrongly interprets *svata eva* as referring to the Sāṅkhya opponent he imagines is the focus of the entire preceding passage: *svata eveti sāṃkhyasya* (cf. Yonezawa 2004: 123, 137 [fol. 2a5]).

243 Cf. Avalokitavrata's comments at PPṬ D 82b1-3, 83a5-83b2; P 96b2-5, 97a8-97b6. Ames (1993: 223f.) translates *para* (*gzhan*) as "different," which is certainly not wrong, but does leave some ambiguity as to whether qualitative or numerical difference is intended. Since this argument and the numerous other Madhyamaka reasonings using *paratva* as ground for the impossibility of effects from causes focus on numerical difference, I prefer to use "other" as a translation equivalent. Seyfort Ruegg's (2002: 60) "from other conditions of theirs" does not quite catch the meaning of *parebhyas tatpratyayebhyaḥ*.

244 The two inferences are presented in Bhāviveka's PP commentary on MMK I.1: *don dam par nang gi skye mched rnams de dag gi rkyen gzhan dag las skye ba med de | gzhan yin pa'i phyir* (D: *phyir |*) *dper na bum pa bzhin no || yang na don dam par gzhan brjod par 'dod pa mig la sogs pa nang* (P: *nad*) *gi skye mched 'grub par byed pa dag rkyen ma yin par nges te | gzhan yin pa'i phyir dper na rgyu spun la sogs pa bzhin no ||* (D 49b4-5; P 59a7-59b1; translated in Kajiyama 1963: 51; Ames 1993: 223f.). PsP Tib's presentation of *yang na don dam par gzhan gyis brjod par 'dod pa* for *yang na don dam par gzhan brjod par 'dod pa* inspired Stcherbatsky (1927: 114 and n. 2) to emend *pare* to *paraiḥ*; he translates, "Thesis: The causes which in the

"[they] are other" and so forth[245] (*paratvādika*) are not established right from [his] (= Bhāviveka's) own [point of view] (*svata evāsiddha*).[246]

§52. And just as [in the case of the opponent's proof, i.e.,]

---

opinion of our opponents, produce mental phenomena are not understood to be causes in the absolute sense" (see also $\mathrm{PsP}_{\mathrm{L}}$ 31, n. 8, where de La Vallée Poussin reconstructs *atha vā paramārthataḥ parair vivakṣitāś cakṣurādyādhyātmikāyatana-sādhakāḥ pratyayā asattvena niścitāḥ* from PsP Tib, adding "La lecture *paraiḥ* est intéressante"). De Jong (1978: 31), however, referring to observations made by Ejima, insists that the reading *pare* be maintained (Hopkins [1983: 519 and n. 441] notes de Jong but nevertheless translates following PsP Tib: "The producers of the internal sources such as eyes, which others want to say [exist] ultimately, are not ascertained as conditions [producing the internal sources] because of being other, as, for example, is the case with threads and so forth"). PPṬ confirms the reading *pare*: *'bras bu mig la sogs pa nang gi skye mched rnams kyi rkyen mer mer po dang nur nur po la sogs pa de dag ni gzhan yang yin | brjod par 'dod pa yang yin | mig la sogs pa nang gi skye mched 'grub par byed pa dag kyang yin no zhes bya ba khyad par gyis* (P: *gyi*) *bsdu bar bya'o* (D 84b1-2; P 98b8-99a2); *gzhan* is commented on in the following sentence: *de la gzhan zhes bya ba ni rkyen mer mer po dang nur nur po la sogs pa de dag 'bras bu mig la sogs pa nang gi skye mched gzhan du gyur pa de dag la ltos* (P: *bltos*) *na gzhan nyid yin pa'i phyir gzhan zhes bya'o* (D 84b2-3; P 99a2-3). *vivakṣitāḥ* is glossed: *brjod par 'dod pa zhes bya ba ni rkyen mer mer po dang nur nur po la sogs pa de dag rkyen du smra ba gzhan dag gis rkyen nyid du brjod par 'dod pa'i phyir brjod par 'dod pa zhes bya'o* ‖ (D 84b3; P 99a3). Seyfort Ruegg (2002: 60) construes the qualification *paramārthena* with *vivakṣitāḥ*: "[Conditions], intended as other in ultimate reality … ."
The logical reason in this argument of Bhāviveka's had already been criticized by Sthiramati as being contradictory; see Kajiyama 1968: 198f.; Ames 244, n. 114; PPṬ D 88a2-89b4; P 103a1-105a1.

[245] "and so forth" refers to the other members of the inference.

[246] Bhāviveka, on the other hand, maintains in the PP that his reason is indeed established inasmuch as he accepts it on the surface level. In response to an opponent who has faulted his subject, the *āyatana*s, for not being established because Bhāviveka does not accept the *āyatana*s in ultimate reality, and thus his reason for being *āśrayāsiddha*, he has responded that he admits both his subject and his reason "[they] are other" (*paratva*, *gzhan nyid*) conventionally: *tha snyad du de'i gzhi bum pa dang mig la sogs pa skye mched rnams dang | gzhan nyid khas blangs pa'i phyir ji skad smras pa'i skyon mi 'thad pas de ni rigs pa ma yin* (PP D 50a5; P 60a4-5; translated in Kajiyama 1963: 53; Ames 1993: 225). See n. 216.

The inner things (*bhāva*) have indeed arisen, because activities are performed by one [i.e., someone] qualified by the objects of those [inner things] (*tadviṣayaviśiṣṭavyavahārakaraṇāt*)[247]

---

[247] This inference of the opponent is presented in the PP as part of Bhāviveka's introduction to MMK II.1, and immediately follows his criticism of Buddhapālita's introduction to the same chapter.
PP: *nang gi dngos po rnams*[1] *skyes pa kho na yin te* | *de dag gi yul dang ldan pa'i tha snyad byed pa'i phyir*[2] *ro* || *'di la gang mi skye ba ni de dag gi yul dang ldan pa'i tha snyad mi byed de* | *dper na mo gsham gyi bu 'gro bar mi byed pa bzhin no* || *lhas byin dang khyab 'jug bshes gnyen ni de ltar 'gro bar mi* (D without *mi*) *byed pa ma yin pas* | *de'i phyir* (P: *phyir na/ni*) *nang gi dngos po rnams skye ba kho na yin no* || (D 63a4-5; P 75b4-5; translated in Ames 1995: 300f.). PsP Tib: [1]*nang gi skye mched rnams* (**ādhyātmikāny āyatanāni*) for *nang gi dngos po rnams* (*ādhyātmikā bhāvāḥ*); [2]*de dag gi yul dang ldan pa'i tha snyad khyad par can byed ba'i phyir* (= PsP Skt) for PP's *de dag gi yul dang ldan pa'i tha snyad byed pa'i phyir*. PsP Tib's subject *nang gi skye mched rnams* may represent an intentional "correction" of PP Tib carried out by the PsP Tib translators (or apprentices assigned the task of copying in citations) owing to their familiarity with the subject *ādhyātmikāny āyatanāni*; alternatively, *āyatanāni* may have stood in place of *bhāvāḥ* in one of their manuscripts. As regards the more elaborate reason in PsP Skt and PsP Tib: it would seem that Candrakīrti revised Bhāviveka's **tadviṣayivyavahārakaraṇāt* to read *tadviṣayaviśiṣṭavyavahārakaraṇāt*; see below, where Avalokitavrata glosses **tadviṣayi*° with **tadviṣayaviśiṣṭa*°: *yul de dag dang ldan pa zhes bya ba ni de dag gis khyad par can du byas pa te*. It is possible that the individual who copied the inference from PP Tib into PsP Tib attempted to incorporate PsP Skt's °*viśiṣṭa*° but misunderstood it as qualifying *vyavahāra*, and thus changed the PP compound to *de dag gi yul dang ldan pa'i tha snyad khyad par can byed ba'i phyir*. *dang ldan pa* may simply indicate that *tadviṣaya* is to be understood as a *bahuvrīhi*. PP Chinese (T 30.1566:59c12f.) translates "because one can speak of the [special] feature(s) of the object sphere of that" (**tadviṣaya-viśeṣa/viśiṣṭavyavahārāt*). At the next instance a few lines later, PP Chinese translates "when there is no arising of this, one cannot speak of the [special] features of the object sphere of that."
I do not see support for Stcherbatsky's (1927: 114 and n. 5) assumption that the concept of *arthakriyā* is relevant to the understanding of the inference; nor does there appear to be support for Hopkins' conjecture (cf. 1983: 519 and n. 442) that a reference to Dignāga's PS is intended with the reason. Hopkins translates the reason as "because of making the special designations of those which possess their objects [that is to say, because of being the reasons why their respective consciousnesses are called 'eye-consciousnesses' and so forth].'" According to Avalokitavrata, *tha snyad* (*vyavahāra*) refers to physical activities such as the going, coming, sitting and eating of a collectivity of bodily parts which facilitate these activities; this collectivity is exemplified by "Devadatta." He dissolves and glosses the members of the compound making up the reason as follows: *de dag gi yul* (**tadviṣaya*) *zhes bya ba ni mig la*

[in regard to which] this [logician Bhāviveka,][248] wanting to bring out the fact that this reason stated by the opponent is not established, has asserted:

> But if it is [sought to be] proved that arising (*utpāda*) and going (*gati*), etc., ultimately exist for the [meditatively] concentrated (*samāhita*) yogi who with the eye of insight (*prajñācakṣu*) beholds the real nature of things (*bhāvayāthātmya*), then the reason, i.e., "activities are performed by one qualified by the objects of those [inner things]" is unestablished, since right with the refutation of arising going is also negated,[249]

---

sogs pa nang gi skye mched de dag gi yul (D: *yul yin*) *te | gzugs la sogs pa gzung ba dang dmigs pa dag go |* (D: ||) *yul de dag dang ldan pa* (**tadviṣayi°*) *zhes bya ba ni de dag gis khyad par can du byas pa te | de dag dang 'brel zhing* (P: *cing*) *ldan pa lus dang mgo dang lkog ma dang mchu dang lag pa dang rkang pa la sogs pa'i tshogs 'gro ba'i byed pa dang ldan pa 'o || de'i tha snyad byed pa'i phyir zhes bya ba ni lus la sogs pa'i tshogs de'i tha snyad | dper na lhas* (D: *lha*) *byin 'gro'o 'ong ngo 'dug go za'o zhes bya la sogs pa lta bu byed pa'i phyir | nang gi dngos po rnams skyes pa kho na yin no zhes bya bar sbyar ro ||* (PPṬ D 219b4-6; P 256a4-7; also summarized in Ames 1995: 337, n. 12).

248 *LṬ's author identifies the referent of the pronoun *anena* as Bhāviveka, and considers the opponent to be the Sāṅkhya (cf. Yonezawa 2004: 123, 137 [fol. 2a6]).

249 PP: *'on te don dam par rnal 'byor pa mnyam par bzhag pa shes rab kyi mig gis dngos po rnams kyi yang dag pa ji lta ba bzhin nyid mthong ba'i skye ba dang |* (D: without |) *'gro ba dang | 'ong ba dag*[1] *yod par sgrub na ni*[3] *de dag gi yul dang ldan pa'i tha snyad byed pa'i phyir*[4] *ro* (P: ||) *zhes bya ba'i gtan tshigs kyi don ma grub pa nyid de*[5] *| 'gro ba yang skye ba dgag pa kho na bzhin du dgag pas 'gro ba bkag pa'i phyir ro*[6] *||* (D 63a6-64b1; P 75b7-8; translated in Ames 1995: 301). PsP Tib: [1]*skye ba dang 'gro ba la sogs pa dag* for *skye ba dang | 'gro ba dang | 'ong ba dag*; [2]*bsgrub*; [3]adds following *de'i tshe*; [4]*tha snyad khyad par can byed pa'i phyir* for *tha snyad byed pa'i phyir*; [5]*ma grub pa'i don nyid de* for *don ma grub pa nyid de*; [6] *'gro ba yang skye ba bkag pa kho nas bkag pa'i phyir ro* for *'gro ba yang skye ba dgag pa kho na bzhin du dgag pas 'gro ba bkag pa'i phyir ro*.

Also of interest is the immediately following sentence in which Bhāviveka addresses—and rejects—the opponent's suggestion that this specific reason be accepted as unspecified in terms of being surface-level or ultimate, i.e., be considered to be of a general nature so that it might be established for both sides of the debate. He rejects the proposal on the ground that since 1) there could not be a positive concomitance and 2) any positive concomitance could occur only with dissimilar examples, the reason would turn out to be contradictory: *spyi'i rnam pa gnyis ka'i phyogs la grags pa gtan tshig su rtog* (D: *rtogs*) *na yang rjes su 'gro ba med pa'i phyir dang | mi mthun pa'i phyogs 'ba' zhig la* (D: *la de*) *rjes su 'gro ba'i phyir gtan*

similarly, in regard to the proof that [he him]self (i.e., Bhāviveka) has formulated (*svakṛtasādhana*),[250] too, [viz.],

> That which has not been traversed (*agata*) is indeed not traversed, because [it] is a path, like a path that has been traversed,[251]

---

tshigs kyi don 'gal ba nyid (PP D 63b1; P 75b1-76a1). Avalokitavrata explains: *spyi'i rnam pas gnyis ka'i phyogs la grags pa gtan tshig su rtog na yang zhes bya bas ni 'di skad bstan te | gal te skye bar smra ba dag 'di skad ces khyed dbu ma pa la yang kun rdzob tu skye ba dang 'ong ba dag yod par grub la | kho bo cag la yang don dam par skye ba dang 'gro ba dang 'ong ba dag yod par grub pas de'i phyir spyi'i rnam pas gnyi ga'i phyogs la grags pa'i gtan tshig yod pas | kho ba cag gi gtan tshigs de dag gi* (P: *gis*) *yul dang ldan pa'i tha snyad byed pa'i phyir ro zhes bya ba de gtan tshigs yin par rtog go zhes zer na | de yang mi rung bar ston to || gal te de ltar rtog na ci'i phyir mi rung zhe na | de'i phyir rjes su 'gro ba med pa'i phyir zhes bya ba smras te | gal te de ltar rtog na de la yang khyod la don dam par skye ba dang 'gro ba dang 'ong ba dag yod par sgrub* (P: *bsgrub*) *pa'i gtan tshigs dang sgrub pa'i rjes su 'gro ba'i dpe med pa'i phyir | khyed kyi gtan tshig kyi don 'gal ba nyid kyis skyon chags pa yin pas mi rung ngo | gal te de ltar* (D: *lta*) *na gtan tshigs kyi don de dpe ma tshang ba nyid yin no zhes brjod par bya ba yin gyi | 'gal ba nyid ces brjod par mi bya'o* (P: ||) *zhe na | de'i phyir mi mthun pa'i phyogs 'ba' shig la | de rjes su 'gro ba'i phyir gtan tshigs kyi don 'gal ba nyid do zhes bya ba smras so || 'di skad bstan te | kun rdzob kyi gtan tshigs kyi sbyor ba gang yin pa de ni don dam pa'i mi mthun pa'i phyogs kun rdzob 'ba' zhig la rjes su 'gro ba'i phyir | des na kun rdzob kho nar skye ba la sogs pa dag yod par sgrub* (P: *bsgrub*) *pa yin pas de'i phyir khyed don dam par 'gro ba la sogs pa yod par 'dod pa nyams pas gtan tshigs kyi don 'gal ba nyid yin no ||* (PPṬ D 221a2-7; P 257b6-258a5).

[250] *LṬ's author identifies the person referred to as Bhāviveka: *svakṛteti bhāvivekakṛtam* (cf. Yonezawa 2004: 123, 137 [fol. 2a6]).

[251] The inference appears in the PP commentary on MMK II.1b which reads *agataṃ naiva gamyate |*.
PP: *ma song ba la 'ang 'gro ba med de* (D: without *de*) *| lam yin pa'i phyir song ba'i lam bzhin no zhes bya bar dgongs so ||* (D 63a3; P 76a3-4; translated in Ames 1995: 302). Bhāviveka asserts that Nāgārjuna initially stated *gataṃ na gamyate tāvat* (MMK II.1a) because this provides an example that is accepted by others. Bhāviveka briefly comments on II.1a: *de la 'gro ba'i bya ba 'das zin pa'i phyir ro || don de ni gzhan dag la yang* (P: without *yang*) *grags pas bsgrub par mi bya'o ||*, and adds: *de smos pa ni gzhan 'dod pa'i dpe nyid du bzhed pa'i phyir ro ||* (D 63b2; P 76a2-3). "A path that has been traversed" is accordingly employed as the example for Bhāviveka's inference which takes MMK II.1b as its thesis, and the property of "that which has been traversed" (*gatam*) of MMK II.1a, namely, "being a path," is used as its reason.

the [logical fault of] non-establishment of the reason "[it] is a path" (*adhvatva*) from [his] (= Bhāviveka's) own [point of view] is applicable.

§53. The [logical fault of] non-establishment of the reason and so forth just from [one's] (= Bhāviveka's) own [point of view] is applicable in regard to the [following] statements:

> It is not the case, ultimately, that an engaged (*sabhāga*) visual [faculty] sees visible form (*rūpa*), because [it] is a visual faculty, just as an unengaged (*tatsabhāga*) [visual faculty does not see visible form].[252]

De La Vallée Poussin (PsP$_L$ 32.7) conjectures that *paramārthato* should be added to the text of the PsP citation of this inference, but it does not appear in the PP or PPṬ, and there is no reason for its inclusion since it is accepted on the surface level that what has not been traversed is untraversed. PsP Tib's translators presumably encountered the (interpolated) word in one of their manuscripts. Stcherbatsky (1927: 115 and n. 3), although his literal translation in his footnote appears to catch the meaning of the proposition, misunderstands the argument as a critique of time as a real entity.

[252] The inference is presented by Bhāviveka in the PP as part of his commentary on MMK III.2cd.
PP: *don dam par brten pa mtshungs pa'i mig ni gzugs la lta bar mi byed de | mig gi dbang po yin pa'i phyir dper na de dang mtshungs pa bzhin no ||* (D 76b7-77a1; P 92b3; translated in Ames 1986: 96; 2001: 11). On *sabhāga* and *tatsabhāga*, see AKBh ad I.39 and AKBh$_{tr}$ I.75-78. AKBh ad I.39d defines a *sabhāga* entity as that which performs its own function: *yaḥ svakarmakṛt sa sabhāga iti*; the text continues: *tatra yena cakṣuṣā rūpāṇy apaśyat paśyati drakṣyati vā tad ucyate sabhāgaṃ cakṣuḥ | evaṃ yāvan manaḥ svena viṣayakāritreṇa vaktavyam* (AKBh$_{ed}$ 28.2-4; AKBh$_{Ej}$ 43.23-25). The visual faculty that is *tatsabhāga* is reported as considered by the Kashmiris to be of four types, viz., the visual faculty that, not having seen visibles, has perished, perishes or will perish, and the visual faculty that is destined not to arise (*tatsabhāgaṃ cakṣuḥ kāśmīrāṇāṃ caturvidham | yad adṛṣṭvā rūpāṇi niruddhaṃ nirudhyate nirotsyate vā yac cānutpattidharmi* [AKBh$_{ed}$ 28.4-5; AKBh$_{Ej}$ 43.26-27]); the "Westerners" add a fifth type based on their dichotomizing of the type "destined not to arise" depending on whether the faculty is connected with consciousness or not. Unlike the other sense faculties, the *manas* that has, is, or will arise invariably has an object, that is, it cannot arise and perish without having grasped its *ālambana*, and thus the *tatsabhāgo manas* can only be a *manas* destined not to arise. Cox (1988: 73, n. 17) remarks: "A distinction between homogeneous (*sabhāga*) and partially homogenous (*tatsabhāga*) sense organs and object-fields was developed in order to distinguish those that have functioned, are functioning, or will function in a moment

Similarly,

> It is not the case that the visual [faculty] perceives visible form (*rūpa*), because [visible form] is derived from the elements (*bhautikatvāt*), like the [visual faculty's] own form (*svarūpa*) [is derived from the elements and is not seen by it].[253]

---

of perception (i.e., homogeneous), from those that do not so function, but are nevertheless of the same nature as those that do (i.e., partially homogeneous)." The words *sabhāga* and *tatsabhāga* are explained as follows: *sabhāga iti ko 'rthaḥ | indriyaviṣayavijñānām anyonyabhajanaṃ kāritrabhajanaṃ vā bhāgaḥ | sa eṣām astīti sabhāgaḥ | sparśasamānakāryatvād vā | ye punar asabhāgās te teṣāṃ sabhāgānāṃ jātisāmānyena sabhāgatvāt tatsabhāgāḥ ||* ($AKBh_{ed}$ 28.22-24; $AKBh_{Ej}$ 44.24-45.3) "What is the meaning of *sabhāga*? *bhāga* means the mutual serving of sense faculty, object and cognition; or, [it means] partaking in an activity. [Thus, the *bahuvrīhi*] *sabhāga* means: they have that [*bhāga*]. Or, because they have the common result of contact. But those which do not have that *bhāga* (*asabhāga*), because they are similar (*sabhāga*) to those having that *bhāga* (*sabhāga*) by way of the commonality which consists in their class (*jātisāmānya*) (i.e., they belong to the same *dhātu*), are similar to them (*tatsabhāga*)"; see also the further comments at AKVy 77.2-12. PP presents the translation equivalents *brten pa mtshungs pa* and *de dang mtshungs pa*, while PsP Tib attests *brten pa dang bcas pa* and *de dang mtshungs pa.* I do not think that *de mthun mthun* of YṢV's sentence *dmigs pa ni chos thams cad de mthun* (v.l. om.) *mthun du sbyar ro* ($YṢV_{ed}$ 66.1-2) should be interpreted as intending *de mthun* (*tatsabhāga*) and *mthun* (*sabhāga*) (cf. $YṢV_{tr}$ 225, n. 410). *de* is probably intended as a semi-final particle and (*mthun*) *mthun du sbyar* may translate *yathāyogam* (cf. Negi 1998: 2115); thus "*ālambana* are all dharmas, respectively corresponding [as regards the individual inner *āyatana*s]." For Yogācāra definitions of *sabhāga* and *tatsabhāga*, see Schmithausen 2014 § 63.4.
*LṬ's author explains *sabhāga* and *tatsabhāga* thus: *sabhāgaṃ savyāpāraṃ savijñānakam ity arthaḥ | tatsabhāgam avyāpāram* (cf. Yonezawa 2004: 123, 137 [fol. 2a6]).

[253] The inference is presented by Bhāviveka as MHK III.41ab: *na cakṣuḥ prekṣate rūpaṃ bhautikatvāt svarūpavat |*. Skt in Lindtner 2001: 11, Heitmann 2009: 57; Skt and Tib in Ejima 1980: 278f.; Iida 1980: 107; English translation in Iida 1980: 107. I understand the *dharmin* for the inference to be visible form (*rūpa*), and the *dharma* to be "not seen by the faculty of vision." I assume that Iida (1980: 107) intends the same with his (not, however, unambiguously formulated) translation "The eye does not behold form, since it has the nature of production from the elements, just as its [eye's] own form." Note that the TJ's author explicitly designates visible form as the *dharmin*. The further reason *sukhādyutpattihetutvāt* and the example *rasādivat* both clearly point to visible form being the *dharmin* (note that visible form is the *dharmin* in the preceding verse MHK III.40).

The author of the TJ clearly appears to understand *svarūpa* of the example to be referring to the fleshy eyeball (*māṃsapiṇḍa*) which is, according to the AKBh, actually the support (*adhisthāna*) of the visual faculty (*cakṣurindriya*). He describes the own-form of the eye as blue like the petal of a lotus, covered with beautiful black eyelashes, etc., a rather unusual interpretation of *svarūpa* which, by implication, could suggest that *cakṣus* of the proposition ought also be interpreted as referring to the eyeball, here metaphorically considered as that which sees. However, such an interpretation seems forced, given that the first *pāda* of the immediately preceding *kārikā*, MHK III.40ab, presents a similar proposition and expressly mentions, as the means of seeing, the visual *faculty* (*na cakṣurindriyagrāhyaṃ rūpaṃ hi paramārthataḥ*). Although the word *cakṣus* is also employed in Buddhist texts to refer to the fleshy eyeball, in contexts where sense perception is dealt with it is used almost exclusively to designate the visual faculty (cp. the explicit clarification in AKVy [re: AKBh ad AK I.35c] in response to an opponent who argues by way of a *sūtra* statement which glosses *cakṣus* with *māṃsapiṇḍa* that the *cakṣurindriya* is hard and thus made of primary matter; AKVy 66.31-33: *tena cakṣurindriyeṇāvinirbhāgavartino 'dhiṣṭhānasya etad vacanam | bhavati hi cakṣuradhiṣṭhāne 'pi cakṣurupacāraḥ | ata eva māṃsapiṇḍa iti grahaṇam | anyathā cakṣuṣīty evāvakṣyat yadīndriyam eveṣyate*). This slightly disturbing interpretation in the TJ becomes suspect when compared with Bhāviveka's commentary on MMK III.2 (III.2: *svam ātmānaṃ darśanaṃ hi tat tam eva na paśyati | na paśyati yad ātmānaṃ kathaṃ drakṣyati tat parān*). Bhāviveka understands *darśana* of the *kārikā* to be designating the faculty of vision, glossing it with *mig gi dbang po* (**cakṣurindriya*), used alternatively throughout the chapter with *mig* (**cakṣus*); he further glosses *rang gi bdag nyid* (**svātman*) of MMK III.2ab with *rang gi ngo bo nyid* (**svarūpa*) (cf. D 76a3; P 91b3) but never explicates the own-form of the eye in a way that might lead one to assume that the eyeball is being referred to. Especially revealing is the opponent's statement in which the own-form referred to in MMK III.2 and in Bhāviveka's various inferences in support of the *kārikā*'s assertion is explicitly indicated to be the own-form of the non-visible *faculty*: "It is correct that the visual faculty does not see itself, because it is invisible (*bstan du med pa*; **anidarśana*), but visible form is visible (*bstan du yod pa*; *nidarśana*); therefore, [the faculty of vision] sees it" (*mig rang gi bdag nyid la lta* [P: *blta*] *bar mi byed pa ni bstan du med pa yin pa'i phyir rung mod kyi | gzugs ni bstan du yod pa yin pas de'i phyir de la lta* [P: *blta*] *bar byed do zhe zer ro* || [D 76b3-4; P 92a5-6]) and Bhāviveka's reply in which he agrees that the visual faculty does not see itself because it is invisible (on his reply, see Ames 1986: 95; 2001: 10). Nowhere in the rather extensive discussion does he refer to *cakṣurindriya* not seeing its support, the *māṃsapiṇḍa*. The apparent disharmony between TJ and MHK, the obvious discrepancy between TJ and PP, and the general agreement between PP and MHK on the referent of *svātman/svarūpa*, is possibly one more piece of internal evidence in support of the hypothesis that at least part of the TJ was authored by a Buddhist scholar other than Bhāviveka. Helmut Krasser suggests that the "author" was a student of Bhāviveka's, and that the "student-level" explanations of the elements of inferences, the discrepancies between the PP and TJ, and the

Earth (*mahī*) does not have the own-being of something solid (*kharasvabhāva*), because it is an element (*bhūtatvāt*), like wind (*anila*).[254]

---

references in the TJ to the "*ācārya*" can be explained on this basis. See Krasser 2011 and 2012a: 569ff.

Hopkins (1983: 520 and n. 445) translates the example following PsP Tib's *dper na gzugs bzhin*: "as, for example, is the case with form." He notes, however, referring to de Jong's correction of the Sanskrit text from *rūpavat* to *svarūpavat*, that "the Tibetan would be better translated as *rang gzugs bzhin*." He nevertheless understands *rang gzugs bzhin* as "'like its form,' meaning the form that the eye sees."

[254] The inference appears as MHK III.27ab. Skt in Lindtner 2001: 10, Heitmann 2009: 55; Skt and Tib in Ejima 1980: 274f.; cf. also Iida 1980: 90. Although not relevant to the immediate PsP discussion, it might again be noted that the commentator's remarks regarding MHK III.27 seem to misrepresent the *kārikā*, or at least fail to clarify its intent. The *kārikā* consists of two reasonings: 1) 3.27ab: *kharasvabhāvā na mahī bhūtatvāt tadyathānilaḥ*, 2) 3.27cd: *dhāraṇam na bhuvaḥ kāryaṃ kṛtakatvād yathāmbhasaḥ*. The commentator states, "Because it has been taught in the world and in the treatises of the Abhidharma, etc., that the characteristic of earth is solidity/hardness and that earth upholds, in order to refute these, a two-fold proof has been brought forth: 1) because there does not exist something called "earth" separate from water and fire and air, that is, [because] it is not possible in any way whatsoever to teach the characteristic of earth separately from those [other elements] which take the form of a composite and 2) [because] the specific function is also like that. Therefore, it is not something that has an own-form." (*'jig rten dang chos mngon la sogs pa'i bstan bcos las sa'i mtshan nyid ni sra ba nyid yin pa la sa ni brtan par byed par bstan pas de dag dgag pa'i phyir tshad ma rnam pa gnyis nye bar bkod de ‖ gang gi phyir chu dang me dang rlung las logs shig na sa zhes bya ba 'ga' yang yod pa ma yin te | 'dus pa'i ngo ba nyid dag las sa'i mtshan nyid logs shig tu bkar te bstan par ni ji ltar yang mi nus la | las kyi bye brag kyang de bzhin pas de'i phyir ngo bo nyid yod pa ma yin no ‖* [cf. Iida 1980: 90]). In both reasonings in the *kārikā*, Bhāviveka, as in *kārikā* 3.41ab, uses a generic property of the subject as the logical reason in order to override and disallow a specific property of the subject, a rather nasty but logically impeccable mode of procedure. The author of the TJ announces a two-fold proof but actually presents a single proof and applies it to both of the *kārikā* reasonings. His argument, i.e., that earth cannot be talked about as something separate from the other three elements, can be linked with the reason in the second argument inasmuch as earth atoms, or more precisely, earth molecules, are only such when solidity (i.e., earth) occurs together with the seven other "qualities" (see AK II.22 and commentary; Frauwallner 1958: 96f.), and must come together with other earth molecules in order to perform the function of upholding, but this seems more an independent reasoning than a clarification of the specific *kārikā* argument. His relating of his reasoning to the first *kārikā* argument seems inappropriate, for the reason *kṛtakatvāt* occurs only in the second. His complete silence as regards the

§54. And this reason, "because [they] are [already] existing" (*sattvāt*), [of the inference put forth by Bhāviveka to prove non-arising from self] is inconclusive (*anaikāntika*) from the [point of view of the Sāṅkhya] opponent,[255] [who will point to the fault with the following question:] "Would the internal bases, because [they] are [already] existing, like consciousness (*caitanyavat*), not arise from self (*svataḥ*) or would they arise from self, like a pot and so forth?"[256]

§55. If [Bhāviveka retorts that] there is not inconclusiveness because a pot and so forth are also similar to the probandum (*sādhyasama*)[257]

---

reason *bhūtatvāt* in the first argument is quite odd. Both the want of explanatory precision and what appears to be the overlaying of a corollary argument may once again speak for independent authorship of these comments in the TJ.

[255] De La Vallée Poussin (PsP_L 33, n. 4) reconstructs *gtan tshigs 'di yang pha rol po'i ltar na | ... | zhes ma nges pa yin no* as *hetur ayam api pakṣavādinaḥ pakṣe | kim ... | iti na niścitaḥ*. I doubt that the mss on which the PsP Tib is based read any differently than the Skt as it has been transmitted. Tibetan *'di*, unlike Sanskrit *ayam*, naturally follows its noun, *yang* translates *ca*, and the translators have merely clarified the meaning of *parataḥ* by adding *ltar na* to *pha rol po*; *ma nges pa* is the usual PsP translation for *anaikāntika*.

[256] The reason is inconclusive because it occurs in both similar cases (*sapakṣa*) and dissimilar cases (*vipakṣa*). Bhāviveka intends the reason *sattvāt* in the sense of "existing already and therefore not requiring arising," a property found in the example *caitanya* which exists eternally and is thus without a time of arising. While the Sāṅkhya opponent holds, on the one hand, that *caitanya* does not arise because it exists (in this case the reason would prove non-arising from self, the *sādhya*), he also maintains that a pot and so forth, which already exist in unmanifest form, do arise; and with this meaning of existing, i.e., existing but requiring manifestation, the reason proves arising from self, the opposite of the *sādhya*.

[257] When the Sāṅkhya adduces pot, etc., as instances of things which, according to him, arise from self and thus, in belonging to the class of dissimilar cases (*vipakṣa*), reveal the inconclusiveness of the reason, Bhāviveka defends his reason by claiming that this example "pot, etc.," is in the same situation as that which is to be proved: pot, etc., like the inner bases, do not arise from self and therefore, contrary to what the Sāṅkhya claims, belong to the class of corresponding cases (*sapakṣa*). Stcherbatsky (1927: 117), interpreting *sādhyasama* in the passage as equivalent to *petitio principii*, translates: "It may be objected (that the adduced example, the identity of matter in physical objects) like jars etc., is a *petitio principii* and therefore the argument is not uncertain, (but wrong)"; on the inappropriateness of the translation *petitio principii* for *sādhyasama*, see Bhattacharya 1974 (Bhattacharya quotes and discusses the present PsP passage on pp. 226-228. I cannot, however, make any sense

[i.e., their situation is the same as the inner bases given that they do not arise from self], [we reply that] this is not so, because [you] did not formulate [your inference] that way.[258]

§56. [Objection:] Yet is it not the case, given that the faulting (*dūṣaṇa*) as it has been expressed in regard to the opponent's (= Bhāviveka's) inferences entails equally for [one's] own inferences (*svānumāna*), that exactly the [same] fault (*doṣa*)—such as [the logical fault that the proposition is] unestablished with respect to its locus (*asiddhādhāra*) and [the logical fault that] the reason is unestablished (*asiddhahetu*)—obtains [for you too]? And therefore, since "And one [party] should not be criticized (*codya*) for that which is a fault of both,"[259] all this faulting (*dūṣaṇa*) turns out to be inappropriate.

---

of his statement, "The principle of *sādhyasama* can be succesfully employed only by a *prāsaṅgika*, not by a *svātantrika*" [1974: 227]); Matilal 1974 (= 1985: 45-58; minor editorial changes in 1985); Bhattacharya et al. 1986: 112, n. 3. Seyfort Ruegg has commented on *sādhyasama* in a number of articles and books; see, e.g., 1981: 22, n. 49; 1983: 210, n. 14; and, more recently, his remarks on *sādhyasama* in 2000: 124, n. 25 (note also the references in 2002: 64, n. 77). Other general illustrations of the fault *sādhyasama* may be found in Buddhapālita's commentary on MMK IV.8 and in Avalokitavrata's *ṭīkā* to PP's commentary on the same. Buddhapālita declares the case of threads adduced by the opponent to prove that cloth is not empty to be *sādhyasama* because exactly the same reasons that prove that cloth is empty prove that threads are empty (cf. BP_{ed} 64.7-14; BP_{tr} 64). *sādhyasama* is employed as a technical term for a logical fault of the *hetu* within the Nyāya school; it is defined at NS I.2.8: *sādhyāviśiṣṭaś ca sādhyatvāt sādhyasamaḥ*. On *sādhyasama* as a *hetvābhāsa* see, e.g., Matilal 1974; Preisendanz 1994: 176f. Tillemans (1990: 278, n. 379), in reliance on Tibetan exegesis, considers CŚ XIII.5cd and Candrakīrti's commentary on it to be focussed on the fallacy of *sādhyasama* as set forth in NS I.2.8.

[258] The *svata evānumāna* that Candrakīrti draws out of Buddhapālita's *prasaṅga* statement has pot, etc., as its subject, i.e., all the things claimed by the Sāṅkhya to manifest from self; the inference therefore cannot be suspected of having an inconclusive reason because there is no dissimilar case the Sāṅkhya might bring forth as having the property of existing and nevertheless arising from self. See §31. *LṬ's author explains *tathānabhidhānāt* with *ghaṭādīty anabhidhānāt* | *adhyātmikānīty abhidhānāc ca* ||; cf. Yonezawa 2004: 123, 138 [fol. 2a7].

[259] De La Vallée Poussin drops the manuscripts' *ca* of *cobhayor* and thus presents Candrakīrti as paraphrasing, and not citing, the *nyāya* "*yaś cobhayor doṣo na tenaikaś codyo bhavati.*" For references, see PsP_L 34, n. 1. Candrakīrti cites the *nyāya*

Reply: This fault (*doṣa*) occurs for those voicing an independent inference (*svatantram anumānam*). We do not employ an independent inference, because our inferences (*anumāna*) result in the negation of the opponent's thesis.[260] To explain: The opponent (*para*) considers that the visual faculty sees.[261] He is rebuffed by way of an inference

---

again at PsP$_{\mathrm{L}}$ 172.11. Cp. ŚV on *śūnyavāda* verse 252: *tasmād yatrobhayor doṣaḥ parihāro 'pi vā samaḥ | naikaḥ paryanuyoktavyas tādṛgarthavicāraṇe* ||.

[260] Both Yotsuya and Seyfort Ruegg integrate Tib's *tsam*, which is not found in Skt but could possibly be assumed as implied by it, into their translations. Yotsuya (1999: 65): "... since the effect of our reasoning is merely to negate the assertion of [our] opponent." Seyfort Ruegg (2002: 64) appears to suggest that the Skt should be emended on the basis of Tib: "But we [Prāsaṅgika Mādhyamikas] formulate (*prayuj-* = *sbyor ba*) no autonomous inference, for our inferences issue solely in negation of an opponent's thesis (*parapratijñāniṣedha<mātra>phalatvād asmadanumānānām*: *gžan gyi dam bca' 'gog pa tsam gyi 'bras bu can*)" (cf. also 2000: 136). None of the manuscripts attest *mātra*, and consideration of it at this point in the argumentation may be premature. Note that Candrakīrti makes known that his opponent-acknowledged inferences bring out only the negation of the opponent's thesis in the next paragraph (*etāvanmātram asmadanumānair udbhāvyate*). It seems that the sentence leading up to the exemplified *paraprasiddhānumāna* (i.e., *na vayaṃ svatantram anumānaṃ prayuñjmahe parapratijñāniṣedhaphalatvād asmadanumānānām*) intends merely to state that a *paraprasiddhānumāna* aims at and is capable of refuting the opponent's thesis. The fact that it does not do more than this (and does not require Candrakīrti's acknowledgment of the *pakṣa*, *hetu*, etc.) is asserted only with *etāvanmātram asmadanumānair udbhāvyate*.
Yotsuya's commentary (1999: 65-66) as regards the logical faults Candrakīrti is rejecting as incurred by his own inferences should be expanded to include *asiddhahetu*. *prasaṅgāpādana* and *svata evānumāna* / *paraprasiddhānumāna* are misleadingly equated/conflated in Seyfort Ruegg 1981: 79 and 1991: 289 (in both cases there is reference to the present passage) but differentiated in Seyfort Ruegg 2000 (cf., e.g., 282f., 286; though see also 251, where employment of *paraprasiddhānumāna* is called "the technique known to the Mādhyamika as *prasaṅgāpādana* ... – or *prasaṅgāpatti* ... – and defined in the *PPMV* (pp. 24 and 34) as simply resulting in the negation of another's thesis ..."). *prasaṅga*s and *paraprasiddhānumāna*s are of course for Candrakīrti quite different, the main difference being, as mentioned earlier, that *pakṣadharmatā* does not apply to the reasons in *prasaṅga*s (see also Yotsuya 1999: 76, n. 10 and 88, n. 58).

[261] De La Vallée Poussin emends the reading *paraḥ cakṣuḥ paśyatīti pratipannaḥ* as found in his three mss to *paraṃ cakṣuḥ paśyatīti pratipannaḥ*, an emendation he admits is not supported by Tib's *gzhan mig lta'o zhes bya bar rtog pa* (cf. PsP$_{\mathrm{L}}$ 34, n. 5). Note that Tib does translate the four instances of Skt's *paradarśana* (referring to the visual faculty seeing what is other) in the following sentences of the same

acknowledged exclusively by him[self] (*tatprasiddhenaivānumānena*): [Mādhyamika:] You maintain[262] that the visual faculty has the property (*dharma*) of not seeing itself (*svātmādarśana*), and it is accepted that [the property of not seeing oneself] is invariably

---

paragraph each time as *gzhan la lta ba*. Mss P and B attest *paraś cakṣuḥ paśyatīti* (the other paper mss, except for ms G which presents *para*, attest *paraḥ* for *paraś*). I reject de La Vallée Poussin's emendation and ms Q's reading *paraṃ*, which appears at first sight to support the emendation, because I understand *paraḥ* as the grammatical subject for the active transitive past participle *pratipannaḥ*, a subject referred back to by the anaphoric *sa* commencing the following sentence and by *tat* in the compound *tatprasiddhenaivānumānena* of the same sentence. If Ms Q's reading is accepted, *pratipannaḥ* is left subjectless (one might expect in place of *pratipannaḥ* neuter *pratipannam*, referring to the nominalized *iti* statement), and it becomes difficult to determine the referent of the following masculine nominative *sa*. The reading *paraś* found in mss P and B (and *paraḥ* in all but Q) is further supported by the fact that the distinction of the object of the visual faculty into self (*svātman*) and other (*para*) becomes topical only during the demonstration of the refutation of the opponent's position, i.e., in the sentences which follow. The argument commences with the opponent maintaining without specification that the eye sees; the Mādhyamika then refutes this view by introducing and using the distinction to his advantage. Cf. PsP on MMK III.1 where the object of *darśana/cakṣu* is given in a general sense as *rūpa*: *iha hi paśyatīti darśanaṃ cakṣuḥ | tasya ca rūpaṃ viṣayatvenopadiśyate* (PsP_L 113.7-8); in MMK III.2 and in PsP on the same *kārikā* it is the Mādhyamika, not the opponent, who bifurcates the object, and this for the sake of refuting the opponent's view.

Vaidya (1960b: 11.7-8) does not comment on de La Vallée Poussin's emendation, but silently emends the text to read *paraḥ cakṣuḥ paśyatīti pratipannaḥ* |. Hopkins (1983: 836, n. 450), noting Vaidya's emendation, reports that the "Four Interwoven Commentaries on (Tsong kha pa's) Great Exposition of the Stages of the Path" also assumes *paraḥ* and indicates that it refers to opponents. Seyfort Ruegg (2000: 248; 2002: 65) presumably relies on PsP_L: "... 'The eye sees an other' ... ."

[262] De Jong (1978: 32) reads *icchadbhi* in ms D and, considering this reading as confirmed by Tib (*mig la rang gi bdag nyid mi lta ba'i chos kyang 'dod la | gzhan la lta*[1] *ba'i chos med na ni mi 'byung ba nyid du yang khas blangs pa yin te*), emends to *icchadbhiḥ*; [1] I emend to *mi lta* (see next note). However, the final *akṣara* of ms D's "*icchadbhi*," ink-blurred as it is, could equally be read as *si*; mss P and Q and the other paper mss attest *icchasi*. It should also be noted that the previous sentence presents the opponent in the singular (*para*, *sa*). Tib's *la* (*'dod la*) more likely represents the addition of the translators than the indication of a case marker (note that the translators appear to have intended the repeated particle *kyang* ... *yang* in the sense of "on the one hand ... on the other"; Skt attests only a single *ca*). De Jong's emendation fails to take the *ca* in *cāṅgīkṛtam* into account; if the Skt is emended as he suggests, *ca* no longer makes sense grammatically or semantically in the sentence.

connected (*avinābhāvitva*) with the property of not seeing [what is] other [than oneself] (*parādarśana*).[263] Therefore, [Exemplification:]

---

[263] The fact that the compound *paradarśanadharmāvinābhāvitvam* as found in all the Sanskrit manuscripts is reflected without distortion in all five versions of the Tibetan translation as *gzhan la lta ba'i chos med na mi 'byung ba nyid* may indicate that *paradarśana°* is the result of an error that had occurred in the Sanskrit manuscript tradition already prior to the Tibetan translation, although one expects that Pa tshab and Mahāsumati, the latter praised as a great logician in the PsP colophon, would have noticed the problem. The particle *tasmāt* introducing the inference indicates that the inference is built upon the two preceding states of affairs, both of which are accepted by the opponent. The property (*dharma*) unconditionally accepted by the opponent, namely, the visual faculty's not seeing itself (to be used as the reason in the inference) having been stated, the property generally accepted as invariably occurring with the former property, namely, not seeing other things (to be used as the probandum), is stated, and it is on account of the fact that the opponent accepts both of these properties and their relationship (thus the word *tasmāt*) that the inference can be formulated. The negation *na* in the inference's *sādhya*, i.e., *paradarśanam api nāsti*, also expects the reading *parādarśanadharmāvinābhāvitvam*. Previous translators have attempted to work with the corrupt reading *paradarśana°*, most considering the opponent to be maintaining that there is an invariable connection between "not seeing itself" and "seeing other." The opponent does not, however, maintain such an invariable connection when it comes to his belief that the visual faculty sees, and is only *made aware* of the connection between not seeing oneself and not seeing others by way of the inference acknowledged by himself (*svaprasiddhānumāna*); the faultiness of his belief that the visual faculty sees is thus brought to light via the inference that contradicts it. Stcherbatsky (1927: 118) understands, as indicated, the opponent to be erroneously maintaining an invariable connection between the attributes "not seeing itself" and "seeing other," but with this interpretation feels forced to translate and supplement *tasmāt* with "Now, (we will assail it by a counter-argument)" (Rizzi [1988: 40] follows Stcherbatsky closely; Sprung's [1979: 41f.] translation, made in reliance on PsP$_{\mathrm{L}}$, is problematic). Seyfort Ruegg's (2002: 65) interpretation is similar to Stcherbatsky's, and deals with the faulty text by adding material in square brackets: "In this way, having supposed (*pratipanna*: *rtog pa*) [the proposition] 'The eye sees an other' [i.e. visible matter (*rūpa*) such as the blue, even though it does not see itself] <[the Substantialist opponent] is confuted (*nirākriyate*) by just the inference acknowledged by him[self] (*tatprasiddhenâivânumānena nirākriyate*)>; and they who maintain [also (*kyaṅ*)] the quality of [the eye's] not seeing itself … [on the other hand still] accept (*aṅgīkṛ-* …) a regular concomitance with the quality [of the eye's] seeing an other (*paradarśanāvinābhāvitva* …) [e.g., the blue]. Therefore, [in reply, Nāgārjuna has advanced the following formal probative inference in *MK* iii.2:] …" (similarly translated in 2000: 248f.). Aware that Nāgārjuna does not in MMK III.2 explicitly assert the inference set forth above, Seyfort Ruegg (2002: 65, n. 81) explains that Candrakīrti "unpacks" MMK III.2's inference in his commentary on the *kārikā* (cf. PsP$_{\mathrm{L}}$ 114.1-2). It should be noted that

Wherever there is not the seeing of oneself there is also not the seeing of [what is] other [than oneself], as in the case of a pot, [which does not see itself or what is other than itself]. [Application:] And [it] is [a fact that] the visual faculty does not see itself; [Conclusion:] Therefore, it also certainly does not see [what is] other [than itself].[264] And thus the seeing of [what is] other [than itself,] such as blue, etc., since it is contradicted by not seeing itself,[265] is controverted by way of an inference acknowledged exclusively by [him]self (= the opponent) (*svaprasiddhenaivānumānena*).

---

although the reason Candrakīrti posits for MMK III.2's inference, namely, because of not seeing itself, is the same as the one he sets forth here, the example adduced there is the auditory faculty, etc. (*śrotrādi*). The fact that Candrakīrti changes the verb form from second person present *icchasi* to passive past participle *aṅgīkṛta* might also provide some, albeit much weaker, support for the emendation. The opponent is directly addressed regarding the property he without hesitation affirms (*icchasi*), while the statement of the invariable connection is construed with the impersonal past participle (*aṅgīkṛta*); the impersonal form relates primarily to the opponent, but (if not merely added for stylistic reasons) may also be intended to include all reasonable persons, among whom the opponent will include himself, who accept the general connection of the attribute of not seeing oneself with the attribute of not seeing others. Seyfort Ruegg's (2002: 65, n. 80) assertion that the words he translates in pointed brackets are not found in the Tibetan is incorrect; the PsP Tib translators simply relocated *tatprasiddhenaivānumānena nirākriyate* (minus *eva*) to the end of the section (*de'i phyir ... sngon po la sogs pa gzhan la lta ba rang la grags pa'i rjes su dpag pa dang 'gal ba yin no* ‖ *zhes de la grub pa'i rjes su dpag pas sel bar byed pa yin no* ‖). Hopkins (1983: 524) appears to have overseen that *med na mi 'byung ba nyid* is the translation for the technical term *avinābhāvitvam* and translates literally, adding "then that an eye sees" in square brackets to bring some sense to the passage: "You assert that an eye [has] the attribute of not seeing its own entity and also assert that if it does not have the attribute of [inherently] seeing other [forms such as blue, then that an eye sees] just does not occur."

[264] Cf. MMK III.2: *svam ātmānaṃ darśanaṃ hi tat tam eva na paśyati* | *na paśyati yad ātmānaṃ kathaṃ drakṣyati tat parān* ‖, and Candrakīrti's commentary on the *kārikā*, as well as CŚ XIII.16: *svabhāvaḥ sarvabhāvānāṃ pūrvam ātmani dṛśyate* | *grahaṇaṃ cakṣuṣaḥ kena cakṣuṣaiva na jāyate* ‖, and Candrakīrti's commentary (Skt and Tib at CŚṬ$_{ed}$ 280f., CŚṬ$_{Ted}$ 92f.; see also CŚṬ$_{tr}$ 190).

[265] Recall Candrakīrti's earlier statement in regard to the reason in the inference he draws out of Buddhapālita's *prasaṅga* statement, where it is made clear that it is the reason that brings out the contradiction (§29, end).

This much [and no more] is brought out by our inferences; how [could there be] ingress of the fault as stated onto our side (*asmat-pakṣa*) so that there would be the same fault [for us]?

§57. [Question:] But is there sublation by inference (*anumāna-bādhā*)[266] even by way of an inference acknowledged [only] by one of the two [parties in the debate] (*anyataraprasiddhānumāna*)?

[Reply:] There is. That [sublation], however, [is effected] by way of a reason (*hetu*) acknowledged only by [one]self (*svaprasiddha*) (= only by the opponent), not by way of [a reason] acknowledged by the other [party] (*paraprasiddha*) (= the Mādhyamika), since [we] look at [sublation] just from the point of view of the world (*lokata eva*).[267] For [in legal disputes] in the world, on some occasions victory (*jaya*) or defeat (*parājaya*) comes about by virtue of the statement of a witness (*sākṣin*) regarded as an authority (*pramāṇīkṛta*) by [both] the plaintiff (*arthin*) and defendant (*pratyarthin*),[268] on [other] occasions

---

[266] As Candrakīrti's following reply shows, the focus remains on the reason (*hetu*), the element that brings out the contradiction and thus performs the sublation. According to the NM, the opponent's inference that is invalidated through presentation of another inference whose members he also accepts is determined to have a pseudo proposition (*pakṣābhāsa*). In addition to the proposition sublated by inference (actually the fourth type of *pakṣābhāsa* listed in the NM), the NM lists that sublated by its own statement (*svavacana*), by authoritative testimony (*āgama*), by what is generally established (*prasiddha*), and by direct perception (*pratyakṣa*). See Tucci 1930: 7 and Katsura 1977: 13. The sublated pseudo proposition develops in the Nyāya tradition into the sublated pseudo reason (*bādhitahetvābhāsa*) or pseudo reason whose object is sublated (*bādhitaviṣayahetvābhāsa*). The historical development of the *pakṣābhāsa* and *bādhitahetvābhāsa* is detailed in Preisendanz 1994: 319-329 (= n. 88).

[267] Stcherbatsky (1927: 119 and n. 1) emends *eva* of *lokata eva dṛṣṭatvāt* to *evaṃ* and translates, "This is what happens in everyday life." All the mss attest *eva* and Tib's *nyid* (*'jig rten nyid du mthong ba'i phyir*) supports the reading *eva*. Given that *eva* construed with *lokataḥ* is an adverbial phrase often employed by Candrakīrti and makes perfect sense here, there is no reason to change the text. Seyfort Ruegg (2002: 66) translates "For it is this that one finds with [the usage of] ordinary folk in the world." Hopkins (1983: 525), disregarding *nyid* and possibly influenced by Stcherbatsky's emendation, translates, "since such is seen in the world."

[268] The qualifications and obligations of witnesses and the examination of witnesses according to the Dharmaśāstra literature are presented in Kane 1973: 330-354. Kane

[it comes about] uniquely by virtue of one's own [= the defendant's] statement, but there is neither victory nor defeat by way of the statement of the other (*para*) [party, i.e., the plaintiff].[269] And just as [it is] in the world, so [is it] also in reasoning/logic (*nyāya*), since worldly procedure (*vyavahāra*) is made a principle (*prastuta*) in the treatises on reasoning/logic (*nyāyaśāstra*).[270]

(ibid., 292) notes, "*Vādin* and *prativādin* generally mean the plaintiff and the defendant, though *vādin* sometimes means 'a litigant' (either the plaintiff or defendant). '*Arthin*' (one who seeks the assistance of the court) and *abhiyoktṛ* (attacker) are synonyms of *vādin*, and *pratyarthin* and *abhiyukta* (attacked) are synonyms of *prativādin*." On the four types of reply (*uttara, pratipakṣa*) allowed a legal defendant, see Lariviere 1989: I, 31 and II, 230; Kane 1973: III, 300-302. Cf. the reference to *parājaya* in verse 5 of the first chapter of the Nāradasmṛti. A *jayapatra* (document of victory) was awarded to the winner of the litigation; cf. verse 43 of the chapter titled "The Plaint" (*bhāṣā*) in the Nāradasmṛti (Lariviere states that this chapter appears in only one of the manuscripts). Lariviere 1989: I, 41: *sabhair eva jitaḥ paścād rājñā śāsyaḥ svaśāstrataḥ | jayine cāpi deyaṃ syād yathāvaj jayapatrakam ||*. Lariviere (ibid., II, 237) translates, "The one whom the judges find guilty must be punished by the king in accordance with the texts; he must give the appropriate document of victory to the winner." See also the entry for *jayapatra* in Sharan 1978: 301.

[269] Candrakīrti focusses here on general courtroom procedure according to which, regardless of the accusation the plaintiff makes of the defendant, it is either the statement of a witness that will decide the case, or the defendant's admission of the veracity of the accusation or his (truthful) denial of it that will decide it. The plaintiff's bare allegation of an offence can never decide the outcome of the case. Candrakīrti intends parallels between the Mādhyamika and the plaintiff and between the Mādhyamika's opponent and the defendant. The Mādhyamika may be the party setting forth the inference but, like the plaintiff in the courtroom, his own acknowledgement of the statement he utters has no bearing on the outcome of the encounter; what matters is the opponent's acknowledgement of the limbs of the inference, for, here in the context of sublation by inference, it is his acknowledgement of them, like the defendant's admission of the misdemeanor he is charged with, that will bring about the defeat of the opponent. Cf. verse 32 of the chapter titled "The Plaint" (*bhāṣa*) in the Nāradasmṛti: *palāyate ya āhūto maunī sākṣiparājitaḥ | svayam abhyupapannaś ca avasannaś caturvidhaḥ ||* (Lariviere 1989: I, 37; the commentary states that these four types of defeated party apply to the party under trial); Lariviere (ibid., II, 235) translates, "There are four types of defeated parties: one who absconds when he has been summoned, one who remains silent, one who is defeated by witnesses, and one who confesses."

[270] Yotsuya's (1999: 37) translation from the Tibetan reads, "For it is transactional usage (*'jig rten pa'i tha snyad*) that is the topic under discussion in a treatise (*bstan bcos*) on [the science of] reasoning (*rigs pa*)." Worldly practice is, however, the

§58. And exactly on account of this certain [scholars] have stated, "There is not sublation by inference due to acknowledgement from the side of the other (= the proponent) because it is precisely the acknowledgement of the other [party] (= the opponent) that is sought to be refuted."[271]

§59. But he (= Dignāga) who considers that "Only that [reason], however, which expresses what is ascertained for both [parties in the debate amounts to] proof / a proving element (*sādhana*) or refutation / a refuting element (*dūṣaṇa*), not [one] expressing doubt or what is established for [merely] one of the two [parties],"[272] also ought to

---

procedure followed, the method assumed in the *nyāyaśāstra*s, and not their topic (see the meaning "voranschicken, an die Spitze stellen" for the entry *pra√stu* in PW). Note that Candrakīrti, in his critique of Dignāga's view which follows, refers to the method as *nyāya*, i.e., a mode of procedure: *tenāpi ... yathokta eva nyāyo 'bhyupeyaḥ*. Stcherbatsky (1927: 119) also understands *prastuta* as pointing out the topic: "because scientific logic is exclusively concerned (with an examination of the principles which underly [sic] purposive action in common life)." Hopkins (1983: 525) understands worldly practice as the orientation, and not the topic, of the texts on logic: "because only the conventions of the world are appropriate in treatises of logic." Seyfort Ruegg (2002: 67) translates: "for in the science of logic ... worldly practice ... is relevant (*prastuta = skabs su bab pa*)."

[271] I have not been able to identify the source of the citation or the individual(s) who propound its point of view. Candrakīrti quotes it as support for his view that the Mādhyamikas do not need to abide by Dignāga's rule that both parties in a debate must accept the elements of an inference; the two references to "other" (*para*) respectively refer to the two individuals involved in a debate. Stcherbatsky (1927: 119) appears to understand both *parataḥ* and *para°* as referring to the same person and thus the statement as a whole as stemming from a party in opposition to the view espoused by Candrakīrti; he translates, "For this very reason some logicians have maintained that an argument cannot be exploded on the basis of the principle admitted by the opponent, because it is just these principles, by him admitted, that it is intended to reject." Seyfort Ruegg (2002: 67) also seems to understand both *para*s as referring to the same individual: "... there is no invalidation of an inference [solely] by the force of what the opponent acknowledges, for [in debate just as in a court of law] there exists a desire to reject what an opponent maintains." Hopkins (1983: 526) translates the sentence as "There is no harm by inference that is through the force of being renowned to the other [party] because [we] wish to refute mere renown to others."

[272] Candrakīrti is citing from Dignāga's NM. See the NM commentary on *kārikā* 2 (Tucci 1930: 15; Katsura 1977: 125f., section 2.4). The text of the PVSV in which

accept, in accordance with worldly establishment, the procedure (*nyāya*) exactly as it has been stated[273] [above by me].[274]

---

this statement of Dignāga's is cited attests (similar to PsP) *nānyataraprasiddha°* instead of *nānyatarāprasiddha°*: *ya eva tūbhayaniścitavācī sa sādhanam, dūṣaṇaṃ vā, nānyataraprasiddhasaṃdigdhavācī* (see PVSV 153). Katsura (1977: 126) emends to *nānyatarāpra°*, apparently on the basis of a negation in the Chinese. PsP Tib accords with PsP Skt: *gang gnyi ga la nges par brjod pa de ni sgrub pa 'am sun 'byin pa yin gyi | gang yang rung ba la grub pa 'am the tshom za ba smra ba ni ma yin no.* Cf. also PS III.12 (Katsura 2009: 160): *nāniṣṭer dūṣaṇaṃ sarvaṃ prasiddhas tu dvayor api | sādhanaṃ* dūṣaṇaṃ vāsti sādhanāpekṣaṇāt punaḥ ‖ (words in Roman reconstructed from the Tibetan) "Not all [*hetus*] are refuting elements [of the proposition] on account of the non-acceptance of [their being an attribute of the locus (*pakṣadharmatā*)] because [such a reason] requires further proving. But a [reason] that is accepted by both [parties in a debate] is a proving [element] or a refuting [element]." Regarding the reason (un)established for one of the two parties, see Tucci 1930: 14 and n. 24; Katsura 1977: 124; PSV ad PS III.11: *gcig la yang bzlog pa ni mngon par gsal bar smra ba la byas pa nyid lta bu'o* (PSV_K P 127b8; PSV_{Kit} 481); Nyāyapraveśa 141: *kṛtakatvād iti śabdābhivyaktivādinaṃ praty anyatarāsiddhaḥ*; on the doubtful reason see Tucci 1930: 14 and n. 25; Katsura 1977: 124; PSV_K ad PS III.11: *gnyi ga la 'am gcig la the tshom za ba ni dper na me bsgrub par bya ba la du ba nyid la the tshom za ba lta bu'o* (PSV_K P 127b8-128a1; PSV_{Kit} 481). Cf. also Steinkellner 1988.

273 PsP Skt's *tenāpi laukikīṃ vyavasthām anurudhyamānena yathokta eva nyāyo 'bhyupeyaḥ* is represented in PsP Tib by *des kyang 'jig rten kyi tha snyad kyi rnam par gzhag pa la brten nas rjes su dpag pa la ji skad smras pa'i tshul 'di nyid khas blang bar bya'o.* At least one of the two Sanskrit manuscripts relied upon by the translators must have carried a reading similar to or the same as the one found in our ms Q, namely, the corrupted *āśrityānumānena* (*āśritya* is a correction in Q) for *anurudhyamānena*, the latter confirmed by ms P and variants of which are found in all of the paper mss. De La Vallée Poussin (PsP_L 35.7), unaware of Q's reading, unnecessarily adds a conjectured *anumāne* after *anurudhyamānena* on the basis of Tib's *rjes su dpag pa la.* Note that Tib's sentence also contains *tha snyad* (*vyavahāra*) and *'di*, neither of which are accounted for by the Skt available to this study.
Yotsuya (1999: 37, n. 41) translates the sentence in reliance on both Sanskrit and Tibetan but, following the Sanskrit, does not translate PsP Tib's *rjes su dpag pa la*: "Even this [person] should base himself on the rules of everyday usage (*'jig rten gyi tha snyad*) and accept this very method mentioned above."

274 Yotsuya's (1999: 37, n. 41) PsP Tib-based translation of this sentence ("Someone thinks that [an argument] expressing what is definitely [established] for both parties is proof (*sgrub pa*) or refutation (*sun 'byin*) ...") and Seyfort Ruegg's section title ("Dignāga on the need for agreement between both parties concerning the terms of an inference-for-other ...") and the note to his translation indicate that both authors understood the main topic of the sentence to be the complete inference. As the NM

§60. For, similarly, sublation by authoritative testimony (*āgamabādhā*) is not exclusively [effected] by authoritative testimony that is acknowledged by both [parties] (*ubhayaprasiddha*). Rather, [it is generally accepted that sublation can be effected] also by [authoritative testimony] acknowledged [only] by [one]self (*svaprasiddha*) [i.e., only by the party whose view is being critiqued].[275] As regards inference for oneself (*svārthānumāna*), on the other hand, in all cases just [one's] own acknowledgement (*svaprasiddhi*) is weightier, not the acknowledgement of both [parties].[276] Precisely on account of this [fact that in each of the above situations it is this own acknowledgement that is the essential factor, not the acknowledgement of both parties], the stating of [technical] definitions pertaining to logic (*tarkalakṣaṇa*) is useless, because the Awakened

makes clear, the subject of Dignāga's statement is the reason, not the whole inference. We see also that Candrakīrti commences the following paragraph with talk of sublation, which is carried out by the reason (there compared with *āgama* citations).

[275] I translate *āgama* as "authoritative testimony" because not all of the "texts" encompassed by the term may have been recorded in writing, i.e., as scripture, and because of the way Candrakīrti describes *āgama* (see below §121). The authoritative/scriptural citations that are accepted only by the debater one aims to defeat, and not necessarily by oneself, may be used to undermine the opponent's proposition. For instance, a Naiyāyika debating with a Buddhist may cite statements attributed to the Buddha to point out a contradiction between them and a certain tenet maintained by the Buddhist. *āgamabādhā* is, of course, a technical term meaning "sublation by authoritative testimony (/ scripture)" and is not intended here, as Seyfort Ruegg (2002: 69) interprets it, as a (non-technical) objective genitive compound in the meaning of "sublation of scripture" ("Thus a scriptural testimony is invalidated not only by scriptural testimony ...").

[276] In Dignāga's system, inference for another is understood as a public announcement focussed on the confirmation of a triply characterized reason, and requires the acceptance of the reason by both parties, whereas inference for oneself involves a subjective, private mental act that confirms the truth of a proposition on the basis of a triply characterized reason, and is not dependent on any opponent's acceptance of the reason. PS II.1ab: *anumānaṃ dvidhā svārthaṃ trirūpāl liṅgato 'rthadṛk* | (Skt cited in Muni Jambuvijayaji 1966: 122). On differences between *svārthānumāna* and *parārthānumāna* according to Dignāga and Dharmakīrti, see, e.g., Tillemans 1984 and 1991.

Ones (*buddha*) aid trainees (*vineyajana*) unacquainted with them[277] (i.e., the technical definitions) by way of reasoning (*upapatti*) that conforms to what [they them]selves acknowledge (*yathāsvaprasiddha*).[278] Enough of this digression; let us [return to] explicating just the main topic.

§61. Nor do things arise from [something] other (*parataḥ*), simply because [something] other does not exist. And [he (= Nāgārjuna)] will explain this here [in the Madhyamakaśāstra:]

> An own-being of things of course does not exist in the conditions and such.[279]

And thus just because other does not exist, [things] do not arise from other, either.

---

[277] PsP Tib: *de kho na mi shes pa'i* for *tadanabhijña*°; de La Vallée Poussin (PsP_L 36, n. 3) reconstructs *atattvajña*°. Hopkins (1983: 526 and n. 457) notes that the Sanskrit "is merely *tadanabhijña* 'who do not know that [or those, which could refer to 'the definitions']' whereas the Tibetan reads *de kho na mi shes pa'i* 'who do not know suchness'"; he refers to Tsong kha pa's presentation of the phrase as "*chos kyi de kho na nyid ma shes pa'i* 'who do not know the suchness of phenomena'" and (thus?) translates PsP Tib as "who do not know suchness." It is possible that he is correct in assuming that the PsP translators understood *tat* in the meaning of *tattva* (n. 457), but since *tattva* has not been topical, it may be more likely that either 1) the translators read *tat*, which they interpreted in the sense of "that," and added the emphatic particle *kho na* (= *nyid*) so that the anaphoric reference to *tarkalakṣaṇa* would be clearer or 2) their manuscript(s) appeared to, or did, read *tatva*, the result of the *akṣara da* (*ta<u>da</u>nabhijña*°) having been read—on account of, possibly, its lower loop having been written larger than usual, or a mark on the palm leaf having caused the right opening to appear as closed—as *tva*. This second possibility may be the less probable one given that Pa tshab usually translates *tattva* as *de kho na nyid*.

[278] Seyfort Ruegg (2002: 70) translates the latter part of the sentence as "… assistance (*anugraha* = *phan btags pa*) comes from the Buddhas (*saṅs rgyas rnams*) by reason of a justified ground in accordance with what is acknowledged by onself"; the translation of *upapatti* as "a justified ground" is in the present context not acceptable. Candrakīrti, here and in other of his works, often uses the word *upapatti* in the sense of "reasoning."

[279] Candrakīrti cites MMK I.3ab: *na hi svabhāvo bhāvānāṃ pratyayādiṣu vidyate* |. Candrakīrti provides two explanations for the *kārikā*; see below.

Further, the negation of arising from other should be ascertained through statements such as [the following from the Madhyamakāvatāra],[280]

> If[281] depending on [something] other (*anya*) [than itself], another (*para*) were to come to be, then from fire thick darkness could arise,
> And there would be the birth of everything, and [that] indeed from everything, because being other (*paratva*) [than the effect] is the same (*tulya*) for every non-producer (*ajanaka*) as well.[282]

---

[280] Only ms Q identifies the source of the verse as the MA. Given that ms P and the paper manuscripts lack the reference, and that the dropping of *madhyamakāvatārād* is difficult to explain paleographically, it can be concluded that this second instance of MA identification also represents an early interpolation. Candrakīrti presumed his audience's familiarity with his other main work; a later scholar or student of the PsP must have deemed the identification of the source to be necessary. Unlike the previous case of an interpolated reference to the MA in Q (see end of PsP_M §21) where the name of the work was written in Q's margin as text to be inserted, in the present case *madhyamakāvatārād* is included within Q's main text. The fact that it is included within Q's main text probably indicates that it was passed on to Q from ms η (see Stemma), which had received the reading from ms δ of γ's line. PsP Tib's reading *dbu ma la 'jug pa las* confirms that *madhyamakāvatārād* also appeared in one of the Skt manuscripts used for the translation, but as the analysis of the manuscripts' variants has demonstrated, this reading probably also goes back to δ. One assumes that it was originally a marginal reading aid that a scribe wrongly interpreted as material needing to be inserted.
De La Vallée Poussin introduces the conjecture *madhyamakāvatārāt* (in square brackets) on the basis of Tib's *dbu ma la 'jug pa las* (see PsP_L 36 and n. 5). He refers back to PsP_L 13 for an earlier reference to the MA that is attested in his three manuscripts, but as explained earlier, this specification of the source text for PsP_L 13.9 (§21) does not appear in ms P and was not in the manuscript used by *LṬ's author; see n. 115.

[281] *LṬ's author notes that *yadi nāma* is to be understood as meaning "if," but adds *yadi nāmeti yadyarthe | nāmābhyupagame vā* "or, alternatively, *nāma* [has been added] in the sense of signalizing acceptance" (cf. Yonezawa 2004: 123, 138 [fol. 2a7]).

[282] MA VI.14: *anyat pratītya yadi nāma paro 'bhaviṣyaj jāyeta tarhi bahulaḥ śikhino 'ndhakāraḥ | sarvasya janma ca bhavet khalu sarvataś ca tulyaṃ paratvam akhile 'janake 'pi yasmāt ||* (Li 2012: 4). Tib at MABh_ed 89.6-7, 15, 19-20: *gzhan la brten nas gal te gzhan zhig 'byung bar 'gyur na ni || 'o na me lce las kyang mun pa 'thug*[1] *po 'byung 'gyur zhing || thams cad las kyang thams cad skye bar 'gyur te*[2] *gang gi*

phyir ‖ *skyed par byed pa ma yin ma lus la yang*[3] *gzhan nyid mtshungs* ‖ [1]PsP Tib: *mthug*; [2]PsP Tib (P): *te* |; [3]PsP Tib: *'ang*.

Quoted in MABh to MA VI.98ab ($MABh_{ed}$ 204.8-11); cf. $MABh_{tr}$ 1910: 286f. (286, n. 6: read *'ndhakāraḥ* for *'dhakāraḥ*). Candrakīrti, in MABh on VI.14ab, cites as further confirmation for the impossibility of arising from other MMK XX.19cd: *rgyu dang 'bras bu gzhan nyid du* ‖ *nam yang 'thad par mi 'gyur ro* ‖ (XX.19cd Skt: *hetoḥ phalasya cānyatvaṃ na hi jātūpapadyate* ‖) and MMK XX.20cd: *rgyu dang 'bras bu gzhan nyid na* ‖ *rgyu dang rgyu min mtshung pas 'gyur* ‖ (XX.20cd Skt: *pṛthaktve phalahetvoḥ syāt tulyo hetur ahetunā* ‖).

De La Vallée Poussin ($MABh_{tr}$ 1910: 286, n. 6) cites the Sanskrit for MA VI.14 but in his translation (287) of 14c he translates freely, ignoring the pair of *ca*s and the word *khalu*: "Toutes choses naîtraient de toutes choses." My translation reflects my understanding of 14c as intending to convey two aspects of a consequence of arising from other. Tilakakalaśa and Pa tshab's translation of MA VI.14c as *thams cad las kyang thams cad skye bar 'gyur te* ... may represent a (not entirely successful) attempt to bring the intent of the Sanskrit into Tibetan verse. Nag tsho's translation of the MA (which was revised by Pa tshab) presents 14c merely as *kun las thams cad skye bar 'gyur te* ... (P 229a5). The Tibetan of MABh on 14c has been translated so that it concurs with the Tibetan translation of the *pāda*: *rgyur gyur pa dang rgyu ma yin par gyur pa thams cad las kyang dngos po 'bras bur gyur pa dang 'bras bur ma gyur pa thams cad skye bar 'gyur ro* ‖. Candrakīrti would appear to elaborate on the two aspects he refers to in 14c, however, in the MABh on 14d: *yang ji ltar sa* ($MABh_{UN}$: *sā*) *lu'i sa bon gzhan du gyur pa las sa* ($MABh_{UN}$: *sā*) *lu'i myu gu skye ba de bzhin du* | *me dang sol ba dang nas kyi sa bon la sogs pa dag las kyang 'gyur ro* ‖ *yang ji ltar sa* ($MABh_{UN}$: *sā*) *lu'i myu gu* ($MABh_{UN}$: *gu'i*) *gzhan du gyur pa sa* ($MABh_{UN}$: *sā*) *lu'i sa bon las 'byung ba de bzhin du bum pa dang snam bu la sogs pa rnams kyang 'gyur ba zhig na* | ($MABh_{ed}$ 90.4-8); the two *yang*s respectively commencing each sentence possibly translate two *ca*s (or two *api*s) which are meant to correspond to the two *ca*s of 14c.

Huntington (1989: 158f.) translates the verse: "If one entity arises in dependence on another, then pitch darkness can arise from a flame. In fact, [if this were the case, then] anything could arise from anything, because it is not simply [the cause] which is different from [its effect] – all non-causes as well are different [from that effect]." Given the structure of 14c and the commentary, it seems that Candrakīrti intends *sarva* to be understood in a comprehensive sense as "all, everything," and the optative *bhavet* in a more definite and dynamic sense of "would be / would come to be" than Huntington's "anything could arise" (for *sarvasya janma ca bhavet*) allows; Candrakīrti uses this consequence to demonstrate that arising from other entails total chaos, not that a pot *could* arise from a rice seed, but that it and everything else definitely would arise, because the condition of being other is fulfilled. Cp. MA VI.99 where he rejects arising without a cause and clearly states that in a world in which things arise without a cause, everything would perpetually (*rtag tu*) arise from everything: *gal te rgyu med kho nar skye bar lta zhig 'gyur na ni* | *de tshe mtha' dag rtag tu tham cad las kyang skye 'byung zhing* |. While one could alternatively trans-

§62. The Master Buddhapālita, for his part, asserts:

> Things do not arise from other, because of the consequence that everything would originate from everything.[283]

§63. The Master Bhāviveka voices criticism in regard to this [statement of Buddhapālita's]:

---

late the consequence in VI.14b as "from fire thick darkness would arise" (cf. LVP_{tr} 1910: 286: "sans doubte une épaisse obscurité naît de la flame") in place of my "from fire thick darkness could arise," my choice of translations for the optatives is based on my interpretation of the verse as intending, for poetic and dramatic purposes, a progression from the first consequence to the second: an unwelcome possibility is presented and then in a second step a stronger, more definite and more devastating consequence of the opponent's view is set forth.
Candrakīrti devotes a substantial section of the sixth chapter of the MABh to the refutation of arising from other, chiefly because arising from other is accepted by the schools of Conservative Buddhism (note that his refution of arising from other commences with the enumeration and definitions of the four conditions (*pratyaya*) maintained by the Sarvāstivāda and Sautrāntika schools [see $MABh_{ed}$ 87.15-89.2]) and by the Yogācāra school. Candrakīrti's argumentation against arising from other in the MABh is too extensive to be included and elucidated here, but mention should be made of the fact that he couches within it, in the framework of explicating why the viewpoint of the world (*loka*) cannot be taken as an authority for proving that things arise from other (cf. $MABh_{ed}$ 101.3ff.), his own presentation of the two truths and a discussion regarding them. This is followed (cf. $MABh_{ed}$ 122.7ff.) by his defense of karmic causality within the Madhyamaka system which eschews the reality of all things and his rejection of, primarily, the *ālayavijñāna* of the Vijñānavāda school, a rejection that leads to the refutation of the possibility of the arising of the world from truly existing *vijñāna/citta* and the rejection of other doctrines of the school. Only after an excursion into an elucidation of *nītārtha* and *neyārtha sūtra*s does Candrakīrti commence the refutation of arising from both self and other ($MABh_{ed}$ 202.6ff.).

[283] Candrakīrti is quoting from Buddhapālita's MMK commentary. BP_{ed} 10.18-19: *gzhan las kyang skye ba med de | ci'i phyir zhe na | thams cad las thams cad skye bar thal bar 'gyur ba'i phyir ro.* The statement is embedded in PP Tib: *'di la gzhan ni dngos po rnams gzhan las kyang skye ba med pa ste | ci'i phyir zhe na | thams cad las thams cad skye bar thal bar 'gyur ba'i phyir ro ||* (D: omits ||) *zhes rnam par bshad pa byed do ||* (D 50a5-6; P 60a5-6). Avalokitavrata identifies *gzhan* of *'di la gzhan ni* as Buddhapālita (D 102a1; P 119b7). PsP Tib reads: *dngos po rnams gzhan las skye ba med de | thams cad las kyang thams cad skye bar 'gyur ba'i phyir ro || zhes rnam par 'chad do ||. sarvasambhavaprasaṅgāt* is again translated merely as *thams cad skye bar 'gyur ba'i phyir* in PsP Tib when Buddhapālita's consequence is repeated in Bhāviveka's critique.

Then, as regards this, because it is a statement of a consequence,[284] when the reversal (*viparyaya*) of the probandum (*sādhya*) and the probans (*sādhana*) is made, contradiction [of the consequence] with [your] original position (*prākpakṣa*) [becomes evident, since the reversal states that] "Things arise from self, from both [self and other] or without a cause (*ahetutaḥ*), because a certain thing (*kasyacit*) arises from a certain thing (*kutaścit*)." Otherwise[285] [that is, if the reversal is not accepted], since this [probans] "because of the consequence that everything would originate from everything" does not fall under[286] [either] proof

---

[284] PsP Tib translates *prasaṅgavākya* as *thal bar 'gyur ba'i ngag*, PP Tib attests *glags yod pa'i tshig*. On Candrakīrti's replacement of *sāvakāśa* with *prasaṅga*, see n. 123. In the present case too, I assume that *sāvakāśavacana* stood in PP Skt and that the PsP translators, upon appropriating the criticism from PP Tib, replaced *glags yod pa'i tshig* with *thal bar 'gyur ba'i ngag* in order to conform with Candrakīrti's preference for and thus use of *prasaṅga* in his reiteration of phrases in PP containing the compound *sāvakāśa*.

[285] De La Vallée Poussin (PsP_L 37, n. 2) considers PsP Tib's *gzhan du na yang* to be reflecting *anyathāpi*, but *gzhan du na yang* is also used elsewhere in the PsP to translate *anyathā*. The PsP Tib translators have in the present case, however, adopted *gzhan du na yang* from PP Tib (see the following notes).

[286] PsP Tib: *de la sgrub pa dang sun 'byin ba nyid med pa'i phyir* for *asya sādhanadūṣanānantaḥpātitvāt*. De La Vallée Poussin (PsP_L 37, n. 3) reconstructs the Skt for PsP Tib as "... *atra sādhana-dūṣaṇatā-abhāvāt*." I doubt that the PsP Tib translators were confronted with such a reading in their Sanskrit manuscripts; it seems more probable that PsP Tib reads as it does because the translators inserted the (slightly modified) version of Bhāviveka's critique as found in PP Tib into their PsP translation; PP Tib attests the phrase as *de la sgrub pa dang sun dbyung ba nyid med pa'i phyir* (see also the following note). The fact that *dūṣaṇāntaḥpātitvāc ca* in Candrakīrti's response is similarly translated as *sun 'byin pa nyid kyang yin pa'i phyir* may only indicate that the translators preferred to employ a verb (*yin*) that would better accord with the verb (*med*) of the PP Tib critique (note that at PsP_L 490.2 *antaḥpātitvāt* is translated more literally as *nang du 'dus pa'i phyir*). Whether de La Vallée Poussin's reconstructed *sādhanadūṣaṇatābhāvāt* could represent the original reading for PP Skt is difficult to know. PPṬ also attests *de la sgrub pa dang sun dbyung ba nyid med pa'i phyir* throughout, but one must keep in mind that it was translated by the same team of scholars that translated the PP; nevertheless, the paraphrase in explanations such as ... *mngon sum la sogs pa dang 'gal ba phyogs kyi skyon rnams las 'ga' yang ma brjod pas | de la gzhan sun dbyung ba nyid kyang med pa yin pa'i phyir nyes pa yod do ||* (PPṬ D 103b3; P 111a7-8) leads one to wonder if Candrakīrti's words might represent a paraphrase or interpretation of Bhāviveka's

(*sādhana*) or refutation (*dūṣaṇa*), this [statement of Buddhapālita's would be] incoherent in meaning (*asaṅgatārtha*).[287]

---

original reason. *LṬ's author cites *sādhanadūṣaṇānantaḥpātitvāt* and explains it with *na sādhanaṃ nāpi dūṣaṇam ity arthaḥ* (cf. Yonezawa 2004: 123, 138 [fol. 2b1]). Stcherbatsky (1927: 120 and n. 8) has not understood the compound and thus suggests emending the text to "*sādhana-dūṣaṇāntaḥ...*, i.e., *ity asya sādhanasya dūṣaṇa...*" in order to arrive at the meaning "because the argument contains its own destruction."

Bhāviveka exemplifies the incoherence he sees in Buddhapālita's argument with a senseless verse (translated in Kajiyama 1963: 54; Ames 1993: 226). Avalokitavrata, prior to citing the verse, explains the incoherence as arising from the dissonance between the two parts of Buddhapālita's assertion: in stating the two parts of his consequence, Buddhapālita ends up first asserting that arising does not exist, and then that everything arises from everything: *de ltar dngos po rnams gzhan las skye ba med do zhes smras la | de'i 'og tu thams cad las thams cad skye bar thal bar 'gyur ba'i phyir ro zhes smras pas | de ltar gyur na rang gis sngar skye ba med par smras pa dang | de'i 'og tu thams cad las thams cad skye bar smras pa gnyis* (P: *nyid*) *don 'brel pa med pa nyid yin pas rnam par bshad pa de ni mi rung ngo ||* (D 103b4-5; P 111a8-111b2).

[287] Candrakīrti is citing from Bhāviveka's PP, the translation of which reads: *des na de la glags yod pa'i tshig*[1] *yin pa'i phyir bsgrub par bya ba dang | sgrub pa*[2] *bzlog pa*[3] *byas na*[4] *dngos po rnams bdag gam gnyis sam*[5] *rgyu med pa las skye bar 'gyur ba dang | 'ga' zhig las 'ga' zhig skye bar 'gyur ba'i phyir phyogs snga*[6] *ma dang 'gal bar 'gyur ro || gzhan du na yang thams cad las*[7] *thams cad skye bar thal bar*[8] *'gyur ba'i phyir ro* (P: ||) *zhes bya ba*[9] *de la sgrub pa dang sun dbyung ba*[10] *nyid* (D: *gnyis*) *med pa'i phyir | de ni don 'brel pa med pa yin te* (D 50a6-7; P 60a6-60b1). [1]PsP Tib: *thal bar 'gyur ba'i ngag* for *glags yod pa'i tshig*; [2]PsP Tib: *sgrub par byed pa* for *sgrub pa*; [3]PsP Tib, PPṬ: *par*; [4]PPṬ: *nas*; [5]PPṬ: *gnyi ga 'am* for *gnyis sam*; [6]PsP Tib: *gong*; [7]PPṬ P: omits *thams cad las*; [8]PsP Tib omits *thal bar*; [9]PsP Tib: *de bas na* for *zhes bya ba*; [10]PsP Tib: *sun 'byin pa* for *sun dbyung ba*. Translated in Kajiyama 1963: 53 and Ames 1993: 225f. The original position contradicted by the reversal is that things do not arise, not the "theses" that result from the reversal, as Seyfort Ruegg's (2002: 72) translation misleadingly suggests. Seyfort Ruegg translates *asaṅgatārtha* as "irrelevant," but it does seem that Bhāviveka intends the meaning "incoherent," since he subsequently, stating that Buddhapālita's consequence is like it, cites a completely incoherent verse (see PP D 50a7-50b1; P 60b1-2).

On the reversal of the *prasaṅga*, see Watanabe 2013 and n. 124. Avalokitavrata describes the reversal of the *sādhya*, viz., "things do not arise from other, either" (*bsgrub par bya ba dngos po rnams gzhan las kyang skye ba med de zhes bya ba*) as resulting in "things arise from self, both, or without cause" (*dngos po rnams bdag gam gnyi ga 'am rgyu med pa las skye bar 'gyur ba dang*), and the reversal of the *sādhana*, viz., "there would be the consequence that everything would arise from everything" as resulting in "a certain thing arises from a certain thing" (*sgrub pa thams cad las thams cad skye bar thal bar 'gyur ro* (P: ||) *zhes bya ba bzlog par byas*

[Reply:] This [critique, like your earlier one] too, is incoherent in meaning,[288] since it has already been explained [that reversal does not

---

na 'ga' zhig las 'ga' zhig skye bar 'gyur); cf. PPṬ D 103a1-2; P 120b1-2. He considers the original position (*phyogs snga ma*; **prākpakṣa*) that would be contradicted through the reversal to be that asserted by Nāgārjuna in MMK I.1: *'di ltar slob dpon gyis phyogs snga ma las | dngos po gang dag gang na yang || skyes pa nam yang yod ma yin || zhes gsungs ... de dang 'gal bar 'gyur* (PPṬ D 103a3-5; P 110b7-111a2; on the misplaced text in P, see Ames 1993: 245, n. 119; correct his point of insertion for P 121a from line 7 to line 4). "Otherwise" (*gzhan tu na yang*), that is, if Buddhapālita refuses to reverse the *sādhya* and *sādhana*, leaving them to stand as stated, Avalokitavrata continues, he can be faulted, because his [consequence's reason], namely, that there would be the consequence that everything would arise from everything, is not a property of the subject; the consequence is, on the one hand, not a proof of his own position. And since his statement has not expressed any faults of the opponent's proposition, i.e., contradiction with direct perception and so forth, it is not a refutation of the opponent's position: *thams cad las thams cad skye bar smras pa de phyogs kyi chos ma yin pa'i phyir | de la rang gi sgrub pa* (P: *ma*?) *nyid kyang med pa yin la | gnas brtan buddhapālita'i rnam par bshad pa de mngon sum la sogs pa dang 'gal ba phyogs kyi skyon rnams las 'ga' yang ma brjod pas | de la gzhan sun dbyung ba nyid kyang med pa yin pa'i phyir nyes pa yod do ||* (PPṬ D 103b2-3; P 111a6-8).
The two inferences set forth by Bhāviveka to prove non-arising from other have already been cited by Candrakīrti and rejected as faulty because their reasons are not accepted by both Bhāviveka and his opponent; see §51.

[288] PsP Tib: *'di yang don 'brel pa med pa ma yin te.* Stcherbatsky (1927: 121 and n. 1) suggests emending the Sanskrit text so that it accords with PsP Tib ("... read *asaṃgārtham nāsti.*" "It is not nonsense!"). De La Vallée Poussin notes Tib's reading and the reading *etadam apy asaṃgatārtha(m)* of his three mss; he emends to *etad apy asaṃgatārtham*, considering as support for his choice Candrakīrti's response *tad etad ayuktaṃ pūrvoditaparihārāt* (PsP_M §68; PsP_L 39.4) to Bhāviveka's *seyaṃ vyākhyā na yuktā prāguktadoṣāt* (PsP_M §67 end; PsP_L 39.2-3). Mss P and Q attest the correct reading *etad apy asaṅgatārtham* (D supports it with *etad apy asaṃgatārtha*). With this statement, Candrakīrti intentionally parrots the final words of Bhāviveka's critique (*asaṅgatārtham etad*). PsP Tib's interpretation is awkward inasmuch as *api* will imply that Buddhapālita's first consequence has also been referred to as incoherent, but there Bhāviveka did not declare that the argument was *asaṅgatārtha*, rather that it was *ayukta*. Cf. also PsP_M §23 (PsP_L 14.4), where Bhāviveka opens his criticism of Buddhapālita's first consequence with the words *tad ayuktam*, and PsP_M §24 (PsP_L 15.3-4) where Candrakīrti, as here, rejects Bhāviveka's critique using his opponent's own words (... *tad ayuktam*). The extra negation in PsP Tib may have been the result of intentional change in one of the manuscripts relied on by the translators which had been made by a previous scholar or student who understood *etat* to refer to Buddhapālita's statement (as Bhāviveka intends his *etat*) and not, as Candrakīrti intends it, to refer Bhāviveka's critique of Buddhapālita's statement.

apply to such consequences] and because [the consequence] falls under refutation (*dūṣaṇa*) in that [it] refutes the matter proposed by the opponent.[289] Thus, there is nothing to this [criticism]; effort is therefore not put forth again [to respond to your complaints].

§64. Nor do things arise from both [self and other], because the faults stated for both positions (*ubhayapakṣa*) would entail,[290] and because

---

[289] PsP Tib, which may be corrupt, appears to understand three reasons: *gong kho nar bstan zin pa'i phyir dang | gzhan gyis dam bcas pa'i don sun 'byin par byed pa yin pa dang | sun 'byin pa nyid kyang yin pa'i phyir.* The Sanskrit expects *yin pas* instead of *yin pa dang.*

[290] Buddhapālita states only this single consequence for the position of arising from both self and other. BP_{ed} 10.19-21: *bdag dang gzhan gnyis las kyang skye ba med de | gnyi ga'i skyon du thal bar 'gyur ba'i phyir ro ||*. Bhāviveka does not criticize this *prasaṅga* statement of Buddhapālita's, presumably because the consequence only refers back to the faults already adduced for arising from self and arising from other. Bhāviveka declares that Nāgārjuna was inspired to include and reject the position of arising from both self and other on account of 1) the Sāṅkhya claim that an effect arises from causes both distinct and not distinct from it, such as, respectively, earth, etc., and a seed: *grangs can dag ni byed rgyu rnam par phye ba dang | rnam par ma phye ba* (D: *bas*) *sa la sogs pa dang | sa bon gyi mtshan nyid dag las 'bras bu myu gu zhes bya ba skye'o zhes smra* (PP D 50b 1-2; P 60b2-3) and 2) the Jaina claim that things arise from self and other, for instance, that a gold ring arises from both gold and fire, etc.: *gcer bur rgyu ba pa'i phyogs dgag phyir yang ... 'di ltar de dag ni gser gyi sor gdub ni gser dang | me la sogs pa las bdag dang gzhan las skye bar smra ba'i phyir ro ||* (D 50b3-4; P 60b6-7; Ames proposes *nirgranthacārin* as the possible Sanskrit for *gcer bur rgyu ba pa* [1993: 246, n. 142]). Bhāviveka argues that the proof for non-arising from both is included in the proofs for non-arising from self and for non-arising from other, and that there does not exist an inference showing that things arise from both self and other; see PP D 50b3; P 60b5-6; Kajiyama 1963: 54; Ames 1993: 226. See also MHK III.192.
Reasons disproving arising from both self and other are set forth by Candrakīrti in MA VI.98: *gnyis las skye ba 'ang rigs pa'i ngo bo ma yin gang gi phyir || bshad zin nyes pa de dag thog tu 'bab pa yin phyir ro || 'di ni 'jig rten las min de nyid du yang 'dod min te || gang phyir re re las ni skye ba 'grub* ($MABh_{ed}$ *grub*) *pa yod ma yin ||* ($MABh_{ed}$ 202.8-9; correct the verse number at $MABh_{tr}$ 1911: 256 and 258 from 95 to 98). Candrakīrti also attributes the position of arising from both self and other to the Jainas, who claim that a pot, for example, in that the pot and the lump of clay from which it is made are not other, arises from self; yet since the activity of the potter, etc., that produce it are different from the pot, it also arises from other (see $MABh_{ed}$ 202.10-18; $MABh_{tr}$ 1911: 256. The Jainas are referred to by Candrakīrti as *tshig gal gnyis su smra ba rnams*; along with de La Vallée Poussin, I do not understand the

there is no capacity for production by either one on its own.[291] For he (= Nāgārjuna) will state [further on in the Madhyamakaśāstra],

> There might be suffering (*duḥkha*) created by both [self and other] if [suffering] could be created by each one singly (*ekaika-kṛta*).[292]

---

meaning of *tshig gal* here). Similarly, Candrakīrti states, they argue that since Maitra is born in the present life with the same soul (*jīva*) as in the previous, he arises from self; but since his birth is determined by his mother, father, merit, demerit and influxes, he arises from other. Thus, assert the Jainas, because they neither claim arising exclusively from self nor arising exclusively from other, they are unaffected by the earlier criticism with respect to arising from self or arising from other (see $MABh_{ed}$ 203.2-12; $MABh_{tr}$ 1911: 256f.).

291 PsP Tib translates the second reason given by Candrakīrti with *skyed par byed pa'i nus pa med pa'i phyir*; I too understand *utpāda* in a causal sense here, i.e., in the sense of production as opposed to its more usual meaning of arising. Cf. MA VI.98d: *gang phyir re re las ni skye ba* (intransitive) *'grub* ($MABh_{ed}$ *grub) pa yod ma yin* ($MABh_{ed}$ 205.2) and $MABh_{ed}$ to 6.98d: *dper na til gcig gis 'bru mar 'byin nus pas* || *mang po rnams kyis kyang 'gyur la* || *nus pa ma mthong ba'i bye ma rnams kyis ni ma yin pa ltar re res bskyed par 'gyur na ni* || *de lta bu'i rang bzhin can mang po rnams kyis kyang 'gyur ba zhig go* || ($MABh_{ed}$ 205.3-6).

292 Candrakīrti is citing MMK XII.9ab: *syād ubhābhyāṃ kṛtaṃ duḥkhaṃ syād ekaikakṛtaṃ yadi* | (Ye 2011a follows the ABh, BP, PP tradition which does not include MMK XII.6 [see Ye 2007b: 166] and thus numbers the verse as XII.8). Suffering, the topic of the twelfth chapter and as made clear by Nāgārjuna in MMK XII.2, refers to the five *skandhas*. In *kārikās* XII.2-6 the *skandhas* and the *pudgala* are individually considered and rejected, each from the point of view of "self" and "other," as that by which suffering, i.e., the *skandhas*, is created. The alternatives of suffering being created by self, by other, by both and without a cause are presented and addressed already in the Canon (suffering in the Canonical contexts refers to "the mass of suffering"); see, e.g. SN II.19.27-20.16: *Kim nu kho bho Gotama sayaṃ-kataṃ dukkhanti* || *Mā hevaṃ Kassapāti Bhagavā avoca* || *Kim pana bho Gotama paraṃkataṃ dukkhanti* || *Mā hevaṃ Kassapāti Bhagavā avoca* || *Kim nu kho bho Gotama sayaṃkatañ ca paraṃkatañ ca dukkhanti* || *Mā hevaṃ Kassapāti Bhagavā avoca* || *Kim pana bho Gotama asayaṃ-kāram aparaṃ-kāram adhicca samuppannaṃ dukkhanti. Mā hevaṃ Kassapāti Bhagavā avoca* || ... *so karoti so paṭisamvediyatīti kho Kassapa ādito sato sayaṃkataṃ dukkhanti iti vadaṃ sassatam etam pareti* || *Añño karoti añño paṭisaṃvediyatīti kho Kassapa vedanābhitunnassa sato paraṃkataṃ dukkhanti iti vadam ucchedam etam pareti* || *Ete te Kassapa ubho ante anupagamma majjhena Tathāgato dhammam deseti* || *avijjāpaccayā saṅkhārā* || *saṅkhārapaccayā viññāṇaṃ* || *pe* || *Evam etassa kevalassa dukkhakkhandhassa samudayo hoti* || (cf. SN_{tr} 545-547). Note that the fourth alternative is presented as *adhicca samuppannaṃ*, thus fortuitous arising. See DN I.28-29, where the Buddha explains that one group of

§65. Nor do [things] arise without a cause (*ahetutaḥ*), because the faults that will be stated by way of [other assertions on the part of Nāgārjuna] would be entailed, such as,

> When the cause (*hetu*) does not exist, neither the effect (*kārya*) nor the [co-operative] cause (*kāraṇa*) exists,[293]

and because of the entailment of faults such as [the following from the Madhyamakāvatāra]:

---

holders of the view of fortuitous arising consists of persons who were previously gods in a realm without consciousness and are thus unable to remember more than the (re-)arising of consciousness. That is, through meditative concentration (*samādhi*) in the present life, these persons, previously *asaññadeva*s, gain memory of the past, but only to the point of the re-arising of consciousness after the *asañña* existence, and they thus think that they came into existence only then and did not exist previously. Such a person thus thinks: "*Adhicca-samuppanno attā ca loko ca. Taṃ kissa hetu? Ahaṃ hi pubbe nāhosiṃ, so'mhi etarahi ahutvā sattattāya pariṇato ti*" (DN I.29.1-3). The other group, the Buddha states, has come to the view of fortuitous arising through reasoning. Cf. also SN II.22-23, 33-35, 38-39, 41-42, 112-114 for the rejection of suffering, pleasure and pain, and the links of dependent-arising created by self, other, both or fortuitously.
The *pudgala* spoken of by Nāgārjuna appears to be the controversial "person" maintained by the Vātsīputrīyas and Sāṃmitīyas (see, e.g., Bareau 1955: 115f., 123; AKBh IX; Schayer 1931: 16, n. 13). Vetter (1992: 496), who assumes that Nāgārjuna spent his early years in a "*pudgalavāda* milieu," writes, "Accepting a person on a preliminary level of truth as having the same reality as the constituents (*skandha*) of a person seems to be the most individual characteristic we know of Nāgārjuna." In certain other chapters of the MMK, it can been seen that Nāgārjuna accepts the reality of the subject or agent on the surface level.

[293] Candrakīrti cites MMK VIII.4ab: *hetāv asati kāryaṃ ca kāraṇaṃ ca na vidyate* |. MMK VIII.3: *karoti yady asadbhūto 'sadbhūtaṃ karma kārakaḥ* | *ahetukaṃ bhavet karma kartā cāhetuko bhavet* ||. I have translated the half-verse following Candrakīrti's interpretation of it; it is questionable whether his interpretation of *kāraṇa* as co-operative cause, which appears to rely on Buddhapālita's interpretation of *kāraṇa* as **pratyaya*, reflects Nāgārjuna's intent. Cf. May 1959: 146, n. 422 for comments on the half-verse. Garfield (1995: 179) translates *kāraṇa* as "cause," but his comments on VIII.4 betray a lack of understanding of VIII.4ab and the verse as a whole. See Bhattacharya 1981 for comments on Candrakīrti's interpretation of the chapter.
In his introduction to VIII.4ab, Candrakīrti makes it known that he considers the proposition of an unreal agent and object, which entails the lack of a cause for both the agent and the object, to be equivalent to asserting a position propounding no cause: *sati ca ahetukavādābhyupagame kāryaṃ ca kāraṇaṃ ca sarvam apoditaṃ syāt.*

And the world would certainly not be perceived if it were devoid of a cause, just like the colour and scent of a sky-lotus [is not perceived].[294]

[294] Candrakīrti cites MA VI.100ab: *gṛhyeta naiva ca jagad yadi hetuśūnyaṃ syād yadvad eva gaganotpalavarṇagandhau* |. MABh$_{ed}$ 207.7-8: *gal te 'gro ba rgyu yis stong par 'gyur na nam mkha' yi* || *ut pa la yi dri mdog ji bzhin bzung du med nyid na* ||. Cf. MABh$_{tr}$ 1911: 260. PsP Tib: *gal te rgyu yis stong na 'gro ba 'di dag gzung bya min* || *ji ltar nam mkha'i utpala yi dri dang kha dog bzhin* ||.
Candrakīrti argues in the MA and MABh from *kārikā* 99 to *kārikā* 103 with the proponent of intrinsic nature (**svabhāvavādin*; *ngo ba nyid smra pa*), first against the arising of the things of the world without any causes, then against the denial of the retribution of acts as regards the *paraloka* (see MABh$_{ed}$ 205.8-212.14; MABh$_{tr}$ 1911: 259-266). The *svabhāvavādin* opens the debate by declaring: *gal te skye ba rgyu las yin na ni de 'bras bu'i bdag tu gyur pa dang* | *gzhan du gyur pa dang* | *gnyi gar gyur pa zhig tu 'gyur bas nyes pa de dag tu 'gyur ba zhig na* | *bdag gis ni rgyu khas ma blangs pas bshad zin pa'i nyes pa'i go skabs med do* || *de'i phyir dngos po rnams kyi skye ba ni ngo ba nyid las 'byung ba kho na yin te* | (MABh$_{ed}$ 205.8-13). The doctrine of intrinsic nature appears to have been common to the Materialists and the Ājīvikas. Silburn (1989: 133) writes, "C'est du jeu de *niyati*, *svabhāva* et des circonstances environnantes que dépend la diversité des êtres et leurs conditions heureuses et malheureuses. Autrement dit, le sort de chacun n'est nullement déterminé par ses actes vertueux et coupables et la transmigration n'obéit en aucune manière aux lois du karman. C'est pour cette raison que les Bouddhistes désignent les doctrines de la nature propre (*svabhāva*) par les termes de *ahetuvāda*, 'production sans cause' ou *adhiccasamuppāda* 'apparition accidentelle.' Pour les Svabhāvavādin les choses surgissent à l'existence sans qu'intervienne une cause finale interne ou externe tels les actes antérieurement accomplis de chacun ou la volonté divin. Les choses évoluent de façon méchanique, de par leur nature propre: si les épines auxquelles je me suis heurté sont ainsi acérées et si elles se trouvent sur mon passage c'est que leur nature est de piquer; ce n'est nullement par décret divin, ni en raison de fautes que j'aurais pu commettre." Regarding *svabhāvavāda*, see Silburn 1989: 133-135; MABh$_{tr}$ 1911: 258, n. 1; May 1959: 122, n. 320; Bhattacharya 2012.
Bhāviveka rejects arising without a cause by arguing that there is no inference demonstrating uncaused arising, and that such a thesis would be in conflict with both inference and what is generally accepted (see PP D 50b5-6; P 61a1-2; Kajiyama 1963: 54f.; Ames 1993: 227; see also MHK III.194-195). Bhāviveka then, moving on to interpret no cause (**ahetu*) as bad cause (**kuhetu*; see n. 298), presents arguments from the side of the *svabhāvavādin*; Avalokitavrata identifies the proponents of the doctrine of *svabhāva* as Lokāyatas, the followers of Maharṣi 'Jig rten mig (see Ames 1993: 247, n. 147). Avalokitavrata further identifies the proponent of no cause called 'Jug stobs can by Bhāviveka as also a disciple of Maharṣi 'Jig rten mig (ibid., 1993: 247, n. 156).

§66. The Master Buddhapālita, for his part, says,

> Things do not arise without a cause, because of the consequence that everything would originate from everything, all the time.[295]

§67. The Master Bhāviveka criticizes in regard to this too:

> Also with respect to this [argument], on account of [its] being the statement of a consequence, if the expression of the reversed probandum and probans is accepted as the meaning of the

---

[295] Candrakīrti cites here Buddhapālita's consequence for the position of arising without a cause, quoting only the first of its two reasons. BP_{ed} 10.21-23: *rgyu med pa las kyang skye ba med de | rtag tu thams cad las thams cad skye bar thal bar 'gyur ba'i phyir dang | rtsom pa thams cad don med pa nyid kyi skyon du 'gyur ba'i phyir ro*. Buddhapālita repeats the reasons (*rtag tu ...*) in his commentary on MMK IV.2 (BP_{ed} 60.10-12). His consequence with the first reason is cited in PP just before Bhāviveka's critique of it (D 53a5; P 64a5): *'di la gzhan ni dngos po rnams rgyu med pa las kyang skye ba med de | rtag tu thams cad las thams cad skye bar thal ba la sogs par 'gyur ba'i phyir*; Avalokitavrata identifies the author of the statement as Buddhapālita (D 153b1; P 176b7). As noted by Ames (1993: 250, n. 197), even though Bhāviveka indicates the second reason only with *la sogs pa*, he does refer to it specifically in his critique, albeit in its reversed form. The translators of PsP Tib have relied on BP Tib or PP Tib for the citation (PsP Tib attests the *kyang* not found in Skt). Cp. MA VI.99ab: *gal te rgyu med kho nar skye bar lta zhig 'gyur na ni | de tshe mtha' dag rtag tu thams cad las kyang skye 'byung* ($MABh_{UN}$: *'gyur*) *zhing* | ($MABh_{ed}$ 206.3-4; $MABh_{tr}$ 1911: 259). According to Candrakīrti's commentary on MA VI.99ab, which constitutes his initial response to the *svabhāvavādin*, things such as the fruits of mango trees and breadfruit trees (Tib: *la ku rtsva* [$MABh_{UN}$: *tsa*]; Skt: **lakuca*, **lakaca*; *Artocarpus lacucha*) would always (**sadā*) be produced because they would no longer be dependent on a ripening process determinative of their appearance at a specific time. The eyes of the peacock's tail-feathers would appear on a crow, and a peacock would have parrot feathers all the time, even while still in the womb, i.e., in its egg (*mngal gyi gnas*) (MABh 206.12-19; Huntington's [1989: 250, n. 125] translation of the section has some problems). Buddhapālita's second reason, which is not cited here in the PsP but referred to via Bhāviveka's cited critique, is exemplified in MA VI.99cd: "And this world would not gather seeds and such by the hundreds with a view to the coming forth of a result" (*'bras 'byung ched du 'jig rten 'di yis sa bon la sogs ni | brgya phrag dag gi sgo nas sdud par byed par yang mi 'gyur*). Huntington (1989: 169) mistranslates the half-verse: "and hundreds of thousands of seeds sown by common people for the purpose of raising crops would result in no harvest whatsoever." Cp. also Padmakara 2002: 82, where *brgya phrag dag gi sgo nas* is related to worldly people's act of gathering of seeds and translated "in all their myriad ways."

statement (*vākyārtha*), then this ends up being asserted: "Things arise from a cause (*hetutaḥ*), 1) because a certain thing (*kasyacit*) arises from a certain thing (*kutaścit*) at a certain time (*kadācit*), and 2) because of the usefulness of undertakings (*ārambha-sāphalya*)." Therefore, that explanation [of Buddhapālita's] is not appropriate because of the fault stated earlier.[296]

§68. Thus others [= Candrakīrti and his party consider] this [criticism of Bhāviveka's] to be inappropriate because [its] refutation was stated previously.[297]

§69. And what has also been asserted [by Bhāviveka, namely, that *ahetutaḥ* can additionally be understood in the meaning of "bad cause"] for the sake of taking into account [opponents' positions which assume the cause of things to be] the Lord (*īśvara*), etc., is also

---

[296] Candrakīrti is citing from Bhāviveka's PP: *de la yang glags yod pa'i tshig*[1] *yin pa'i phyir gal te | bsgrub par bya ba dang | sgrub pa*[2] *bzlog* (P: *zlog*) *pa'i tshig gi don*[3] *mngon par 'dod na des*[4] *'di skad bstan par 'gyur te | dngos po rnams rgyu las skye bar 'gyur ba dang | lan 'ga' kha cig las kha cig skye bar 'gyur ba dang | rtsom pa 'bras bu dang bcas pa nyid du 'gyur ba'i phyir*[5] *de*[6] *ni mi rigs te | sngar smras pa'i skyon du 'gyur ba'i phyir ro ||* (D 53a5-7; P 64a5-7).
[1]PsP Tib: *thal bar 'gyur ba'i ngag* for *glags yod pa'i tshig*; [2]*sgrub par byed pa* for *grub pa*; [3]*bzlog pa gsal ba ngag gi don du* (following PsP Skt) for *bzlog pa'i tshig gi don*; [4]*de'i tshe*; [5]*phyir ro || zhes bstan par 'gyur na* (PP Tib places *bstan par 'gyur te* before the reversed probandum and probans); [6]*bshad pa de*.
Bhāviveka concludes the critique as he did his critique against Buddhapālita's consequence for arising from other, i.e., by referring back to his earlier criticism: *ji ste gzhan du na yang don 'brel pa med pa yin te | snga ma bzhin no*. Translated in Kajiyama 1963: 62 and Ames 1993: 234. The translators of PsP Tib, citing from PP Tib, as usual, replace *glags yod pa'i tshig* with *thal bar 'gyur ba'i ngag* and *sgrub pa* with *sgrub par byed pa* and make other minor adjustments. They adhere to PP Tib's format in listing the reversed *sādhya* and *sādhana* and connecting them with *dang*s. PPṬ Tib also follows the PP Tib format.
Bhāviveka refers to the fault he explained in regard to Buddhapālita's consequence refuting arising from other, namely, that the reversal of the *sādhya* and *sādhana* contradicts the earlier position that things do not arise; if the reversal is not accepted, the statement does not fall under either proof or refutation. See PPṬ D 154b7-155a7; P 178b1-179a2.

[297] Candrakīrti refers again to his refutation of Bhāviveka's critique of Buddha-pālita's consequence for arising from self.

not reasonable, because the Lord and so forth—depending on [the specific cause] maintained—are included in the positions of self, other, and both [self and other].[298]

§70. Therefore, this has been proven, [namely,] that there is no arising. And since arising is impossible, dependent-arising qualified by non-arising, etc., is established.

§71. In regard to this, [the Conservative Buddhist] states: If you determine that dependent-arising is in this way qualified by non-arising, etc., [i.e., in the sense that nothing arises,] then [as regards] that which has been stated by the Exalted One, [to wit,] —

> With ignorance as condition (*avidyāpratyaya*), the impulses (*saṃskāra*)[299] [come to be]; from the cessation (*nirodha*) of ignorance, the impulses cease;[300]

---

[298] Bhāviveka considers *ahetu* to have the alternative meaning of "bad cause" (**kuhetu*). In support of *ahetu* interpreted as *kuhetu*, he cites the example *abhāryā*, which, he states, besides meaning "not a wife," can also mean "bad wife": *yang na rgyu med ces* (P: omits *ces*) *bya ba ni rgyu ngan pa ste | chung ma med pa zhes bya ba la sogs pa bzhin no ||* (PP D 50b7; P 61a4); cf. AKBh ad AK III.29ab: *yathā tarhi kubhāryā abhāryety ucyate kuputraś cāputraḥ* ($AKBh_{ed}$ 141.8-9). Bhāviveka includes under "bad cause" intrinsic nature (**svabhāva*; *ngo bo nyid*), the Lord (**īśvara*; *dbang phyug*), spirit / Cosmic Man (**puruṣa*; *skyes bu*), primordial matter (**pradhāna*; *gtso bo*), time (**kāla*; *dus*), Nārāyaṇa, and so forth (*ādi*); see Ames 1993: 247, n. 146 for Avalokitavrata's identification of the members alluded to with "and so forth." Bhāviveka refutes these "bad causes" individually and at length; see PP D 51a1-52b6; P 61a6-63b5; Kajiyama 1963: 55-60; Ames 1993: 227-233; for his refutation of *īśvara*, see PP D 51a7-52b5; P61b7-62a7; MHK III.215-223. *LṬ: *ahetor īśvarādeḥ* (Yonezawa 2004: 123, 139 [fol. 2b1]).
Candrakīrti has asserted in his MABh that since those holding the positions of arising from / caused by *īśvara*, etc., would consider *īśvara* to be the same as, other than, or both the same as and other than the things that arise, they do not escape the faults associated with arising from self, other or both, and therefore there can be no fifth alternative for / conception of a productive cause: *gang dag dbang phyug la sogs pa dag las dngos po rnams skye bar mngon par 'dod pa de dag gi ltar na yang dbang phyug la sogs pa de dag bdag tu gyur pa'am | gzhan du gyur pa'am | gnyi gar gyur pa zhig tu 'gyur bas dbang phyug la sogs pa rgyur smra ba dag kyang bshad zin pa'i skyon las mi 'da' ste | de'i phyir skyed par byed pa'i rgyu'i rnam par rtog pa gzhan lnga pa yod pa ma yin no ||* ($MABh_{ed}$ 214.20-215.5).

similarly,

---

[299] As Schmithausen (2000d: 65-66) has observed, *saṃskāra* appears to have originally been closely connected in meaning with the wish and wishful imagining, and with the desire, indeed the firm resolve, for a specific sort of rebirth, and in this latter sense was seen to serve as the preliminary or preparatory act for the securing of consciousness (*vijñāna*) in the womb of one's future mother (see also Vetter 2000: 45f.). Certain descriptions of chains of dependent-arising in the Canon that were not expanded to include all 12 members reveal that the link *saṃskāra* in such chains had a meaning quite close to thirst (*tṛṣṇā*, *tanha*); thus as a functionally equivalent term, *saṃskāra* was used in place of *tṛṣṇā* as the second member of the twelve-linked chain of dependent arising (see Vetter 2000: 66; also Vetter 1988: 51). *cetanā*, intent (more appropriately translated, according to Vetter [2000: 30], as "decision") was on occasion used as a definition for *saṃskāra*; *saṃskāra* understood as intention brought the concept into the domain of *karma*, with the result that *karma* in fact became the general later interpretation of *saṃskāra* of the 12 links; see, e.g., AK III.21b: *saṃskārāḥ pūrvakarmaṇaḥ* and its commentary: *pūrvajanmany eva yā puṇyādikarmāvasthā seva* (read *saiva*) *saṃskārā[ḥ]*. Candrakīrti, following this interpretation as set forth by Nāgārjuna in MMK XXVI.1 (*punarbhavāya saṃskārān avidyānivṛtas tridhā | abhisaṃskurute yāṃs tair gatiṃ gacchati karmabhiḥ*), comments: *avidyayā nivṛtaḥ chāditaḥ pudgalaḥ punarbhavāya punarbhavārthaṃ punarbhavotpattyartham abhisaṃskaroti utpādayati* [*yān*] *kuśalādicetanāviśeṣāṃs te* [*punarbhavābhisaṃskārāt*] *saṃskārāḥ | te ca trividhāḥ kuśalā akuśalā ānejyāś ca | yadi vā kāyikā vācikā mānasāś ceti* (PsP_L 542.12-543.2). Cf. also $YṢV_{tr}$ 204, n. 347. I follow Vetter in translating *saṃskārāḥ* as "impulses"; see his enlightening discussion on *saṃskāra* and on *abhisaṃ(s)√kṛ* and its derivatives in Vetter 2000: 27-63. On *abhisaṃ(s)√kṛ* and its derivatives see also the important comments in Schmithausen 1987b: 156.

[300] The citation presented is the first of five *āgama* citations considered by the Conservative Buddhist to refute specific characterizations of dependent-arising as set forth in the MMK *maṅgala ślokas*. This first citation is intended as authoritative evidence against the characterization of dependent-arising as "without cessation" (*anirodha*). Only the first two links of 12-membered dependent-arising as they respectively appear in presentations of the formula describing coming into being (*samudaya*) and cessation (*nirodha*) are mentioned in the citation, the focus being on the fact that the Buddha stated that ignorance ceases. Cf. SN II.1.10-11: *Avijjāpaccayā bhikkhave saṅkhārā || saṅkārapaccayā viññānaṃ* ..., passim; SN II.9.5-6: *avijjānirodhā saṅkāranirodho* ..., passim. Bodhi (2000: 725, n. 1) notes that the SN-aṭṭha explains that *avijjapaccayā saṅkhārā* should be understood in the meaning *tasmā avijjāpaccayā saṅkhārā sambhavanti*.
See also $ŚSV_{ed}$ 245.1-8 ($ŚSV_{tr}$ 83, and n. 825) where the Mādhyamika is accused of distorting the original teaching of *pratītyasamutpāda*.

Impermanent, alas, are the constituent elements (*saṃskāra*)[301] which are subject to arising (*utpāda*) and perishing (*vyaya*),
For having arisen, they cease; their calming is happiness (*sukha*);[302]

likewise,[303]

---

301 On the word *saṅkhārā* used to indicate external objects, see Vetter 2000: 53-63. For instances in addition to the verse cited above where *saṅkhārā* appears to refer to the five *skandhas*, see ibid., 61f. As the context from which Candrakīrti has taken the verse is unknown, I have translated *saṃskārāḥ* here as referring to the five *skandhas* (see Vetter 2000: 62).

302 Udānavarga I.3: *anityā bata saṃskārā utpādavyayadharmiṇaḥ | utpadya hi nirudhyante teṣāṃ vyupaśamaḥ sukham* ||; see Bernhard 1965: 96. Candrakīrti places this Canonical citation in the mouth of the opponent representing the Buddhists of the Conservative schools primarily because it affirms arising (*utpāda*) and thus contradicts and sublates the MMK *maṅgala ślokas*' declaration that dependent-arising is "without arising" (*anutpāda*). The previous Canonical statement was cited for the sake of contradicting *anirodha* of the *maṅgala ślokas*, and the present statement secondarily addresses cessation with the words *vyaya* and the verb *nirudhyante*. Cp. DN II.157.8-9: *aniccā vata saṃkhārā uppādavayadhammino, uppajjitvā nirujjhanti, tesaṃ vūpasamo sukho' ti*; DN II.199.6-7; SN I.158; SN I.200 attests the variant reading *aniccā sabbe saṅkhārā*; AKBh_{ed} 80.15; other parallels in Bernhard 1965: 96; Pāsādika 1989: 40; Vetter 2000: 61, n. 127; see also Bodhi 2000: 348, n. 20 and Seyfort Ruegg 2002: 77, n. 107. The same verse is cited by Candrakīrti in the YṢV (once only the first quarter, later the entire verse); see YṢV_{ed} 27 and 60, references at YṢV_{tr} 123, n. 66.

303 PsP_{L} presents after the previous *anityā bata* statement (intended by the Conservative Buddhist as evidence contradicting the MMK *maṅgala ślokas*' characterization of dependent-arising as "without arising" [*anutpāda*]) and before the following *eko dharmaḥ* citation (intended as evidence contradicting the MMK *maṅgala śloka*'s characterization of dependent-arising as "without one thing" [*anekārtha*]) a further citation from *āgama*. This citation in PsP_{L} reads: *utpādād vā tathāgatānām anutpādād vā tathāgatānāṃ sthitaivaiṣā dharmāṇām dharmatā*; it can be translated "[Regardless of] whether the Tathāgatas arise or the Tathāgatas do not arise, this [real] nature (*dharmatā*) of things (*dharma*) definitely abides (*sthita*)." It was included in PsP_{L} because all three of the manuscripts used by de La Vallée Poussin (my L, M and N) attest the citation. The other paper manuscripts used for the present study as well as ms Q also attest the citation (ms Q's citation has *sthitiraiṣā* for *sthitaivaiṣā* and an additional *dharmmadhātus* as its last word), and PsP Tib presents the translation *de bzhin gshegs pa rnams byung yang rung | de bzhin gshegs pa rnams ma byung yang rung | chos rnams kyi chos nyid 'di ni gnas pa kho na ste*. The well-known citation was assumed by previous scholars to have been included by Candrakīrti for the sake of providing representative *āgama* evidence from the Con-

servative Buddhist side that contradicts the MMK *maṅgala ślokas*' assertion that dependent-arising is not eternal (*aśāśvata*). I do not include the citation in my edition because I am convinced that it is an accretion. Both manuscript and contextual evidence speak against its being intrinsic to the work. On the side of the manuscript evidence, ms P does not appear to have attested the citation. There is damage in P that starts with the final *m* of *sukham* of the *anityā bata* citation (the diplomatic reading for P is (*sukh*)*ạ*+) and continues on, such that P lacks approximately the next 10-11 *akṣaras*. When the text becomes readable again, the words *yaduta catvāra* ("namely, the four") appear (only the *ā* of *āhārāḥ* is visible); these are the final three words of the citation that is cited for the sake of contradicting dependent-arising characterized as "without one thing." There is thus only enough space in the damaged area for the words *tathā eko dharmaḥ sattvasthitaye*, i.e., for the introductory *tathā* and the words which precede *yaduta catvāra āhārāḥ*. Ms Q, as stated, does attest the citation, but it does not occur in Q's main text: the entire citation has instead been written in Q's lower margin. This citation in Q is followed (also in the lower margin) by a second citation, which appears to read *kāmābhāvaḥ paraṃ sukham* ("The non-existence / absence of desire is the highest happiness"). This latter citation is surely intended as authoritative proof from the Conservative side against the MMK *maṅgala ślokas*' assertion that dependent-arising is without annihilation (*anuccheda*). The appearance of the two citations in Q's margin caused me to wonder if perhaps mss P's and Q's exemplars had attested the two citations and both P's and Q's scribes had by chance committed exactly the same eyeskip, i.e., both had jumped from the final *sukham* of the *anityā bata* citation to the final *sukham* of the *kāmābhāvaḥ* citation—a rather unlikely scenario but certainly not impossible. If this had happened, Q's marginal material would indicate that Q's scribe (or his proofreader) noticed the mistake and added the two missing citations in the margin. The paper manuscripts, on the other hand, contain the *dharmatā* citation within their main text but lack the *kāmābhāvaḥ* citation, and it seems unusual that they too would have dropped an entire citation at this point; even an eyeskip from the *tathā* introducing the *kāmābhāvaḥ* citation to *tathā* introducing the *eko dharmaḥ* citation has to be excluded because the paper manuscripts all lack the expected *tathā* before the *eko dharmaḥ* citation. The fact that a postulation of three independent eyeskips, each of entire citations, seemed suspicious suggested that other avenues needed to be explored. There are of course a number of possible alternatives for transmission of text from ms β to mss ε and ζ and on to P, Q, and ms ι (and possibilities for its omission), but I will not detail them here because none are convincing and because they all pale in the light of further evidence and analysis. From the point of view of context, a main point to be noted is that even though Candrakīrti has the Conservative Buddhist present scriptural passages that refute the individual qualifiers of dependent-arising in the *maṅgala śloka*, the primary goal of the opponent is to establish that individual things exist, and that they come into and pass out of being; his aim is definitely not to convince the Mādhyamikas that anything exists eternally or that the annihilation of things is to be accepted. The Conservative Buddhists would in fact heartily agree that dependent-arising is non-eternal (*aśāśvata*) and without annihilation (*anuccheda*). Attention can be drawn to Bhāviveka's presentation in his PP of a group of Conservative Buddhists who argue that they accept all eight negations stated in the MMK's *maṅgala śloka* (of course according to their own interpretation of the negations) and who expressly state that they accept that dependent-arising is without annihilation and permanence because the result arises in dependence on a cause and because when the result arises, the cause ceases (cf. PP D 48a5-6; P 75a6-7; Ames 1993: 220). It is highly improbable that Candrakīrti had the intention, especially in the present context, to introduce as his interlocutor a group of Conservative Buddhists who would be so bold as to argue that dependent-arising, i.e., dependently arisen things, are characterized by eternality and annihilation. While it is certainly true that the *dharmatā* citation was employed in Canonical and Conservative circles, its point, when used in regard to dependent-arising by members of these circles, was that things arise in dependence on conditions; it is only the *fact* that they arise in this way—i.e., that it is their real nature (*dharmatā*) to arise in dependence on conditions whether or not a Buddha turns up to realize and then teach this truth—that endures. (For the Conservative schools that considered dependent-arising to be *asaṃskṛta*; see Bareau 1955: 285).

Finally, were the two citations in question to have been original, one expects that Candrakīrti would have arranged them so that they too would follow the order of the related words in the first *maṅgala śloka*: unlike all of the other manuscripts' Canonical statements for the present passage, Q's pair addressing *aśāśvata* and *anuccheda* are in the wrong order (the first *maṅgala śloka* reads *anirodham anutpādam anucchedam aśāśvatam*).

We have little choice but to conclude that Ms Q's, the paper manuscripts' and PsP Tib's citation is an accretion. It is easy to imagine that later scribes or readers of the PsP might have been puzzled by the fact that the content of the scriptural statements of the present PsP passage lines up with only six, and not all eight, of the famous negations in the first *maṅgala śloka*. At some point, one or more individuals must have decided to "repair" the text by introducing citations that would address *aśāśvata* and *anuccheda*. The addition of the first and second citations probably occurred at two separate times since the second citation was obviously not in the manuscript relied upon the copyist of ms ι (the closest common ancestor of the paper manuscripts) or in the manuscripts relied upon by the translators of PsP Tib. The paper manuscripts' and PsP Tib's lack of an introductory *tathā* before the *eko dharmaḥ* citation is also explained by the interpolation: the *tathā* before the *dharmatā* citation originally introduced the *eko dharmaḥ* citation, but when the *dharmatā* citation was inserted after this *tathā*, a following *tathā* was not, and this left the *dharmatā* citation and the two following citations (which can be seen as a pair) to be introduced by a single *tathā*.

The main text of ms Q, which does not attest either of the two citations, has to be accepted as correct, and its two marginal citations have to be seen as later extraneous additions. Ms P's text strongly supports this conclusion; the fact that it is missing 10-11 *akṣaras* at the critical point is hardly a hindrance, since the lack of (required) space speaks for itself. I hypothesize that Q received both of the citations from ms θ,

There is one factor (*eko dharmaḥ*) for the support of beings, namely, the four nutriments (*āhāra*);[304]

Two *dharmas* (*dve dharmau*) protect the world: shame (*hrī*) and embarrassment (*apatrāpya*);[305]

---

since they would have been in its main text had they been received from ms δ over ms η. The occurrence in the paper manuscripts of the first citation is due to ms ι having also received it from ms δ (see infra Manuscript Relationships, where I explain that ms ι has also received readings from ms δ, though far fewer than ms Q). PsP Tib's translation of the citation is explained by the fact that one of the manuscripts relied on by the PsP Tib translators carried the readings of a manuscript related to ms δ. The translators must have concluded, as they did in a number of other cases when they encountered one of ms δ's interpolated readings, that the citation was inherent to Candrakīrti's text and thus deserved to be included in their translation.
For textual references for the *utpādād vā tathāgatānām anutpādād vā tathāgatānāṃ sthitaivaiṣā dharmāṇām dharmatā* citation, see Appendix X.

[304] The citation as presented by Candrakīrti reads: *eko dharmaḥ sattvasthitaye yaduta catvāra āhārāḥ*. It is considered by the opponent to be Canonical evidence contradicting the MMK *maṅgala ślokas*' assertion that dependent-arising is "without one thing" (*anekārtham*). Cp. MN I.261.5-12: *Cattāro 'me bhikkhave āhārā bhūtānaṃ vā sattānaṃ ṭhitiyā sambhavesīnaṃ vā anuggahāya, katame cattāro: kabaḷiṃkāro āhāro oḷāriko vā sukhumo vā, phasso dutiyo, manosañcetanā tatiyā, viññāṇaṃ catutthaṃ. Ime ca bhikkhave cattāro āhārā kiṃnidānā kiṃsamudayā kiṃjātikā kiṃpabhavā: ime cattāro āhārā taṇhānidānā taṇhāsamudayā taṇhājātikā taṇhāpabhavā. Taṇhā cāyaṃ bhikkhave kiṃnidānā ... : taṇhā vedanānidānā ...* . Ñāṇamoli and Bodhi (cf. MN_{tr} 353) translate: "Bhikkhus, there are these four kinds of nutriment for the maintenance of beings that already have come to be and for the support of those seeking a new existence. What four? They are: physical food as nutriment, gross or subtle; contact as the second; mental volition as the third; and consciousness as the fourth. Now, bhikkhus, these four kinds of nutriment ... have craving as their source, craving as their origin; they are born and produced from craving. And this craving has what as its source ...? Craving has feeling as its source ..." (and so on down to ignorance). See also SN II.11-13, 98-104; MN_{tr} 1185, n. 120 and SN_{tr} 731, n. 18 and 19. Cp. $AKBh_{ed}$ 153.8-9: *catvāra ime āhārā bhūtānāṃ sattvānāṃ sthitaye yāpanāyai saṃbhavaiṣiṇāṃ cānugrahāyeti* (see Pāsādika 1989: 66). See the discussion focussed on the four nutriments at AKBh ad AK III.38d-41 ($AKBh_{ed}$ 152.8-154.26). Further references at PsP_L 40, n. 3.

[305] The quotation cited, namely, *dvau dharmau lokaṃ pālayato hrīś cāpatrāpyaṃ ca*, in the view of the opponent, contradicts the *maṅgala* verses' declaration that dependent-arising is "without separate things" (*anānārtham*), i.e., without diverse things. Cf. AN I.51.19-21: *dve 'me bhikkhave sukkā dhammā lokaṃ pālenti. Katame*

and,

> Coming (*āgamana*) here from the other world, and going (*gamana*) to the other world from this world[306]

—how is that dependent-arising qualified by cessation and so forth which the Exalted One[307] taught in this [above] way not contradicted?

[It is] of course (*hi*) precisely because cessation and so forth are perceived for dependent-arising [by your party and others] that the Master [Nāgārjuna], for the sake of teaching the distinction (*vibhāga*) between [*sūtra*s] with provisional meaning and *sūtra*s with definitive meaning (*neyanītārthasūtrānta*),[308] composed this Madhyamakaśāstra.

---

dve? Hiri ca ottappañ ca. Cf. also AN I.83, 95; Iti 36; AK II.32; further references at PsP_L 40, n. 4.

[306] The statement brought forth by the opponent, namely, *paralokād ihāgamanam ihalokāc ca paralokagamanam*, is considered to confute the *maṅgala śloka*s' declaration that dependent-arising is without coming or going (*anāgamam anirgamam*). Cf. $YṢV_{ed}$ 26.9-10: *'jig rten pha rol nas 'dir 'ongs pa dang | 'jig rten 'di nas 'jig rten pha rol tu 'gro bar bstan pa ...* . An equivalent passage does not occur in the Pāli Canon; the citation may belong to the Canon of another school or be drawn from a *muktaka-sūtra*; Candrakīrti could alternatively be paraphrasing or summarizing a scriptural statement; cp. Udānavarga 3.12: ... *saṃsāre tv āgatiṃ gatim* (parallels in Pāli Tripiṭaka Concordance under *āgati*).

[307] The group of citations is introduced in the Sanskrit by *yat tarhi bhagavatoktam* but in the Tibetan only by equivalents for *tarhi* and *bhagavatā*. The Sanskrit's *yat ... sa* construction is anacoluthic, in this case with a transition from a neuter to masculine subject (on *yat tarhi* and *yadā tarhi* in elliptical usage, see Schmithausen 1987a: 570, n. 1492). The PsP Tib translators may have revised the sentence because they were disturbed by the change of subject. They present a relative–co-relative construction that refers to *pratītyasamutpāda* (*'o na bcom ldan 'das kyis* [citations] *zhes de ltar rten cing 'brel par 'byung ba 'gag pa la sogs pas khyad par du byas pa bstan pa gang yin pa de ji ltar 'gal bar mi 'gyur zhe na*); the pronoun *gang*, the relative for the demonstrative *de* (= *sa*), lacks a Skt equivalent. The translators' re-structuring resulted in *bhagavatā* of the question after the citations not being translated, because *bhagavatā* before the citations serves as the instrumental agent for the (nominalized) verb *bstan*.

[308] According to the Mādhyamikas, all *sūtra*s but those which teach emptiness, non-arising, etc., fall into the category of *sūtra*s with provisional meaning, that is, *sūtra*s whose assertions require further interpretation and explanation. The *sūtra*s with provisional meaning are of value inasmuch as they serve the more propaedeutic

In this regard, these [i.e.], the arising and so forth asserted for dependent-arising [in the above Canonical statements, have] not [been asserted] with reference to a [purported] own-being of the object (*viṣaya*) of uncontaminated gnosis (*anāsravajñāna*)[309] of those [persons] whose *timira* of ignorance has vanished. Rather, [they are

---

purpose of gradually introducing to the path those whose minds are not yet ready to comprehend the teaching of emptiness (see also the following Akṣayamatisūtra quotation). Cf. YṢV where Candrakīrti compares the situation to that in the world where certain things, even though they may be true, are not taught if they are not necessary, and certain other things, although false, if considered necessary, are taught (*'jig rten na bden yang mi dgos na ni kha cig mi bstan to ǁ brdzun yang dgos pa yod na ni la la bstan dgos te*); because there exists a need for a means of entry to the ultimate (*don dam pa la 'jug pa'i thabs*; **paramārthāvatāropāya*), the *skandha*s and *dhātu*s are taught in the beginning, but true reality (*de kho na*; *tattva*), emptiness, etc., are not because it would be pointless (see YṢV$_{ed}$ 70.1-15; YṢV$_{tr}$ 235f.). In the CŚṬ Candrakīrti quotes Pañcatantra I.389 in support of the idea that only persons fit to be vessels of the teaching of selflessness are to be instructed in it: "For fools, teaching [leads] to anger, not calm. For snakes, the drinking of milk only increases their venom" (*upadeśo hi mūrkhāṇāṃ prakopāya na śāntaye | payaḥpānaṃ bhujaṅgāṇāṃ kevalaṃ viṣavardhanam*; see CŚṬ$_{ed}$ 265.5-8 and 410). See also PsP$_{L}$ 276.1-3 where Candrakīrti asserts that doctrines such as the *vijñānavāda*, like the *pudgalavāda* of the Sāṃmitīyas, were taught by the Exalted One out of great compassion because they are a means of attaining the ultimate view (*paramārthadarśanopayabhūtatvāt*; the section is translated in Schayer 1931: 77). Interesting is the extended discussion with the Yogācāra school at MABh$_{ed}$ 181.11-202.4, in which Candrakīrti demotes the *sūtra*s considered by it to be definitive to the status of *sutra*s with provisional meaning. Cf. MA VI.97: *evaṃ jñātvā prakriyām āgamasya vyākhyātārthaṃ yac ca neyārtham uktam | sūtraṃ buddhvā nīyatāṃ yan na tattvaṃ nītārthaṃ ca jñāyatāṃ śūnyatārtham* ǁ (Li 2012: 14); *de ltar lung gi lo rgyus shes byas te* ǁ *mdo gang de nyid ma yin bshad don can* ǁ *drang don gsungs pa'ang rtogs nas drang bya zhing* ǁ *stong nyid don can nges don shes par gyis* ǁ (MABh$_{ed}$ 199.13-16; MABh$_{tr}$ 1911: 253) Huntington's (1989: 168) translation of the first *pāda* as "One must therefore proceed according to these guidelines when interpreting doctrinal passages ..." is very free. Cf. also the commentary: *mdo sde gang dag skye ba med pa la sogs pas khyad par du byas pa'i rten cing 'brel par 'byung ba dngos su gsal bar byed pa ma yin pa de dag ni ji ltar rang bzhin med pa la 'jug pa'i rgyur 'gyur ba de ltar bshad par bya ste* | (MABh$_{ed}$ 199.17-20; MABh$_{tr}$ 1911: 253f.). On *neyārtha* and *nītārtha*, see, e.g., May 1959: 298, n. 1089 (ref.); YṢV$_{tr}$ 235, n. 449; Erb 1997: 200, n. 965; PsP$_{L}$ 597 (addition to 41, n. 1); see also Seyfort Ruegg 1985.

309 Stcherbatsky's (1927: 125, n. 1) suggestion for the emendation of the text from *anāsrava* to *āsrava* is based on de La Vallée Poussin's corrupt text and is thus inadmissible.

stated] with reference to the object of cognition of those [beings] whose mind's eye is impaired by the *timira* of ignorance.

§72. In reliance on [his] vision of reality (*tattva*),[310] the Exalted One has, on the other hand, said:

> For this, O monks, is the ultimate truth, namely, *nirvāṇa*, which does not have a deceiving nature (*amoṣadharma*); all conditioned things (*saṃskāra*),[311] however, are false (*mṛṣā*), of a deceiving nature.[312]

---

[310] Candrakīrti provides a grammatical gloss of *tattva* in his commentary on YṢ 30 (YṢ 30: *sarvam astīti vaktavyam ādau tattvagaveṣiṇaḥ* ‖ *paścād avagatārthasya niḥsaṅgasya viviktatā*): *de'i dngos po ni de nyid do* ‖ *brjod par 'dod pa'i don spyi'i dngos po dang 'brel pa can de'i zhes bya ba 'di dang sbyar ro* ‖ *dngos po ni rang gi ngo bo ste* | *gang gi rang gi ngo bo gang yin pa de ni de'i dngos po ste* | *de kho na'o* ‖ *rang gi ngo bo'o* ‖ *ngo bo nyid do* ‖ *de bzhin nyid do* ‖ *gzhan ma yin pa nyid do* ‖ *zhes bya ba'i tha tshig go* ‖ (YṢV$_{ed}$ 71.3-5). The newly found folio of the YṢ (transcribed in Ye 2013) starts shortly after this. Scherrer-Schaub reconstructs: *tasya bhāvas tattvam* ‖ *vivakṣitārthaḥ sāmānya-bhāva-saṃbandhī 'tasya' ity anena saṃbadhyate* ‖ *bhāvo hi svarūpaṃ* | *yad yasya svarūpaṃ tad dhi tasya bhāvaḥ* | *tattvam* (see YṢV$_{tr}$ 237 and n. 457). Cf. PsP$_L$ 373.6-7: *evam aparapratyayaṃ bhāvānāṃ yat svarūpaṃ tat tattvam*. See also La Vallée Poussin 1933: 38-47.

[311] On *saṅkhārā* used in the sense of "conditioned things/factors," see Vetter 2000: 62f. Candrakīrti's commentary on MMK XIII.1 indicates that he understands *saṃskārāḥ* of the *kārikā* and of the citation as equivalent to *sarvadharmāḥ/sarvabhāvāḥ*.

[312] Cp. MN III.245.16-21: *Taṃ hi bhikkhu musā yaṃ mosadhammaṃ taṃ saccaṃ yaṃ amosadhammaṃ nibbānaṃ ... . Etaṃ hi bhikkhu paramaṃ ariyasaccaṃ yad idam amosadhammaṃ nibbānaṃ*. Bodhi (MN$_{tr}$ 1093) translates: "For that is false, bhikkhu, which has a deceptive nature, and that is true which has an undeceptive nature – Nibbāna". The Canonical statement cited here in the PsP is quoted again in Candrakīrti's commentary on MMK XIII.1: *etad dhi khalu*[1] *bhikṣavaḥ paramaṃ satyaṃ yad idam*[2] *amoṣadharmaṃ*[3] *nirvāṇaṃ sarvasaṃskārāś ca mṛṣā moṣadharmāṇaḥ* (PsP$_L$ 237.11-12); [1]the PsP chapter one citation lacks *khalu*; [2]the PsP chapter one citation presents *yaduta* for *yad idam*; [3]emended from *amoṣadharma* following mss P, B and D. MMK XIII.1 is explained by Candrakīrti as being a reformulation of the Canonical statement (MMK XIII.1: *tan mṛṣā moṣadharmaṃ*[1] *yad bhagavān ity abhāsata* | *sarve ca moṣadharmāṇaḥ saṃskārās tena te mṛṣā* ‖; [1]on the emendation *moṣadharmaṃ*, see n. 325. MMK XIII.1 will be cited in §73). On *moṣadharma(ka)*, see n. 314. Versions of the Canonical statement quoted by Candrakīrti appear six times in the YṢV; cf. YṢV$_{ed}$ 27.16-18 where the single full YṢV citation reads *dge slong dag 'di lta ste* | *mi bslu ba'i chos can mya ngan las 'das pa 'di ni bden pa'i mchog gcig pu'o* ‖ *'du byed thams cad ni brdzun pa bslu ba'i chos can no* (PsP Tib for the

Similarly,

> There is no truth (*tathatā*) or inerrancy (*avitathatā*) here;[313] this has a deceptive nature (*moṣadharmaka*)[314] and is as well subject

---

statement in both chapter 1 and 13 differs). Scherrer-Schaub translates, "Mendiants, ceci est la meilleure, l'unique vérité: à savoir, ce qui a pour nature de ne pas tromper: l'extinction. Mais tous les *saṃskāra* sont faux et de nature trompeuse" ($YṢV_{tr}$ 122). See $YṢV_{tr}$ 122, n. 65 for further references. Candrakīrti quotes the statement in full in MABh (see $MABh_{ed}$ 119.17-19) and alludes to the same citation or cites a similar one in CŚṬ: *ata eva tan mṛṣāmoṣadharmakaṃ yad etat saṃskṛtaṃ ity uvāca śāstā* ($CŚṬ_{ed}$ 164.8-9). De La Vallée Poussin (PsP_L 41, n. 2) refers to the statement as cited in BCAP ad BCA IX.2 (see BCAP 363.1-2 and note 1). Cp. Sn 147-148 (vv. 757-758).

[313] The present context's reference to there not being *tathatā* here, i.e., in regard to dependently arisen things, intends to advert to the fact that things are not truly as they appear to be; their actual nature is otherwise. The *tathatā* and *avitathatā* of dependent-arising are mentioned in the Pāli Canon (and thus assumed by the Conservative Buddhist); cf. SN II.25.24-26.6: *Jātipaccayā bhikkhave jarāmaraṇam ... avijjāpaccayā bhikkhave saṅkhārā uppādā vā tathāgatānaṃ anuppādā vā tathāgatānaṃ* || *ṭhita vā sā dhātu ... idappaccayatā .... Avijjāpaccayā bhikkhave saṅkhārā* || *Iti kho bhikkhave yā tatra tathatā avitathatā anaññathatā idappaccayatā* || *ayaṃ vuccati bhikkhave paṭiccasamuppādo* ||; Schmithausen (1969: 105, n. 46) translates: "Die hier [vorliegende] Wahrheit, Nichtunwahrheit, Nichtandersheit (d.h. die sich immer bewahrheitende, niemals unzutreffende, unabänderliche Regel), [sc.] die Tatsache, dass [etwas gerade] dies zu seiner Ursache hat: das nennt man das 'Entstehen in Abhängigkeit.'" De La Vallée Poussin (La Vallée Poussin 1929: 743) comments: "Le sense est probablement celui indiqué par Buddhaghosa, Visuddhi, p. 518: 'le Pratītyasamupāda est nommé *tathatā* parce qu'il y a production de tel et tel Dharma en raison de telles et telles causes déterminées; *avitathatā*, parce que la production ne manque jamais quand les causes sont présentes; *anaññathatā*, parce qu'un Dharma ne naît des causes d'un autre Dharma.'" Cf. Bodhi 2000: 742, n. 54.
In other instances, Candrakīrti employs the word *tathatā* to describe the ultimate nature of things; the *tathatā* of things refers to the fact of their being without own nature. Asked in his commentary on MMK XV.2 whether a real, independent own nature of things exists, Candrakīrti replies that it neither exists nor does not exist by own nature, but that for the sake of soothing the fear of hearers, it is said that one—it having been superimposed from the point of view of surface truth—exists. PsP_L 264.11-265.2: *yā sā dharmāṇāṃ dharmatā nāma saiva tatsvarūpam* | *atha keyaṃ dharmāṇāṃ dharmatā* | *dharmāṇāṃ svabhāvaḥ* | *ko 'yaṃ svabhāvaḥ* | *prakṛtiḥ* | *kā ceyaṃ prakṛtiḥ* | *yeyaṃ śūnyatā* | *naiḥsvābhāvyam* | *kim idaṃ naiḥsvābhāvyam* | *tathatā* | *keyaṃ tathatā* | *tathābhāvo 'vikāritvaṃ sadaiva sthāyitā* | *sarvadānutpāda eva hy agnyādīnāṃ paranirapekṣatvād akṛtrimatvāt svabhāva ity ucyate*. See the excursuses on *tathatā* in La Vallée Poussin 1929: 743ff. and $YṢV_{tr}$ 213-215 (= n. 378). On *tathatā* described in a positive sense, see Schmithausen 1976: 260 and references. On *dharmatā* (as a synonym for *dharmadhātu*), see Schmithausen 1969: 145f.

to ruin (*pralopa*);[315] this is also false (*mṛṣā*); an illusion (*māyā*) is this, a deceiver of fools (*bālalāpinī*).[316]

Likewise,

Bodily material (*rūpa*) is like a clump of foam, feeling (*vedanā*) similar to a bubble,

---

According to de La Vallée Poussin, the citation should also appear in Candrakīrti's commentary on MMK XIII.1. He inserts *nāsty atra tathatā vā avitathatā vā* (PsP_L 237.12-238.1) in square brackets before the citation *moṣadharmakam apy etat | pralopadharmakam apy etat*, but notes that his insertion does not appear in his manuscripts or in PsP Tib (PsP_L 238, n. 1). Vaidya (1960b: 104 and n. 1) misinterprets de La Vallée Poussin's n. 1 as referring only to the *vā* after *tathatā*, and incorporates the inserted material into his text (without brackets), noting that de La Vallée Poussin has "*tathatā vā* for *tathatā* against Mss. and T." Neither ms P nor the paper manuscripts attest de La Vallée Poussin's inserted material (I do not have access to Q's reading). Galloway (2001: 325 and n. 16) removes the inserted material.

[314] Candrakīrti tends to understand *moṣadharma(ka)* as if it would be derived from √*muṣ* and thus in the sense of "having a deceptive nature" (cf. PsP_L 238.4 where he equates *moṣadharmaka* with *visaṃvādaka*). It would, however, seem that its meaning "liable to decay" "destined to vanish" (possibly intended by the original statement) would also, given its placement, fit even here in the PsP, especially because the deceptive nature of things is brought out by the words after *pralopadharmaka*, namely, *mṛṣā*, *māyā* and *bālalāpinī*.
Pāli *mosa* (of *mosadhamma*) is formed from Pāli *musā* (*musā* = Skt *mṛṣā*, from √*mṛṣ* "to neglect" [von Hinüber 2001: § 122 notes that *mṛṣā* cannot be derived from √*muṣ*]; cf. PTSD s.v. *mosa*; BHSD s.v. *moṣa*). One expects a semantic difference between *mosa*/*moṣa* and *musā*/*mṛṣā* since the derivation of the former from the latter would otherwise be tautological. Oberlies (1995: 133) notes *mosadharma* in the sense "liable to decay or loss" (with reference to Johnson's Saundarananda, where *moṣadharma* is translated as "subject to loss"); see also MN-aṭṭha IV: 56 ad MN II 261: *mosadhammā ti nassanasabhāvā* and Oberlies 2001: § 12 (16). One notes that *mṛṣā* can mean "in vain" "to no purpose" as well as "falsely."

[315] *moṣadharmakam apy etat | pralopadharmakamam apy etat* is cited again at PsP_L 238.1. De La Vallée Poussin adverts to SN IV.205.4-6: *Etaṃ dukkhan ti ñatvāna | mosadhammam palokinaṃ | Phussaphussavayam* (read, following $SN_{Nāl}$ *Phussa phussa vayam*) *passaṃ | evaṃ tatha virajjatīti* (PsP_L 598 to 41, n. 5; on the verse, see also SN_{tr} 1432, n. 228).

[316] Cf. BHSD s.v. *ullāpana* (2): "deceitful, deceptive"; on *bālalāpinī* and its various spellings, see Deleanu 2006: I, 321, n. 53. Cf. SN III.143.6-7: *Etādisāyaṃ santāno || māyāyam bālalāpinī || vadhako eso akkhāto || sāro ettha na vijjati ||*. SN-aṭṭha glosses: *ayaṃ bālamahājanaṃ lapāpanika-māyā nāma*. Bodhi (2000: 953) translates *bālalāpinī* as "beguiler of fools."

Ideation (*sañjñā*) is like a mirage, the impulses (*saṃskāra*) similar to a plantain trunk,
[Primary] awareness (*vijñāna*) is like a magical illusion; [so] has [it] been explained by the Kinsman of the Sun (*ādityabandhu*).[317]

Observing factors (*dharma*) thus, the monk with energy aroused,
Whether by day or in the night, aware (*samprajāna*) [and] mindful (*pratismṛta*),
Would reach the peaceful place (*padaṃ śāntam*), the calming of the constituent elements[318] (*saṃskāropaśama*), [ultimate] welfare (*śiva*),
And [the understanding] that all dharmas are without self (*nirātman*).[319]

---

[317] Cp. SN III.142.29-31: *pheṇapiṇḍūpamam rūpaṃ* ‖ *vedanā bubbuḷupamā* ‖ *marīci-kūpamā saññā* | *saṅkhārā kadalūpamā* ‖ *māyūpamañ ca viññāṇaṃ* ‖ *dīpitādicca-bandhunā* ‖.
Cited again at PsP_L 549.2-4; also found at $MABh_{ed}$ 22.3-5 and in CŚṬ (D 61b7-62a1): *gzugs ni dbu ba rdos pa 'dra* ‖ *tshor ba chu yi chu bur bzhin* ‖ *'du shes smig rgyu lta bu ste* ‖ *'du byed rnams ni chu shing bzhin* ‖ *rnam par śes pa sgyu ma ltar* ‖ *nyi ma'i gnyen gyis bka' stsal to* (cp. PsP Tib). Cp. $MABh_{ed}$ 165.9-12: *rnam shes sgyu ma dang mtshungs par* ‖ *nyi ma'i gnyen gyis gsungs pa yin* ‖ *de yi dmigs pa'ang de bzhin te* ‖ *nges par sgyur ma'i dngos dang 'dra* ‖.
Cited also in the PSP (see Lindtner 1979: 117.26-28), which has been ascribed by Lindtner (ibid., 91-92) to the author of the PsP but is more probably a composition by Candrakīrtipāda (eighth c.); the *prajñā* section, however, in which the verses are cited, may have been authored by Candrakīrti the author of the PsP. Of the four verses from the SN cited in the PSP, this specific verse, the initial one of seven in the SN, appears as the third. This verse is also found in the TJ: *gzugs ni dbu ba rdos pa 'dra* ‖ *tshor ba chu bur dag dang mtshungs* ‖ *'du shes smig rgyu 'dra ba ste* ‖ *'du byed rnams ni chu shing bzhin* ‖ *rnam shes sgyu ma lta bu zhes* ‖ *de nyid gzigs pas bka' stsal to* (P 77b2-3) and the Madhyamakaratnapradīpa: *gzugs ni dbu ba rdos pa 'dra* ‖ *tshor ba chu yi chu bur 'dra* ‖ *'du shes smig rgyu 'dra ba ste* ‖ *'du byed rnams ni chu shing bzhin* ‖ *rnam par shes pa sgyu ma ltar* ‖ *nyi ma'i gnyen gyis gsungs pa yin* (P 335b1-2). See also May 1959: 257, n. 924; Lamotte 1966: 358, n. 1 and 370, n. 2; PsP_L 41, n. 9. The Sanskrit is also cited in the Paramārtha-gāthā; see Wayman 1961: 170 (v. 17-18); my thanks to Yoshiaki Niisaku for this reference.
Ādityabandhu/Ādiccabandhu is frequently used as an epithet of the Buddha. According to Malalasekera (1974: 245 [see his other references]), the Vimanavatthu Commentary states that like the Buddha, Ādicca, the sun, belonged to the Gotamagotta.

[318] Given that *dharma*s, not the *skandha*s as in the Pāli version of the verse, are the monk's object of observation in this Sanskrit verse, it is possible that Candrakīrti understands *saṃskārāḥ* here in the sense of "the conditioned."

[319] Cp. SN III.143.8-9: *evaṃ khande avekkheyya* ‖ *bhikkhu āraddhavīriyo* ‖ *divāvāya divārattiṃ* (read: *divā vā yadi vā rattiṃ*) ‖ *sampajāno paṭissato* ‖. The three *pāda*s *pratividhyet padaṃ śāntaṃ saṃskāropaśamaṃ śivam* | *nirātmatvaṃ ca dharmāṇām* ‖ do not appear in Pāli. I have tentatively appended as the present verse's final *pāda* the emendation *nirātmatvaṃ ca dharmāṇām* (P and Q read *iti* | [Q: ‖] *nirātmatvāc ca dharmāṇām* while the paper manuscripts read *iti nirātmakatvāc ca dharmāṇām*). P and Q's *nirātmatvāc ca dharmāṇām* forms a *pathyā pāda*, but as a separate citation intended to support Candrakīrti's viewpoint it is quite strange: the ablative has been torn out of context, and the *ca* does not connect to anything. Also unusual is the lack of a *tathā* introducing it: Candrakīrti usually introduces citations from new sources with the word *tathā*, and there is not a *tathā* in any of the manuscripts before *nirātma(ka)tvāc ca dharmāṇām*. PsP Tib, as de La Vallée Poussin has noted, presents the verse in prose: *de bzhin du* | *dge slong brtson 'grus brtsams pa dran pa dang shes bzhin dang ldan pa nyin dang mtshan du chos la so sor rtog par byed pa na* ‖ *'du byed thams cad ni nye bar zhi ba'i go 'phang zhi ba* | *chos rnams bdag med pa nyid rtogs par 'gyur ro* ‖. It appears to be based on the reading *nirātmatvaṃ ca dharmāṇām* (= my emendation for the Skt) and includes this within the scope of the verb *pratividhyet*, i.e., as part of the verse (cf. BHSD s.v. *pratividhyati* "*penetrates*... reaches, *attains* (a place) ... usually fig., *penetrates* intellectually, *understands*"). Lambert Schmithausen informs me that the Chinese version of the *sūtra* (T vol 2: 69a22) contains a reference to *nairātmya* in its translation of the verse corresponding to the second verse in the Pāli version (*rittakaṃ tucchakaṃ* ...); it adds to the verse the Chinese characters for "There is no self (**ātman*) or anything belonging to a self (**ātmīya*)." This addition of course by no means proves that Candrakīrti's source-verse for the present PsP citation contained the line I append to it, or even that Candrakīrti had access to a version of the second Pāli verse like the one on which the Chinese is based, but it does suggest that the conjecture may have some basis. Certainly from the point of view of context the appended *pāda* transforms the verse into much stronger scriptural support for the Mādhyamika viewpoint: with it, not only is the goal of the reflecting monk, i.e., the "peaceful place," which is characterized as the "calming of the constituent elements," a main subject, but the *content* of the monk's realization, the intellectual understanding that serves as the *means* for his attainment of the "peaceful place," namely, the insight into the selflessness of *dharma*s, is brought to the stage and spotlighted. The *dharma*s of the final *pāda*, which are realized to be without self, are no other than the *dharma*s of the first *pāda*. It is possible that PsP Tib was copied in from another Tibetan translation of the verse, i.e., was not translated directly from PsP Skt, but this fact does not seem to detract from the arguments that support the inclusion of the final *pāda* as part of the verse, and may even provide them with further support.

The PSP, interestingly, presents the verse with two different *pāda*s attached to it: *de ltar phung po la rtog pas* ‖ *nyin mo dang ni mtshan rnams su* ‖ *brtson 'grus brtsams pa'i dge slong gis* ‖ *shes bzhin so sor dran pa yis* ‖ *'du byed nyer zhi zhi ba yi* ‖ *zhi ba'i go 'phang rab tu 'thob* ‖ *bde ba bla med dang ldan pa'i* ‖ *mya ngan 'das pa 'gro bar 'gyur* ‖ (see Lindtner 1979: 117.29-32). The first four *pāda*s, given as verse six in

§73. [It was] for both [types of] trainees (*vineyajana*), [that is, on the one hand, the trainee] who, inasmuch as [he] is unacquainted (*anabhijña*) with the intent of the teachings, would in this way be uncertain (*sandeha*) [and ask himself:] "Which here then is the teaching with the meaning of true reality (*tattva*) [and] which [one] can it be that is intentional (*ābhiprāyika*)?",[320] and also [on the other hand, the trainee] who, being of weak intellect, understands a teaching with provisional meaning as having definitive meaning, that the Master [Nāgārjuna], for the sake of clearing away [their respective] doubt (*saṃśaya*) and wrong understanding (*mithyājñāna*)

---

the Pāli group, are presented in the PSP as the fourth verse. The verse is quoted by Candrakīrti at CŚṬ P 62a1-2 (again with *chos rnams* instead of *phung po*, but without the final emended *pāda* of the present text or the final two of the PSP): *de ltar chos rnams rtog pa yi* ‖ *dge slong brtson 'grus brtsams ldan zhing* ‖ *nyin nam gal te mtshan mo'ang rung* ‖ *shes bzhin so sor dran ldan pa* ‖ *'du byed nyer zhi zhi ba yi* ‖ *go 'phang zhi ba rtogs par 'gyur* ‖. The Sanskrit is cited again at PsP_L 549.5-7 (PsP Skt and Tib again with *dharmān/chos* in place of Pāli *khande*; cf. also May 1959: 257, n. 925). De La Vallée Poussin states that "le pāda *evaṃ dharmān vīkṣamāṇo* est très incorrect" but the quarter is in fact in *ra-vipulā*. I doubt that the Sanskrit on which PsP Tib is based differed as drastically as de La Vallée Poussin's reconstruction of the Sanskrit would have it (see PsP_L 41, n. 10), and think rather that *vīkṣamāṇo* was translated as *so sor rtog par byed pa na* (possibly to stress the meaning "respectively" of the prefix *vi*), and *pratividhyet* as *rtogs par 'gyur*, a translation equivalent that occurs not infrequently for *prati√vidh*. The positioning of *zhi ba* suggests that *śivaṃ* was indeed in the Sanskrit (de La Vallée Poussin assumes it to be a translation for *śāntaṃ* and that *śivaṃ* was lacking). The *thams cad* for which an equivalent Skt *sarva* is missing could be evidence that the entire PsP Tib verse was copied from another Tibetan translation of the verse (which had mistranslated the fifth and sixth *pāda*s or was based on Sanskrit that attested a slightly different fifth and sixth *pāda*) or, alternatively, could indicate that *śāntaṃ* in at least one of the PsP Tib exemplars had suffered damage or had been misread by an earlier scribe: *śa* and *sa* can be misread for each other in Śārada and other north Indian scripts of the eleventh and twelfth centuries, the *akṣara nta* may have appeared as *vva*, and the final *anusvāra* may have been interpreted as superscript *r*, all of which together may have led to a discounting of the *ā* in *śā/sā*. The change of the final *pāda* to an independent citation could have been caused by a number of factors, such as the reading or interpretation of °*tvañ ca* as °*tvāñ ca* and/or familiarity with the verse, only without the final seventh *pāda*. Once separated from the verse, an *iti* was added to close the verse but, as stated, a *tathā* to introduce the new "citation" was not.

320 For references, cf. Seyfort Ruegg 2002: 80, n. 116.

by way of reasoning (*yukti*) and authoritative testimony (*āgama*),[321] undertook this [treatise].[322] Among these, reasoning is indicated by statements such as, "Not from self" (*na svataḥ*).[323] Authoritative testimony is indicated by way of statements such as,

> The Exalted One has declared that that which has a deceiving nature (*moṣadharma*) is false (*mṛṣā*),[324]
> and all conditioned things (*saṃskāra*) have a deceiving nature; therefore, they are false.[325]

---

[321] On the term *yukti*, see Scherrer-Schaub 1981, and 1991: xi-xiii. For a discussion of *āgama* from the point of view of the epistemological school and as commented on in the CŚ, see Tillemans 1990: I, 23-35.

[322] Scherrer-Schaub (1991: xii-xiii) integrates a paraphrase of this sentence into her discussion of *yukti* in the Avant-Propos to her edition and translation of the YṢV: "Le recours au raisonnement et à l'Ecriture (*yuktyāgamābhyām*) a pour but d'écarter le doute et la connaissance fausse de ceux qui en proie à l'incertitude ne reconnaissent pas l'intention de l'enseignement du Bouddha et se demandent si tel enseignement se réfère au sens vrai (*tattvārtha*) ou bien s'il a été dit avec une intention; et pour ces êtres niais qui comprennent comme de sens déterminé un enseignement qui est à interpréter." One might merely note that "connaissance fausse" is a characteristic only of the second sort of trainee. A large part of the paragraph is freely translated in Thurman 1991: 258.

[323] Candrakīrti is referring to MMK I.1.

[324] PsP Tib for MMK XIII.1ab, both here in chapter one and in chapter thirteen, presents *bcom ldan 'das kyis chos gang zhig* ‖ *slu ba de ni brdzun zhes gsungs* ‖, with *slu ba* (*moṣa*) not compounded with *chos* (*dharma*), but rather used predicatively. It is compounded with *chos* in the third *pāda*: *'du byed thams cad slu ba'i chos*. The *kārikā* has been copied in from Jñānagarbha and Klu'i rgyal mtshan's translation but Pa tshab has slightly revised *pāda*s a and b; ABh, BP, and PP read *chos gang slu ba de brdzun zhes* ‖ *bcom ldan 'das kyis de skad gsungs* ‖ (for variants, see Ye 2011a: 210).

[325] Candrakīrti is citing MMK XIII.1: *tan mṛṣā moṣadharmaṃ yad bhagavān ity abhāṣata* | *sarve ca moṣadharmāṇaḥ saṃskārās tena te mṛṣā* ‖. The *kārikā* is translated, e.g., in Schayer 1931: 26, Saito 1984: 179, Oetke 1992: 206, Ames 1996: 126, Garfield 1995: 35, 207, Galloway 2001: 338, Seyfort Ruegg 2002: 80. Nāgārjuna and his commentators understand (falsely sanskritized) *moṣa* to be a derivative of √*muṣ* "to rob, steal"; see MMK XIII.2. At PsP_L 238.4 Candrakīrti equates *moṣadharmaka* with *visaṃvādaka*. Retorting to his opponent in his introduction to MMK XIII.2, he states: *satyaṃ moṣadharmakāḥ sarvasaṃskārāḥ ye 'dyāpi bhavantaṃ muṣnanti* "It is true that all the conditioned factors have a deceiving nature, [to the extent] that they

The Great Sage (*mahāmuni*) has said that an initial point (*koṭi*) is not known,
For *saṃsāra*[326] is without lower or upper [limit] (*anavarāgra*); it has neither a beginning (*ādi*) nor an end (*paścima*).[327]

---

fool you even today!" See the references and discussion of *moṣadharma* in Schayer 1931: 26, n. 20; see also Saito 1984: 277f., n. 6; Oetke 1992: 206ff.
Even though Candrakīrti unambiguously indicates with his employment of *moṣadharmaka* when he paraphrases and elaborates on the *kārikā* that he understands *moṣadharmaṃ* of XIII.1 to be a *bahuvrīhi* compound, Galloway (2001: 334, n. 8 and 9) rejects that it is a *bahuvrīhi* and translates (338) the compound as a *karmadhāraya* (with a plural final member): "What are deceptive (*moṣa*) dharmas are false (*mṛṣā*), the Lord has said; All the *saṃskāra*s are deceptive dharmas, therefore they are false." Galloway also translates *(a)moṣadharma* of Candrakīrti's citation of the Canonical statement reflected in MMK XIII.1 as a *karmadhāraya*. Garfield (1995: 35, 207), without explanation, does not translate *dharma/chos* and adds an unattested "all" to the final *pāda*. He (ibid., 207, n. 69) points out Kalupahana's wrong understanding of *saṃskāra* as "dispositions," but chooses the infelicitous yet widely used translation "compounded phenomena" for *saṃskāra* in its broader sense. *saṃskāra* in this sense refers rather to all phenomena that are formed/fashioned/activated (*saṃskṛta*) by causes. According to Abhidharma scholasticism, the individual atom-like "free-floating" qualities—which are also *saṃskāra*s—of which molecules are composed are caused (*saṃskṛta*) but are partless, i.e., they are not "compounded." "Conditioned things/factors" is thus a more accurate translation for *saṃskāra* in such contexts.
On the metrically required emendation *moṣadharmaṃ* for PsP_L's *moṣadharma* (in both MMK XIII.1a and XIII.2a), see MacDonald 2007: 34f. The version of the *sūtra* Nāgārjuna relied upon may additionally have attested this reading (the nominative plural *moṣadharmāṇaḥ* of XIII.1c, on the other hand, accords with Pā 5.4.124: the word *dharma*, when preceded by a single word in a *bahuvrīhi* compound, becomes *dharman*). Candrakīrti provides the *sūtra* citation in his commentary on MMK XIII.1: *sūtra uktam tan mṛṣā moṣadharmaṃ*[1] *yad idaṃ saṃskṛtam* | *etad dhi khalu bhikṣavaḥ paramaṃ satyaṃ yad idam amoṣadharmaṃ*[2] *nirvāṇam* | *sarvasaṃskārāś ca mṛṣā moṣadharmāṇaḥ iti* (cp. PsP_L 237.11-12); [1]emended following mss P, B and D; [2]emended following mss P, B and D.

[326] *saṃsāra* literally means "the rushing through, the wandering through [a series of places or states]." It refers to the crossing over of a being into ever new existences and thus to the chain of existences experienced (cf. L. Schmithausen, *Historisches Wörterbuch der Philosophie*. Ed. J. Ritter u. K. Gründer. Band 8, R-Sc., Basel 1992, s.v. *saṃsāra*). The opponent in Candrakīrti's PsP introduction to MMK XVI.1 explains the word *saṃsāra* as follows: *iha saṃsaraṇaṃ saṃsṛtiḥ gater gatyantaraga-manaṃ saṃsāra ity ucyate* (PsP_L 280.3-4). The Conservative Buddhist in YṢV asserts that *saṃsāra* exists having the nature of an entity because it has the own nature of the five constituent elements; just these, propelled from destiny to destiny by action and defilements, are called *saṃsāra*: *'khor ba ni nye bar len pa'i phung po*

lnga'i rang gi ngo ba yin pas dngos po'i ngo bo ste | nye bar len pa'i phung po lnga po de dag nyid las dang nyon mongs pas 'phangs nas | 'gro ba rnams su 'gro ba nas 'gro ba gzhan du 'gro ba'i phyir | 'khor ba zhes bya bas na de yang yod do ‖ (YṢV$_{\mathrm{ed}}$ 33.6-10; YṢV$_{\mathrm{tr}}$ 135f.). Although often translated as "cyclic existence" or "round of existence" these translations are, strictly speaking, actually more appropriate for *saṃsāracakra*, "the wheel of *saṃsāra*," the reference being to the (sometimes pictorially represented) group of five or six destinies continuously and repeatedly wandered through by beings in an order determined by the respective *karma* of the individual being. "Cyclic existence," "round of existence," etc., however, tend to be used to translate *saṃsāra* because the idea of wandering around within a closed system is often implicitly or secondarily intended. See n. 336.

[327] Candrakīrti is citing MMK XI.1: *pūrvā prajñāyate koṭir nety uvāca mahāmuniḥ | saṃsāro 'navarāgro hi nāsyādir nāpi paścimam* ‖. Translated, e.g., in May 1959: 170. The unemended Tibetan for the first two quarters of the *kārikā* here in the first chapter differs: *sngon mtha' sngon nam zhes zhus tshe* ‖ *thub pa chen pos min zhes gsungs* ‖. May (170, n. 540) notes the same discrepancy between PsP Skt and PsP Tib (he used P and N; D and C also read *sngon*) for the *kārikā* in the eleventh chapter and reconstructs (literally, not with a view to creating a metrically correct *śloka*) "'*pūrvakoṭiḥ pūrvam asti?' iti pṛṣṭe mahāmunir nety uvāca*" and translates, "à la question: 'y a-t-il une extrémité antérieure, un 'avant'?' le grand Anachorète répond: 'non'." Given that the differences between PsP Skt and PsP Tib are difficult to explain in terms of misreadings of the Sanskrit, I think it is more reasonable to assume that the Tibetan translators (here the reference is to Jñānagarbha and Klu'i rgyal mtshan, since the citation has been copied into PsP Tib) found the same Sanskrit text in their manuscript and only expanded on it, that is, they added *nam zhus tshe* in order to clarify their understanding of *pūrvā prajñāyate koṭiḥ* as a question; the *sngon* which May considers to be translating an original *pūrvam* is probably merely the result of an auditory or carving error for *mngon*, a common equivalent for *prajñāyate*. A glance at MMK XI.1 as preserved in MMK$_{\mathrm{T}}$ D, and in ABh and BP confirms this: all attest the correct reading *sngon mtha' mngon nam zhes zhus tshe* (see MMK$_{\mathrm{T}}$ D 7a7; ABh$_{\mathrm{ed}}$ 358.13; BP$_{\mathrm{ed}}$ 159.18; MMK$_{\mathrm{T}}$ P attests, as PsP Tib does, the faulty *sngon*).
Candrakīrti presents in his commentary on MMK XI.1 the *sūtra* quotation he considers Nāgārjuna to be referring to: *uktaṃ ca bhagavatā anavarāgro hi bhikṣavo jātijarāmaraṇasaṃsāra iti* (PsP$_{\mathrm{L}}$ 218.2-3; 219.5-6; references for *jātijarāmaraṇasaṃsāraḥ* in BHSD under *anavarāgra*). Cp. SN II.178.8-10, 186.13-15; III.149.25-27, 151.3-5, etc. (see also PsP$_{\mathrm{L}}$ 218, n. 3): *Anamataggāyam bhikkhave saṃsāro pubbakoṭi* (SN: *pubbākoṭi*) *na paññāyati avijjānīvaraṇānaṃ sattānaṃ taṇhāsaṃyojanānaṃ sandhāvataṃ saṃsarataṃ* ‖. Bodhi (2000: 651, etc.) translates, "Bhikkhus, this *saṃsāra* is without discoverable beginning. A first point is not discerned of beings roaming and wandering on hindered by ignorance and fettered by craving" (at 795, n. 254, he notes that the SN-aṭṭha explains that *saṃsāra* is the uninterrupted succession of the aggregates, etc.). For *anamatagga* see PTSD, CPD. For *muni*, see YṢV$_{\mathrm{tr}}$ 106, n. 11; May 1959: 170, n. 539; Candrakīrti elaborates on the word *muni* in

And in the Advice to Kātyāyana, both "[it] exists" (*asti*) and "[it] does not exist" (*nāsti*) have been negated by the Exalted One who understands[328] existence (*bhāva*) and non-existence (*abhāva*).[329]

§74. And it is stated in the Noble Akṣayamatisūtra,

Which *sūtra*s have a provisional meaning (*neyārtha*), which a definitive meaning (*nītārtha*)? Those *sūtra*s that have been taught for entry (*avatāra*) onto the path are called [*sūtra*s] with provisional meaning. Those *sūtra*s that have been taught for entry into

---

CŚṬ with *aśaikṣyakāyavāṅmanomaunayogān munir buddho bhagavān* ($CŚṬ_{ed}$ 164.13).
Garfield (1995: 197) translates the *kārikā* rather freely from the Tibetan as "When asked about the beginning, [t]he Great Sage said that nothing is known of it. Cyclic existence is without end and beginning. So there is no beginning or end." The first quarter actually translates, as May has already shown, "When asked, 'Is a prior point known?' ... ." Garfield's overinterpretation of the simple *min* ("[one] is not") with "nothing is known of it" is misleading, for it implies that the Buddha does indeed affirm the existence of a beginning, but that not even he has access to details about it (Garfield's "So" is also unsupported; the third quarter commences with *de la* [= *asya*]). PsP Tib's equivalent for *hi* might be represented by the semi-final particle of the preceding *pāda*; for comments on *hi* represented by semi-final particles, see Schmithausen 2014 § 349.

[328] I translate *vibhāvinā* as "who understands" (PsP Tib: *mkhyen*) but "who discloses/teaches [the truth regarding] …" is also possible (ABh and BP: *ston pa*). Kumārajīva's translation (T 30.1564: 20b1) suggests "who causes to disappear" ("The Buddha destroys existence and non-existence").

[329] Candrakīrti is citing MMK XV.7: *kātyāyanāvavāde cāstīti nāstīti cobhayam* | *pratiṣiddhaṃ bhagavatā bhāvābhāvavibhāvinā* ||. Translated, e.g., in Schayer 1931: 69. See SN II.17: *Dvayanissito khvāyaṃ Kaccāyana loko yebhuyyena atthitañ ceva natthitañ ca* || ... *Sabbam atthīti kho Kaccāyana ayam eko anto* || *Sabbaṃ natthīti ayaṃ dutiyo anto* || *Ete te Kaccāyana ubho ante anupagamma majjhena Tathāgato dhammam deseti* || *Avijjāpaccayā sankhārā* || *saṅkhārapaccayā viññāṇam* || *pe* ||. Candrakīrti commences his commentary on the *kārikā* as follows (punctuation revised): *uktaṃ hi bhagavatā āryakātyāyanāvavādasūtre yadbhūyasā kātyāyana ayaṃ loko 'stitāṃ vā abhiniviṣṭo nāstitāṃ ca* | *tena na parimucyate jātijarāvyādhimaraṇa-śokaparidevaduḥkhadaurmanasyopāyāsebhyo, na parimucyate pāñcagatikāt saṃsāracārakāgārabandhanāt, na parimucyate pitṛmaraṇasaṃtāpaduḥkhāt, na parimucyate pitṛmaraṇasaṃtāpaduḥkhād iti vistaraḥ*. The *kārikā* is also cited at $MABh_{ed}$ 22.13-14 (minus PsP Tib's semantically empty but potentially misleading *'ang* in the final quarter; *gnyi ga'ang* is equivalent to *ubhāv api* "both of them").

the result (*phala*) are called [*sūtra*s] with definitive meaning.[330]

---

[330] Ms Q, unlike ms P and the paper manuscripts, includes after *yāvad ye sūtrāntāḥ* a sentence detailing the topics of *neyārthasūtra*s: *ātmasatvajīvapoṣapudgalamanujamānavakārakavedaka* (read *vedakā*) *nānārutabhāṣā asvāmikāḥ svāmikavan*[1] *nirddiṣṭās ta ucyaṃte neyārthāḥ yāvad ye sūtrāntāḥ.* [1]read *sasvāmikavan*? PsP Tib: *bdag po dang bcas pa*(*r*). PsP Tib also includes the entire sentence: *mdo sde gang dag bdag dang | sems can dang | srog dang gso ba dang | skyes bu dang | gang zag dang | shed las skyes dang | shed bu dang | byed pa po dang | tshor ba po dang | sgra rnam pa sna tshogs su bshad pa dang | bdag po med pa la bdag po dang bcas par bstan pa de dag ni drang ba'i don zhes bya'o* ||. De La Vallée Poussin assumes that Candrakīrti (or a scribe?) abridged the text ("Le copiste abrège" [PsP_L 43, n. 3]); he reconstructs the Sanskrit from the Tibetan (cf. ibid.) but does not include the reconstruction in his main text. Like the majority of the citations in our chapter, PsP Tib has, however, been copied in from its source text, in the present case the Tibetan translation of the Akṣayamatisūtra (cf. Braarvig 1993: 117f.; [tr. 451]), and thus does not necessarily indicate that the sentence was originally in PsP Skt. It is even possible that the extra sentence was copied into PsP Tib by mistake; see MacDonald 2015, where it is hypothesized that apprentice translators or assistants may have been responsible for searching out source texts and copying in citations, and that missing or extra text in the copied-in citations could be due to their oversights. On the other hand, the fact that ms Q presents the same sentence appears to indicate that this sentence also stood in one of manuscripts relied upon by Pa tshab and the *paṇḍita*s helping him, and was thus included when the larger citation was copied from the Tibetan translation of the Akṣayamatisūtra. The complete lack of the sentence, however, in ms P and in the paper manuscripts raises suspicions, especially because one expects that if Q had received the sentence from ms β over ms ζ, P would have it too, via either ms ζ or ms ε, or via both ms ζ and ms ε. It could be argued that the lack of the sentence in P and the paper manuscripts can be explained as due to a simple eyeskip on the part of ms ε's scribe from *ye sūtrāntāḥ* (*ātma*°) to *ye sūtrāntāḥ* (*śunyatā*°), and due to the fact that P's scribe was relying solely on ms ε, i.e., was not checking the readings in ms ζ at this point in his copying. These and other arguments for inclusion of the sentence in question in the main PsP text, however, weaken considerably when Q's wording is taken into account. Q's sentence describing the topics of provisional *sūtra*s commences with *yāvad ye sūtrāntāḥ*, and its next sentence detailing the topics of definitive *sūtra*s begins with *yāvad ye sūtrāntāḥ*. The *yāvat* before *ye sūtrāntāḥ śunyatā*° has obviously been included by Candrakīrti for the purpose of indicating that he has *abridged* the citation and left out the sentence commenting on the topics of provisional *sūtra*s (i.e., *yāvat* is used in its BHS sense indicating omission of part of a citation). His emphasis at this stage in the discussion is on the fact that only *sūtra*s which teach that things do not arise, etc., are definitive, and he has purposely excluded the sentence detailing the subjects of provisional *sūtra*s because it is not pertinent to the point he is making. Q's sentence must therefore represent an interpolation. It is possible that the individual who decided to add the "missing" sentence to the manuscript he was using or copying simply forgot to delete the word *yāvat*

... The *sūtra*s [i.e., those in which] the doors to release (*vimokṣamukha*)[331] have been taught—[such as] emptiness (*śunyatā*), the absence of marks/phenomena (*ānimitta*), the lack of something to long for (*apraṇihita*), the lack of making effort toward [anything involving *prapañca*] (*anabhisaṃskāra*), the unborn (*ajāta*), non-arising (*anutpāda*), non-existence (*abhāva*), [the fact that one] lacks a self (*nirātman*), lacks a being (*niḥsattva*), lacks a soul (*nirjīva*), lacks a person (*niḥpudgala*),

---

before *ye sūtrāntāḥ* and the added sentence. The fact that *yāvad ye sūtrāntāḥ* also introduces the sentence dealing with definitive *sūtra*s in ms Q may indicate that the sentence was brought into the main text without much thought; it may have originally been written in the margin (without *yāvat*) and was later added by a scribe who did not delete the main text's *yāvat* and who again copied *yāvad ye sūtrāntāḥ* as the introductory words for the sentence dealing with definitive *sūtra*s.

[331] Normally only the three forms of concentration mentioned first in the list, i.e., *śūnyatā*, *ānimitta*, and *apraṇihita* are referred to as the "doors to release" (*vimokṣa-mukha*); see Lamotte 1970: 1213-1232; May 1959: 148, n. 436; Conze 1967: 59-69; further references in Tillemans 1990: 241, n. 193. Candrakīrti describes the characteristics of the three *vimokṣamukha*s in MA VI.208cd-209 and his commentary: *śūnyatā* as a *vimokṣamukha* has the characteristic of isolation (**vivikta*) because, since things/existence are/is not perceived, one is not soiled by the stain of conceptuality (MABh_{ed} 319.1-3: *dngos po ma dmigs pas rnam par rtog pa'i dri mas nye bar ma sbags pa'i phyir na | rnam par thar pa'i sgo stong pa nyid ni rnam par dben pa'i mtshan nyid can no ||*). *ānimitta* as a *vimokṣamukha* has the characteristic of calm (**śānta*) inasmuch as a mark/phenomenon is not perceived (MABh_{ed} 319.7-8: *rnam par thar pa'i sgo mtshan ma med pa ni mtshan ma ma dmigs pa'i sgo nas zhi ba'i mtshan nyid can no ||*). *apraṇihita* as a *vimokṣamukha* has the characteristic of absence of suffering and of confusion/disorientation (**duḥkha, *moha*) because when one accurately examines conditioned things which have the nature of suffering and sees by way of insight conditioned things' [true] own-being, one does not wish [for them] (see Tauscher 1981, 148, n. 249, where he explains, following Jayānanda, that from the point of view of the surface-level truth, things are not desired because they are seen as suffering; MABh_{ed} 319.9-13: *rnam par thar pa'i sgo smon pa med pa 'di ni sdug bsngal dang gti mug med pa'i mtshan nyid can te | 'du byed sdug bsngal gyi bdag nyid can rnams la yang dag par rjes su lta zhing shes rab kyis 'du byed kyi rang bzhin la lta ba na smon par mi byed pa'i phyir na |*). The section is translated in Tauscher 1981: 81f. See also PsP_{L} 246.6-8. In the CŚṬ, Candrakīrti proclaims *śūnyatā* as the unrivalled door to release: *yady api śūnyatānimittāpraṇihitākhyāni trīṇi vimokṣamukhāni tathāpi nairātmyadarśanam eva pradhānam [/] vidita-nairātmyasya hi bhāveṣu parikṣīṇasaṅgasya na kvacit kācit prārthanā kuto vā nimittopalambha ity advitīyam eva śivadvāram etan nairātmyam* (CŚṬ_{ed} 270.2-6; cf. CŚṬ_{tr} 127). On *apraṇihita*, see Schmithausen 1987b: 153f.; Deleanu 2000: 93, n. 23.

> lacks a ruler (*asvāmika*)—[all those] are called definitive.[332] This, O Bhadanta Son of Śāradvatī, is called reliance on definitive *sūtra*s, not reliance on *sūtra*s with provisional meaning.[333]

And similarly, in the Noble Samādhirājasūtra,

> He knows the distinguishing feature of definitive *sūtra*s to be emptiness as taught by the Well-gone One (*sugata*).
> But where the person (*pudgala*), being (*sattva*) [and] soul / [enduring] individual (*pūruṣa*) [are taught], all these *dharma*s (= *sūtra*s) he knows to be of provisional meaning.[334]

---

[332] The sentence listing the topics of definitive *sūtra*s is problematic, for it is difficult to know how to construe °*mukhā* with *nirdiṣṭāḥ*. PsP Tib (= Akṣayamatisūtra Tib) appears to understand *nirdiṣṭāḥ* in an active sense, even though *nirdiṣṭāḥ* of the previous two sentences has been understood in the expected passive sense. De La Vallée Poussin (PsP_L 43, n. 4), citing the end of the sentence in PsP Tib (*gang zag med pa dang | bdag po med pa dang | rnam par thar pa'i sgo'i bar du bstan pa de dag ni nges pa'i don zhes bya ste | 'di dag ni nges pa'i don gyi mdo sde la rton gyi | drang ba'i don gyi mdo sde la mi rton pa zhes bya'o*), remarks "La syntaxe de cette phrase paraît troublée"; he reconstructs the extra sentence in PsP Tib dealing with provisional *sūtra*s in the form *yeṣu sūtrānteṣu … te neyārthāḥ*. I translate *nirdiṣṭāḥ* in its passive sense and in reliance on BHSG § 7.14 add the bracketed words at the beginning of the sentence. Understanding the sentence like this requires assuming that °*mukhā* is an error for °*mukhāni*, or that it is to be understood as a neuter plural. Braarvig (1993: 451) does not comment on either the Sanskrit or the Tibetan syntax, and for the sentence dealing with the topics of definitive *sūtra*s translates *nirdiṣṭāḥ* in an active sense: "… the scriptures teaching emptiness … and the gates of liberation are called explicit." The problem with assuming that °*vimokṣamukhā* is the final item in the list is that *śūnyatā*, *ānimitta*, and *apraṇihita are* the "gates of liberation." Seyfort Ruegg (2002: 81) does not comment on the syntax of the sentence, but obviously aware of the difficulty, translates, "When in Sūtrāntras there are taught Emptiness …, these are termed of definitive meaning."

[333] The PsP manuscripts have preserved the Sanskrit for these sentences of the Akṣayamatisūtra. Braarvig (1993: 167) includes the PsP_L 43 citation in his list of fragments, but in his translation (ibid., 451) presents both it and de La Vallée Poussin's reconstruction from the Tibetan of the sentence dealing with provisional *sūtra*s (the latter should not be marked in bold as a Sanskrit fragment [ms Q, however, now provides us with the Sanskrit]). On the four reliances as described in the Akṣayamatisūtra, see ibid., 443-453; see also de La Vallée Poussin's comments on the *pratisaraṇa*s at PsP_L 598 for 43, n. 5.

[334] Cf. SR chapter 7, verse 5 (SR p. 36.1-4). Cited again by Candrakīrti at PsP_L 276.5-8. Cited in MABh in the context of a discussion on distinguishing *nītārtha*- and

§75. Therefore, the Master [Nāgārjuna] undertook the explication of dependent-arising in order to demonstrate that the teaching of arising, etc., has a false meaning (*mṛṣārtha*).[335]

§76. [Objection:] But if, in consideration of the fact that arising, etc., do not exist, the Master [Nāgārjuna] undertook this [explanation] for the sake of demonstrating that all factors (*dharma*) are false (*mṛṣā*), [then] it being thus [i.e., that things are false], since that which is false does not exist, isn't it the case that unwholesome (*akuśala*) actions do not exist, [and] due to their non-existence the bad destinies (*durgati*) do not exist, [and] wholesome (*kuśala*) actions [as well] do not exist, [and] due to their non-existence the good destinies (*sugati*) do not exist, and on account of the impossibility of good and bad destinies[336]

*neyārtha-sūtra*s (see $MABh_{ed}$ 200.7-10 and $MABh_{tr}$ 1911: 254). I follow de La Vallée Poussin in understanding *dharma*s to be referring to *sūtra*s: "il connaît que tous ces dharmas (= sūtras) sont de sens provisoire." Somewhat disturbing is the fact that *upadiṣṭa* would seem to complete the predicate of the *yasmin* sentence in the second line but is included in an attributive element in the first line (emptiness, as the Sugata taught it). One wonders if *yatho*° might be the secondary Sanskritization (metri causa) of Middle Indian *yattho*° = *yatro*°, and if the line might originally have been understood as "He knows that the special kind of *sūtra*s which are of definitive meaning are those where emptiness has been taught by the Sugata" or "He knows the distinguishing feature of *sūtra*s which are of definitive meaning to be [the fact] that in them emptiness has been taught by the Sugata."

[335] *mṛṣārtha* modifies *utpādādideśanā* and thus has to be understood as meaning that the teaching has, from the ultimate perspective, a false object/content. When *mṛṣārtha* appears again a few lines later (*mṛṣārthatā bhāvānāṃ*), however, it seems to mean no more than *mṛṣā*.

[336] On the terms *kuśala* and *akuśala*, see Schmithausen 2013. Candrakīrti concurs with the AK in considering *saṃsāra* to consist of five *gatis* (AK III.4ab: *narakādi-svanāmoktā gatayaḥ pañca teṣu* [*teṣu* refers to the three realms]); they are listed at $AKBh_{ed}$ 114.7: *narakās tiryañcaḥ pretā devā manuṣyā* (cp. PsP_L 218.1-2: *pāñcagatike saṃsāre*; $YṢV_{ed}$ 32.23: *'gro ba lngar 'khor ba*). Six *gati*s are mentioned at $MABh_{ed}$ 175.17 but here Candrakīrti is quoting another text (see $MABh_{tr}$ 1910: 356). Bhāviveka refers to six *gati*s in MHK I.19: *kṛtapuṇyatayodyānayātrām iva ca ṣaḍgatim | paśyantas trāsam āyānti na te saṃsāracārakāt* || (Lindtner 2001: 3; Heitmann [2009: 47] reads *api* instead of *iva* [Tib: *ltar*]). On the *gati*s, see $YṢV_{tr}$ 134, n. 89; Lamotte 1976: 1953-1959 and 1988: 630.

saṃsāra does not exist? Therefore all undertakings would be absolutely (*eva*) futile (*vaiyarthya*)![337]

Reply: Taking reference to surface truth, we teach the falseness (*mṛṣārthatā*) of things as an antidote to worldly attachment to [things] as true (*idaṃsatyābhiniveśa*).[338] But the Nobles, by whom the task has

---

337 The Conservative Buddhist opponent objects that should *saṃsāra*, consisting of good and bad destinies which are arrived at by way of wholesome and unwholesome acts, not exist, there would be no point in cultivating wholesome mental, verbal, and physical behaviours and avoiding unwholesome ones. Not explicitly stated in the opponent's objection but certainly implied is the accusation that the Mādhyamika is a nihilist. In its classical Indian sense the nihilist label (*nāstika*) characterizes a person who denies the causal efficiency of *karma* and thus rebirth as the result of wholesome and unwholesome actions. Candrakīrti responds variously in his works to the charge that the Mādhyamika is a nihilist, on occasion arguing that a nihilist deserving of the name denies something he has earlier affirmed, and this the Mādhyamika does not do. Here in PsP chapter one, he first clarifies to his opponent that the things the world perceives out of ignorance and clings to because of the belief in their reality have actually never existed, but are spoken of by the Mādhyamika and taught as being false solely for the sake of breaking the world's attachment to them. He then confines his response to the ultimate level, speaking from the point of view of the Nobles who see reality, those beings who have "completed the task" (*kṛtakāryāḥ*; according to Candrakīrti in his commentary on YṢ, the task the Nobles have completed is not to perceive any thing and not to perceive arising and perishing; this is known as *nirvāṇa* in seen things [see YṢV_{ed} 47.1-14; YṢV_{tr} 171]). Inasmuch as the Nobles perceive nothing at all, there is not an object of which it might be predicated that it "is false" or "is not false" and that as a result might be deemed inexistent or existent. For the Nobles, whose realization of the lack of existence of things has freed them from the bonds of *karma* and released them from *saṃsāra*, actions and the various destinies they lead to have become irrelevant.

338 The compound *idaṃsatyābhiniveśa* (Pāli: *idaṃsaccābhinivesa*) appears in the Canon as one of the four "bodily knots" (*kāyagrantha*; Pāli: *kāyagantha*); see DN III.230; SN V.59; DS 201 (§ 1135) (further references in Erb 1997: 152, n. 500, YṢV_{tr} 249, n. 483). The other three "knots" are covetousness (*abhidhyā*; Pāli: *abhijjhā*), malevolence (*vyāpāda*; Pāli: *byāpāda*), and clinging to observances and vows (*śīlavrataparāmarśa*; Pāli: *silabbataparāmāsa*). DS 202 (§ 1139) elucidates the *kāyagantha idaṃsaccābhinivesa* as follows: *tattha katamo idaṃsaccābhiniveso kāyagantho? Sassato loko idam eva saccaṃ moghaṃ aññan ti vā; asassato loko, idam eva saccaṃ mogham aññan ti vā; antavā loko, idam eva saccam mogham aññan ti vā; anantavā loko, idam eva saccaṃ mogham aññan ti vā* ... (referred to are the extreme views [*dṛṣṭi*: the world is permanent, not permanent, the world has an end, does not have an end, etc.] in regard to which the Buddha tended to maintain silence; see, e.g., Oetke 1994, Vetter 1988 [chapter eleven], May 1959: 277, n. 1015). *idaṃsaccābhi-*

been completed (*kṛtakārya*), certainly do not perceive something that might be false or not false. Moreover, do acts (*karman*) exist or does *saṃsāra* exist for the one who has discerned the falseness of all factors (*dharma*)?[339] [Definitely not!] Nor is it the case that this one perceives the existence (*astitva*) or non-existence (*nāstitva*) of any factor.

As stated by the Exalted One in the Noble Ratnakūṭasūtra,

> For the mind (*citta*), Kāśyapa, being searched for, is not found. That which is not found is not perceived. That which is not

nivesa, according to the DS, is expressed in the stubborn holding to such views with the belief and attitude "only this (*idaṃ*) is true (*sacca*), [everything] other [than this view I hold] is false (*mogha*) (cf. also MN I.484f., 498f.). The same words are found in ŚSV$_{ed}$ 226.5-7 (... *mngon par zhen pas 'di dag kho na bden par yod la gzhan ni rmongs pa'o zhes 'di dag la bden par mngon par zhen pa mchog tu 'dzin pa lus kyi mdud pa skyed pas 'khor bar 'khor*); the view held as true by the opponents in this ŚSV context, however, is not found among those appearing in Canonical literature and is rather, according to the Mādhyamikas who target it, the soteriologically disastrous view held by common persons that things, here specifically the eye, truly exist. Erb (1997: 56f.) translates: "Durch das Festhalten an dieser [Vorstellung] erzeugen sie die Bindung an den Körper [in Gestalt] des Sich-Anklammerns (*mchog tu 'dzin pa*; **parāmarśa*), d.h., des hartnäckigen Festhaltens an dieser [Vorstellung] als wahr, in dem Gedanken: 'Nur diese [Vorstellung] ist wahr, [alles] andere ist falsch', und kreisen dadurch im Kreislauf der Existenzen." As Erb notes (ibid. 152, n. 500), here, as in other cases, an older concept has been appropriated and filled with a new content: in the Canonical literature, the permanence of the world is doubted, but never its reality, and it is just this belief in its reality that Candrakīrti applies as the content of *idaṃsatyābhiniveśa* (for a detailed description of another case of the re-filling of old Canonical "skins" with new content, see Schmithausen 1976). *idaṃsatyābhiniveśa* as a *kāyagrantha* is similarly mentioned in the commentary on YṢ *kārikā* 32 in which, following Candrakīrti, Nāgārjuna states that in the beginning the Exalted One taught the existence of the results of actions and the existence of the various destinies and afterwards taught their non-arising and that one ought to attain thorough knowledge of their [true] nature; see YṢV$_{ed}$ 73.16-17: *'di bden no snyam du mngon par zhen pa mchog tu 'dzin pa lus kyi mdud pa 'di'i gnyen por* |; see YṢV$_{tr}$ 251 and n. 483 and Erb's comments on **parāmarśa* (**idaṃsatyābhiniveśaparāmarśakāyagrantha*) as it appears in ŚSV and YṢV.

[339] I understand the *hi* in the sentence to indicate the rhetorical character of the question, and thus the sentence as equivalent to the negative construction *na hi yena ... tasya karmāṇi santi ...*; I therefore add the rhetorical question's implied negation in square brackets.

perceived is neither past, nor future, nor present. That which is neither past, nor future, nor present does not have own-being (*svabhāva*). There is no arising (*utpāda*) of that which does not have own-being. There is no perishing (*nirodha*) of that which does not have arising.[340]

But he who, on account of being steeped in [subjective] error (*viparyāsa*), does not understand that things (*dharma*) are false, [who] is attached to an own-being of dependently [arisen] things (*pratītya-*

---

[340] On the name of the *sūtra*, see KP$_{ed}$ Preface, pp. V-VI; I refer to the *sūtra* as KP here in the annotation. The KP citation presented by Candrakīrti is shorter than the corresponding section of Staël-Holstein's Skt edition. Candrakīrti was either relying on an earlier version of the KP or abbreviated the section. KP$_{ed}$ § 102 (punctuation reflects the ms' punctuation style; see Vorobyova-Desyatovskaya [henceforth VD] 2002: 36): *cittaṃ hi kāśyapa parigaveṣamāṇaṃ na labhyate yan na labhyate tan nopalabhyate*[1] *tan nātītaṃ*[2] *nānāgataṃ na pratyutpannaṃ • yan nātītaṃ*[3] *nānāgataṃ na pratyutpannaṃ*[4] *tatradhvasamatikrāntaṃ* (read, following Weller 1965: 122, n. 1: *tat tryadhva°*) *yatryadhvasamatikrāntaṃ* (read, following Weller 1965: 122, n. 1: *yat tryadhva°*) • *tan naivāsti neva nāsti • yan naivāsti na nāsti • tad ajātaṃ yad ajātaṃ • tasya nāsti svabhāvaḥ yasya nāsti svabhāvaḥ tasya nāsty utpāda*[5] • *yasya nāsty utpādaḥ tasya nāsti nirodhaḥ yasya nāsti nirodhaḥ tasya nāsti vigamaḥ avigamas*[6] *tasya rna*[7] *gatir nāgatir na cyutir nopapattiḥ yatra na gatir nāgatir na cyutir nopapattiḥ tatra na kecit saṃskārāḥ yatra na kecit saṃskārāḥ tad asaṃskṛtaṃ* • ... .
[1]*yan nopalabhyate* follows in PsP Skt and PsP Tib, and is also found in KP$_{ed}$ Tib. KP$_{ed}$ Skt's *tan nātītaṃ* would seem to expect it; it may have dropped from KP Skt as the result of an eyeskip or, alternatively, after not having been attested in earlier versions of the *sūtra*, it may have been added to Candrakīrti's version and the version KP$_{ed}$ Tib is based on because it was felt that a relative clause was needed. Weller's translation of the Han version of the *sūtra* reveals that the Skt manuscript used for the Chinese translation lacked as much as *yan nopalabhyate tan nopalabhyate tan nātītaṃ nānāgataṃ na pratyutpannaṃ yan nātītaṃ nānāgataṃ na pratyutpannaṃ tat tradhvasamatikrāntaṃ yat tryadhvasamatikrāntaṃ* (cf. Weller 1987a: 1215 and n. 2). Weller (1965: 121f.) translates, without comment, the Tibetan equivalent of *yan nopalabhyate* in his Sanskrit- and Tibetan-based translation; [2]PsP Skt: *naivātītam*; [3]PsP Skt: *naivātītam*; [4]PsP Skt and PsP Tib skip from here to *tasya nāsti svabhāvaḥ*; [5]read *utpādaḥ*; the loss of *visarga* is probably merely due to scribal negligence and not because the non-inclusion of *visarga* is allowed in BHS (BHSG 8.22); [6]see Weller 1965: 122, n. 6; [7]read: *na*.
PsP Tib corresponds exactly with the KP$_{ed}$ Tib translation, but has been abbreviated to conform to PsP Skt. The passage is translated in Weller 1965: 121f., Pāsādika 1979 (7): 30 and Chang 1983: 400. Further references at PsP$_{L}$ 45, n. 1. See also the passage as commented on in Steinkellner 1992: 401f.

bhāva),[341] in being attached to things (*dharma*) as one whose attachment [takes the form] "this is true" (*idaṃsatyābhiniveśin*), both performs acts and wanders in *saṃsāra*, [and][342] because he is entrenched in error he is not fit to attain *nirvāṇa*.

§77. [Question:] But do things (*padārtha*) even with a false own-being become the cause of defilement (*saṅkleśa*) and purification (*vyavadāna*)?

[Answer: Yes,] they do, like an illusory young woman (*māyāyuvati*) [conjured up by a magician becomes a cause of defilement] for those who are not aware of her [true] nature (*svabhāva*) and [like a person] created by the Tathāgata (*tathāgatanirmita*) [becomes a cause of purification] for those who have gathered wholesome roots (*kuśala-mūla*).[343]

For it is stated in the Dṛḍhādhyāśayaparipṛcchāsūtra,

> For example, O son of good family, a certain [man], his mind overcome by desire upon having seen a woman created by a magician (*māyākāra*) during the presentation of the magician's

---

[341] PsP Tib presents *dngos po rnams rang bzhin yod par rtogs nas mngon par zhen pa* for *pratītyabhāvānāṃ svabhāvam abhiniviśate*; that is, the translators understood *pratītya* as a verb and *svabhāvam* as its object. Although the compound *pratītyabhāva* is, to the best of my knowledge, not found elsewhere in the PsP, the formulation *pratītya svabhāvam*, especially in the present context, would be unusual. PsP Tib's *rtogs* (for *pratītya*) does not inspire confidence in the translators' interpretation because *rtogs* usually denotes a positively assessed understanding or insight and not an error.

[342] I do not accept ms Q's *tu*, because a contrast is not intended between the final part of the sentence, i.e., between *viparyāsāvasthitatvān na bhavyo nirvāṇam adhigantum*, and the preceding part; the only contrast intended is between the preceding KP citation and this sentence.

[343] The word *kuśala* here probably refers to *puṇya* (karmic "merit"), or to spiritual maturity, and possibly less to moral virtues, though these might be secondarily presupposed. On the word *kuśala*, see Schmithausen 2013. The PsP Tib translators, lacking the "square bracket" option, have chosen to expand the sentence for the sake of clarity: *de'i rang bzhin mngon par mi shes pa rnams kyi kun nas nyon mongs pa'i rgyu yin la* | *de bzhin gshegs pa'i sprul pa ni dge ba'i rtsa ba bsags pa rnams kyi rnam par byang ba'i rgyur 'gyur ba bzhin no* ||.

show, after leaving his seat on account of the anxiety and shyness [he feels from being in such a state] in public, would exit [the show]. Having left, he would reflect on that very woman as repulsive (*aśubha*), [he] would reflect [on her] as impermanent (*anitya*),[344] as suffering/unpleasant (*duḥkha*), as empty (*śūnya*), [and] as without self (*anātman*).[345]

---

[344] PsP Tib attests six, not five, modes of reflection, adding *mi gtsang ba* (impure) as the second mode, before *anityataḥ* and in place of *manasikuryāt*. **aśucitaḥ* is also not found in the citation of the same *sūtra* passage in Candrakīrti's commentary on MMK XXIII.14. The PsP Tib translators may be citing from a proto-Canonical version of the *sūtra*, or they may have revised the pertinent section (in a version of the *sūtra* similar to the one found in the Canon) by adding *mi gtsang ba* in order to remove the syntactical oddness of *mi sdug pa yid la byed* as against *bdag med par yid la byed*. See the following note.

[345] The quotation is assigned by the PsP manuscripts to the Dṛḍhādhyāśaya-paripṛcchāsūtra. De La Vallée Poussin reconstructs the title Lhag pa'i bsam pa bstan pa'i mdo, attested in the Tibetan editions of the PsP and in the Golden Manuscript, as Adhyāśayanirdeśasūtra, and perhaps because of this, adds a reference to the Adhyāśayasaṃcodanasūtra (cf. PsP_L 46, n. 1). I have not been able to locate a similar citation in the Lhag pa'i bsam pa bskul ba (Derge no. 69) and thus assume that *bstan pa* of the PsP Tib title is a carving error for *brtan pa* (= *dṛḍha*). A version of the citation is in fact found in the Tibetan Canon in the *sūtra* entitled ('Phags pa) lhag pa'i bsam pa brtan pa'i le'u (Derge no. 224). The possibly reconstructed Sanskrit title is given as Āryasthīrādhyāśayaparivarta (sic) at the beginning of the translated *sūtra*. A very similar section is cited within a larger citation in Candrakīrti's commentary on MMK XXIII.14 (the quotation appears at PsP_L 463.10-13). There the *sūtra* from which the citation is taken is also called the Dṛḍhādhyāśayaparipṛcchā (de La Vallée Poussin corrects the title given at PsP_L 462.15 at PsP_L 605), a title given by the PsP translators as 'Phag pa lhag pa'i bsam pa brtan pas zhus pa. This citation in the commentary on MMK XXIII.14 (cf. PsP_L 463.10-13) is nearly identical with the Canonical version. The Canonical version of the quotation reads: *rigs kyi bu 'di lta ste dper na | mi*[1] *la la zhig gis sgyu ma mkhan gyi rol mo byung ba'i tshe | sgyu ma mkhan gyis sprul pa'i bud med mthong na*[2] *'dod chags kyi sems bskyed de | de*[3] *'dod chags kyis sems dkris nas 'khor gyis 'jigs shing*[4] *bag tsha ste stan las langs nas song ste | de song nas bud med de nyid la mi sdug pa yid la byed cing*[5] *| mi rtag pa dang | sdug bsngal ba dang | stong pa dang | bdag med par yid la byed na |* (D Taipei edition fol. 330.3-5; D 165b). [1]PsP Tib chapter 1, in accord with chapter 1 Skt: omits *mi*; PsP Tib chapter 23, in accord with chapter 23 Skt, includes *mi*. [2]PsP Tib chapter 1 and 23: *nas*. [3]PsP Tib chapter 1, in accord with chapter 1 Skt: omits *'dod chags kyi sems bskyed de | de*; PsP Tib chapter 23, in accord with chapter 23 Skt: includes *'dod chags kyi sems bskyed de | de*. [4]PsP Tib chapter 23: *nas*; PsP Tib chapter 1: *shing*.

And so on [in the *sūtra*].

And in the Vinaya, a mechanical woman (*yantrayuvati*) made by a builder of [such] devices (*yantrakāra*), which was empty of a real (*sadbhūta*) woman, appears to be a real young woman, and became the object of the lust and desire of the painter (*citrakara*).[346]

In the same way, things (*bhāva*) even with a false own-being become the cause of the defilement[347] of the [spiritually] immature.[348]

---

[5]PsP Tib chapter 1, against chapter 1 Skt: *mi gtsang ba dang* for *yid la byed na*; PsP Tib chapter 23, in accord with chapter 23 Skt: *yid la byed na.*

[346] The Vinaya reference is probably not a direct citation but rather Candrakīrti's summary of a story in the Vinaya. The story can be found in the Mūlasarvāstivāda Vinaya; for references, see Panglung 1981: 51. In the tale as recorded in the Gilgit manuscript (Skt in Dutt 1947: 166f.), a painter (*citrakarācārya*) from Madhyadeśa who had traveled to a Greek area (*yavanaviṣaya*) went to the place of a builder of mechanical devices (*yantrācārya*) and was there served by a mechanical woman (*yantraputrikā*). He wanted to enjoy himself with her but when she didn't respond he grabbed her hand and pulled her, which caused her to fall into a heap of parts. When he realized she was just a mechanical woman he felt extremely embarrassed. To get back at the mechanic, he drew a picture on the wall of himself having committed suicide out of shame by hanging – and then hid in order to watch the mechanic's reaction. The mechanic was shocked when he saw the hanged "man." He reported the suicide to the king, who then came to the mechanic's place. The king, however, perceived that the hanged man was only a drawing on the wall, and as a result, the mechanic was very embarrassed. The story also occurs at CŚṬ D 131b1ff.

[347] PsP_{L} Skt: *saṃkleśavyavadānanibandhana* "the cause of the defilement and purification"; PsP Tib without an equivalent for *vyavadāna*. I reject the Sanskrit manuscripts' *vyavadāna* and consider PsP Tib to preserve the uncorrupted original reading. The two examples just given, viz., the magically created woman and the mechanical woman, are examples of unreal things that cause defilement; only the KP quotation that Candrakīrti subsequently inserts provides an example for unreal things that cause purification. The sentence following the KP quotation reads *evaṃ mṛṣāsvabhāvābhyāṃ tathāgatanirmitābhyāṃ bhikṣubhyāṃ pañcānāṃ bhikṣuśatānāṃ vyavadānanibandhanaṃ kṛtam*, and thus refers exclusively to the KP quotation and its presentation of unreal things that cause (only) purification. The word *vyavadāna* of the sentence *tathā mṛṣāsvabhāvā api bhāvā bālānāṃ saṅkleśavyavadāna-nibandhanaṃ bhavanti* here after the Vinaya reference, however, does not relate back to material in either the Dṛḍhādhyāśayaparipṛcchāsūtra quotation or the Vinaya reference just presented, for both depict situations in which unreal things cause only defilement. Given that Candrakīrti, in his initial response to the opponent's question, has announced the two, namely, a magical young woman and a being created by the

§78. Likewise, in the Noble Ratnakūṭasūtra,[349]

Tathāgata, as examples of unreal things that respectively cause defilement and purification, the appearance of *vyavadāna* in the Sanskrit sentence after the Vinaya reference seems premature. It appears to be an insertion, probably added because a scribe was struck by the similarity of the sentence *tathā mṛṣāsvabhāvā api bhāvā bālānāṃ saṅkleśanibandhanaṃ bhavanti* to the opening question *kiṃ punar mṛṣāsvabhāvā api padārthāḥ saṅkleśavyavadānanibandhanaṃ bhavanti* and concluded that the sentence was the final answer to that question and that *vyavadāna* had dropped out. De La Vallée Poussin, on the other hand, is of the opinion that when the magically created woman of the first example is reflected upon as impermanent, suffering/unpleasant, etc., she is additionally a cause of the purification of the man who took her to be real and experienced desire for her (he states, "°*vyavadāna*° manque dans Tib., se rapporte en effet à l'example précédent" [PsP_L 46, n. 5]); he therefore retains *vyavadāna*. The magical woman might—although even this is a stretch—be considered as such if the man, his mind finally calmed, learned from his experience with her and, applying what he had gleaned from his experience with her to real women, similarly reflected upon them as impermanent and empty, but I hardly think that the poor fellow's desperate attempt to calm his mental and physiological reactions to her makes her a cause of his purification. He simply forces himself to focus on lust-neutralizing thoughts in regard to her; she does not, as the magical monks in the following long KP quotation do, effect anyone's release from defilement.

[348] Although *bāla* is often translated in similar contexts as "fools" (Seyfort Ruegg [2002: 84] translates it in the present context as "the foolish"), the word is more often used by Candrakīrti in the PsP, MABh, YṢV, CŚṬ and ŚSV to refer to the counterpart to the *ārya*s (Nobles). See, e.g., PsP_L 371.8-9: *tatra bālajanāpekṣayā sarvam etat tathyam | āryajñānāpekṣayā tu sarvam etan mṛṣā.* The *bāla*s are those who, inasmuch as their "mind's eye" is impaired by the "*timira* of ignorance," are attached to things that actually lack own-being (*niḥsvabhāva*) because they are convinced that these things have own-being, i.e., are real. They include those who speak of a characteristic (*lakṣaṇa*) of things, such as heat as the characteristic of fire (see PsP_L 261.3-6). The word *bāla* sometimes appears conjoined with or glossed by the compound *pṛthagjana*, also used as a synonym for *anārya*. *pṛthagjana* is used to refer to ordinary persons, sometimes indeed to uninstructed ones, in general (see, e.g., the Canonical citation at PsP_L 137.5-8 and de La Vallée Poussin's n. 3) but in the more specific soteriological context the word designates persons who have not yet attained the path of seeing (*darśanamārga*), and thus includes Buddhist practitioners as advanced as the *prayogamārga* (cf. $YṢV_{tr}$ 115, n. 39; 137, n. 97).

[349] The corresponding KP passage is found at KP_{ed} § 141.3-149.5; VD 2002: 49-53. The first sentence of this PsP chapter 1 citation bears some similarity with the Sanskrit as found at KP_{ed} § 138.3-5 (*paṃca* ...) and KP_{ed} § 139.2-4. The citation appears in a more extensive form at PsP_L 336.3-339.2 (see Kragh 2003: 93ff.); this version commences with text found at KP_{ed} § 139.2 and its initial section (not cited here in the first chapter) corresponds quite closely with the Sanskrit for KP_{ed} § 139-141.

Note that Kragh (2003: 93, n. 3) points out that the PsP chapter 17 citation appears to be an interpolation: it is not included in PsP chapter 17 Tib, and in PsP chapter 17 Skt it is misplaced.

In comparing KP_{ed} Skt with PsP Skt, I have noted only the most important variants, and have focussed primarily on the presence or absence of entire words and/or phrases. A perusal of these variants as attested for the KP citation as found in PsP chapter 1 vis-à-vis KP_{ed} Skt reveals that Candrakīrti relied on a more condensed and somewhat different version of the text of the KP than that contained in the manuscript used by Staël-Holstein for his edition of the KP, a manuscript written in Brāhmī script and possibly copied in Khotan around the seventh-eighth centuries (see VD 2002: vii; Staël-Holstein judged that the manuscript dates from around the ninth to tenth centuries; see KP_{ed} Preface, p. VII); the manuscript is kept in St. Petersburg and has been assigned the call number SI P/2. As can be noticed immediately upon comparing the Sanskrit and Tibetan for the paragraphs in Staël-Holstein's edition, KP_{ed} Tib frequently differs substantially from KP_{ed} Skt. PsP Skt, interestingly, on a number of occasions agrees, against KP_{ed} Skt, with KP_{ed} Tib, thus suggesting that Candrakīrti is citing from a version of the KP closer to the one from which the KP_{ed} Tib translation was made than to that found in ms SI P/2. Seemingly indicative of the fact that the manuscript relied on for KP_{ed} Skt contains accretions is the reference to 500 nuns (*paṃcānāṃ ca bhikṣunīśatānāṃ*) at the end of KP_{ed} § 149 Skt, a reference not appearing in KP_{ed} Tib or in PsP Skt or PsP Tib. The PsP Tib translators have, as is their practice, inserted the pre-made KP Tib translation of the citation; thus PsP Tib largely reproduces KP_{ed} Tib (the variants between PsP Tib and KP_{ed} Tib in the passages cited are minimal and usually insignificant). PsP Tib—perhaps because the translators inserted the sections of the long citation en bloc without meticulously collating it against the PsP Skt citation—includes a number of passages and sections found in KP_{ed} Tib but not in PsP Skt.

Lamotte (1936: 288, n. 1) does not translate the KP citation in his PsP chapter 17 translation, referring there to the translation of the section in Stcherbatsky's rendering of PsP chapter 1 (cf. Stcherbatsky 1927: 129-131). The sections in the more extensive PsP chapter 17 citation which do not appear in Stcherbatsky's chapter 1 translation are translated in an Appendix in May 1959 (299f.). The entire chapter 17 citation has more recently been translated in an Appendix in Kragh 2003: 266ff. A partial translation of the citation as found in the first chapter of the PsP appears in Lamotte 1987: 174, n. 66. The KP section is translated in Weller 1965: 145-152 and in Pāsādika 1979 (9). Of comparative interest are Weller's translations from the Han version of the KP (see Weller 1987a: 1229-1234) and from the Sung version of the KP (see Weller 1987b: 1440-1447); see also Chang 1983: 407.

Those five hundred monks,[350] not understanding[351] the Exalted One's teaching of the Doctrine (*dharmadeśanā*), not fathoming [it], not being convinced [by it], rose from [their] seats and went forth.[352] Then the Exalted One created two [magical] monks on the path on which these monks were going. Those five hundred monks came near where those two monks were.[353] Having come near, they said to the two [magical monks], "Where are the

---

[350] PsP Tib (cp. PsP$_M$ §78, PsP$_L$ 47.1) and the second citation of the passage at PsP$_L$ 336.3 additionally contain the epithet *dhyānalābhīni* / *bsam gtan thob pa* ("attainers of the concentrations"), which is also found in KP$_{ed}$ Skt and KP$_{ed}$ Tib (see KP$_{ed}$ § 139.2; VD 2002: 48); *dhyānalābhī* is also found earlier in KP$_{ed}$ Skt and KP$_{ed}$ Tib in a similarly constructed sentence (see KP$_{ed}$ § 138.4; VD 2002: 48). Ms P for PsP$_L$ 336.2 also presents *dhyānalābhīni* but does not attest it for our first chapter citation. The first sentence for chapter 17's citation reads *pañca ca bhikṣuśatāni dhyānalābhīny utthāyāsanebhyaḥ prakrāntāni imāṃ gambhīrāṃ dharmadeśanām anavabudhyamānāny anavataranty anavagāhamānāny anadhimucyamānāni* | (cp. KP$_{ed}$ § 138.3-5; KP$_{ed}$ § 139.2-4). Candrakīrti's manuscript may not have contained the compound, or he may be abbreviating.

[351] The KP manuscript (see KP$_{ed}$ § 139.3 Skt; VD 2002: 48) for the sentence after which this first sentence in the PsP appears to be modelled reads *avataraṃto*, which is corrected by Weller (1965: 145, n. 7) to *nāvataraṃto* on the basis of KP Tib *mi 'jug*; he corrects to *nāva°* and not *anava°* presumably because the KP manuscript presents the immediately following negated participle in the form *nāva°* (masculine plural forms appear in KP Skt because the monks are men; the grammatically correct neuter plural forms in PsP Skt seem to have resulted from standardization). PsP$_L$ 337.1: *dharmadeśanām ana[va]budhyamānāny anavataranty anavagāhamāny anadhimucyamānāni*. KP Tib and PsP Tib place a *shad* after *mi 'jug ste* (KP Skt: *nāvataraṃto*). The Sanskrit on which KP Tib is based may have read *nāvataranti*, with *avataranti* being interpreted by the translators of KP Tib not as a neuter nominative plural participle but as a third person plural finite verb. Alternatively, the Sanskrit may have read *nāvataranto* (as KP Skt probably did), but the vertical stroke making up part of the *o* of *°nto/°ṃto akṣara* was read as a *daṇḍa* and the superscript part of the *o* interpreted as an *i*.

[352] The KP citation that commences at PsP$_L$ 336.3 now includes, after its version (similar to KP$_{ed}$ § 139.2-4 Skt) of this first sentence, passages not found here in the KP citation of PsP chapter 1 but found in KP$_{ed}$ Skt; see PsP$_L$ 337.3-338.5 and cp. KP$_{ed}$ § 139.4 - § 141.3; see also Weller 1965: 145; May 1959: 299f.

[353] PsP Tib: *dge slong lnga brgya po de dag dge slong de gnyis lam gang nas dong ba'i lam der dong*. Weller (1965: 146 and n. 13) translates the KP$_{ed}$ Tib sentence: "Dann kamen die fünfhundert Mönche dorthin, wo die zwei hervorgezauberten Mönche auf dem Wege gingen," noting "Das Verb steht im Tibetischen."

Venerable Ones about to go?" The [magical monk] creations said, "We are about to go to places in the forest. There we shall abide in states of comfort consisting in the happiness of meditation (*dhyānasukhasparśavihāra*).[354] For we do not understand, do not fathom, are not convinced of the Doctrine the Exalted One teaches; we are afraid, are terrified [of it], we fall into [a state of] dread."[355] Then those five hundred monks said this: "We too, O Venerable Ones, do not understand the Exalted One's teaching of the Doctrine, do not fathom [it], are not convinced [by it], are afraid, are terrified [of it], fall into dread. Therefore we shall, at places in the forest, abide in states of comfort consisting in the happiness of meditation." The [magically] created [monks] said, "Then, Venerable Ones, we shall confer together,[356] we shall not dispute; for the duty of the

[354] Weller (1965: 146, n. 18) notes that although KP_{ed} Skt presents *sukhaṃ phāṣaṃ vihariṣyāmaḥ* ("we shall dwell happily, comfortably") at this point and *sukhaṃ vihariṣyāmaḥ* where the magical monks repeat their intent (KP_{ed} § 141.11 Skt), KP_{ed} Tib attests *bsam gtan gyi bde ba la reg par gnas pa rnams kyis gnas par bya*, i.e., the translation for *dhyānasukhasparśavihārair vihariṣyāmaḥ* for both instances. PsP Skt and PsP Tib attest respectively *dhyānasukhasparśavihārair vihariṣyāmaḥ* and its Tibetan equivalent for the first instance (PsP Skt does not include an equivalent sentence for the one containing *sukhaṃ vihariṣyāmaḥ*, but PsP Tib does, and reads as KP_{ed} Tib). PsP Skt further attests *dhyānasukhasparśavihārair vihariṣyāmaḥ* where KP_{ed} § 142.3-4 Skt presents *dhyānasukhavihārair vihariṣyāmaḥ* (PsP Tib, based on KP Tib, presents *bsam gtan gyi bde ba la reg par gnas pa rnams kyis gnas par bya*). Seyfort Ruegg (2002: 85) interprets *sukha* in the PsP Skt compound adjectivally ("we shall abide in the abode of blissful contact in meditation") but does not explain with what the "blissful contact" might be. The Tibetan and BHSD (s.v. *sparśavihāratā*) speak against the adjectival interpretation. On *vihāra*, *vihārati*, see Maithrimurthi 1999: 17-19, especially nn. 14 and 15; Wezler 1990: 134ff. Cf. PsP_L 47, n. 4.

[355] PsP Tib adds: *kho ba cag dgon pa'i gnas rnams su bsam gtan gyi bde ba la reg par gnas pa rnams kyis gnas par bya'o*. This sentence appears as the final sentence of KP_{ed} § 141 Tib. KP_{ed} Skt reads: *tāv āvām āraṇyāyataneṣu sukhaṃ vihariṣyāmaḥ*.

[356] Weller considers KP_{ed} Skt's typically BHS future form *saṃgāyiṣyāma* (PsP Skt presents the classical form *saṅgāsyāmaḥ*) as properly reflected in KP_{ed} Tib's *yag dag par bgro bar bya* (PsP Tib in all four Canonical editions and the Golden Manuscript is presented as *yag dag par 'gro bar bya*, probably the result of an auditory error), which he translates in a note "wir wollen auf rechte Weise erörtern, betrachten" (cf. Weller 1965: 147, n. 2); cf. Jäschke s.v. *bgro ba*: "to argue, discuss, deliberate, consider." Weller translates *saṃgāyiṣyāma* in his main text as "Wir wollen uns

ascetic (*śramaṇadharma*) consists principally in [being] without strife (*avivādaparama*)[357].[358] For the sake of abandoning what have the Venerable Ones engaged in practice?" They said, "We have engaged in practice for the abandoning of desire (*rāga*), hatred (*dveṣa*) and disorientation (*moha*)."[359] The created

---

zusammen beraten." He notes that Edgerton differs in his interpretation of the verb: BHSD entry for *saṃgāyati*: "lit.: '*sings in union*' = *is concordant*, avoids quarreling, opp. of vivadati" (Edgerton's single reference is to this KP passage). Pāsādika (1979 [9]: 26) translates "let us be united." See, in support of Weller's main text translation, PW s.v. *sam√gā*: "gemeinschaftlich besingen" which, applied to the KP situation makes sense as "talk/discuss together."

[357] KP_{ed} § 142.5: *avivāda paramo hi śramaṇadharmaḥ* for *avivādaparamo hi śramaṇadharmaḥ*, but correctly presented in VD 2002: 50. Weller (1965: 147) translates, "Ist doch die Streitlosigkeit das höchste Gesetz für die Religiosen." KP_{ed} Tib reads *rtsod pa med pa lhur len pa ni dge sbyong gi chos*, and PsP Tib presents the synonymous *rtsod pa med pa lhur byed pa ni ...* (both *lhur len* (*pa*) and *lhur byed* (*pa*) are often seen representing *parama* as the final member of a compound). If Jäschke's rendering of *lhur len pa* as "to apply oneself" is correct, it may be that the translators interpreted the Sanskrit slightly differently, i.e., as "[to be] one who applies oneself to [being] without strife is the duty of ascetics." In line with this, Weller (1965: 147, n. 3) translates KP_{ed} Tib's *rtsod pa med pa lhur len pa ni dge sbyong gi chos* as "Sich der Streitlosigkeit zu befleissigen ist das Gesetz der Religiosen." De La Vallée Poussin comments on *avivāda* at PsP_L 47, n. 5. Noteworthy are Vetter's (2001: 72f. and n. 44) comments on the meaning of "one dwelling without strife" in this KP passage (**araṇavihārin*; his focus is Lokakṣema's Chinese translation). Cp. the reference to *samaṇadhamma* at AN III.371.

[358] PsP Tib includes the continuing text found in KP_{ed} § 142 Tib (KP_{ed} Skt contains similar, more extensive text) but not found in PsP Skt. It also reproduces the text, with minor variants, as it is found in KP_{ed} § 143 Tib (KP_{ed} Skt differs from KP_{ed} Tib).

[359] The two sentences *kasyāyuṣmantaḥ prahāṇāya pratipannāḥ* | *tāny avocan rāgadveṣamohānāṃ prahāṇāya vayaṃ pratipannāḥ* do not appear in KP_{ed} Skt, KP_{ed} Tib, or PsP Tib. There also does not appear to be enough space in the corresponding damaged part of the PsP chapter 17 citation in ms P for the two sentences. This damaged part in ms P's chapter 17, however, provides exactly enough space for the KP_{ed} Skt (not found in our PsP chapter 1 Skt) which follows the compound *śramaṇadharmaḥ*: *yad iha-m-āyuṣmanta ity ucyate parinirvāṇam iti* | *katamaḥ sa dharmo yaḥ pari*(*nirvā*)*syati* (KP_{ed} § 142.5-7; see VD 2002: 50; ms P's chapter 17 text in fact begins again with *nirvāsyati*). PsP Tib (chapter 1), not attesting the two sentences found in our PsP Skt, accords with KP_{ed} Tib in including the rest of KP_{ed} § 142 Tib. PsP Tib carries on with KP_{ed} § 143 Tib, which lacks an equivalent for KP_{ed} § 143.1-4 Skt. PsP Skt ends for KP_{ed} § 142 with *śramaṇadharmaḥ* (KP_{ed} § 142.5) and picks up again at KP_{ed} § 143.6. KP_{ed} § 143.4-5 Skt: (*kiṃ*) *puna sākṣīkṛyāyā parinirvāsyatīti* | *te*

[monks] said, "But do desire, hatred and disorientation [actually] exist for the Venerable Ones so that you might destroy them?" They replied, "Neither internally, nor externally, nor [somewhere] in between the two are they perceived;[360] nor do they, unless one imagines them (*aparikalpita*), arise." The [two] created [monks] said, "Therefore, O Venerable Ones, do not construct, do not conceptualize. And when you, O Venerable Ones, do not construct, do not conceptualize, you will not feel desirous, you will not become free from desire.[361] And it is said that he who is not desirous, is not desireless, is at peace (*śānta*). Morality (*śīla*), O Venerable Ones, does not wander [in *saṃsāra*] (*na saṃsarati*), does not enter full *nirvāṇa* (*na parinirvāti*); concentration (*samādhi*), insight (*prajñā*), liberation (*vimukti*), and the knowledge and the vision of liberation (*vimuktijñānadarśana*),[362] O Venerable Ones, do not wander in *saṃsāra*, do not

āhuḥ | *rāgakṣayāya dveṣakṣayāya mohakṣayāya āyuṣmanta parinirvāṇaṃ* (see VD 2002: 50). KP_{ed} Tib and PsP Tib present *gang zad pas yongs su mya ngan las 'da'* | *de dag gis smras pa* | *'dod chags zad zhe sdang zad gti mug zad pas yongs su mya ngan las 'da'o.*

360 A parallel expression occurs in the Pratyutpannabuddhasaṃmukhāvasthitasamādhisūtra (see Harrison 1990: 42), and in the Vimalakīrtinirdeśasūtra (*nāpattir adhyātmaṃ na bahirdhā nobhayam antareṇopalabhyate*; see Lamotte 1987: 174). KP_{ed} Tib (and PsP Tib following it) translates *nobhayam antareṇa* as *gnyi ga med pa la yang* (PsP Tib *par* for *pa la*), that is, as "also not in the absence of the two." Harrison (1990: 42, n. 24) considers a desire for intelligibility as the reason for this translation choice, stating: "Certainly 'neither inside nor outside' is more readily understood than 'between inside and outside.'" PsP Tib for the following Vajramaṇḍadhāraṇī quotation likewise translates *sa ca paridāho nādhyātmaṃ na bahirdhā nobhayam antareṇa sthitaḥ* as *de yang nang na 'ang mi gnas phyi rol na 'ang mi gnas gnyi ga med par yang mi gnas.*

361 Lamotte (1987: 174, n. 66) translates *na raṃkṣyatha na viraṃkṣyatha* as "vous n'éprouverez ni amour ni haîne" but I think that the author of the KP probably wishes to convey the idea that when conceptualizing has ceased, there is no desire, and when there is no desire, there can be no relinquishing of it. The non-existence of desire implies that there is nothing there, i.e., no desirous feeling or emotion, that could be given up. Cf. Seyfort Ruegg 2002: 86; Pāsādika 1979 (9): 27.

362 As de La Vallée Poussin notes, morality, concentration, insight, liberation, and the knowledge and vision of liberation are the five *lokottaraskandhas*. For references, see Lamotte 1987: 139, n. 30; PsP_L 48, n. 1; 292, n. 4. Candrakīrti refers to this grouping of *skandhas* in his commentary on MMK XXII.1 where he states that if the

enter full *nirvāṇa*. And *nirvāṇa*, O Venerable Ones, is indicated by these *dharma*s, but these *dharma*s are empty (*śūnya*), isolated by nature (*prakṛtivivikta*). Give up, O Venerable Ones, this notion (*sañjñā*), namely, 'full *nirvāṇa*.' Neither form a notion in regard to a notion nor see through a notion by way of a notion; because for the one who sees through a notion by way of a notion this becomes nothing but bondage to notions.[363] O Venerable Ones, accomplish the absorption of the cessation of [all] notions and feelings (*sañjñāvedayitanirodhasamāpatti*).[364] We assert that there is nothing left to be done by the monk who has accomplished the absorption of the cessation of [all] notions and feelings."

Then the minds (*citta*) of those five hundred monks, not clinging (*anupādāya*), became liberated from the influxes/impurities (*āśrava*). Those [monks] of liberated mind went near to where the Exalted One was, [and] come near, [and] having paid homage with their heads to his feet, sat to one side. Then the Venerable Subhūti said this to those monks: "Where did the Venerable Ones go? Or from where did you come?" They replied, "Not for going somewhere, not for coming from somewhere, O Reverend Subhūti, did the Exalted One teach the Doctrine." [Subhūti] said, "Who, then, is the teacher of the Venerable Ones?" They said, "The one who has not arisen, [who] will not enter full *nirvāṇa*." [Subhūti] said, "How (i.e., expecting what) have you listened to the Doctrine?" They said, "Not for bondage, not for liberation." [Subhūti] said, "By whom have you been trained?" They said, "[By the one] who has no body, no mind." [Subhūti] said, "How

---

Tathāgata really existed, he would exist having either the own-being of the five *skandha*s [bodily] matter, feeling, ideation, impulses, and consciousness, the own-being of the five listed here, or one different from these. He goes on to say that only the first set of *skandha*s is considered in the chapter, since the second is not comprehensive, included as it is in the first set (*avyāpakatvād eṣāṃ pūrvakair antarbhāvitatvāt*; see PsP_L 432.14-433.3)

[363] *pari√jñā* "to know thoroughly," thus by extension "to see through," often implies that that which is seen through is also cleared away, eliminated.

[364] On *sañjñāvedayitanirodhasamāpatti*, see Schmithausen 1981: 214ff.; Griffiths 1991 (Index s.v. Attainment of Cessation).

have you practised?" They said, "Not for abandoning ignorance, not for generating knowledge (*vidyā*)."[365] [Subhūti] said, "Whose auditors (*śrāvaka*) are you?" They said, "[We are the auditors of the one] who has not attained [anything], who has not awakened to [anything]."[366] [Subhūti] said, "Who are your fellow disciples (*sabrahmacārin*)?" They said, "[Those] who do not range in the triple world (*tridhātu*)." [Subhūti] said, "After how long a time will the Venerable Ones enter into full *nirvāṇa*?" They said, "When the [magical monks] created by the Tathāgata will enter into full *nirvāṇa*." [Subhūti] said, "Have you done what is to be done?" They said, "Owing to seeing through the notions of 'I' and 'mine' (*ahaṅkāramamakāra*)." [Subhūti] said, "Are your defilements (*kleśa*) exhausted?" They said, "Owing to the complete exhaustion of all phenomena (*dharma*)." [Subhūti] said, "Has Māra been overpowered by you?" They said, "Owing to the non-perception of Māra [represented by] the [five] constituent elements (*skandha*)."[367] [Subhūti] said, "Has the teacher been honoured by you?" They said, "Not with the body, not with speech, not with the mind." [Subhūti] said, "Has the ground (*bhūmi*) of those worthy of gifts (*dakṣiṇīya*) been purified by

---

[365] The PsP Skt text here agrees with KP_{ed} Tib, against KP_{ed} Skt; see Weller's (1965: 149, n. 13) comments on KP_{ed} Skt for this passage. PsP Tib includes the final sentences of KP_{ed} § 146.

[366] KP_{ed} Skt reads: *yasya na prāpto nā[bhi]saṃbuddhaḥ* (see VD 2002: 52). Cf. CPD (s.v. *abhi* -2.) on the prefix *abhi* lending a transitive sense to intransitives: "as preverb to verbs and their derivatives expresses: movement towards or against or over; intensivity; or gives a transitive meaning to intransitive verbs." Weller (1965: 149) translates, "[Dessen,] von dem keiner [als Schüler] erlangt wird und der nicht die völlige Erleuchtung gewann." PsP Tib and KP_{ed} Tib: *gang gis thob pa med cing mngon par rdzogs par sangs rgyas pa med pa'i'o.*

[367] The four Māras found in later literature are *skandhamāra*, *kleśamāra*, *mṛtyumāra*, and *devaputramāra* (noted at PsP_L 49, n. 4); on the Māras, see Dayal 1978: 306-317; Lamotte 1966: 339-346; Lamotte 1987: 204, n. 121; $AKBh_{tr}$ II.124, n. 5 (ref.). Candrakīrti refers to the four Māras at PsP_L 442.3 and 451.7; cp. YṢ *kārikā* 36ab and Candrakīrti's commentary where he describes the Māra referred to in the *kārikā* as *'phags pa'i shes rab kyi dbang po'i srog gi bar chad byed pa* ($YṢV_{ed}$ 76.8-15; see also $YṢV_{tr}$ 264f., nn. 511-513).

you?"[368] They said, "From not taking, from not receiving." [Subhūti] said, "Have you crossed over *saṃsāra*?" They said, "On account of non-annihilation (*anuccheda*), on account of non-eternity (*aśāśvata*)."[369] [Subhūti] said, "Have you attained the ground of those worthy of gifts?" They said, "From the release of all grasping (*grāha*)." [Subhūti] said, "Where do the Venerable Ones intend to go?" They said, "Where the [monks] created by the Tathāgata intend to go." Right then as the Venerable Subhūti was questioning [them] and as those monks were responding, the minds of eight hundred monks in that assembly, not clinging, were liberated from the influxes/impurities, and of thirty-two thousand beings the Dharma-eye (*dharmacakṣu*) in regard to the teachings was purified (*viśuddha*), [to the point of being] dustless (*virajas*), delivered of [all] dross (*vigatamala*).[370]

---

[368] KP Skt presents *sthitā yuṣmākaṃ dākṣiṇeyabhūmau* : (the two final dots represent punctuation; see VD 2002: 52. KP_{ed} mistakenly presents *bhūmauḥ*), as compared to PsP's *viśodhitā yuṣmābhir dakṣiṇīyabhūmiḥ*. Weller (1965: 151, n. 9) reconstructs *śuddhā yuṣmābhir dākṣiṇeyabhūmiḥ* from KP_{ed} Tib's *khyed khyis sbyin pa'i gnas kyi sa sbyangs sam* (PsP Tib: *khyod kyis yon gnas kyi sa sbyangs sam*), noting that the Djin and Sung Chinese translations also support the reading *śuddhā*, not *sthitā*.

[369] I do not know why Seyfort Ruegg (2002: 88) translates *anucchedato 'śāśvatataḥ* as "Neither from non-destruction nor from non-eternity". "Neither" is not supported by PsP Skt or PsP Tib.

[370] On the Dharma-eye, see ASBh 78.6: *yad uktaṃ virajo vigatamalaṃ dharmeṣu dharmacakṣur utpadyata iti tad darśanamārgam adhikṛtyoktam, tatprathamataḥ satyeṣv āryaprajñācakṣuḥsvabhāvatvāt* | *tatra dharmakṣāntibhir virajaḥ, tābhiḥ kleśa-rajaḥprahāṇāt* | *dharmajñānair vigatamalam, teṣāṃ prahāṇatadāvaraṇamalāśrayotpādāt*[1] | *punar anayor eva kṣāntijñānāvasthayor yathākramaṃ parijñayā prahāṇena ca mārgasya viśuddhatām adhikṛtya virajo vigatamalaṃ veditavyam* ||; [1]Tatia (n. 2) notes that the Tibetan and Chinese appear to have the better reading **tadāvaraṇa-malaprahāṇāśrayotpādāt*. One might instead suggest *prahīṇatadāvaraṇa*° (Tib [P 704b]: *de dag ni de'i sgrib pa'i dri ma* <u>*spangs pa*</u>*'i gnas su skyes pa'i phyir ro*). The Canonical Pāli texts tend to present the construction *virajaṃ vītamalaṃ dhamma-cakkhum udapādi*. Both PTSD and BHSD refer to the definition *dhammesu vā cakkhuṃ dhammamayam vā cakkhuṃ* for *dhammacakkhu* of DN-aṭṭha I.237. Walshe (1987: 547, n. 140) notes that the opening of the Dharma-eye is "a term for 'entering the stream' and thus being set irrevocably on the path." He continues, "As RD [= Rhys Davids] points out, it is superior to the divine eye (*dibba-cakkhu* ...) which is a superior kind of clairvoyance, and below the wisdom-eye (*pañña-cakkhu*), which is the wisdom of the Arahant." Bodhi (2000: 1404, n. 40), in reference to the formulaic

In this way, a cause of purification was effected for the five hundred monks by way of the [two] monks created by the Tathāgata, [both of whom] had a false own-being.

§79. And it is stated in the Noble Vajramaṇḍadhāraṇī,[371]

> "Just as, O Mañjuśrī, in dependence on a stick (*kāṇḍa*), in dependence on a churning stick (*mathanī*),[372] and[373] in dependence on a man's manual exertion (*hastavyāyama*), smoke appears, [and] fire comes forth—but that burning heat (*santāpa*) of the fire is not located in the stick, not located in the churning stick, not located in the man's manual exertion—exactly so, O

---

virajaṃ vītamalaṃ dhammacakkhum udapādi appearing at SN IV.47, states, "The arising of the vision of the Dhamma (*dhammacakkhu*) means the attainment of one of the three lower stages of awakening, usually stream-entry." On the five kinds of eyes (especially the heavenly eye), see Lamotte 1987: 168f., nn. 57 and 58.

[371] De La Vallée Poussin (PsP_L 50, n. 3) states that a fragment of this same citation of the Vajramaṇḍadhāraṇī (VMD) is cited at PsP_L 462.4-5. The *sūtra*, which is not preserved in Sanskrit, is found in P vol. 32 (no. 807; 300b3-312a4) and D vol. 56 (no. 139; 278a1-289b4) under the name 'Phags pa rdo rje'i snying po'i gzungs (shes bya ba theg pa chen po'i mdo); its Sanskrit name is given as Āryavajramaṇḍanāma-dhāraṇī(mahāyānasūtra). PsP Tib frequently differs from the Canonical translation. This, together with the fact that readings in PsP Tib also diverge from PsP Skt, point to the Tibetan having been quoted from a proto-Canonical translation of the VMD. I note only the major variants between PsP Skt and PsP Tib. The VMD Tib text up to the "etymological" explanation of *moha* is found at P fol. 304b8-305a3. The text for the section discussing the hells is found at P fol. 306b6-308a4.

[372] I suspect that *mathanī* refers to the churning stick and not to the act of rotating the first-mentioned stick (*kāṇḍa*), for otherwise the "manual exertion" (*hastavyāyāmam*) would be redundant. Cp. R.L. Turner, *A Comparative Dictionary of Indo-Āryan Languages*, London: Oxford U. Press, 1966, p. 561 s.v. *mathana*, where *mahanī* is translated as "churning stick." *kāṇḍa* would appear, then, to be the counterpart to the churning stick. I do not know exactly how it was used together with the churning stick. PsP Tib translates *mathanī* with *gtsub stan* ("a basis for the [fire]churning stick"). TCD explains *gtsub shing gtsub stan* with *me 'byin pa'i shing yas mas gnyis*. The translators may have had a slightly different set of tools in mind than the author of the *sūtra*. Seyfort Ruegg (2002: 89), in translating *mathanī* as "a rubbing surface," appears to be following the Tibetan.

[373] The *ca* appears only in ms Q, and I accept it for my edition. P's (and the paper mss') reading without *ca* is, however, also possible if one assumes that the sticks are already lying there and the physical activity of the hand is the catalyst.

Mañjuśrī, does the burn (*paridāha*) of desire (*rāga*), the burn of hatred (*dveṣa*), the burn of disorientation (*moha*) arise for a person (*puruṣapudgala*)[374] who is disoriented by [subjective] error in regard to what is unreal. And that burn is not inside, not outside, not [somewhere] in between the two. But, Mañjuśrī, why is 'disorientation' (*moha*) called 'disorientation'? Because disorientation is completely deprived (*atyantamukta*) of [the true nature of] all phenomena (*dharma*), O Mañjuśrī; therefore it is called 'disorientation.'[375] Similarly, all phenomena have [a source like] the source of the hells (*narakamukha*), O Mañjuśrī; this is a formulaic phrase (*dhāraṇīpada*)."[376] [Mañjuśrī] said,

---

[374] *LṬ's author comments on *puruṣapudgala* as follows: *puruṣa ity ātmāpi syād ataḥ pudgala ity āha*; "'*puruṣa*' could also mean the Self/soul (*ātman*); therefore he says [i.e., adds,] '*pudgala*'" (cf. Yonezawa 2004: 123, 140 [fol. 2b2]). The compound is composed of quasi-synonyms, and has the sense "a human person." Cp. PTSD s.v. *purisapuggalo*: "a man, a human character."

[375] The *sūtra* presumes an etymological connection between the substantive *moha* (in classical Sanskrit derived from √*muh*) and the past passive participle *mukta* (in classical Sanskrit derived from √*muc*). Specifically, *moha* is interpreted as derived from √*muc*, possibly because the word explanation originated within a middle-Indic linguistic environment or because the author of the *sūtra* had a middle-Indic development in mind. One might hypothesize that the substantive **mo⁽ʸ⁾a*—from **moca* or **moka* (derived from √*muc*)—was written as *moha*, with *h* serving as a glide, as in certain other Prākrit words; on the *h* glide, cf. von Hinüber 2001: 211. *LṬ's author glosses *sarvadharmaiḥ mukto* with *sarvadharmmaiḥ śūnyatvādibhir mukto bahiṣkṛtaḥ* (ms: *bahiḥkṛtaḥ*) "[disorientation is] deprived of [that is,] separate from all *dharma*s, that is, [separate from] emptiness and so forth" (cf. Yonezawa 2004: 123, 141 [fol. 2b2]). Candrakīrti explains *moha* (from √*muh*) elsewhere as readily understood in both a *bhāvasādhana* and a *karaṇasādhana* sense: *mohanaṃ mohaḥ saṃmohaḥ padārthasvarūpāparijñānaṃ muhyate vānena cittam iti mohaḥ* (PsP_L 457.5; cf. May 1959: 186). The general meaning of *moha* is nicely exemplified in the compound *digmoha* "confusion with respect to the directions." Included is the idea of a confusion that is disturbing to the person experiencing it. The compound does not necessarily imply, but may take into account the idea that one has mixed up the directions, i.e., that in taking north to be south one has become misoriented. The primary idea is one of disorientation. PsP Tib presents *'jam dpal gti mug ni chos thams cad rab tu grol ba ste* for *atyantamukto hi mañjuśrīḥ sarvadharmair mohas*.

[376] Some texts suggest that a *dhāraṇīpada* is a formulaic phrase containing the essence of the/a Buddhist teaching in condensed form. Cf. BhoBhū 272.12ff.; see also Hartmann 1985. I understand the "source/origin" (*mukha*) of phenomena intended by the *sūtra* to be conceptuality (*vikalpa*), i.e., ideational error (*sañjñāviparyāsa*). I

"How, O Exalted One, is this a formulaic phrase?" [The Exalted One] said, "The hells, O Mañjuśrī, fabricated by [subjective] error in regard to what is unreal by [spiritually] immature ordinary persons, have come about through [these persons'] own conceptuality (*vikalpa*)." [Mañjuśrī] said, "Where, O Exalted One, are the hells gathered together?" The Exalted One said, "The hells are gathered together in space, O Mañjuśrī. Then what do you think, O Mañjuśrī, have the hells come about by virtue of [these persons'] own conceptuality or have they come about by [their] own nature?" [Mañjuśrī] said, "Only by virtue of [their] own conceptuality, O Exalted One, do all [spiritually] immature ordinary persons know the hells and the animal [realm] and the

---

concur with *LṬ's author in taking *narakamukhāḥ* as an *upamā bahuvrīhi* compound. *LṬ's author, however, offers an interpretation of the sentence that slightly differs from my undertanding of its meaning. He begins his comments on the formulaic phrase (*dhāraṇī*) by glossing *mukha* of *narakamukhāḥ* of the citation with *āśrayaḥ*, (even though the *LṬ manuscript could be interpreted as reading *mukhyatā* here and Yonezawa [2004: 123, 141] accepts this reading, the continuing explication makes clear that *mukham* is being glossed; one should perhaps read *mukham āśrayaḥ*). He explains that in the present context that which is the source, i.e., the basis, is [empty] space (*tac cātrākāśaṃ*). After dissolving *narakamukhāḥ* of the *sūtra* citation as, as stated, an *upamā bahuvrīhi* (*narakamukham iva mukhaṃ yeṣāṃ sarvadharm{m}ā-ṇāṃ*), *LṬ's author concludes his explanation by stating that the *sūtra*'s sentence thus means that just as the hells have [empty] space as their basis, so do all phenomena (*yathā narakā ākāśāśrayās tathā sarvadharmā apīty arthaḥ*). He adds that a *dhāraṇī-pada* is called such because it contains the teaching of all the Buddhas (alternatively, "the entire teaching of the Buddhas"): *sarvabuddhadharm{m}adhāraṇād dhāraṇī-padaṃ* (cf. Yonezawa 2004: 123, 141 [fol. 2b2]).
Seyfort Ruegg (2002: 89) understands the sentence *tathā narakamukhā mañjuśrīḥ sarvadharmā idaṃ dhāraṇīpadam* differently, and translates, taking the Tibetan into consideration: "Thus, Mañjuśrī, all *dharma*s being entries for (the denizens of) hells (*narakamukha* = *sems can dmyal ba'i sgo*), this is a Formulaic Phrase (*dhāraṇīpada* = *gzuṅs gi tshig*)." It is true that *sems can dmyal ba* can have the meaning "hell-being," but given the context and the fact that *naraka* occurs a number of times in the citation and is consistently translated throughout as *sems can dmyal ba*, it is better understood as referring to the hells. It is also difficult to know what the *sūtra* author might have intended if he really meant that *dharma*s are "entries for the denizens of hells." Stcherbatsky's (1927: 131) free translation "The axiom of this Dhāraṇī is that all elements are like the hells" indicates that he understood the sentence as expressing an equivalence of the hells and all other phenomena.

world of Yama.[377] And they, on account of [their] superimposition of the unreal, feel painful feeling, and experience [imagined] pain in all three bad destinies (*apāya*)."

"And just as, O Exalted One, I see the hells [as unreal], so [do I see] hellish pain (*duḥkha*) [as unreal].[378] For example, O Exalted One, a certain man, asleep, in a dream, experiences[379] himself as gone to hell. There, he would experience himself as cast into a boiling, glowing iron pot of many fathoms.[380] Inside it, he would feel harsh, sharp, acute, agonizing pain; in it, he would experience mental anguish, he would be afraid, would be terrified, would fall into [a state of] dread. Then, upon awakening,[381] he

---

377 *LṬ's author glosses *yamaloka* with *pretāḥ* (hungry ghosts) (cf. Yonezawa 2004: 124, 141 [fol. 2b3]).

378 Even though PsP Tib and VMD Tib support ms Q's reading *nāham*, ms P's (and B, J and L's) *cāham* is preferable on stylistic grounds: Were the negation itself to be emphasized, *na* would stand at the beginning of the sentence (right after *yathā* [= Q]), but should the stress be on *narakān* and *nārakaṃ duḥkham*, one would expect it to be placed before *paśyāmi*. The fact that it does not stand before *paśyāmi* in Q leads one to suspect that Q's *na* is either a scribal mistake or the result of deliberate change. As stated earlier, PsP Tib has been copied in from VMD Tib.

379 *sam√jñā* covers a broad field of concepts, some of which can be challenging to find English equivalents for. The two aspects prominent in the present section are conscious experience (*sam√jñā* in its sense of apperception) and imagining, and the emphasis on one or the other varies throughout. I translate *sañjānīte* as "experiences" above because the aware experience of being in hell stands in the foreground at this point, and it is clear that this experience occurs in a dream; one could alternatively consider "imaginarily experiences."

380 PsP Skt reads *anekapauruṣāyāṃ lohakumbhyāṃ* ("into a … iron pot of many fathoms") but PsP Tib reads *lcags kyi bum pa skyes bu du ma dang ldan pa* ("[into] a … iron pot *with many people* in it"). VMD Tib has been corrected to read *lcags kyi bum pa … 'dom du ma mchis pa'i nang na*, which corresponds with PsP Skt. See the following note. Seyfort Ruegg (2002: 90), taking the Tibetan into consideration, translates, "There he might conceive of himself as precipitated into a boiling and fiery iron cauldron large enough for many men."

381 The VMD citation, which was copied into PsP Tib, presents *de de nas sad par gyur zhing rlom pa dang bcas pas* for *sa tatra prativibuddhaḥ samānaḥ*, with *samāna* thus interpreted in the sense of "prideful/arrogant." *samānaḥ* is, however, here not intended in its classical meaning. It rather represents a Middle Indian medial present participle from *√as* ("being") that survived in Buddhist Hybrid Sanskrit; in the present context it can be translated as "upon" (thus "he, upon awakening") (cf.

would cry out, would lament, would wail, 'Oh, the pain! Oh, the pain!' His friends, acquaintances and relatives would then inquire, 'What is this pain of yours from?' He would speak to those friends, acquaintances and relatives thus, 'I have experienced the pain of the hells!' He would [then] scold, would rebuke them [saying], 'Really![382] I experience the pain of the hells, and you [go on to] ask me, 'What is this pain of yours from?!' Then those friends, acquaintances and relatives would speak to that man in the [following] way, 'Ah, [good] fellow, don't be afraid, don't be afraid, for you were sleeping; you did not depart from this house for somewhere [else].' Once again his memory would surface [and he would realize:] 'I was asleep! This which I assumed [to be happening] is false (*vitatha*), unreal (*abhūta*).' [And] once again he recovers [his] contentedness (*saumanasya*)."

"Just as, O Exalted One, that man, through the superimposition of the unreal (*asat*), asleep, in a dream, would experience himself as gone to hell, in exactly the same way, O Exalted One, do all [spiritually] immature ordinary persons, ensnared by unreal desire, construct the appearance (*nimitta*)[383] of a woman. Having

BHSD s.v. *samāna*). The erroneous *rlom pa dang bcas pa* in the translation of the VMD relied upon by the PsP Tib translators does not appear in the version of the *sūtra* found in the Canon or in the sTog, Gondhla and Phug brag collections. This and other errors and inconsistencies have led me to hypothesize that the PsP translators relied on an early and unrevised version of the VMD. For more details, see MacDonald 2015.

[382] I understand *nāma* in its sense of indicating anger or censure (cf. Apte s.v. *nāma*, meaning 7.)

[383] The word *nimitta* in the context of the citation refers to the entity woman in her entirety, and not, as it does in many other contexts, to a quality or a characteristic feature of an entity, such as the breasts of a woman (e.g., as in passages in which monks are advised not to grasp, i.e., give attention to, the female *nimitta* [= breasts] because if the *nimitta* are not grasped, there will be no formation of *saṃjñā* in regard to them and thus no resulting unwholesome mental, verbal or physical action on the part of the monk). PsP Tib supports this interpretation of *nimitta* as the entire entity with *bud med la mtshan mar rtog par bgyid*. As Schmithausen has noted, the expression *nimitta* means first of all "characteristic" ("Merkmal"; he calls attention to the series of quasi-synonyms *yair ākārair yair liṅgair yair nimittaiḥ* recorded in the Aṣṭādaśasāhasrikā Prajñāpāramitā, ed. E. Conze, Rome 1962: 149.3), but, similar

constructed the appearance of a woman, they experience themselves playing amorously with those [women]. The [spiritually] immature ordinary person comes to think thus, 'I am a man, this is a woman, this woman is mine.' His mind, inasmuch as that mind is possessed by yearning and desire (*chandarāga*),[384] goes in search of enjoyment (*bhoga*). For that reason he provokes arguments, quarrels and disputes. Because his [mental] faculty is corrupted, enmity (*vaira*) arises in him. He, on account of that ideational error (*sañjñāviparyāsa*), upon[385] dying imagines himself as feeling agonizing pain in the hells for many thousands of aeons (*kalpa*)."[386]

---

to the way in which *dharmas* are held to be independent characteristics or states, without there being a substance bearing them, the *nimittas* too are often considered to be independent, and not merely the attributes of their bases, the attribute-bearers (see his further comments in Schmithausen 1969: 120, n. 67). Erb (1990: 146) comments, "*nimitta* wird aber nicht nur für rein nominelle Erscheinungen wie Zahlen, Zeitstufen oder für Eigenschaften wie *śubha*, *strī*, *puruṣa* usw. verwendet, sondern bezeichnet auch durchaus konkretere Gegenstände: RĀ Vers 91-92; MMK XXV.24ab: *sarvopalambhopaśamaḥ*; Paraphrase dazu in Pras. S. 538.5: *iha hi sarveṣāṃ prapañcānāṃ nimittānāṃ ya upaśamo* ...". See, similarly, YṢV on YṢ 6cd (*srid pa yongs su shes pa ni* ‖ *mya ngan 'das shes brjod pa yin* ‖), where it is stated in regard to the thorough knowledge of existence, i.e., the knowledge that [occurs] in the mode of thorough non-knowledge of existence's being without arising, that "*de nyid mtshan ma thams cad rab tu zhi ba'i ngo bo yin pas*" ("just that has the nature of the calming of all appearances"; cp. Scherrer-Schaub's translation "C'est elle qui constitue la forme (*ngo ba*) de l'apaisement de toutes les déterminations (*mtshan ma* = *nimitta*) [qui caractérisent les objects de la connaissance empirique]." See YṢV$_{\text{ed}}$ 37.23-25; YṢV$_{\text{tr}}$ 147. *LṬ's author interprets *strīnimitta* to mean the fact of being endowed with the characteristics of a woman, such as the mouth/face: *strīnimittaṃ mukhādivaiśiṣṭyaṃ* (cf. Yonezawa 2004: 124, 141 [fol. 2b3]).

384 De La Vallée Poussin takes note of a scholastic definition of *chanda* and *rāga* recorded in the AKVy: *aprāpteṣu viṣayeṣu prārthanā chandaḥ prāpteṣu rāgaḥ* (PsP$_{\text{L}}$ 52, n. 3). I believe that the *sūtra* cited above intends the two as quasi-synonyms.

385 As earlier in the same VMD citation, *samāna* is translated as *rlom pa dang bcas pa*. See n. 381.

386 Seyfort Ruegg (2002: 91) appears to assume that the desirous man just described is the same man who dreamed he went to hell: "And, with this conceptual misapprehension (*saṃjñāviparyāsa*), he conceives of himself as, being dead, feeling a sensation of pain in hells for many thousands of aeons. For example, Lord, his friends, relations and kinsmen address this man as follows: "Do not fear, good fellow do not fear! You were asleep, you have gone nowhere outside this house." The two

"Just as, O Exalted One, the friends, acquaintances and relatives of that man [who dreamed he went to hell] speak thus, 'Ah, [good] fellow, do not be afraid, do not be afraid, for you were sleeping; you did not depart from this house for somewhere [else],' in just the same way, O Exalted One, do the Buddhas, the Exalted Ones, teach the Doctrine to beings who are mistaken due to an error of the mind (*cittaviparyāsaviparyasta*) thus: 'There is no woman (*strī*) here, there is no man (*puruṣa*), no being (*sattva*), no living being (*jīva*), no individual (*puruṣa*), no person (*pudgala*).[387] All these phenomena (*dharma*) are untrue (*vitatha*), all these phenomena are inexistent (*asat*). All these phenomena are fabricated (*viṭhapita*); like a magical illusion are all these phenomena, like a dream are all these phenomena, like magically created [things] are all these phenomena, like the moon [reflected] in water are all these phenomena,' and so on in detail. They, having heard this the Tathāgata's teaching of the Doctrine, see all phenomena as [things] for which desire (*rāga*) has faded, they see all phenomena as [things] in regard to which hatred (*doṣa*) has faded, they see all phenomena as [things] with regard to which disorientation (*moha*) has faded, as without own-being, without obstruction (*anāvaraṇa*). They die with the mind situated

---

men are not identical: the first only dreamed he went to hell, but the second actually did end up in hell. Because the latter believes in the reality of things, he does feel agonizing pain in hell; it is stated that he "imagines" himself as feeling the agonizing pain only because all things, from heaven and heavenly pleasure to hell and hellish pain are imagined by spiritually immature beings. The introduction to the paragraph makes clear that the experience of ordinary persons is being compared to a dream.

[387] Given that in the present passage the references to *puruṣa* and *strī* suggest that a negation of conventional concepts is primary, I translate the second occurrence of *puruṣa* in the sentence as "individual" and not as "soul," and also *pudgala* as "person," not as "[enduring, holistic] person." I also assume that *jīva* is merely intended as equivalent to *sattva* and therefore in the present context means "living being," as opposed to "life principle" and thus "soul." However, the Śrāvakas listening to or reading the *sūtra*'s statements would probably also make an association with the traditional negation of metaphysical entities like "soul" and "[enduring, holistic] person."

in space.[388] After death they enter the sphere of *nirvāṇa* without remainder. [It is] in this way, [i.e., arisen from conceptuality and thus like a dream, etc.,] that I, O Exalted One, see the hells."

§80. And it is stated in the Noble Upāliparipṛcchā,[389]

The peril of hell I have shown — many thousands of beings have become upset.[390]
But there exists in this world no being[391] who, having died, goes to a horrific bad destiny.

---

[388] *LṬ glosses *ākāśasthitena* with *anālambanena* (cf. Yonezawa 2004: 124, 141 [fol. 2b3]).

[389] Candrakīrti cites Upāliparipṛcchā 67-70. The same verses are cited again at PsP$_L$ 191.2-9 and PsP$_L$ 234.10 (de La Vallée Poussin does not reproduce the Sanskrit for the final citation and instead refers back to the previous two). Python (1973: XI) writes, "Les abondantes citations de l'*Upāli*° prouvent son autorité aussi bien pour le Vinaya mahāyāniste—dont il paraît être le texte de base—que pour la doctrine métaphysique du Mādhyamika: il est cité par Candrakīrti presque autant que le Samādhirājasūtra." Sanskrit (based on PsP$_L$) and Tibetan in Python 1973: 59f., translation 128f. PsP Tib's citation has been copied in from the premade Upāliparipṛcchā Tib translation. The PsP's citations of the verses are translated in Stcherbatsky 1927: 133; May 1959: 156f.; Schayer 1931: 22f., Seyfort Ruegg 2002: 92f. The *sūtra* forms part of the larger Ratnakūṭa collection. The Sanskrit for the text exists only in fragments and citations which, according to Python (1973: 1), cover approximately a third of the work. The PsP provides the only known Sanskrit for verses 67-70; thus again the importance of the readings attested in our manuscripts.

[390] I translate *darśita* as "shown" (and not as "taught," as the Tibetan and other translators have) because it is possible that the author of the *sūtra* wanted to convey the idea that a terrifying vision of hell had been created by the Buddha (cf. also Seyfort Ruegg 2002: 92). Stcherbatsky (1927: 133) takes *darśita* as a non-causative form and translates, "I have seen the many terrors of the hell, by which thousands of creatures are tormented"; similarly Schayer (1931: 22): "Ich habe manche Höllenschrecken geschaut, von denen Tausende von Wesen gequält werden." The first line of PsP Tib and Upāliparipṛcchā Tib reads *sems dmyal 'jigs pa nga yis bstan byas te*. May (1959: 156): "J'ai enseigné la terreur de l'enfer: bien des milliers d'êtres en sont bouleversés." Python (1973: 128): "Bien qu'à mon enseignement sur les terreurs des enfers [d]es milliers et des milliers d'êtres sont accablés." Lang (2001: 239): "I have explained the fear of hell. A hundred beings have trembled, not [just] one." Seyfort Ruegg (2002: 92): "Hellish (*nairayika* = *sems dmyal*) fear was shown by me, and thousands of sentient beings fell into shock." I understand *bhaya*, which means "fear" but also what one is afraid of, i.e., "danger," as intended here in the latter sense ("danger, risk, hazard"; cf. Apte s.v. *bhayaṃ* #3).

Nor do the torturers[392] [in hell], by whom swords, lances and daggers are used, exist.[393]
Yet by the power of [mental] construction one sees there, in a bad existence, those daggers plunge down on the body.[394]

---

[391] PsP Tib, Upāliparipṛcchā Tib: *gang dag shi 'phos ngan song drag 'gro ba'i* ‖ *'gro ba de dag nam yang yod ma yin* ‖ for *na ca vidyati kaściha* (to be understood as *kaśc'iha*) *satvo yo cyutu gacchati ghoram apāyam* ‖. The translators of Upāliparipṛcchā Tib may have read *karhi ta sattvā* instead of *kaściha satvo*, or possibly *karhi sa satvo* (their *dag* indicating a collective understanding of the singular).

[392] Python (cf. 1973: 128, n. 6) emends *kāraku kāraṇa* to *kāraṇakāraka* on the basis of the Upāliparipṛcchā Tib (*gnod pa byed pa*) and Chinese, noting that the final *ā* of *kāraṇā* has been dropped metri causa. (On *kāraṇā* "torture," "torment," cf. BHSD s.v. *kāraṇā*, and Gustav Roth, Bhikṣuṇī-Vinaya. Manual of Discipline for Buddhist Nuns, Tibetan Sanskrit Works Series XII. Patna: K.P. Jayaswal Research Institute, 1970, p. 130 § 154). The reading *kārakakāraṇa* as found in ms Q and in all three instances of the citation in ms P, as well as in D, J and L (ms B reads *kāraka-kāraṇaṃ*), may have entered the PsP ms tradition due to a scribe's unintentional transposition of *kāraka* and *kāraṇa* or because someone understood *kāraṇa* in the sense of "cause" and not as *kāraṇā* ("torture") and felt *kāraka* should stand in first position (but should we assume that the person responsible for the change also located and "corrected" the other two instances later in the PsP?). May (1959: 156) translates following PsP_L: "Il n'y a ni agent ni cause qui produise épées, javelots, couteaux." Stcherbatsky (1927: 133) attempts to deal with the problematic text by translating, "There are there no swords, no arrows and no spears, by which torture is inflicted" (Schayer [1931: 23] translates similarly). Lang (2001: 239), also reading *kārakakāraṇa*, translates: "There are no instruments [of torture] and no agents who brandish knives, spears, and swords." Seyfort Ruegg (2002: 92): "There are no slaughterers [?] by whom swords, javelins and knives are brandished." See the following note.

[393] The *pāda* reads *yehi kṛtā asitomaraśastrāḥ*. I tend to doubt that the author intended to lay stress on the idea that the torturers *made* their weapons and thus assume that *asi*, etc., plus √*kṛ* should be understood along the lines of *astrāṇi* √*kṛ* (MW s.v. √*kṛ*) "to practice the use of weapons." See also, e.g., *bhesajjaṃ karoti* (cf. CPD s.v. *karoti*), which may, in addition to "to prepare medicine," mean "to treat with medicine." The Tibetan presents *gang dag ral gri mda' chen mtshon 'byin pa'i* ‖; *'byin pa* can also mean "to pull out (a sword)."

[394] PsP Tib, Upāliparipṛcchā Tib: *rtog pa'i dbang gis ngan song de dag na* ‖ *lus la 'bab mthong de na mtshon cha med* ‖. Stcherbatsky (1927: 133) and Schayer (1931: 23) translate following the Tibetan: "... there are no real weapons"; "... diese Waffen existieren nicht." PsP_L presents *... patanti apāyita śāstrāḥ*, which Python corrects to *apāyi ta* (= *apāye te*). Python (1973: 128, n. 8) considers Upāliparipṛcchā Tib to be translating *apāyitāḥ* "ceux qui sont entrés dan les enfers" and that de La Vallée

Adorned[395] with multi-coloured, delightful flowers,[396] lovely
golden palaces shine [in the heavenly realms],
[Yet] for these, too, there is not some agent here; and these too
have been set up by the power of [mental] construction.

By the force of [mental] construction the world is conceptualized; through grasping at ideation a [spiritually] immature
[person] is conceptualized;[397]

Poussin was influenced by the Tibetan; de La Vallée Poussin (PsP$_L$ 53, n. 6), however, retranslates PsP Tib for the verse (very literally) as *ye asi-tomara-śastra-
kṣepaṇa-apaghāta-kārakāḥ, [te] na santi; kalpavaśena durgatiṣu tāsu kāye patanti
[śastrāṇi] paśyati; tatra śastrāṇi na santi.* I doubt that the difference between the
Tibetan and Sanskrit was so extreme; perhaps the Tibetan is a result of *apāyi ta
śastrāḥ* having been read as *apāyi na śastrāḥ.*

[395] All the manuscripts attest *saṃjñita*, I presume a wrong reading for *sajjita*, given
that *jj* of *sajjita* could be easily confused with—at least in old Nepalese and forms of
old Bengālī script—graphically similar *jñ. sajjita* must be based on √*sajj* (cf. MW
s.v. *sajjita*: fastened or attached to; equipped, prepared; ornamented), whereas Tib's
kha bye seems to be based on a form like *phullita*. PsP Tib, Upāliparipṛcchā Tib: *sna
tshogs yid dga' me tog kha bye zhing ‖ gser gyi khang mchog 'bar ba yid 'ong ba ‖.*
Stcherbatsky (1927: 133): (And in the heavens) delightful golden palaces decorated
with beautiful variegated flowers appear before us." Schayer (1931: 23): "[Und im
Himmel] erscheinen schöne, goldene Päläste, geschmückt mit lieblichen, bunten
Blumen." May (1959: 156): "[Dans les paradis,] de beaux châteaux dorés étincellent,
où s'épanouissent d'exquises fleurs multicolores." Python (1973: 129): "Des fleurs
de toutes couleurs, plaisantes, épanouies, (Avec) des palais d'or attrayants qui
resplendissent: Pour ces choses ... ." Seyfort Ruegg (2002: 92): "Lovely golden
pavilions shine, with bright and charming flowers blooming."

[396] In accord with de La Vallée Poussin, Python and Upāliparipṛcchā Tib, I have
emended the manuscripts' *śreṣṭhāḥ* to *puṣpāḥ* (the confusion/change is paleographically explainable), although *śreṣṭhāḥ* is not metrically impossible if it is read as
ś‚eṣṭhāḥ (cp. *g‚aho*, i.e., *gaho*) The compound is difficult to explain, especially
because even with *puṣpāḥ* one expects °*puṣpasajjitāḥ*, not °*sajjitapuṣpāḥ*; was the
order reversed for the sake of the metre?

[397] One is tempted to translate *vikalpitu bāla* as "the [spiritually] immature [person]
conceptualizes," but this would demand understanding *vikalpitu* (= *vikalpita*) in an
active sense, and thus differently than in *pāda* a, where it has its usual passive sense
(Seyfort Ruegg [2002: 92f.] translates both *vikalpitu*s actively). PsP Tib (=
Upāliparipṛcchā Tib), however, has *rtog pa'i dbang gis 'jig rten rnam brtags te ‖ 'du
shes 'dzin pas byis pa rnam par phye ‖.* The Chinese (T 12.325: 42a5) translates
"Clinging to *sañjñā* makes immature persons wander around [in *saṃsāra*?]." May
(1959: 156f.): "par la force de l'imagination, le vulgaire hypostasie; par croyance en

But that grasping is non-grasping, unreal;[398] for conceptuality is similar to a magical illusion and a mirage.

Thus in this way it is established that things with an unreal own-being, which are fabricated by [one's] own [subjective] error, become causes of defilement for the [spiritually] immature in *saṃsāra*.

And the way in which things with a false own-being are causes of defilement and purification should be determined in detail from the Madhyamakāvatāra.[399]

(son) aperception, le simple différencie." Cp. Lang (2001: 239): "A fool is conceptualized through grasping at ideas."

[398] All other translators of the verse have understood the intent of *so ca gaho agaho asabhūto* to be that grasping and non-grasping are unreal, e.g., Python (1973: 129): "Mais appréhension et non-appréhension sont sans existence propre"; Seyfort Ruegg (2002: 93): "unarisen (*asadbhūto* = *'byuṅ min te*) is this grasping (*graha*) and non-grasping (*agraha*)." The Upālipariprcchā Tib translator understood the statement in the same way: *'dzin dang 'dzin med de yang 'byung min te* ‖. It would seem, however, that the *sūtra* author only intends to convey the message that the realms of existence and all grasping at them is unreal; whether non-grasping as well is unreal is in the present context irrelevant.

[399] Candrakīrti may have in mind, among other passages, the section in the MABh which commences with an opponent asserting that when attachment (**abhiniveśa*) to real existence is being cut off, the fearful person is inevitably attached to the truth of worldly practice (*vyavahāra*), because he thinks that the cause of defilement and purification necessarily arises with some substantial own-being (*ci ste yang de ltar dngos po la mngon par zhen pa'i bdog pa thams cad kun nas gcod pa na bred sha thon pa tha snyad kyi bden pa la mngon par zhen pa 'di gang zhig kun nas nyon mongs pa dang rnam par byang ba'i rgyur gyur pa rdzas kyi bdag nyid 'ga' zhig skye bar 'gyur bar bya dgos so zhes smra na* | (MABh$_{ed}$ 122.7-11). De La Vallée Poussin, who has not understood that *bred sha thon pa* refers to a person, translates: "Mais, dira-t-on, cette adhésion (*abhiniveśa*) à la vérité pratique, qui expulse crainte et désir quand on abandonne tous ses biens,—et qui est adhésion aus choses,—qui, en général, est cause de souillure (*saṃkleśa*) et de purification (*vyavadāna*), il est nécessaire qu'elle naisse avec quelque réalité" (MABh$_{tr}$ 1910: 315). Candrakīrti responds (MA VI.36) that arising from self or other on the level of worldly practice is not tenable for the same reasons it is not tenable with regard to the ultimate. After explaining that all things arise from causal complexes and are thus, like mirages, etc., which arise from causal complexes, empty of own-being, he focusses the discussion on karmic causality, with the aim of demonstrating that even without acceptance of the reality of karmic acts and their fruits—and especially without unnecessary constructs like the *ālayavijñāna* of the Yogācāra school, *avipraṇāśa* (rejected

§81. At this point [the opponent] says, "If things do not arise from self, from other, from both or without a cause, then why did the Exalted One say, 'With ignorance as condition (*avidyāpratyaya*), the impulses (*saṃskāra*) [come to be]'?"[400]

Reply: This is the surface [level] (*saṃvṛti*), not true reality (*tattva*).

§82. [Question:] Is it, [in the case] of the surface level,[401] not necessary to point out how it is established [i.e., in terms of *svataḥ*, etc.]?

[Answer:] The surface [level's] establishment (*siddhi*) through mere conditionality (*idampratyayatāmātra*) is accepted [by us]; not, however, [an establishment] through acceptance of the four-fold position (*pakṣacatuṣṭaya*), because [that] would entail [our admitting] a doctrine [which posits that things are] endowed with own-being (*sasvabhāvavāda*), and because that [acceptance of any of the four positions] is inappropriate. For when mere conditionality is accepted, owing to the mutual reliance (*anyonyāpekṣa*) of cause (*hetu*) and effect (*phala*), there is no establishment implying own-being (*svābhāvikī siddhiḥ*).[402] Thus, a doctrine [whereby things are posited as] endowed with own-being is not [maintained by us].

---

ultimately but accepted on the surface level by Nāgārjuna; cf. MMK XVII.13-20), and *prāpti* of the Sarvāstivādins—karmic retribution is possible. In the course of the discussion, Candrakīrti cites the Bhavasaṃkrāntisūtra's example of a great king who dreams of being with a beautiful woman and who later, awake, remembering her, becomes obsessed with her and tortured by his loss. In the same way, the *sūtra* continues, do ordinary persons, having seen [unreal] objects, become attached to them, develop desire for them, and confer energy (**abhisaṃ(s)√kṛ*) to actions arising from desire, hatred and disorientation by way of their body, voice and mind (cf. $MABh_{ed}$ 127.17-128.13).

400 Cf. §71 and n. 300.

401 Or: "Is it, [in the case] of [dependent-arising on] the surface level, not necessary … ."

402 Candrakīrti clarifies that on the surface level things "exist" only through their being conditioned by something else, exemplifying this by way of the mutual reliance (*anyonyapekṣā*) of cause and effect. Mutual reliance is in fact the second of the three meanings ascribed by Candrakīrti to the word *saṃvṛti* (PsP_L 492.11): *parasparasaṃbhavanaṃ vā saṃvṛtir anyonyasamāśrayeṇety arthaḥ* "Or, *saṃvṛti* is reciprocal coming into being; [this] means [coming into being] by way of mutual

Just on account of that [Nāgārjuna] has stated,

> Logicians (*tārkika*) maintain that suffering (*duḥkha*) is created by self (*svayaṅkṛtam*), created by other, created by both, [created]

---

relation/contingence." On the possible logic behind statements in Nāgārjuna's MMK which demand the reciprocal existence of, e.g., cause and effect, and yet reject the real existence of such mutually reliant entities, see Oetke 1990. According to Oetke (ibid., 103), who proposes a "condition-merger-hypothesis", real existence is shown by Nāgārjuna to be impossible when atemporal logical conditions, such as those of cause and effect—where the concept of cause logically requires the concept of effect, and vice-versa (thus mutual dependence)—are assimilated to, applied to, temporal "real" conditions, since the "real"—in the case of cause and effect also "causal"—conditions can be demonstrated to not admit of the temporally prior existence of any one of the (pair, triad, etc., of) conditions under consideration. MMK VIII.12 is included in the verses cited after the present paragraph because its presentation of the pair action (*karma*) and agent (*kāraka*) confirms Candrakīrti's claim that mere mutual reliance is the only mode of establishment that can be acknowledged on the surface level. As Candrakīrti points out in his introduction to this same eighth-chapter *kārikā*, the surface level attains, when one acquiesces to worldly subjective error, its "establishment" exclusively through the acceptance of the mere conditionality of surface level things, which are similar to water in a mirage (PsP_L 189.1-3: ... *laukikaṃ viparyāsam abhyupetya sāṃvṛtānāṃ padārthānāṃ marīcikājalakalpānām idaṃpratyayatāmātrābhyupagamenaiva*). For Candrakīrti's explanation of the meaning of *saṃvṛti* and also of *saṃvṛtisatya*, see additionally MA VI.28 and its commentary. In the context of responding to an opponent who argues that the Mādhyamika, in rejecting arising from self or other, actually asserts only one level of truth, and not two, Candrakīrti replies that although this lack of reality of things on the surface level does indeed imply that there is in fact only one level of truth, the surface truth, unanalyzed and in conformity with the world, is accepted because it is the means for entering into ultimate truth (cf. $MABh_{ed}$ 119.14-120.4: *ci ste de ltar mi 'dod na ni bden pa gnyis ci ste brjod de | bden pa gcig kho nar 'gyur ro || ... 'di la bshad par bya ste | 'di bden mod kyi don dam par na bden pa gnyis yod pa ma yin te | dge slong dag bden pa dam pa 'di ni gcig ste | ... de'i phyir kun rdzob kyi bden pa gang yin pa de ni don dam pa'i bden pa la 'jug par bya ba'i thabs yin pa'i phyir | bdag dang gzhan dag las skye ba ma dpyad par 'jig rten pa'i lugs kyis khas len par byed pa yin no ||*). Shortly thereafter Candrakīrti states that one should merely accept that which the world thinks, namely, "When this is present, this comes to be" ($MABh_{ed}$ 120.15-17: *'jig rten pas yongs su mthong ba 'di yod na 'di 'byung ngo zhes bya ba 'di tsam zhig gzhan la rag las pa'i 'jug pa'i sgo nas khas blang bar bya ste |*; de La Vallée Poussin tentatively reconstructs *gzhan la rag las pa'i 'jug pa'i sgo nas* as *parādhīnavṛttidvāreṇa* and translates "subordonnant ainsi sa manière de faire au prochain" [$MABh_{tr}$ 1910: 314]). On *idampratyayatā*, see n. 85. For comments on the argumentation in MMK VIII, see Bhattacharya 1981.

without cause. You, however, have [merely] stated that it originates in dependence (*pratītyaja*).[403]

Also here [in the Madhyamakaśāstra he] will say,

---

[403] Candrakīrti cites Lokātītastava 21: *svayaṅkṛtaṃ parakṛtaṃ dvābhyāṃ kṛtam ahetukam | tārkikair iṣyate duḥkhaṃ tvayā tūktaṃ pratītyajam* ||. Sanskrit, Tibetan and translation in Lindtner 1982b: 134f. Nāgārjuna devotes MMK XII to a refutation of suffering created by self, other, both, and without a cause (suffering is explicated by Candrakīrti as being the five appropriated *skandhas*). Candrakīrti again cites Lokātītastava 21 in his commentary on the final *kārikā* of MMK XII, again in the context of a response to a questioner who has asked what kind of establishment suffering and external things might have if they are not possible in any of the four ways. He answers: ... *tasmāt svabhāvato na santi duḥkhādīnīty avasīyate | atha viparyāsamātralabdhātmasattākāyā duḥkhādisaṃvṛteḥ pratītyasamutpādavyavasthā mṛgyate tadā karmakārakaparīkṣāprakaraṇavihitavidhinā yathoditapakṣacatuṣṭayatiraskāreṇedaṃpratyayatāmātrārthapratītyasamutpādasiddhyā siddhir abhyupeyā* ||. "... Therefore, it is ascertained that suffering, etc., do not exist by own-being. But if a determination of the dependent-arising of surface [level things] such as suffering—the existence of which is arrived at through mere [subjective] error—be sought, then one ought to maintain an establishment according to the manner prescribed in the chapter on the examination of act and agent, [i.e.,] without the stated four-fold position, that is, by way of the establishment of dependent-arising in the meaning of mere conditionality" (PsP_L 234.3-6; the Lokātītastava verse is cited immediately after this statement).

Discussions that consider the way in which suffering arises occur already in the Canon. Cp. SN II.19-21, where the Buddha explains to Kassapa, who has asked if suffering is self-made, made by other, made by both, or fortuitously comes into being, that if one thinks the person who acts is the same as the person who experiences the result of actions [in the next life], one maintains self-created suffering and thereby holds an eternalistic view. If one thinks the actor and experiencer are different persons, one holds the view of annihilation. The Tathāgata, he states, without veering toward either extreme, teaches the Dhamma by way of the middle: "With ignorance as condition, the impulses [come to be]; with the impulses as condition, consciousness comes to be ... such is the origin of this whole mass of suffering" (... *Ete te Kassapa ubho ante anupagamma majjhena Tathāgato dhammam deseti* || *Avijjāpaccayā saṅkhārā* ...). See also the following *sutta*'s (SN II.22f.) similar explanation in regard to pain and pleasure (*sukhadukkha*) and SN II.112f. for the dismissal of aging and death—down to consciousness and name and form—as arisen from self, other, both or fortuitously. It is stated at SN II.33ff. that "some ascetics and brahmins, proponents of *kamma*" (*samaṇabrāhmaṇa kammavādā*) are holders of one or another of the four views in regard to suffering. These Canonical discussions of course presume the real existence of the respective links of dependent-arising.

In dependence on action (*karma*), an agent (*kāraka*) [exists], and dependent on that agent
Action comes to be. We do not see another cause of establishment (*siddhikāraṇa*).[404]

Just this much has been stated by the Exalted One, too: "As concerns this, this is the conventional explanation of things (*dharmasaṅketa*),

---

[404] Candrakīrti cites MMK VIII.12: *pratītya kārakaḥ karma taṃ pratītya ca kārakam* | *karma pravartate nānyat paśyāmaḥ siddhikāraṇam* ||. Candrakīrti cites the same *kārikā* in his MABh in the comparable context of responding to an opponent who has asked how the surface-level arising of consciousness, etc., and a sprout, etc., from respectively ignorance and the impulses, and a seed, is determinable if arising from self, other, both and without a cause is negated from the point of view of both the surface and ultimate levels (cf. $MABh_{ed}$ 226.1-4; $MABh_{tr}$ 1911: 276). There Candrakīrti states that one bases oneself on just the principle "*'di la brten nas 'di 'byung ba zhig*" (**idaṃ pratītyedaṃ bhavati*) ($MABh_{ed}$ 226.14-15); for when one explains dependent-arising which consists in mere conditionality, not only are the concepts of arising without a cause, etc., impossible, but also other concepts such as eternity and annihilation, permanence and impermanence, etc., are completely impossible (*de ltar rkyen nyid 'di pa tsam gyi rten cing 'brel par 'byung ba bshad pa na* | *rgyu med par skye ba la sogs pa'i rtog pa 'di dag mi srid pa 'ba' zhig tu ma zad kyi* | *rtag pa dang chad pa dang rtag pa dang mi rtag pa dang dngos po dang dngos po med pa gnyis la sogs pa rtog pa gzhan dag kyang mi srid pa nyid do* || [$MABh_{ed}$ 227.14-18; $MABh_{tr}$ 1911: 277f.]).
Candrakīrti's commentary on the following *kārikā* (MMK XII.9) makes clear that the mutual reliance deemed by him to allow for a so-called establishment of the surface level is to be related to mutually reliant pairs; it in no way implies dependence on a "causal nexus" or even the *inter*dependence of all things, an idea that is bereft of any textual support but still propagated by a number of scholars—and applied to the ultimate level(!): PsP_L 190.5-8: *karmakārakopādeyopādātṛvyatiriktā ye 'nye bhāvā janyajanakagantṛgamanadraṣṭavyadarśanalakṣyalakṣaṇotpādyotpādakāḥ tathāvayavāvayaviguṇaguṇipramāṇaprameyādayo niravaśeṣā bhāvās teṣāṃ kartṛ-karmavicāreṇa svabhāvato 'stitvaṃ pratiṣidhya parasparāpekṣikīm eva siddhiṃ prājño nirmumukṣur jātijarāmaraṇādibandhanebhyo mokṣāya vibhāvayet* || "The intelligent person who wants release [from *saṃsāra*], having refuted—by way of the analysis of act and agent—the existence by own-being of other things, i.e., [things] other than act and agent, appropriated and appropriator, [things, that is, such as] the originated and the originator, goer and [act of] going, what is seen and sight, what is characterized and characteristic, that produced and producer [and] similarly, part and whole, quality and qualificand, means of valid cognition and what is cognized, and so forth, [in short,] all things, should regard, for the sake of release from the bonds of birth, old age and death, their establishment to be solely one of mutual reliance."

namely, 'When this is present, that comes to be, from the arising of this, that arises,' namely, 'with ignorance as condition, the impulses [come to be], with the impulses as condition, consciousness [comes to be]'."[405]

§83. At this point, certain [Naiyāyika opponents] critique:[406]

---

[405] The same citation occurs at MABh_{ed} 226.16-18: *ji skad du bcom ldan 'das kyis de la chos kyi brda ni 'di yin te | 'di lta ste | 'di yod na 'di 'byung | 'di skyes pas 'di skye ste | gang 'di ma rig pa'i rkyen gyis 'du byed rnams zhes bya ba la sogs pa gsungs so* ‖. De La Vallée Poussin identifies the MABh citation as an extract from the Paramārthaśūnyatāsūtra, noting that a version of the extract occurs in the BCAP and that the beginning of the version of the citation as found in the BCAP is cited in the Sūtrālaṃkāra and that the *sūtra* is identified there by name (cf. MABh_{tr} 1911: 277, n. 2). Mahāyānasūtrālaṅkāra (ed. Sylvain Lévi, Paris 1907: 158.20-22): *paramārtha-śūnyatāyām asti karmāsti vipākaḥ kārakas tu nopalabhyate ya imāṃś ca skandhān nikṣipati anyāṃś ca skandhān pratisaṃdadhāti | anyatra dharmasaṃketād iti deśitaṃ* |. BCAP 474.15-18: *uktaṃ caitad bhagavatā | iti hi bhikṣavo 'sti karma | asti phalam | kārakas tu nopalabhyate ya imān skandhān vijahāti | anyāṃś ca skandhān upādatte | anyatra dharmasaṃketāt | atrāyaṃ dharmasaṃketo yad asmin sati idaṃ bhavaty asyotpādād idam utpadyata iti* |.

[406] Candrakīrti does not name the opponents. *LṬ's author neither identifies the opponents nor comments on any of the words or phrases in the citation. Most scholars who have translated or studied this section of the PsP assign the critique to Dignāga and/or representatives of the Buddhist logical-epistemological school; some others consider the opponent to be Bhāviveka.
The ascription to Dignāga of the view, expressed at three different points in the objection, that all things exist, is unacceptable. Dignāga would have been fully aware that the Madhyamaka negation of things is made from the point of view of the ultimate, and he would not have engaged with his fellow Mahāyānists in a debate focussed on the final nature of things in which he would utter pronouncements incongruous with his own Yogācāra stance. Dignāga shares with the Mādhyamikas the view that worldly things exist only on the surface level and are actually unreal, differing from them primarily in maintaining that ultimately nothing but self-cognizing consciousness exists. In encounters where the topic of conversation was the ultimate status of things, the declaration *sarvabhāvāḥ santi* would have been as sharply denounced by him as it was by the Mādhyamikas.
Although a passage with the exact wording of the objection could not be located, I have been able to find similar, but less elaborated, versions of the objection's arguments at two places in Uddyotakara's NV (NV on NS IV.1.40 and NV on NS IV.2.27) and in one passage in Pakṣilasvāmin Vātsyāyana's NBh (NBh on NS IV.2.30). Uddyotakara, for example, in his commentary on NS IV.2.27, critiques the opponent's assertion that all things are not possible by stating: *sarvabhāvānupapattir iti ca bruvāṇaḥ pramāṇaṃ paryanuyojyaḥ | yadi pramāṇaṃ bravīti, vyāhataṃ bhava-*

Does this ascertainment (*niścaya*), namely, "things have not arisen" (*anutpannā bhāvā iti*)[407] stem from a means of valid cognition (*pramāṇaja*) or does it not stem from a means of valid cognition (*apramāṇaja*)?[408] Among those [two alternatives], if it is maintained that it stems from a means of valid cognition, then this needs to be disclosed [by you]: How many means of valid cognition are there? What characteristics (*lakṣaṇa*) do they have? What are their objects (*viṣaya*)? Have they arisen from self? [Have they arisen] from other, from both, or [have they arisen]

---

ti | *atha na bravīty artho 'sya na sidhyati pramāṇābhāvāt* | *athāprāmāṇikī siddhiḥ sarvabhāvānām upapattir ity asya kasmān na siddhiḥ* | (cf. NV 487.17-488.1). For the NV on NS IV.1.40, the NBh passage and further details, see below Appendix XI. See also MacDonald 2011.

It is interesting but not surprising that Candrakīrti takes time to deflect the Naiyāyika critique given the school's long history of attacking the Mādhyamikas; the fact that Uddyotakara's lifetime may have intersected with his own might also have played a role (Steinkellner [1961: 153] has suggested 550–610 for Uddyotakara's lifetime). Given that Candrakīrti does on occasion slightly alter the wording of passages he is citing from the *śāstra*s of others, it is possible that he relied on the arguments in Vātsyāyana's and/or Uddyotakara's commentaries and revamped them to suit his own agenda. On the other hand, it is possible that Candrakīrti had at his disposal another Nyāya text that contained this more extensive, fleshed-out version of the well-known and frequently utilized critique. If this is the case, the PsP has preserved for us a lengthy citation from a lost Nyāya treatise.

The transition in the PsP from the discussion with the Naiyāyika to the longer one with Dignāga is in fact quite clear, or at least would have been for the philosophers making up Candrakīrti's audience. His explanation of the purpose of the MMK, a response to the final critique in the above objection, neatly winds up the discussion, and his new opponent's reference to the "treatise" (*śāstra*) in which worldly dealing with means of cognition and that which is cognized is topical unambiguously announces that the confrontation with the Yogācāra proponent Dignāga and his influential work, the PS, has begun.

[407] The Naiyāyika opponent may be referring with *anutpannā bhāvāḥ iti* to the declaration of a specific Mādhyamika, or may consider it to represent the Madhyamaka view in general. It is is possible that the reference is specifically to MMK I.1's *na … utpannā … vidyate bhāvāḥ*.

[408] Tib takes only *pramāṇa* as the scope for the negation and thus translates *apramāṇaja* as *tshad ma ma yin pa las skyes pa*. The next occurrence of *apramāṇaja* has also been translated this way.

without a cause?[409] But if [you maintain that this ascertainment] does not stem from a means of valid cognition, [we will respond that] that [ascertainment derived in such a way] is not tenable, because the apprehension of an object of valid cognition (*prameyādhigama*) relies on a means of valid cognition (*pramāṇādhīna*); for a thing / state of affairs that has not [yet] been apprehended cannot be apprehended without [one or another of] the means of valid cognition. Thus, when there is no apprehension of a thing / state of affairs on account of the non-existence of means of valid cognition, how [can] that [sort of ascertainment be] for you a reasonable ascertainment? Therefore, this [claim that] things have not arisen is not tenable. Or, [alternatively,] on the basis of exactly that [same non-reliance on a means of valid cognition] owing to which the ascertainment that things have not arisen may occur for you, [there may occur] also/equally for me [the ascertainment] that all things exist.[410]

---

[409] It goes without saying that the Mādhyamika will reject this first alternative which demands acceptance of the arising of means of valid cognition from one of the four alternatives. Cf. VV 51: *naiva svataḥ prasiddhir na parasparataḥ parapramāṇair vā* | *na bhavati na ca prameyair na cāpy akasmāt pramāṇānām* || (VV_{ed} 72).

[410] Cf. n. 406 and Appendix XI for the argument as set forth by Uddyotakara. Cf. the comparable argumentative style in VV 18: *yadi cāhetoḥ siddhiḥ svabhāvavinivartanasya te bhavati* || *svābhāvyasyāstitvaṃ mamāpi nirhetukaṃ siddham* ||. The commentary reads (VV_{ed} 53): *atha manyase nirhetukī siddhir niḥsvabhāvatvasya bhāvānām iti yathā tava svabhāvavinivartanaṃ nirhetukaṃ siddhaṃ tathā mamāpi svabhāvasadbhāvo nirhetukaḥ siddhaḥ* |.
Garfield's (2008: 512, n. 8) translation (from the Tibetan) of the latter half of the objection, starting with the present one, is problematic. The construction *gang las … 'di nyid las* (in the sentence *yang na khyed kyi dngos po rnams skye ba med do zhes bya ba'i nges pa 'di gang las gyur pa 'di nyid las nga'i dngos po thams cad yod pa yin no zhes bya ba yang yin la* |), which translates *yataḥ … tata eva*, certainly does not mean "to the extent that." The following sentence's *nga'i … yang*—for *mamāpi*—(the sentence reads: *yang ji ltar khyod kyi dngos po thams cad skye ba med do zhes bya ba'i nges pa 'dir 'gyur ba de kho na ltar nga'i dngos po thams cad skye bar yang 'gyur ro* ||) has been incorrectly construed by Garfield (ibid.) with *dngos po thams cad*, which has resulted in the unusual translation "In the same way that you are certain of your statement 'all phenomena are unarisen' I can be certain that all of my phenomena are arisen." The final sentence *des na dngos po thams cad bkag pa med par yod pa yin no*, translating *iti santy apratiṣiddhāḥ sarvabhāvāḥ*, has also been wrongly translated as "Therefore, the existence of no entities has been refuted!"

> And just as there is this ascertainment for you that all things have not arisen, so indeed can there also be for me the arising of all things. But if this ascertainment that all things have not arisen does not exist for you,[411] then, because it is impossible to convince another of something that has not been ascertained by oneself,[412] undertaking the [Madhyamaka-]treatise would be absolutely pointless. Thus, all things, unrefuted, do exist.

Reply: If something called ascertainment existed for us,[413] it would either stem from valid cognition or not stem from valid cognition. But [it] does not exist. Why [not]? According to our system (*iha*), if non-ascertainment (*aniścaya*) were possible, there might be its counterpart (*pratipakṣa*), [i.e.,] the ascertainment which relies on that [non-ascertainment].[414] Yet when, first of all, [that] very non-

---

[411] It should be noted that with this third alternative the opponent is not assuming that the Mādhyamika now retreats and retracts his assertion, i.e., denies that he has ascertained the true status of things, as Dan Arnold's translation of the first part of the sentence leads one to presume: "Or [perhaps you will say] you *have* no certainty [to the effect that] 'all existents are unproduced.' In that case, ..." (cf. Arnold 2005b: 420; 2005a: 146). Garfield (2008: 512, n. 8) follows the same interpretation: "If, however, you,[sic] have no certainty about the idea that all phenomena are unarisen ....". Seyfort Ruegg's (2002: 96) translation is worded more ambiguously: "But if, for you, there is no ascertainment that all entities are unoriginated, ...". In fact, the opponent is allowing the Mādhyamika to maintain his view of the non-existence of the physical, linguistic and conceptual components of the world (note the placement of *asti*) but, putting an elegant twist on things, points out the devastating consequence that the Mādhyamika's insistence on consistency entails.

[412] Tib interprets *niścitasya* as a subjective genitive indicating the person: *de'i tshe rang nyid kyis kyang ma nges pas gzhan khong du chud par byed pa mi srid pa'i phyir* ... ("then, because it is not possible for someone who himself does not have any certainty to convince another ...").

[413] PsP_M §83 reply (PsP_L 56.4): *yadi kaścin niścayo nāmāsmākaṃ syāt*. Cp. VV 29ab_1: *yadi kācana pratijñā syān me*. For comments on the latter, see n. 136.

[414] Tenets held receive their legitimacy, in the opinion of the Naiyāyika, from means of valid cognition. The attempt to verify a thing / state of affairs has as its starting point uncertainty about and non-ascertainment of this thing / state of affairs; non-ascertainment is replaced by ascertainment when direct perception or another *pramāṇa* is able to provide confirmation. Candrakīrti is thought to have been cornered into having to admit a means of valid cognition that has arisen from self or other, etc., i.e., an existent means of valid cognition, which will contradict the statement that nothing

whatsoever arises, or into having to abandon his position. He skillfully and easily extracts himself from the Naiyāyika trap by pointing out that from the ultimate point of view, from which the assertion that things have not arisen is made, not even the starting point of an investigation, i.e., non-ascertainment, exists. And when not even this can exist, then an ensuing ascertainment definitely cannot exist. For Candrakīrti, *aniścaya* is a worldly concept which has its counterpart in the concept *niścaya* (for Mādhyamikas, concepts are also considered to be constituents of the world); ultimately neither exist. The conceptual pair *niścaya/aniścaya* is comparable to the conceptual pair *śubha/aśubha* (for the MMK argument refuting the conceptual pair *śubha/aśubha*, see the following note).
Previous interpretations of *niścaya* and *aniścaya* and of the first sentences of the passage include the following. According to Stcherbatsky (1927: 137, n. 1), "*aniścaya* evidently means a problematic judgment." Sprung (1979: 50) translates *niścaya* as "assertion" and *aniścaya* as "negative assertion": "In your thinking, where there is a negative assertion (*aniścaya*) there would have to be a counter assertion which, with reference to the first, would be positive." Siderits (1981: 123), who speaks of "conviction" and "non-conviction," attempts to understand *aniścaya* by taking reference to the VV: "We are reminded here of Nāgārjuna's statement (VV 30) that he neither affirms nor denies any thesis. We may then take 'aniścaya' to refer to any statement which is metaphysical in nature, i.e., is intended as a characterization of the ultimate nature of reality, and which contradicts the claim that all existents are empty. In this case Candrakīrti is claiming that there is no aniścaya which the Mādhyamika is called upon to refute." Although I would not disagree that the claim under attack here in the PsP, namely, *anutpannā bhavāḥ*, reminds one of the claim *śūnyāḥ sarvabhāvāḥ* under attack in the VV, and would agree that Candrakīrti's procedure here in the PsP resembles, to a certain degree, that of Nāgārjuna's in VV 29, I see no grounds for assuming that *aniścaya* is intended to relate to statements contradicting the Madhyamaka claim. Huntington (2003: 78) renders *niścaya* and *aniścaya* of our passage as "certainty" and "uncertainty," but, denying Candrakīrti his denial of the world and seeing the Madhyamaka project as merely encouraging and aiming to fully enable a life lived without clinging, superimposes meaning onto the pair unintended by Candrakīrti. He writes, "According to Candrakīrti, it is absolutely essential that this compulsive desire, or need, for certainty—and its contrary, the fear of uncertainty—be seen for what they are, insurmountable obstacles to any real appreciation of Nāgārjuna's philosophy, for they only serve to reinforce the tendency to crave and cling." Arnold (2005a: 146ff.), considering the opponent to be Dignāga, is of the opinion that Candrakīrti is stating that he has no "doubt" or "certainty" because he (Candrakīrti) rejects that his claim of non-arising requires the *a posteriori* justification, via *pramāṇa*s, the Epistemologist deems necessary for establishment of the claim. According to Arnold, seeking this sort of justification is incoherent because the *pramāṇa*s that Dignāga holds provide certainty "are themselves possible only given the truth of Candrakīrti's claim (that is, that everything is empty-qua-interdependent)—a fact that must therefore be knowable *prior* to the exercise of any such epistemic factors. This is the point of Candrakīrti's

ascertainment does not exist for us, then how could there be its opposite, [i.e.,] ascertainment, since it (= ascertainment) would not be reliant on something related to [it], like the shortness and longness of a donkey's horn [do not rely on each other].[415] And when in this way

---

rejoining that there is no possibility of doubt with respect to his claim." To understand Arnold's interpretation one needs to be aware of the fact that he does not consider Candrakīrti to be denying the existence of things but rather to maintain the view that things, including concepts and statements, do indeed really exist, but do so only in (inter)dependence. It is difficult to defend Arnold's position, and my own view of the general Madhyamaka stance stands in contradistinction to it. Garfield's (2008: 512, n. 8) non-foundationalist interpretation of Madhyamaka that, like Arnold's, allows him to preserve the existence of the world may explain his translating *pratipakṣa* as "antidote"; he translates the passage beginning with *ihāniścayasambhave sati* as: "Since, according to us, where there is uncertainty, in dependence on that, certainty is achieved as its antidote in the case where there is no uncertainty, how can certainty arise as its opposite, since it depends on its opposite? This is just like a donkey's horn being long or short!"

[415] The logic behind the idea that ascertainment cannot exist if its counterpart, non-ascertainment, does not exist, because its existence requires the existence of another related to it, is set forth in somewhat more detail in a parallel case in Candrakīrti's commentary on MMK XXIII.10 (XXIII.10: *anapekṣya śubhaṃ nāsty aśubhaṃ prajñapayemahi | yat pratītya śubhaṃ tasmāc chubhaṃ naivopapadyate ||*: "Repulsive, in dependence on which we might designate attractive, does not exist independent of attractive. Therefore, attractive is simply not logically possible"). Candrakīrti comments (the underlined compounds find partial correspondences in the passage under discussion in the first chapter): *iha yadi śubhaṃ nāma kiṃcit syān niyataṃ tad aśubham apekṣya bhaved pārāvāravad bījāṅkuravad hrasvadīrghavad vā śubhasya sambandhyantarapadārthasāpekṣatvāt | tac cāpy apekṣaṇīyam aśubhaṃ śubhena vinā nāsti | anapekṣya śubhaṃ aśubhaṃ nāsti | śubhanirapekṣam aśubhaṃ nāstīty abhiprāyaḥ | yad aśubhaṃ pratītya yad aśubhaṃ apekṣya śubhaṃ prajñapayemahi vyavasthāpayemahi | ... yataś caivaṃ śubhasya prajñaptau saṃbandhyantaram apekṣaṇīyam aśubhākhyaṃ padārthāntaraṃ nāsti tasmāc chubhaṃ naivopapadyate hrasvāsaṃbhavād iva dīrgham pārāsaṃbhavād ivāvāram ity abhiprāyaḥ* (PsP$_L$ 458.13-459.5; corrected following mss P, D, B and de Jong 1978: 239. De Jong corrects *padārthāntaram* to *padārtham*, but does not mention that his manuscript reads *padārthāntaraṃ padarthaṃ*, and seems to have overlooked that a nominative form is required. P is severely damaged at this point, but attests the remains of the *akṣara*s in question. Tib reads *gang gi phyir de ltar na sdug par gdags pa la | mi sdug pa zhes bya bar bltos par bya ba dngos po 'brel pa can gzhan yod pa ma yin pa |*. In the parallel construction at PsP$_L$ 459.14, B and D attest *padārthāntaram nāsti* [the text in P is missing; Tib as above]). Candrakīrti argues that repulsive does not exist on its own, independent of attractive, i.e., as an independently established entity in regard to which attractive could then be named/designated in dependence, i.e., be

ascertainment does not exist, then for the sake of the establishment of what will we postulate means of valid cognition? Or how might there be their number (*saṅkhyā*), characteristic (*lakṣaṇa*) [and] object (*viṣaya*) [or their] arising from self, from other, from both, or without a cause? None of this need be asserted by us.

§84. [Opponent:] If ascertainment thus does not exist for you, still, why is this assertion (*vākya*) "not from self, nor from other, nor from both or without a cause, do things come to be,"[416] which has the form

---

dependently established, for repulsive, in its turn, requires that attractive be established independently so that it can be established in dependence on it (see also MMK XXIII.11). The same vicious circle will hold for the conceptual pair ascertainment and non-ascertainment. Ascertainment can be designated/established only in dependence on an independently existing counterpart, and since this does not exist, ascertainment is not logically possible. In the example, shortness and length are meant to parallel non-ascertainment and ascertainment. If non-ascertainment, like the (impossible) shortness of something non-existent, does not exist, then ascertainment cannot exist, in the same way that length, deprived of its counterpart, shortness, cannot exist (and vice-versa). See also the comments and references in Seyfort Ruegg 2002: 97, n. 159. Oetke has argued convincingly against allegations that certain arguments in the MMK that appear to take the step from "If p, then q" to "If not p, then not q" violate the "law of contraposition"; see Oetke 1992.
Candrakīrti's reply provides an appropriate answer to the critique, and is in strict conformity with the Madhyamaka stance; any characterization of the move as evasive is to misunderstand Candrakīrti. He will, however, with his reply to the next question say that the assertion (*vākya*) that nothing arises is ascertained by the world. Still, the constructs of the surface level cannot be applied to the ultimate level; from the point of view of the ultimate, *prameya*s and *pramāṇa*s and the issue of the latter are impossible.
It might be noted that Candrakīrti argues in other of his works that cognition (*vijñāna*)—in the form of which or in conjunction with which worldly means of valid cognition function—stops when the ultimate is realized, for cognition (and thus any ascertainment connected with or derived from it) is impossible when one is in the state where nothing appears. He does, however, reveal in his commentary on MMK XXV.16 that gnosis (*jñāna*), which he qualifies as non-existing and non-arisen, but also as transcending all manifoldness (*sarvaprapañcātītarūpa*), has emptiness as its object-support; see MacDonald 2009.

[416] The opponent includes MMK I.1ab (*na svato nāpi parato na dvābhyāṃ nāpy ahetuto*) in his version of the Mādhyamikas' *vākya*. PsP Tib does not translate *bhavanti*; a *shed* followed by *iti* closes its citation of MMK I.1ab.

of something that has been ascertained (*niścitarūpa*), found among you?[417]

Reply: This assertion is ascertained by world (*loka*) by way of reasoning (*upapatti*) acknowledged exclusively by [the world it]self; [it is] not [ascertained] by the Nobles (*ārya*).

§85. [Opponent:] Does there really not exist [any] reasoning for the Nobles?[418]

[Reply:] Who says this: "[Reasoning] exists" or "[Reasoning] does not exist"? For the ultimate (*paramārtha*) is noble silence (*āryas*

---

[417] Now that it has become clear to the opponent that the Mādhyamikas deny even ascertainment, he asks why one nevertheless finds them setting forth the thesis that nothing exists. *katham* can have the meaning of either "how" or "why," and in the present sentence it is intended in the latter sense. The unexpected switch in the sentence from *bhavataḥ* to *bhavatām*, if not due to early interference or scribal error, appears to indicate that in the initial instance the opponent addresses his comment directly to Candrakīrti, his immediate partner in conversation, but in the second refers to the use of the statement by Mādhyamikas in general. The interpretations of the sentence by previous translators are less satisfactory. Huntington (2003: 78): "… then why does your statement … appear to be certain?"; Garfield (2008: 512, n. 8): " … how can you be certain that you understand the purport of the statement … ?"; Arnold (2005b: 421): "… then how is your own statement … understood?"; Seyfort Ruegg (2002: 98): " … how does your honour apprehend … the [following sentence] …?". Interestingly, Stcherbatsky (1927: 137) understood the question correctly; he paraphrases: "But we hear from you a proposition which looks like a definite assertion … . How is that (to be explained)?".

[418] I understand the inclusion of *khalu* in the sentence as intending insistence on the part of the opponent, to the effect of "Would you make yourself clear, please!" Seyfort Ruegg (2002: 99, n. 166) suggests that the sentence is probably not an opponent's objection and rather a question posed by a student of Candrakīrti's, or alternatively a question that "Candrakīrti as a philosopher might ask himself." I see no reason not to understand the question as part of the continued discussion with the Naiyāyika. Arnold (2005b: 421), who incorporates the sentence into Candrakīrti's previous response and thus has Candrakīrti rhetorically ask himself the question, would seem to share Seyfort Ruegg's opinion. Stcherbatsky's (1927: 137) interpretation is similar to mine, and is in fact perhaps more to the point as regards *khalu*: "Do you really mean to say that these Saints (believe in) no argument?"

tuṣṇībhāvaḥ);[419] thus how is there [any] possibility of [disquieting subjective] proliferation (*prapañca*) in that [silence], so that there might be reasoning or [its counterpart,] non-reasoning (*anupapatti*)?[420]

---

[419] PsP Tib: *'phags pa rnams kyi don dam pa ni cang mi gsung ba yin te* for *paramārtho hy āryas tūṣṇībhāvas*. De Jong (1978: 33) writes, "Tibetan *'phags pa rnams kyi* (*āryāṇām*) is an interpretation and not a translation." As he notes, the expression *ariyo tuṇhībhāvo* is common in Pāli texts. Cf. the Kolitasutta of the SN, where Mahāmoggallāna explains noble silence in connection with the second concentration which lacks thought and reflection: *Idha mayhaṃ āvuso rahogatassa patisallīnassa evaṃ cetaso parivitakko udapādi* || *Ariyo tuṇhībhāvo ariyo tuṇhībhāvo ti vuccati* || *Katamo nu kho ariyo tuṇhībhāvo ti* || *Tassa mayham āvuso etad ahosi* || *Idha bhikkhu vitakkavicārānaṃ vūpasamā ajjhattam sampasādanaṃ cetaso ekodibhāvaṃ avitakkam avicāraṃ samādhijam pītisukhaṃ dutiyaṃ jhānam upasampajja viharati* || *Ayaṃ vuccati ariyo tuṇhībhāvoti* (SN II.273). Bodhi (SN_{tr} 713) translates, "Here, friends, while I was alone in seclusion, a reflection arose in my mind thus: 'It is said, "noble silence, noble silence." What now is noble silence?' Then, friends, it occurred to me: 'Here, with the subsiding of thought and examination, a bhikkhu enters and dwells in the second jhāna, which has internal confidence and unification of mind, is without thought and examination, and has rapture and happiness born of concentration. This is called noble silence.'" In the MN, in a different context, monks are advised by the Buddha to do either of two things when they assemble: they should hold discussion on the Dharma or maintain noble silence: *Sannipatitānaṃ vo bhikkhave dvayaṃ karaṇīyaṃ: dhammī vā kathā ariyo vā tuṇhībhāvo* (MN I.161.33-34; cf. MN_{tr} 254). Bodhi (MN_{tr} 1215, n. 298) notes that the MN-aṭṭha "points out that the second jhāna and one's basic meditation subject are both called 'noble silence.'" De Jong (1978: 33) refers to the Pāli Tipiṭakaṃ Concordance (Vol. II, p. 244b) for further references for *ariyo tuṇhībhāvo*; see also BHSD s.v. *tūṣṇī*. Here in the PsP, as Candrakīrti makes known in the next clause, "noble silence" refers to the state in which subjective *prapañca*, i.e., mental speech (*abhidhāna*; *manojalpa*) has ceased, along with, of course, the verbal expression of this. *prapañca* in the present instance seems clearly, in being contrasted to the calm of silence, to contain nuances of disquiet, restlessness, and disturbance. On the silence of the awakened ones, see, e.g., Nagao 1955; Gomez 1976; Oetke 1994; Seyfort Ruegg 2000: 154f.; 1977: 12, 19; 1981: 34f.; La Vallée Poussin 1933: 40.

[420] Candrakīrti has stated that logical reasoning (*upapatti*) is employed only by the world, and that it brings about, solely for the world, the ascertainment (*niścaya*) that things do not arise. In the present paragraph he explains to the opponent that the spiritually attained have achieved a state that transcends all linguistic and conceptual activity and is as a result free from all mental agitation and unrest. As he explains in other passages, it is a state without objective support, and in the absence of any

§86. [Opponent:] [Well, the question is] obvious:[421] How indeed, if the Nobles do not formulate [any] reasoning, will they now bring the world to understand the ultimate?

[Reply:] The Nobles certainly do not formulate [any] reasoning [of their own] by way of worldly linguistic practice (*lokasaṃvyavahāra*);[422] but adopting, for the sake of the comprehension of others,

---

objective support the application of predicates like "exists" or "does not exist" is impossible.
Many of the previous translators of the paragraph have understood the sentence *kenaitad uktam asti vā nāsti veti* to mean that it is not possible to know if the Nobles take recourse to reasoning/arguments or not; cf. Stcherbatsky 1927: 137; Huntington 2003: 78: "Who can say whether they do or they don't?"; Garfield 2008: 512, n. 8; Arnold 2005b: 421 (the exception is Seyfort Ruegg [cf. 2002: 99]). Lamotte (1987: 317, n. 43), commenting on Vimalakīrti's silence, translates following Stcherbatsky: "Qui donc pourrait dire si les saints ont ou n'ont pas d'argument? En effet l'absolu, c'est le silence des saints. Comment donc une discussion avec eux sur ce sujet serait-elle possible [et comment pourrions-nous savoir] s'ils ont ou n'ont pas d'argument en cette matière?" The point of the rhetorical question *kenaitad uktam asti vā nāsti veti*, as is made clear by the sentence following it, is that mental activity does not occur at all when ordinary consciousness has come to rest, i.e., has ceased; it certainly does not intend to convey the idea that the Nobles *might* be mentally active and might spend time formulating arguments but that we as ordinary beings do not have access to this information. On the various interpretations of the Buddha's silence, see Oetke 1994.
PsP Tib reads *de'i phyir gang la 'thad pa dang 'thad pa ma yin pa mi mnga' bar 'gyur ba de dag la spros pa mnga' bar ga la 'gyur* ||: "Therefore, how could those who do not have reasoning or non-reasoning have *prapañca*?" instead of the expected *de'i phyir gang las 'thad pa dang 'thad pa ma yin par 'gyur ba de la spros pa yod pa ga la 'gyur* for *tataḥ kutas tatra prapañcasambhavo yata upapattir anupapattir vā syāt*. The sentence as it appears in the Tibetan does not make much sense. De La Vallée Poussin (PsP_L 57, n. 2) has noted the discrepancy and reconstructs the Sanskrit as *tasmād yatropapattyanupapattyasaṃbhavas tatra prapañcasaṃbhavaḥ kutaḥ*. Possibly the translators read *tataḥ kutas tatra prapañcasambhavo yatra upapattir anupapattir vā syāt*, i.e., read *yatra* for *yata(ḥ)* and added a negation in order to try to make some sense of the sentence.

421 I understand *hi* as expressing the obviousness of the problem posed by the opponent. My translation may give too much emphasis to the *hi* but I have not been able to come up with a better solution.

422 In general, *vyavahāra* refers to physical, verbal and/or mental activity/practice. Here, *saṃvyavahāra*, qualified by *loka*, refers to the linguistic activity engaged in and focussed on by the persons of the world (conceptual activity is not excluded, but it

does not stand in the foreground in the present context). *lokavyavahāra* is in fact the third meaning Candrakīrti gives for *saṃvṛti* in his commentary on MMK XXIV.8: *atha vā saṃvṛtiḥ saṃketo lokavyavahāra ity arthaḥ* | *sa cābhidhānābhidheya-jñānajñeyādilakṣaṇaḥ* ‖ (PsP$_{\mathrm{L}}$ 492.11-12) "Or, *saṃvṛti* is convention, the meaning is: worldly practice. And it has the characteristic of name and what is named, cognition and what is cognized, etc." Seyfort Ruegg (1981: 74) paraphrases this definition as "worldly transactional usage (*lokavyavahāra*) defined in terms of the relation of a designation to its designatum and of a cognition to the object of cognition." One might understand the definition as referring to worldly linguistic practice as it relates to the dependent pairs referred to in Candrakīrti's second etymologically based definition of *saṃvṛti* (*parasparasaṃbhavanaṃ vā saṃvṛtir anyonyasamāśrayeṇety arthaḥ* | [PsP$_{\mathrm{L}}$ 492.11]).

The compound **lokavyavahāra* (*'jig rten snyad*) of ŚS *kārikā* 1 is elucidated in the ŚSV. According to the ŚSV, the compound's first word "world" (**loka*) refers to the person (**pudgala*, *gang zag*) who/which is designated in reliance on the [five] constituents (**skandha*, *phung po*). Persons are differentiated into two groups, namely, those whose sense organs are not impaired by the *timira* visual condition, etc., and those whose sense organs are impaired (cp. MA VI.24 and commentary). Only the former group is called the "world," for the latter is not an authority from the point of view of the world. "Linguistic practice" (**vyavahāra*) is said to be that which brings about in the continuum of another the understanding of things—things whose manifoldness is [merely] imagined—that one wants the other to understand (... *gzhan gyis khong du chud par 'dod pa'i dngos po kun nas rtog pa'i dngos po sna tshogs pa gzhan gyi rgyud la rtogs pa 'jug par byed pa la tha snyad ces brjod do* ‖; ŚSV$_{\mathrm{ed}}$ 213.14-16). The commentary also alludes to the conceptual aspect of *vyavahāra* (thus *vyavahāra* understood as including thought and mental "speech"), stating that in the way worldly persons bring about [via speech] the mutual understanding of the things they want understood, or understand [directly] the things they want to know, so, i.e., correspondingly, do they establish in regard to those things the relationship of the thing to be named with [its] name (**abhidheyābhidhāna*), and the relationship of the thing to be cognized with [the] cognition [that knows it] (**jñeyajñāna*), so that at a another time conventional linguistic practice is not disturbed. Thus "linguistic practice" is stated in regard to the [respective] object that has the characteristic of, i.e., consists in, name and what is named and cognition and what is cognized, whose coming into existence is produced by mere error (*ji ltar 'jig rten pa rtogs par 'dod pa'i don phan tshun du rtogs par byed pa'am* | *shes par 'dod pa'i don khong du chud pa de bzhin du don de la brjod bya rjod byed kyi 'brel pa dang* | *shes bya shes byed du rnam par 'jog par byed cing* | *dus gzhan du yang tha snyad kyi gdams pa mi 'chad pa'i don du* | *de la 'di ltar rjod byed dang brjod bya dang* | *shes pa dang shes bya'i mtshan nyid can gyi don phyin ci log tsam gyis nye bar bskyed pa'i dag nyid kyi dngos po la tha snyad ces brjod* ...; ŚSV$_{\mathrm{ed}}$ 213.17-22; cf. ŚSV$_{\mathrm{tr}}$ 37f. and notes).

reasoning which is acknowledged only from the side of the world, they—through it alone—cause the world to understand.[423] For [it is] just as [in the following example]: Desirous persons who are involved in error (*viparyāsānugata*)[424] do not perceive the impurity (*aśucitā*) of the body even though [this impurity] exists [right in front of them], and having superimposed an unreal aspect of attractiveness (*śubhākāra*) [onto the body, they] are defiled.[425] For the sake of their [reaching] a state of dispassion (*vairāgya*), [a magical being] created by the Tathāgata, or a god, would describe the faults of the body which had previously been hidden by the notion (*sañjñā*) of attractiveness, with [the statement], "There are hairs on this body," etc.[426] And on account of the disappearance of that notion of attractiveness they would reach a state of dispassion. [It is] like that here too: Ordinary persons (*pṛthagjana*), having superimposed—inasmuch as the eye of their minds is impaired by the *timira* of ignorance—an

---

[423] Cf. Candrakīrti on MMK XXII.11 (XXII.11abc: *śūnyam ity apy avaktavyam aśūnyam iti vā bhavet | ubhayaṃ nobhayaṃ ceti*): *sarvam etan na vaktavyam asmābhiḥ | kiṃ tu anuktaṃ yathāvadavasthitaṃ svabhāvaṃ pratipattā pratipattuṃ na samartha iti | ato vayam api āropato vyavahārasatya eva sthitvā vyavahārārthaṃ vineyajanānurodhena śūnyam ity api brūmaḥ aśūnyam ity api śūnyāśūnyam ity api naiva śūnyaṃ nāśūnyam ity api brūmaḥ* (PsP_L 444.3-6; corrected following ms P and de Jong 1978: 236; ms P reads ... *kin tūktaṃ yathāvad* ...).

[424] PsP Tib takes *anugata* to be intended in an active sense: *phyin ci log gi rjes su song ba'i 'dod chags can rnams kyis* "Desirous persons who follow perverted views (*viparyāsa*) ...", which seems equally acceptable.

[425] Cf. PsP to MMK XXIII.7: *tad eṣāṃ kleśānāṃ rūpādikaṃ ṣaḍvidhaṃ vastv ālambanaṃ bhavati | tatra śubhākārādhyāropeṇa yathā rūpādibhyo rāga upajāyate* ... (PsP_L 457.6-7).

[426] Cp. MN I.57.13-20: *Puna ca paraṃ bhikkhave bhikkhu imam eva kāyaṃ uddhaṃ pādatalā adho kesamatthakā tacapariyantaṃ pūran nānappakārassa asucino paccavekkhati: Atthi imasmiṃ kāye kesā lomā nakhā dantā taco maṃsaṃ nahāru aṭṭhī aṭṭhimiñjā vakkaṃ hadayaṃ yakanaṃ kilomakaṃ pihakaṃ papphāsaṃ antaṃ antaguṇaṃ udariyaṃ karīsaṃ, pittaṃ semhaṃ pubbo lohitaṃ sedo medo assu vasā kheḷo siṅghāṇikā lasikā muttan ti*. Ñāṇamoli and Bodhi (1995: 147) translate: "Again, bhikkhus, a bhikkhu reviews this same body up from the soles of the feet and down from the top of the hair, bounded by skin, as full of many kinds of impurity thus: 'In this body there are head-hairs, body-hairs, nails, teeth, skin, flesh, sinews, bones, bone-marrow, kidneys, heart, liver, diaphragm, spleen, lungs, large intestines, small intestines, contents of the stomach, feces, bile, phlegm, pus, blood, sweat, fat, tears, grease, spittle, snot, oil of the joints, and urine.'"

erroneous own-being of things, which has the nature of not being perceived in any way whatsoever by the Nobles, and [also having superimposed, once own-being has been imagined,] some quality (*viśeṣa*) onto cases (*kvacit*) [of imagined own-being], become extremely defiled.[427] Now, the Nobles cause them to fully understand by way of reasoning acknowledged only by those [ordinary persons, such as]:[428] "Just as it is accepted [by you] that there is no [re-]arising from clay, etc., of a pot that [already] exists, so should it be ascertained that there is no arising of a pot [claimed to] exist prior to arising, because it [already] exists. And just as it is accepted [by you] that there is not the arising of a sprout from a flame or a glowing coal and so forth, [i.e., from things] that are other [than the sprout], so should it be determined that there is not [the arising of a sprout] from

---

[427] As regards the meaning of "a certain quality onto cases [of imagined own-being]," see also below §88 where Candrakīrti declares that the first chapter of the MMK was composed as an antidote to the superimposition of an own-form (*svarūpa* = *svabhāva*) of things and that the rest of the chapters were composed to refute any qualities (*viśeṣa*) that might further be superimposed in various cases of this imagined own-being. Clarifying that he intends all possible qualities which might be applied to dependent-arising, he exemplifies them with three qualities refuted in the second chapter of the MMK, to wit, "goer, what is gone [over] and going." Arnold (2005b: 422) translates *parikliśyanti* (and the previous *parikliśyante*) as "suffer," but the word is intended in its BHS meaning (cf. BHSD s.v. *kliśyati* "becomes soiled"); that is, people are defiled, or as Seyfort Ruegg (2002: 100) translates, "sullied," by the wrong views. That they will suffer at some point as a consequence of their superimposition of *svabhāva* is an expected result, but this future suffering is not relevant in the present context.

[428] The sentence in PsP Tib begins with *de dag da ltar 'phags pa rnams kyis*, which is immediately followed by the two arguments (*bum pa yod pa ... nges par gyis shig ... me dang sol ba ... nges par gyis shig* ||). The translation for *tatprasiddhayaivopapattyā paribodhayanti* does not appear either at the beginning of this sentence or, as might be expected, after the two exemplifications of arguments, but rather has been added to the end of Candrakīrti's reply to the objection concerning experience (*anubhava*: see the text's next paragraph). This section closes: ... *bsgrub par bya ba dang mtshungs pa nyid yin pa'i phyir des phyir bzlog par rigs pa ma yin no zhes de dag la grags pa nyid kyis khong du chud par mdzad pa yin no* || (*upapattyā* has not been translated). The translators (or a scribe in the tradition of one of their Sanskrit manuscripts) may have considered the reasoning in the *anubhava* section to belong generally to the exemplification of reasonings used to convince the world, and thus decided that the phrase's proper place was at the close of the *anubhava* section, and not after the argument against the arising of a sprout from a seed.

a seed and so forth, even though [these are] alleged (*vivakṣita*) [to be conditions]."[429]

§87. Even if there would be [the objection]: [But] this is our *experience*![430]

---

[429] Both of these arguments, that is, the argument against arising from self and the argument against arising from other, were presented earlier in the chapter; see above §29 and §51.

[430] Compare the defense found in NBh on NS IV.2.33. The Buddhist opponent has argued in NS IV.2.31 that the imagining of means of valid cognition and what is cognized is like the (erroneous) imagining of objects in a dream (NS IV.2.31: *svapnaviṣayābhimānavad ayaṃ pramāṇaprameyābhimānaḥ*; cf. NBh 273). Commenting on NS IV.2.33, which rejects the Buddhist proposition because there is no reason that supports it (IV.2.33: *hetvabhāvād asiddhiḥ*), Vātsyāyana has the Buddhist present the reason "because of non-perception when one is awake" (NBh 274.1: *pratibodhe 'nupalambhād iti cet*). He responds to this by stating that this reason is in fact capable of proving the opposite of what the Buddhist wants to prove, i.e., that the things perceived when one is awake do exist because they are perceived: *pratibodhaviṣayopalambhād apratiṣedhaḥ | yadi pratibodhe 'nupalambhāt svapne viṣayā na santi tarhi ya ime pratibuddhena viṣayā upalabhyante te upalambhāt santīti | viparyaye hi hetusāmarthyam | upalambhāt sadbhāve saty anupalambhād abhāvaḥ siddhyati | ubhayathā tv abhāve nānupalambhasya sāmarthyam asti yathā pradīpasyābhāvād rūpasyādarśanam iti tatra bhāvenābhāvaḥ samarthyata iti |* (NBh 274.1-5). "There is not refutation [of our view that things exist] because there is the perception of objects when one is awake. If the objects in a dream do not exist on account of the non-perception [of them] when one is awake, then these objects that are perceived by one who is awake do exist, [precisely] because of [their] perception; for the reason is capable [of proving] the opposite [of your thesis]. [Only] when real existence on the basis of perception is [accepted] can non-existence on the basis of non-perception be established. But when [as you maintain] there is the non-existence [of objects] in both cases [i.e., in dreams and when one is awake], non-perception is not suitable. It is like not seeing colour in the absence of lamplight: in this case, the non-existence [of colour] is determined by way of [its] existence [when there is light]." This argument is certainly more elaborate than the PsP sentence, but it too grounds itself in the view that direct perception, or, as the PsP opponents put it, "experience," is trustworthy, and it provides reasoned justification for this position in the light of the Buddhist's argument: the things that we both agree are unreal can be determined to be such only in dependence on the truly existing correlates given to us by direct perception. *LṬ's author explains that that which is experienced is the arising of a sprout from a seed, etc. (*anubhava iti | bījādibhya evāṅku*[*ra*]*syotpattir ity eṣaḥ* (Yonezawa 2004: 124, 141 [fol. 2b3]).

[we will reply that] this too is unreasonable, since this experience (*anubhava*) is false (*mṛṣā*),[431] because it is experience (*anubhavatvāt*), like the experience of a double moon and so forth by those with [the visual disorder] *timira* [is false]. And therefore, since experience as well is similar to the probandum (*sādhyasama*), an objection by way of it is not appropriate.[432]

§88. Therefore, to begin with, the initial chapter [of the Madhyamakaśāstra] commences thus [i.e., by declaring that] "Things have not arisen,"[433] [that is,] with an antidote to the superimposition of erroneous own nature. Now [after that],[434] in order to refute whatever qualities have been superimposed in cases [of imagined own nature], the rest of the chapters are undertaken, for the sake of demonstrating that no quality either, such as goer, what is gone [over], or going (*gantṛgantavyagamana*),[435] exists for dependent-arising.[436]

---

[431] The Tibetan does not present a literal translation for *yasmād anubhava eṣa mṛṣā* and instead attests *'di ltar nyams su myong ba ni brdzun pa'i don can yin te*. The Sanskrit and Tibetan *sādhya*s set forth different claims, the former focussed on experience itself, the latter on its object. The manuscript on which this sentence is based may have been damaged at this point; *eṣa* appears to have been read as *artha*.

[432] Candrakīrti sets forth an inference acknowledged only by the opponent. On the logical fault *sādhyasama*, see n. 257.

[433] Seyfort Ruegg (2002: 101) follows the Tibetan in translating the following *pratipakṣeṇa* as "as a counteragent" (PsP Tib: *gnyen por*).

[434] The Tibetan's *de nas* for *idānīm* expresses the implication of the Sanskrit's "now." The translators, not using a convention like square brackets, on occasion chose to present the sense of a word instead of its literal translation. *LṬ's author glosses *idānīm* with *prathamaprakaraṇānantaraṃ* (cf. Yonezawa 2004: 124, 142 [fol. 2b3]).

[435] *gantṛ*, *gantavyam* and *gamanam* are refuted in MMK II. On the argumentation in this chapter, see especially Oetke 2001a: 59-88 (for his critique of Garfield's translation of the chapter, see 184-191) and Oetke 2004. Dan Arnold (2005b: 424 and n. 41), in contradistinction to Seyfort Ruegg (2002: 102), interprets de La Vallée Poussin's half-*daṇḍa* at the end of PsP 58.11 as a full stop and thus reads the part of the sentence beginning with *gantṛgantavyagamanādikaḥ* as a new sentence, with the result that he must supply (misleading) material in brackets: "Now, the remainder of the treatise is undertaken for the sake of refuting some qualifications that are imputed in particular cases. Dependent origination does not have any single qualification, not even such as being the agent, the locus, or the action of motion — [this treatise is undertaken] for the sake of showing [that]"; the focus, however, in the second part of

the sentence is still on what is refuted in the rest of the chapters, and not in the entire treatise, i.e., including chapter one.

[436] The paragraph is intended as Candrakīrti's conclusion to his extended conversation with the Naiyāyikas, but it can also be seen as a response to the concluding sentence of the original critique he cited to commence the discussion. The Naiyāyikas ended this critique by asserting that things are indeed established as arisen (*santy apratiṣiddhāḥ sarvabhāvāḥ*) and that the composition of the treatise, namely, the MMK, is pointless (*śāstrārambhavaiyarthyam eva*). Candrakīrti, having earlier refuted their arguments, now reiterates the Madhyamaka position, i.e., that things are unarisen (*anutpannā bhāvāḥ*) and connects it with the first chapter of the MMK, explaining that this chapter serves to counter the erroneous superimposition of own-being; he then declares the subject matter and purpose of the rest of the chapters of the MMK. The MMK thus defended as having an extremely important purpose, he commences his offensive against Dignāga by pronouncing that the effort put into *his* treatise was pointless.
The transition from the discussion with the Naiyāyikas to the attack on Dignāga thus appears, from the perspective just described, to be quite smooth. Stcherbatsky (1927: 140, n. 4), on the other hand, surmises that the first chapter originally ended with the present paragraph, adding that the discussion which follows "looks like a later addition." Stcherbatsky's (ibid., 139) free translation accordingly indicates that he understood *idānīm* as signalling the commencement of the rest of the chapters: "The remaining parts of the treatise are now (concerned with details)." Of course, as the chapter is now structured, Candrakīrti has only commented on the first of the fourteen *kārikā*s of the first chapter of the MMK, but Stcherbatsky's observation may have some merit. One has to agree that the employment of *idānīm* here is unusual, and that the sentence including it or one similar to it would not be out of place introducing the second chapter of the MMK. I do not think that we need to go as far as Stcherbatsky and assume that the altercation with Dignāga is a later addition, i.e., material inserted by a later scholar (if this is what he meant), but it is possible that Candrakīrti, in the course of composing the first chapter, or the larger PsP, revised the first chapter's material, re-locating sentences and paragraphs, adding new sentences and even entire sections. As a result of the revisions, some of the originally seamless transitions between passages may have been disturbed, as in the present case, where the remaining *idānīm* seems misplaced (compare also, e.g., PsP_{M} §70 [PsP_{L} 39.8], where the concluding statement links up better with the *maṅgala śloka*s than with MMK I.1). We must also keep in mind that information related to the process of the creation and composition of the Indian works is extremely sparse. Helmut Krasser hypothesizes that some texts that have been held to represent direct compositions by Indian masters are actually student class notes; see Krasser 2011 and Krasser 2012a: 569ff.
Sprung (1979: xiii-xv), following up on Stcherbatsky's idea that the first chapter ended with the present paragraph, opines that "[t]he lengthy and unfocussed first chapter of the Sanskrit is so unmistakably composed of discrete sections that we must suspect careless editing some time before the extant manuscripts came into being."

§89. If [the following objection] were [brought forth by Dignāga]: Exactly this worldly practice regarding means of valid cognition and the object cognized (*pramāṇaprameyavyavahāra*) has been described by us with [our] treatise (*śāstra*),[437]

[we would reply:] Then the advantage (*phala*) of its description should be stated.

§90. [Opponent:] It [i.e., worldly practice regarding means of valid cognition and the object cognized] has been ruined by poor logicians (*kutārkika*) through [their] assertion of an erroneous characteristic

---

He therefore considers the "sections" of the PsP up to the present paragraph "to have been, at one time, an introductory chapter in their own right" and separates the refutation of the views of the opponent ("either Dignāga or Bhāvaviveka") which follow as Chapter II of his translation, setting off "the normal commentary on Nāgārjuna's *kārikā*s concerned with causal conditions" as Chapter III. It is certainly an exaggeration to call the chapter "unfocussed," and to blame the chapter's length and the perceived lack of focus on "careless editing" is too cavalier. Rather than breaking the chapter into three parts, it may be more prudent to merely be aware that revision appears to have taken place. Felix Erb (1997: 7) comments on the "gross[e] Freiheit des Kommentarstils Candrakīrtis" in his introduction to his translation of the ŚSV, stating that in his commentary on the first two *kārikā*s of the ŚSV, Candrakīrti takes advantage of Nāgārjuna's choice of (the Buddha's) statements concerning the self, non-self, etc., which Nāgārjuna uses to illustrate the *nītārtha/neyārtha* theory, in order to refute the Hindu systems' *ātman* theory, and in particular, to refute the Hīnayāna and Yogācāra schools', as well as Bhāviveka's, views of *śūnyatā*. The result is that the commentary on the first two *kārikā*s takes up a quarter of the entire ŚSV (Candrakīrti's commentary on the first chapter of the MMK makes up approximately one sixth of the PsP).

[437] The treatise referred to is the Pramāṇasamuccaya. Candrakīrti cites from it in the following discussion on direct perception. *LṬ's author identifies "us" as Dignāga, etc.: *asmābhi*[*r*] *dignāgādibhiḥ*. He also notes that this assertion by Dignāga, etc., is made in regard to the position that worldly usage in regard to means of valid cognition and the object cognized, while not applicable on the ultimate level, is accepted on the worldly level: *laukika eva pramāṇaprameyavyavahāro yukto na pāramārthika ity asmin pakṣa* (ms: *pakṣe*) *āha* | (cf. Yonezawa 2004: 124, 142 [fol. 2b4]). See also Siderits 1981: 130f. On Dignāga's affiliation with the Yogācāra school and the development of his ideas and argumentation in regard to the ultimate non-existence of external things, see Frauwallner 1959; cf. also Dreyfus and Lindtner 1989; Tosaki 1987. Cf. Steinkellner 1990 on Dharmakīrti's ultimate view, as well as, e.g., Dunne 2004: 53ff.

(*lakṣaṇa*).[438] We have stated its (= *pramāṇa* and *prameya*'s) correct characteristic.[439]

---

[438] The "poor logicians" spoken of by the opponent are considered by most scholars to be the Naiyāyikas (cf., e.g., Stcherbatsky 1927: 140; Sprung 1979: 53, n. 2; Siderits 1981: 127; Arnold 2005a: 151). According to Tillemans (1990: 39, n. 89), the *kutārkika*s are other philosophers "such as the Naiyāyikas"; he refers exclusively to the Naiyāyikas in his next sentence ("In other words, the only justification for the Epistemologist's program would be if the Naiyāyika account of worldly truth was inadequate, but, argues Candrakīrti, such is not the case" [the sentence quoted is on p. 40]). The majority of scholars who claim that the Naiyāyikas are the adversaries criticized base their judgement on the fact that Candrakīrti later on in this PsP chapter (PsP_M §119-§122 [PsP_L 75.2-8]) defends a four-*pramāṇa* system (versus Dignāga's two-*pramāṇa* system), asseverating that direct perception (*pratyakṣa*), inference (*anumāna*), authoritative testimony (*āgama*) and comparison (*upamāna*) are to be accepted on the surface level. While it is true that these four correspond to the *pramāṇa*s of the Nyāya school, I expect that Candrakīrti's Dignāga is making a general statement here and doubt that it should be connected with Candrakīrti's four-*pramāṇa* presentation; in addition to the epistemological theories of the Naiyāyikas, Dignāga refutes those of the Vaiśeṣikas, Sāṅkhyas and Mīmāṃsakas (and that of the Vādavidhi) in his PS. It can further be noted that the *Upāyahṛdaya documents that **pratyakṣa*, **anumāna*, **āgama/śabda/āptaśruti* and **upamāna* were posited within the Buddhist fold for a strand of the pre-(and parallel?)Vasubandhu–pre-Dignāga tradition: *atha katividhaṃ pramāṇam* | *caturvidhaṃ pramāṇam* | *pratyakṣam anumānam upamānam āgamaś ceti* (reconstructed from Chinese by Tucci; cf. Tucci 1981: 13. See also Kajiyama 1991: 109 and Nagasaki 1991: 221). I therefore hesitate to assert that Candrakīrti intends to defend specifically (or exclusively) the Nyāya *pramāṇa*s. For the descriptions/definitions of the four *pramāṇa*s provided by Candrakīrti, see PsP_M §119-§122 (PsP_L 75.2-8); for disparities between these definitions and the Naiyāyika definitions, see n. 541. The same four *pramāṇa*s are listed and refuted in the VV (Lindtner [1982b: 70, n. 110] is of the opinion that the opponent in the VV is a Buddhist, and gives as one of his reasons the fact that the third *pramāṇa* is designated *āgama* in the VV, not *śabda* as it is more commonly, but not exclusively, designated in Nyāya works). Dignāga asserts in the NM that *śabda*, *upamāna* and so forth are not separate means of valid cognition, because they are included in *pratyakṣa* and *anumāna*; cf. Tucci 1930: 50; Katsura 1982: 82. On the *pramāṇa*s accepted by other schools, see Hattori 1968: 78, n. 1.12.

[439] It would seem that in the present context the term *lakṣaṇa* refers primarily to the essential characteristic of *pramāṇaprameyavyavahāra*, but secondarily to the words that formulate and express this characteristic. *lakṣaṇa* as the verbally formulated specification of the existential characteristic may thus secondarily intend a definition. It can probably be assumed that the correct characterization of *pramāṇaprameya-vyavahāra* depends above all on the correct characterization, and thus also the

[Reply:] This too is not reasonable. For if, caused by [the fact that these] poor logicians have adduced an erroneous characteristic, the world would be mistaken in regard to the object characterized (*lakṣya*),[440] [then] for its (= the world's) sake [your] endeavour (*prayatna*) would be advantageous—but this is not the case (i.e., that worldly practice has been detrimentally affected by the assertions of these logicians).[441] Thus, this endeavour [of yours to provide a so-called corrected account of the matter] is simply pointless.[442]

---

correctly formulated definitions, of *pramāṇa* and *prameya*, of which the characterization and definition of *pramāṇa* would be primary.

[440] *LṬ's author exemplifies *lakṣya* of the compound *lakṣyavaiparītyaṃ*, i.e., what might be misunderstood if the world were mistaken in regard to the object characterized: *lakṣye dhūmād vahnipratītau* (cf. Yonezawa 2004: 124, 142 [fol. 2b4]).

[441] I follow Ms B's and PsP Tib's text and thus read *yadi hi kutārkikair viparītalakṣaṇapraṇayanakṛtaṃ lakṣyavaiparītyaṃ lokasya syāt* instead of PsP_L's ... *viparītalakṣaṇapraṇayanaṃ kṛtaṃ ... syāt*; that is, I read the sentence up to *lokasya syāt* as a single conditional phrase. PsP Tib reads: *gal te 'jig rten la rtog ge ngan pas mtshan nyid phyin ci log brjod pas byas pa'i mtshon bya phyin ci log yod par 'gyur na ni ...* . Were the text with the *anusvāra* to be correct, one would expect, given the *syāt* after *lokasya*, a *syāt* after *kṛtaṃ*. Ms P's and ms Q's *anusvāra* may have been passed on to them by ms ζ, unless it was already in ms β and ms B's lack of it merely represents a scribal omission. Vaidya (1960b: 20) emends de La Vallée Poussin's text in his own edition by appropriating (without reference!) de La Vallée Poussin's reconstruction (PsP_L 59, n. 2) of PsP Tib's *brjod pas byas pa* as °*praṇayanāt kṛtaṃ*.
Candrakīrti responds to Dignāga's justification for composing his treatise by saying that if the "poor" logicians have misled the world by giving a wrong characterization, thereby causing it to deal with the objects of the world in a confused and self-detrimental way, then Dignāga's setting forth of a corrected presentation could be of value inasmuch as the world could then rely on it. However, he continues, the world has not been misled by the conclusions of these logicians. Implicit in the response is the idea that logicians' statements on means of cognition, etc., be they correct or incorrect, have little relevance for the everyday world; the world relies on its own consensually established understanding of *prameya* and *pramāṇa*.

[442] Tillemans (1990: 39, n. 89), referring to PsP_L 58.14-59.3 (PsP_M §89-§90), argues that Candrakīrti aims to "characterize the Epistemologist's program as a mere description of worldly truth," a program the Epistemologist considers justified because philosophers like the Naiyāyikas have bungled their own descriptions. Tillemans remarks, "In fact, this is a somewhat too facile and inaccurate characterization of what the Epistemologist is up to and blurs the fact of his reductionism: he is not trying to do a better inventory of the worlds' (sic) notions, he is explaining and criti-

§91. Moreover, the fault [as regards your view] has been assigned in the Vigrahavyāvartanī through statements such as "If apprehension of the object cognized (*prameyādhigama*) is dependent on means of valid cognition (*pramāṇādhīna*), by what are those means of valid cognition determined?"[443] Since [you] have not refuted that [fault, you] do not clarify, for its part, the correct characteristic.

---

cizing them by reducing unrealities to more ontologically fundamental elements." Candrakīrti is, however, very aware of the Epistemologist's reductionist program, but is commencing his argumentation with an allusion to his own stance that Buddhist philosophers, when dealing with the *saṃvṛti* level, should undertake no more than a description of worldly things and concepts. While it is true that at this point he has Dignāga professing to do only this, with this first step Candrakīrti shows that any presentation that aims to correct the world—which is finding and working with its objects unproblematically—will have no impact on it (see previous note). He will in the following harshly critique Dignāga for bringing his reductionism into play on the everyday level, since analysis has no place on this level and in fact can have only detrimental effects.

[443] Candrakīrti now argues that even though Dignāga claims to have provided the correct characteristic, he has failed to do so, since he has not answered the critical question of how the *pramāṇa*s are ascertained.

The citation that Candrakīrti states derives from the VV is not found in these words in the VV as it has been transmitted to us; it is also not in verse. It appears that Candrakīrti is making reference to and re-phrasing VV 31 to reflect the discourse of the Epistemologist. VV 31 reads: *yadi ca pramāṇatas te teṣāṃ teṣāṃ prasiddhir arthānām | teṣāṃ punaḥ prasiddhiṃ brūhi kathaṃ te pramāṇānām* || (de La Vallée Poussin paraphrases the verse at PsP_L 59, n. 3). The author of the VV poses the question for the sake of refuting the view that means of valid cognition exist ultimately. It is, however, acceptable for Mādhyamikas to speak of surface level *prameya*s and *pramāṇa*s, but they must be understood as existing in mutual dependence; it is not correct to speak of only one of the pair as being established by the other. Candrakīrti is using the paraphrased VV *kārikā* to reject Dignāga's position on *pramāṇa* and *prameya* on the *surface* level. Hattori (1968: 76, n. 1.10), referring to Dignāga's Yogācāra affiliation, asserts that Dignāga's "theory does not conflict with Nāgārjuna's argument against the substantiality of *pramāṇa* and *prameya*." He adds that "a later extreme transcendentalist, Candrakīrti, makes an attack on Dignāga's proposition '*pramāṇādhīnaḥ prameyādhigamaḥ*,' asserting that there is nothing to be apprehended in the ultimate sense; see *Prasannap.* p. 58.14ff., but this criticism does not fundamentally affect Dignāga's standpoint." On the contrary, Candrakīrti's focus in this discussion is not the nature of the *pramāṇa*s and *prameya*s on the ultimate level, but rather Dignāga's fault-ridden presentation of them on the *worldly* level.

Candrakīrti will next take as his target just one of the *prameya*s, the particular characteristic (the general characteristic, conceptualized on the basis on the particular

§92. Furthermore, if in conformity with the pair of characteristics, namely, the particular and the general (*svasāmānyalakṣaṇa*), a pair of means of valid cognition is asserted, does the object characterized (*lakṣya*), of which these two characteristics [constitute its characteristics], exist or not?[444] If it exists, then, since an object of cognition (*prameya*) other than those [two characteristics] exists, why [is there only] a pair of means of valid cognition? But if an object characterized does not exist, then the characteristic too, [being]

---

characteristic, can be left aside), because its refutation serves to invalidate Dignāga's view of direct perception, one of his primary interests in the following long debate.

[444] Dignāga's two means of valid cognition, namely, direct perception (*pratyakṣa*) and inference (*anumāna*), respectively have as object the particular characteristic (*svalakṣaṇa*) and the general characteristic (*sāmānyalakṣaṇa*). Cf. PS I.1: *pratyakṣam anumānaṃ ca pramāṇe lakṣaṇadvayam* | *prameyam* (Sanskrit in Hattori 1968: 76, n. 1.11 and Appendix, and Steinkellner 2005: 1; Tib in Hattori 1968: 176f.; translation p. 24). The *svavṛtti* to PS I.1 reads: *na hi svasāmānyalakṣaṇābhyām anyat prameyam asti* | *svalakṣaṇaviṣayaṃ ca pratyakṣaṃ sāmānyalakṣaṇaviṣayam anumānam iti pratipādayiṣyāmaḥ* | (Hattori 1968: 79, n. 1.14 and Steinkellner 2005: 1). According to Dignāga, the *svalakṣaṇa* is the particular, inexpressible (*avyapadeśya*; cf. the *svavṛtti* to PS I.2cd) perceptible, which is apprehended without conceptual overlay (*kalpanā* is described in PS I.3d as *nāmajātyādiyojanā*, i.e., that "which has an association with name, genus and so forth," see Hattori 1968: 82, n. 1.25 and 83, n. 1.27.) or, as Tillemans (1990: 39, n. 89) puts it, "what one *really* sees in direct perception – all the rest is mental fabrication coming from conceptualizing." The *sāmānyalakṣaṇa* is conceptually constructed through generalizing from many individuals; the *svalakṣaṇa* is real, the *sāmānyalakṣaṇa* not. Dharmakīrti thus asserts "but what is [really] cognized is the particular characteristic alone" (PV III.53cd: *meyaṃ tv ekaṃ svalakṣaṇam*). Hattori (1968: 80), making reference to PV III.54cd (*tasya svapararūpābhyāṃ gater meyadvayaṃ matam*), writes: "That there are two sorts of *prameya* implies that *sva-lakṣaṇa* is apprehended in two ways, as it is (*sva-rūpeṇa*) and as something other than itself (*para-rūpeṇa*), but not that there is real *sāmānya* apart from *sva-lakṣaṇa*. Thus, the distinction between *sva-lakṣaṇa* and *sāmānya-lakṣaṇa* is the result of a changed perspective." On *svalakṣaṇa* and *sāmānyalakṣaṇa*, and Dharmakīrti's characterization of them, see, e.g., Hattori 1968: 79, n. 1.14; Tillemans 1990: 273, n. 366; Dunne 2004: 79ff. Dignāga denies that a third *pramāṇa* is required for cognizing things such colour, etc., as impermanent or for cases of recognition (cf. PS I.2cd-3b; Hattori 1968: 24f.).

without a basis (*āśraya*), does not exist; thus, how [can you maintain] a pair of means of valid cognition?[445] For he [= Nāgārjuna] will say:

> And when there is not the proceeding of a characteristic, an object characterized is not logically possible;
> And when an object characterized is not logically possible, a characteristic as well is impossible.[446]

---

[445] Candrakīrti commences his attack on Dignāga's view that there are two means of valid cognition (*pramāṇa*) by pointing out that when these two means of valid cognition, namely, direct perception and inference (= *pramāṇa* #1 and #2) respectively and restrictively take as object the two characteristics, i.e., the particular and the general (= *prameya* #1 and #2), Dignāga is obliged to consider what is characterized (*lakṣya*) by them. Implicit in Candrakīrti's argument is the assumption that a *lakṣaṇa* cannot exist without a *lakṣya*: if Dignāga agrees that a *lakṣya*, i.e., a basis for the *lakṣaṇa*s, exists, then a third *pramāṇa*, i.e., one that perceives the *lakṣya* (= *prameya* #3), will be have to be admitted (*LṬ's author notes that *lakṣyam* should be understood as *prameyam*; cf. Yonezawa 2004: 124, 142 [fol. 2b4]); but if Dignāga rejects the existence of a *lakṣya* where the *lakṣaṇa*s come to appear or, so to speak, take their foothold, then the *lakṣaṇa*s will be without a basis. *lakṣaṇa*s without a basis, i.e., not characterizing anything, cannot exist, and thus cannot serve as objects of cognition. The two means of valid cognition are therefore impossible. MMK V.4 is subsequently cited by Candrakīrti to support this second argument.
Arnold (2005b: 427, n. 51) criticizes Seyfort Ruegg's translation of *lakṣya* in the present paragraph as "characterized *definiendum*." I agree that definitions and the objects they define are not immediately relevant, but, as I indicated earlier, the ideas "characteristic" and "definition" are closely connected and often interwoven, a definition being nothing more than the verbal formulation of a characteristic. Arnold (ibid.) also criticizes Seyfort Ruegg's translation of *svalakṣaṇa* as "particular characteristic" inasmuch as he considers that it suggests, against Dignāga's understanding and intent, that such characteristics characterize something else; he translates the word as "unique particular." I acknowledge that the word bears this meaning in Dignāga's epistemology but retain the translation "particular characteristic" because Candrakīrti's argumentation focusses on its being exactly this. That Candrakīrti here and in the following discussion takes the implications of Dignāga's *svalakṣaṇa* as "characteristic" as focal point does not, however, mean that he is merely bickering about word choices and ignoring or overlooking Dignāga's conception of *svalakṣaṇa*. As will be seen in the following, Candrakīrti deals with the meaning and implication of the word as "characteristic" in order to show just how inappropriate it is for a Mahāyānist to posit unique particulars on the surface level.

[446] MMK V.4: *lakṣaṇāsaṃpravṛttau ca na lakṣyam upapadyate | lakṣyasyānupapattau ca lakṣaṇasyāpy asaṃbhavaḥ* ||. Nāgārjuna has argued in MMK V.2ab that no thing without a characteristic exists anywhere (*alakṣaṇo na kaścic ca bhāvaḥ saṃvidyate kvacit*); there is nothing existing in an indefinite, murky state which only subsequent-

§93. If there were [the following objection from the side of the Epistemologist:] It is not a characteristic (*lakṣaṇa*) because [something, i.e., a *lakṣya*] is characterized by it (*lakṣyate anena*). Rather, taking the [affix] *lyuṭ* (= *ana*) [of the word *lakṣaṇa*] in [its function of denoting] the object (*karman*) [on the basis of the grammatical rule:] "Secondary affixes and *lyuṭ* affixes [are allowed to occur] variously" (*kṛtyalyuṭo bahulam*),[447] [we maintain that it is] a characteristic (*la-*

---

ly attains delineation and distinctiveness through the application of a characteristic. When things without any characteristic do not exist, there is nowhere for a characteristic to apply itself, to "set foot" (MMK V.2cd: *asaty alakṣaṇe bhāve kramatāṃ kuha lakṣaṇam*). A characteristic is also not admissible when a thing is already endowed with its characteristic (*salakṣaṇa*), for such a thing does not need to be characterized again, and no third thing, i.e., something other than an *alakṣaṇa* or *salakṣaṇa* thing, exists (MMK V.3). Thus, when a characteristic has, so to speak, nowhere to go, no fundament in which to appear or constitute itself, a thing characterized (*lakṣya*) is impossible, for a *lakṣya* is defined by a *lakṣaṇa*; the characteristic must be able to apply itself to something in order to make this a characterized thing. And when a thing characterized is impossible, so too a characteristic, for a characteristic is only such in relation to the thing it characterizes (MMK V.4); note that Candrakīrti in his commentary on MMK V.4cd, as in his argumentation here against a non-existing *lakṣya*, grounds the argumentation in the *pāda* with the statement that the characteristic would be without a basis (*nirāśraya*). Garfield's translation of these verses is unreliable. Garfield (1995: 14, 150) translates MMK V.2 as "A thing without a characteristic [h]as never existed. If nothing lacks a characteristic, [w]here do characteristics come to be?" (the translation in Samten and Garfield 2006 retains the mistakes) and comments (150): "So we can conclude that everything has characteristics." Unfortunately, his interpretation of the entire chapter is flawed, failing to reflect Nāgārjuna's intent.

447 Candrakīrti allows Dignāga to defend his theory of the two characteristics by way of a grammatical argument. According to hypothetical Dignāga, the word "characteristic" (*lakṣaṇa*) as used in his system does not denote an instrument (*karaṇa*), but rather an object (*karman*) and as such it is unaffected by Candrakīrti's contention—applicable only to "characteristic" as an instrument—that a characteristic, as a "characterizer," i.e., that by which something is characterized, requires a thing characterized (*lakṣya*). Dignāga's defense finds legitimation in the grammatical rule that allows the affix "*ana*"—termed *lyuṭ* in the Pāṇinian system—more than one function. As Candrakīrti's interpretation of the word *lakṣaṇa* reflects, this affix may have the function of denoting the instrument (he will state that the word is commonly accepted as derived in an instrumental sense); this function, along with an alternative function of denoting the location, is expressed in Pā 3.3.117: *karaṇādhikaraṇayoś ca* "[The affix *lyuṭ* denotes] the instrument or locus."

kṣaṇa) because that [characteristic itself] is characterized (*lakṣyate tat*).

[Reply:] Even so, because the instrument (*karaṇa*) by which that [characteristic] is characterized [has to be] something different (*arthāntara*) from the object (*karman*) since something cannot be characterized by itself, precisely that fault [remains, i.e., that the characteristic cannot exist because it cannot stand alone, in this case, without something characterizing it].[448]

The Kāś slightly expands: *karaṇe 'dhikaraṇe ca kārake dhātor lyuṭ pratyayo bhavati* "The affix *lyuṭ* occurs after a root in [the function of denoting] a *kāraka* as an instrument or locus"; among the examples provided by the Kāś are *idhmapravraścana*, an axe, that is, an instrument (*karaṇa*) for cutting wood, and *godohanī*, a milk-pail, that is, a receptacle (*adhikaraṇa*) into which milk is milked. Pā 3.3.115 (*lyuṭ ca*) further authorizes usage of the affix *lyuṭ* to form verbal nouns (Kāś provides, among others, the examples *hasana* "laughing" and *jalpana* "chattering"). The rule that Dignāga avails himself of to substantiate his interpretation of *lakṣaṇa* as object (*karman*) is Pā 3.3.113: *kṛtyalyuṭo bahulam* (my translation is based on Cardona's [1988: 233]; cf. also Böthlingk [2001: 126]: "Die kṛtja genannten Suffixe und das Suffix *ana* ... haben häufig andere Bedeutungen als diejenigen, die ihnen zugetheilt wurden"). The Kāś comments: *kṛtyasaṃjñakāḥ pratyayā lyuṭ ca bahulaṃ artheṣu bhavanti ... karanādhikaraṇayoḥ bhāve ca lyuṭ | anyatrāpi bhavati* "The affixes termed *kṛtya* and *lyuṭ* occur in various senses. ... *lyuṭ* [is applied] in [denoting] an instrument [or] locus and [to form] a verbal noun [but] it occurs [denoting] other [grammatical forms] as well." Cardona (1988: 233) illustrates Pā 3.3.113 as it pertains to *lyuṭ* with the verb √*bhuj*: "Again, *bhojana*, with *lyuṭ* after *bhuj*, can signify not only eating but also an object that is eaten, food." Thus on this interpretation, Dignāga's *lakṣya*-like *lakṣaṇa* will not require a *lakṣya*.

See also the reference to Pā 3.3.113 in the MABh (MABh$_{ed}$ 261.9: *krit dang luṭ ni phal cher*) which occurs in the course of Candrakīrti's refutation of the Buddhist opponent's view that *ātman*, the appropriator (*upādātṛ*), which is claimed to be nothing more than the composite of the *skandha*s, i.e., what is appropriated (*upādāna*), does not exist (cf. MABh$_{ed}$ 260.12-261.14; MABh$_{tr}$ 1911: 306).

[448] *lakṣaṇa* understood as having a *lyuṭ* affix in its function of denoting the object would have to be characterized by something, and that which characterizes is a *lakṣaṇa*, the latter in its function of instrument. The single object-*lakṣaṇa* cannot additionally be an instrument, cannot self-characterize, and when it is not characterized it is incapable of existing as an object-*lakṣaṇa*. That things cannot act on themselves is an argument used by Candrakīrti in various contexts, and one he will apply in the upcoming refutation of self-cognition. Cf., e.g., the argument in his commentary on MMK II.2 against the visual faculty seeing itself: *tatra tad eva darśanaṃ svātmānaṃ na paśyati svātmani kriyāvirodhāt* | (PsP$_L$ 114.1).

§94. If it were [argued:] This is not a fault, because cognition (*jñāna*) is an instrument and because it is included as a particular characteristic (*svalakṣaṇa*).[449]

Reply: According to general agreement (*iha*), the individual (*ātmīya*) own form (*svarūpa*) of things not common to other [things] (*anyāsādhāraṇa*) is the particular characteristic (*svalakṣaṇa*), for example, earth's solidity (*kāṭhinya*), feeling's (*vedanā*) experience (*anubhava*), consciousness' (*vijñāna*) awareness of the respective object (*viṣayaṃ prati vijñaptiḥ*)[450]—considering that (*iti kṛtvā*) [the entity] which pos-

---

[449] Dignāga responds to Candrakīrti's demand by asserting that there is also a *svalakṣana*-cum-*lakṣaṇa* which is capable of performing the function of an instrument (*karaṇa*), and as an instrumental particular characteristic it characterizes the particular characteristic considered by him to have the function of *karman*. Thus the particular-characteristic-cum-object indeed has a characteristic characterizing it, and, inasmuch as this characteristic is the separate entity known as cognition, the instrument (*karaṇa*) is indeed something other than the object (*karman*). As Siderits (1981: 133f.) remarks, with the stress laid on cognition being itself a particular characteristic, "the opponent is seeking to meet the objection that lakṣaṇa and lakṣya must be thought of as distinct ... without admitting to his ontology anything other than the unique svalakṣaṇa."
It would seem that Dignāga's response also takes into consideration another nuance of the verb √*lakṣ*, namely, √*lakṣ* in the sense of "to perceive," intending with it support for his view: the *svalakṣaṇa* as object perceived (*karman*) is perceived by the instrument (*karaṇa*) perception (*jñāna*).

[450] The examples Candrakīrti provides are found in the AK and AKBh. AKBh_{ed} 8.19 (= AKBh_{Ej} 12.15) leads into AK I.12d's listing of the own nature of the four elements with: *svabhāvas tu yathākramaḥ*. AK I.12d: *kharasnehoṣṇateraṇāḥ* (AKBh_{ed} 8.21 [=AKBh_{Ej} 12.17]: *kharaḥ pṛthivīdhātuḥ*). AKBh ad AK I.12ab: *ete catvāraḥ svalakṣaṇopādāyarūpadhāraṇād dhātavaś catvāri mahābhūtāny ucyante* (AKBh_{ed} 8.13 [= AKBh_{Ej} 12.6-7]) "These four *dhātu*s, [so named] because [they] bear their own [particular] characteristic and [bear] secondary matter, are called the four great elements"; AKVy 32.33-33.2: *svalakṣaṇopādāyarūpadhāraṇād dhātava* iti kāṭhinyādi*svalakṣaṇaṃ cakṣurādyupādāyarūpaṃ* ca dadhātīti (read: dadhatīti) *dhātavaḥ* (cf. MW s.v. √*dhā*: bear, hold, support). Further references to *kāṭhinya* as the particular characteristic of earth are given by de La Vallée Poussin at PsP_{L} 60, n. 5. Cf. also AK I.14c: *vedanā 'nubhavaḥ*; AK I.14d: *saṃjñā nimittodgrahaṇātmikā*; AK I.16a: *vijñānaṃ prativijñaptiḥ* (AKBh ad I.16a: *viṣayaṃ viṣayaṃ prati vijñaptir upalabdhir vijñānaskandha ity ucyate* [AKBh_{ed} 11.7 = AKBh_{Ej} 17.7]; AKVy ad I.16a [38.23f.]: *vijñāna*skandhaḥ *prativijñaptir* ity arthaḥ skandhādhikārāt. pratir vīpsārthaḥ. viṣayaṃ viṣayaṃ pratīty arthaḥ. *upalabdhir* vastumātragrahaṇam. Cf. also AKBh_{ed} 108.11-12, where the first two of the three types of mental attention

sesses that [characteristic] (*tadvān*) is naturally (*hi*) characterized by that [characteristic]. But [he who] (= Dignāga), having rejected the derivation (*vyutpatti*) [of the word *lakṣaṇa*] which conforms with what is generally acknowledged (*prasiddhi*), maintains[451] [that *lakṣa-*

[*manaskāra*] are given as *svalakṣaṇamanaskāraḥ* and *sāmānyalakṣaṇamanaskāraḥ* [AKBh$_{tr}$ II.325]). Candrakīrti lists the respective *lakṣaṇa*s of the five *skandha*s at PsP$_L$ 343.9: *rūpaṇānubhavanimittodgrahaṇābhisaṃskaraṇaviṣayaprativijñaptilakṣa-ṇāḥ pañcaskandhāḥ*. Erb (1997: 166, n. 656) notes, "Schliesslich unterscheidet Ca zwei Arten von Merkmalen der Daseinsfaktoren: Die spezifischen Wesensmerkmale (*svalakṣaṇa*), wie die Festigkeit usw. als spezifisches Wesensmerkmal der Elemente Erde usw. (s. Pras 126,1), und die allgemeinen Merkmale der *dharma*, womit meist die allgemeinen Wesensmerkmale des Verursachten (*sāmanya-saṃskṛta-lakṣaṇa* [read: *sāmānya°*]) Entstehen, Bestehen und Vergehen (vgl. 7. *parīkṣā* in der Pras) gemeint sind." Candrakīrti further refers to an interpretation of *sāmānyalakṣaṇa* in his commentary on MMK XV.1ab in which *anityatva* and so forth are referred to as *sāmānyalakṣaṇa*s: *evam ... bālā ... lakṣaṇam ācakṣate agner auṣṇyaṃ svalakṣaṇaṃ tato 'nyatrānupalambhād asādhāraṇatvena svam eva lakṣaṇam iti kṛtvā | bālajana-prasiddhyaiva ca bhagavatā tad evaiṣāṃ sāṃvṛtaṃ svarūpam abhidharme vyava-sthāpitam | sādhāraṇaṃ tv anityatvādikaṃ sāmānyalakṣaṇam iti coktam* (PsP$_L$ 261.3-7; presumably meant are *anitya*, *duḥkha*, and *anātman*, or *anitya*, *śūnya* and *anātman*). See also de Jong 1949: 4, n. 14.

451 De La Vallée Poussin (PsP$_L$ 60.6-7), relying on his three manuscripts and PsP Tib, edited the passage to read: ... *vijñānasya viṣayaprativijñaptiḥ* (half-*daṇḍa*) *tena hi tal lakṣyata iti kṛtvā prasiddhānugatāṃ ca vyutpattim avadhūya karmasādhanam abhyupagacchati | vijñānasya ca ...* . Stcherbatsky (1927: 143, n. 4) considers the *iti kṛtvā* phrase as belonging to the Mādhyamika's statement, and thus asserts that a full *daṇḍa* needs to be placed after *iti kṛtvā*. Stcherbatsky's assigning of the *iti kṛtvā* phrase to the Madhyamaka side is of course correct (cf. also Seyfort Ruegg 2002: 106), for the Mādhyamika justifies his stance regarding (*sva*)*lakṣaṇa*s as instruments via this statement. Vaidya (1960b: 20.30) adopts de La Vallée Poussin's text for his edition, but he sets, in place of de La Vallée Poussin's half-*daṇḍa*, a full *daṇḍa* after PsP$_L$'s *viṣayaprativijñaptiḥ* (I accept the manuscript reading *viṣayaṃ prati vijñaptiḥ*) thereby assigning the *iti kṛtvā* phrase to the sentence describing the opponent's view on the word *lakṣaṇa*; Siderits' translation (cf. 1981: 134), which is based on Vaidya's edition, has been influenced by the latter's punctuation. Dan Arnold (2005b: 430, n. 64) notes that there are problems with de La Vallée Poussin's text, even mentioning that emending *abhyupagacchati* to *abhyupagacchatā* would make the passage clearer, but he (reluctantly) accepts *tena* in the meaning of "therefore" and takes the *ca* following *prasiddhānugatāṃ*, which is intended as an adversative, as a continuative, so that he construes, like Vaidya and Siderits, the *iti kṛtvā* phrase with the description of the Epistemologist's slant on things; he translates (ibid., 429) "... Therefore, taking [*svalakṣaṇa*] in the sense of 'what is characterized,' and [thus] disregarding the etymology that follows the familiar sense, [our interlocutor] takes it as denoting

ṇa is used in the sense of] denoting the object (*karmasādhana*),[452] and [further] regards consciousness (*vijñāna*) as the instrument (*karaṇa*), ends up asserting this, [namely, that] the particular characteristic (*svalakṣaṇa*) itself is the object (*karman*) and [that] another particular characteristic is the instrument (*karaṇa*). As concerns this, if the particular characteristic consciousness is the instrument, there has to be a separate object (*karman*) for it (i.e., for consciousness), [and since you have not asserted one,] just that fault [i.e., that the characteristic cannot exist because it will stand alone, without that which it characterizes, remains].[453]

---

an object. And by positing [at the same time] … ." The sense of the *iti kṛtvā* phrase was of course obfuscated by de La Vallée Poussin's PsP Tib-based (*des de mtshon par byed pas*) emendation of his manuscripts' reading *tena hi tadvāna lakṣyate* to *tena hi tal lakṣyate*. None of the manuscripts attest a *daṇḍa* after *viṣayaṃ prati vijñaptiḥ* (or after *iti kṛtvā*, for that matter) and both mss P and D (Q is not available for this section) attest the instrumental present active participle *abhyupagacchatā* in place of de La Vallée Poussin's *abhyupagacchati*. The uncorrupted textual tradition thus understood the instrumental participles *abhyupagacchatā* and *pratipadyamānena* as signaling the logical subject for the second sentence. De La Vallée Poussin's *abhyupagacchati*, it might be noted, is bereft of a subject.

452 The compound *karmasādhana* is a technical term of the grammatical tradition which, when used in reference to a word as a whole, indicates that the word referred to is derived in its passive, or object-denoting, sense, as opposed to being derived in its active sense (*bhāvasādhana*). Renou (1957: 125) translates *karmasādhana* as "qui a l'objet-transitif (i.e. une notion passive) pour mode de réalisation," *bhāvasādhana* as "qui a pour mode de réalisation la production (d'un phénomène nouveau)." Cf., e.g., Patañjali's Bhāṣya to Pā 1.1.58, where the two senses of the word *vidhi* are glossed as *vidhīyate*, "that which is taught/enjoined," i.e., *vidhi* in its object-denoting sense, and *vidhāna*, "the teaching/enjoining (of something)," i.e., *vidhi* in its active sense (*ayaṃ ca vidhiśabdo 'sty eva karmasādhano vidhīyate vidhir iti | asti bhāvasādhano vidhānam vidhir iti*; translated and discussed in Filliozat 1978: 127f.). The term *karmasādhana* can also be used in regard to an affix, in which case it signals that the addition of the affix effects or establishes an object-denoting sense for the word derived; see, e.g., Patañjali's Bhāṣya to Pā 2.1.51, where the affix *ghañ*, added to the root *hṛ* preceded by *sam* and *āṅ* is said to effect the object-denoting sense, that is, the derived word *samāhāra* means *samāhriyate*, "what is grouped together," and does not serve to create an action noun meaning *samāharaṇa* "grouping together" (translated and discussed in Joshi and Roodbergen 1971: 6-9).

453 Candrakīrti lets it be known that the Mādhyamika accepts the Abhidharmic position according to which *svalakṣaṇa* is properly understood only in its instrumental sense, as characterizing its *lakṣya*, that to which it is said to belong. Solidity, for example, the essential and distinctive feature of earth, thus possessed, so to speak, by

§95. If it were [argued:] There is, indeed, an object for it [i.e., for consciousness], namely, the solidity (*kāṭhinya*) and so forth pertaining [respectively] to earth, etc., which are accessible to consciousness; and that (= solidity, etc.) is not [something] separate from the particular characteristic (= earth, etc.).[454]

---

earth, characterizes earth. Dignāga, on the other hand, has claimed that he understands *svalakṣaṇa* in its object sense, but that cognition (*jñāna*), also a *svalakṣaṇa*, can be considered as and can perform the function of an instrument. Candrakīrti retorts that the consequence of this view is that consciousness (*vijñāna*; note the switch from the noun *jñāna*, commonly employed in the treatises of the Epistemologists, to its synonym *vijñāna* for the sake of bringing out the comparison with the Abhidharma example), in now being claimed as an instrumental-*svalakṣaṇa*, will need yet another *svalakṣaṇa* for its object. More precisely: according to the Ābhidharmikas, the essential, basic feature of consciousness (*vijñāna*) is its awareness of individual objects, and due to this, *viṣayaṃ prati vijñapti* is considered the (*sva*)*lakṣaṇa* of the *lakṣya vijñāna*. *viṣayaṃ prati vijñapti* as instrumental-*lakṣaṇa* (= *karaṇa*) thus characterizes *vijñāna*, its *lakṣya* (= *karman*). Dignāga, who is responding to Candrakīrti's demand for an instrument which would characterize his object-denoting *svalakṣaṇa*, states that (*vi*)*jñāna* can serve as this *karaṇa*. However, argues Candrakīrti, if (*vi*)*jñāna* is now a *karaṇa* instead of a *lakṣya*/*karman*, i.e., if it assumes the function allotted by the Ābhidharmikas to *viṣayaṃ prati vijñapti*, then (*vi*)*jñāna* will have to have—like the Ābhidharmikas' *viṣayaṃ prati vijñapti* does—a *lakṣya*, that is, it will have to be assigned a *lakṣya*, and this *lakṣya* cannot again be (*vi*)*jñāna*. If it doesn't have a *lakṣya*, then it stands alone, and a *lakṣaṇa* without a *lakṣya* is not acceptable.

Dan Arnold (2005a: 154f.; 2005b: 432, n. 66) is of the view that the fault (*doṣa*) Candrakīrti sees in Dignāga's position is one of infinite regress. Candrakīrti will point out in his next reply that Dignāga's positing of a *svalakṣaṇa* which functions as both a *karaṇa* and *karman* will involve infinite regress, but in the present response he is merely reiterating the problem he indicated at the beginning of the discussion about (*sva*)*lakṣaṇa*s, namely, that they cannot stand alone.

[454] Dignāga responds to the demand for a separate object-*svalakṣaṇa* by asserting that the solidity of earth and so forth are consciousness' object, and attempts to avoid further criticism by pointing out that this solidity is not related to earth as the Ābhidharmikas (and Candrakīrti, at least as regards the *saṃvṛti* level) understand it to be, i.e., as an instrumental-*svalakṣaṇa*, but merely represents the nature of earth and is thus nothing other than earth.

The Buddhists of the Conservative schools were the heirs and developers of an anti-substantialist or anti-foundationalist line of thought—the beginnings of which, quite possibly inspired by the historical Buddha himself, can be found in early Buddhism—that emphasized the fleeting, evanescent nature of things. Attention was thus intentionally diverted away from the idea of a firm and enduring core of

[Reply:] Then, it being so, because the particular characteristic consciousness is not an object (*karman*), [consciousness] would not be an object of cognition (*prameya*), since only the particular characteristic that has the form of the object (*karmarūpa*) is an object of cognition. And therefore, this [tenet of yours] that the object of cognition (*prameya*) is of two types, [viz.] the particular characteristic (*svalakṣaṇa*) and the general characteristic (*sāmānyalakṣaṇa*), has to be [re]formulated after it has been qualified (*viśeṣya*) [with the following]: "A certain particular characteristic, which is intended thus [i.e., 'it] is characterized' (*lakṣyate*), is an object of cognition (*prameya*), [and] a certain [other particular characteristic], which is intended [in the sense of] 'it characterizes' (*lakṣyate 'nena*), is not an object of cognition (*aprameya*)."[455] But if that [latter sort of particular

---

persons, such as an *ātman*, and from concepts of a bearer of the qualities of things, and as a result, qualities came to be viewed as the sole existing entities. Within the category of matter (*rūpa*), odour, for example, held in non-Buddhist schools to be the quality (*guṇa*) of the substance (*dravya*) earth, was, so to speak, "liberated" from earth and set off as an independent entity, and earth was identified with its nature of solidity; earth as solidity as well as odour were afforded the status of fundamental elements of the inner and outer world (see the discussion of the Buddhist theory of atoms in Frauwallner 1958: 96-100). However, the conventional distinguishing of characteristic and object characterized was still applied by the scholastics in regard to, e.g., the individual element-quality earth, even as they rejected the notion of substance as posited by the non-Buddhists. As pointed out in the previous paragraph by Candrakīrti, who is following, as he states, general consensus, the individual own-form of an object that is not common to other things is considered this object's particular characteristic.
Stcherbatsky (1927: 144) interprets Dignāga's response, as he did his previous response, to be from the point of view of the theory of the object's aspect appearing in consciousness and thus interprets *svalakṣaṇa* of *svalakṣaṇāvyatirikta* to be referring to consciousness. The *ākāra*-theory is, however, not relevant here, and Candrakīrti has demanded a separate object for consciousness; were *svalakṣaṇāvyatirikta* intended as Stcherbatsky interprets it, one would expect a retort or remark from Candrakīrti at some point in the following discussion. Candrakīrti does not comment on the Epistemologist's equating of earth and solidity in his response because he has been steering the argumention to the issue of self-cognition, but he will return to this.

[455] Dignāga's positing of consciousness as an instrument and of another, separate *lakṣaṇa* as its object leads to an unwanted consequence: there would have to exist two mutually exclusive types of *svalakṣaṇa*s, one an object of cognition, and one not

characteristic] is also [considered as having] the sense of an object (*karmasādhana*), then there will have to be a further instrument for it—but when another cognition is postulated as the instrument, the fault of a succession without end (*aniṣṭhādoṣa*) is incurred.[456]

§96. But if you think: There is self-awareness (*svasaṃvitti*).[457] Therefore, given that [consciousness] is an object (*karman*) by virtue

---

an object of cognition, with the *svalakṣaṇa* cognition (*vijñāna*) falling into the latter category.

Both Seyfort Ruegg and Arnold construe *viśeṣya* with the foregoing (Seyfort Ruegg 2002: 107: "Therefore, it having been specified that the *prameya* is twofold ..."; Arnold 2005b: 432: "And thus, since you have specified (*ity etad viśeṣya*) that two kinds of things ..."), but it seems more reasonable that the content of the qualification indicated with the word *viśeṣya* is presented in the following part of the sentence. PsP Tib basically understands the sentence as I do, although its *khyad par 'di tsam zhig brjod par bya dgos* suggests that the translators read something like **etāvad viśeṣaṇaṃ vaktavyam* instead of *etad viśeṣya vaktavyam*; PsP Tib for the sentence reads: *de'i phyir gzhal bya ni rnam pa gnyis te rang gi mtshan nyid dang spyi'i mtshan nyid do zhes bya bar | rang gi mtshan nyid cung zad cig ni gzhal bya yin te | mtshon par bya bas na zhes de ltar bsnyad pa gang yin pa'o || cung zad cig ni gzhal bya ma yin te 'dis mtshon par byed pas na zhes brjod pa gang yin pa'o zhes khyad par 'di tsam zhig brjod par bya dgos so* ||.

456 This second consciousness, imagined by the opponent as the instrument for, i.e., characterizing, the first consciousness characterizing the *svalakṣaṇa* earth, will also have to be accepted as both an instrument and an object and will thus require a third consciousness as its instrument, and this third instrument- and object-consciousness will require its own instrument, and so on into infinity.

457 Dignāga and his followers, like the Sautrāntikas and Yogācāras, posit that cognitions cognize themselves in order to explain how awareness of cognition occurs; the theory of self-awareness sidesteps the problem of infinite succession entailed by any theory positing awareness of cognition via yet another cognition. See PS I.12ab: *jñānāntareṇānubhave 'niṣṭhā tatrāpi hi smṛtiḥ* (cf. Steinkellner 2005: 5; Steinkellner et al. 2005: 84f.); Hattori (1968: 30) translates: "If a cognition were cognized by a separate cognition, there would be an infinite regression, because there is a recollection of this [separate cognition] too." See also the Yogācāra explanation presented by Candrakīrti of *svasaṃvitti* as necessary for the avoidance of the fault of *anavasthā* at $MABh_{ed}$ 167.18-168.11 ($MABh_{tr}$ 1910: 350f.). Self-awareness applies to every cognition, regardless of whether the cognition is devoid of or involves conceptuality. The theory of self-awareness is further used to explain the phenomenon of memory: a person's, e.g., visual cognition of an object also involves the awareness of the cognition of the object, and on the basis of this awareness of the cognition of the object one can later remember the experience of the cognition and express it with the

of [its] being grasped by self-awareness, [consciousness] is indeed included among objects of cognition (*prameya*),[458]

[we would] reply: Due to the fact that self-awareness has [already] been refuted in extenso in the Madhyamakāvatāra,[459] [your contention

---

words, "I saw [this or that] object" (see Candrakīrti's presentation of the Yogācāra arguments on the necessity of *svasaṃvitti* for memory at MABh$_{\mathrm{ed}}$ 167.11-18 and the proving of *svasaṃvitti* from the fact of memory at 168.11-18. MABh$_{\mathrm{ed}}$ 167.11-17 [MABh$_{\mathrm{tr}}$ 1910: 350]: *gang zhig mi 'dod pa des kyang gdon mi za bar rang rig pa khas blang bar bya dgos te | gzhan du na mthong ngo zhes dus phyis 'byung ba'i dran pas yul dran pa nyid dang | ngas mthong ngo snyam du yul gyi nyams su myong ba dran par mi 'gyur ro || ci'i phyir zhe na | dran pa ni nyams su myong ba'i yul can yin na shes pa yang nyams su ma myong bas dran pa pa* [MABh$_{\mathrm{UN}}$: without *pa*] *yod par mi 'gyur ro ||*). According to Dignāga, each cognition has a dual form, namely, a subjective form (*svābhāsa* = *grāhakākāra*) and an objective form (*viṣayābhāsa* = *grāhyākāra*); the self-awareness is considered the result (*phala*) of the act of the cognition (PS I.9a: *svasaṃvittiḥ phalaṃ vātra*. PSV: *dvayābhāsaṃ hi jñānam utpadyate svābhāsaṃ viṣayābhāsaṃ ca | tasyobhayābhāsasya vijñānasya yat svasaṃvedanaṃ tat phalam*). On *svasaṃvitti*, see Hattori 1968: 100ff., notes 1.60-1.80; Moriyama 2010; Kellner 2010; Keira 2004: 39-43 (= n. 75); Arnold 2010; on *svasaṃvitti* as it pertains to *mānasapratyakṣa*, cf. Nagatomi 1979; on later Tibetan discussions of *svasaṃvitti*, see Williams 1998.

[458] The translators of PsP Tib have not accommodated the locative absolute phrase and merely set forth and join the two consequences interpreted to result from the grasping of consciousness by self-awareness (the *phyir* phrase) with the connective *dang*: *ci ste rang rig pa yod de des na rang rig pas de 'dzin pa'i phyir las nyid yin dang | gzhal bya'i khongs su 'du ba yod pa yin no snyam du sems na*. Consciousness's being a *karman* and being *prameya*, however, are not consequences of equal weight in the Sanskrit sentence; the stress of this defense ought to be, as it is in the Sanskrit, on the fact that consciousness as the opponent defines it can also be a *prameya*.

[459] The refutation of *svasaṃvitti* is found at MA VI.72-76 and in the corresponding MABh, where its refutation serves to disprove the existence of the dependent nature of the world (in the *trisvabhāva* scheme, *paratantrasvabhāva*), the causally connected stream of consciousness devoid of *grāhya* and *grāhaka* posited by the Yogācāra opponent. Candrakīrti commences his attack on dependent nature (*paratantra*) by asking by what sort of consciousness the opponent knows it (MA VI.72): *grāhyaṃ vinā grāhakatāviyuktaṃ dvayena śūnyaṃ paratantrarūpam | yady asti kenāsya paraiṣi sattām agṛhyamāṇaṃ ca sad ity ayuktam ||* (Li 2012: 11; MA Tib: *gal te bzung med 'dzin pa nyid bral zhing | gnyis kyis stong pa'i gzhan dbang dngos yod na | 'di yi yod par gang gis shes par 'gyur | ma bzung bar yang*[1] *yod ces byar mi rung ||* [1]MABh$_{\mathrm{ed}}$: without *yang*; MABh$_{\mathrm{ed}}$ 166.6: *de khyod kyis shes pa gang gis dmigs*). According to Candrakīrti, dependent nature definitely cannot perceive itself, for it is contradictory that something acts upon itself (**svātmani kriyāvirodhāt*): the blade of a knife does

that] the particular characteristic (e.g., solidity-cum-earth) is characterized by another particular characteristic (i.e., consciousness), that [latter] further by self-awareness (*svasaṃvitti*), is not tenable. Moreover, not even that cognition (*jñāna*), which [according to you] is not established as [an entity] separate from its particular characteristic,

---

not cut itself, the tip of a finger does not touch itself, and even a well-trained and flexible acrobat is not able to mount his own shoulders. Subsequent to the Yogācāra response in which it is claimed that *svasaṃvitti* is the cognizer and an inherent aspect of cognition—*svasaṃvitti* purportedly being the illumination of consciousness by itself, comparable to a lamp which illuminates both a pot and itself simultaneously, without entering into a state of duality—and that *svasaṃvitti* is the aspect of cognition that accounts for memory, Candrakīrti replies (MA VI.73 and respective MABh) that memory is not caused by self-cognition, and thus cannot be used as a reason to prove self-cognition, in the same way that one cannot infer the existence of a magical water-producing jewel from the mere seeing of water, for even without a magical jewel, an accumulation of water occurs as a result of rain, etc. Even if, Candrakīrti continues (MA VI.74 and corresponding MABh), it is accepted that cognition knows both the object and itself, it cannot be accepted that there is a cognition which remembers them, for this remembering cognition is something other than the original cognition that experienced the object. Just as a cognition of aversion does not remember an earlier experience of the self-cognition of a cognition of love or the object of this cognition of love, similarly, since a cognition arisen at a later time in one's own continuum does not experience the earlier cognition and its object because it is something other than that earlier cognition, like one arisen in a continuum of one who has not known them, it would not remember them. Even if the Yogācāra opponent argues that memory as described by his school is indeed possible because it occurs within one continuum and in a relationship of cause and effect, Candrakīrti's comprehensive reason "because of being other" (*paratvāt*) will override this qualification too, for the later cognition which is claimed to remember is not a component of the unique continuum of cognitions that actually experience the object, and thus does not stand in a relationship of cause and effect; it is, in fact, other than the cognitions that experience the object, like a cognition in a completely different continuum. He closes his refutation of *svasaṃvitti* (MA VI.76 and corresponding MABh) with the argument that the agent (*kartṛ*), object (*karman*), and action (*kriyā*), like a hewer, a tree and the act of hewing, cannot exist as a single thing, and they would exist like this in the case of dependent nature (*paratantra*) being known through self-cognition: as both object to be known and knower, it would be simultaneously the *karman* and the *kartṛ*, and the agent's act of knowing (*kriyā*) would not be distinct from the agent, i.e., the knower.

For translations of MA VI.72-76, see, e.g., MABh$_{tr}$ 1910: 349ff.; Fenner 1983: 257ff. (the translation and explanation are not always reliable); Huntington 1989: 166 and respective notes. On explanations of memory in the Abhidharma schools, see, e.g., Cox 1988: 59-61, 67 and the essays by Cox and Jaini in Gyatso 1992.

[namely, awareness of the respective object (*viṣayaṃ prati vijñaptiḥ*)], exists in any way, given that [this characteristic] is impossible when an object characterized (*lakṣya*) does not exist, since it is not possible that a characteristic occurs without a basis (*āśraya*); thus how [could] there [be] self-awareness![460]

---

[460] After referring to his argumentation against self-awareness in the MA, Candrakīrti clinches his refutation of it by demonstrating the impossibility of the existence of a cognition that might be said to self-cognize. Relying on Dignāga's earlier characterization of solidity as not being something other than earth, Candrakīrti, by way of the modifier *svalakṣaṇavyatirekeṇāsiddha*, calls attention to the fact that *jñāna* will similarly not be something different from its characteristic (*svalakṣaṇa*), viz., awareness of the respective object (*viṣayaṃ prati vijñaptiḥ*). Dignāga maintains that the object (*karman*) in the case of self-cognition is *jñāna*, but since *jñāna* is nothing but its characteristic, i.e., awareness, in this case self-awareness, there will not be an object for this self-awareness; that is, *jñāna*-cum-*svasaṃvitti* cannot additionally be posited as a *lakṣya*. And when a separate *jñāna* as *karman* does not exist, it is absolutely impossible for self-awareness to exist.
The translators of PsP Tib have understood the sentence slightly differently, and appear to have taken *asambhavāt* as the reason for cognition not existing (thus: ... *jñānaṃ ... asambhavāl ... sarvathā nāsti*), and *lakṣyābhāve* as a conditional phrase to be construed with *nirāśrayalakṣaṇapravṛttyasambhavāt*, understanding this as an explanatory gloss to the tersely expressed reason *asambhavāt* of the main clause. PsP Tib: *shes pa de yang mi srid pa'i phyir rang gi mtshan nyid las tha dad par ma grub la* | *mtshan gzhi med na rten med pa'i mtshan nyid 'jug pa med pa'i phyir rnam pa thams cad du yod pa ma yin pas rang rig pa ga la yod* |.
*LṬ's author glosses *jñānaṃ svalakṣaṇavyatirekeṇāsiddham* with *svalakṣaṇaṃ svasaṃvedyarūpatvaṃ* | *tadvyatirekeṇāsiddhaṃ jñānaṃ lakṣyabhūtaṃ* | (cf. Yonezawa 2004: 124, 143 [fol. 2b5]). He explains that with *svalakṣaṇa* reference is made to cognition's autoluminosity, and that cognition is viewed as the *lakṣya* for *svasaṃvitti*. Stcherbatsky (1927: 144, n. 4) appears to correctly understand that Candrakīrti is arguing that consciousness is impossible because it does not exist independently of the (object-related) particular characteristic (his free translation however brings in ideas not expressed by Candrakīrti). Sprung (1979: 55), whose understanding of the passage otherwise remains obscure to me, interprets the word cognition (*jñāna*) as referring to self-awareness (*svasaṃvitti*). Siderits (1981: 137) understands *jñāna* of the sentence to refer to cognition, not self-awareness, but complicates matters by interpreting the argument in the light of the concept of the *ākāra* of the object appearing in cognition. Dan Arnold (2005b: 434) understands cognition (*jñāna*) to refer to self-awareness. He translates: "Moreover, this latter cognition doesn't exist at all, since—given that there's no subject to be characterized (*lakṣya*), owing to the impossibility of [its] establishment by a separate *svalakṣaṇa*—there is no possibility of the operation of a characteristic without a locus" (he does not translate *kutaḥ svasaṃvittiḥ*). Arnold (ibid., n. 76) criticizes Seyfort Ruegg for reading the sentence

And as it is stated in the Noble Ratnacūḍaparipṛcchā:[461]

> Not perceiving (i.e., not finding) the mind (*citta*),[462] he inquires into the mindstream (*cittadhārā*), thinking, "Whence does it (= the mind) arise?" He reflects thus: "When there is an objective support (*ālambana*), the mind arises. Then is the objective support one thing (*anya*) [and] the mind another (*anya*), or is exactly that which is the objective support the mind? If, first, the objective support is one thing (*anya*), the mind another, then one will have two minds [when the mind, occasioned by the objective support, arises]. But if the objective support is the mind, then how does the mind perceive the mind? But it is not the case that the mind perceives the mind. For example, the blade of a sword is not able to cut that very [same] sword-blade; the tip of a finger

---

as having two reasons. See Seyfort Ruegg (2002: 109, n. 194) for Chos dbang grags pa'i dpal's interpretation of the argument. It should be added that all of the previous translators have been disadvantaged by PsP_L's corrupt *svalakṣaṇavyatirekeṇāsiddher* (for *svalakṣaṇavyatirekeṇāsiddham*).

461 The Ratnacūḍaparipṛcchā (RCP) is the forty-second tract of the Ratnakūṭa cycle (cf. PsP_L 62, n. 3). Part of this same citation attested in the PsP, with introductory sentences not included here, is found at BCAP 392.10-393.5, also in the context of the refutation of *svasaṃvedana*, and at ŚiS 235.1-8 (translated in Bendall and Rouse 1990: 221). The translators of PsP Tib, as usual, rely on a Tibetan translation of the *sūtra*. The translation they have used is, with the exception of a few negligible variants, none of which affect the sense, identical with the Canonical version of the RCP.

462 Stcherbatsky (1927: 145, n. 6), against PsP Tib and RCP Tib, but in line with the manuscripts, states that he prefers to read, with Burnouf (1844: 561) *cittaṃ samanupaśyan*, arguing: "*asamanupaśyan* could only mean 'not having yet fully realized what consciousness is (i.e. not having yet attained *vipaśyana*), he investigates ...'." He translates (ibid., 145), "Considering consciousness he (the Bodhisattva) investigates the stream of thought, and asks where it comes from." Sprung (1979: 55) translates in reliance on Stcherbatsky's reading. The introductory sentences to the citation attested in BCAP and ŚiS read however: *sa cittaṃ parigaveṣamāno nādhyātmaṃ cittaṃ samanupaśyati | na bahirdhā cittaṃ samanupaśyati | na skandheṣu cittaṃ samanupaśyati | na dhātuṣu cittaṃ samanupaśyati | nāyataneṣu cittaṃ samanupaśyati.* It is only logical that the next sentence must read *sa cittam asamanupaśyaṃś cittadhārāṃ paryeṣate* ... . Dan Arnold (2005b: 435, n. 78) corrects Siderits' assumption that *tasyotpattir*, instead of the pronoun *sa*, is the sentence's subject, but translates *tasyaivaṃ bhavati* commencing the next sentence as "Its [arising] is thus." *tasya* in this case refers back to the pronoun *sa*, thus to the person, not the mind.

is not able to touch that very [same] fingertip. In exactly the same way, the mind is not able to see that very [same] mind." If he correctly applies [himself] in this way, he knows and sees—in a way that corresponds to truth (*tathatā*)—that stream of mind (*cittadhārā*), creeper of mind (*cittalatā*), the real nature (*dharmatā*) of mind, the non-fixedness (*anavasthitatā*) of mind, the not coming forth (*apracāratā*) of mind, the imperceptibility (*adṛśyatā*) of mind, mind's not having a particular characteristic (*asvalakṣaṇatā*), the non-abiding (*anavasthānatā*) of mind, [its] being without annihilation, without eternity, [its] not being immutable (*kūṭasthatā*), [the mindstream's] not [being] without a cause (*ahetukī*),[463] [its] not [being] opposed to conditions, [its] not [being] from it[self] (*tataḥ*) or from another (*anyataḥ*), not [being] the same (*saiva*) or other (*anya*)—and he does not resist [this insight]. And he knows, he sees, that state of isolation (*vivekatā*) of mind.[464] This, O son of good family, is the concentration of awareness (*smṛtyupasthāna*) consisting in, in regard to the

[463] The transition from abstract forms (*anavasthānatānucchedāśāśvatatā*, *kūṭasthatā*) to adjectives (*nāhetukī*, *na pratyayaviruddhā*, etc.) and their unclear reference is somewhat problematic, but the author of the RCP apparently intends the adjectives as attributes of *cittadhārā* and *cittalatā*. The understanding of the *LṬ's author supports this: *nāhetukī* (or *kā*? ms *ka*) *cittasya dhāreti śeṣaḥ* (cf. Yonezawa 2004: 124, 143 [fol. 2b5]). The transition from *cittadhārām* and *cittalatām* to the abstract forms *cittadharmatām*, *cittānavasthitatām*, *cittāpracāratām*, *cittādṛśyatām*, *cittāsvalakṣaṇatām* and *cittavivekatām* is also curious but would seem to indicate a transition from the superficial level of reality to the ultimate level.

[464] Dan Arnold (2005b: 435) for reasons unexplained translates *citttavivekatā* as "analysis of thought," even though Seyfort Ruegg (2002: 111) has translated the compound correctly as "Isolatedness [i.e. Emptiness] of thought" (cf. BHSD s.v. *viveka*); the words *viveka* and *vivikta* (additionally *viviktatā*), having the senses of "isolation" and "isolated," are used practically as synonyms of emptiness but usually retain some of the sense of being separated from something, e.g., in cases where things are explained as being "separate/isolated" from real existence, or from other *dharma*s (because they do not exist), from qualities (i.e., because neither the qualities nor that to which they might apply exist) or from own-being. In the YṢV, Candrakīrti, comparing things, i.e., *bhāva*s, to ascetics who live isolated from society, states that things are "isolated" in the hermitages of non-arising; Scherrer-Schaub reconstructs **anutpādasya araṇyeṣu viviktāḥ* (cf. $YṢV_{tr}$ 218, n. 388). See Scherrer-Schaub's comments on *vivikta* and *viviktatā* in $YṢV_{tr}$ 218, n. 387 and n. 388, and 244, n. 468.

mind [as object of concentration], the observation of the mind (*citte cittānupaśyanā*).[465]

Therefore, in this way, there is not self-awareness. Since it does not exist, what is characterized by what?

§97. Furthermore, that characteristic (*lakṣaṇa*) would exist either as [something] distinct (*bhedena*) from the object characterized (*lakṣya*) or as [something] not distinct (*abhedena*) [from it].[466] Of those [two

---

[465] On the *smṛtyupasthāna*s, see especially Schmithausen 1976; on their application within Mahāyāna, pp. 259ff.; on *tathatā* representing the content of the initial insight of the spiritual experience of Mahāyānist liberation and its integration into the structure of the four concentrations of awareness, cf. p. 260: "Es ist einleuchtend, dass dieses höchste Sein—die *tathatā*, die das wahre Wesen des (als solches unwirklichen) leidvollen Daseins und seiner Entstehungsursachen ist und zugleich die Befreiung davon, das Nirvāṇa, metaphysisch antizipiert, und die somit im Mahāyāna anstelle der (gewissermassen in ihr verschmolzenen) vier 'Edlen Wahrheiten' des älteren Buddhismus den Inhalt der das spirituelle Ereignis der Erlösung initiierenden Einsicht bildet—auch im Rahmen der vier 'Konzentrationen der Aufmerksamkeit' zur Geltung kommen musste." Schmithausen refers to and translates the relevant sections of the Ratnacūḍaparipṛcchā concerned with the concentrations of awareness as applied to feeling (261) and to the body (261f.).

[466] Candrakīrti takes up a fresh line of argumentation against Dignāga's *svalakṣaṇa* by considering it from the point of view of the *svalakṣaṇa*'s numerical (as opposed to qualitative) difference from or identity with a *lakṣya*. The *svalakṣaṇa* is thus bombarded from a new direction in order to reach Candrakīrti's objective of demolishing this cornerstone of Dignāga's epistemology. Although the argumentation deals with the topic of the relationship of *lakṣaṇa* and *lakṣya* in a general manner, Candrakīrti may also have the specifics of the preceding discussion in mind. The PsP's Dignāga, as has been demonstrated, maintains a *(sva)lakṣaṇa* that is to be understood as having an object sense (*karmasādhana*), which translates to it being a *lakṣaṇa* that is free from the need for a *lakṣya*; compare the example of solidity-cum-earth. Candrakīrti points out that the positing of a *lakṣaṇa* that is independent of and thus exists as something separate from a corresponding *lakṣya* is not tenable, because a *lakṣaṇa* of this sort would be like any other thing that also exists separately from the relevant corresponding *lakṣya* and that does not qualify as a *lakṣaṇa*. Candrakīrti may also be intending to critique the idea of *jñāna* in the role of instrumental *(sva)lakṣaṇa*, since solidity-cum-earth is indeed able to exist separately from *jñāna* and vice versa. *jñāna* therefore cannot be considered the *lakṣaṇa* of earth because as something that can exist separately, it is not earth's *lakṣaṇa* any more than some other thing that exists separately from earth and is not a *lakṣaṇa* (such as another *lakṣya*); and independently existing solidity-cum-earth cannot be a *lakṣya* by very reason of its independence,

alternatives], if, first, [the characteristic exists] as [something] distinct, then because it is distinct from the object characterized, like [something that is] not a characteristic (*alakṣaṇavat*),[467] [that] characteristic [would] also not [be] the characteristic of that [object characterized]. And because it is distinct from the characteristic, the object characterized, like something that is not an object characterized (*alakṣyavat*), [would] also not [be] an object characterized. In the same way, owing to the fact that [under this alternative] the characteristic is distinct from the object characterized, the object characterized would be independent (*nirapekṣa*) of the characteristic, and therefore [would] not [be] a [real] object characterized, because of being independent of the characteristic, like a sky-flower [which is independent of a characteristic and not a real object characterized]. But if the object characterized and the characteristic are not distinct [from one another, i.e., are one and the same thing], then because [the object characterized] is not separate (*avyatirikta*) from the characteristic, like the own self (*svātman*) of the characteristic [is not separate from the characteristic and is not a *lakṣya*],[468] the object characterized

like all other things that do not qualify as *lakṣya*s. As support from the side of authoritative testimony (*āgama*) for the argument against a separate *lakṣaṇa* and *lakṣya*, Candrakīrti will cite Lokātītastava 11, in which, according to Nāgārjuna, the Buddha himself asserts that a *lakṣaṇa* cannot be (numerically) distinct from its *lakṣya*. Should Dignāga want to rescue his *svalakṣaṇa* by claiming that it is not distinct from, but is rather identical with the *lakṣya*, he is shown that this too is impossible. For Candrakīrti, *lakṣaṇa* and *lakṣya* can only exist (on the surface level) in a relationship of mutual dependence, a relationship that excludes both distinctness and identity.

[467] The examples in the inferences in the above paragraph have not been understood as logical examples in Arnold 2005b. The present example *alakṣaṇavat* has been translated (ibid., 436) as "as though it were a non-characteristic" ("In this regard, if, on the one hand, it's by virtue of difference, then because of being different from the *subject characterized*, the *characteristic* wouldn't be a characteristic, either, as though it were a *non*-characteristic").

[468] Arnold (2005b: 437, n. 84) notes Seyfort Ruegg's misleading translation of *lakṣaṇasvātmavat* (Seyfort Ruegg 2002: 112: "... the *lakṣya*'s condition of being a *lakṣya* would be lost, in the same way as the nature of the *lakṣaṇa*") but translates instead: "... the subject's being a subject (*lakṣyatā*) is forfeited, as though [the subject] were itself the *characteristic*." The logical example *lakṣyasvātmaval* of the next sentence has correspondingly been translated (Arnold 2005b: 437): "as though it were itself the *subject*."

[will] forfeit its status as an object characterized. And since [the characteristic] is not separate from the object characterized, like the own self of the object characterized [is not separate from the object characterized and is not a *lakṣaṇa*], the characteristic as well [will] not have the nature (*svabhāva*) of a characteristic.

And as it is stated [in the Lokātītastava],[469]

> If the characteristic [were something] other (*anya*) than the object characterized, that object characterized would be without a characteristic (*alakṣaṇa*).
> When there is no otherness (*ananyatva*), the two are non-existent. [This] You have clearly stated.

And aside from identity (*tattva*) and otherness (*anyatva*), another option (*gati*) for the establishment of object characterized and characteristic does not exist.

And similarly, [in the Madhyamakaśāstra] he (= Nāgārjuna) will say,[470]

---

[469] Candrakīrti cites Lokātītastava 11: *lakṣyāt lakṣaṇam anyac cet syāt tal lakṣyam alakṣaṇam | tayor abhāvo 'nanyatve viṣpaṣṭaṃ kathitaṃ tvayā ||*. Tibetan in La Vallée Poussin 1913b: 8; Sanskrit and Tibetan in Lindtner 1982b: 132. Translated in La Vallée Poussin 1913b: 12; Lindtner 1982b: 133. On the Catuḥstava and its editions and translations, see Lindtner 1982b: 121-124. Candrakīrti's purpose in citing the verse, given that the discussion in the present context focusses on the *saṃvṛti* level, is of course not to prove that *lakṣaṇa* and *lakṣya* are impossible, but rather to provide scriptural support in order to convince Dignāga that neither *lakṣaṇa* nor *lakṣya*, especially in the present case a *svalakṣaṇa*, can exist on its own, i.e., both are necessary, and that they can only exist in a relationship of mutual dependence. Cp. Lokātītastava 7 and 8, where it is made clear that two other pairs, i.e., designation (*saṃjñā*) and its object (*artha*), and agent (*kartā*) and action (*karman*), cannot exist either as things that are numerically different or as the same thing, but from the point of view of the surface level, such pairs are asserted as existing in mutual dependence. Lokātītastava 7: *saṃjñārthayor ananyatve mukhaṃ dahyeta vahninā | anyatve 'dhigamābhāvas tvayoktaṃ bhūtavādinā ||*, Lokātītastava 8: *kartā svatantraḥ karmāpi tvayoktaṃ vyavahārataḥ | parasparāpekṣikī tu siddhis te 'bhimatānayoḥ ||*.

[470] Candrakīrti cites MMK II.21: *ekībhāvena vā siddhir nānābhāvena vā yayoḥ | na vidyate tayoḥ siddhiḥ kathaṃ nu khalu vidyate ||*. Oetke (2001a: 79) translates, "Wie soll man denn wohl die Existenz von Dingen etablieren können, die sich beide weder

How indeed is there the establishment of two [things]
Of which there is no establishment either by way of identity (*ekībhāva*) or difference (*nānābhāva*)?

§98. But if [Dignāga argues:] There could be establishment (*siddhi*) by way of inexpressibility (*avācyatā*).[471]

[We reply:] This is not the case, for so-called "inexpressibility" comes into play when clear knowledge of the distinction of one [thing] from another (*parasparavibhāga*) is lacking. And [in cases] where there is no clear knowledge of the distinction [between two things], when discrimination (*pariccheda*) from the point of view of [their] difference [in the form] "this is the characteristic, this is the object characterized" is impossible, both of them are simply non-existent. Therefore, there is no establishment even by way of inexpressibility.

§99. Moreover, if cognition (*jñāna*) is the instrument (*karaṇa*), what is the agent (*kartṛ*) in the discrimination of the object (*viṣaya*)? And without an agent there is no possibility of an instrument and so forth[472]—as in [the case of] the act (*kriyā*) of cutting [where the

---

als identisch noch als verschieden etablieren lassen?" Cp. PsP Tib: *gang dag dngos po gcig pa dang* ‖ *dngos po gzhan pa nyid du ni* ‖ *'grub par 'gyur ba yod min na* ‖ *de gnyis grub pa ji ltar yod* ‖.

[471] Candrakīrti now proceeds to consider the case for the establishment of *lakṣaṇa* and *lakṣya* as entities that cannot be defined in terms of identity or difference, a line of defense utilized by certain Conservative Buddhists for the *pudgala* as regards its relationship to the *skandhas*. According to them, *pudgala* cannot be analyzed in terms of identity with or difference from the *skandhas*, because the relationship is inexpressible (de La Vallée Poussin [PsP_L 64, n. 3] cites BCAP 297.9: ... *skandhebhyas tattvānyatvābhyām avācyaṃ pudgalanāmānam ātmānam icchanti*). See also Candrakīrti's argumentation against *ātman* as inexpressible as identical with or other than the *skandhas*, together with argumentation against *ātman* as inexpressible as permanent or impermanent (*nityānityatvenāvācya*) and inexpressible as existent or non-existent (*astitvanāstitvenāvācya*) at PsP_L 288.9-17.

[472] "and so forth" of "instrument and so forth" (*karaṇādīnām*) refers to the other four *kārakas* basic to the Pāṇinian theory of *kārakas*, to wit, 1) the object/patient (*karman*), 2) the point of departure (*apādāna*), 3) that which the agent intends as goal through the object of the action (*saṃpradāna*), 4) the locus (*adhikaraṇa*). As Ganeri

instrument, e.g., an axe, requires an agent who performs the act of cutting]. But if it is postulated that the mind (*citta*) is the agent in this case,[473] that too is not correct, because the mind operates in the perception (*darśana*) of the mere thing (*arthamātra*), the mental factors (*caitasa*) with respect to the distinguishing features (*viśeṣa*) of the object (*artha*), since it is accepted that:

> Of those [two], consciousness (*vijñāna*) is perception (*dṛṣṭi*) of the object (*artha*), while the mental factors (*caitasa*) [are directed] toward its distinguishing features (*tadviśeṣa*).[474]

(1999: 52) states, "The term *kāraka*, derived from the verb *kṛ* ('to do, make'), literally means *that which makes* the event." Things are *kāraka*s when, being viewed in relation to an action, they play specific roles in regard to the accomplishment of that action (cf. Nath 1987: 145: "what makes a thing a *kāraka* is the power (*śakti*) of bringing an action towards completion"). For example, in the sentence *devadatto rathena vanaṃ prāsādād gacchati*, four types of *kāraka*s are involved in the accomplishment of the action of going. The agent (*kartṛ*) is defined as "[that *kāraka* which is] independent [relative to others involved in an action]" (*svatantraḥ kartā*), the independence of which is explained by Bartṛhari as due to, among other reasons, the fact that it "suppresses the agency of other *kāraka*s, whose participation is subordinated to [it]" and due to the fact that "a sentence may denote no other *kāraka* but denote an agent alone" (Cardona 1974: 239). See also Butzenberger 2000.

[473] According to the AK, the words mind (*citta*), mental [faculty] (*manas*) and consciousness (*vijñāna*) are synonymous: AK II.34ab: *cittaṃ mano 'tha vijñānam ekārtham*. For Candrakīrti in this section of the PsP, *caitta*, *caitasa* and the opponent's *jñāna* represent a second group of synonyms. *LṬ's author notes that the mental factors are by implication stated to be the instrument: *cittasya kartṛtvam ity ukte arthāc caittānāṃ karaṇatvam uktaṃ* (cf. Yonezawa 2004: 124, 144 [fol. 2b5]; Yonezawa reads *cittānāṃ* but the *LṬ manuscript clearly reads *caittānāṃ*).

[474] Candrakīrti cites MAV 1.8cd. MAV 1.8 as cited in MAVṬ (30.2, 45.8): *abhūtaparikalpaś tu cittacaittās tridhātukāḥ | tatrārthadṛṣṭir vijñānaṃ tadviśeṣe tu caitasāḥ ||* (MAVBh: *abhūtaparikalpaś ca ...*). MAVBh to 1.8cd: *tatrārthamātre dṛṣṭir vijñānam | arthaviśeṣe dṛṣṭiś caitasā vedanādayaḥ ||* (MAVBh 20.19-20). If MAVBh is followed, MAV 1.8 should be translated as "Of those [two], consciousness (*vijñāna*) is perception (*dṛṣṭi*) with respect to the object (*artha*), while the mental factors (*caitta*) [are perception] with respect to its distinguishing features (*tadviśeṣa*)." MAVṬ on *tatrārthamātre dṛṣṭir vijñānam*: *mātraśabdo viśeṣanirasanenāgṛhītaviśeṣā vastusvarūpamātropalabdhir ity arthaḥ |* (MAVṬ 31.16-17); underlined words reconstructed by Yamaguchi. Stanley (1988: 38, n. 199) reconstructs *viśeṣāpanayanāyāgṛhītaviśeṣā*. Arnold (2005b: 438, n. 91) notes that Seyfort Ruegg (2002: 113) erroneously ascribes the MAV to Sthiramati.

For when one principal activity (*pradhānakriyā*) is to be accomplished, there is the instrumentality, etc., of the instrument and so forth on account of [their] becoming ancillary [to the principal action] by virtue of effectuating the subsidiary actions (*guṇakriyā*), each individually (*yathāsvam*).[475] But in the present case (*iha*), there is not

---

Cp. AKVy 38.23-25 (ad AK I.16a: *vijñānaṃ prativijñaptiḥ*; AKBh: *viṣayaṃ viṣayaṃ prati vijñaptir upalabdhir vijñānaskanda ity ucyate*): *vijñāna*skandha *prativijñaptir* ity arthaḥ ... . *upalabdhir* vastumātragrahaṇam. vedanādayas tu caitasā viśeṣagrahaṇarūpāḥ (Wogihara adds *viśeṣā* after *caitasā* but notes that *viśeṣā* only occurs in the Tibetan and is not attested in the AKVy mss; Śāstri does not add *viśeṣā*). MAVṬ on *arthaviśeṣe dṛṣṭiś caitasā vedanādayaḥ*: ... *evaṃ caiṣām āśrayālambanakāladravyasamatābhiḥ samprayuktatvaṃ na tv ākārasamatayāpi vijñānāviśeṣaprasaṅgāt* | (MAVṬ 31.15-17). Mind and its mental factors are taught in the AK as being similar in five ways: AK II.34cd: *cittacaitasāḥ sāśrayālambananākārāḥ samprayuktāś ca pañcadhā* (the concept of *ākāra* in this *kārikā* is apparently different from that just referred to in the MAVṬ); $AKBh_{ed}$ 62.9: *pañcabhiḥ samatāprakārair āśrayālambanākārakāladravyasamatābhiḥ* (see $AKBh_{tr}$ II.177f.; on the *caitta*s, $AKBh_{tr}$ II.150, n. 2; Tillemans 1990: 285, n. 427). More references at PsP_L 65, n. 3.
On the role of the MAV in Bhāviveka's works, see Saito 1998.

[475] In general, the term "principal action" (*pradhānakriyā*) denotes the activity indicated by a verbal root, such as the verbal root √*pac*. In the case of √*pac*, the accomplishing of the cooking involves various individual subsidiary actions (*guṇakriyā*), such as the internal conscious effort of the agent (*kartṛ*), the placing of a pot on a stove or hearth, the placing of water and grains in the pot, blowing, heating, etc. Pāṇinīyas thus consider that all activities are composites, and hold, given that the subsidiary actions occur sequentially, that the unity of the principal action is a mental construct (see Cardona 1974: 237).
In the case of a sentence that expresses Devadatta's act of cooking rice in a pot with firewood (*devadattas taṇḍulān edhaiḥ sthālyāṃ pacati*), Devadatta is the principal agent (*pradhānakartṛ*) of the principal activity of cooking; in the process, he makes the decisions as the activity proceeds, places the rice in the pot and the pot over the firewood, ignites the firewood, etc. The firewood is the instrument of the activity of cooking, the pot its locus, and the rice grains the object. Although Devadatta the principal agent lights the firewood, sentences such as *edhāḥ pacanti* "the firewood cooks" are also acceptable because firewood can be seen as participating as instrument in the principal activity of cooking (on sentences like *edhāḥ pacanti*, where the instrument of the principal activity is assigned its own agency, constituted by its burning until the food is cooked, see Cardona 1974: 263; on the subsidiary agents [*guṇakartṛ*] of the individual subsidiary actions being considered as suppressed by the principal agent, see 264). On the *kāraka*s, see also Deshpande 1990.

one [single] principal activity for cognition (*jñāna*) and consciousness (*vijñāna*) [which you allege function respectively as instrument and agent]. Rather, the principal activity of consciousness (*vijñāna*) is discernment of the mere object (*arthamātra*), whereas [that] of cognition (*jñāna*) [is] the discernment of the distinguishing features of the object;[476] thus there is neither the instrumentality of cognition nor the

---

In the present passage, Candrakīrti calls attention to the fact that the instrument is responsible for a subsidiary action; for example, in the case of cooking, the firewood burns, thereby contributing to the principal activity of cooking.
De La Vallée Poussin (PsP$_L$ 65, n. 4) considers PsP Tib's *byed pa la sogs pa rnams ni bdag nyid ji lta bu'i bya ba phal pa sgrub pa'i sgo nas | gtso bor gyur pa'i bya ba cig bsgrub par bya ba la yan lag gi ngo bor gyur pa las byed pa la sogs pa nyid du 'gyur na* to reflect *karaṇādīnāṃ yathāsvaṃ guṇa ... dvāreṇa ekasyā ... sādhyāyā* (sic) *aṅgībhāvopagamāt karaṇāditvam*. The translators have merely re-ordered the sentence.

[476] In the previous argumentation in this larger section, Dignāga attempted to rescue his position that (*sva*)*lakṣaṇa* should be understood in the sense of an object (*karman*) by positing *jñāna* as an instrument. Candrakīrti attacked this idea by considering *jñāna* from the point of view of its being equivalent to *vijñāna*, specifically *vijñāna* understood as equivalent to its *lakṣaṇa viṣayaṃ prati vijñaptiḥ*. The present argument may also implicitly intend reference to Dignāga's earlier assertion that *jñāna* as instrument has as its object the solidity and so forth (*kāṭhinyādi*) of earth, because this ability of Dignāga's *jñāna* to discriminate earth's aspects, i.e., its distinguishing features such as solidity—as opposed to cognizing the mere object earth—means that *jñāna* must be a mental factor (*caitta*). Cf. above n. 474, citing AKVy on AKBh ad AK I.16a: *vedanādayas tu caitasā viśeṣagrahaṇarūpāḥ*, and MAVBh on MAV 1.8cd *arthaviśeṣe dṛṣṭiś caitasā vedanādayaḥ*. See also AK II.24, where Vasubandhu presents the *mahābhūmika caitta*s as: *vedanā cetanā saṃjñā cchandaḥ sparśo matiḥ smṛtiḥ | manaskāro 'dhimokṣaś ca samādhiḥ sarvacetasi ||*; Vasubandhu presents the same group of *caitta*s (the first five classified as *sarvatraga*, the last five as *pratiniyataviṣaya*) in his Pañcaskandhaka as: *sparśo manaskāro vedanā saṃjñā cetanā cchando 'dhimokṣaḥ smṛtiḥ samādhiḥ prajñā* (Li and Steinkellner 2008: 4f.). Candrakīrti appears to be identifying Dignāga's *jñāna* with the mental factor *sañjñā*, since *sañjñā*'s function is, as Candrakīrti states above for *jñāna* understood as a mental factor, the discernment of the distinguishing features of the object. AKBh$_{ed}$ 54.20-21 (ad AK II.24) on *sañjñā*: *saṃjñānaṃ viṣayanimittodgrahaḥ*; AKVy 127.24-25: *viṣayanimittagrahaḥ* iti *viṣaya*-viśeṣa-rūpa-*grāha* ity arthaḥ; Pañcaskandhaka on *sañjñā*: *sañjñā katamā | viṣayanimittodgrahaṇam |* (Li and Steinkellner 2008: 4). Cf. also AKBh$_{ed}$ 10.17-18 (ad AK I.14cd, corrected following AKBh$_{Ej}$ 16.5-6): *yan nīlapītadīrghahrasvastrīpuruṣamitrāmitrasukhaduḥkhādinimittodgrahaṇam asau saṃjñāskandhaḥ*.
Dignāga's attempt to defend his positing of *jñāna* as the instrument (*karaṇa*) for the (*sva*)*lakṣaṇa* (interpreted in the sense of an object) by asserting that the mind (*citta*)

agency of mind (*citta*) [in this case of cognition characterizing the particular characteristic], and therefore, just that fault [remains, namely, that an agent is lacking].[477]

§100. If there were [this objection]: Because—since according to authoritative testimony (*āgama*) "All phenomena are without self" (*anātmānaḥ sarvadharmāḥ*)[478]—an agent (*kartṛ*) does not exist in any way whatsoever, linguistic usage (*vyavahāra*) of activity (*kriyā*), etc., [can] certainly occur even without an agent.

[We reply:] This too is not [acceptable], because [you have] not determined the correct meaning of the *āgama*. But this has been explained in the Madhyamakāvatāra.[479]

---

serves as the agent (*kartṛ*) for the activity (*kriyā*) of cognizing, e.g., the solidity, etc., of earth is therefore shown by Candrakīrti to be nonsensical, since the mind that cognizes the mere object and the mental factor(s) cognizing its features do not function within the context of one and the same activity, but rather perform two completely separate activities.

[477] Candrakīrti, as might be expected, does not go into the grammarians' discussion about sentences such as *asiś chinatti* "the sword/axe cuts" (in place of *asinā chinatti devadattaḥ*) or *sthālī pacati* "the pot is cooking (something)" (in place of *devadattaḥ sthālyāṃ pacati*) being acceptable given that that sword/axe and pot can also be seen as functioning as agents of cutting and cooking. Cardona writes (1974: 235), "Whether one speaks of swords and pots as agents of cutting and cooking, however, the fact remains that these implements do not function totally independently (*svatantra*); even when one uses [these sentences], one understands that the sword cuts when wielded by someone and the pot cooks when someone has put food in it and set it to cooking. Moreover, ... such implements are not agents without simultaneously functioning as instrument and locus."

[478] The statement appears in the Pāli Canon as *sabbe dhammā anattā* and there has the meaning "all phenomena are not the self." Cf., e.g., SN III.132.22-133.2: *Evaṃ vutte therā bhikkhū āyasmantaṃ Channam etad avocuṃ | Rūpaṃ kho āvuso Channa aniccaṃ | vedanā aniccā | saññā aniccā | saṅkhārā aniccā | viññāṇam aniccaṃ | Rūpam anattā | vedanā | saññā | saṅkhārā | viññāṇam anattā | Sabbe saṅkhārā aniccā sabbe dhammā anattā ti* |; MN I.228, 230. "Not the self" is said to be the third of the three marks (*trilakṣaṇa/tilakkhaṇa*) of phenomena (cf., e.g., PTSD s.v. *lakkhaṇa*; Conze 1967: 34ff.; for an explanation of why suffering is not mentioned in the SN and MN passages just referred to, see Bodhi 2000: 1084, n. 180).

[479] *LṬ's author, commenting on the sentence *etad api nāsti, āgamasya samyagarthānavadhāraṇāt*, explains that the *āgama* cited by the Epistemologist has the intention of rejecting the agency of the *ātman*, but not additionally the agency of the

mind: *anavadhāraṇād iti* {|} *ātmanaḥ kartṛtvam tatra vāritaṃ na tu cittasyāpi* | (cf. Yonezawa 2004: 124, 144 [fol. 2b5]; Yonezawa reads *cāritaṃ* for *vāritaṃ*). He adds, regarding the PsP's mention of the MA: *tatraivāvadhāryo 'tra nokta iti* (cf. Yonezawa 2004: 124, 144 [fol. 2b5]). The reference appears to be to MA VI.137 and the respective MABh, and further to MABh ad MA VI.159a-c. Just before MA VI.137, the opponent attempts to escape the consequence that agent (**kartṛ*) and object (**karman*), that is, appropriator (**upādātṛ*) and appropriated (**upādāna*), will be the same thing if he holds to his view that *ātman* exists as the shape/arrangement (*dbyibs*; **ākāra*, **saṃsthāna*) of the *skandhas* by arguing that this appropriator-cum-agent is not really some thing, because it is nothing more than the mere composite of the *skandhas* (*gang zhig byed pa po nyid du 'gyur ba nye bar len pa po ni 'ga' yang yod pa ma yin pa nyid de* | *'di ni nye bar len pa 'dus pa tsam zhig tu zad do*; MABh$_{ed}$ 260.12-13). Candrakīrti responds with MA VI.137cd: *byed po med las yod snyam blo yin na* || *ma yin gang phyir byed po med las med* || "If [your] idea is that [even if] the agent (**kartṛ*) does not exist, the object (**karman*) does exist, it is not [so], because [if] the agent does not exist, the object [also] does not exist." Referring to MMK VIII.13, he explains in his *bhāṣya* that the object cannot exist alone, because the agent serves as its reason (*rgyu*, **hetu*) for being: *gal te byed pa po mi 'dod na rgyu med pa'i las kyang 'dod par mi bya'o* || (MABh$_{ed}$ 260.18-19); something is designated as object only in dependence upon an agent, and vice versa: *de'i phyir ji ltar byed pa po la brten nas las su gdags par bya la* | *las la brten nas kyang byed pa po yin pa de bzhin du* ... . He closes by pointing out that the scripture which states that an agent is not perceived but that the act and its maturation exist (*byed pa po ni ma dmigs kyi las kyang yod la rnam par smin pa yang yod do*) has the purpose of communicating that the agent does not exist by own-being; it does not communicate that the agent designated in dependence, which is an element of conventional linguistic usage (**vyavahārāṅgībhūta*), is negated: ... *brten nas gdags par bya ba tha snyad kyi yan lag tu gyur pa yang bkag go zhes bya bar* (MABh$_{UN}$: *pa*) *ni shes par mi bya'o* || (see MABh$_{ed}$ 261.20-262.4; Huntington 1989: 257, n. 167. The entire section is found in MABh$_{tr}$ 1911: 305-7; on p. 307, n. 2 de La Vallée Poussin refers to the Paramārthaśūnyatā). Again, toward the end of the *ātman* critique (ad MA VI.159a-c), Candrakīrti criticizes the person who, having understood certain discourses in a mistaken way, incorrectly asserts worldly *saṃvṛti* thus: "the mere collection of parts (**aṅga*) exists, but the whole (*aṅgin*) does not exist in any way at all, because it is not perceived separate from it ... solely the act (*karman*) exists, the agent (*kartṛ*) does not exist ...," for the unwanted consequence of this person's reasoning is that the mere parts, etc., will also not exist: *gang 'ga' zhig gsung rab kyi don phyin ci log tu rtogs pas yan lag tshogs pa tsam zhig yod kyi yan lag can ni rnam pa tham cad du yod pa ma yin te* | *de las tha dad par ma dmigs pa'i phyir ro* || ... *las 'ba' zhig kho na yod kyi byed pa po ni med do* || ... *zhes de lta bur rnam par gnas pa'i* (MABh$_{UN}$: *pa ni*) *'jig rten gyi kun rdzob phyin ci log tu smra ba de'i ltar na gtan tshigs de nyid kyis yan lag la sogs pa tsam yang med par thal bar 'gyur bas* ... (MABh$_{ed}$ 278.9-18; MABh$_{tr}$ 1911: 321).

§101. Even if there were [this objection:] There is, for example, a relationship of qualifier (*viśeṣaṇa*) and qualificand (*viśeṣya*) [between the members of genitive constructions like] "the pestle's body"[480]

Stcherbatsky (1927: 149, n. 7) points to "e.g. Madhy. avat., 6.68ff." as the passage Candrakīrti is alluding to here in the PsP, but MA VI.68cd and the citations presented in the related MABh merely declare the non-existence of all things. Seyfort Ruegg (2002: 114 and n. 205) erroneously understands *artha* of *āgamasya samyagarthāna-vadhāraṇāt* as "object" and thus translates "For no correct intentional object has been specified … by the [cited] scriptural testimony" but does refer to MA VI.76. However, as Arnold (2005b: 440, n. 96) has already indicated, MA VI.76 simply asserts that the notion of *svasaṃvedana* is incoherent. One might add that although MA VI.76 mentions the *kāraka*s *kartṛ*, *karman* and *kriyā*, Candrakīrti introduces them for the sake of demonstrating that they cannot be a unity and thus to prove that *paratantra* cannot be known by itself. MA VI.76: *tasmāt svasaṃvedanam asti naiva kenānyatantragrahaṇaṃ tava syāt* | *kartuś ca karmakriyayoś ca naikyaṃ tenaiva tasya grahaṇaṃ na yuktam* || (Li 2012: 12).
Siderits (1981: 141) comments on our main text's objection and response as follows: "We can already see what Candrakīrti has in mind here, however, for we know that the Yogācāra-Sautrāntika proposes to provide a correct definition of the worldly practice with respect to pramāṇa and prameya; that is, his analysis is purported to be nothing more than a description of conventional epistemic practice. As such, this account is thoroughly ensconced on the side of saṃvṛti, that species of truth which is determined by conventional linguistic behavior. Now it is well known that the Mādhyamikas reinterpret the doctrine of anātman as the doctrine of niḥsvabhāvatā, the denial that there are ultimately any self-existent reals. Anātmavāda thus belongs on the side of paramārtha or absolute truth .... the epistemologist may not legitimately employ the anātman doctrine in defense of some feature of his analysis, for that analysis must proceed within the boundaries of those structures which govern our linguistic behavior, and anātmavāda is not among these." One might qualify this by stating that while it is true that things disappear when one moves to the ultimate level, for Candrakīrti, even on the *saṃvṛti* level things are empty of real existence, and it is this lack of real existence, of a real nature of things, that allows for dynamic existence, because truly existing things could never change. On the *saṃvṛti* level things can only exist in dependence, e.g., an agent exists in dependence on an action, an instrument in dependence on an agent, etc., and vice-versa, and nothing exists independently, i.e., an action or instrument cannot exist without an agent.

[480] De La Vallée Poussin and some of the modern translators of the present section of the PsP understand *śilāputrakasya śarīram* to mean "body of a statue," and not "body of a pestle." Pa tshab translates *śilāputrakasya śarīram* into Tibetan as *mchi gu'i lus*, thus taking *śilāputraka* in the meaning of pestle. Cf. TCD, where *mchi gu* is explained as *rang 'thag gi yas rdo* (the upper mill-stone) and *mchig gu* as *rang 'thag gi yas rdo* but also as *sgog gtun gyi yas rdo* (the upper pestle); cf. also Jäschke (s.v.

mchig), where *mchig gu* is said to be "a small mortar," "a pestle." MW translates *śilāputra* literally as "little rock" and assigns to it the meanings "a grindstone" and "a torso"; these same meanings are given for *śilāputraka*. It should be noted, however, that the Sanskrit texts noted in MW as attesting *śilāputra* and *śilāputraka* in the meaning "torso," namely, the Sāṅkhyapravacanabhāṣya and the Bṛhadāraṇyakopaniṣadbhāṣya, respectively, only present the example *śilāputrakasya śarīram*, without further explanation. According to Apte, both *śilāputra* and *śilāputraka* refer to a lower stone: "a small flat stone for grinding condiments on." BHSD mentions that *śilāputra* = *niśādāputra*, i.e., upper millstone or pestle, noting that Pāli *nisadapota* is glossed in the Visuddhimagga as *silāputtako* and that the Mahāvyutpatti translates *śilāputra* as *gtun bu* (misprinted as *gtur bu*), i.e., as pestle. Only PW attests *śilāputraka* in the (single) meaning "eine Figur, eine Statue von Stein" (*śilāputra*, on the other hand, is said to mean "Reibstein"), but the text reference given as supportive of the meaning of "statue" is the same as that supplied in MW for the meaning "torso," namely the Bṛhadāraṇyakopaniṣadbhāṣya's sole attestation of *śilāputraka* in the uncommented example *śilāputrakasya śarīram*. It is perhaps worth mentioning that Cakrapāṇi, in Carakasaṃhitā Cikitsāsthāna 1.57.2, comments on the word *kūrcanna* with *jarjarīkaraṇasādhanaṃ śilāputrakamusalādi*, which indeed confirms that at least there *śilāputraka* means pestle (my thanks to Philipp Maas for this reference). One might add that Apte states that *śarīra* refers to the body of both animate and inanimate objects.

The example *śilāputrakasya śarīram* is also found, e.g., in the AKBh in the Sautrāntika refutation of the Sarvāstivāda view which holds that the mark of the conditioned (*saṃskṛtalakṣaṇa*) known as arising (*jāti*) is a real entity. The Sautrāntikas state that it is only for the sake of qualifying matter that the genitive construction "matter's origination" (*rūpasyotpāda*) is employed, adding that this construction is used so that one understands that the arising specifically refers to matter, lest the arising of something else be understood. The situation is similar to that reflected by other expressions, such as "sandalwood's odour, etc." or "*śilāputrakasya śarīram*" (where odour and body are not something different from the sandalwood or the *śilāputraka* but appear with them in genitive constructions for the sake of qualifying them) (*tasya viśeṣaṇārthaṃ rūpasyotpāda iti ṣaṣṭīṃ kurvanti yathā rūpasaṃjñaka evotpādaḥ pratīyeta mā 'nyaḥ pratyāyīti | tadyathā candanasya gandhādayaḥ śilāputrakasya śarīram iti* [AKBh$_{ed}$ 80.1-3]). Jinamitra and dPal brtsegs, the translators of the AKBh, like Pa tshab in the present section, render *śilāputrakasya śarīram* of the cited AKBh passage into Tibetan as *mchi gu'i lus*, thus understanding the phrase to be referring to the body of a pestle (cf. AKBh Tib P 96a2; D 84a3). The fact that Pa tshab translates *śilāputraka* as pestle quite possibly indicates that the tradition of the PsP transmitted to his *paṇḍita* collaborator Mahāsumati in Kashmir also interpreted *śilāputraka* as pestle, and not as "statue." On the basis of the above, I have decided to translate *śilāputraka* as pestle. Nevertheless, the rendering of *śilāputraka* as "statue" in many of the modern translations of the PsP does not detract from the point being made by Dignāga, since a statue can of course also be understood as something that is not different from its body.

[and] "Rāhu's head"[481] even when a qualifier (i.e., a pestle, Rāhu) [as some entity] separate from the body and head does not exist.

The translation equivalents for *śilāputraka* employed by modern translators of the PsP section vary. Siderits (1981: 142) translates the compound as "statue." Thurman (1991: 292, n. 11) states that he prefers, against Stcherbatsky, who translates *śilāputraka* as "statue," to rely on Tibetan *mchi gu* in the sections of the PsP he translates. Seyfort Ruegg (2002: 115) takes a middle path and translates "the body of a torso/pestle." Arnold (2005b: 440, n. 97) writes, "the primary sense of *śilāputraka* is 'millstone' or 'pestle,' which is reflected in the Tibetan (*mchi gu*)" but argues that understanding *śilāputraka* in this way might not be optimal: "If … we take it that way, the point of this example would differ slightly from that of the other — and indeed, would not be altogether clear. The point would perhaps be that, insofar as the word involves a semantic unit that ordinarily refers to persons (i.e., *putra*, such that the word's *nirukti* makes it mean something like 'stone boy'), one might be inclined to suppose that the *body* of such is, like the body of a person, *animate* — hence, the force of the subsequent part where we're told that the *ākāṅkṣā* that goes with this word is *buddhi*, 'intellect.' Thus, the reason a *śilāputraka just is* a body is that it is *inanimate* (whereas a statue would only *be* a "body" if it happened to be a headless statue). However, it seems to me preferable to follow Stcherbatsky (1927: 158) in reading this to mean 'statue'— in which case the point of the example is exactly the same as that of the 'Rāhu's head' example … ." I doubt that considerations of animate stone bodies and headless statues are relevant here. Arnold (and all of the previous translators of the passage, in fact) has in part been misled by the idea that the other associated thing (*sahabhāvipadārthāntara*—see Candrakīrti's response) that is implied by the mention of "body" is "intellect, etc." (*buddhyādi*) rather than, as I understand it, an individual who possesses or has control over the body (see n. 482). As will be seen, with *buddhyādi…vat* Candrakīrti merely compares "body" to "intellect" because the mention of these words and others like them suggests an owner or possessor.

[481] Rāhu, according to Indian mythology, was a Daitya who, subsequent to the gods' churning of the ocean to retrieve the stolen *amṛta*, the nectar of immortality, sat amongst the gods and drank a portion of the *amṛta*. Sūrya and Candra, the gods of the sun and moon, revealed the fraud, upon which Viṣṇu beheaded the Daitya. The head and trunk of the Daitya settled in the heavens as the immortalized Rāhu and Ketu. Rāhu seeks to avenge Sūrya and Candra's exposure of him by pursuing them through the stellar sphere, and when he catches them, he swallows them, thereby causing eclipses; but since Rāhu only exists as a head, they reappear when they pass out of his neck. Within Indian astrology, Rāhu and Ketu represent the ascending and descending nodes of the moon (Basham 1988: 491). On Rāhu in eclipse mode as susceptible to the influence of the chanting of Buddhist verses, see SN I.50-51.
Rāhu as a mere head is set forth by hypothetical Dignāga as a second example of things that are actually one but that may nevertheless be spoken of as existing in a relationship of qualifier and qualified. Hypothetical Dignāga for now leaves aside his earlier postulation of a *karmasādhana lakṣaṇa*-cum-*lakṣya* which has cognition

Similarly, even when earth [as some entity] separate from [its] particular characteristic (*svalakṣana*) does not exist, there will be [a relationship of qualifier and qualificand for the members of the genitive construction] "earth's particular characteristic."

[Reply:] This is not so, because [the case you intend to prove] is not the same [as the other two]. For given that the words "body" and "head" [respectively] presuppose another associated (*sahabhāvin*) thing, in the same way that intellect (*buddhi*), etc., [presuppose someone who possesses them] and hands, etc., [presuppose an individual to whom they belong], when a thought (*buddhi*) which has the mere word "body" or "head" as objective support (*ālambana*) is produced [in someone], [this] person (*jana*) [will] certainly expect the other associated thing, [wondering] "Whose body?" [or] "Whose head?"[482] It is reasonable that the other [person], for his part, wanting

---

acting as its instrument, and with this new argument focusses on the *viśeṣya* solidity and its merely nominally existent *viśeṣaṇa* earth, again attempting to circumvent Candrakīrti's demand for a separately existing *lakṣya*.

[482] My understanding of the sentence differs slightly from that of previous translators for two reasons. First, I do not consider "intellect, etc., and hands, etc." (*buddhyādi-pāṇyādi*) to be the referents of either *sahabhāvipadārthāntara* or *sahacāripa-dārthāntara*, but rather understand these items simply as further examples of things like "body" and "head" which on their own imply or lead one to presuppose—in the case of body and intellect, etc.—a "possessor" of them or—in the case of head and hands, etc.—a whole person who is constituted by these body parts and to whom they thus belong. That is, on my understanding, the referent of *sahabhāvipadārthāntara* is nothing other than the referent of *sahacāripadārthāntara*, namely, an "owner," the existence of whom/which is assumed and expressed by the questions that enter the mind of the person who has just heard the words "body" or "head." Compare, e.g., Siderits' (1981: 142) translation, which takes the referent of *sahabhāvipadārthāntara* to be *buddhyādipāṇyādi* and that of *sahabhāvipadārthāntara* to be the person who possesses *buddhyādipāṇyādi*: "In the case of the words 'body' and 'head', their occurrence being related to other associated things like intellect and hands, when the object consisting of just the words 'body' or 'head' is productive of intellection, it occurs having the requirement (expectation) of some other associated thing to complete the sense: 'The body of whom?' 'The head of whom?'" It is not entirely clear to me if Seyfort Ruegg (cf. 2002: 115f.) understands *sahabhāvipadārthāntara* and *sahacāripadārthāntara* to have the same or separate referents; his translation, which further unexpectedly associates 'head' with *buddhyādi* and 'body' with *pāṇyādi*, reads: "For—given that in the case of the words 'body' and 'head' there operates a [semantic] dependency on a further, accompanying, thing … such as a

thought, etc., (*buddhyādi*) [in relation to a head], and a hand, etc. (*pāṇyādi*) [in relation to a body]—there is present the additional production of a thought having as its object the words 'body' and 'head' (*śarīra-śiraḥśabdamātrālambano buddhyupajananaḥ* [?] = *lus daṅ mgo'i sgra tsam la dmigs pa'i blo skyes pa lta žig*), and involving precisely the (syntactic-semantic) expectation of a further, accompanying, thing ..., [this expectation taking the form of the enquiry] 'the body of whom/what?', 'The head of whom/what?', etc." Arnold assumes that the referent of both *sahabhāvipadārthāntara* and *sahacāripadārthāntara* is *buddhyādipāṇyādi*, and, like Seyfort Ruegg, associates "head" with *buddhyādi* and "body" with *pāṇyādi*. Arnold (2005b: 441) translates: "For the use of words like 'body' and 'head' depends on other associated categories, such as, [in the case of 'heads'], intellect, etc., and, [in the case of bodies,] hands, etc. That being the case, the production of an idea based on the words 'body' or 'head' creates a semantic expectation regarding the other associated categories, [such that one expects to know] *whose* body? *whose* head?" *LṬ's author similarly appears to have mistakenly understood Candrakīrti to be saying that the mention of a body (*śarīra*) implies things like *buddhi*: *śarīram ity ukte* {|} *buddhyādisahabhāvipadārthāntarasāpekṣatā bhavati* | (cf. Yonezawa 2004: 124, 144 [fol. 2b6]).

Second, earlier translators have had to struggle with PsP_L's almost surely corrupt text *śarīraśiraḥśabdamātrālambano buddhyupajananaḥ*, a reading also attested by the manuscripts. I am grateful to Lambert Schmithausen for suggesting the emendation *janaḥ*. The emendation assumes that a scribe's early, pre–ms-P eyeskip was responsible for the loss of the *akṣara ne* of my critical text's °*upajanane* and of the *ja* of the subject *janaḥ* (eyeskip *na* to *na*[*ḥ*]). I further assume that the preceding compound, which reads *śarīraśiraḥśabdamātrālambano* in PsP_L and the manuscripts, originally read °*ālambana* and was compounded with *buddhyupajanane*.

*LṬ's author's comment on the word *sākāṅkṣaḥ* of the compound *sahacāripadārthāntarasākāṅkṣaḥ*, to wit, [*s*]*ākāṅkṣa iti pratipattā* (the original *s* of *sākāṅkṣa* was wrongly copied as initial *a*), makes explicit the reference to the *person* who understands the words "body" and "head." The *LṬ thus supports the emendation *buddhyupajanane janaḥ*. Yonezawa, on the other hand, considers the *LṬ ms's *ākāṅkṣa* to represent the citation of the PsP's following *kāṅkṣām* and therefore emends PsP_L's *kāṅkṣām* to *ākāṅkṣām*, a change that cannot be accepted; cf. Yonezawa 2004: 124, 144 (fol. 2b6).

Lack of access to the subject *janaḥ* left Seyfort Ruegg and Arnold with little choice but to understand *upajananaḥ* as the sentence's subject (Seyfort Ruegg: "... there is present the additional production of a thought having as its object the words 'body' and 'head' ...") and probably explains Arnold's free translation of *vartate* as "creates" ("... the production of an idea based on the words 'body' or 'head' creates a semantic expectation ..."). Siderits' (1981: 142) assumption that *buddhi* of *buddhyupajananaḥ* is the subject of the verb *vartate* and his presentation of PsP_L's °*ālambano* (the masculine form clearly indicating that it is the final member of a *bahuvrīhi* compound) as if it were part of a locative absolute construction is, however, inexplicable ("when the object consisting of just the words 'body' or 'head' is productive to prevent a connection [of the word "body" or "head"] with [any] other qualification, removes the expectation (*kāṅkṣā*) of the comprehending person (*pratipattṛ*) by [stating] the qualifying word (*dhvani*) "pestle" or "Rāhu," [both of] which are in conformity with worldly convention (*laukikasaṅketa*). But in this case [of particular characteristic], where earth, etc., separate from solidity, etc., do not exist, a relationship of qualification and qualificand is not tenable.[483]

---

of intellection, it occurs having the requirement (expectation ...)." It should be mentioned that Stcherbatsky (1927: 150, n. 3), apparently also puzzled by PsP_L's text, noted that °*ālambano* might have originally read °*ālambana* and been connected to the following compound, an idea that I accept: "*buddhyupajananaḥ* for *upajāta-buddhiḥ* or °*ālambana-buddhy-upajananaḥ* (sc. *puruṣaḥ*)"; he presents as his literal translation (ibid., 150, n. 5): "... a man who produces a thought intent upon only the words body and head is always (*eva*) in expectation of the coexisting other things, 'whose the body', 'whose the head'?"
De La Vallée Poussin (PsP_L 66, n. 3) comments on PsP Tib's *sgra tsam la dmigs pa'i blo skyes pa lta zhig gang gi lus* ... with "Si *lta-zhig* peut remplacer *hga-zhig*, *la-la-zhig*, il s'oppose à [*g*]*cog-ços* (itara = eka-tara), et nous avons: 'Un homme intelligent (*blo-skyes-pa*? *buddhimān janaḥ*) entend pronouncer le mot tête et se demande: la tête de qui? ...'." It is difficult to reconstruct what the PsP Tib translators might have read in their manuscript(s). On the meaning and usage of *lta zhig*, see Hahn 1994: 289ff.

483 Candrakīrti makes the point that head and body, for example, in contradistinction to solidity, which according to Dignāga is not something different from earth, presuppose and imply other things (*antarapadārtha*), that is, numerically different things, these "things" being the "possessors" or "owners" of head and body. Rāhu is just one of the innumerable possessors of heads in this world, and it is the mention of his name that reveals, for the person for whom the mention of the word "head" has sparked a desire to know exactly whose head is being referred to, the identity of the owner of this specific head. The fact that Rāhu has lost the rest of his body and can be considered, as Dignāga intends to present him, as nothing more than his head is more or less irrelevant here: in the world, Rāhu is accepted as someone/something different from the mere head inasmuch as he is acknowledged as the possessor of his head, like all other possessors of heads. The case of the pestle is the same: the mention of "body" brings about the hearer's desire to know who or what possesses said body. The information that the possessor of the body is a pestle excludes everyone and everything but a pestle; that the reference is only to a pestle and not to some person by no means detracts from the fact that on the level of worldly convention a pestle is acknowledged as having a body. As indicated by Candrakīrti, similar to Rāhu and his head, a pestle is conventionally accepted as something different from its mere body and thus appropriate to be characterized as in a relationship of qualifier and qualificand with it. In the case of earth and solidity, on the other hand, which are

§102. If [Dignāga argues:] Since the non-Buddhists (*tīrthika*) accept a separate object characterized (*lakṣya*), [our] assertion of a qualification (*viśeṣaṇa*), which is in conformity with that [acceptance], is without fault.[484]

---

envisioned by Dignāga as existing in a relationship of qualifier and qualificand even though he holds them to be one and the same thing, a relationship of qualifier and qualificand is excluded, because such a relationship can only occur between two separate things. Thus the argument brought forth by Dignāga to preserve some semblance of a *lakṣya*, be it only nominal (that is, earth is the merely nomimal *lakṣya* of the (*sva*)*lakṣaṇa* solidity), is faulty because Dignāga's *lakṣya* does not exist separately from the *lakṣaṇa*; there is simply no qualifier for the opponent's *lakṣaṇa*.

Arnold's summation of the paragraph slightly misses the point. He states (2005b: 442, n. 103), "Thus, adjectival 'qualification' (*viśeṣaṇa*) is called for only when there is some syntactic 'expectation' (*ākāṅkṣā*), such that we need to know more in order to know precisely which token of some type is being picked out. In contrast, since there cannot meaningfully be any earth which is not 'earth' *by definition*—which is not, that is, possessed of the characteristic that makes it an instance *of* 'earth'—we do not, when encountering some instance of 'resistance,' wonder what it belongs to; for when one encounters an instance of 'earth,' one *just is* encountering an instance of 'resistance.' This is just what it means for the latter to be a defining characteristic of the former." Candrakīrti's emphasis, however, is less on qualification being demanded by "expectation" than on qualification requiring separate things. And as Candrakīrti has made very clear, the view of the non-difference of earth and its characteristic is the opponent's view, not his own. Arnold's subsequent contention that the argument presented in the paragraph counters Dignāga's stance that perception (*pratyakṣa*) has access to uninterpreted data because it "advances the point that we invariably encounter things *as they are defined*. That is, tokens of the type 'earth' are invariably encountered *under a description* (viz., as 'hard' or 'resistant')" is an overinterpretation.

[484] Non-Buddhists such as the Vaiśeṣikas and Naiyāyikas posit a categorical difference between substance (*dravya*) and quality (*guṇa*), the coalescence of which is facilitated by the separate category inherence (*samavāya*); see, e.g., Halbfass 1992: 75, where it is stated, "At any rate, classical Vaiśeṣika considers *samavāya* as a principle that is supposed to account for the cooccurrence and coalescence of different and ontologically distinct world constituents within concrete things. In a sense, it restores the unity and concreteness of things after their categorical decomposition" (see also ibid., 70-72, and chapters five and six).

Dignāga argues here that his positing of earth as a *viśeṣaṇa*, and indeed as one that is in a relationship with its *viśeṣya*, is legitimate because non-Buddhists like the Vaiśeṣikas and Naiyāyikas posit substance (*dravya*) as something separate from its quality (*guṇa*), even though the two have been caused to coalesce by inherence. Neither Seyfort Ruegg nor Arnold explains the argument. Stcherbatsky (1927: 150f.)

[We reply:] This is not so. For it not proper (*nyāyya*) to accept into [your] own doctrine (*svasamaya*)[485] the entities (*padārtha*) bereft of reasoning that are postulated by the non-Buddhists, because this would entail that [you would] also accept other means of valid cognition (*pramāṇa*) and such.[486]

§103. Moreover, like designations (*prajñapti*) such as the person (*pudgala*), [which actually exist as appropriators of things such as the *skandha*s],[487] a pestle actually exists as the appropriator (*upādātṛ*) of

---

wrongly understands Dignāga to be speaking ironically and intending the acceptance of the qualification to be from the Madhyamaka side (150, n. 9: "it is a jeer at the fact that the Mādhyamika prefers the realistic logic of the Naiyāyikas and rejects the reforms of the Buddhist logicians"). Arnold (2005b: 443) does not explain why he translates *viśeṣaṇābhidhāna* as "[our] definition of characteristic."
The Jainas likewise posit substance (*dravya*) and quality (*guṇa*) as distinct categories (Halbfass 1992: 78). The Mīmāṃsakas also maintain the existence of substance separate from its qualities (see, e.g., Bhatt 1989: 362-364). Classical Sāṅkhya appropriates the Vaiśeṣika doctrine of the categorical distinction between substance and quality (see, e.g., Frauwallner 1984: 313-315).

485 Arnold (2005b: 443, n. 106) considers Seyfort Ruegg's (correct) translation of *svasamaye* as "into one's own doctrine" to be based only on PsP Tib ("Ruegg [2002: 116] ... reading *svamata* per the Tibetan *rang gi gzhung lugs*") and thus translates *svasamaye* as "with regard to your own occasion," which does not make much sense in the present context.

486 Should Dignāga accept any of the entities or views posited by the non-Buddhist schools, he would be met with the consequence that he would also have to admit, along with other unacceptable entities and doctrines, the means of valid cognition (*pramāṇa*) by which the objects propounded by the respective school are known and validated. For example, in addition to direct perception and inference, authoritative testimony (*śabda*) and comparison (*upamāna*) are accepted by the Vaiśeṣikas and Naiyāyikas (implication [*arthāpatti*] is additionally accepted by the Prabhākara-Mīmāṃsakas, negation [*abhāva*] by the Bhāṭṭa-Mīmāṃsakas and the Vedāntins, and possibility [*sambhava*] and tradition [*aitihya*] by the Paurāṇikas; see, e.g., Hattori 1968: 78, n. 1.12; Randle 1976: 305). The tenet fundamental to Dignāga's system of the existence of only two *pramāṇa*s and two corresponding *prameya*s would therewith be demolished. Cf. also PsP_L 67, n. 1 and Siderits 1981: 141.

487 Cp. Candrakīrti's MA argument against the thesis that the *ātman* is the same thing as the *skandha*s in which he states that the appropriator must be something different from that which is appropriated, because otherwise act and agent would also be the same thing: *len po rang nyer len gcig rigs dngos min | de lta na las byed po gcig nyid 'gyur ||* (MA VI.137). Ultimately, neither appropriator nor appropriated exists, but on

that [which is] appropriated (*upādāna*), viz., [its] own body, [that is, actually exists] as a qualifier (*viśeṣaṇa*) that is a component of worldly linguistic practice (*laukikavyavahāra*) [inasmuch as that pestle is] generally established without analysis, and Rāhu actually exists as appropriator of [his] head, the appropriated; therefore, this example (*nidarśana*) [of pestle and Rāhu as substantiation for your claim that earth—which you maintain does not actually exist as something separate from its particular characteristic—is a qualifier of the particular characteristic] is inappropriate.[488]

---

the surface level, both appropriator and appropriated are accepted as existing; they exist on the surface level in mutual dependence (MABh$_{ed}$ 261.12-14), and if one does not exist, the other cannot exist. Candrakīrti substantiates his argumentation for an agent which exists as an element of worldly linguistic activity in MABh ad MA VI.137 with authoritative testimony (*āgama*) that asserts the existence of the person (*pudgala*, *gang zag*): "This person caught up in ignorance also creates good/wholesome impulses" (*ma rig pa dang rjes su 'brel pa'i gang zag 'di ni bsod nams mngon par 'du bya ba yang mngon par 'du byed do* [MABh$_{ed}$ 262.4-6]).
*LṬ's author comments on the example of *pudgala* and its relationship to the example of the pestle as follows: *yathā* {|} *avidyamāne pi pudgale rūpādyupādānā pudgalaprajñapti*[*s*] *tadvat śarī*[*ra*]*m upādānaṃ kṛtvā* {|} *śilāputraka upādātā upādīyate prajñapyate* | (cf. Yonezawa 2004: 124, 144 [fol. 2b6]).
I agree with Arnold (2005b: 443, n. 108) that Seyfort Ruegg's qualification "designational" is uncalled for and detracts from the point Candrakīrti is making (cf. Seyfort Ruegg 2002: 116: "Moreover, given the [designational] existence of a *śīlaputraka* …").

488 Just as the *pudgala* actually exists as a legitimate element of conceptual activity and linguistic discourse on the non-analyzed worldly level in the form of the appropriator of the *skandhas*, so do pestles and Rāhu actually exist as the appropriators of respectively their bodies and head on this level. Dignāga has, however, expressly stated that the *lakṣya* (= earth, etc., his intended qualifier) does *not* actually exist, and thus any comparison of this non-existent *lakṣya*-cum-proposed-qualifier with the examples of the existing qualifiers pestle and Rāhu is unacceptable.
*LṬ's author states that the examples of pestle and Rāhu are incorrect because a relationship of qualifier and qualificand is not possible when there is not a qualifier: *ayuktam iti* | *viśeṣaṇābhāve pi viśeṣaṇaviśeṣ*[*y*]*abhāva iti na yuktaṃ* | (cf. Yonezawa 2004: 124, 145 [fol. 2b7]). He explains: *saṃvyavahārasiddhasya viśeṣaṇasya bhāvād eva* (cf. ibid., 124, 145 [fol. 2b7]; Yonezawa [p. 145] erroneously associates this sentence with the following paragraph in the PsP).
De La Vallée Poussin (PsP$_L$ 67, n. 3) reconstructs PsP Tib as *api ca śarīra-upādāna-viśeṣaṇa*[*sya*] *laukikavyavahārāṅgībhūta-avicāra-prasiddha*[*sya*] *upādātṛ-śilāputraka*[*sya*], *śira-upādāna*[*sya*] *upādātṛ-rāhoś ca pudgala-ādi-prajñapti-vat sadbhāvān nidarśanam etad ayuktam*, but Pa tshab has merely changed the word-order, con-

§104. If [Dignāga retorts:] The example is indeed established, because another thing separate from body or head is not established since there is the perception (*upalambha*) of only that [body or head].[489]

[We reply:] This is not the case, because [first,] analysis (*vicāra*) does not take place in this manner in worldly practice, and [second,] worldly things (*laukikapadārtha*) exist from the non-analytical point of view. For exactly as the self (*ātman*), being analyzed, is not possible as [an entity] different from the body (*rūpa*), etc., and yet from the point of view of worldly convention (*lokasaṃvṛti*) it exists [as something] based on (*upādāya*) the constituent elements (*skandha*), so also [do] Rāhu and the pestle [exist from the point of view of worldly convention]; therefore, [your] example is not established. Thus, even if in the case of earth, etc., an object characterized (*lakṣya*), when analyzed, does not exist separately from solidity, etc., and a characteristic (*lakṣaṇa*) separate from the object characterized (*lakṣya*) [would be] without a basis (*nirāśraya*), nevertheless, in view of [the fact that] this is (i.e., that we are dealing with) the surface [level], the Masters have determined that there is establishment (*siddhi*) by virtue of an establishment (*siddhi*) [that consists in] mere mutual reliance (*parasparāpekṣā*).[490] And it certainly has to be

---

densed the two *sadbhāvāt*s into one, and omitted *sva*. De La Vallée Poussin seems also to have overlooked that *khyad par du byed pa* (*viśeṣaṇasya*) is to be construed with *rten pa po* (*upādātuḥ*).

[489] PsP Tib reverses the two reason clauses (*gal te de tsam zhig dmigs pas lus dang mgo las tha dad pa'i don gzhan ma grub pa'i phyir dpe grub pa nyid do zhe na* |), but the Sanskrit can also be read this way, and in fact makes more sense when construed thus. Both Seyfort Ruegg (2002: 117) and Arnold (2005b: 444) read *śarīraśirovyatiriktasyārthāntarasyāsiddhiḥ* as giving the reason for *tanmātrasyopalambhaḥ*.

[490] Cf., e.g., MMK VIII.12 (cited earlier in §82): *pratītya kārakaḥ karma taṃ pratītya ca kārakam* | *karma pravartate nānyat paśyāmaḥ siddhikāraṇam* ||. Arnold (2005b: 445, n. 118) considers *ācāryāḥ* to be employed as an honourific plural intending Nāgārjuna ("The teacher [Nāgārjuna] ..."). This is certainly possible, but since Candrakīrti otherwise regularly uses *ācārya* in the singular when he is referring to Nāgārjuna, I have chosen to interpret *ācāryāḥ* as including Nāgārjuna and (at least) Āryadeva. Both Arnold and Seyfort Ruegg read the *iti* before *ācāryāḥ* as indicating a full stop (Arnold 2005b: 445: "nevertheless, this is the convention. The teacher [Nāgārjuna] settled the matter ...."; Seyfort Ruegg 2002: 118: "even so [there is here] this [existence on the] surface-level. Teachers have propounded ..."), but I

accepted that this is so: for otherwise, the surface [level] (*saṃvṛti*) would not be divorced from reasoning (*upapatti*), [and it would follow,] then, [that] this (= the alleged surface level) would be exclusively true reality (*tattva*), [thus] not [at all] the surface [level].[491] And not only are the pestle and so forth, when analyzed with reasoning, impossible, but, by dint of argumentation (*yukti*) that will be stated [in later chapters], bodily matter, feeling, and so forth, are also not possible. Thus it would have to be maintained that they too, like the pestle, etc., do not exist on the surface level [if, following your procedure, the ultimate state of affairs is applied to the surface], but this is not the case (i.e., you do not maintain that that which is appropriated, i.e., the object qualified, does not exist on the surface level).[492] Therefore, this [comparison with the two examples] is fallacious.[493]

---

understand it as intended in a connective sense, specifically, as indicating that the previous clause provides the reason for the subsequent statement.

491 *LṬ's author comments on the paragraph to this point as follows: *yady avicā{sa?}ra saṃvṛtir na bhavetadātvam eva na bhavet* (read: *yady avicārā saṃvṛtir na bhavet tadā tattvam eva bhavet* ?) | *tata upapat[t]yā na viyujyeta* | (cf. Yonezawa 2004: 124f., 145 [fol. 2b7]; Yonezawa [p. 145] edits the comment as: *yady avicāraḥ saṃvṛtinā bhavet tadā tvam eva na bhavet* | *tata upapattyā na viyujyeta* |).

492 Candrakīrti chides Dignāga for jumbling the levels of reality and applying reasonings and conclusions associated with ultimate analysis to the surface level. On the surface level, the level where critical analysis is set aside and everyday linguistic practice is given priority and granted credibility, things, which include the self and the *skandha*s, pestles and their bodies, and Rāhu and his head, are accepted as existing. When examined by reasoning, however, not only the appropriating self, pestles, and Rāhu, but also the appropriated *skandha*s, bodies and head are revealed to be ultimately non-existent. Candrakīrti argues that the opponent who maintains that a *lakṣya* is in a relationship of qualified-qualificand with its *lakṣaṇa* is dealing with the surface level and must therefore accept the real existence of the *lakṣya*. When, as here, Dignāga claims that the appropriating entities pestles and Rāhu, etc., do not really exist, he is speaking from the ultimate point of view, and from this point of view the objects appropriated, qualified, etc., are as non-existent as the appropriator, qualifier, etc.
Arnold (2005b: 445, n. 123) rejects de La Vallée Poussin's emendation *teṣām api saṃvṛtyā śilāputrakādivan nāstitvam āstheyam syān na caitad evam ity asad etat* for the reading ... *śilāputraka ivāstitvam āstheyam syān* ... found in the three manuscripts used for PsP_L, and translates: "hence, their existence, too, like that of the statue, would have to be accepted as conventional. And this is not how [you accept them]; hence, [your position is] false." Seyfort Ruegg (2002: 118) apparently accepts de La

Vallée Poussin's emendation *śilāputrakādivat* but rejects the emendation *nāstitvam*: "Hence, as in the case of the *śīlaputraka*, etc., on the surface-level (*saṃvṛtyā*) their existence is to be accepted … . But since it is not [really] so, [in ultimate reality] it is non-existent (*asat* = *yod pa ma yin*)." Arnold argues that the attestation in "some versions of the Tibetan," viz., in P, N and G, of *yod pa ma yin pa nyid*, on which de La Vallée Poussin based the emendation *nāstitvam* (D and C attest *yod pa yin pa nyid*), may represent a corrupt reading, and is of the opinion that his translation "seems more straightforwardly to follow what precedes it, as Candrakīrti's point is instead that the merely 'conventional' existence of the *skandha*s is *precisely* what we have to accept. I take this as stated counterfactually, then, insofar as it is a conclusion that Candrakīrti thinks his interlocutor wishes to avoid (though of course Dignāga's generally Ābhidharmika idea that there is an enumerable set of 'ultimately existent' entitites involves only *svalakṣaṇa*s, not the *skandha*s)." However, exactly the emendation suggested by de La Vallée Poussin is attested by ms Q (ms P attests *śilāputrasyevāstitvam*), and it has to be accepted as correct because Candrakīrti is obviously referring with *na caitad evam* to the fact that the assertion in the previous clause, to wit, that one would have to maintain that the *skandha*s as well do not exist on the surface level, is not accepted by Dignāga, because he, like his fellow Mahāyānist Candrakīrti, maintains their non-existence only ultimately. Arnold, presumably because his interpretation of Dignāga's views overlooks his Yogācāra affiliation and thus his final denial of all things but the mind, considers Dignāga to maintain that things ultimately exist, and hence has the clause emphasize the mere surface-level existence of the *skandha*s. However, their conventional existence is not at all in question here, since it is accepted by Dignāga. Candrakīrti exposes with this part of the sentence the consequence entailed by Dignāga's denial of a constituent part of the surface level, namely, that if he denies that pestles and Rāhu exist, then he will have to maintain that all the things appropriated, such as the *skandha*s, also do not exist.

[493] As noted in my Sanskrit edition, ms Q includes another, following sentence: *eṣā copādāyaprajñaptivyavasthā vistareṇa madhyamakāvatāre vihiteti tata eva paryanveṣyā* "And since this establishment by way of dependent designation has been set forth in detail in the Madhyamakāvatāra, it should be sought right there." PsP Tib supports ms Q's reading with: *brten nas btags par rnam par gzhag pa 'di yang dbu ma la 'jug pa las rgyas par bstan pas de nyid las yongs su btsal bar bya'o.* The topic of dependent designation is, however, really not relevant to the present flow of argumentation or to the point Candrakīrti is making. As my discussion regarding the PsP manuscripts indicates, ms Q attests a number of words and sentences that do not occur in ms P but do appear in the Tibetan translation, which demonstrates that at least one of the manuscripts relied on by the Tibetan translators was closely related to Q's manuscript tradition. Since there is usually no paleographical support in ms P for a loss of these words and sentences, and since the majority of them can be shown to supply explanatory or extra material, I consider them additions made by post-Candrakīrti scholars, students and/or scribes. Arnold (2005b: 445f.), who could not have known of the complexities of the manuscript tradition when his work on the section was published, includes the sentence in his translation. Seyfort Ruegg (2002:

§105. If there were [this objection]: What use is this trifling examination (*sūkṣmekṣikā*)?! For we definitely do not assert that all that ordinary practice with regard to valid cognition and what is cognized (*pramāṇaprameyavyavahāra*) is true; rather, this general establishment by the world is validated by way of this procedure (*nyāya*) [i.e., by way of our determining, defining, and explicating the means of valid cognition and their respective objects, etc.].[494]

[Reply:] We too assert [the situation to be] such: What use is this trifling examination that leads [us] into worldly practice? Let this surface [level], which has reached its own [real] existence (*ātmabhāvasattā*) through mere error (*viparyāsa*) [but which is nevertheless] the cause of the accumulation of wholesome roots conducive to liberation (*mokṣa*) for those desiring liberation, stand [as valid] as long as one has not penetrated true reality (*tattva*).[495] You, however, [who] have

---

119, n. 218) cites and translates the Tibetan sentence in a note, but does not include this translation in his main text. The sentence is not commented on in *LṬ and, on the basis of evidence which indicates that the manuscript relied upon by *LṬ's author may have been closer to ms P's tradition than ms Q's, it is quite possible that it also did not appear in *LṬ's PsP exemplar.

[494] Dignāga retorts that he doesn't need to be tutored about the ultimate and surface levels: he, like Candrakīrti, accepts that things do not exist ultimately and exist only superficially. He emphasizes that his focus is merely what the world accepts: he inquires into, defines and, where appropriate, elucidates the epistemologically relevant entities already accepted by the world on the strength of its perception. I have translated, following Candrakīrti's interpretation of the situation, *vyavasthāpyate* as "validated." From Dignāga's actual point of view, "adjusted" might be more appropriate.

[495] Seyfort Ruegg (2002: 119) translates *hetu* as "motivating cause," possibly considering *saṃvṛti* as equivalent to *saṃsāra* attended by *duḥkha*. It seems, however, that Candrakīrti is intending to convey the idea that even though the everyday level of existence is actually an illusion erroneously brought about by the ordinary person's mind/ignorance, this illusion is to be accepted as general consensus maintains it because it is on its basis and in relationship to the objects in it that the spiritual life can be taken up and spiritual development can occur (cp. MMK XXIV.10). The illusion itself is thus the cause that allows for spiritual activity. As Candrakīrti declares in the following sentence, Dignāga, in depriving—via his revisionary insistence on mere (*sva*)*lakṣaṇa*s—the everyday level of half of its components, i.e., of its *lakṣya*s, is destroying *saṃvṛti*.
Arnold (2005b: 447) construes *tiṣṭhatu* as a separate sentence that relates to the preceding sentence ("We, too, say, What's the use of this hair-splitting, which delves into ordinary discourse? Let it be!") but it should be taken, as PsP Tib does, as the

introduced reasoning (*upapatti*) in certain cases (*kvacit*)—inasmuch as [your] thinking is sloppy (*durvidagdha*) as regards the distinction between surface [truth] and ultimate truth—inappropriately (*anyāyataḥ*)[496] ruin this [surface level].[497] Owing to [my] proficiency (*vaicakṣaṇya*) in the determination of the surface truth, I [on the other hand], [in] situating [myself] exclusively on the worldly side [and in] invalidating, by way of other reasonings [of my own] the various reasonings (*upapattyantarāntara*) [you have] adduced for the sake of denying one aspect of the surface [level], obstruct—like an elder in the world (*lokavṛddha*) [someone] straying from [proper] worldly conduct (*lokācāra*)—only *you*, certainly not the surface [level].[498]

---

verb for the longer, following sentence. Cp. Stcherbatsky's (1927: 154) free translation: "As to phenomenal reality, leave it alone ... !" Seyfort Ruegg (2002: 119) understands the sentence's structure as I do, but translates the *bahuvrīhi viparyāsamātrāsāditātmabhāvasattākā* as "wherein the existence of an entity is acquired through mere misapprehension."

496 Stcherbatsky (1927: 154, n. 4), translating *anyāyataḥ* as "wrong logic," suggests the reading *anyāyato 'nyato nāśayati* for *anyāyato nāśayati*. His suggestion does not make much sense, and the text *anyāyato nāśayati* as found in PsP_L is supported by all six manuscripts consulted and by PsP Tib.

497 Arnold (2005b: 447, n. 127) argues that *upapatti* is the referent of PsP_L's *etām* but the position of this pronoun (emended on the basis of manuscript evidence to *enām*) in the sentence indicates that it refers to the preceding *saṃvṛti*. Candrakīrti argues in the subsequent sentence that he (unlike Dignāga) does *not* harm *saṃvṛti*. Seyfort Ruegg (2002: 120) also takes *upapatti* to be the referent of *enām*: "However, because [your] intellect (*buddhi*) is not expert in making the distinction (*vibhāga*) between *saṃvṛti* and *paramārtha*, your honour ruins (*nāśayati* = *'jig par byed pa*) without reason (*anyāyatas* = *rigs pa ma yin pa las*) the justification (*upapatti* = *'thad pa*) after having [nevertheless] introduced it in some place (*kva cid ... avatārya*)."

498 I understand the complete phrase *lokavṛddha iva lokācārāt paribhraśyamānam* to be intended as a comparative example, and do not, as Stcherbatsky, Siderits, Seyfort Ruegg and Arnold do, take Candrakīrti to be directly referring to Dignāga as *lokācārāt paribhraśyamānaḥ* (Seyfort Rugg [2002: 120]: "... in the manner of an elder of the world ..., I confute (*nivartayāmi* = *zlog par byed pa*) only you who have fallen away from the way of the world"; Arnold [2005b: 447]: "Like a respected elder (*lokavṛddha*), I overturn one argument dedicated to the refutation of one part of the conventional by another argument—and in so doing, I refute only *you,* who are deviating from the conduct of the world."). Rather, Dignāga, in denying *lakṣya*s as constituent elements of *saṃvṛti*, is *like* someone who strays from the worldly moral code and is stopped by a wise elder. In the example, *lokācāra* (worldly conduct/practice) has a moral sense and thus in its primary meaning does not perfectly

Therefore, if [the focus is] worldly practice, then there absolutely must be, like the characteristic (*lakṣaṇa*), also the characterized (*lakṣya*); and thus, [since you do not posit the latter,] that very fault [pointed out earlier, namely, that the characteristic would be without a basis, remains].[499] But if [the focus is] the ultimate, then because the characterized does not exist [on this level], the pair of characteristics (*lakṣaṇadvaya*) also do not exist. Thus how [can there be] the pair of means of valid cognition (*pramāṇadvaya*)?

§106. But if [you argue]: A derivation (*vyutpatti*) of words which in this way presupposes a connection of action and *kāraka* (*kriyākāraka-sambandha*) is not accepted [by us].[500]

---

match the object of comparison, but of course secondarily it fits the comparison to the worldly *vyavahāra* under discussion.

[499] Arnold (2005b: 448, n. 129), in contrast to PsP Tib, Stcherbatsky and Seyfort Ruegg, but in conformity with Siderits (cf. 1981: 147), prefers to read *lakṣaṇaval lakṣyeṇa* as a compound: "then there must also be a subject that possesses a characteristic (*lakṣaṇavallakṣyeṇāpi bhavitavyaṃ*)." He argues, "Given that Candrakīrti has wanted all along to show that Dignāga's conception of *svalakṣaṇa* founders on the necessity of admitting that there must be some *lakṣya* in which it is instantiated, the reading I have chosen seems to make more sense." Candrakīrti did earlier state that in the world an entity that possesses a particular characteristic is held to be characterized by it, but there he was arguing against Dignāga's declaration that a (*sva*)*lakṣaṇa* is to be understood in the object sense (*karmasādhana*). His main point throughout this larger section has been that if there is a *lakṣaṇa*, there must also be a *lakṣya*, certainly not that there has to be a *lakṣya* that *possesses* a *lakṣaṇa* or one *in* which a *lakṣaṇa* is instantiated. The stress is on the fact that there must be *two* things, and that they exist in a relationship of mutual dependence.

[500] Dignāga makes a final attempt to rescue his pair of characteristics (*svasāmānya-lakṣaṇa*) with an outright rejection of the normative Pāṇinian theory according to which words presume a connection to an action and functional activity related to one of the six *kāraka*s, the reference in the above being specifically to the word *lakṣaṇa* understood as an instrumental *kāraka* (= *karaṇa*) in connection with a characterizing event. By liberating the word *lakṣaṇa* from the constraints of the *kāraka* system, Dignāga considers that he has exempted it from Candrakīrti's demand for the *lakṣya* required by the existence of an instrumental *lakṣaṇa*. Seyfort Ruegg (2002: 121) and Arnold (2005b: 448) translate *kāraka* here and in the following paragraph as "agent" but the collective group of *kāraka*s are meant ("agent" is represented by the word *kartṛ* within the *kāraka* categorization).

[We reply:] Then this is more than wrong (*atikaṣṭa*). You transact linguistically by way of exactly those words that start from a connection of action and *kāraka*, but do not want a meaning for a word (*śabdārtha*) such as action (*kriyā*), instrument (*karaṇa*), etc. Unbelievable—your procedure is contingent on nothing but [your own] wish[ful thinking]![501]

§107. And when in this way the pair of objects cognized (*prameya-dvaya*) are unestablished, then authoritative testimony (*āgama*) and so forth, inasmuch as they [can] no [longer be maintained as] having general characteristics (*sāmānyalakṣaṇa*) as [their] object (*viṣaya*),[502]

---

[501] Siderits (1981: 148) translates, "This is quite unfortunate, you conduct yourself by means of those very words whose functioning is by means of the verb-case relation and yet do not wish the meaning of a word to be derived from verb, case, etc.; amazing, this practice of yours, which is entirely contradicted by the wish!" It should be noted that *kāraka*s are not equivalent to the nominal declension groups. Ganeri (1999: 52), referring to Matilal's translation of part of NBh ad NS II.1.16 ("In this way it is neither the thing itself nor the action itself that is a *kāraka*. What then? *When a thing is a participant in an action or when it is endowed with a special functional activity* [*kriyāviśeṣayukta*], *it becomes a kāraka*"; cf. NBh 64.1-2), writes, "A *kāraka* is clearly conceived of here as a specific causal role. It is now widely recognized that it would be a mistake to identify the *kāraka* categories with the purely grammatical cases, by which I mean the nominal declension groups. ... Although, if one excludes the vocative and the genitive, which is a noun-noun relation, there is a superficial correspondence between *kāraka*s and declensional groups, it is clear from the above that the *kāraka*s are semantic, not syntactic, relations." It is unclear why Arnold (2005b: 448) translates *pravṛtti* of the final sentence as "sense" ("You fool! Your sense is bound to a mere fancy"). Stcherbatsky (cf. 1927: 155 and n. 3; 156 and n. 1) overinterprets Dignāga's objection as hinting at *apoha* theory and thus formulates Candrakīrti's reply accordingly.

[502] *āgama* is, according to Dignāga, not an additional means of valid cognition because it is subsumed under inference (*anumāna*). Hattori (1968: 78, n. 1.12) explains that a cognition based on word (*śābda*) knows its object through the exclusion of other objects (*anyāpoha*), a process which is the function of *anumāna*. Cf. PS V.1: *na pramāṇāntaraṃ śābdam anumānāt tathā hi saḥ* | *kṛtakatvādivat svārtham anyāpohena bhāṣate* ||; Skt in Pind 2009: Appendix 1; Hattori 2000: 139. See also, e.g., Tucci 1930: 50; Katsura 1979b; Katsura 1982; Pind 2009; Hattori 2000. Pind (2009: 76) translates: "[V]erbal cognition] is not a means of cognition separate from inference (*anumānāt*). That is, a [word] denotes (*bhāṣate*) its own referent (*svārtham*) by exclusion of other [referents] (*anyapohena*) like [the general property] 'being produced,' and the like." Both *anumāna* and *śābda* are concerned with concepts, i.e.,

[will] *not* be[, as you claim they are,] not further means of valid cognition (*pramāṇāntara*).[503]

§108. Moreover, [your] definition (*lakṣaṇa*) [of *pratyakṣa*] has insufficient extension (*avyāpitā*), because [it] does not include worldly linguistic usage like "the pot is *pratyakṣa*" (i.e., a direct perceptible) and because [you allegedly] accept the linguistic practice of non-

---

the general, conceptually constructed and linguistically tinted characteristics of their objects (cf. Hattori 1979: 61f.). See also PS II.5ab: *āptavādāvisaṃvādasāmānyād anumānatā* | (cf. Lasic et al. 2012: 29; Lasic 2010: 521). For translations and interpretations of the verse-half, see Tillemans 1990: 18ff., Krasser 2012b; Lasic 2010; Eltschinger 2007: 70, 218ff. *upamāna* is likewise classified under inference: when an authority states a sentence such as "a *gavaya* is similar to a cow," this, according to Dignāga, is verbal cognition (*śābda*); also when one cognizes the similarity oneself based on later observation of the two objects the understanding of the similarity functions like *anumāna*. PSV ad PS V 50d: *upamānaṃ tāvad gogavayādiṣu sārūpyapratipattyartham. tatra parata upaśrutya yā pratītiḥ sā śābdam. svayam tu dvayārthaṃ <pramāṇāntareṇā>dhigamya manasā sārūpyaṃ <yadā> kalpayati, <tadā> tad api na pramāṇāntaram. nāpy evam adhigamyamānam sārūpyam prameyam. evam anyāny apy anumānavikalpāvyatiriktatvāt parikṣiptavyāni* (translation in Pind 2009: 116f.; see his n. 643 for PSṬ's Skt text and its English translation; PSV Tib cited in Hattori 1968: 79, n. 1.12). Candrakīrti argues here in the PsP that since the pair of objects of cognition, namely, the particular characteristic and the general characteristic, have been shown by him to be impossible, *āgama* can be accepted as having as its object something other than the general characteristic assigned to it by Dignāga, and that as a means of valid cognition based on an object other than the general characteristic, *āgama* will have to be admitted as an independent type of cognition. The same will hold for *upamāna*. As Candrakīrti will later indicate, he accepts both *āgama* and *upamāna* as means of valid cognition on the *saṃvṛti* level.
De La Vallée Poussin conjectures [*sva*]*sāmānya*° on the basis of PsP Tib's *rang dang spyi'i mtshan nyid*; none of the Skt manuscripts, however, attest *sva*. It is true that *pratyakṣa*'s object is the *svalakṣaṇa*, but *pratyakṣa* is not topical in the present argument. Although one might argue that Candrakīrti includes *svalakṣaṇa* in order to exclude it as a possible or indirect object of *āgama*, I follow the Skt manuscripts because the argument is more specific and cleaner without it. PsP Tib's *rang dang* may, however, be the legitimate translation of an interpolated *sva* that was attested in one of Pa tshab's manuscripts, the inclusion of which would have been inspired by the mention of *prameyadvayam* in the preceding clause.

503 *LṬ's author clarifies the double negative construction with *āgamādeḥ pramāṇāntaratvaṃ yuktaṃ* (cf. Yonezawa 2004: 125, 145 [fol. 2b7]).

Nobles [i.e., ordinary people]; therefore, this [definition] is not tenable.[504]

§109. If there were [this argument from Dignāga's side]: Blue and so forth, i.e., the appropriated [substratum] (*upādāna*) of the [notion] pot, [may be designated] *pratyakṣa* (i.e, direct perceptibles) because [they] are what is distinguished (*paricchedya*) by the means of valid cognition *pratyakṣa*. And therefore, just as, when metaphorically

---

[504] Candrakīrti commences his refutation of Dignāga's definition of *pratyakṣa*, which will focus to a large extent on the etymological understanding of the word itself. The definition of *pratyakṣa* given by Dignāga at PS I.3c makes it clear that for him, *pratyakṣa* refers to a type of consciousness: *pratyakṣam kalpanāpoḍham* (cf. Steinkellner 2005: 2; Hattori 1968: 25 and 82, n. 1.25, 1.27; the definition occurs already at NM 15a: see Katsura 1982: 84; Tucci 1930: 50; Tillemans 1990: 274, n. 367). PSV Tib ad I.3c explains: *shes pa gang la rtog pa med pa de mngon sum mo* (cf. Hattori 1968: 176); Steinkellner (2005: 2) reconstructs: *yasya jñānasya kalpanā nāsti, tat pratyakṣam*. See also Jinendrabuddhi's commentary (cf. Steinkellner et al. 2005: 37): *svabhāvavipratipattinirākaraṇāyāha* – ***pratyakṣam*** *ityādi | pratigatam akṣaṃ pratyakṣaṃ prādisamāsaḥ | etal lakṣyam |* ***kalpanāpoḍham*** *iti lakṣaṇam | kalpanāyā apoḍham apagataṃ kalpanayā vāpoḍhaṃ rahitaṃ kalpanāpoḍham | kalpanāpoḍhanirdeśāc ca jñānātmakaṃ tad iti gamyate | yato jñānasyaiva kalpanāsaṃsargo 'sti, atas tatpratiṣedhena tad eva pratīyate*. Candrakīrti criticizes the definition as being too narrow because Dignāga's definition thus excludes regular worldly usage according to which pots, etc., not consciousness, are *pratyakṣa*.

Arnold (2005b: 449, n. 135) notes, "He begins by stating the main point he will be concerned to make: that on the conventional use of the word *pratyakṣa*, it is the adjectival sense ('perceptible') that is primary. ... In fact, *pratyakṣa* must be an adjective in the example adduced by Candrakīrti; the noun form of the word is neuter, and in Candrakīrti's example it has taken the masculine gender of the word (*ghataḥ*) that it modifies"; it is correct that Candrakīrti understands *pratyakṣa* as an adjective, but as we shall see, Dignāga also considers it an adjective. See also CŚṬ$_{\mathrm{Ted}}$ 64.10 where the Epistemologist opponent, when asked what he holds *pratyakṣa* to be, replies: *shes pa mngon sum yin*; see Tillemans 1990: 274, n. 367. Arnold (2005b: 449, n. 136) rightly critiques Seyfort Ruegg's translation of *avyāpitā* (Seyfort Ruegg 2002: 122: "Furthermore, this is without foundation since, for the [postulated] *lakṣaṇa*, there exists no [logical-epistemological] pervasion ...").

*LṬ's author records that Candrakīrti states that the definition is not tenable because it is not broad enough, explaining that the world calls a pot *pratyakṣa* and yet Dignāga says that according to the linguistic practice of ordinary people *pratyakṣa* is cognition: *kiñ ca pramāṇalakṣaṇam ayuktam avy*[*ā*]*pitvāt | yato loke ghaṭa*[*ḥ*] *pratyakṣa ucyate | tvayā tu anārya*(ms: *ācārya*)*vyavahāreṇa jñānam* (cf. Yonezawa 2004: 125, 145f. [fol. 2b7-3a1]; Yonezawa does not correct *ācārya*° to *anārya*°).

applying the effect to the cause, one designates as "happy the birth of the Buddhas" (*buddhānāṃ sukha utpādaḥ*),[505] in the same way, metaphorically applying the cause to the effect, [one] designates a pot *pratyakṣa*, even though [its] causes (*nimitta*), blue and so forth, are [all that is actually] directly perceived.[506]

---

[505] De La Vallée Poussin refers to *buddhānāṃ sukha utpādaḥ* as an "exemple classique." This *pāda* and the rest of the verse appear in the AKBh ad AK I.10d: *buddhānāṃ sukha utpādaḥ sukhā dharmasya deśanā | sukhā saṃghasya sāmagrī samagrāṇāṃ tapaḥ sukham ||* (AKBh$_{ed}$ 7.13-14; AKBh$_{Ej}$ 10.9-10). The source of the verse is Udānavarga XXX.22, where the first *pāda* reads *sukhaṃ buddhasya cotpādaḥ* (the other three *pāda*s are identical to those in the AKBh; parallels in Pāsādika 1989: 21). The verse in the AKBh is used to exemplify the metaphorical usage of the effect, there hunger (*jighatsā*), in regard to the cause, the tangible that produces desire for food: *jighatsā bhojanābhilāṣakṛt | kāraṇe kāryopacārāt | yathā | buddhānāṃ sukha utpādaḥ* ... (AKBh$_{ed}$ 7.12f.; AKBh$_{Ej}$ 10.7f.). Yaśomitra cites the same example in regard to the case of the metaphorical understanding of *sparśa* by the Sarvāstivādins (AKVy 305.16: *yathā sukho buddhānām utpāda iti*; cf. AKBh$_{ed}$ 143.20-23). At PsP$_{L}$ 70, n. 2, de La Vallée Poussin quotes H.C. Warren's free translation of a passage in VM XVII: "Karma is called existence because it causes existence, just as the birth of a Buddha is called happy because it results in happiness" (Buddhism In Translations. Cambridge, Mass.: Harvard University, 1906, p. 194). The passage occurs at VM 571: *Kammaṃ pana yathā sukhakāraṇattā: sukho Buddhānaṃ uppādo ti vutto, evaṃ bhavakāraṇattā phalavohārena bhavo ti veditabban ti.* VM$_{tr}$ 697: "Karma aber ist mit Rücksicht auf die Wirkung als der Werdeprozess zu verstehen, da es eben den Werdeprozess erzeugt, genau wie die Geburt eines Erleuchteten als ein Glück bezeichnet wird, weil sie ein Glück erzeugt."
Siderits, Seyfort Ruegg and Arnold translate *sukhaḥ* as a noun, but it is an adjective (Siderits [1981: 149]: "Thus just as the birth of the Buddha is termed 'pleasure'"; Seyfort Ruegg [2002: 122]: "Hence, just as the Buddha's birth is designated ... as bliss"; Arnold [2005b: 450]: "Hence just as it is taught that "the birth of buddhas is bliss"; cp. Stcherbatsky [1927: 157, n. 1]: "Hence, ... it is said that the birth of Buddha is agreeable"). I have translated *vyapadiśyate* actively to avoid breaking the quotation.

[506] Dignāga refers to the primary and secondary meanings of *pratyakṣa* in PSV on PS I.41cd (PS I.41cd: *sarvathā nārthavijñāne sthitā pratyakṣadhīr bhavet ||*). Steinkellner (2005: 22) presents the PSV text as: *pratyakṣaśabdo hi triṣu vartate* pramāṇajñānaviṣayeṣu. tatra *pramāṇe mukhyo* 'nyayor upacāritaḥ. tatra viṣaye *pratyakṣa*meyatvāt pratyakṣopacāraḥ (reconstructed Sanskrit text italicized; for Jinendrabuddhi's comments, see Steinkellner et al. 2005: 177ff.). Arnold (2005b: 450, n. 139) translates from the Tibetan (Tibetan in Hattori 1968: 233): "The word *pratyakṣa* is used with respect to three things: the reliable warrant, the awareness [that results from the exercise thereof], and the object [of this awareness]. With respect to these, [the usage designating] the reliable warrant is primary, and the others are secondary (*nye bar*

[Reply:] Metaphorical usage (*upacāra*) in regard to such an object (= pot) is not appropriate. For in the world birth is perceived to be different from happiness; and because [the birth of a future Buddha] has as its cause many hundreds of hardships since it has as its nature

---

btags = Skt. *aupacārika*). In this regard an object is [figuratively] characterized as '*pratyakṣa*' since it is cognized by [the reliable warrant called] *pratyakṣa*."

Compare the stance of the PsP's hypothetical Dignāga with the position of Epistemologist opponents (identified as *rtog ge pa rnams*) in Candrakīrti's commentary on CŚ XIII.1 (CŚṬ$_{Ted}$ 63.21-64.1): *'di la rtog ge pa rnams*[1] *na re bum pa la mngon sum nyid yod pa ma yin pa kho na ste* | *gzugs la sogs pa rnams kyi rang gi mtshan nyid ni bstan du med pa yin la* | *mngon sum gyis bsnyad par bya ba'i mig la sogs pa'i rnam par shes pa'i yul yin pa'i phyir mngon sum zhes bya bar 'dogs so* ‖ ([1]CŚṬ$_{Ted}$ reads *rtog ge ba rnams*). Tillemans (CŚṬ$_{tr}$ 176) translates, "On this point the logicians (*rtog ge pa* = *tārkika*) argue as follows: The vase is not at all *pratyakṣa*; the particular character (*rang gi mtshan nyid* = *svalakṣaṇa*) of [visual] form and the other [eight substances] are inexpressible and are designated as '*pratyakṣa*' because they are the objects of the visual consciousnesses, etc., which is what is [really] said to be *pratyakṣa*." Thus the Epistemologists referred to in both the PsP and the CŚṬ prioritize consciousness and only secondarily designate sense data as *pratyakṣa*. Having come under fire for his too narrow definition of *pratyakṣa*, the PsP's hypothetical Dignāga goes one step further and also allows for the metaphorical designation of things like pot as *pratyakṣa*. Compare the explanation of the CŚṬ opponents, who present their school's customary view on the matter (CŚṬ$_{Ted}$ 64.1-4): *bum pa ni blos yongs su brtags pa tsam yin pa'i phyir rang gi mtshan nyid du yod pa ma yin la* | *gang la rang gi mtshan nyid yod pa ma yin pa de la ni dngos kyi gnas pas mngon sum nyid mi srid pa 'ba' zhig tu ma zad kyi de la btags pa'i mngon sum nyid kyang mi rung ngo* ‖. Tillemans (CŚṬ$_{tr}$ 176f.) translates, "Because the vase is merely something completely imaginary, it does not exist as a particular character, and whatever lacks a particular character cannot in reality be *pratyakṣa*, not only that but it cannot even be metaphorically designated as *pratyakṣa*." A pot cannot be metaphorically designated *pratyakṣa* because the idea of a pot is nothing but conceptual overlay, superimposed onto the perceived sense data.

Cp. the Yuktidīpikā's explanation (YD 78.13-16) as to why the object of perception may be termed *pratyakṣa*: *āha: yadi tarhi adhyavasāyaḥ pramāṇaṃ kathaṃ laukikaḥ prayogo 'rthavān bhavati pratyakṣaṃ vastv iti* | *ucyate: ... yathā prasthapramito vrīhirāśiḥ prasthaśabdavācyo bhavati* | *evaṃ pratyakṣapramito 'rthaḥ pratyakṣaśabdavācyaḥ syāt* |. Schmithausen (1972: 160f.) translates (following Chakravarti's ed., p. 40.25ff.): "Objection: If 'means of knowledge' (lit.: 'measure') [and therefore also *pratyakṣam*] is [defined as] determination (i.e. activity of the *buddhiḥ*), how [can you explain as] making sense the common usage that a thing is *pratyakṣam*? Answer: Just as a heap of rice which has been measured by a *prastham* (= a certain measure of capacity) is [itself] called a *prastham*, thus an object cognized (lit.: measured) by means of *pratyakṣam* (= direct perception) may [itself] well be called *pratyakṣam* (= directly perceived), [too]."

the mark of the conditioned (*saṃskṛtalakṣaṇa*),[507] it is nothing if not unhappy (*asukha*). When it is designated as "happy," it is [in reality] not at all connected [with happiness], so that (*iti*) metaphorical usage in such a case is appropriate.[508] However, in this [case of] "the pot is *pratyakṣa*," there is of course not an *apratyakṣa* (i.e., imperceptible) [thing] called pot that is apprehended separately (*pṛthak*) [i.e., apart from its *upādāna*], which might, on account of metaphorical usage, be [termed] *pratyakṣa* (i.e., a direct perceptible).[509]

---

[507] PsP Tib reads *'dus byas kyi mtshan nyid kyi rang bzhin yin pa'i phyir* dang | *dka' ba brgya phrag du ma'i rgyu can yin pa'i phyir* for *saṃskṛtalakṣaṇasvabhāvatvād anekaduṣkaraśatahetutvāt*. It is possible that one of the Sanskrit manuscripts relied on by Pa tshab and his *paṇḍita* collaborators contained a *ca* (*°hetutvāc ca*), or they may have added it themselves because they did not think that the mere fact that birth has the nature of a *saṃskṛtalakṣaṇa* was suitable as a ground for it being occasioned by many hundreds of difficulties. I have not emended the Sanskrit because one can still make sense of the sentence without the addition of *ca*. I do, however, in contrast to Seyfort Ruegg and Arnold, accept PsP Tib's understanding of *anekaduṣkaraśata-hetu* as a *bahuvrīhi*, because I am not familiar with *duṣkara* being commonly referred to in texts as the *consequence* of mere birth, and because it is often stated that a bodhisattva on the path must carry out many difficult tasks (*duṣkaracārya*), such as self-sacrifice. Additionally, the reference to birth as the *cause* of many hardships as concerns the birth of a (future) Buddha is problematic. One could, on the other hand, following Seyfort Ruegg's and Arnold's interpretation, possibly consider that with *saṃskṛta* Candrakīrti had in mind *saṃskāraduḥkhatā* and with *anekaduṣkaraśata* was thinking of *duḥkhaduḥkhatā* (on the three-fold *duḥkhatā*, see Schmithausen 1977).
Arnold (2005b: 450) uses the infelicitous but unfortunately ubiquitous translation "compounded" for *saṃskṛta* (*saṃskṛtalakṣaṇasvabhāvatvāt* "which is because of its having as its nature the characteristic of [being] compounded"). *saṃskṛta* is properly translated as "conditioned," not least because atoms, which are certainly not composites, are also included in this category. See n. 325.

[508] *asambaddha*, which I render as "not connected," is translated by Seyfort Ruegg (2002: 122) as "inappropriate" ("Being described as bliss is indeed inappropriate …"); Arnold (2005b: 450) translates it as "incoherent" ("With respect to the sort of object where what is being taught – 'it [i.e., birth] is happiness' – is *incoherent* …"). It is possible that the Sanskrit formulation is somewhat inexact, but grammatically *asambaddha*(*ḥ*) has to refer to *utpāda*, not to what *utpāda* is described as, i.e., *sukha*.

[509] Candrakīrti accepts Dignāga's example illustrating the metaphorical transfer of the designation of an effect to a cause but rejects his explanation of the transfer of the designation *pratyakṣa* to a pot. In the case of the example, the effect, namely, the "happy" state experienced upon liberation from the cycle of birth and death, is applied to the cause, namely, the very unpleasant situation of birth within *saṃsāra*. The cause (i.e., *utpāda*) taken in its primary sense (*mukhyārtha*) is exactly the oppos-

§110. If [Dignāga argues]: Because a pot does not exist separately from blue, etc., [it is] metaphorically *pratyakṣa*.

[Reply:] Even in this way, metaphorical usage is still more (*sutarām*) unreasonable, since there is no basis (*āśraya*) to which it (= the status of being *pratyakṣa*) could be metaphorically applied;[510] for sharpness is not metaphorically applied to the horn of a donkey!

§111. Moreover, pot is part of worldly discourse (*lokavyavahāra*). If [you], considering [a pot] not to exist as [something] separate from blue, etc., postulate that its perceptibility is metaphorical, [then] this being the case, should [it] not [additionally] be supposed, since blue,

---

ite (= *asukha*) of the effect (= *sukha*), and thus metaphorical application sublates the primary meaning of birth in this instance of reference to the birth of Buddhas. On Dignāga's explanation of *pratyakṣa*, to arrive at pot metaphorically designated as *pratyakṣa*, there would have to be two instances of metaphorical designation. First, as he indicates in the first sentence of his objection, *pratyakṣa* in its primary meaning consciousness is applied to consciousness' object, the sense data, namely, blue, etc. (see n. 506). The *pratyakṣa* status received by the sense data, which constitute pot's material cause, is then in a second step transferred to their effect, i.e., their appropriator, the pot. Candrakīrti asserts that to speak of this latter instance as metaphorical designation is misinformed because there is simply no recipient for the transference: contrary to unhappy birth in the world which is able to receive the qualifier "happy," an (existing but) imperceptible pot separate from blue, etc., the imperceptibility of which would be sublated by perceptibility (*pratyakṣatva*), does not exist. See also the explanation in Arnold 2005b: 451, n. 140.
The final Sanskrit sentence in Candrakīrti's PsP response has been simplified by Pa tshab: "... [a thing] called pot that is *apratyakṣa* is also(? *yang*) not apprehended separately ... ." He has turned the negative existence statement into a negative predication; it is unlikely that he and his collaborators had a different Sanskrit text. PsP Tib: *bum pa mngon sum zhes bya ba 'dir ni gang zhig btags nas mngon sum nyid du 'gyur ba bum pa zhes bya ba mngon sum ma yin pa logs shig tu dmigs pa yang ma yin no* ||.

[510] Seyfort Ruegg (2002: 123) translates the reason *upacaryamāṇasyāśrayasyābhāvāt* as "because there exists no base [such as colour] that is transferred." *āśrayasya* refers to pot, not colour, and *upacaryamāṇasya* is its adjectival attribute, taken not in the sense of "which is being metaphorically applied" but rather "to which something is metaphorically applied." Arnold (2005b: 451) translates imprecisely with "since there is no basis which is being figuratively described." Seyfort Ruegg also translates *hi* of the following clause as "indeed" but here it is used in its common sense of indicating a reason.

etc., as well do not exist separately from earth (*pṛthivī*), etc., that the perceptibility of blue, etc., is also metaphorical?[511]

As it is stated [in the Catuḥśataka]:

> Just as a pot does not exist separately from the visible, etc.,
> So does the visible not exist separately from wind, etc.[512]

---

[511] Candrakīrti points out that when Dignāga insists on an analytical approach to surface-level things like pots which takes them as not existing as anything beyond their blue colour, etc., and thus deems them "perceptible" only by way of the metaphorical transfer of the perceptibility of their basis (i.e., the visible blue colour, etc.), consistency demands that Dignāga also regard the blue colour, etc., as only metaphorically perceptible, because the blue colour, etc., like the pot, do not exist as anything different from their basis. This challenges Dignāga's (surface-level) view that sense data, i.e., *svalakṣaṇa*s such as blue colour, really exist and are directly perceptible. He maintains that visual sense data like blue are not conceptual constructions, i.e., not mere designations made in dependence on molecules consisting of the elements and their derivatives, but are visible aggregations of atoms, i.e., aggregations of atoms (structured into molecules) of the elements and their derivatives. See PSV ad I.4cd (Steinkellner 2005: 2): *anekadravyotpādyatvāt tat svāyatane sāmānyaviṣayam uktam, na tu bhinneṣv abhedakalpanāt.* Hypothetical Dignāga's quirky application of metaphorical usage to the result of his misplaced surface-level analysis of pots would thus lead to serious consequences for his system. According to the AK, the things of the world are made up of molecules which are minimally composed of one atom of each of the four elements, viz., earth, water, fire and wind—which within the Buddhist schools are no longer viewed, as in, e.g., the Vaiśeṣika school, as substantial bearers of their qualities, but as qualities themselves, thus solidity, moistness, heat and movement—and one atom of each of the four types of derivative (*bhautika*) matter (previously the qualities "borne" by the primary elements), viz., olfactory, gustatory, visible, and tangible matter. Only aggregates of the molecules are perceived; individual atoms and individual molecules are not visible. See AK I.12, II.22, 65; Frauwallner 1959: 97f.; May 1959: 88, n. 184, 91, n. 189; Tillemans 1990: 251, n. 236; 279, n. 386-7.
Siderits (1981: 150ff.) suggests that Candrakīrti may with his PsP response be "pointing out an inconsistency between PS I.1.4cd and Ālambanaparīkṣā" and showing that the opponent's argument will entail his admitting "what is universally denied, namely that atoms are perceived." I do not think that Candrakīrti intends any of this with his response, especially because he would be aware that the explanation in the PS relies on the Sautrāntika view of atoms and their perceptibility, whereas the Ālambanaparīkṣā argues from a Yogācāra standpoint for the impossibility of the perception of external things.

[512] Candrakīrti is quoting CŚ XIV.15: *rūpādivyatirekeṇa yathā kumbho na vidyate* | *vāyvādivyatirekeṇa tathā rūpaṃ na vidyate* ‖. Cf. Lang 1986: 131. Cited in MABh$_{ed}$

Therefore, because such worldly usage (i.e., *ghataḥ pratyakṣaḥ*) is not included by [your] definition (*lakṣaṇa*), the definition unequivocally has insufficient extension. Of course, from the point of view of an [individual who] knows true reality (*tattvavid*), [it] is not maintained that pot, etc., and blue, etc., are *pratyakṣa*; from the point of view of worldly convention, however, [it] definitely has to be accepted that pot, etc., are *pratyakṣa*.[513]

224.9-11; cf. MABh$_{tr}$ 1911: 274f. Candrakīrti comments on the verse in his CŚṬ (CŚṬ$_{ed}$ 340.11-13) as follows: *rūpādivyatirekeṇa yathā kumbho na siddhaḥ* {|} *evaṃ kumbhaprajñaptyupādānā api rūpādayo vāyvādimahābhūtacatuṣṭayavyatirekeṇa na yujyante* | *nirhetukatvaprasaṅgāt* |. "Just as a pot is not established separately from visible form, etc., so too are visible form, etc., the appropriated bases of the designation pot, not tenable [as things] separate from the four elements, wind and so forth, due to the consequence that [the visible form, etc., would thereby be] without a cause."

[513] Candrakīrti also argues for the world's view of *pratyakṣa* in his CŚṬ, declaring that it is illogical to reject worldly conventions when one is speaking from the worldly point of view. Cf. CŚṬ$_{Ted}$ 67.4-7: *de'i phyir de ltar 'jig rten pa'i tha snyad gnas pa yin* (sic) *dang 'jig rten kho na las bum pa mngon sum mo zhes bya bar brjod par rigs kyi* | *rang bzhin tshol ba'i dus su de nyid rig pas de skad du smra bar 'os pa ma yin te* | *bum pa'i rang gi ngo bo rnam pa thams cad du ma dmigs pa'i phyir ro* ||. Tillemans translates (CŚṬ$_{tr}$ 178): "So then, as there is a worldly convention [for objects being *pratyakṣa*], then just because of the world it is correct to say that a vase is *pratyakṣa*. But should one look for any nature, then he who understands the truth cannot make this type of an assertion, for in no respect is any nature of a vase perceived." Candrakīrti continues by saying that for the world, a pot, visual form, etc., and what is appropriated by the visual form (as *upādāyarūpa*), i.e., aggregations of atomic molecules, are accepted as *pratyakṣa*: *'jig rten pa'i rnam par shes pa la ni bum pa la yang mngon sum yin zhing gzugs la sogs pa dag kyang mngon sum yin la de'i nye bar len pa rnams kyang mngon sum yin pas nyes pa med do* || (CŚṬ$_{Ted}$ 67.7-9); Tillemans translates (CŚṬ$_{tr}$ 178): "For a worldly consciousness vases are *pratyakṣa* (i.e., perceptible), (visual) form and the like are also *pratyakṣa* and the material causes (*nye bar len pa* = *upādāna*) of such [things] are *pratyakṣa* too. Thus there is no fault (here)." Thus Candrakīrti, in contradistinction to the PsP's hypothetical Dignāga, does not maintain that a pot (or visible form) is only metaphorically designated *pratyakṣa*. For Candrakīrti "situated on the side of the world," a pot, as appropriator, exists (cp. the earlier case of Rāhu and pestle), and is as much a perceptible thing as that which it appropriates. At CŚṬ$_{Ted}$ 62.8-16, he explains that even though pots do not ultimately exist, on the worldly level they are held to be established and perceptible: *'byung ba chen po bzhi dang rgyur byas pa'i gzugs bzhi ste* | *rdzas brgyad po de dag la brten nas bum pa 'dogs te* | *ji ltar bud shing la brten*

nas me dang | rtswa dang shing la sogs pa la brten nas khyim dang phung po dag la brten nas bdag tu 'dogs la | de yang rang gi rgyu las rnam pa lngas btsal na ma dmigs pa de bzhin du rang gi rgyu la brten nas sbrang rtsi dang chu dang 'o ma 'chu zhing 'dzin par nus pa mthong ba'i dbang pos go bar bya ba yin pas 'jig rten gyi mngon sum du gyur pa'i bum pa nye bar len pa po nyid du rnam par gzhag gi | ji skad bshad pa'i brten nas btags pa 'di khas ma blangs par rtog pa gzhan gyis bum par rnam par gzhag par nus pa ni ma yin no ||. Tillemans translates (CŚṬ$_{tr}$ 175f.): "The vase is designated in dependence (*brten nas 'dogs pa = upādāya prajñapti*) upon the eight substances (*rdzas = dravya*), i.e. the four elements (*'byung ba chen po = mahābhūta*) and the four [types] of form which depend upon [the elements]. Just as fire is designated in dependence on fuel, houses in dependence upon grass and wood, and the self in dependence upon the aggregrates, but if one searches [for these entities] among their causes by means of the fivefold [reasoning] one will not perceive them, so too a vase, which is something perceptible for the world because it is understood by the sense faculty which sees that it can scoop up honey, water and milk, is established in dependence on its causes as being the appropriator (*nye bar len pa po = upādāt*ṛ) [of the eight substances]. However, rival conceptions, which do not hold that [things] are dependently designated as just explained, are unable to establish [anything] as being a vase."
Cf. also CŚṬ$_{Ted}$ 63.5-10, the last part of Candrakīrti's response to opponents who have argued that things like pots are not perceived separately from visible form, etc., and are thus completely imagined: *de'i phyir bum pa la sogs pa rnams sems dang sems las byung ba lta bu dang | 'byung ba chen po bzhin du rten cing 'brel par 'byung ba 'am brten nas btags par ci ste khas mi len te | de'i phyir bum pa rdzas brgyad kyi nye bar len pa can rang gi nye bar blangs pa'i nye bar len pa por gyur cing nye bar len pa'i bya ba byed pa po 'jig rten gyi mngon sum du gyur pa'i yan lag can de ltar rnam par gnas pa yin dang 'di rnam par dpyad de* |. Tillemans translates (CŚṬ$_{tr}$ 176): "Therefore, why don't they accept that vases, just like the mind and the mental or the elements, are dependent arisings or [in other words] are dependently designated? So the vase, which has the eight substances as substrata, is the appropriator of what it appropriates, and the agent of the action of appropriation (*nye bar len pa'i bya ba*); the whole, which is something perceptible for the world, exists in this manner, [but] should one analyse it … ."

§112. [514]Furthermore, because the word *pratyakṣa* denotes objects that

[514] Antecedent to this sentence, Ms Q and the four paper manuscripts collated attest the introductory words *yathoktaṃ śatake*, which are followed by two verses, namely, CŚ XIII.1 and XIII.2 and a final closing *iti*: (CŚ XIII.1) *sarva eva ghaṭo 'dṛṣṭo rūpe dṛṣṭe hi jāyate | brūyāt kas tattvavin nāma ghaṭaḥ pratyakṣa ity api* || (CŚ XIII.2) *etenaiva vicāreṇa sugandhi madhuraṃ mṛdu | pratiṣedhayitavyāni sarvāṇy uttamabuddhinā* || *iti* (for CŚ XIII.1, cf. $CŚṬ_{Ted}$ 61 and $CŚṬ_{tr}$ 175; Lang 1986: 118; for CŚ XIII.2, cf. $CŚṬ_{Ted}$ 68 and $CŚṬ_{tr}$ 179; Lang 1986: 118f.). PsP Tib attests a translation for the introduction and for both verses, and closes with *zhes bshad do* ||. PsP_L naturally includes the Sanskrit text. Ms P, however, lacks the introduction, both of the verses and the final *iti*. Given that ms Q contains interpolated material that it has passed on to the paper manuscripts and the fact that the Tibetan translation has also incorporated interpolated readings from a manuscript in Q's line (see Stemma), ms P's non-attestation of the verses demands attention. I do not include the two verses in my edition because I am convinced that they were not included by Candrakīrti and rather represent later additions—they were possibly originally marginal notes—made by a scholar studying or teaching this chapter of the PsP. My reasons are as follows. First, it is difficult to explain ms P's non-attestation of the material as due to scribal error, because a hypothesis in this direction is not paleographically supported. I initially wondered if an eyeskip might have occurred from *nā* of *ghaṭādīnām* (last word of the sentence before Q and the paper manuscripts' *yathoktaṃ śatake*) to *nā* of *uttamabuddhinā* (last word of the second CŚ verse), but rejected this idea because ms P does not attest the citation-closing *iti* after *uttamabuddhinā*, which certainly would have been copied if we are merely dealing with an eyeskip. Ms Q and the four paper manuscripts further meld *uttamabuddhinā* and *iti* via *sandhi* to read *uttamabuddhineti* (the coalescing of the final word/compound in a quotation with the closing *iti* is common in the manuscripts), which makes a *nā* to *nā* eyeskip impossible. Second, when one considers Candrakīrti's discussion and the point he is making, it becomes obvious that the two verses simply do not belong in the text. The two verses translate (CŚ XIII.1:) "The entire pot is of course unseen when the visible (*rūpa*) is seen. What knower of reality (*tattvavid*) would also say, 'The pot is perceptible'?" (CŚ XIII.2:) "With this very analysis the fragrant, the sweet, the soft—all [of these]—should be refuted by one of superior intelligence." It is true that Candrakīrti refers to knowers of reality (*tattvavid*) in the prose of the sentence immediately before ms Q's CŚ verses and to the fact that from the vantage point of the ultimate level, on which no things whatsoever exist, pots are naturally not *pratyakṣa*, but this is merely intended as a tipping of the hat to the final viewpoint, for Candrakīrti is by no means interested in instructing Dignāga in ultimate analyses that deny the perceptibility of pots. Throughout the entire previous section he has been pressing home to Dignāga that when he deals with the *saṃvṛti* level, the level of everyday discourse, he has to accept—especially because Dignāga maintains that he *does* accept everyday conceptual and linguistic practice—that pots are *pratyakṣa*. Within this context it would indeed be counterproductive for Candrakīrti to cite

are not beyond the ken of the senses (*aparokṣa*), an object (*artha*) accessible to the sense (*akṣābhimukha*) is *pratyakṣa*. In consideration of [the fact that the compound word *pratyakṣa* is etymologized as] "this [is what] the sense has gone toward" (*pratigatam akṣam asmin*),[515] it becomes established that [objects] not beyond the ken of the senses—pots, blue, and so forth—are *pratyakṣa*.[516] The cognition

---

verses which argue for the *non*-existence of pots. I expect that an individual engaged in studying or teaching the PsP's first chapter copied the two CŚ verses into the margin because the talk of pots and knowers of reality brought them to mind (they would certainly be worthy of a digression in a teaching situation) and that a later scribe assumed that the verses and CŚ ascription belonged to the main text, and thus copied the marginalia into it. The addition of the citation must have occurred sometime before the late eleventh century for it have been attested in one or both of the manuscripts relied upon by Pa tshab and his collaborators. The two CŚ verses were also present in the PsP manuscript relied upon by *LṬ's author given that he comments on the words *madhuram* and *mṛdu*: *madhuram iti rasaḥ* | *mṛdu iti sparśaḥ* | (cf. Yonezawa 2004: 125, 146 [fol. 3a1]).
Candrakīrti explains *api* of CŚ XIII.1's final *pāda* as indicating the inclusion of the blue colour as well as the other substances in the question (cf. CŚṬ$_{Ted}$ 60.16-17 and CŚṬ$_{tr}$ 175). Arnold (2005b: 452) translates CŚ XIII.1 as: "The whole jar, unseen, is present even when only its color is seen." *jāyate* (Arnold's "is present") has instead the meaning "occurs," i.e., the pot occurs as something unseen, i.e., is not seen; Pa tshab renders *adṛṣṭo jāyate* with *mthong mi 'gyur.*

[515] With his presentation of the etymology *pratigatam akṣam asmin* (literally "towards this the sense has gone") Candrakīrti reveals that he endorses the interpretation of the word *pratyakṣa* which considers it to be a *bahuvrīhi*, specifically a *prādi bahuvrīhi*, the more standard dissolution of which would be *pratigatam akṣaṃ yasmin*.
PsP Tib presents *'di la dbang po mngon du phyogs pas* for *pratigatam akṣam asminn iti kṛtvā*. Pa tshab justifiably employs *mngon du phyogs pa* instead of a literal equivalent for *pratigata* because the Tibetan word being etymologized is *mngon sum* (an etymology with *mngon* appearing in it is thus expected). The idea is not—at least not according to the Buddhist conception of sense perception—that the sense literally departs from its *āśraya* and "goes" anywhere, but that the sense has "gone toward" (*pratigata*) the object in that it is "turned toward" it (*mngon du phyogs pa*), i.e., takes the object as its focus.

[516] The view that *pratyakṣa* refers to the object and not to cognition, or only secondarily to cognition, is found in other works. Schmithausen draws attention to the fact that the AS's definition of *pratyakṣa* has to be understood as referring to the object. The AS definition is: *pratyakṣaṃ svasatprakāśābhrānto 'rthaḥ*. Schmithausen (1972: 161) translates, "[The means of proof (*sādhanam*) consisting in] what is directly perceived (*pratyakṣam*) is an object (*arthaḥ*) which is proper [to the

(*jñāna*) that discerns them is [secondarily] designated *pratyakṣa*, because [it] has as its cause the *pratyakṣa* [objects], [just] as a grass [fire] and a chaff fire [have as their respective causes grass and chaff and are accordingly named after them].[517]

---

respective sense-faculty] (*sva-*), [really] existent (*sat-*), manifest (*prakāśa-*), and non-erroneous (*abhrānta-*)." He translates the ASBh's comments as follows (ibid., 159): "In this [definition of *pratyakṣam*], 'its own object' (*svo 'rthaḥ*) is, for example, the visible in the case of the sense of sight. [The attribute] 'real' (*sat-*) is used in order to state that things like pot etc. which in ordinary life are considered to be *pratyakṣa-* are not *pratyakṣa-* [in reality] because they are mere denominations. [The attribute] 'manifest' (*prakāśa-*) is used in order to exclude objects (*viṣaya-*) which are not in the range of sight on account of being hidden or [on account of] any other cause of non-perception. [The attribute] 'non-erroneous' (*abhrānta-*) is used in order to exclude [erroneous objects] like a wheel [manifested by brandishing] a fire-brand, a magical apparition, or a mirage" (ASBh 152.27-30: *tatra svo 'rthas tadyathā cakṣuṣo rūpam* | *sadgrahaṇaṃ ghaṭādidravyāṇāṃ loke pratyakṣasammatānāṃ pratyakṣatva-vyudāsārthaṃ prajñaptimātratvāt* | *prakāśagrahaṇam āvṛtatvādibhir anupalabdhi-kāraṇair anābhāsagataviṣayavyudāsārtham* | *abhrāntagrahaṇam alātacakramāyā-marīcikādivyudāsārtham iti* ||). Schmithausen further records a presentation which associates *pratyakṣa* with the object at Carakasaṃhitā III.8.39: *pratyakṣaṃ nāma tad yad ātmanā pañcendriyaiś ca svayam upalabhyate; tatrātmapratyakṣāḥ sukha-duḥkhecchādveṣādayaḥ, śabdādayas tv indriyapratyakṣāḥ*; he translates (ibid., 160), "*pratyakṣam* (= directly perceived) is that which is perceived by oneself through the soul and the five sense faculties. [Psychical qualities] like pleasure, pain, desire or aversion are directly perceived through the soul; [exterior objects] like sound are *pratyakṣa* (= directly perceived) through the sense faculties." Schmithausen (ibid., 161) notes, "Still more important is the fact that our explanation of the definition of *pratyakṣam* in the AS is also supported by the main source on which the AS is based, viz. the Yogācārabhūmiḥ. This text contains a chapter on the theory of discussion in which (as in the AS which obviously has made use of this chapter) *pratyakṣam* is discussed among the 'means of proof' (*sādhanāni*), and there are at least two passages in which *pratyakṣam* is clearly defined as the <u>object</u> perceived: 1) Y_m 97b4 = $ŚrBh_m$ 2A.8-5f.: *anabhyūhitam anabhyūhyaṃ pratyakṣaṃ katamat? yo grahaṇamātra-prasiddhopalabdhyāśrayo viṣayaḥ, yaś ca viṣayapratiṣṭhitopalabdhyāśrayo viṣayaḥ* and 2) Y_m 98a5 = $ŚrBh_m$ 2B.8-6: *rūpīndriyapratyakṣaṃ katamat? rūpiṇāṃ pañcānām indriyāṇāṃ yo gocaro viṣayaḥ*." He concludes, "Thus, in the AS *pratyakṣam* differs from the other 'means of proof' (*sādhanāni*) in so far as the *object itself* is the means of the proof of its existence or of its special character ... ."

[517] *LṬ's author explains the example of grass and chaff fire by stating that the chaff itself when it is burned is (metaphorically) called "fire": *yathā tuṣa eva dagdho 'gnir ity ucyate* (cf. Yonezawa 2004: 125, 147 [correct his *tu sa* to *tuṣa*] [fol. 3a1]). Arnold (2005b: 453, n. 145) rightly critiques Seyfort Ruegg for having wrongly understood the first three sentences as expressing the view of the opponent, i.e., Dignāga (cf.

§113. The etymology, on the other hand, of the one (= Dignāga) who etymologizes the word *pratyakṣa* as "[cognition that] occurs with regard to the respective senses" (*akṣam akṣaṃ prati vartate*) is not correct,[518] because cognition does not have the sense faculty as object

---

Seyfort Ruegg 2002: 124, n. 231). The first three sentences of the PsP passage are also translated in Siderits 1981: 152, Tillemans 1990: 277, n. 374 and Thakchoe 2010: 107 (the Sanskrit of the PsP passages presented in Thakchoe's footnotes is unreliable).

[518] Dignāga's etymology is attested in his commentary on NM 15. The TSP preserves the Sanskrit of the sentence containing the etymology: *tatrāyaṃ nyāyamukhagranthaḥ yat jñānārtharūpādau* (read: *yaj jñānam arthe rūpādau*) *viśeṣaṇābhidhāyakābhedopacāreṇāvikalpakaṃ tad akṣaṃ akṣaṃ prati vartata iti pratyakṣam* (TSP 456, ad TS *kārikā* 1236; see Tucci 1930: 50 and n. 85; Katsura 1982: 84; Tillemans 1990: 274, n. 367); the Sanskrit (beginning with *yat*) translates: "The cognition in regard to an object such as visible form which is without conceptuality through superimposition of an identity [of the object] with a qualification (*jāti*, etc.) or a denomination is *pratyakṣa*, [etymologized as] '[it] occurs with regard to the respective senses.'" Tillemans' (1990: 274, n. 367) translation from the Chinese of the NM is slightly different. Jinendrabuddhi, commenting on PS I.3c (*pratyakṣaṃ kalpanāpoḍham*) remarks that *pratyakṣa* is a *prādi* compound; he states (cf. Steinkellner et al. 2005: 37): *pratyakṣam ityādi. pratigatam akṣaṃ pratyakṣaṃ prādisamāsaḥ.* Thus for Jinendrabuddhi, and for Dignāga, *pratyakṣa* is a *prādi tatpuruṣa*, with *akṣam* of the *vigraha pratigatam akṣaṃ pratyakṣam* understood as an accusative. The word is placed in the neuter gender because it modifies *jñāna*. Cf. also the grammatical explanation given by Dharmottara in the Nyāyabinduṭīkā as presented and translated in Kajiyama 1998: 29, n. 23.

The view that the compound word *pratyakṣa* is a *prādi tatpuruṣa* is documented in other Indian texts. The Nyāyapraveśa presents the same etymology as Dignāga: *tatra pratyakṣaṃ kalpanāpoḍhaṃ yaj jñānam arthe rūpādau nāmajātyādikalpanārahitaṃ tat | akṣam akṣaṃ prati vartata iti pratyakṣam* (see Tachikawa 1971: 144; Katsura 1982: 84). See also Hattori 1968: 76, n. 1.11. Uddyotakara, like Jinendrabuddhi, explicitly states that *pratyakṣa* is a *prādi tatpuruṣa*. He notes that Pakṣilasvāmin has presented it in the NBh as an *avyayībhāva* (*akṣasyākṣasya prativiṣayaṃ vṛttiḥ pratyakṣam* "the functioning of the respective senses in regard to each object"), but that he has done so only to explain the intent of the *sūtra*, i.e., to indicate the distributive sense intended. But since the genitive *akṣasya* cannot be used in the explanation of an *avyayībhāva* that would end in *akṣam*, Uddyotakara asserts that *pratyakṣa* is properly a *prādisamāsa*, to be analyzed as *pratigatam akṣam* ("gone toward the sense") similar to the *prādisamāsa upaguḥ* "near cows" which is analyzed as *upagato gobhiḥ* "approached by / furnished with cows" (NV 26.15-18: *akṣasyākṣasya prativiṣayaṃ vṛttiḥ pratyakṣam iti | ayaṃ ca sūtravivakṣāyām avyavībhāvaḥ samāsaḥ | anyathā tu vastunirdeśo na samāsaḥ | samāse hi akṣasyeti ṣaṣṭī na śrūyeta | kaḥ punar atra*

(*viṣaya*) and because [cognition] takes as its object the object (*viṣaya*); [thus the word Dignāga uses should not be *pratyakṣa*], but should [instead] be *prativiṣaya* or *pratyartha* [and his corrected etymology should read *viṣayaṃ viṣayaṃ prati vartate* or *artham arthaṃ prati vartate* "(cognition that) occurs with regard to the respective objects"].[519]

§114. But if there were [this objection:] For example, even though consciousness proceeds in dependence on both [the object and the basis (*āśraya*), i.e., the sense],[520] since consciousnesses undergo modification through the modification of those [bases] (*tadvikāravikāritvāt*) on account of the fact that they conform to the sharpness or dullness (*paṭumandatānuvidhānāt*) of the basis (*āśraya*), there is designation only in terms of the basis—[thus the designation] "visual

---

samāsaḥ? prādisamāso 'yaṃ drṣṭavyaḥ pratigatam akṣaṃ pratyakṣam iti yathopagato gobhir upagur iti). For these and other interpretations of the compound *pratyakṣa*, see Sharma 1985.

[519] Candrakīrti rejects Dignāga's *prādi tatpuruṣa* interpretation of the compound *pratyakṣa* on the grounds that its focus is confused and rectification of the mistake would momentously and preposterously require changing the name of this fundamental *pramāṇa* of the Indian schools from *pratyakṣa* to *prativiṣaya* or *pratyartha*.
In the PSV introduction to PS I.4ab, Dignāga has an interlocutor ask the question why *pratyakṣa*, given that it is dependent on both the sense and the object, is not called *prativiṣaya*. Dignāga responds in PS I.4ab that it is named after its specific cause: *atha kasmād dvayādhīnāyām utpattau pratyakṣam ucyate na prativiṣayam* (PS I.4ab:) *asādhāraṇahetutvād akṣais tad vyapadiśyate* | (PSV:) *na tu viṣayai rūpādibhiḥ* (cf. Steinkellner 2005: 2; Hattori 1968: 25f.; 86, n. 1.31 and 87, n. 1.32). Candrakīrti will make reference to this response in Dignāga's next PsP objection.
For partial or complete translations of the paragraph, see Stcherbatsky 1927: 159; Siderits 1981: 152; Tillemans 1990: 277, n. 374; Seyfort Ruegg 2002: 125; Arnold 2005b: 452f.; Thakchoe 2010: 107). Arnold (2005b: 454, n. 149) notes that Seyfort Ruegg's (2002: 125f.) translation of the final part of the sentence as "But let there stand [the expression] *prativiṣayam*, or [the expression] *pratyartham*" indicates that Seyfort Ruegg takes this statement to be Candrakīrti's preferred account. It should be added that Seyfort Ruegg (ibid., 126, n. 234) calls attention to PsP Tib's negative construction *yul so so ba 'am don so so ba nyid ces bya bar ni mi 'gyur ro* ||, possibly because he was disturbed by the Sanskrit as he had interpreted it.

[520] *LṬ's author notes that "both" refers to the sense faculty and the object: *ubhayādhīnendriyaviṣayau* (read: *ubhayādhīnetīndriya°*?) (cf. Yonezawa 2004: 125, 147 [fol. 3a1]).

consciousness."[521] Similarly, even if [it does] occur with regard to the respective objects (*artham arthaṃ prati vartate*), consciousness, which occurs based on the respective senses (*akṣam akṣam āśritya*), will nonetheless be what is called *pratyakṣa* because there is designation in terms of the basis. For it is observed [in the world] that there is designation by way of the specific (*asādhāraṇa*) cause [for example,] kettledrum sound (*bherīśabdo*) [and] barley sprout (*yavāṅkura*), [which are named after their specific causes, not after any of their causes common to other things].[522]

---

[521] The reason why the six consciousnesses are named after their respective senses, and not after their objects, is explained in AK I.45: *tadvikāravikāritvād āśrayāś cakṣurādayaḥ | ato 'sādhāraṇatvāc ca vijñānaṃ tair nirucyate* (AKBh$_{ed}$'s *ato 'sādhāraṇatvād hi* [the ms reading] has been corrected following AKBh$_{Ej}$, which corrects on the basis of AKVy. AKBh 34.25 expects *ca*). Vasubandhu comments (AKBh$_{ed}$ 34.20-22; AKBh$_{Ej}$ 54.21-23; AKBh$_{tr}$ I.96): *cakṣurādīnāṃ hi vikāreṇa tadvijñānānāṃ vikāro bhavaty anugrahopaghātapaṭumandatānuvidhānāt | na tu rūpādīnāṃ vikāreṇa tadvikāraḥ | tasmāt sādhīyas tadadhīnatvāt ta evāśrayā na rūpādayaḥ*. See also AKVy 87.2-17 for a discussion focussed on the compound *anugrahopaghātapaṭumandatānuvidhānāt*, in which it is stated that no matter how clear the object might be, if the visual sense faculty is affected by jaundice, *timira* or old age, the visual consciousness will also be affected. PsP Dignāga's introductory words *ubhayādhīnāyām api vijñānapravṛttau* call to mind his PSV formulation *dvayādhīnāyām utpattau* (lead-in to PS I.4ab) but also remind one of *ubhayādhīnāyāṃ vijñānotpattau* of the AKBh sentence leading into AK I.45ab: *kiṃ punaḥ kāraṇam ubhayādhīnāyāṃ vijñānotpattau cakṣurādaya evāśrayā ucyante na rūpādayaḥ*. The question of why visual consciousness is named after the sense, and not after the object, is inspired by the frequently encountered statement attributed to the historical Buddha that visual consciousness arises in dependence on [both] the visual faculty and visible form (*cakkhuṃ ca paṭicca rūpe ca uppajjati cakkhuviññāṇam*; SN II.72ff., passim). See Hattori 1968: 86, n. 1.31.

Arnold (2005b: 454) takes the two reasons to stand in apposition, the second elucidating the content of the first ("Even given that the functioning of perceptual cognition (*vijñāna*) is dependent upon both [the sense faculty and an object], it is based on conformity with the acuity of the basis (*āśraya*)—i.e., because perceptual cognitions have the quality of changing as that [basis] changes—that there is designation [of the epistemic faculty] precisely in terms of the *basis* [thereof]"), but I understand the first as giving the reason for the second; this interpretation is supported by the AKBh ad AK I.45ab: *cakṣurādīnāṃ hi vikāreṇa tadvijñānānāṃ vikāro bhavaty anugrahopaghātapaṭumandatānuvidhānāt* | (AKBh$_{ed}$ 34.20-21; AKBh$_{Ej}$ 54.21-22).

[522] Candrakīrti's sentence *dṛṣṭo hy asādhāraṇena vyapadeśo bherīśabdo yavāṅkura iti* closely echoes PSV ad PS I.4ab (Steinkellner 2005: 2): *asādhāraṇena ca vyapadeśo*

[Reply:] This [case of *pratyakṣa*] is not the same as the previous [concerning the designation of consciousness]. For there [in the case of consciousness], if consciousness were designated in terms of the

---

dṛṣṭo yathā bherīśabdo yavāṅkura iti (cf. Hattori 1968: 87, n. 1.33; see also Jinendrabuddhi's comments in Steinkellner et al. 2005: 39f.). Dignāga asserts in PS I.4ab that *pratyakṣa* is named after the sense because the sense is its specific cause: *asādhāraṇahetutvād akṣais tad vyapadiśyate* |, explaining in PSV (Steinkellner 2005: 2): *tathā hi viṣayā manovijñānānyasantānikavijñānasādhāraṇāḥ* | *asādhāraṇena ca vyapadeśo dṛṣṭo yathā bherīśabdo yavāṅkura iti* "To explain, objects are common to consciousnesses belonging to the continuum of another [person] and to mental consciousness; and designation by way of the specific [cause] is observed [in everyday life], as [in the cases of] 'kettledrum sound' and 'barley sprout'." The reason **asādhāraṇahetutvāt* is attested also in NM ad 15ab; see Tucci 1930: 50; Hattori 1968: 87, n. 1.32; Katsura 1982: 84; Tillemans 1990: 274, n. 367. The point of reference is AK I.45cd: *ato 'sādhāraṇatvāc ca vijñānaṃ tair nirucyate* and AKBh ad AK I.45cd (AKBh$_{ed}$ 34.27-30; corrected on the basis of AKBh$_{Ej}$ 55.3-6, see AKBh$_{tr}$ I.96): *na hi cakṣur anyasya vijñānasyāśrayībhavitum utsahate* | *rūpaṃ tu manovijñānasyālambanībhavaty anyacakṣurvijñānasyāpīti ... tasmād āśrayabhāvād asādhāraṇatvāc ca vijñānaṃ tair eva nirdiśyate na rūpādibhiḥ* | *yathā bherīśabdo yavāṅkura iti* "For it is not the case that the eye is able to become the base for another consciousness. Visible form, on the other hand, becomes the object support for mental consciousness as well as for another visual consciousness. ... Therefore, due to the existence of the basis and because [the basis] is the specific [cause], consciousness is indicated by way of those [bases], not by way of visual form, etc. [It is] the same as 'kettledrum sound' [and] 'barley sprout' [being named after their respective specific causes]." Yaśomitra explains in the AKVy that one speaks of a "kettledrum sound," not a "stick-sound," because a stick is the instrument for a *paṭaha*-drum, etc., as well; and one speaks of a "barley sprout," not a "field sprout," because a field is the common [cause] also for a rice sprout and a wheat sprout; AKVy 87.24-26: *asādhāraṇatvāt tābhyāṃ bherīyavābhyāṃ yathā nirdeśo loke bherīśabdo yavāṃkura iti na tu daṇḍaśabdaḥ kṣetrāṃkura iti vā* | *daṇḍo hi paṭahādiśabdasyāpi kāraṇībhavet. kṣetraṃ ca śāligodhūmāṃkurasyāpīti sādhāraṇatvāt na tābhyāṃ nirdeśaḥ kriyate* |.

Hattori (1968: 87, n. 1.33) criticizes Candrakīrti for relying on the first reason given in the AK (= AK I.45ab) to explain why consciousness is named after the sense and then inappropriately employing the examples kettledrum sound and barley sprout, the examples used by Dignāga and Vasubandhu in support of the *second* reason (= AK I.45cd). This critique is misplaced. Candrakīrti's Dignāga presents Vasubandhu's explanation (i.e., AK I.45ab) as to why visual consciousness is named after the sense as a point of comparison for the case of *pratyakṣa*. The conclusion in the case of consciousness is that consciousness is designated by way of its basis. This *conclusion* is then applied to the case of *pratyakṣa* (*āśrayeṇa vyapadeśāt*), and the reason Dignāga actually uses in PS (= AK I.45cd), together with its examples, is presented.

The passage is discussed briefly in Siderits 1981: 152f. See also Seyfort Ruegg 2002: 126f. and Arnold 2005b: 454f.

object (*viṣaya*), a differentiation (*bheda*) of the six-fold consciousness (*vijñānaṣaṭka*) could not be indicated by way of [expressions] like "visible-form consciousness" (*rūpavijñāna*), because mental consciousness occurs with regard to the same object as visual consciousness, etc.[523] To explain: When [someone,] with respect to the six-fold consciousness of blue and so forth,[524] utters [the word] "consciousness," an expectant thought arises [in the mind of the hearer, viz.,] "Has this consciousness arisen from a material sense faculty (*rūpīndriyaja*) or is it a mental (*mānasa*) [consciousness]?"[525] However

---

[523] The objects of the senses are also perceived by mental consciousness. Cf. AK I.48a: *pañca bāhyā dvivijñeyāḥ* and its commentary ($AKBh_{ed}$ 36.24-25; $AKBh_{Ej}$ 57.16-20): *rūpaśabdagandharasaspraṣṭavyadhātavo yathāsaṃkhyaṃ cakṣuḥśrotraghrāṇajihvākāyavijñānair anubhūtā manovijñānena vijñāyante | evam ete pratyekaṃ dvābhyāṃ vijñānābhyāṃ vijñeyā bhavanti | śeṣās trayodaśa dhātavaḥ pañcānāṃ vijñānakāyānām aviṣayatvād ekena manovijñānena vijñeyā ity ākhyātaṃ bhavati* (the thirteen *dhātu*s perceived only by *manovijñāna* are the six senses, the six consciousnesses, and the *dharmadhātu*). Candrakīrti accordingly asserts that mental consciousness takes as its object the same object apprehended earlier by the preceding visual, auditory, etc., consciousness; cf. $CŚṬ_{ed}$ 292.10-12: *iha cakṣuḥ pratītya rūpaṃ ca cakṣurvijñānam utpadya nirudhyamānaṃ sahendriyaviṣayair nirudhyate | tasmin niruddhe pūrvadṛṣṭo yo 'rthaḥ sa eva paścān manasā gṛhyate* | (see $CŚṬ_{tr}$ 193). Nagatomi (1979: 253) writes, "*Mano-vijñāna*, as traditionally understood, is capable of cognizing objects that are not amenable to *indriya-jñāna*, and involves emotive and conceptual elements."
mānasapratyakṣa of Dignāga's system is modelled after *manovijñāna* but does not involve conceptuality. *mānasapratyakṣa* is described in PS I.6ab as *akalpaka* and in PSV as *avikalpaka*; PSV ad PS I.6ab (Steinkellner 2005: 3): *mānasam api rūpādiviṣayālambanam avikalpakam anubhavākārapravṛttam* … . Hattori (1968: 27) translates: "The mental [perception] which, taking a thing of color, etc., for its object, occurs in the form of immediate experience (*anubhava*) is also free from conceptual construction …" (see also ibid., 93, n. 1.46). On *mānasapratyakṣa*, see, e.g., Nagatomi 1979; Kobayashi 2010. On later discussions on *mānasapratyakṣa*, see Tillemans 1989 and 1990: 286, n. 428.

[524] The expression *nīlādivijñānaṣaṭke* in the present context is somewhat unusual – one expects *rūpādi°* instead of the much more specific *nīlādi°*. The manuscript readings diverge at this point and I have not been able to come up with a better solution than de La Vallée Poussin's *nīlādivijñānaṣaṭke*.

[525] As stated, the object apprehended by mental consciousness is the object that has been apprehended by the preceding sense consciousness. Were consciousness to be designated in reliance on its object, with the result that consciousness of, e.g., sound and odour would be termed "sound consciousness" and "odour consciousness," not

when there is designation in terms of the basis (*āśraya*), even given the possibility of mental [consciousness] occurring with respect to the object of a visual consciousness, etc., the difference [of the consciousnesses] from each other ends up [clearly] established. But here [in the case of *pratyakṣa*], when [you]—with a view to asserting definitions for the means of valid cognition (*pramāṇalakṣaṇa*)—maintain that only [consciousness] devoid of conceptuality (*kalpanāpoḍha*)[526] is *pratyakṣa*, [then,] because that [sort of consciousness] is admitted [by you] to be different exclusively from conceptual [consciousness] (*vikalpaka*), [we] do not see any point in there being[527] designation in terms of the specific cause [since no ambiguity exists between the two types of consciousnesses which might be clarified thereby].[528]

"auditory consciousness" or "olfactory consciousness," one would not know, upon hearing the assertion "sound consciousness," whether the consciousness indicated would be an auditory consciousness, i.e., one reliant on the auditory sense, or the mental consciousness of a sound initially perceived by the auditory sense.

[526] Candrakīrti refers to Dignāga's definition of *pratyakṣa* as presented in PS I.3c: *pratyakṣaṃ kalpanāpoḍham*. See n. 444.

[527] Arnold (2005b: 456, n. 160) emends *vyapadeśe sati* to *vyapadeśe*, but *sati* occurs in all the manuscripts and the locative absolute makes good sense. De La Vallée Poussin (PsP_L 73, n. 8) is not, as Arnold thinks he is, suggesting that *sati* ought to be dropped; he is simply pointing out that Tib lacks it (it would anyway hardly be expressible in Tibetan). PsP Tib reads *thun mong ma yin pa'i rgyus bstan pa la* for *asādhāraṇakāraṇena vyapadeśe sati*.

[528] Consciousness has the name of its *āśraya* appended to it in order to differentiate a consciousness generated by any of the senses from mental consciousness, which takes as its object the aspect (*ākāra*) of the object apprehended by the specific sense consciousness. In the present situation concerning the etymology of *pratyakṣa*, however, Dignāga's aim is to set forth definitions for the various means of valid cognition, and although this requires distinguishing them from each other, the only distinguishing necessary in the case of *pratyakṣa* is the delineating of it from conceptual consciousness. Thus given that there is no potential overlap with other means of valid cognition, even from the point of view of Dignāga's own system there is absolutely no benefit in or justification for relying on an etymology that connects *pratyakṣa* with the senses instead of objects.
*LṬ's author adds to his comments on the sentence that a delineation from conceptuality is also established by the etymology relied upon by Candrakīrti. He writes (cf. Yonezawa 2004: 125, 147 [fol. 3a2]): *vikalpakāt* (ms: *vikalpyāta*) *sakāśāt* | *tadviśeṣasya pratyakṣasya yo bhedas* [|] *tasya asādhāraṇakāraṇena akṣam akṣaṃ pra*[*ti*] *vartate ity anena* | *pratigatam asminn iti vyutpat*[*t*]*yāpi vikalpād bhedaḥ siddhaḥ* | (in

And given that the occurrence (*pravṛtti*), as regards their number, of means of valid cognition is dependent (*paratantra*) on the objects cognized (*prameya*),[529] and because there is the establishing of the own-form (*svarūpa*) of the [two] means of valid cognition (= *pratyakṣa* and *anumāna*) whose individual existence (*ātmabhāvasattā*) has been reached through nothing but conformity (*anukāritā*) to the [specific] form (*ākāra*) of the [respective] object cognized, designation in terms of sense faculty does not serve anything at all. Thus, designation solely by way of the object is right (*nyāyya*) in every respect.[530]

§115. If [Dignāga objects:] Since the word *pratyakṣa* is generally established in [its] intended meaning in the world, and since "*pratyartha*" is not generally established, [we] resort to an etymology just in terms of the basis.[531]

Reply: It is [true] that this word *pratyakṣa* is generally established in the world.[532] Yet we [unlike you] really use it the way it [is used] in

---

contrast, Yonezawa reads the first word as *vikarṇṇāt* [emended to *vikarṇāt*] and unnecessarily emends *vyutpatyāpi* to *vyutpattiḥ api*).

[529] Cf. PS I.2ab$_1$ (Steinkellner 2005: 1): *pratyakṣam anumānaṃ ca pramāṇe* with PSV ad PS I.2ab$_1$: *te dve eva yasmāt*, and PS I.2b$_2$c$_1$: *lakṣaṇadvayaṃ prameyam*. Arnold's (2005b: 456) translation "function" for *pravṛtti* of *pramāṇasaṅkhyāpravṛttau* ("given that the function and number of reliable warrants") is not acceptable because the function of the *pramāṇa*s is not topical. Stcherbatsky (1927: 161, n. 2) translates, "since the existence of the number of the sources of cognition"; Seyfort Ruegg (2002: 128): "given that the number of *pramāṇa*s operates."

[530] Arnold (2005b: 456, n. 161) notes, "Again, Candrakīrti here accepts, *ex hypothesi*, Dignāga's goals, noting that according to these one ought to want a *nirukti* that etymologizes *pratyakṣa* in terms of its *object*, since the whole point of Dignāga's account is that *pramāṇa* follows/corresponds to *prameya*. But of course, if Candrakīrti wins this concession, then he's well on the way to advancing the trivialization of Dignāga's privileged epistemic faculty."

[531] Dignāga justifies his etymology by arguing that he is merely following common usage: the general populace relies on the word *pratyakṣa*, in full comprehension of its intended meaning, and never uses the word *pratyartha* in its place; there thus is no reason for Candrakīrti to insist that Dignāga should switch to *pratyartha*.

[532] Seyfort Ruegg (2002: 129) translates, "There is this word *pratyakṣa* which is current among ordinary folk in the world … ." *asti* has, however, been placed at the

the world [i.e., we relate the word to the object, not the sense].[533] But since it is etymologized [by you] by setting aside (*tiraskāra*) worldly things as they stand (*yathāsthita*), [you] should also set aside the generally established word [*pratyakṣa*]. And therefore [the word you use] should indeed be *pratyartha*.[534]

---

beginning of the sentence to emphasize the agreement with Dignāga's assertion (thus my "It is [true]"). Arnold (2005b: 457) adds "indeed" to indicate the stress: "This word 'perceptible' is indeed well-known in the world."

533 Arnold (2005b: 457, n. 164) critiques Seyfort Ruegg's (2002: 129) translation of *tu* as "indeed."

534 PsP Tib at this point attests *de'i phyir mngon sum zhes bya ba de ltar mi 'gyur ro* for *tataś ca pratyartham ity eva syāt*, which is found in all six Sanskrit manuscripts used for this part of my edition. Relying on the Tibetan, de La Vallée Poussin emends the reading *pratyartham ity evaṃ syāt* as found in at least one of his manuscripts (he refers to "mss." at PsP_L 74, n. 2; his Cambridge manuscript, my ms L, attests *eva*, and not *evaṃ*) to *pratyakṣam ity evaṃ* [*na*] *syāt*. The reading attested in the Cambridge manuscript and the other manuscripts used for the present edition is preferable. Dignāga has just defended himself by arguing that he retains the word *pratyakṣa* (etymologizing it as *akṣam akṣaṃ prati vartate*)—even though Candrakīrti has pointed out that his etymology ought to be corrected to *artham arthaṃ prati vartate* and that the word he should be using to accommodate the corrected etymology should be *pratyartha*—because the world uses the word *pratyakṣa*, not *pratyartha*. Candrakīrti retorts that since Dignāga intentionally ignores the fact that people understand the word *pratyakṣa* to refer to the object when he etymologizes it, he shouldn't have any qualms about ignoring the word *pratyakṣa* itself, and thus should definitely replace it with *pratyartha*. This is the unwanted conclusion Candrakīrti has been forcing on Dignāga all along and it is certainly expected in the final sentence. The translation yielded by PsP Tib and de La Vallée Poussin's conjectured Sanskrit, viz., "Therefore, there would not in this way be [that called] *pratyakṣa*," robs the concluding sentence of its continuity and its nice punch, and leaves us with the weak and redundant conclusion that the opponent would simply give up using the word *pratyakṣa*. It fails as a response to the opponent's defence focussed on the acceptability of his use of *pratyakṣa* as opposed to *pratyartha*.

The manuscript used by the PsP Tib translators may have read *pratyakṣam* where *pratyartham* originally stood, thus forcing them, like de La Vallée Poussin, to conjecture a *na*, or it may have presented the dittography *eva*(*ṃ*)*va*, the latter *va* of which looked like *na* and caused the translators to emend *pratyartham* to *pratyakṣam*. Siderits (1981: 154), who has been misled by Vaidya's (= PsP_L's) faulty text, notices that the argument as it stands (and as he has interpreted it) is a weak one, and adds to his explanation of the passage the judgement "Candrakīrti is not at his best in this debate over the derivation of 'pratyakṣa'." Both Arnold's (2005b: 457) and Seyfort Ruegg's (2002: 130) translations of the sentence are naturally also based on PsP_L. Mention might additionally be made of Arnold's (2005b: 457) unexpected translation

§116. Additionally, one visual consciousness, which has as [its] support a [single] moment (*kṣana*) of one sense faculty, would not be *pratyakṣa*, because there is not the distribution (*vīpsārtha*) [expected by the word etymologized as *akṣam akṣaṃ prati vartate*]. And when a single [moment of visual consciousness] is not *pratyakṣa*, neither would many [i.e., a continuum of such moments] be [*pratyakṣa*].[535]

---

of the final clause of the previous sentence as "[then] there would also be disregard for the expression 'well-known'!"; he does, however, in a note (ibid., 457, n. 165) provide an alternative translation for the compound *prasiddhaśabdatiraskāraḥ* which is comparable to mine above. Thakchoe (2010: 107) follows Arnold in taking *prasiddha* (*rab tu grags pa*) as the referent of *śabda*.

535 Candrakīrti argues on the basis of the etymology requiring the involvement of more than one sense (*akṣam akṣam*). Cp. the argumentation in CŚṬ (CŚṬ$_{\text{Ted}}$ 64.15-18): *'o na dbang po'i rnam par shes pa skad cig ma gcig ji ltar mngon sum nyid yin* | *de ni dbang po dang dbang po la brten nas 'jug pa ma yin te* | *thun mong ma yin pa'i phyir dang* | *dbang po dang rnam par shes pa'i skad cig dag skyes ma thag tu 'jig pa nyid kyi phyir ro* || "But how is one moment of a sense consciousness *pratyakṣa*? It does not occur in dependence on various senses, because it is specific and because the single moment of [respectively] sense and consciousness perishes as soon as it has arisen" (cf. also CŚṬ$_{\text{tr}}$ 177). The discussion in the CŚṬ continues with the opponent defending the case of one moment of consciousness being *pratyakṣa* by arguing that the atoms making up the sense faculty are individually causes for the consciousness, thereby implying that the distributive meaning contained in *akṣam akṣaṃ prati* should be understood as related to the various atoms of the (single) sense faculty. After rejecting this solution, Candrakīrti considers the opponent's objection that the requirements of the etymology are fulfilled because he maintains that the collection (*tshogs*) of the various consciousnesses occurs in relation to their corresponding sense faculties. He replies: *'di yang yod pa ma yin no* || *gang las she na* | *mig gi rnam par shes pa'i skad cig ma gcig la de ltar bye brag tu bshad pa mi srid pa'i phyir la* | *tshogs pa rdzas su med pa la yang dbang po la brten pa nyid med pa'i phyir ro* (CŚṬ$_{\text{Ted}}$ 66.5-9; see CŚṬ$_{\text{tr}}$ 178).
Candrakīrti's etymology *pratigatam akṣam asmin* is not distributive and is thus not threatened by a focus on only one moment of consciousness.
Seyfort Ruegg (2002: 130) understands Candrakīrti to be arguing that one moment of visual consciousness would not be visible: "And a single eye-cognition having a single moment of the sense-faculty for its sense-base would not [then] possess the condition of being directly perceptible." Arnold (2005b: 458) translates *vīpsārthābhāvāt* as "since there would be no point in repetition" but Candrakīrti intends it as "because there is not the meaning of distribution." Arnold (cf. ibid., 458, n. 167 and 168), considering *vīpsā* in the present context to imply continuity or successiveness, appears to take Candrakīrti to be arguing that Dignāga's etymology is impossible since there cannot be the *successiveness* of the moments of a specific sense (called

§117. And because [you] maintain that only cognition devoid of conceptuality (*kalpanāpoḍha*) is *pratyakṣa*—yet since with that [definition] there is no [reflection of] worldly usage and since worldly usage regarding means of valid cognition and object cognized is supposed to be explained—[your] conception (*kalpanā*) of the means of valid cognition *pratyakṣa* turns out to be absolutely useless (*vyartha*).

§118. And neither is it the case that according to authoritative testimony (*āgama*) only consciousness free of conceptuality is *pratyakṣa*, because in the case of the *āgama* [that you adduce as support for this idea, namely,] "One endowed with visual consciousness cognizes [the object] blue but not '[this is] blue,'"[536] the [discussion] point

---

for, following Arnold, by the etymology's *akṣam akṣam*) when only one moment of consciousness is taken into consideration. It is true that a lack of succession entails when the focus is restricted to one moment of a sense, but Candrakīrti's point is that distribution over more than one sense (as indicated by *akṣam akṣam*)—be it various senses or later moments of the same sense—is not possible when the topic is one moment of a sense consciousness.

[536] The same *āgama* statement is cited by Dignāga in PSV ad PS I.4ab as support for *pratyakṣa* being free of conceptuality (see Steinkellner 2005: 2; Hattori 1968: 26). Dignāga indicates that the statement comes from an Abhidharma treatise. Jinendrabuddhi (cf. Steinkellner et al. 2005: 43) comments on Dignāga's citation as follows: *na kevalaṃ pratyakṣeṇaiva kalpanāpoḍhatvaṃ siddham, api tv āgamenāpīti darśayann āha – abhidharme 'pītyādi. samaṅganaṃ samaṅgaḥ saṅgatir ity arthaḥ. cakṣurvijñānena samaṅgaḥ so 'syāstīti cakṣurvijñānasamaṅgī, cakṣurvijñānena saṅgata iti yāvat. nīlaṃ vijānātīti nīlam arthasvarūpeṇa jānāti, no tu nīlam iti na tan nāmato nīlam etad iti jānāti.* See Hattori 1968: 88, n. 1.36. It is to be noted that for Candrakīrti, the category *āgama* includes canonical Abhidharma works; see too his commentary on MMK I.8 where a quotation from the Prakaraṇa is referred to as *āgama*.
De La Vallée Poussin (AKBh$_{tr}$ I.28, n. 1) notes that the equivalent for *cakṣurvijñānasamaṅgī nīlaṃ jānāti no tu nīlam iti* is found in the Vijñānakāya of the Sarvāstivāda school (see also Frauwaller 1964: 90; Frauwallner 1995: 29 and Muni Jambuvijayaji 1966: 61). Lambert Schmithausen informs me that Hsüan tsang's translation of the Vijñānakāya (cf. T 26:559b27f.) lacks an equivalent for °*samaṅgī*. AKBh on AK III.30cd presents the expanded reading *cakṣurvijñānena nīlaṃ vijānāti no tu <nīlaṃ>*[1] *manovijñānena nīlaṃ vijānāti nīlam iti ca vijānātīti* | [1]re: <nīlaṃ>: the right margin of the manuscript is missing but there is space for (only) two *akṣara*s (AKBh$_{ed}$ 144.3-4; see Pāsādika 1989: 63). The same citation as found in the PSV and PsP is cited by Yaśomitra in the AKVy (AKVy 64.22-23: *cakṣurvijñānasamaṃgī*

'formulation of a definition for *pratyakṣa*' is not topical,[537] and because [this particular *āgama* merely] teaches that the five sense

---

nīlaṃ vijānāti nohati [read with AKVy mss *no tu*] *nīlam iti vacanāt*). One expects a second *iti* in Candrakīrti's text to mark the end of the citation (thus *no tu nīlam ity iti cāgamasya*) but none of the manuscripts attest one; PsP Tib, however, assumes one: *mig gi rnam par shes pa dang ldan pas sngon po shes kyi sngon po'o snyam du ni ma yin no zhes bya ba'i lung*. Hsüan tsang's Vijñānakāya translation has been rendered in a way that suggests that *nīlam* was construed with an *iti* (Vijñānakāya Chinese: "... but it does not cognize 'This is blue'"). Hsüan tsang translates AKBh$_{ed}$ 144.2-4 the same way, i.e., the translation of *no tu nīlaṃ* implies the construal of *nīlaṃ* with a following *iti* (AKBh Chinese: "cognizes blue, [but] does not cognize '[It] is blue'"); cp. the AKBh sentence focussing on *manovijñāna*, where *nīlam iti* expresses the cognitive determination of the object (*manovijñānena nīlaṃ vijānāti nīlam iti ca vijānātīti*). The AKBh's reading *cakṣurvijñānena nīlaṃ vijānāti no tu* <*nīlaṃ*> is strange because the sentence as it stands contradicts itself. Its second *nīlaṃ* might be intended predicatively, but even so one expects, for the sake of clarity, *nīlataḥ* or *nīlatayā*/*nīlatvena*; note the clear opposition *nīlam* / *nīlam iti* when *manovijñāna* is explained. On the other hand, the fact that the AKVy and the PsP manuscripts present only one *iti* after *no tu nīlaṃ* may indicate that this single *iti* was understood as serving a double function, that is, it acts as 1) part of the citation, and 2) the citation marker. The question nevertheless remains open as to whether an *iti* has dropped out in the above cases. *ca* of *iti cāgamasya* is presumably not an error (cp. PsP$_L$ 74, n. 6 where de La Vallée Poussin, noting the missing *iti*, reconstructs PsP Tib's Sanskrit as *nīlam iti* [*sñams du*] *ity āgamasyāpi*) but—standing in second place in the sentence (the citation is a unit)—is rather intended as a sentence-connector; the second *ca* serves to coordinate the two reasons.

The AKVy citation occurs in the context of answering the AKBh question regarding how the five consciousnesses can be without conceptuality (*avikalpika*) if they are *savitarka* and *savicāra* (= introductory sentence to AK I.33ab. See AKBh$_{ed}$ 22.20-22 where it is stated that according to the Vaibhāṣikas, only one of the three types of *vikalpa* applies to the five consciousnesses and therefore, just as a horse with one foot is said to be "without feet," so are the consciousnesses said to be *avikalpika*. Yaśomitra supplies the Sautrāntika view). In the PSV Dignāga continues his citation: *arthe 'rthasaṃjñī, na tv dharmasaṃjñī iti* (not cited by Candrakīrti; see Steinkellner 2005: 2); as Hattori (1968: 88, n. 1.37) notes, "To have *dharma-saṃjñā* in respect to an object means to apprehend the object by its name." Jinendrabuddhi explicates (cf. Steinkellner et al. 2005: 43): *arthe 'rthasañjñīty arthe svarūpasañjñī. na tv arthe dharmasañjñīti nārthe nāmasañjñīty arthaḥ.*

537 The PsP Tib translators have understood *pratyakṣalakṣaṇābhidhānārthasya* of *pratyakṣalakṣaṇābhidhānārthasyāprastutatvāt* as a *bahuvrīhi*: *mngon sum gyi mtshan nyid brjod pa'i don can gyi skabs ma yin pa nyid kyi phyir* ("because it is not a case of [an *āgama*] which has the purpose of stating a definition of *pratyakṣa*") but it may be better understood as a subjective genitive. Seyfort Ruegg (2002: 131), in reliance on the Tibetan *bahuvrīhi* interpretation, translates: "For (i) there is no relevance [here]

consciousnesses [in contradistinction to mental consciousness] are insentient (*jaḍa*) [i.e., are not capable of making the determination "blue"].[538] Thus, this [assigning the status of *pratyakṣa* to non-conceptual consciousness] is not tenable.

§119. Therefore, everything in ordinary life—be it [something] characterized (*lakṣya*) or a characteristic (*lakṣaṇa*), a particular characteristic or a general characteristic (*svasāmānyalakṣaṇa*)—through being directly (*sākṣāt*) apprehended is not beyond the ken of the senses (*aparokṣa*) [and] is thus established as [that which is] *pratyakṣa*, along with the cognition which has that [directly perceived thing] as its object.[539] Yet with respect to the cognition of [persons] without

---

of the Āgama which has the sense expressing the defining characteristic of direct perception." As Arnold (2005b: 459, n. 175) has already pointed out, Candrakīrti's rebuttal as Seyfort Ruegg understands it would fail to effectively counter Dignāga's claim, for it has Candrakīrti accepting that the *āgama* cited does indeed deal with direct perception; he states, "Ruegg tries to salvage Candrakīrti's point by taking the sentence to mean that this passage, though defining 'perception,' is not relevant here." My (and Arnold's) interpretation of this reason reflects Candrakīrti's intent: he is rejecting that the *āgama* used as support for Dignāga's claim that *pratyakṣa* is free of conceptuality has anything at all to do with the topic of *pratyakṣa* — and he is justified in doing so, because both the Vijñānakāya and the AKBh are merely differentiating sense consciousness from mental consciousness. Arnold (ibid.) notes that "Yaśomitra's citation of the passage … recommends Candrakīrti's point; for Yaśomitra adduces the quotation in commenting on the part of Vasubandhu's text that treats the cognitive outputs of the five *non-mental* senses — and the point of the passage is (as Candrakīrti goes on to say) thus to urge simply that the outputs of the five sense faculties are not meaningful until they have become the objects, as well, of the *manovijñāna*. This quotation, as deployed by these Ābhidharmikas, therefore indeed does not state a definition of perception, but instead makes a characteristically Ābhidharmika point about the relationship between the five bodily '*vijñānas*' and the *manovijñāna*."

*LṬ's author explains that the reason *aprastutatvāt* has been used because the *pratyakṣa* free of conceptuality is not a part of everyday practice inasmuch as it is spoken of with respect to the ultimate state: *aprastutatvād iti paramārthāpekṣayoktatvena vyavahārānaṅgatvāt* (cf. Yonezawa 2004: 125, 148 [fol. 3a2]). The point may also be that it is therefore not useful in the framework of everyday practice.

538 *LṬ: *jaḍatveti* | *yathābhūtānavabodhāt* (cf. Yonezawa 2004: 125, 148 [fol. 3a3]).

539 All previous translators of this section only had recourse to PsP_L's faulty reading *yadi lakṣyaṃ yadi vā svalakṣaṇaṃ sāmānyalakṣaṇaṃ vā* for *yadi lakṣyaṃ yadi vā lakṣaṇaṃ svasāmānyalakṣaṇaṃ vā*. PsP Tib has been influenced by the same faulty

the *timira* [disorder], a double moon and so forth are not *pratyakṣa*; however, with respect to [persons] who have *timira*, etc., [the double moon and so forth are] indeed *pratyakṣa*.[540]

---

reading, passed on to it by a manuscript in ms Q's transmission line: *de'i phyir gal te mtshan gzhi 'am rang gi mtshan nyid dam spyi'i mtshan nyid kyang rung ste* |. Seyfort Ruegg's (2002: 131) translation is problematic: "Therefore, for ordinary folk in the world (*loka*), if [as claimed by you, there indeed exists] a *lakṣya*, or if [there indeed exists both] a *svalakṣaṇa* and a *sāmānyalakṣaṇa*, all will in fact be not unamenable to perception (*aparokṣa* = *lkog tu ma gyur pa*), for there will [then] be immediate apprehension (*sākṣād upalabhyamānatvāt*). And [by you] the *pratyakṣa* is accordingly set out systematically (*vyavasthāpyate*) along with the (*vi*)*jñāna* having it for its object." *yadi* in the construction *yadi ... yadi vā* is not a conditional in the sense of "if" (Seyfort Ruegg assumes an implicit *tadā* before *sarvam*) but rather means "whether." The assignment of the part of the sentence commencing with *ataḥ* to Dignāga is unexpected and mistaken, for Candrakīrti is setting forth his own view here, and secondarily designating consciousness as *pratyakṣa*. Stcherbatsky's (1927: 163) translation was much closer to the intended sense: "Therefore from the empirical, (not from the transcendental), point of view, everything without exception is called present, (i.e., a perception), when it is directly perceived (by the senses), whether it be (your strictly) particular essence or the general essence of the thing (possessing both these essences). A perception is thus determined (as meaning) the object of perception together with its cognition." Arnold (2005b: 460), who appears to have been influenced by Siderits' (1981: 155) translation takes the first *yadi* in a conditional sense and construes it with *ataḥ*; he translates "Therefore, in the world, if *any* (*sarvam eva*) subject of characterization (*lakṣya*) — whether it be a *svalakṣaṇa* or a *sāmānyalakṣaṇa* — is visible, because of being directly apprehended, then it is established as perceptible, along with the cognition that has it as its object [which is derivatively called *pratyakṣa*]." Although Arnold has in part been misled by PsP_L's faulty text, his classification of *svalakṣaṇa* and *sāmānyalakṣaṇa* as subcategories of *lakṣya* (verging on Dignāga's presentation! [see *LṬ]) would certainly be rejected by Candrakīrti.

*LṬ's author also errs in his interpretation of the sentence, identifying, like Siderits and Arnold, *svalakṣaṇam* and *sāmānyalakṣaṇam* as subtypes of *lakṣyam*. I suspect that his PsP exemplar had been influenced by the reading *yadi lakṣyaṃ yadi vā svalakṣaṇaṃ sāmānyalakṣaṇaṃ vā* which appears in ms Q: *lakṣ*[*y*]*am iti* | *prameyaṃ tac ca svalakṣaṇaṃ* | *sāmānyalakṣaṇam vā* (cf. Yonezawa 2004: 125, 148 [fol. 3a3]).

[540] Candrakīrti sums up his discussion on *pratyakṣa* by reiterating his own view on this important *pramāṇa*: *pratyakṣa* is properly the *thing* that is apprehended; the object itself is the means of knowledge and the establisher of its existence and characteristics. The consciousness that apprehends the *pratyakṣa* is only secondarily, in reliance on the actual *pramāṇa*, i.e., the object, designated *pratyakṣa*. Further, even though everything that is directly apprehended can be classified as *pratyakṣa*, a certain thing's being determined as such depends on the individual apprehending it.

§120. In contrast, the cognition whose object is beyond the ken of the senses [and] which has arisen from a sign (*liṅga*) that does not deviate from the probandum is inference (*anumāna*).[541]

Thus even objects like the imaginary flies, hairs and double moon seen by persons afflicted by the *timira* visual disorder, though not *pratyakṣa* for someone not visually impaired, cannot be denied their place in the *pratyakṣa* category.
Cp. Candrakīrti's closing comments from his attack on the Epistemologist in the CŚṬ: *gang yang 'dis dbang po'i rnam par shes pa 'di mngon sum nyid du sgro btags nas gzhan tshad ma nyid du rtog par byed* (read, following P: *byed pa*) *de yang ches shin tu ma 'brel pa zhig go* ‖ *mi slu ba'i shes pa ni 'jig rten na tshad ma nyid du mthong na rnam par shes pa yang bcom ldan 'das kyis 'dus byas yin pa'i phyir brdzun pa bslu ba'i chos can dang sgyu ma lta bur gsungs so* ‖ *gang zhig brdzun pa bslu ba'i chos can dang sgyu ma lta bu yin pa de ni mi bslu ba ma yin te* | *rnam pa gzhan du gnas pa'i dngos po la rnam pa gzhan du snang ba'i phyir ro* ‖ *de lta bur gyur pa ni tshad ma nyid du brtag par rigs pa ma yin te* | *rnam par shes pa thams cad kyang tshad ma nyid du thal bar 'gyur ba'i phyir ro* ‖ (CŚṬ$_{\text{Ted}}$ 67.10-17). "And also this [opponent's] conception that this sense consciousness is another means of valid cognition—[the consciousness] having wrongly had [the status of] *pratyakṣa* attributed to it—is extremely incoherent." (my translation; Tillemans translates the sentence as: "He who fabricates the notion that this sense consciousness is *pratyakṣa* and then also imagines that it is a means of valid cognition (*tshad ma* = *pramāṇa*) is completely beside the point," but Candrakīrti is not characterizing the opponent himself as "beside the point." Continuing on with Tillemans' translation:) "While a nonbelying (*mi slu ba* = *avisaṃvādin*) consciousness is regarded as being a *pramāṇa* in the world, the Illustrious One said that consciousness, since it is conditioned (*'dus byas* = *saṃskṛta*), is false and deceptive and is like an illusion (*sgyu ma* = *māyā*). Whatever is false and deceptive and is like an illusion is not non-belying, for it is an entity which exists in one way and appears in another. Something like that should not be imagined to be a *pramāṇa* in that [if it were] it would follow that every consciousness would also have to be a *pramāṇa*" (CŚṬ$_{\text{tr}}$ 179).
Seyfort Ruegg (2002: 132) understands the entire PsP paragraph as continuing the critique of Dignāga (see also the previous note) and thus translates his final sentence as: "However, [following your doctrine,] in respect [even] to those who are affected by eye-disease and the like (*taimirikādyapekṣayā*) there will indeed be direct perceptibility."

[541] Most modern scholars assert at this point that Candrakīrti accepts the *pramāṇa*s inference, authoritative testimony and comparison as posited by the Nyāya school; cf., e.g., Stcherbatsky 1927: 163, n. 6; Siderits 1981: 156; 2011: 172 and n. 12. Arnold (2005a: 182) asserts, "Having thus argued that his interlocutor's account of *pratyakṣa* contradicts the conventional usage, Candrakīrti effectively states—by endorsing (with typically Naiyāyika definitions) the list of *pramāṇa*s admitted by Naiyāyikas—that the epistemology of the Brahmanical Nyāya school better describes our epistemic practices as they are conventionally understood." Although the Nyāya

school does accept these three *pramāṇa*s, I am not convinced that Candrakīrti intends to directly endorse the Naiyāyika presentation, or that he is necessarily paraphrasing the definitions asserted by that school. The definition he provides for inference, i.e., *parokṣaviṣayaṃ jñānaṃ sādhyāvyabhicārilingotpannam anumānam*, bears no resemblance to the older definition *atha tatpūrvakaṃ trividham anumānaṃ pūrvavaccheṣavatsāmānyatodṛṣṭaṃ ca* given at NS I.1.5, and it would be a stretch to consider it to represent a paraphrase or extremely abbreviated version of the explanation given by Pakṣilasvāmin in his commentary on NS I.1.5: *tatpūrvakam ity anena liṅgaliṅginoḥ sambandhadarśanam liṅgadarśanaṃ cābhisambadhyate. liṅgaliṅginoḥ sambaddhayor darśanena liṅgasmṛtir abhisambadhyate. smṛtyā liṅgadarśanena cāpratyakṣo 'rtho 'numīyate* (NBh 12.4-6; translated in Oberhammer 1991: 48; see also Junankar 1978: 117). A characterization offered by Uddyotakara, namely, *(bhavatu vāyam artho) laiṅgikī pratipattir anumānam* (NV 26.21-27.1) is, in its brevity and with its reference to a subjective act and a sign (although here the subjective act is not explicitly presented as resulting from the sign), somewhat closer, but this explanation makes no reference to the fact that the *liṅga*, i.e., the *hetu*, must not deviate from the *sādhya*, i.e., must be absent from dissimilar cases, nor does it make reference to a *parokṣa* object. As regards the next *pramāṇa* presented here in the PsP, namely, *āgama*, the definition set forth by Candrakīrti appears to be structured to present *āgama* as conveying information solely about objects / states of affairs out of the range of the senses. NS I.1.8, on the other hand, states that *śabda* is of two kinds (note the difference in terminology; Uddyotakara, however, employs the word *āgama* as a synonym for *śabda* in his commentary on this *sūtra*): relating to seen things and to unseen things (NS I.1.8: *sa dvividho dṛṣṭādṛṣṭārthatvāt*). Pakṣilasvāmin explains that seen and unseen things refer to things perceived respectively in this world and in the next; accordingly, he states, there is a division of the statements of worldlings and *ṛṣi*s. In his comments on NS I.1.7 (*āptopadeśaḥ śabdaḥ*), Pakṣilasvāmin counts *ṛṣi*s, *ārya*s and even *mleccha*s as persons who may have the characteristic of reliability (*āpti*), the characteristic required for them to be termed *āpta*s (cf. NBh 14.4-5; Oberhammer 1991: 119). That he considers the statements of ordinary persons who have gained their knowledge of the things they describe by ordinary means to be a valid form of *śabda* is clear from a later statement: *loke ca bhūyān upadeśāśrayo vyavahāraḥ. laukikasyāpy upadeṣṭur upadeṣṭavyārthajñānena parānujighṛkṣayā yathābhūtārthacikhyāpayiṣayā ca prāmāṇyam, tatparigrahāc cāptopadeśaḥ pramāṇam iti* (NBh 97.12-14). Translated in Oberhammer 1991 (119f.): "Auch im normalen Weltgeschehen basiert der Umgang [der Menschen miteinander] meist auf Mitteilungen [durch Glaubwürdige]. Die Massgeblichkeit eines, der im alltäglichen Leben etwas mitteilt, ergibt sich [ebenso wie beim nicht profanen Lehrer] dadurch, dass er das, was er mitteilen will, [selbst] erkannt hat, dadurch, dass er [sein Wissen] mit dem anderen teilen möchte und dadurch, dass er die Sache so darzulegen wünscht, wie sie wirklich ist. Die Mitteilung eines [profanen] Glaubwürdigen ist [daher ebenfalls] Erkenntnismittel, weil [sie] das umfasst." Uddyotakara, in his refutation of the claim that *śabda* as described in NS I.1.7 can be classified, depending on how the *sūtra* is interpreted, as either *pratyakṣa* or *anumāna* and thus should not be

§121. The statement (*vacana*) of persons of authority (*āpta*) who know directly objects / states of affairs out of the range of the sense faculties (*atīndriya*) is authoritative testimony (*āgama*).

---

considered as another *pramāṇa*, describes *śabda* as relating to objects both connected and not connected with the sense faculties (*nāyaṃ sūtrārthaḥ āptopadeśaḥ śabda iti api tv indriyasaṃbaddhāsaṃbaddheṣv artheṣu yā śabdollekhena pratipattiḥ sā āgamasyārthaḥ* | [NV 57.6-8]). Finally, the definition Candrakīrti gives for the fourth *pramāṇa upamāna* (presented in the NS as the third *pramāṇa*, *śabda* is given as the fourth), namely, *sādṛśyād ananubhūtārthādhigama upamānaṃ gaur iva gavaya iti yathā*, also cannot accurately be called a paraphrase of *prasiddhasādharmyāt sādhyasādhanam upamānam* (NS I.1.6). Even though it contains the same example that Pakṣilasvāmin provides, Candrakīrti's definition markedly differs from Pakṣilasvāmin's explanation of the NS definition, namely, *prajñātena sāmānyāt prajñāpanīyasya prajñāpanam upamānam iti* | *yathā gaur evaṃ gavaya iti* | (NBh 13.11-12). On *upamāna*, see, e.g., Oberhammer 1996: 43-49.
Although conclusive evidence is lacking, I am inclined to think that, similar to the case of *pratyakṣa* for which we can assume that Candrakīrti draws on a Buddhist source for his explanation of it (see n. 516), Candrakīrti has taken over the definitions of *anumāna*, *āgama* and *upamāna* he cites or paraphrases here from Buddhist materials. We know from the *Upāyahṛdaya (the extant Chinese version was translated in 472 CE; an earlier translation is lost) that the four *pramāṇa*s **pratyakṣa*, **anumāna*, **āgama/śabda/āptaśruti* and **upamāna* were indeed posited within the Buddhist fold (cf. Kajiyama 1991: 109; Nagasaki 1991: 221); the older *Upāyahṛdaya definitions, however, differ from those set forth by Candrakīrti; see Tucci 1981: 13f. (Sanskrit reconstruction). The Kuṣāṇa-period Spitzer manuscript investigated by Eli Franco also strongly suggests the admission of four *pramāṇa*s on the part of some Buddhists. Franco (2010: 121) writes, "As far as I know, this manuscript is the only Sanskrit source that testifies to the fact that certain Buddhists, probably affiliated to the Sarvāstivāda school, accepted a theory of four *pramāṇa*s. It confirms thereby the testimony of *Upāyahṛdaya/*Prayogasāra which is available only in Chinese translation." The Spitzer manuscript's discussion about *pratyakṣa* is lost, but fragments of the discussion on inference (*anumāna*) have been preserved (Franco assumes that the *pratyakṣa* discussion preceded it). A discussion on comparison or analogy (*aupamya*) follows the consideration of inference. Franco presumes that a discussion on verbal testimony (possibly *aitihya*) closed the presentation of the *pramāṇa*s. He (ibid., 126) notes: "The sequence of the discussion is significant because it shows that the exposition followed the same tradition as that of the Nyāyasūtra and the *Upāyahṛdaya as opposed to the one followed in the Carakasaṃhitā, where comparison and verbal testimony are discussed in reverse order. However, in terminology the discussion follows the same tradition as that of the Carakasaṃhitā, and uses the terms *aupamya* and, possibly, *aitihya* rather than *upamāna* and *śabda*." See Eltschinger 2010: 48, n. 79 for comments on the varying number of *pramāṇa*s in the Buddhist tradition. Future research may shed more light on the matter as it relates to Candrakīrti and his sources.

§122. The apprehension of an object not [previously] experienced [that comes about] due to similarity (*sādṛśya*) [with another object] is comparison (*upamāna*), as [when one has been told] "a gavaya is like a gaur."[542]

§123. Thus the world's apprehension of objects is in this way established as being from the four-fold means of valid cognition. And those [means of valid cognition and their objects] are established in reliance on each other.[543] Therefore, just let worldly [things] be, the way [they are] observed.

---

[542] A gayal (Skt. *gavaya*; *Bos gaurus frontalis*) is often referred to as a subspecies of the gaur (*Bos gaurus*: a type of wild ox, also referred to as Indian bison), and is thought to be the result of the interbreeding of gaur and domestic cattle. Gayals are smaller than the gaur and are without the gaur's massive shoulder hump. Both have horns and dewlaps (cf. International Wildlife Encylopedia, Third Edition, New York: Marshall Cavendish Corporation, 2002, pp. 936ff.). As Seyfort Ruegg (2002: 133, n. 258) notes, the example comparing a gayal to a gaur is found already in Patañjali's Mahābhāṣya II.i.55. Franco (2001: 10) reports that the example also appears in the discussion of the *pramāṇa aupamya* (= *upamāna*) in the Buddhist Kuṣāṇa-period Spitzer manuscript.

[543] Two sentences have been written in Ms Q's lower margin (presumably by the same scribe as that of the main text) and are marked to be inserted after *tāni ca parasparāpekṣayā sidhyanti*, viz., *satsu pramāṇeṣu prameyārthāḥ satsu prameyeṣu pramāṇāni* | *no tu khalu svāṅgavikī* (read: *svābhāvikī*) *pramāṇaprameyayoḥ siddhir iti* "When the means of valid cognition exist, the objects cognized (*prameyārtha*) [exist]; when the objects cognized exist, the means of valid cognition [exist]. But there is absolutely not establishment by way of own-being (*svābhāvika*) of the means of valid cognition and what is cognized." The four paper manuscripts (B, D, J, L) attest (with minor variants) both of the sentences and also include the word *artheṣu* after *prameyeṣu*. PsP Tib attests the Tibetan translation of the two sentences: *tshad ma dag yod na gzhal bya'i don dag tu 'gyur la* | *gzhal bya'i don dag yod na tshad ma dag tu 'gyur gyi* | *tshad ma dang gzhal bya gnyis ngo bo nyid kyis grub pa ni yod pa ma yin no* ‖. De La Vallée Poussin includes, along with ms L's *artheṣu*, the two sentences in PsP_L. Ms P, however, does not attest either of the sentences. The PsP exemplar relied upon by *LṬ's author also seems not to have attested the sentences, because *LṬ's author misunderstands *tāni* ("those") to refer only to the means of valid cognition (*tānīti pramāṇāni*; cf. Yonezawa 2004: 125, 148 [fol. 3a3]). Had the sentences been attested by his PsP exemplar he would surely have understood that the mutual dependence intended is between the *pramāṇa*s and the *prameya*s, and not nonsensically beween the individual *pramāṇa*s (even if one assumes that Candrakīrti intends the *pramāṇa pratyakṣa* as the object, and not the consciousness, a coherent presentation of the mutual dependency of the *pramāṇa*s is still impossible).

I doubt that the two sentences were originally part of Q's text; that is, I think it quite unlikely that they were in the main text of Q's exemplar and accidentally overlooked by Q's scribe during the process of copying, but then added in the margin when the scribe noticed his mistake. One might attempt to explain the fact that exactly the same two sentences are missing from the main text of both ms P and ms Q by conjecturing that ms P's and ms Q's scribes dropped precisely the same textual material owing to an eyeskip from *nti* of *sidhyanti* to *ti* of *iti*, but this hypothesis is somewhat weakened by the fact that *nt* and *t* do not resemble each other. The sentences become more suspicious when their content and the argumentative flow of the PsP are taken into consideration. The sentence *satsu pramāṇeṣu prameyārthāḥ satsu prameyeṣu pramāṇāni* indeed spells out what is meant by *tāni ca parasparāpekṣayā sidhyanti*, but this information is certainly not necessary for understanding the sentence *tāni ca parasparāpekṣayā sidhyanti*, especially because both *pramāṇa*s and objects were just mentioned in the previous sentence. Candrakīrti's immediate reading audience would have been familiar with the Madhyamaka presentation of the surface-level mutual establishment of things like *lakṣya* and *lakṣaṇa* (just discussed in the PsP), *kāraṇa* and *kārya*, etc., and would also have been acquainted with the VV's *pramāṇa* and *prameya* discussion inclusive of—even though the aim there is to refute ultimate establishment—its references to the mutual reliance of the *pramāṇa*s and *prameya*s (cf. VV 46-56), and would thus not have required further clarification. The second sentence *no tu khalu svābhāvikī pramāṇaprameyayoḥ siddhir iti*, in calling attention to the ultimate nature of the *pramāṇa*s and *prameya*s, further seems quite unnecessary, and almost intrusive in the present worldly-focussed context; note that the connecting and final sentence *tasmāl laukikam evāstu yathādṛṣṭam* follows much more smoothly after *tāni ca parasparāpekṣayā sidhyanti* than it does after *no tu khalu svābhāvikī pramāṇaprameyayoḥ siddhir*. Thus, given the above and our knowledge about ms Q's contamination, not least the fact that it has been possible to demonstrate that a number of the readings written in its margins have been appropriated from the contaminated manuscript ms θ, I am convinced that the sentences *satsu pramāṇeṣu prameyārthāḥ satsu prameyeṣu pramāṇāni* | *no tu khalu svāṅgavikī* (read: *svābhāvikī*) *pramāṇaprameyayoḥ siddhir iti* are foreign to the PsP. A teacher or educated scribe or reader must have added them, presumably in the margins, as clarificatory information, perhaps because a student or the reader himself stumbled just as *LṬ's author did, erroneously thinking that *tāni* of *tāni ca parasparāpekṣayā sidhyanti* referred only to the *pramāṇa*s. The fact that PsP Tib attests a translation for the sentences shows that the foreign material had made its way into ms γ's line sometime before the late eleventh century. Although the paper manuscripts received the two sentences via ms δ, the sentences were probably not passed on to ms η from ms δ because had this happened they would have been incorporated into the main text of Q's exemplar (ms η or a descendant of η), and would thus have been directly copied by Q's scribe into Q's main text, and not set in the margin. It thus seems reasonable to assume that Q's scribe added the marginal material when he checked Q against ms θ.

Enough of this digression. We shall focus our explanation on the primary subject matter.[544]

It may be worth mentioning that even though Candrakīrti emphasized in the preceding discussion with Dignāga that the *pramāṇa pratyakṣa* is the *object*, and that the consciousness apprehending the *pratyakṣa*-object is only secondarily designated *pratyakṣa*, in the present paragraph, in—and for the sake of—describing the mutual reliance of the *pramāṇa*s and their *prameya*s, he appears to intend the *pramāṇa pratyakṣa* in its secondary meaning of consciousness.

[544] Following the sentence closing the discussion with Dignāga (*alaṃ prasaṅgena prastutam eva vyākhyāsyāmaḥ*), all of the manuscripts present the sentence *laukika eva darśane sthitvā buddhānāṃ bhagavatāṃ dharmadeśanā* ("The Buddhas, the Exalted Ones, teach the norm(s) [of conduct] (*dharma*) by situating themselves in (i.e., starting from) the view of ordinary life/people"). The sentence has been included in PsP_L. Ms P continues with an unidentified BHS verse composed in *dodhaka* metre (for P's unemended reading, see PsP_M): *et' upamābhi nidarśanā vakṣye kin tu na teṣā samo iha kaścit* | *paṇḍitavijñajanā...* ("This has been taught by way of similes: I say, [or: I will explain this which has been taught by way of similes:] but there is not someone in this world equal to them ..."); unfortunately, the leaf breaks off after *paṇḍitavijñajanā* (P's text for the final third of the leaf is thus unavailable). Ms P's text resumes at the beginning of the next line of writing with a *pāthya śloka* that can be identified as verse 37 of Mātṛceṭa's Prasādapratibhodbhava (= Śātapañcāśatka = Adhyarddhaśataka; see Shackleton Bailey 1951: 61; see also Hartmann 1987: 23ff.): *ajñānatimiraghnasya jñānālokasya te mune* | *na ravir viṣaye bhūmiṃ khadyotīm api vindatītyādi* || (all but the first two *akṣara*s, i.e., *ajñā*, are attested in ms P; the vowel-marker *u* in *mune* is missing. Shackleton Bailey emends *khadyotīm* to *khādyotīm*). Shackleton Bailey (ibid., 159) translates, "Before the light of your knowledge, O Sage, which destroys the darkness of ignorance, the sun does not even attain the level of a firefly." That the PsP exemplar used by *LṬ's author contained at least the first verse can be ascertained by *LṬ's citation and gloss of some of its words. *LṬ: *etat*[*] *upamayābhi darśitaṃ teṣāṃ buddhānāṃ samo na kaścid asti yo jānāti* | (cf. Yonezawa 2004: 125, 148 [fol. 3a3]; Yonezawa reads *samo* as *satya*). The word he glosses next is *tāni*, which begins the paragraph asserting the mutual dependence of the *pramāṇa*s and their *prameya*s; all the PsP manuscripts used for my edition place the sentence *laukika eva darśane sthitvā buddhānāṃ bhagavatāṃ dharmadeśanā* after the closing statement announcing the return to the main subject matter, i.e., the explanation of MMK I. But this placement of the *laukika eva darśane sthitvā buddhānāṃ bhagavatāṃ dharmadeśanā* sentence after the announcement of the resumption of the main subject matter makes little sense, given that it provides support for the idea that things on the *saṃvṛti* level should be accepted as ordinary people maintain them to be, which was the topic in the *pramāṇa* discussion. This problem with the location of the sentence, together with the fact that the PsP exemplar used by *LṬ's author seems to have had the sentence *laukika eva darśane sthitvā buddhānāṃ bhagavatāṃ dharmadeśanā* and at least one of the verses found in ms P *before* the sentences asserting the mutual dependence of the *pramāṇa*s and

§124. Here, [some] belonging to [our] own group (= fellow Buddhists) (*svayūthya*)[545] say: This which has been stated, [namely,] "Things do not arise from self,"[546] is correct, because arising from self is pointless. And what is also stated, [namely,] "[Things do] not [arise] from both [self and other]" is correct, because of the ruin (*hāni*) of one part (i.e., arising from self has been rejected). On the other hand, the thesis [that things arise] without a cause (*ahetupakṣa*) is completely base; thus its refutation as well is appropriate.[547] But as a matter of fact[548] this statement, [namely,] "Nor [do things arise]

prameyas—also an inappropriate placement—leads one to think that the *laukika eva darśane sthitvā buddhānāṃ bhagavatāṃ dharmadeśanā* sentence, and the verses in ms P and *LṬ's PsP exemplar, quite possibly represent marginalia that were brought into the main PsP text by different scribes, one deeming that the sentence belonged after the *pramāṇa*-discussion section, another determining that it should be placed before the sentences on mutual dependency, one deciding to include the verses, the other to leave them in the margin. The complete absence of the *laukika eva darśane sthitvā buddhānāṃ bhagavatāṃ dharmadeśanā* sentence and of the verses in PsP Tib indicates that they were not attested in either of the manuscripts used by Pa tshab and his Indian collaborators, and thus renders them even more suspicious. I have therefore not included them in my edition.

545 Bhāviveka likewise identifies the speakers of MMK I.2 and its PP introduction as **svayūthyāḥ* (*rang gi sde pa dag*). Avalokitavrata identifies these fellow Buddhists as "all the Śrāvakas, Sautrāntikas, Vaibhāṣikas and so forth" (*nyan thos mdo sde pa dang bye brag tu smras ba la sogs pa thams cad* [PPṬ D 156b1-2; P 180a5-6]).

546 The reference here, as with the following *na dvābhyām*, *ahetu(pakṣas tu ekāntanikṛṣṭaḥ)* and *nāpi parataḥ* is, of course, to the negated alternatives of MMK I.1.

547 Candrakīrti has formulated his MMK I.2 introduction along the lines of Buddhapālita's introduction to the same *kārikā*: *dngos po rnams bdag las skye ba med de | 'di ltar myu gu de nyid myu gu de nyid las ji ltar skye zhes bshad pa gang yin pa dang | bdag las skye ba med na bdag dang gzhan gnyis las skye ba de yang mi rigs te | phyogs gcig nyams pa'i phyir ro zhes bya ba dang | 'di ltar rgyu med pa las skye'o zhes bya ba'i phyogs de ni tha chad yin pas de dag ni re zhig khas mi len to* (BP_{ed} 11.3-7).

548 It is sometimes difficult to find a single English word that is able to capture the meaning of certain Sanskrit particles. I understand *khalu* in the present context to mean something like "now pay attention / now we come to the actual problem" and thus translate it as above.

from other," is incorrect, because the Exalted One has taught that precisely *others* produce things.[549]

[MMK I.2]

> There are four conditions (*pratyaya*): the cause [condition] (*hetu*), the object [condition] (*ārambaṇa*),[550] the immediately preceding [condition] (*anantara*)
> And similarly, the dominant [condition] (*ādhipateya*).[551] There is not a fifth condition.[552]

---

[549] Cp. with Candrakīrti's PsP introduction to MMK I.2 the argument for arising from other in the MABh where the opponent, citing from scripture, states: *'di ltar gzhan du 'gyur ba'i* ($MABh_{UN}$: *gyur pa'i*) *rkyen bzhi po rgyu dang dmigs pa dang de ma thag pa dang de bzhin du bdag po ste | rkyen rnams dngos po rnams kyi skyed par byed pa'o ||* ($MABh_{UN}$: without ||) *zhes bya ba'i gsung rab la bltos* ($MABh_{UN}$: *ltos*) *nas mi 'dod pa bzhin du yang gzhan las skye bar khas blang bar bya'o ||* ($MABh_{ed}$ 87.19-88.3).

[550] The manuscripts consistently read *ārambaṇa*, not *ālambana*. Cf. BHSD s.v. *ārambaṇa*. I therefore retain the manuscripts' readings (see also de Jong 1978: 35 [referring to PsP_L 76.5]) but sometimes use the designation *ālambana* in my notes, especially when citing from other text editions which attest this spelling.

[551] De La Vallée Poussin (PsP_L 87, n. 2, see also 76, n. 7) spells *ādhipateya* as *adhipateya*, noting that Bendall states that it is "a Palicism not hitherto noted in Sanskrit"; the spelling *adhipateya* has been adopted by various other scholars (cf., e.g., Oetke 2001a: 54, n. 30; 55). See, however, BHSD s.v. *ādhipateya*.

[552] Candrakīrti cites MMK I.2: *catvāraḥ pratyayā hetur ārambaṇam anantaram | tathaivādhipateyaṃ ca pratyayo nāsti pañcamaḥ ||* (intentionally presented in Ye 2011a as MMK I.3; see infra. n. 560). The author of the Akutobhayā attributes this assertion of four conditions to Ābhidharmikas; his introduction to the *kārikā* reads: *'dir chos mngon pa shes pa dag gis smras pa* (**atrābhidharmajñā āhuḥ*) (ABh_{ed} 253.20). Buddhapālita states in his commentary that with the assertion that there is not a fifth condition, "a certain Master" (*slob dpon kha cig*) ascertains that all conditions spoken of that are other than these four are included in these four (*lnga pa yod pa ma yin zhes bya bas ni slob dpon kha cig gis rkyen bzhi po 'di las gzhan gang dag tha snyad du brjod pa de dag thams cad kyang rkyen bzhi po 'di dag tu 'du so || zhes nges par 'dzin par byed do ||* [BP_{ed} 11.14-16]). In the next sentence, Buddhapālita states that for the sake of teaching this, he (= the certain Master) taught that those four conditions are the conditions that produce things (*de rab tu bstan pa'i phyir rgyu la sogs pa rkyen bzhi po de dag dngos po rnams skyed pa'i rkyen du bstan te |* [BP_{ed} 11.16-18]). Bhāviveka's fellow Buddhists state that the "Teacher," i.e., the Buddha, proclaimed in the *sūtra*s and Abhidharma treatises that there are [only] these four conditions in the Buddhist and other systems and in the heavenly domain and on

earth (*ston pas mdo sde dang chos mngon pa'i bstan bcos las | rang dang gzhan gyi gzhung lugs dang | lha yul dang | sa'i steng dag tu bka' stsal to ||* [PP D 53b2; P 64b2-3]). Candrakīrti's fellow Buddhists likewise claim that the Buddha himself asserted the four conditions, and by implication that things are produced from other.

A *sūtra* on the four conditions is cited in AKBh ad AK II.61c: AK II.61c: *catvāraḥ pratyayā uktāḥ*; $AKBh_{ed}$ 98.5-6: *kvoktāḥ | sūtre | catasraḥ pratyayataḥ | hetupratyayatā samanantarapratyayatā ālambanapratyayatā adhipatipratyayatā ceti* |. Peter Skilling (1998: 141ff.) has investigated the *sūtra* and concluded that it belongs to the section on fours in the (Mūla-)Sarvāstivādin Ekottarikāgama. On the basis of Śamathadeva's AK commentary, he reconstructs the *sūtra*'s title as *Pratyayasūtra. The set of four *pratyaya*s proclaimed in the *Pratyayasūtra, namely, *hetupratyaya*, *ālambanapratyaya*, *samanantarapratyaya* and *adhipatipratyaya*, appears in the early Abhidharma literature of the (Mula-)Sarvāstivāda school, being encountered already in Devaśarman's Vijñānakāya where they are discussed in relation to cognition (cf. Frauwallner 1995: 27f.; Willemen et al. 1998: 203). Skilling (1998: 143) asserts, "The theory of four conditions seems to have been the kernel from which more elaborate theories of causal relations grew. It is presented in the canonical (Mūla-) Sarvāstivādin Abhidharma, occurring first in the Vijñānakāya (where it is applied to the six types of consciousness: *cakṣurvijñāna*, etc.), followed by the Prakaraṇapāda and the Jñānaprasthāna. The latter text is generally held to be the latest of the seven Sarvāstivādin Abhidharma treatises, and dated to the 1st century BCE. If this dating is correct, the theory of four conditions must have evolved by the end of the 2nd century BCE." The four *pratyaya*s also occur in later (Mūla-)Sarvāstivādin works such as the Abhidharmahṛdaya; further references in Skilling 1998: 144.

The Sarvāstivādins additionally set forth a separate classification of *hetu* into six (cf. AK II.49: *kāraṇaṃ sahabhūś caiva sabhāgaḥ saṃprayuktakaḥ | sarvatrago vipākākhyaḥ ṣaḍvidho hetur iṣyate* ||), a classification that is first seen in the Jñānaprasthāna. Skilling (1998: 144) states: "Thus the four conditions were a fundamental category of the (Mūla-)Sarvāstivāda-Vaibhāṣikas. An alternate theory of causation within the same tradition propounded a list of six causes (*hetu*). That the six causes were a later development is shown by the fact that, unlike the four conditions, they are not mentioned in any *sūtra* – a point which was not ignored, and which left their authenticity open to challenge. According to the Vaibhāṣikas themselves, the six causes first appeared in the Jñānaprasthāna of Kātyāyanīpūtra. Later scholastics attempted to reconcile and coordinate the two originally independent lists." The first of the six *hetu*s, namely, *kāraṇahetu*, the "cause [for being]" *hetu*, refers to *hetu* in its broadest possible application: all *dharma*s which do not obstruct the arising of a specific *dharma* are its *kāraṇahetu* (AK II.50a: *svato 'nye kāraṇaṃ hetuḥ*); allowance is made, however, in the AKBh for "predominant" *kāraṇahetu*s, for example, the visual sense faculty and the visible are the main *kāraṇahetu*s for the visual consciousness, food the main one for the body, and seeds, etc., for spouts, etc. ($AKBh_{ed}$ 83.8-9: *yas tu pradhānaḥ kāraṇahetuḥ sa utpādane 'pi samartho yathā cakṣūrūpe cakṣurvijñānasyāhāraḥ śarīrasya bījādayo 'ṅkurādīnām*; AKVy 190.27-28: *yo hi pradhāno janakaḥ sa kāraṇahetuḥ.* sa sutarāṃ avighnabhāvenāvatiṣṭhate na kevalam itaraḥ). *sahabhūhetu*, "simultaneous cause," refers to causes that serve as each others' causes, e.g., the simultaneously arising elements in a molecule, or consciousness and the mental factors which accompany it (AK II.50b-d: *sahabhūr ye mithaḥphalāḥ | bhūtavac cittacittānuvartilakṣaṇalakṣyavat*). *sabhāgahetu*, "homogeneous cause," is the cause that accounts for the production of a like result, e.g., from a previous moment of corn a subsequent moment of corn, not rice, arises (AK II.52ab: *sabhāgahetuḥ sadṛśāḥ svanikāyabhūvo 'grajāḥ*); *saṃprayuktahetu*, "concomitant cause," refers to consciousness and mental factors that arise together sharing the same support; they are considered as similar in five ways (AK II.53cd: *saṃprayuktakahetus tu cittacaittāḥ samāśrayāḥ*). *sarvatragahetu*, "universal cause," refers to the universal *anuśaya*s and their influence; they are the causes of defiled *dharma*s (AK II.54ab: *sarvatragākhyaḥ kliṣṭānām svabhūmau pūrvasarvagāḥ*; AK V.12 sets forth the universal *anuśaya*s: *sarvatragā duḥkhahetudṛggheyā dṛṣṭayas tathā | vimatiḥ saha tābhiś ca yāvidyāveṇikī ca yā*). Finally, *vipākahetu*, "maturation cause," is the cause of the different ripenings experienced (AK II.54cd: *vipākahetur aśubhāḥ kuśalāś caiva sāsravāḥ*); cf., e.g., Hirakawa 1990: 179-184; La Vallée Poussin 1913a: 54-56; Lamotte 1980: 2174-2179; Conze 1967: 154-156. The *pratyaya* scheme encompasses that of the *hetu*s: the latter five causes are included in *hetupratyaya*, and the first, *kāraṇahetu*, is equivalent to *adhipatipratyaya*; *samanantarapratyaya* and *ālambanapratyaya* find no equivalent in the *hetu* model (AK II.61d: *hetvākhyaḥ pañca hetavaḥ*; $AKBh_{ed}$ 98.8: *kāraṇahetuvarjyāḥ pañca hetavo hetupratyayaḥ*; for an alternative opinion, see $AKBh_{tr}$ II.299, n. 1).

As Skilling (1998: 147) notes: "Schools that accepted the *Pratyayasūtra could not expand the system of relations by adding further conditions to the original four, as did the Theravādins who did not accept the discourse; rather, they had to subdivide the four basic conditions, and correlate them with sets of causes (*hetu*)." The four *pratyaya*s are included in the list of ten *pratyaya*s given in the Śāriputrābhidharmaśāstra, thought by some scholars to belong to the Dharmaguptaka school (cf. Frauwallner 1995: 97 and n. 1 and 2, 105-107; Hirakawa 1990: 179, 182f.; Skilling [1998: 145] states the *śāstra*'s school affiliation remains unknown), and in the list of twenty-four *pratyaya*s in the Paṭṭhāna, a Theravāda Abhidharma text (cf. Frauwallner 1995: 50f.; Conze 1967: 150-153; La Valleé Poussin 1913a: 51f.; Hirakawa 1990: 179, 183f.; Skilling 1998: 145). The Paṭṭhāna includes both an *anantarapratyaya* and a *samanantarapratyaya*; according to Buddhaghosa, these two have been explained variously; see VM 534f. and Nyanatiloka 1975: 625f. Garfield's (1995: 108f.) presentation of the conditions in his commentary on MMK I.2 is unreliable.

Cf. also de La Vallée Poussin's references for *pratyaya* at PsP_L 76, n. 7. Further references in $AKBh_{tr}$ II.244, n. 4; Lamotte 1980: 2164-2167; Skilling 1998.

The Akutobhayā and the Chung Lun switch the order of MMK I.2 and I.3 (see ABh_{ed} 252, 254); Frauwallner (1958: 178f.) translates the *kārikā*s according to the order found in these texts.

Among these [four, as regards the *hetu*], because the [defining] characteristic[553] (*lakṣaṇa*) [has been formulated as] "The cause (*hetu*) is that which brings forth (*nirvartaka*)," [it] obviously (*hi*) [follows that] the [thing] which brings forth something [i.e.,] is available as the seed (*bīja*), is the cause condition (*hetupratyaya*) of that [other thing].[554] The [specific] object support (*ārambaṇa*) by virtue of which the factor (*dharma*) in the process of arising arises is the object

---

[553] I usually translate *lakṣaṇa* in the present section as "[defining] characteristic" even though—especially in the case of "*nirvartako hetuḥ*"—"definition" might also be appropriate. *lakṣaṇa* primarily denotes the essential and constitutive *ontological* characteristic of a thing—the *lakṣaṇa* of a thing makes that thing what it is, constitutes its "Sosein." "*nirvartako hetuḥ*" considered as a definition can therefore be understood to represent the formulation, the *linguistic* indication, of the essential characteristic of the *hetupratyaya*; that is: *lakṣaṇam ucyate*. I have refrained from translating *lakṣaṇa* in the present section as "definition" because, as will become clear in his arguments against the individual four conditions, Candrakīrti's focus is primarily on the actual essential characteristic of each condition.

[554] Reference to the formulation *nirvartako hetuḥ* also appears in MMK I.7c. In Bhāviveka's commentary on MMK I.7, fellow Buddhists attribute this definition to the Buddha (*de ltar yang bcom ldan 'das kyis rgyu ni sgrub par byed pa'o* [PP D 58b4; P 70b1]). Candrakīrti sets forth two presentations of conditions in the MABh (the first attributed to *kha cig*, the second to *gzhan dag*); the *hetupratyaya* as elucidated here in the PsP appears in the second presentation (*sgrub par byed pa ni rgyu yin no zhes bya ba'i mtshan nyid las gang zhig gang gi skyed pa sa bon gyi ngo bor gnas pa de ni de'i rgyu'i rkyen yin la |* [MABh$_{ed}$ 88.10-12]). In the first presentation, the *hetupratyaya* is explained as *rgyu'i rkyen ni byed rgyu ma gtogs pa'i rgyu lnga*, i.e., as it is described in the AK and AKBh (AK II.61d: *hetvākhyaḥ pañca hetavaḥ*; AKBh$_{ed}$ 98.7: *kāraṇahetuvarjyāḥ pañca hetavo hetupratyayaḥ*). Bhāviveka also explains the *hetupratyaya* of MMK I.2 as it is described in the AK, listing the five types of *hetu* it includes: *de la rgyu'i rkyen ni lhan cig 'byung ba dang | skal ba mnyam pa dang mtshungs par ldan pa dang | kun tu 'gro ba dang | rnam par smin pa zhes bya ba ni rgyu lnga po dag* (PP D 53b3-4; P 64b4-5); Ames (1994: 93) translates, "As to that, the causal condition [which is] the cause (*hetu-pratyaya*) [consists of] the five [types of] cause [known as] the simultaneously arisen (*saha-bhū*), the similar (*sabhāga*), the conjoined (*samprayukta*), the universal (*sarvatraga*), and [the cause of] maturation (*vipāka*)." The author of the ABh makes the brief comment: *rgyu'i rkyen ni bskyed pa'i don gyis* (ABh$_{ed}$ 254.10-11). Buddhapālita does not offer definitions for any of the conditions at this point.
On *hetupratyaya*, see also n. 552.

condition (*ārambaṇapratyaya*) of that [factor].[555] The immediately preceding (*anantara*) cessation (*nirodha*) of the cause (*kāraṇa*) is the condition for the arising of the effect; for example, the immediately preceding cessation of a seed is the condition for the arising of a sprout.[556] The [condition] owing to the existence of which [some-

---

[555] The defining characteristic of the object condition is formulated as *utpadyamāno dharmo yenārambaṇenotpadyate sa tasyārambaṇapratyayaḥ*. The word *dharma* (factor) in the formulation/definition also appears in MMK I.8, the *kārikā* that refutes the possibility of an *ārambaṇapratyaya*. That *dharma* here in the definition is restricted to consciousnesses and mental factors is made clear in Candrakīrti's commentary on MMK I.8. (on consciousnesses and mental factors relying on an *ālambana*, cf. AK II.34bc: *cittacaitasāḥ* | *sāśrayālambanākārāḥ* and AKBh$_{ed}$ 62.5-6: *sālambanā viṣayagrahaṇāt*).
According to the AK, *ārambaṇapratyaya* comprises all factors of existence, for whereas the visual, auditory, gustatory, olfactory and tangible consciousnesses have limited spheres of activity, mental consciousness apprehends all factors; AK II.62c: *ālambanaṃ sarvadharmāḥ*; AKBh$_{ed}$ 100.4-6: *yathāyogaṃ cakṣurvijñānasya sasaṃprayogasya rūpam* | *śrotravijñānasya śabdaḥ ... manovijñānasya sarvadharmāḥ*. This description of *ārambaṇapratyaya* as comprising all factors is reflected in the first presentation of the *pratyaya*s in the MABh: *de la dmigs par bya bas* (MABh$_{UN}$: *byas* for *bya bas*) *na dmigs pa ste* ‖ *ci rigs par rnam par shes pa drug gi dmigs pa chos thams cad ni dmigs pa'i rkyen no* ‖ (MABh$_{ed}$ 88.5-6). The second presentation in the MABh contains a definition of *ārambaṇapratyaya* that is similar to, but more elaborate than the one appearing in the PsP: *skyes bu rgan po ldang ba ltar sems dang sems las byung ba rgyu las skye* (MABh$_{UN}$: *skyes*) *bzhin pa rnams rten mkhar* (MABh$_{UN}$: *khar*) *ba dang 'dra ba'i dmigs pa gang gis bskyed par 'gyur ba de ni dmigs pa'i rkyen te* | *skye bzhin pa'i chos kyi rten yin no* | (MABh$_{ed}$ 88.12-15; de La Vallée Poussin translates, "le point d'appui, semblable à un bâton d'appui, grâce auquel sont engendrés la pensée et ses succédanés naissant de la cause, semblables à un homme âgé qui se lève, c'est l'*ālambana pratyaya*, car il est le point d'appui de la chose naissante" [MABh$_{tr}$ 1910: 286; de La Vallée Poussin's "car" is not in MABh Tib). Candrakīrti relies on this example to explain *ārambaṇa* in his commentary on YṢ 26: *brten par bya bas dmigs pa ste* ‖ *ldang mi nus pa rnams ldang bar byed pa'i 'khar ba bzhin no* ‖ (YṢV$_{ed}$ 65.15-16). Bhāviveka cites the AK in regard to this *pratyaya*: *dmigs pa'i rkyen ni chos thams cad* (PP D 53b4; P 64b5). The author of the ABh comments: *dmigs pa'i rkyen ni rten gyi don gyis* (ABh$_{ed}$ 254.11-12).

[556] The defining characteristic of the immediately preceding condition is formulated as *kāraṇasyānantaro nirodhaḥ kāryasyotpattipratyayaḥ*. Of interest here is Candrakīrti's example, according to which (*sam*)*anantarapratyaya* refers to the cessation of a material object, and not specifically to mental *dharma*s. The views expressed in the AK and AKBh restrict *samanantarapratyaya* to consciousness and mental factors (AK II.62ab: *cittacaittā acaramā utpannāḥ samanantaraḥ* "Arisen consciousnesses and mental factors, with the exception of the final ones [of Arhats entering *nirvāṇa*],

thing] comes into being is the dominant [condition] for that [thing] (*yasmin sati yad bhavati tat tasyādhipateyam*).[557] These are the four

are the *samanantara* [condition]"). This restriction is explained as entailed by the prefix *sam*, understood in the sense of *sama*: *samaś cāyam anantaraś ca pratyaya iti samanantarapratyayaḥ | ata eva rūpaṃ na samanantarapratyayo viṣamotpatteḥ* ($AKBh_{ed}$ 98.10-11; AKVy 232.18: *samānārthe saṃśabdaḥ*). The cause and result of material *dharma*s are not "equal" in the cases where an individual produces from one material cause such as the Prātimokṣa vow not one, but two, *avijñaptirūpa*s at the same time in two different spheres, i.e., in Kāmadhātu and Rūpadhātu (see $AKBh_{tr}$ II.300f. and n. 5) or when a lesser or greater effect arises from its cause, such as a small heap of ashes from a pile of straw (cf. $AKBh_{ed}$ 98.12-17). This view that (*sam*)*anantarapratyaya* applies only to consciousness and mental factors is found in the first group of explanations of the *pratyaya*s set forth by Candrakīrti in the MABh: *phung po lhag ma med par mya ngan las 'das par 'jug pa'i sems las gzhan pa'i sems dang sems las byung ba rnams ni de ma thag pa'i rkyen no* || ($MABh_{ed}$ 88.7-9; $MABh_{tr}$ 1910: 285). The second presentation, however, contains the description of (*sam*)*anantarapratyaya* as it is set forth in the PsP: *rgyu 'gags ma thag pa ni 'bras bu skye ba'i rkyen yin te | dper na sa bon 'gags ma thag pa myu gu'i tshungs pa de ma thag pa'i rkyen yin pa lta bu'o* || ($MABh_{ed}$ 88.15-17; $MABh_{tr}$ 1910: 286). Bhāviveka's explanation of (*sam*)*anantarapratyaya* conforms to the AK's: *de ma thag pa'i rkyen ni sems dang sems las byung ba skyes pa rnams las tha ma ma gtogs pa'o* (PP D 53b4; P 64b5). The author of ABh comments: *de ma thag pa'i rkyen ni bar du ma chod pa'i don gyis* (ABh_{ed} 254.12-13). On *samanantarapratyaya* in the Sarvāstivāda school, see also Cox 1995: 117f.
The author of the *LṬ states that the definition for this condition derives from the Vaibhāṣika school: *hetor nirodho vaibhāṣikeṇotpat*[*t*]*ipratyaya uktaḥ* (cf. Yonezawa 2004: 125, 148 [fol. 3a3]).

[557] The *adhipatipratyaya* (= *ādhipateya*) is equated to the *kāraṇahetu* (the "general cause"; see also n. 552) in the AK and AKBh: AK II.62d: *kāraṇākhyo 'dhipaḥ smṛtaḥ*; the AKBh states that although the *adhipatipratyaya* and the *ārambaṇa-pratyaya* have equal extension, i.e., encompass all *dharma*s, *dharma*s that arise together with [another] factor are never the *ārambaṇa* condition, whereas all *dharma*s do serve as the *adhipatipratyaya* for a single *dharma* coming into existence (cf. $AKBh_{ed}$ 100.14-16: *ālambanapratyayo 'pi sarvadharmāḥ adhipatipratyayo 'pīti kim asty ādhikyam | na jātu sahabhuvo dharmā ālambanaṃ bhavanti | bhavanti tv adhipatipratyaya ity asyaivādhikyam*; AKVy 236.8: *ālambanapratyayo 'pi sarvadharmā* iti manovijñānāpekṣayā). The AK definition of the *adhipatipratyaya* is found in the first group of explanations of the four *pratyaya*s in the MABh: *byed rgyu ni bdag po'i rkyen yin no* ($MABh_{ed}$ 88.9). As in the case of the other *pratyaya*s Candrakīrti describes in the PsP, he does not rely on the AK for his explanation of this *pratyaya*, turning instead to another source. The description found in the second group of explanations of the *pratyaya*s in the MABh corresponds with that of the PsP: *gang zhig yod na gang 'byung ba de ni de'i bdag po'i rkyen yin no* ($MABh_{ed}$ 88.17-18). Bhāviveka relies on the AK for his explanation of this *pratyaya*: *bdag po'i rkyen ni*

conditions. And others, such as the prenascent (*purojāta*), the conascent (*sahajāta*), the postnascent (*paścājjāta*), and so forth, are included in just these [four].[558] The Lord (*īśvara*) and so forth, on the

---

byed pa'i rgyu (PP D 53b4; P64b5); however, in his commentary on MMK I.7 and his introduction to MMK I.10, his "fellow Buddhist" asserts the definition given by Candrakīrti. The author of the ABh comments: *bdag po'i rkyen ni dbang byed pa'i don gyis* (ABh_{ed} 254.13-14). Although Buddhapālita does not define this *pratyaya* at this point, he introduces MMK I.10 with the objection of an opponent who defines the *ādhipateyapratyaya* in a way similar to that found in the PsP: *bdag po nyid ni yod do || bdag po'i dngos po ni bdag po nyid de | de yang mdor bsdu na gang yod na gang 'byung ba dang | gang med na gang mi 'byung ba de ni de'i bdag po nyid* (BP_{ed} 24.19-21).

[558] The *purojāta*, *sahajāta* and *paścājjāta pratyaya*s constitute three of the twenty-four *pratyaya*s of the Theravāda Paṭṭhāna (Pāli: *purejāta*, *sahajāta*, *pacchājāta*, respectively numbers 10, 6 and 11 of the list); see Conze 1967: 283, n. 11; Hirakawa 1990: 183f. The same list is found in VM 532 (see Nyanatiloka 1975: 622f.). The *sahajātapratyaya* is explained in the VM as the condition which through its simultaneous generation acts as a supportive factor, like lamplight for illumination (*uppajjamāno va saha uppādanabhāvena upakārako dhammo sahajātapaccayo, pakāsassa padīpo viya*); *purojātapratyaya* as a previously arisen condition which through its existence is a supportive factor, like the visual sense faculty for visual consciousness (*paṭhamataraṃ uppajjitvā vattamānabhāvena upakārako dhammo purejātapaccayo*); the *paścajjātapratyaya* as a non-material factor which supports through supporting the material factors, like the desire for and a will [to eat] food the bodies of young vultures (*purejātānaṃ rūpadhammānaṃ upatthambhakattena upakārako arūpadhammo pacchājātapaccayo, gijjhapotakasarīrānaṃ āhārāsā cetanā viya*; see VM 535-538; Nyanatiloka 1975: 626-630). The *sahajātapratyaya* corresponds to the *sahabhūhetu* of the Sarvāstivādin *hetu* list (Skilling 1998: 145, n. 28); it is found as the sixth *pratyaya* in the list of ten *pratyaya*s in the Śāriputrābhidharmaśāstra (cf. Hirakawa 1990: 183). A statement similar to that of the PsP appears in the MABh: *yang rkyen gzhan gang dag lhan cig skyes pa dang phyi nas skyes pa la sogs pa de dag kyang 'di rnams kyi nang du 'dus pa yin no* || ($MABh_{ed}$ 88.19-20).
Bhāviveka, commenting on MMK I.2d, refers to *purojātapratyaya* and two other *pratyaya*s, namely, *atthipratyaya* and *natthipratyaya*, also found in the Paṭṭāna list, stating, like Candrakīrti, that such additional *pratyaya*s are included in the four asserted by Nāgārjuna: *sde pa gzhan gyis* (P: *gyi*) *yongs su brtags pa'i rkyen mdun du skyes pa dang | yod pa dang | med pa rnams kyang 'di dag nyid du 'dus pa'i phyir* (PP D 53b3; P 64b3-4). As Ames (1994: 122, n. 3) notes, Avalokitavrata specifies the "other" school as the Ārya-Sthaviras. On *atthipratyaya* and *natthiprayaya*, see VM 540f. and Nyanatiloka 1975: 633f.
*LṬ's author uses the example of the *timira* disorder to show that *purojātapratyaya* is subsumed under *ādhipateyapratyaya*: *timir*[*ā*]*dhipatyena keśoṇḍ*[*u*]*kadarśanam* (ms: *keśoṇḍūka°*) *iti adhipatiḥ*. He states that *sahajātapratyaya* is referred to by the Vai-

other hand, are simply not possible as conditions.[559] Just on account of this, [the Exalted One] makes the restriction, "There is not a fifth condition." Therefore, because things arise from these [four conditions that are] other, there is arising from other.

§125. Regarding this, we reply: There is of course *no* arising of things from conditions that are other. Because,

[MMK I.3]

> An own-being (*svabhāva*) of things of course does not exist in conditions and such;
> When own-being does not exist, other-being (*parabhāva*) does not exist.[560]

---

bhāṣikas as *sahabhūpratyaya*, and appears to subsume *paścajjātapratyaya* under *ādhipateyapratyaya* (cf. Yonezawa 2004: 125f., 148f. [fol. 3a3-4]).

[559] After stating in the MABh that the *sahajāta* and *paścājjāta pratyaya*s, etc., are included in the four *pratyaya*s, Candrakīrti denies that things such as the Lord are conditions, citing MMK I.2d as support (cf. $MABh_{ed}$ 88.20-89.2).

[560] Candrakīrti cites MMK I.3: *na hi svabhāvo bhāvānāṃ pratyayādiṣu vidyate | avidyamāne svabhāve parabhāvo na vidyate ||* (given in Ye 2011a as MMK I.2). This *kārikā* appears in ABh and Chung Lun as MMK I.2; MMK I.2 of BP, PP and PsP appears in these two texts as MMK I.3. The author of the ABh sees his second *kārikā* (= PsP's MMK I.3) as explaining MMK I.1's assertion that no things ever arise anywhere from self, other, both or causelessly. He explains: 1) because an own-being of things does not exist in the conditions, etc., it is not tenable that things arise from self; 2) because other-being does not exist owing to own-being not existing, it is not tenable that things arise from other; 3) because [both] own-being and other-being do not exist, it is not tenable that things arise from both; and 4) because [the thesis of arising] causelessly is simply base, it is not tenable that things arise in this way (ABh_{ed} 253.10-19: *gang gi phyir dngos po rnams kyi rang bzhin rkyen la sogs pa dag la yod pa ma yin pa de'i phyir dngos po rnams bdag las skye bar mi 'thad do || gang gi phyir bdag gi dngos po yod pa ma yin na | gzhan gyi dngos po yod pa ma yin pa de'i phyir dngos po rnams gzhan las skye bar mi 'thad do || bdag gi dngos po dang gzhan gyi dngos po yod pa ma yin pas dngos po rnams gnyis la* (read as D and C: *las*) *skye bar mi 'thad do || rgyu med pa ni tha chad kho na yin pas de las kyang dngos po rnams skye bar mi 'thad do*); see also Oetke 2001a: 42, n. 18. This explication is quite different from that given by Buddhapālita, Bhāviveka and Candrakīrti, all of whom view the *kārikā* as refuting only the thesis of arising from other. One has to admit that the ABh commentary, in interpreting the *kārikā* as an elucidation of MMK I.1, seems somewhat forced.

For if there would be the existence (*sattva*), prior to [their] arising, of things [i.e.], of effects, somewhere—in the conditions that are other, such as in the cause, [that is], [either] in the collective (*samasta*) [conditions], in the individual (*vyasta*) [conditions], in the collective and individual (*vyastasamasta*) [conditions], or in something other than the collection of cause and conditions—there might be arising from those [conditions]. But it is not like this, [i.e.,] that there would be existence (*sadbhava*) prior to arising. If there were [prior existence], it would be apprehended, and arising would be pointless. Therefore, there is not own-being in the conditions and such[561] of things.[562] And when own-being does not exist, there is not other-being

---

Oetke (2001a: 40) rejects Weber-Brosamer and Back's translation of MMK I.3's *hi* as "bekanntlich," stating that it is questionable whether *hi* ever has this sense, and that even if it might, *hi* almost exclusively means "denn" ("for") in philosophical texts, especially in the MMK. I agree that Nāgārjuna does usually intend *hi* in the meaning "for" in the MMK (there are no cases in which it is merely a verse-filler) but it is quite clear that Candrakīrti often employs *hi* in the meaning "of course," "naturally," i.e., as indicating that something is logically or empirically obvious, and sometimes interprets the particle as used by Nāgārjuna, as in the case of MMK I.3, in this way. See Oetke 2001a: 40ff. for further comments on MMK I.3. Garfield's (1995: 112f.) interpretation of MMK I.3 as having the purpose of demonstrating that conditions are simply useful explanans because "[w]hat we are typically confronted with in nature is a vast network of interdependent and continuous processes" overlooks the fact that Nāgārjuna nowhere appeals to the idea of "nature" or anything else as a network, nor to the idea of the world as an interdependent complex.

[561] Both the author of the ABh and Buddhapālita claim that the word *ādi* in *pratyayādiṣu* of MMK I.3 refers to the conditions taught by non-Buddhists. Bhāviveka explains it in two different ways, in accord with the two explanations of MMK I.3 he provides: he first explains *ādi* as referring to other conditions such as the [causal] collection (*tshogs*) and the Lord, etc., and then as referring to the collection of causes and common and uncommon conditions and other [conditions] (*rgyu dang byed rgyu thun mong dang | thun mong ma yin pa tshogs pa dang gzhan*; see Ames 1994: 96 and n. 26).

[562] Although not exactly the same, a comparable argument is found in BP: *'di ltar gal te dngos po rnams kyi rang bzhin rkyen rnams la 'am rkyen rnams las gzhan pa la 'am | gnyi ga la yod par gyur na | yod pa la skye ba ci zhig bya ste dngos po rang bzhin gyis yod pa rnams la yang skye bar brtag pa don med pa nyid du 'gyur* (BP_{ed} 13.7-11).
For a comprehensive refutation of the possibility of effects either existing or not existing in the causal complex of cause and conditions, see PsP on MMK XX.1-4.

(*parabhāva*). "Being" (*bhāva*) [of "other-being" in the *kārikā* means] "becoming" (*bhavana*), [that is,] "arising" (*utpāda*); "other-being" [means] "arising from others"—that [arising from others] does not exist.[563] Therefore, this [tenet of yours] is not tenable, [namely, that there is] the arising of things from [things] that are other.

§126. Alternatively, [the *kārikā* may be understood as meaning that] there is not an own-being of things, [that is,] of effects such as a sprout and so forth when the conditions such as a seed and so forth exist [but are still] in an unmodified (*avikṛta*) form [i.e., have not started to germinate], because of the consequence that [the effects, i.e., the sprout and so forth] would be without a cause (*nirhetuka*) [because the seed had not reached the state of causal efficacy]. In reliance on what, then, would there be the otherness of conditions, etc.?[564] For only when two things exist [at the same time, for example

---

Cp., e.g., the MMK XX.3 argument that an existing effect would be perceived: *hetoś ca pratyayānāṃ ca sāmagryām asti cet phalam | gṛhyeta nanu sāmagryāṃ sāmagryāṃ ca na gṛhyate ||*; PsP$_L$ 392.8-9: *yad yatrāsti tat tatra gṛhyate tadyathā kuṇḍe dadhi | yac ca nāsti na tat tatra gṛhyate tadyathā sikatāsu tailaṃ maṇḍūkajaṭāyāṃ śiromaṇiḥ ||*.

[563] Bhāviveka also explains *parabhāva* as meaning "arising from others." Commenting on MMK I.3cd, he states: *rkyen la sogs pa la bdag gi dngos po yod pa ma yin na'o || gzhan gyi dngos po ni gzhan dag las 'byung ngo || 'byung ba ni skye ba ste rkyen rnams la med do* (PP D 54a3-4; P 65a5-6). Considering MMK I.3ab as providing two reasons (*chos = phyogs kyi chos*), and I.3cd as expressing the probandum (*sgrub par bya ba'i don*), he constructs two inferences based on this interpretation of the *kārikā*: *don dam par mig la sogs pa skye mched rnams khu chu dang khrag la sogs pa rkyen rnams las skye ba med de | de dag la med pa'i phyir dper na bum pa bzhin no | de bzhin du don dam par khu chu dang khrag la sogs pa'i rkyen rnams mig la sogs pa'i skye mched rnams skyed par byed pa ma yin te | de dag gis stong pa'i phyir dper na thag bzangs la sogs pa bzhin no* (PP D 54a4-5; P 65a7-65b1); "'Ultimately, the bases, the visual faculty, etc., do not arise from conditions such as semen and blood, etc., because they do not exist in those [conditions], [just] as a pot [does not exist in them and arise from them]'; similarly, 'Ultimately, conditions such as semen and blood, etc., do not produce the bases such as the visual faculty, etc., because they are empty/devoid of them, [just] as a loom, etc., [are empty/devoid of them and do not produce them]'" (also translated in Ames 1994: 95).

[564] The same argument is found in the commentary on MA VI.17 (MA VI.17: *asty aṅkuraś ca na hi bījasamānakālo kutaḥ paratayāstu vinā paratvam | janmāṅkurasya na hi sidhyati tena bījāt saṃtyajyatāṃ parata udbhavatīti pakṣaḥ ||*; (Li 2012: 5; the

the persons] Maitra and Upagupta, is there otherness with regard to each other; but there is not similarly the simultaneity of seed and sprout. Therefore, when an own-being of effects is not existing, there is not other-being (*parabhāva*), [i.e.,] the otherness (*paratva*) of seeds and so forth. Thus, precisely on account of [the fact that] a designation as "other" is not [possible], there is not arising from other.[565]

---

first *pāda* of the verse as cited in the Subhāṣitasaṅgraha is unmetrical [cf. $MABh_{tr}$ 1910: 290, n. 2]), in which Candrakīrti cites and explicates MMK I.3. He asserts that when the conditions, etc., have an unmodified own-being, an own-being of effects absolutely cannot exist, because it has not arisen; and if that does not exist, there is not other-being of the conditions, that is, their being other than the effect is not possible: *'dir rkyen la sogs pa zhes bya ba ni rgyu'am rkyen dag gam | rgyu dang rkyen gyi tshogs pa'am de las gzhan yang rung ste | rang bzhin rnam par ma gyur pa na 'bras bu rnams kyi rang bzhin yod pa ma yin pa kho na ste ma skyes pa'i phyir ro || de med na rkyen la sogs pa rnams la gzhan nyid yod pa ma yin no ||* ($MABh_{ed}$ 93.9-13). Candrakīrti explains in the following sentence that the locative of MMK I.3's *pratyayādiṣu* should be understood according to Pā 2.3.37, that is, as a locative absolute: *yasya ca bhāvena bhāvalakṣanam* "By the action of whatsoever the time of another action is indicated, that takes the seventh case-affix" (Vasu 1980: 292; correct de La Vallée Poussin's reference "Pāṇini iii, 3, 37" in $MABh_{tr}$ 1910: 291, n. 2 to "Pāṇini ii, 3, 37". The Kāś clarifies that *bhāva* refers to an action [*bhāvaḥ kriyā | yasya ca bhāvena yasya ca kriyayā kriyāntaraṃ lakṣyate, tato bhāvavataḥ saptamī vibhaktir bhavati*], and supplies the examples *goṣu duhyamānāsu gataḥ, dugdhāsv āgataḥ, agniṣu hūyamāneṣu gataḥ, huteṣv āgataḥ*).
*LṬ's author displays a similar understanding of the second interpretation of MMK I.3 as that presented above: *nirhetukatvam iti {|} yady asti svabhāvas tadā hetunā kim kartavyam | svabhāvotpādanārthaṃ hetur anvi{ne}ṣyate |* (cf. Yonezawa 2004: 126, 149 [fol. 3a4-5]).
See also MA VI.18 and 19 for Candrakīrti's refutation of the opponent's assertion that the perishing of the seed and arising of the sprout occurs simultaneously, a simultaneity that, according to the opponent, would allow for the otherness of condition and effect.

565 Candrakīrti again relies on his commentary on MA VI.17 for the reference to Maitra and Upagupta: *'di na byams pa dang nyer sbas yod bzhin pa dag kho na phan tshun bltos nas gzhan nyid du mthong gi | sa bon dang myu gu dag ni de ltar cig car dmigs pa yang ma yin te | sa bon rnam par ma gyur par myu gu med pa'i phyir ro || gang gi tshe de ltar sa bon dang dus mnyam du myu gu yod pa ma yin pa de'i phyir sa bon la myu gu las gzhan nyid yod pa ma yin la | gzhan nyid med na gzhan las myu gu skye'o zhes bya ba 'di yod pa ma yin no ||* ($MABh_{ed}$ 92.16-93.3). A similar argument, with the points of comparison Caitra and Gupta instead of Maitra and Upagupta, appears in BP: *'di la dngos po yod pa rnams gcig la gcig ltos nas gzhan nyid du 'gyur ba ni dper na cai-tra las gub-ta gzhan du 'gyur la | gub-ta las kyang cai-tra gzhan du 'gyur ba lta bu yin na | gnas skabs gang na sa bon la sogs rkyen rnams yod pa'i gnas*

§127. Therefore, the opponent (*para*) is simply unaware of the intent of the *āgama* [when it declares the four conditions], for the Tathāgatas do not utter a statement contradicted by reasoning (*yuktiviruddha*); and the intent of *āgama* [in this connection] was already given earlier.[566]

§128. Then when the proponent of arising from conditions has been rebuffed in this way, the proponent of arising from activity (*kriyā*) conjectures, "It is not the case that conditions such as the visual

---

skabs de na myu gu la sogs pa dngos po rnams yod pa ma yin te | de'i phyir rgyu la sogs pa rkyen rnams yod pa na myu gu la sogs pa dngos po rnams kyi rang bzhin yod pa ma yin no || de rnams kyi bdag gi dngos po yod pa ma yin na rgyu la sogs pa dag ji ltar gzhan du 'gyur | de lta bas na rgyu la sogs po (read: *pa*) *rkyen rnams myu gu la sogs pa dngos po rnams las gzhan nyid yin par mi 'thad do* (BP_{ed} 12.7-15; see BP_{tr} 12). Buddhapālita presents this interpretation of the *kārikā* as the first of the two interpretations provided by him.

The sentence *ayuktam etat parata utpadyante bhāvā iti* is written in ms Q's upper margin, and is marked to be inserted after *paravyapadeśābhāvād eva na parata utpāda iti.* Ms P's folio has broken off after *tasmād avidyamāne svabhāve kāryā*[*nām*] and its reading thus cannot be accessed. None of the paper manuscripts (B, D, J, L) attest the sentence. A translation for the sentence, however, appears in PsP Tib: *dngos po rnams gzhan las skye'o zhes bya ba 'di ni mi rung ngo* ||. The sentence indeed reflects and rejects the concluding statement given by the opponent for arising from other, i.e., *tasmād ebhyaḥ parabhūtebhyo bhāvāvām utpatter asti parata utpattir.* It seems, however, unnecessary and redundant: Candrakīrti already responded to the reason given in the opponent's concluding statement at the end of his first interpretation of MMK I.3 with *tasmād ayuktam etat parabhūtebhyo bhāvānām utpattir.* After presenting his alternative interpretation of MMK I.3, Candrakīrti ends with the words *na parata utpādaḥ.* The resultant redundancy and the fact that the sentence *ayuktam etat parata utpadyante bhāvā iti* is missing from the paper manuscripts and only occurs in Q's margin inclines one to suspect that it is an interpolation which was received by Q from ms θ. It must have been in ms δ for PsP Tib to have received it, but like other interpolated readings in ms δ that were not appropriated by ms ι (or one of ms ι's ancestors), it did not enter the paper manuscript line. For the above reasons, I have not included the sentence in my edition. I do, however, admit that from a paleographical standpoint, an eyeskip from *iti* of *utpāda iti* to *iti* of *bhāva iti* is possible.

566 See the discussion at PsP_M §71-§75 (PsP_L 39.8-44.7). *LṬ's author states: *vyavahāramātreṇoktaṃ | na tu tat*[*t*]*vata ity āgamābhiprāyaḥ* (cf. Yonezawa 2004: 126, 149 [fol. 3a5]).

faculty, visual form, etc., directly generate consciousness.[567] Rather, one speaks of conditions because [they] effect the activity of the originating of consciousness (*janikriyā*). And that activity generates consciousness.[568] Therefore, the activity consisting in the originating

---

[567] The opponent here and in the following takes as his point of reference assertions based on the Canonical statement *cakṣuḥ pratītya rūpāṇi cotpadyate cakṣurvijñānam.* Cf. n. 67.

[568] The activity of originating (*jani*) occurs, according to the Buddhist opponents, in an entity that is in the process of originating (*jāyamāna*). The entity in the process of originating is not merely a "half-arisen" thing (*ardhajātaḥ*) but is recognized as the state just prior to that of the fully arisen thing; cf. Candrakīrti's introduction to CŚ XV.19: *yasya nirodhena jātaḥ padārtho bhavati sa jāteḥ prāgavasthārūpo*[1] *'rtho jāyamāna ity ucyata iti* (CŚṬ$_{ed}$ 364.2-3), [1]Suzuki notes that ms B reads *jātaprāg°*, HPS *jāta(taḥ) prāg°*, CŚṬ$_{ed}$ Tib: *skyes pa'i snga rol gyi*; CŚ XV.19: *jāyamāna-nirodhena jāta utpadyate yataḥ | tato 'nyasyāpi sadbhāvo jāyamānasya dṛśyate ||*. When the CŚṬ opponent is forced by Candrakīrti to admit that a *jāyamāna* thing is actually something originated (*jāta*), i.e., something arisen, the opponent states that the *jāyamāna* thing, although unoriginated (*ajāta*), is [only] called originated (*jāta*) because it is "turned toward origination" (*janmābhimukha*), that is, is about to arise (cf. CŚṬ$_{ed}$ 366.1-2). Compare AKBh ad AK III.28ab, where the Sautrāntika view of arising is defended against Grammarians who have stated that the gerund suffix in *pratītya* of *pratītyasamutpāda* implies that an already *existing* thing depends (on its conditions). The Grammarians are informed that that which arises is something future (*anāgataḥ*) which is "turned toward arising," i.e., is about to, ready to, arise (cf. AKBh$_{ed}$ 138.14-15): *kim avasthaś cotpadyate | utpādābhimukho 'nāgataḥ | tadavastha eva pratyayaṃ pratyetīty ucyate |*. In response to the Grammarian's complaint that an agent (*kartṛ*) as well as an action/activity (*kriyā*), expressly stated as "becoming" (*bhūti*), is expected, it is replied that there is not an action of becoming different from the agent (*bhavitṛ*), but that there is no fault in such linguistic usage (cf. AKBh$_{ed}$ 138.15-17). See, on the other hand, n. 572 for instances where Candrakīrti refers to the thing arising as both the agent (*kartṛ*) of and the basis (*āśraya*) for the activity (*kriyā*).

In Candrakīrti's introduction to CŚ XV.22ab, the opponent states that a thing in the process of originating is affected by, under the influence of, the activity of arising: *utpattikriyayāviśyamāno hi padārtho jāyamāna iti* (CŚṬ$_{ed}$ 366.12-13). The CŚṬ opponent further states that a previously unoriginated thing becomes something that is originating when it comes under the influence of the activity of originating (*ato 'py ajāta eva jāyamāno bhavati janikriyāveśakāle* (CŚṬ$_{ed}$ 368.11-12). See also the description of the process of arising in the opponent's defense at PsP$_{L}$ 158.11-13: *yasmād ihotpattikriyāyuktam utpadyamānam iti vyapadiśyate | tasmād utpattau satyām utpattiṃ pratītyotpadyamānasiddher utpadyamānam evotpadyate* (cf. also PsP$_{L}$ 158.6: *utpadyate iti vartamānakriyāviṣṭaḥ*). The activity of arising (*utpattikriyā*) does not occur in something arisen, for the activity fulfils its purpose with the comof consciousness, which possesses the conditions (*pratyayavatī*), is the generator of consciousness, not the conditions, [just] as for boiled rice the activity of cooking (*pacikriyā*) [produces it, not the conditions, such as the pot or fire, etc.]."[569]

---

pletion of the entity's arising (*utpanna ity uparatotpattikriya ucyate* [PsP_L 158.6]). At PsP_L 405.5-6, reference is made to the opponents' view that the effect is the agent of the activity of arising (*utpattikriyākartṛtvaṃ phalasya*) and that the cause is the instigator of the activity of arising of the result (*hetoḥ phalotpattikriyāprayojaka-tvam*). It is not clear if these statements represent the views of a single Buddhist school or if some should be attributed to separate or sub-groups. In the PP on MMK I.5, Bhāviveka expressly attributes to the Sautrāntika school the view that conditions that have activity assist each other only at the time when the result originates (PP D 56b5-6; P 68a7: *mdo sde pa dag na re | 'bras bu skye ba'i dus kho na rkyen bya ba dang ldan pa rnams gcig la gcig phan 'dogs pas rkyen nyid du khas blangs pa'i phyir |* ...). Cf. Ames 1994: 103.

In the PP on MMK I.4b where Guṇamati's comments are rejected, someone (*kha cig na re*)—according to Avalokitavrata, Bhāviveka himself—asserts in regard to the process of arising that immediately after and as a result of the causal conditions assisting each other, activity (**kriyā*) capable of producing the result comes into being and brings the thing on the point of arising into existence; and because this sequence of events is not rejected on the everyday level, activity is also not rejected on this level: *kha cig na re rkyen rnams gcig la gcig phan 'dogs pas | de ma thag pa'i skad cig la 'bras bu bskyed nus pa'i bya ba bdag nyid thob pa'i skad cig gis dngos po skye par 'dod pa skyed pa tha snyad du ma btang bas med pa nyid ma yin la |* (PP D 55b6-7; P 67a5-6) "Since the conditions assist each other, immediately following [the mutual assistance of the conditions], the next moment [of the conditions] in which the activity capable of producing the effect comes into being produces the entity that has been on the verge of origination. Since [we] do not reject [this] conventionally, it is not the case that [the activity of origination] does not exist [on the surface level]." See also Ames 1994: 100.

It may be finally mentioned that in the PsP on MMK VII, in which the real existence of the three characteristics (*lakṣaṇa*) propounded by the Sarvāstivādins, namely, *utpāda*, *sthiti* and *anityatā/nirodha*, is rejected, the activity (*kriyā*) of *utpadyamāna* is given as *utpatti* and that of *tiṣṭhan/tiṣṭhamāna* as *sthiti*.

[569] Candrakīrti relies on his commentarial predecessors for the objection as found here in the PsP: it appears in both BP and PP (see BP_{ed} 13.21-14.8; PP D 55a3-5, P 66a8-66b2). An abbreviated version of Buddhapālita's presentation of the argument and his refutation of it is cited and criticized by Bhāviveka within his commentary on MMK I.4a; Bhāviveka rejects Buddhapālita's critique as being a mere proposition (*dam bcas pa tsam*; **pratijñāmātra*). As Ames (1994: 125, n. 41) notes, Avalokitavrata identifies the opponents as the Vaibhāṣikas and the Sautrāntikas. Bhāviveka's opponent, setting forth his objection in the form of an inference, specifies that the activity of origination of visual consciousness possesses the conditions visual faculty,

§129. Reply:

[MMK I.4a]

> Activity (*kriyā*) that possesses conditions (*pratyayavatī*) does not [exist].[570]

If some activity existed, [then] it, possessing conditions by way of conditions such as the visual faculty, might generate consciousness. But it does not exist. Why [not]? This activity accepted in [your] system (*iha*) is maintained in regard to either consciousness that has [already] originated (*jāta*), [consciousness] that has not [yet] originated (*ajāta*) or [consciousness which is in the process of] originating (*jāyamāna*). Among those [three alternatives, activity] is not appropriate in regard to [consciousness] that has [already] originated, for activity brings about things; if the thing (*bhāva*) has [already] been brought about, of what use is activity for it? And this has been explained in the Madhyamakāvatāra by way of [statements] such as:

---

visible form, light, space and mental attention, and the activity of cooking the pot, water, rice, fire and fuel. Buddhapālita refers to the person cooking, the pot, water, fire, stove and so forth as the conditions which, each performing their respective activities, effect the activity of cooking for the object cooked, i.e., boiled rice.

[570] Candrakīrti cites MMK I.4a: *kriyā na pratyayavatī.* I translate the *kārikā* following Candrakīrti's interpretation of it. The entire *kārikā* reads: *kriyā na pratyayavatī nāpratyayavatī kriyā | pratyayā nākriyāvantaḥ kriyāvantaś ca santy uta ||*. A variety of translations have been offered by classical and modern translators. Pa tshab, following Candrakīrti's interpretation, presents MMK I.4 as *bya ba rkyen dang ldan pa med || rkyen dang mi ldan bya ba med || bya ba mi ldan rkyen ma yin || bya ba ldan yod 'on te na ||*. He has merely slightly revised Jñānagarbha and Klu'i rgyal mtshan's earlier translation, which presents *ma yin* instead of *pa med* at the end of I.4a, and *yod* instead of *nam* in I.4d. *kriyā* has been translated in different ways by modern translators, e.g., as "energies" (Stcherbatsky 1927: 168), "Wirkung" (Frauwallner 1958: 179), "force" (Wood 1994: 284), "power to act" (Garfield 1995: 113); the last three translations do not take the commentaries into consideration. Oetke (2001a: 43f.) takes issue with Weber-Brosamer and Back's (1997: 3) translation "Wirkkraft" and considers Frauwallner's translation "Wirkung" (MMK I.4a: "Die Wirkung hat keine Ursache ...") to render the thought more understandable, but admits that it is arguable whether *kriyā* can be said to represent the same concept as *phala*. Kajiyama (1963: 105) and Ames (1994: 98) respectively translate the PP's *bya ba* as "Tätigkeit" and "activity."

> And the origination (*janma*) once again of what has [already] originated is simply not reasonable.[571]

[Activity] is also not appropriate in regard to [a thing] that has not [yet] originated, because of statements such as

> And without an agent (*kartṛ*) this [activity of] originating (*jani*) is not tenable.[572]

Activity is also not possible in regard to a thing [which is in the process of] originating, because something [in the process of] originating, apart from what has [already] originated and what has not [yet] originated, does not exist.[573]

---

[571] Candrakīrti cites MA VI.8cd: *jātasya janma punar eva ca naiva yuktam* ||. The verse was cited earlier at PsP_M §21 (PsP_L 13.7).

[572] Candrakīrti cites MA VI.19d: *kartrā vinā janir iyaṃ na ca yuktarūpā* || (Li 2012: 5; MA VI.19 is cited in full at PsP_L 545.9-12). Taking in his commentary on MA VI.19 the case of a sprout that is about to originate, Candrakīrti explains that the agent of the activity of originating is the sprout; the sprout, however, being a thing of the future, does not exist. The activity of originating, lacking a support (*āśraya*), thus cannot exist: *skye ba'i bya ba gang yin pa de'i byed pa po myu gu ni ma 'ongs pa yin pa'i phyir yod pa ma yin pa nyid do* || *de med na yang rten med par 'di yod pa ma yin* ($MABh_{ed}$ 96.1-3). Cp. Candrakīrti's argument against *kriyā* in his commentary on MMK VII.17: *athāghaṭāśrayeṇa kriyā prārabhyeta tad vaktavyaṃ yo asāv aghaṭaḥ sa kiṃ bhavitum arhati paṭa uta naiva kiṃcit* | *yadi paṭa utpadyamānaḥ sa kathaṃ utpannaḥ [san] ghaṭo bhaviṣyatīti* | *atha naiva kiṃcit kathaṃ tadāśrayā kriyā pravartate* | *kathaṃ vā sa utpannaḥ san ghaṭo bhaved* (PsP_L 161.6-9). See also his commentary on CŚ XV.23abc, where the opponent points out that a thing in the process of originating (*jāyamāna*) is indispensable as the support for the activity of originating, for what has not originated is incapable of providing support: *na cābhūtasyālabdhātmabhāvasya nirāśrayā janikriyā prava[rtitum u]tsahate* ($CŚṬ_{ed}$ 368.13-14). *LṬ's author also refers to the agent as the support for the activity of originating: *vijñānaṃ kartṛ tadabhāve tadāśritā kriyā kathaṃ bhavet* (ms: *bhaveda*) | (cf. Yonezawa 2004: 126, 150 [fol. 3a5]).

[573] Candrakīrti follows Buddhapālita in refuting activity by considering it with reference to consciousness already originated, not yet originated and in the process of originating. Buddhapālita argues that activity does not function in consciousness already originated because something already originated does not originate again, or in consciousness not yet originated because then activity would be without a support (*gnas pa med*), or in consciousness in the process of originating because there is not something in the process of originating separate from what has already originated

As it is stated [in the Catuḥśataka],

> Because something [in the process of] originating (*jāyamāna*) is half-originated, something [in the process of] originating does not originate.
> Alternatively, it follows that absolutely everything is [in the process of] originating.[574]

---

and what has not yet originated (see BP_{ed} 14.15-15.5). Bhāviveka briefly summarizes this refutation of Buddhapālita's as *rnam par shes pa skyes pa dang ma skyes pa dang | skye bzhin pa la rnam par shes pa skyed pa'i bya ba mi 'thad pa'i phyir*, criticizing it (and the opponent's argument as presented by Buddhapālita), as he is prone to, as a "mere thesis" (see PP D 55a7-55b3; P 66b5-8). Of interest in Bhāviveka's commentary on MMK I.4b is his citation of comments by Guṇamati, according to whom MMK I.4a should be interpreted as a response to opponents who maintain that the activity of origination is the nature of consciousness. MMK I.4a would thus teach that when consciousness does not yet exist, activity, being its nature, also cannot exist, and therefore the possessive affix "*vat*" (of *pratyayavatī*), is inappropriate (see PP D 55b5-6; P 67a3-4; PPṬ D 171b1-6; P 198b8-199a8; Kajiyama 1964: 106f.; Ames 1994: 99f.).
This refutation of the possibility of activity in things of the three times is found in various forms in Madhyamaka literature (see, e.g., the refutation of *gati/gamana* in MMK II, of *utpatti* and *sthiti* in MMK VII). See also CŚ XV.17 for a refutation of *kriyā*, and ŚS *kārikā* 5 and the ŚSV for arguments against the possibility of arising in the three times ($ŚSV_{ed}$ 237f.)

[574] Candrakīrti cites CŚ XV.16: *jāyamānārdhajātatvāj jāyamāno na jāyate | atha vā jāyamānatvaṃ sarvasyaiva prasajyate ||*. See Lang 1986: 140f. Candrakīrti, in his commentary on the *śloka*, explains that if something in the process of originating is conceived of as something partly originated and partly not originated, it does not exist, because this would correspond to the already originated (**jāta*) and that not yet originated (**ajāta*); there is not another third temporal aspect. If it is said to have the nature of both something already originated and something not yet originated, then the part that has originated does not originate, since it has just been stated in CŚ XV.14 and commentary that what is existent does not originate; and the part that has not originated likewise does not originate, since it has also been stated in CŚ XV.14 that what is not existent does not originate. On the other hand, if there is the process of originating for what has already originated and what has not yet originated, then the past and the future will be in the process of originating: *gal te gang cung zad cig skyes shing cung zad cig ma skyes pa de skye bzhin pa yin na | de ltar na ni 'o na skye bzhin pa de yod pa ma yin te skyes pa dang ma skyes pa dag la rjes su zhugs pas gzhan gsum pa skye bzhin pa'i dus kyi rnam pa med do || de'i phyir med pa nyid kyis skye bzhin pa mi skye'o | gal te gnyi ga'i ngo bo skye* (P: *skyes*) *bzhin pa yin na ni de'i phyir de'i gang cung zad gcig skyes pa de ni skyes pa'i khongs su gtogs pa'i phyir mi skye ste | dngos po ni mi skye'o zhes brjod pa'i phyir ro || de'i cung zad ma skyes pa*

And because in this way the activity of originating is impossible in the three times, it does not exist. Precisely on account of that, [Nāgārjuna] asserts, "Activity that possesses conditions does not [exist]." This has been explained in the Madhyamakāvatāra with statements such as,

> There is not a qualifier without a qualificand.[575]

For one does not say that the son of a barren woman possesses a cow (*gomān*).

---

gang yin pa de yang mi skye ste dngos po med pa mi skye'o zhes brjod pa'i phyir ro || *ci ste skyes pa dang ma skyes pa dag la skye bzhin pa nyid* (D: adds *du*) *rtog na* | *de lta yin na* | *'das pa dang ma 'ongs pa gnyis kyang skye bzhin pa nyid du 'gyur ro* (CŚṬ P 258a8-258b3). See the continued discussion in CŚ XV.18-24 in which Āryadeva rejects the opponent's attempts to rescue *jāyamāna*; in the commentary on CŚ XV.23 there is reference to the concept of *utpattikriyā*, the endowment with which, according to the opponent, distinguishes something in the process of originating from something not originated: *yathājātāj jāyamāno bahiṣkṛtaḥ kriyāveśād evaṃ jātād api bahiṣkṛta evāniṣpannarūpatvāt* ($CŚṬ_{ed}$ 368.1-2).

575 Candrakīrti cites MA VI.57c: *viśeṣaṇaṃ nāsti vinā viśeṣyam* (cf. Li 2012: 9). Here in the PsP, the qualificand (*viśeṣya*) is activity (*kriyā*) and its qualifier (*viśeṣaṇa*) is "possessing conditions" (*pratyayavatī*). *kriyā*, having been shown to be impossible, cannot be qualified by conditions, i.e., cannot possess conditions.
MA VI.57c in the context of the MA and MABh can only mean "There is not a qualificand without a qualifier," because there the argumentation demonstrates that the *qualifier*, not the qualificand, does not exist. The verse occurs in the refutation of *śakti* as that which induces consciousness, and Candrakīrti explicitly states in his commentary on MA VI.57c that consciousness is the qualifier and *śakti* the basis of the qualification, i.e., the qualificand. In MA VI.57ab, he asserts that there cannot be *śakti* either for a consciousness that has originated or for one that has not originated. In his commentary on MA VI.57cd he takes as subject a consciousness that has not yet originated, i.e., one not existing, stating that a consciousness which has not originated cannot be taught either as something affirmed or negated, i.e., as "consciousness" or "non-consciousness" (*gang ma skyes pa de ni rnam par shes pa 'am* | *rnam par shes pa ma yin zhes bya bar dgag pa dang sgrub pa'i ngo bos bstan par mi nus so* ||) and as such cannot be the qualifier for *śakti*. If one nevertheless attributes *śakti* to consciousness which has not originated, then *śakti* could also be attributed to the son of a barren woman (see $MABh_{ed}$ 148.7-17).
Pa tshab presumably copied MA VI.57c directly from MA Tib, for PsP Tib reads: *khyad par med par khyad par can yod min* ||.

§130. [The opponent argues:] If in this way [activity possessing conditions does not exist], then [activity] will exist as [something] that does not possess conditions.

§131. Since this is also not tenable, [Nāgārjuna] states,

[MMK I.4b]

Activity that does not possess conditions does not [exist].[576]

When [activity] that possesses conditions does not exist, then how would [activity] that does not possess conditions, [that is, activity] without a cause, exist? For if it is thought that it is not tenable that cloth is made from threads, it is not [then] maintained that it is made from fragrant grass![577] Therefore, activity is not the generator of things (*bhāvajanika*).

---

[576] Candrakīrti cites MMK I.4b: *nāpratyayavatī kriyā* |.

[577] Candrakīrti interprets MMK I.4b as meaning that the opponent's proposal of activity without conditions is absurd because this would mean that it has no cause, and nothing exists without a cause. The example of cloth made from threads is meant to provide a parallel for activity with conditions, and cloth made from fragrant grass (used to make mats, not cloth) is meant as a parallel for activity without conditions. The fragrant grass is presumably intended in the sense of no cause, that is to say, cloth without threads as conditions would be without a cause (*nirhetuka*), and nothing else, such as fragrant grass, can serve as cloth's conditions. *apratyayavatī* of I.4b is thus taken to be a possessive adjective with alpha privative (*a* + *pratyayavatī*). This interpretation of the quarter considers I.4b to parallel I.4d. Pa tshab seems to have understood Candrakīrti as I do, for he does not tamper with Jñānagarbha and Klu'i rgyal mtshan's translation of the quarter (*rkyen dang mi ldan bya ba*). One could also consider that *apratyayavatī* is a possessive adjective composed of a *nañ-karmadhāraya* and a possessive suffix (*apratyaya* + *vatī*); in the latter case, the verse-quarter would mean "Activity that possesses non-conditions does not exist." Fragrant grass would then illustrate a non-condition, and the quarter would be rejecting the possibility that activity might possess conditions that are not its *own true* conditions. The interpretation of the quarter which takes *apratyayavatī* as a possessive adjective with alpha privative, however, better suits the consequence pointed out by Candrakīrti, namely, that activity would be without a cause (*nirhetuka*). Candrakīrti provides only general remarks on MMK XX.24b (MMK XX.24ab: *na sāmagrīkṛtaṃ tasmān nāsāmagrīkṛtaṃ phalam* |): *yadā sāmagrīkṛtaṃ phalaṃ na saṃbhavati tadā katham atyantaviruddham asāmagrīkṛtaṃ bhaviṣyati* | *asāmagrīkṛtam iti phalaṃ na saṃbhavati* || (PsP_L 407.3-4), and in this case PsP Tib translates *asāmagrīkṛtaṃ* as *tshogs min byas pa*. It might be noted that when Candrakīrti comments on MMK I.1's rejection

§132. In regard to this, [the opponent] says: If activity is thus impossible, then conditions will be the generators (*janaka*) of things.

§133. Reply:

[MMK I.4c]

Conditions that do not possess activity do not [exist].[578]

When activity does not exist, then how without activity, [that is,] not possessing activity, [and thus] without a cause (*nirhetuka*), [could] conditions be generators?[579]

---

of things arising from no cause (*ahetutaḥ*), no cause is taken to refer to no cause at all and also to non-causes.
Buddhapālita interprets the quarter as meaning that activity without conditions does not exist, and repeats his arguments on MMK I.1 against arising from no cause: *'di ltar rkyen dang mi ldan pa'i bya ba med do ‖ gal te yod par gyur na rtag tu thams cad las thams cad skye bar 'gyur ro ‖ de lta yin na rtsom pa thams cad don med pa nyid du 'gyur bas de yang mi 'dod de | de'i phyir rkyen dang mi ldan pa'i bya ba yang mi 'thad* (BP_{ed} 15.9-12). Bhāviveka interprets the quarter to mean that activity without conditions, i.e., not characterized by the possession of causal conditions, does not exist.

[578] Candrakīrti cites MMK I.4c: *pratyayā nākriyāvantaḥ.*

[579] Candrakīrti has presented an opponent who acquiesces to the refutation of activity set forth in the two previous verse-quarters but argues for conditions as the primary generators of things. Candrakīrti rejects this position on the ground that conditions require activity in order to be generators; given that activity has been proven to be non-existent, conditions lack the cause that would render them generators. *LṬ's author, on the other hand, understands *nirhetuka* to mean without causal function: *nirhetukāḥ* {|} *ahetava ity arthaḥ* (cf. Yonezawa 2004: 126, 150 [fol. 3a6]).
Buddhapālita addresses an opponent who attempts to rescue the establishment of things and their arising by arguing from the existence of conditions (BP_{ed} 15.13-14: *re zhig rkyen rnams ni yod do ‖ de dag yod pas dngos po 'grub po ‖ de grub pas skye ba 'grub po*). Buddhapālita, like Candrakīrti, explains the quarter by relying on the earlier refutation of activity, stating that the visual faculty and so forth might be the conditions of visual consciousness through their bringing about the activity of origination, but since activity does not exist, there is obviously not something that brings it about; therefore the visual faculty and so forth cannot be conditions for the activity of originating. He adds that should they be considered conditions even without the existence of activity, everything would be the condition of everything and everything would arise from everything (see BP_{ed} 15.17-16.2). Bhāviveka addresses an opponent who sets forth the inference that conditions such as the visual faculty produce visual consciousness because they possess activity, like a seed, etc., produces a sprout. He

§134. But if [the opponent argues:] Only [conditions] that possess activity [are] generators, [Nāgārjuna] replies,

[MMK I.4d]

And [conditions] that possess activity definitely do [not] exist.[580]

[The negative particle] "not" (*na*) [of "do not [exist]" of the previous quarter has] a connection with the topic of discussion [i.e., this quarter]. The word "definitely" (*uta*) is [used] here in [the sense of] restriction.[581] There [in the first two quarters] the non-existence of

---

responds that because origination has been refuted on the ultimate level, and since the activity of origination does not exist, conditions do not possess activity, and not possessing it, they are not suitable as conditions: *'di la don dam par skye ba bkag pa'i phyir bya ba med pas sa bon la sogs pa rkyen rnams de dang ldan pa ma yin la | bya ba dang mi ldan pa rnams ni rkyen du mi rung ...* (PP D 56b2-3; P 67b1-2).

580 Candrakīrti cites MMK I.4d: *kriyāvantaś ca santy uta* ||.

581 The commentators on MMK I.4d elucidate the quarter in different ways. Buddhapālita states that the negation *na* is to be supplied from I.4.c, but does not comment on *uta*; he may understand *na … uta* in its natural sense of "also … not" / "not … either" (thus, "And [conditions] that possess activity also do not exist" / "And [conditions] that possess activity do not exist either"). He states: *ma yin zhes bya ba'i skabs de dang sbyar te rkyen rnams bya ba dang ldan pa ma yin no || bya ba rkyen dang ldan pa ma yin pa dang rkyen dang mi ldan pa med pa de ni sngar rab tu bstan pa kho na yin no || bya ba med na ji ltar rkyen rnams bya ba dang ldan par 'gyur* (BP_{ed} 16.7-10). As Saito (1984: 224, n. 16) has asserted in his remarks on the commentators' interpretations of the particle *uta*, this explanation of Buddhapālita's indicates that MMK I.4d as found in the canonical editions of BP should be corrected from *bya ba ldan nam 'on te na* to read *bya ba ldan yod 'on te na*, as it is found in the PsP. That the quarter appears as it does in BP is a consequence of Jñānagarbha and Klu'i rgyal mtshan having inserted the translation of the MMK they had made in reliance on PP and PPṬ into their subsequent translation of BP (see Saito 1984: xviif.). Bhāviveka presents the quarter twice (PP Tib: *bya ba ldan nam 'on te na*), initially without commenting on *uta* but possibly understanding it in a restrictive sense (see Saito 1984: 224, n. 16; Ames 1994: 126, n. 58) or in the more natural sense of "also" "either." Bhāviveka then explains *uta* as indicating an alternative (*'on te na zhes bya ba'i sgra ni rnam par brtag pa'i don*), such that, according to Saito (1984: 224, n. 16), MMK I.4cd would mean "Conditions are neither without action, nor in possession of action" (see also Ames' [1994: 102] translation following PPṬ). Avalokitavrata provides yet another interpretation of the quarter (in regard to Bhāviveka's initial citation of it), according to which *uta* is to be taken as indicating an alternative within MMK I.4d itself, with the quarter thus expressing a question directed toward the opponent. The quarter would translate, "Do [conditions] that

activity was asserted; [so] how [could] the conditions possess activity? And also things (*bhāva*) such as the activity of cooking (*pacikriyā*) should be understood as having been declared [to be] the same as the activity of originating (*janikriyā*) of consciousness. Therefore, there is not the arising of things even from activity. Thus, it turns out that the expression "arising" (*utpāda*) is empty of meaning.

§135. Here [the opponent] says: What use is this examination (*vicāra*) with respect to "conditions possess activity" and so forth for us (*naḥ*)? Since things such as consciousness originate in dependence on conditions such as the visual faculty, the visual faculty and so forth are conditions, and consciousness, etc., arise from them.[582]

§136. Because this too is incorrect, [Nāgārjuna] states,

[MMK I.5]

> It is alleged (*kila*) that these are conditions because in dependence on them [an effect] arises.

---

possess activity exist or [not]?"; *na*, taken over from I.4c, supplies, according to Avalokitavrata, the answer to the question: "Do [conditions] that possess activity exist or [not? They do not.]." See Saito 1984: 224, n. 16; Ames 1994: 101 and n. 57.

[582] Candrakīrti appears to have reworked Buddhapālita's introduction to MMK I.5. Buddhapālita writes: *'dir smras pa | ci rkyen rnams bya ba dang mi ldan no zhe 'am | bya ba dang ldan no zhes bya ba mi dgos pa bsam pa 'dis ci bya | gang gi phyir rnam pa thams cad du rgyu la sogs pa'i rkyen bzhi po de dag la brten nas dngos po rnams skye bas de'i phyir de dag dngos po'i rkyen yin no* (BP_{ed} 16.13-16). Bhāviveka uses a Sautrāntika objection as the lead-in to MMK I.5. In his alternative interpretation of MMK I.4d he stated that the opponent's reason "because they possess activity" is not established because (conventionally) it is not maintained that the conditions of a result that is *not* on the point of arising possess activity (PP D 56b4-5; P 68a6-7: *'di la rkyen rnams bya ba dang ldan pa nyid du ni 'bras bu skyed* [P: *bskyed*] *pas bstan pa yin na | de yang 'bras bu skye ba la mngon du phyogs par ma gyur pa la ni mi 'dod pas* ...). In his introduction to MMK I.5 he has the Sautrāntikas argue that conditions do possess activity right at (but not before) the time of the arising of the effect (PP D 56b5-6; P 68a7: *mdo sde pa dag na re | 'bras bu skye ba'i dus kho na rkyen bya ba dang ldan pa rnams gcig la gcig phan 'dogs pas rkyen nyid du khas blangs pa'i phyir | gtan tshigs kyi don ma* [P omits *ma*] *grub pa yang ma yin la* |; cf. Ames 1994: 103).

> [But] as long as [the effect] has not arisen, how are these not non-conditions (*apratyaya*)?[583]

If, since consciousness arises in dependence on conditions such as the visual faculty, these are said to be the conditions of this [consciousness], how indeed, as long as that effect called consciousness has not arisen, are these, the visual faculty and so forth, not non-conditions? The intent [of the rhetorical question of 1.5d] is "[they are] nothing but non-conditions."[584] And there is no arising from non-conditions, [just] as [there is no arising] of oil from sand.

§137. But if [you] think that [those]—existing first as non-conditions—attain the status of conditions (*pratyayatva*) when [they] rely on something, [i.e.,] on another condition, [we reply that] this too is unreasonable: also that other condition postulated as the condition for the non-condition['s becoming a condition] becomes a condition for this [only] when [it attains] the status of a condition. Thus exactly this same consideration (*cintā*) applies to this [other condition] as well.

---

[583] Candrakīrti cites MMK I.5: *utpadyate pratītyemān itīme pratyayāḥ kila | yāvan notpadyata ime tāvan nāpratyayāḥ katham ||*. De La Vallée Poussin (PsP$_{L}$ 81, n. 3) states that BP, PP and ABh read *ji srid mi bskyed* ("= *yāvan notpādayantīme*") but BP$_{ed}$ and PP D and P read, like PsP Tib, *ji srid mi skye*; according to ABh$_{ed}$, the Tibetan editions D, C, P, and N for ABh read *ji srid mi bskye* (obviously an error, although Huntington has not corrected the reading; see ABh$_{ed}$ 255.20). Saito accepts BP D and C's *grags* (for *kila*) and rejects P and N's *grag*, noting that ABh and PP attest *grag* (PsP Tib and MMK$_{T}$ D and P also attest *grag*); see TCD s.v. *grag*: *lo grag zer gsum gyi grag ste mi 'dod pa dang | ma rangs pa'i tshig shugs ston pa'i phrad cig*. See Oetke 2001a: 44f. for comments on the meaning of the *kārikā*.

[584] Whereas Candrakīrti merely paraphrases *kila* of MMK I.5ab with *ucyante*, Bhāviveka clarifies that its inclusion shows that Nāgārjuna does not accept the assertion: *grag ces bya ba'i sbyor ba ni 'dir slob dpon mi bzhed par ston pa yin* (PP D 56b7; P 68b1). Bhāviveka also explains the intent of the rhetorical question in 1.5d but adds another rhetorical question as an analogous example: "As long as one is unread, how is one not not a scholar?" (PP D 57a 1; P 68b2-3: *'di dag la rkyen nyid med do zhes bya ba'i tshig gi don to || dper na ji srid du mi klog pa de srid du mkhas pa ma yin par ji ltar mi 'gyur zhes bya ba bzhin*).

Therefore this [position of yours that things arise from conditions] is not tenable.[585]

§138. Moreover, these, [i.e.,] the visual faculty and so forth, that are being postulated here as the conditions of consciousness, would be postulated with respect to either an existent (*sataḥ*) or inexistent (*asataḥ*) [consciousness].[586] But because [a condition of either type of consciousness] is not in any way tenable, he [= Nāgārjuna] says,

[MMK I.6ab]

> Neither for an inexistent nor an existent thing (*artha*) is a condition tenable.[587]

[With MMK I.6cd] he states why:

> [If the thing] is inexistent: of what is the condition? And [if it's] existent: what use is a condition?[588]

---

585 Similar argumentation is found in BP, but only after Buddhapālita asserts that if non-conditions later became conditions everything would end up the condition of everything: *ci ste sngar rkyen du ma gyur pa phyis rkyen du 'gyur bar sems na | de yang mi 'thad de | ci'i phyir zhe na | thams cad kyi rkyen du thams cad thal bar 'gyur ba'i phyir de yang mi 'dod* (BP_{ed} 17.5-7); he continues: *ci ste rkyen ma yin pa dag kyang gzhan 'ga' zhig la ltos nas rkyen du 'gyur te | des na thams cad kyi rkyen du thams cad thal bar mi 'gyur bar sems na | de la yang de nyid do || gang yang rung ba la ltos nas rkyen ma yin pa yang rkyen nyid du 'gyur na | rkyen nyid de la yang rkyen yod par 'gyur zhing | de la yang de ltar bsam dgos so || thug pa med pa'i skyon du yang 'gyur te |* ... (see BP_{ed} 17.7-15). Bhāviveka concerns himself with responding to the Sautrāntikas who claim they do not maintain that conditions are conditions prior to the arising of the effect; he argues that conditions such as a seed grain (*'bras bu*) are not conditions even when the effect originates because they are neither exactly the same as nor different from the effect: *don dam par 'bras bu* (P: *'bu for 'bras bu*) *la sogs pa ni myu gu skye pa'i dus na rkyen gyi ngo bo nyid ma yin te | de nyid dang gzhan nyid du brjod par bya ba ma yin pa'i phyir dper na skad cig snga ma la de dag nyid bzhin* (PP D 57a2-3; P 68b4-5).

586 It is difficult to include *asya* in the English translation; I compensate by placing the referent of *asya* in square brackets. More literally, the sentence would read: "Moreover, these … would be postulated of this (*asya*) [consciousness maintained] as either [something] existing or not existing."

587 Candrakīrti cites MMK I.6ab: *naivāsato naiva sataḥ pratyayo 'rthasya yujyate |*.

For how could there be a condition of an inexistent thing [i.e.,] of [something] not existing (*avidyamāna*)?

§139. If [the opponent argues that] there will be the designation [condition] in consideration of the future thing, [we reply that] it is not so, because of the fault asserted by statements such as [the following from the Madhyamakāvatāra]:

> If [you] maintain there is the designation [of *śakti*] in consideration of the future [consciousness, this is wrong,] for without *śakti* there is not the futurity of this [consciousness].[589]

---

[588] Candrakīrti cites MMK I.6cd: *asataḥ pratyayaḥ kasya sataś ca pratyayena kim* ‖. PsP Tib: *med na gang gi rkyen du 'gyur* ‖ *yod na rkyen gyis ci zhig bya* ‖. Saito (1984: 226, n. 21) is of the opinion that *asataḥ* and *sataḥ* were understood as genitive absolutes, but it would seem rather that they are intended as elliptical conditional clauses, viz., *asataś* [*cet*] … *sataś* [*cet*]… .

[589] Candrakīrti is citing MA VI.58ab: *bhaviṣyatā ced vyapadeśa iṣṭaḥ śaktiṃ vinā nāsti hi bhāvitāsya* | (cf. Li 2012: 10). The opponent in the MABh maintains that consciousness arises from *śakti*. In response to Candrakīrti's statement that anyone who maintains that there is *śakti* of a consciousness that has not originated would also have to maintain it of the son of a barren woman, the opponent argues that the *śakti* he maintains is not intended to be related to a non-existent consciousness, but rather to a future consciousness (and thus, in refutation of MA VI.57cd, this future consciousness can be considered the qualifier of its *śakti*; see n. 575); for in the world one also speaks of future things, as in, "Cook the boiled rice" and "Weave the cloth" (cf. $MABh_{ed}$ 148.18-149.7). Candrakīrti replies that there could be the futurity of something which will come into existence at some point, but things such as the son of a barren woman, space, etc., which never arise, cannot be future [things]. Thus, in the case at hand, if *śakti* would exist, there might be a future consciousness (for *śakti* makes its existence possible). But when, inasmuch as a future consciousness does not exist (on account of the fact that it is future), *śakti* does not exist (since it requires its qualifier in order to exist as the qualified), then without *śakti*, consciousness, like the son of a barren woman, etc., cannot be future. Cf. $MABh_{ed}$ 149.11-18: *res 'ga' gang zhig tu 'gyur na ni de 'byung bar 'gyur gyi* | *rtag tu 'byung ba ma yin par nges pa mo gsham gyi bu la sogs pa'am nam mkha' la sogs pa ni mi 'gyur ro* ‖ *de'i phyir 'dir gal te nus pa yod par 'gyur na ni* | *rnam par shes pa 'byung bar 'gyur ba nyid du 'gyur ba zhig na gang gi tshe rnam par shes pa ma 'ongs pa yod pa ma yin pa nyid kyis nus pa med pa nyid yin pa de'i tshe* | *mo gsham gyi bu la sogs pa rnams* ($MABh_{UN}$: without *rnams*) *bzhin du nus pa med par de'i 'byung bar 'gyur ba nyid yod pa ma yin no* ‖. Candrakīrti adds that the example of boiled rice is also explained accordingly.
An objection not dissimilar to that here in the PsP, in which it is said that because cloth comes into being from threads, it is appropriate to teach threads as the

§140. Also for something existent, [that is,] for something existing (*vidyamāna*), whose origination has [already] resulted (*labdhajanma*), the postulation of a condition is absolutely useless (*niṣphala*).

§141. It having been brought out in this way that the collective (*samasta*) conditions, through [their] lack of capability to produce an effect, are not conditions, it is subsequently explained that the individual (*vyasta*) [conditions] are not conditions.

§142. At this point [the opponent] says: Even if conditions are thus impossible, there certainly is, nonetheless, the general establishment of [the individual] conditions, because their [defining] characteristics (*lakṣaṇa*) are taught. Among them, the [defining] characteristic [disclosed by the formulation] "the cause is that which brings forth" (*nirvartako hetuḥ*) has been stated for the cause condition (*hetu-pratyaya*). And teaching a [defining] characteristic for something that does not exist does not make sense, just as [teaching the defining characteristic] of the son of a barren woman [would not].[590]

---

conditions of cloth by reason of [the latter's] later origination, appears in BP: *smras pa | rgyu spun dag las snam bu 'byung bas phyis 'byung ba'i tshul gyis rgyu spun dag snam bu'i rkyen yin par bstan du rung* (BP_{ed} 18.7-8). Buddhapālita retorts that a condition cannot be established in reliance on something that arises later, i.e., something not arisen (see BP_{ed} 18.9-17). A similar objection turns up again in PP, where the opponent argues that he does not maintain the arising of the non-existent (such as a sky-flower), but rather maintains the arising of that which possesses arising (**utpattimat*). Bhāviveka responds that even in the case of a pot, cloth and hut, etc., which have the characteristic of non-existence prior to arising, the alleged conditions will not be *of* anything, since the pot, cloth, etc., are non-existent prior to arising (see PP D 57b2-4; P 69a5-8; see also PPṬ D 183b7-185a3). Bhāviveka additionally reinterprets MMK I.6a's *naivāsato naiva sataḥ* as referring to a thing neither existent nor inexistent (thus: "For a neither-existent-nor-inexistent thing a condition is not tenable") in order to refute Sautrāntikas who accept that conditions are not tenable either for something existent or for something inexistent, but argue that conditions attain the status of conditions right when the effect is in the process of arising, that is, when it cannot be defined as either non-existent or existent (see PP D 57b7-58a4; P 69b3-8 and Ames 1994: 107).

[590] A similar argument introduces MMK I.7 in BP (BP_{ed} 19.9-11: *'dir smras pa | 'di la dngos po rnams ni mtshan nyid las 'grub la | rgyu ni sgrub par byed pa'o || zhes rgyu'i mtshan nyid kyang bstan pas de ltar mtshan nyid yod pa'i rgyu yod do*). Bhāviveka introduces his alternative interpretation of the *kārikā* with a fellow Buddhist's objec-

§143. Reply: There might be a cause condition if its [defining] characteristic existed. But it does not exist, because,

[MMK I.7]

> When neither an existent (*sat*), nor an inexistent (*asat*), nor a [both] existent and inexistent (*sadasat*) factor (*dharma*) comes forth (*nirvartate*),
> How is the cause [condition] (*hetu*) that which brings forth (*nirvartaka*)?[591] Such being the case, [a cause condition] is not reasonable.[592]

---

tion in the form of a five-part inference arguing for the existence of the four conditions because they have been taught by the Tathāgata (see PP D 58b3-5; P 70a7-70b3; see also n. 236). The Tathāgata, the opponent Buddhist states, taught the cause [condition] to be that which brings forth (*rgyu ni sgrub par byed pa'o*).

[591] PsP Tib presents *ji ltar sgrub byed rgyu zhes bya* for *kathaṃ nirvartako hetuḥ*, i.e., "How is there an effectuator called 'cause'?" Saito (see BP_{tr} 19) does not translate *zhes bya*. Ames (1994: 108), relying on Bhāviveka's commentary, translates MMK I.7c as "How is the cause 'that which brings about?'"

[592] MMK I.7, according to de La Vallée Poussin (both at PsP_L 83.7-8 and at PsP_L 31.6 and 8) and all the manuscripts (here and at their equivalent for PsP_L 31.6 and 8), reads: *na san nāsan na sadasan dharmo nirvartate yadā | kathaṃ nirvartako hetur evaṃ sati hi yujyate ||*. PsP Tib, however, presents: *gang tshe chos ni yod pa dang || med dang yod med ni 'grub pa || ji ltar sgrub byed rgyu zhes bya || de lta yin na mi rigs so ||*. De La Vallée Poussin notes that PsP Tib would reflect *kathaṃ nirvartako hetur ity evaṃ sati na yujyate* (PsP_L 83, n. 2; the *iti* of de La Vallée Poussin's reconstruction unmetrically adds a *mātrā* to the *pāda*). ABh, BP, PP, PPṬ and MMK_T also present the final quarter as *de lta* (BP: *ltar*) *yin na mi rigs so* (Huntington [1986: 39] reports that CL corresponds with ABh). All five of these texts were translated by Jñānagarbha and Klu'i rgyal mtshan (some of the verses in MMK_T were later revised by Pa tshab). Before concluding that the individual Sanskrit manuscripts relied on for the five translations must have each read *evaṃ sati na yujyate* for MMK I.7d, it is important to recall that Saito has determined, through a comparison of the *kārikās* in ABh, BP and PP with the respective commentators' interpretations of them, that Jñānagarbha and Klu'i rgyal mtshan first translated the PPṬ, which contains the PP and the MMK, and then extracted the MMK (translated in reliance on the PP and PPṬ's interpretation of it) and inserted it into their translations of BP, ABh and PP ([Saito 1984: xvii:] "... Jñānagarbha and Klu'i rgyal mtshan always gave the same translation of MK embedded in ABh, BP, PP, and PPṬ even though these commentaries obviously differ in their interpretation of the *kārikās*"; see also Saito 1995). We may nevertheless assume that the Sanskrit manuscripts of the PPṬ and PP relied upon by Jñānagarbha and Klu'i rgyal mtshan presented MMK I.7d as *evaṃ sati na yujyate*. We may also assume that one, possibly both, of the PsP manuscripts used

approximately 250 years later for the PsP translation read *evaṃ sati na yujyate*, because PsP Tib for MMK I.7d reads *de lta yin na mi rigs so*. Even though Mahāsumati and Pa tshab elected to insert Jñānagarbha and Klu'i rgyal mtshan's earlier MMK translation into their PsP translation instead of translating the MMK embedded in the PsP of their Sanskrit manuscript—they did carefully check the inserted MMK translation against the PsP's MMK, and made any emendations or revisions deemed necessary, including occasional changes to bring it into accord with Candrakīrti's commentarial interpretation of it (for two instances in which they did not make the necessary changes, see Saito 1995).

The stand-alone version of MMK_T in the Tanjur was, as Saito has noted, originally the version made by Jñānagarbha and Klu'i rgyal mtshan in reliance on the PP and PPṬ. According to the MMK_T Derge colophon, this MMK_T translation underwent two later revisions: the first was made in Kashmir by the translator team Mahāsumati and Pa tshab in reliance on the MMK embedded in the PsP, the second in Lhasa by Kanakavarman and Pa tshab in reliance on the MMK embedded in a second PsP Sanskrit manuscript. Mahāsumati and Pa tshab applied the revisions they had made to the MMK they had "pasted" into their PsP translation to the stand-alone MMK_T. Kanakavarman and Pa tshab's MMK_T revisions would similarly have reflected the revisions—if any—they made to the MMK contained in the PsP translation when they checked this translation against the second PsP manuscript. It is possible—though evidence is lacking—that they also checked the MMK_T translation in reliance on a stand-alone manuscript of the MMK available in Lhasa (that the MMK circulated in India as stand-alone work has been confirmed by Luo Zhao and Shaoyong Ye's discovery of two MMK Sanskrit manuscripts; see Ye 2009: 309f.). The translator teams responsible for, respectively, the translation and revisions of MMK_T accepted each time the translation *de lta yin na mi rigs so* for MMK I.7d.

For the sake of further ascertaining the correct reading for MMK I.7d, it may prove worthwhile to examine the Indian commentators' reactions to MMK I.7cd. 1) The author of the ABh, known for his restatement of the *kārikā*s in his commentary, glosses I.7cd thus: *de'i tshe ji ltar sgrub par byed pa rgyu zhes bya ste | de lta yin na mi rigs so* (ABh_ed 257.8-10). Given that this is little more than the Tibetan version of the *kārikā* in prose form, it seems fairly certain that *na*, and not *hi*, stood in the ABh's Sanskrit citation of MMK I.7d and in the MMK manuscript relied on by the author of the ABh. 2) Buddhapālita comments on I.7cd with the words: *de ltar yin na sgrub par byed pa rgyu zhes bya ba de mi rigs so* (BP_ed 20.14). It is true that this comment could equally apply to the rhetorical question with *hi*, but it may well be intended as the explanation of 1.7cd attesting *evaṃ sati na yujyate*, and *mi rigs so* may be a citation. 3) Bhāviveka presents MMK I.7ab, then adds his own words *de yi tshe na don dam par*, and immediately afterward cites I.7c (I.7c: *ji ltar sgrub byed rgyu zhes bya*). His commentary on I.7c reads: *de ni sgrub par byed pa ma yin pa kho na* "That [alleged cause condition] is certainly not that which brings forth (*nirvartako*)" (PP D 58b1; P 70a5). It is thus clear that he considered MMK I.7c and I.7d to be two independent statements, with only MMK I.7c presenting the rhetorical question; MMK I.7d would simply sum up the situation with *evaṃ sati na yujyate*. He subsequently presents the

As regards the [*kārikā*], that which brings forth (*nirvartaka*) [is] the producer (*utpādaka*). If a factor (*dharma*), [that is,] the [thing] to be brought forth, came forth, the producing cause would produce it. But

---

objection of Buddhists who claim the Tathāgata taught the cause condition and again cites I.7ab, followed by I.7cd. His comment on I.7cd is: *de ni sgrub par byed pa'i rgyu ma yin pa kho na'o zhes bya ba'i tshig gi don* "The meaning of the words is that it is certainly not a cause that brings forth" (PP D 58b7; P 70b5-6). 4) Avalokitavrata quotes MMK I.7cd from the PP and Bhāviveka's above-cited comment on it, referring to I.7cd as follows: ... *de'i tshe ji ltar rgyu'i* (D: *rgyu*) *rkyen ces bya ste* | *de lta yin na don dam par rgyu'i rkyen mi rigs so zhes bya'i tha tshig go* (**tadā kathaṃ hetupratyaya ity evaṃ sati paramārthato hetupratyayo na yujyate* ...) "... then, how is there a cause condition? It being thus, ultimately a cause condition is not [logically] possible" (PPṬ D 192b5; P 225a4-5); Avalokitavrata seems quite definitely to have read I.7c and d as two independent sentences. 5) Candrakīrti's comment on MMK I.7cd as cited in PsP_{M} §50 (PsP_{L} 31.8) is limited to: *naivāsau nirvartako hetu iti vākyārthaḥ*, a statement that could be related to I.7cd construed with either *na* or *hi*. On the other hand, the final words of his commentary on MMK I.7 are precisely *evaṃ sati na yujyate*, which we might presume to be a citation of I.7d.
Thus, to conclude: the MMK manuscript used by the author of the Akutobhayā as well as the MMK manuscript used by Bhāviveka attested MMK I.7d as *evaṃ sati na yujyate*; Avalokitavrata's manuscript of Bhāviveka's PP attested MMK I.7d as *evaṃ sati na yujyate*; the PPṬ manuscript and the PP manuscript used by the translator team Jñānagarbha and Klu'i rgyal mtshan attested *evaṃ sati na yujyate*; one or both of the PsP manuscripts used by the PsP translator teams Mahāsumati and Pa tshab and Kanakarvarman and Pa tshab likewise attested *evaṃ sati na yujyate*. It seems possible that the MMK manuscript used by Buddhapālita also attested MMK I.7d as *evaṃ sati na yujyate*, and that the one used by Candrakīrti read *evaṃ sati na yujyate*, because he closes his commentary on MMK I.7 with exactly these words. I thus consider it justifiable, on the basis of MMK I.7c and d as cited, glossed and paraphrased by the Indian commentarial tradition, and on the basis of the Tibetan translation *de lta yin na mi rigs so* accepted by all three translator teams, to emend to *evaṃ sati na yujyate*.
It must, however, be acknowledged that the reading *evaṃ sati hi yujyate*, attested by both P and Q, was the accepted reading for the present study's manuscript tradition already by the twelfth century. According to our manuscripts, MMK I.7cd (*kathaṃ nirvartako hetur evaṃ sati hi yujyate*) would have been read as a single sentence, with *kathaṃ* construed with *hi*, in the sense "[Then] obviously (*hi*) how, this being the case, could a cause that brings forth be [logically] possible?" (the construction *kathaṃ hi* would be similar to Pāli *kathaṃ hi nāma* used to introduce a rhetorical question expressing wonder or amazement: "How could it be that ...?! [cf. PTSD and CPD s.v. *katham*]). In Kumārajīva's translation (T 30.1564: 3a3) the rendering of MMK I.7cd is made with one *pāda* (d): "How then can one say that there are [for it, the effect,] conditions?" See also Bocking 1995: 133. Compare Oetke's (2001a: 46) attempt to find meaning for *hi*.

[a factor] does not come forth, because [a thing] to be brought forth which has the form of [either] an existent, an inexistent, or an existent and inexistent [factor] does not exist. Among these [three alternatives], an existent [factor] does not come forth because [it already] exists. Nor does an inexistent [factor come forth], because [it] does not exist. Nor does an existent and inexistent [factor come forth], because a mutually contradictory single thing does not exist, and because there would be the faults stated for both alternatives. Because in this way there is no arising of an effect, there is thus no cause condition either. And therefore, it being thus, that which has been asserted [by the opponent], [namely, that] the cause condition exists because [its defining] characteristic exists, is not tenable.[593]

§144. Now, for the sake of the refutation of the object condition (*ārambaṇapratyaya*), he [= Nāgārjuna] states,

[MMK I.8]

> This existent (*sat*) factor, indeed without an object [condition] (*anārambaṇa*), is taught[594] [by you as having an object condition];

---

[593] Devaśarman's commentary on MMK I.7 has been preserved in Bhāviveka's PP (Avalokitavrata informs that his commentary was entitled *dkar po 'char ba*; Ames [1994: 129, n. 105] suggests **Śuklābhyudaya* as the Sanskrit title). Devaśarman claims that the Mādhyamika has two objects of refutation, namely, attachment to objects of expression (**abhidheya*) and attachment to expressions (**abhidhāna*). Attachment to objects of expression has already been refuted via the refutation of arising, and thus Nāgārjuna aims to refute attachment to expressions by way of MMK I.7. He does this by demonstrating that it is impossible for something to come forth. Effects thus being impossible, a reason (*byed rgyu*; **kāraṇa*) for the expression "cause" does not exist (*rgyur brjod pa la 'jug pa'i byed rgyu med pa'i phyir*) (see PP D 59a1-4; P 70b6-71a2; Ames 1994: 110). Bhāviveka also briefly summarizes and attacks, according to Avalokitavrata (Bhāviveka refers to the opponent[s] only as *gzhan dag*), Buddhapālita's commentary on MMK I.7. Avalokitavrata explains Bhāviveka's somewhat laconic critique (PP D 59a5; P 71a4: *de ni bzang po ma yin te | lan btab zin pa'i phyir*) as referring to the fact that Buddhapālita attempts to refute the coming forth of something existent, something inexistent and something both existent and inexistent by utilizing only theses; in each case he fails to present reasons and examples (see PPṬ D 195a1-195b1; P 227a1-227b2).

[594] Candrakīrti and Buddhapālita understand the subject of the verb *upadiśyate* to be the opponent (see BP_{ed} 20.20-24). The author of ABh understands its subject to be

When a[n existent] factor is without an object [condition], how is there nevertheless an object [condition]?[595]

---

the Bhagavat, who has stated in the Prajñāpāramitā that the 84,000 *dharmaskandha*s are of one savour, indeed without an object support (... *ro gcig dmigs pa med pa kho na yin*; cf. ABh_{ed} 257.20-22). Bhāviveka likewise understands its subject to be the Bhagavat; see Saito 1984: 227, n. 28. Bhāviveka provides scriptural support for MMK I.8 with quotations from the Suvikrāntavikrāmiparipṛcchā (see PP D 59b7-60a3; P 71b8-72a4; Ames 1994: 113).

[595] Candrakīrti cites MMK I.8: *anārambaṇa evāyaṃ san dharma upadiśyate | athānārambaṇe dharme kuta ārambaṇaṃ punaḥ ||*. Saito and Huntington note that MMK I.8 and I.9 are reversed in CL (cf. Saito 1984: 228, n. 31; Huntington 1986: 39 [the corresponding *kārikā*s are numbered 10 and 11 in the latter's edition of ABh]); see also Bocking 1995: 114f. Saito points out that the CL presents the four *kārikā*s refuting the individual four conditions (= MMK I.6-9) in the order the conditions are presented in AK II.61cd and 62, and not in the order they appear in MMK I.2, and suggests that Kumārajīva may have relied on the AK order and therefore be responsible for the switch. ABh, BP, PP and PPṬ present *de ltar* for I.8c's *atha*. PsP Tib attests *ci ste*, and MMK_T has been corrected by Pa tshab to read *ci ste*. Ames (1994: 131, n. 119) suggests that Jñānagarbha and Klu'i rgyal mtshan, the translators of the MMK (the version used and lightly revised by Pa tshab), read *tathā*. As Saito has pointed out, their MMK translation was influenced by the readings in their PP and PPṬ manuscripts. Given that Jñānagarbha and Klu'i rgyal mtshan merely inserted their PP and PPṬ-influenced translation of the MMK into BP, it is not surprising that we also find *de ltar* in the BP *kārikā*; what is disconcerting, however, is the fact that Buddhapālita, like Candrakīrti, explains the word as indicating a question (*de ltar zhes bya ba'i sgra ni dri ba'o*), an explanation more reasonably connected with *atha* (cf. Apte s.v. *atha* meaning 5: *praśna*). One thus conjectures that Buddhapālita read *atha*. The fact that *de ltar* also appears in Buddhapālita's commentarial gloss on the *kārikā* word would seem to indicate that either the BP manuscript used by Jñānagarbha and Klu'i rgyal mtshan attested the corrupt reading *tathā* or that the translators noted that Buddhapālita was citing from the *kārikā* and therefore consciously translated the commentary's *atha* to accord with their translation of the *kārikā*'s *atha* (there are two other instances of *de ltar* in BP which occur in combination with the other words of I.8c [see BP_{ed} 21.13; 21.24]). Bhāviveka does not gloss the word in his PP.
De La Vallée Poussin notes that *san* is not translated in MMK I.8 in ABh (PsP_L 84, n. 2) but he has mistaken the beginning of I.8c (*de ltar chos 'di*) for the beginning of 1.8a (*yod pa'i chos 'di*). The *kārikā* in ABh, however, like that of PsP but unlike that of PP and BP which read *yin pa'i chos 'di*, does read *yod pa'i chos 'di* ... (see Saito's [1984: 227, n. 28] comments on the translation of I.8ab). De La Vallée Poussin further notes that *ayam* is not translated in BP; the reading *yin pa'i chos ni* as found in D, C, P and N has been corrected by Saito to *yin pa'i chos 'di* on the basis of the commentary (see BP_{ed} 20, n. 9).

In this system [of the opponent]—owing to authoritative testimony (*āgama*) [which states:] "Which factors have an object [support]? [answer:] All the consciousnesses and mental factors (*citta-caitta*)"[596]—[it is held that] an object [support] such as visual form, by virtue of which the consciousnesses and mental factors, as appropriate (*yathāyogam*), arise, is their object condition (*ārambaṇa-pratyaya*).[597] And this [object condition] would be postulated [by you either] for [consciousnesses and mental factors] that exist or for non-existing [consciousnesses and mental factors]. Among these [two alternatives, as regards the first, i.e., already] existing [consciousnesses and mental factors], there would be no use for their object [condition]; for an object [condition] would be postulated for the sake of the arising of a factor (*dharma*), but that [existent factor] already exists prior to the object [condition]. Now when in this way a factor is established by its own nature (*svātman*) without an object [condition], what is the point in postulating its association (*yoga*) with an object [condition]? Thus, this existent, [that is,] existing, factor such as consciousness is indeed without an object [condition]. You alone, based on [your] own fancy (*svamanīṣikā*), say that it has an object [condition] (*sārambaṇa*).[598] It does not, however, have any connection with an object [condition].

§145. But if [on the other hand,] it is postulated that a non-existent [factor] has an object [condition], that [idea] is not reasonable either, [because Nāgārjuna states:] "[T]his ... indeed without an object," etc. (*anārambaṇa evāyam ityādi*); for there is no association of a non-

[596] The citation is from the Prakaraṇa (T Vol. 26, 715c26), a canonical Abhidharma work of the Sarvāstivāda school traditionally said to have been authored by Vasumitra. It is more likely a compilation. The Prakaraṇa passage cited by Candrakīrti is also cited by Bhāviveka: *dmigs pa dang bcas pa'i chos rnams gang zhe na | 'di lta ste | sems dang sems las byung ba rnams so* (P: ||) *zhes* (PP D 59b5; P 71b5-6). On the Prakaraṇa see, e.g., Frauwallner 1995: 32ff.; Willemen et al. 1998: 212ff. Cf. also AK II.34bc: *cittacaitasāḥ | sāśrayālambanākārāḥ*.

[597] The object condition is explicitly associated with *cittacaitta* here; see n. 555.

[598] Cp. BP_{ed} 20.22-23: ... *khyod kyis rang gi blos dmigs pa dang bcas pa zhes brjod.*

existing [factor] with an object [condition].[599] [The alternative reading of MMK I.8ab is thus:]

---

[599] Candrakīrti views MMK I.8ab as amenable to two interpretations. In the first interpretation, *sat* is taken as an attributive adjective of *dharma*; the statement composed of the first five words of the verse-half is thus connected with the first of the two alternatives presented in Candrakīrti's commentary, viz., that existing consciousnesses and mental factors have an object condition (the first alternative: *ayaṃ ca vidyamānānāṃ vā parikalpyeta ...*). This interpretation may be clarified as: *anārambaṇa evāyaṃ san* (= *vidyamāno*) *dharmaḥ* ... . In the second interpretation, *sat* of the *kārikā* is understood as marking the predicative function of *anārambaṇa*; the first five words of the *kārikā* are thus connected with Candrakīrti's second alternative, viz., that non-existing consciousnesses and mental factors have an object condition (the second alternative: *ayaṃ ca ... parikalpyetāvidyamānānāṃ vā*). This interpretation may be clarified as: *anārambaṇa eva sann ayam* [*avidyamāno*] *dharmo* ... . Candrakīrti refers to this second interpretation with *anārambaṇa evāyam ityādi*. PsP Tib presents a full and revised translation of 1.8ab at this point, with the revisions reflecting the second interpretation: *chos 'di dmigs pa med pa ni* ‖ *yin pa kho nar nye bar bstan* ‖ (*yin pa* renders *san* in its function as a predicate-marker). See also the comments in Saito 1984: 227, n. 28.
This second interpretation of the *kārikā* as found in the PsP corresponds with Buddhapālita's interpretation of MMK I.8. Buddhapālita thus interprets I.8ab to mean "This [inexistent] factor which is indeed without an object [condition], ..." Buddhapālita's comments on the *kārikā* in this meaning are more elaborate than Candrakīrti's. He argues that an existent *dharma* could have an object [condition], but a non-existing *dharma*, i.e., one that has not yet come into existence, could not. Since prior to having an object [condition] a *dharma* is without an object condition, it is therefore without an object condition. It is the same as a person and wealth: only a person who exists can be a possessor of wealth: *chos yod pa ni dmigs pa dang bcas par 'gyur gyi med pa ni mi 'gyur ro* ‖ *dmigs pa dang bcas pa'i sngon rol na dmigs pa med pas de ni dmigs pa med pa yin no* ‖ *'di lta ste* | *dper na nor yod pa ni nor dang bcas pa ste nor can zhes bya'o* ‖ *'ga' zhig yod na nor dang bcas par 'gyur gyi* | *med na mi 'gyur ro* ‖ *nor dang bcas pa'i sngon rol na nor med pas de ni nor med pa yin pa bzhin no* (BP_{ed} 21.2-6). Saito states that Bhāviveka appears to criticize this example of a person and wealth when he clarifies that a consciousness is said to have an object [condition] because it arises having the appearance of the object [condition] by virtue of which it arises, and not because there is a simultaneous connection, as in the case of someone having wealth (see Saito 1984: 228, n. 30); Bhāviveka states: *dmigs pa gang gis skye ba na* | (D: ‖) *der snang ba skye ba'i phyir dmigs pa dang bcas pa zhes bya'i* | *nor can bzhin du dus gcig kho nar 'brel pa'i* (P: *ba'i*) *phyir ni ma yin* (PP D 59b1-2; P 71a8-71b1). While it is possible that Bhāviveka's critique of the example is meant as an indirect criticism of BP, it should also be remarked that Buddhapālita uses the example in the context of refuting the *ārambaṇapratyaya*, whereas Bhāviveka critiques it in the context of explaining the *ārambaṇapratyaya* on the surface level; Bhāviveka may have thus merely been inspired by Buddhapālita's commentary

> This [inexistent] factor, which is (*sat*) indeed without an object [condition], is taught

The [unexpressed] rest of the sentence is: "by you as having an object [condition]."[600]

---

to refer to the example. Buddhapālita subsequently presents an opponent who critiques the example of wealth as inappropriate for the illustration of *sārambaṇa*. The corrected view of *sārambaṇa* set forth by the opponent, according to Buddhapālita, is answered by the last two quarters of MMK I.8 (see BP_{ed} 21.15-19; 21.23-22.5; BP_{tr} 21).

Bhāviveka understands I.8ab (translated in PP Tib as *yin pa'i chos 'di dmigs pa ni* || *med pa kho nar nye bar bstan* ||) to be referring to statements of the Buddha's in which he has taught (*upadiśyate*) or alluded to the fact that past and future *dharma*s, as well as *dharma*s in the process of arising, do not have an object condition. Bhāviveka states that the reason consciousnesses and mental factors do not have an object [condition] is that their arising on the ultimate level has been negated. Only for the sake of setting forth the superficial level of truth is cognition said to have an object condition. According to Avalokitavrata, since all things are momentary and because the object has already ceased when cognition of it occurs, i.e., when consciousness appears in its (i.e., the object's) aspect (*ākāra*), even on the surface level consciousnesses and mental factors do not have a concurrent object condition. Bhāviveka glosses *sat* of MMK I.8ab with a Sanskrit word that has been translated into Tibetan as *gyur pa*: *yin pa'i zhes bya ba ni gyur pa'i zhes bya ba'i tha tshig* (PP D 59a6; P 71a5). Ames (1994: 111) suggests that *gyur pa* reflects *bhūta* and translates this gloss as "'is' (*yin pa* = *san*) has the meaning of being [such-and-such]." It is possible that PP Skt attested instead *bhavan*, which is attested in our ms Q as a gloss for *sat* (*bhavan* appears to be an interpolation in Q). Avalokitavrata considers Bhāviveka to understand *sat* as a predicate-marker that is to be construed with a compound not expressed in the *kārikā*; he informs that what has not been stated is **anārambaṇa*. He, like Bhāviveka, interprets the verse to mean "This factor (*dharma*) which is [without an object condition (*anārambaṇa*)] is taught [by the Buddha] to be indeed ultimately (*paramārthata*) without an object [condition] (*anārambaṇa*)." He comments on the verse-half as follows: *de la yin pa'i chos 'di zhes bya ba ni khyad par gyi gzhi yin la* | *dmigs pa ni* | (P: without |) *med pa kho nar nye bar bstan* | (P: without |) *zhes* (P: *ces*) *bya ba ni de'i khyad par yin te* | *dmigs pa med pa yin pa'i chos mig gi rnam par shes pa la sogs pa blo la bzhag pa 'di ni don dam par dmigs pa med pa kho nar bcom ldan 'das kyis* (P: *kyi*) *nye bar bstan to zhes bya bar sbyar ro* || *yin pa'i zhes bya ba ni gyur pa'i gzhi zhes bya ba'i tha tshig go zhes bya ba ni* | *dmigs pa med pa yin pa'i zhes bya ba ni dmigs pa med par gyur pa'i zhes* (P: *ces*) *bya ba'i tha tshig* (PPṬ D 195b4-6; P 227b6-8).

[600] PsP Tib reads *chos 'di dmigs pa med pa ni* || *yin pa ste gyur pa kho na khyed kyis nye bar bstan te* | *dmigs pa dang bcas par zhes bya ba ni tshig gi lhag ma'o* for *anārambaṇa evāyaṃ san dharma upadiśyate, bhavadbhiḥ sārambaṇa iti vākyaśeṣaḥ*.

When a[n inexistent] factor is without an object [condition], how is there nevertheless an object [condition]?

The word *atha* is [employed] in [the sense of indicating] a question;[601] *kuta* ("how") [is employed] in [the sense of indicating] a reason (*hetu*). Therefore, this is the sense: Thus, when a factor that is inexistent (*asat*) [i.e.], is not existing (*avidyamāna*), is without an object [condition] (*anārambaṇa*), how can there still (*bhūyas*) [be] an object [condition]? The intent is: Since something that has an object [condition] does not exist, an object [condition] also does not exist.[602]

§146. [Question:] Why then [is it asserted that] consciousnesses and mental factors have an object [condition] (*sārambaṇāś cittacaittāḥ*)?

PsP Tib appears to have been influenced by the interpolated reading *bhavan* in a manuscript at the translators' disposal which was connected with ms Q's tradition: ms Q reads at this point *anārambaṇa evāyaṃ san bhavan dharma upadiśyate …* . De La Vallée Poussin (PsP$_L$ 85, n. 1) reconstructs PsP Tib's Sanskrit as *dharmo 'yam anālambanaḥ san bhūta eva bhavadbhir upadiśyate; sālambana iti vākyaśeṣaḥ*; it is more likely that Pa tshab and his collaborators' manuscripts read—with the addition of Q's *bhavan*—as our edition does. Note that Pa tshab revises MMK I.8ab to read *chos 'di dmigs pa med pa ni* ‖ *yin pa kho nar nye bar bstan* ‖ (from *yod pa'i chos 'di dmigs pa ni* ‖ *med pa kho na nye bar bstan* ‖) for the sake of conveying the meaning of the second interpretation.

601 Candrakīrti relies on Buddhapālita's commentary for this explanation (BP$_{ed}$ 21.12-13: *de ltar zhes bya ba sgra ni dri ba'o* ‖ *ga la 'gyur zhes bya ba gtan tshigs bstan pa*). *atha* in its sense of indicating a question, here in combination with the interrogative particle *kuta*, cannot be translated into English.

602 Buddhapālita cites MMK I.8cd twice, constructing his commentary such that the second instance of citation is presented as the response to an opponent who rejects the simultaneous relationship of a *dharma* and its object condition (exemplified in his commentary on MMK I.8ab by a person and wealth, the first citation of I.8cd representing the logical conclusion to I.8ab's commentary) and instead argues that the object condition is the basis (*gzhi*; Saito suggests **nidāna* [BP$_{tr}$ 21]) that produces a *dharma*. In his comments on the second citation of I.8cd, Buddhapālita responds that when a *dharma* does not exist, i.e., has not come into being (*mngon par ma grub*), then what is termed "the *dharma*'s object [condition]" has also not come into being; and thus, given that the object condition does not exist, it does not produce the *dharma* (see BP$_{ed}$ 21.23-22.5).

[Answer:] This is a surface-level characteristic, not an ultimate [one]; therefore, there is not a fault.[603]

§147. Now, for the sake of refuting the immediately preceding condition (*samanantarapratyaya*), he [= Nāgārjuna] says:

[MMK I.9]

> When factors (*dharma*) have not [yet] arisen, cessation (*nirodha*) [of the cause] is not possible,
> Thus, the immediately preceding [condition] (*anantara*) is not [logically] possible. And when [the cause] has ceased, what is the condition?[604]

There [in MMK I.9], the quarters in the last half of the verse should be regarded as [being in] an inverted order, and the word "and" (*ca*) as being in the wrong place [that is, instead of *niruddhe pratyayaś ca kaḥ* one should understand] *niruddhe ca* [*pratyayaḥ kaḥ*]. Therefore, the reading [should be] thus: "And when [the cause] has ceased, what is the condition? Thus, the immediately preceding [condition] is not [logically] possible." For the sake of verse composition, however, it has been put like this.[605]

As concerns the [content], the immediately preceding (*anantara*) cessation (*nirodha*) of the cause (*kāraṇa*) that is the condition for the arising of the effect is the [defining] characteristic of the immediately

---

[603] Both Bhāviveka and Candrakīrti affirm that consciousnesses and mental factors have an object condition on the surface level. Bhāviveka states: *dmigs pa dang bcas pa zhes bya ba ni tha snyad kyi bden pa'i lugs rnam par gzhag pa'i phyir* (PP D 59a1; P 71a8).

[604] Candrakīrti cites MMK I.9: *anutpanneṣu dharmeṣu nirodho nopapadyate | nānantaram ato yuktaṃ niruddhe pratyayaś ca kaḥ* ||.

[605] Candrakīrti follows Buddhapālita in considering the last two quarters of the *kārikā* as requiring reversal for proper comprehension of Nāgārjuna's intent. The Tibetan for the second verse-half reads: *de phyir de ma thag mi rigs* || *'gags na rkyen yang gang zhig yin* || (Pa tshab does not emend Jñānagarbha and Klu'i rgyal mtsan's translation). Buddhapālita writes (cf. BP_{ed} 22.13-16): *de la rtsa ba 'og ma gnyis* || *'gags na rkyen yang gang zhig yin* || *de phyir de ma thag mi rigs* || *zhes bsnor bar blta bar bya'o* ||. The author of ABh and Bhāviveka interpret the *kārikā* as it stands.

preceding condition (*samanantarapratyaya*).[606] Here [the *kārikā*] takes into account the fact that when factors, [i.e.,] effects (*kārya*), [namely,] a sprout and so forth, have not [yet] arisen, the cessation of the cause (*kāraṇa*), [i.e.,] a seed and so forth, does not make sense.[607] When this is the case, then since there is no cessation of a cause, what is the immediately preceding condition for the sprout? But if [you] maintain that even if the effect has not arisen, the seed ceases, [then] in this case, when the seed has ceased, [i.e.,] has become non-existent, what is the condition for the sprout? Or what is the condition for the cessation of the seed? Since both of these [i.e., the cessation of the seed and the sprout,] will be without a cause (*ahetuka*), he [= Nāgārjuna] states, "And when [the cause] has ceased, what is the condition?"[608] The word "and" (*ca*) [of I.9d] takes reference to the

---

[606] Candrakīrti refers to the defining characteristic of the immediately preceding condition as formulated in his commentary on MMK I.2; see n. 556.

[607] Candrakīrti understands *dharma*s of MMK I.9a to refer to effects; Buddhapālita also understands the reference to be to effects. Bhāviveka, on the other hand, is of the opinion that with the mention of *dharma*s in MMK I.9a, Nāgārjuna intends reference to all things, and specifically to causes. Bhāviveka explains that when all *dharma*s are in ultimate reality unarisen, their cessation is not possible, just as the cessation of an unarisen second head is not possible: *'di la don dam par chos thams cad rnam pa thams cad du bkag pa'i phyir chos rnams ma skyes so* (P: ||) *zhes de bstan zin pas de'i phyir* ... (MMK I.9ab) ... *ma skyes pa'i phyir mgo gnyis pa dgag pa bzhin* (PP D 60a4; P 72a4-6). Both Candrakīrti and Buddhapālita present this interpretation as a secondary, alternative approach to the *kārikā*; see BP_{ed} 24.5-18, BP_{tr} 24.

[608] Candrakīrti initially argues that an effect would need to exist for the cessation of its cause to make any sense, because otherwise the effect would not have a cause. Since the cessation of the cause should not occur when the effect is still not there, cessation as the immediately preceding condition is not possible. He then moves on to reject the idea that cessation of the cause could occur even if the effect has not yet arisen, arguing that if the cause, i.e., seed, no longer exists, the effect, the sprout, in not having a cause (*ahetuka*), could not arise. He adds that if one holds that the effect has not arisen before the seed ceases, the perishing of the cause (*kāraṇa*), e.g., a seed, would be without a cause (*ahetuka*), that is, there would be no cause for its perishing. Candrakīrti has appropriated the argumentation from the corresponding section of Buddhapālita's commentary on the *kārikā*. Cp. BP_{ed} 23.4-10: *de la gal te myu gu skye ba'i sngon rol du sa bon 'gags par 'gyur na ni sa bon 'gags te med na myu gu skye bar 'gyur ba gang yin pa de'i rkyen yang gang zhig yin | yang na sa bon 'gag pa'i rkyen yang gang zhig yin | sa bon 'gags te med pa yang ji ltar myu gu skye ba'i rkyen du 'gyur | myu gu ma skyes pa'i rkyen du sa bon 'gag pa ji ltar 'gyur | de lta bas na sa*

bon 'gags nas myu gu skye bar rtog na de gnyi ga rgyu med par thal bar 'gyur te | *rgyu med par ni mi 'dod.* "As regards that, if prior to the arising of the sprout the seed has ceased, what, when the seed has ceased, i.e., is non-existent, is the condition for the arising of the sprout? Or what is the condition for the cessation of the seed? How could the seed, having ceased, [and] although [now] non-existent, be the condition for the arising of the sprout? How could the cessation of the seed be the condition for the sprout which has not [yet] arisen? Thus, if it is imagined that the sprout arises once the seed ceases, it follows that those both [i.e., cessation and arising] are without a cause (**ahetuka*). [But] being without a cause is not maintained [by you the opponent]." In the objection that follows in BP the opponent argues that the seed ceases immediately after the sprout has arisen and therefore the arisen sprout is the condition for the perishing of the seed; Buddhapālita states that even in this case both would be, as in the earlier case, without a cause [**ahetuka*] (see BP_{ed} 23.11-13 and Buddhapālita's response at 23.14-18). Bhāviveka presents I.9d as rejecting the Conservative Buddhists' theory that the cessation of consciousness and mental factors represents the immediately preceding condition; he argues by way of an inference that this cessation of consciousness and mental factors is just like a cessation of consciousness and mental factors that occurred long ago or like matter (according to Avalokitavrata: cessations of matter), neither of which can serve as the immediately preceding condition for a consciousness that is about to arise (see PP D 60a5-7; P 72a6-8; Kajiyama 1964: 120; Ames 1994: 114). Here and in the rest of his commentary on the *kārikā*, Bhāviveka discusses the immediately preceding condition in the context of the explication given in the AK, i.e., as restricted to consciousnesses and mental factors. Both Buddhapālita and Candrakīrti discuss the immediately preceding condition by adverting to the material entities seed and sprout. Although Bhāviveka critiques Buddhapālita's interpretation of MMK I.9cd and speaks of consciousnesses and mental factors in the course of the critique, he does not specifically attack Buddhapālita's discussing the immediately preceding condition in terms of material objects such as seed and sprout.

As indicated, Bhāviveka summarizes and criticizes Buddhapālita's commentary on MMK I.9cd. Repeating a now familiar complaint, he claims that Buddhapālita merely provides a *prasaṅga* argument when he asserts that both cessation and arising would be without a cause (**ahetuka*) because the seed that has ceased and the effect that has not arisen are non-existent, and declares that when the probandum and probans of the *prasaṅga* are reversed, one is confronted with the affirmative statements that what has not ceased is a condition, because it has a cause, and that arising has consciousnesses and mental factors which have not ceased as cause, because it (= arising) has a cause. Thus, the reason "because it has a cause" will be either unestablished (*asiddha*) or contradictory (*viruddhārtha*) (see Ames 1994: 115). Candrakīrti ignores Bhāviveka's charges, in all likelihood because he has already, in his commentary on MMK I.1, defended Buddhapālita's employment of such *prasaṅga* statements by pointing out that they do not imply their opposite. Candrakīrti's own reiteration of Buddhapālita's comments in the face of Bhāviveka's critique is ob-

word[s] "not arisen" (*anutpanna*) [of I.9a].[609] Therefore [one should understand]: And (*ca*) even if you maintain the cessation of seeds and so forth when the sprout has not [yet] arisen (*anutpanna*), these both [i.e., the cessation of the cause and the arising of the effect] end up without a cause (*ahetuka*); thus, the immediately preceding [condition] is not logically possible.

§148. Alternatively, having in mind that arising has been refuted with "Not arisen from self, nor from other" [= MMK I.1], etc., he [= Nāgārjuna] says,

> When factors [without exception] have not arisen, cessation [of the cause] is not possible,
> Thus, the immediately preceding [condition] is not [logically] possible.

Moreover,

> And when [the cause] has ceased, what is the condition?

Here, the explanation [for MMK I.9d] is just as the previous [one for I.9d].

§149. Now, for the sake of the refutation of the own nature (*svarūpa*) of the dominant condition (*adhipatipratyaya*), he [= Nāgārjuna] states,[610]

---

viously intended as implicit sanction of Buddhapālita's style of argumentation and its content, and thus as an indirect rejection of Bhāviveka's complaints.

[609] Candrakīrti has taken the lead for his interpretation of "and" (*ca*) of MMK I.9d from Buddhapālita's explanation: *yang zhes bya ba'i sgra ni 'dir ma skyes pa la ltos par blta bar bya'o* || *de yang ma skyes pa'i sgra la ltos nas* | [I.9d:] *'gags na rkyen yang gang zhig yin* || *ma skyes pa'i rkyen gang zhig yin* || *zhes bya bar sbyar ro* || (BP_{ed} 22.16-20). Bhāviveka states that the *ca* is employed for the sake of including two negations, namely, that what has ceased is not an immediately preceding condition, nor a condition in general; PP D 60a7; P 72a8-72b1: *kyang* (read: *yang*) *zhes bya ba'i sgra ni de ma thag pa'i rkyen nyid ma yin pa dang* | *spyi'i rkyen kyang* (read: *yang*) *ma yin no* (P: ||) *zhes dgag pa bsdu ba'i phyir ro* ||; see Kajiyama 1964: 121; Ames 1994: 115.

[610] PsP Tib presents *da ni bdag po'i rkyen bsal bar bzhed nas bshad pa* for *idānīm adhipatipratyayasvarūpaniṣedhārtham āha*. *svarūpa* does not occur in the similarly

[MMK I.10]

> Because there is no existence (*sattā*) of things that are without own-being (*svabhāva*),
> This [statement] "when this exists, that comes to be" is definitely not tenable.[611]

In this system [of the opponent], the [defining] characteristic of the dominant condition (*adhipatipratyaya*) is [formulated as]: The [condition] owing to the existence of which [something] comes into being is the dominant [condition] for that [thing] (*yasmin sati yad bhavati tat tasyādhipateyam*). But when, because things are dependently arisen (*pratītyasamutpanna*), own-being (*svabhāva*) does not exist, how does what is designated as the cause, [expressed by] "[when] this" (*asmin*), [exist] and how does what is designated as the effect, [expressed by] "that" (*idam*), [exist]? Therefore, there is not, also from the point of view of the [defining] characteristic, the establishment of the [dominant] condition.[612]

---

constructed introductory sentences to MMK I.8 and I.9. It has ostensibly been included in MMK I.10's introductory sentence because both I.10 and Candrakīrti's commentary on it make reference to the lack of own-being (*svabhāva*) of the *adhipatipratyaya*.

[611] Candrakīrti cites MMK I.10: *bhāvānāṃ niḥsvabhāvānāṃ na sattā vidyate yataḥ* | *satīdam asmin bhavatīty etan naivopapadyate* ||. Garfield (1995: 119) renders the Tibetan translation of MMK I.10 (*dngos po rang bzhin med rnams kyi* || *yod pa gang phyir yod min na* || *'di yod pas na 'di 'byung zhes* || *bya ba 'di ni 'thad ma yin* ||) as "If things did not exist [w]ithout essence, [t]he phrase, 'when this exists so this will be,' [w]ould not be acceptable," arguing that the translations by Inada, etc., (in general in line with mine) are "not supported by the dialectical structure of the chapter and force an excessively negative interpretation on the chapter as a whole." In his attempt to force an unwarranted positive interpretation on the *kārikā*, Garfield overlooks that his translation is not supported by its wording or grammar. His translation ignores *gang phyir*, assumes *na* to indicate a conditional construction (*na* should be construed with *gang phyir*) and treats the second half of the verse as though it were the apodosis of a conditional sentence. Nor is it acceptable to turn a blind eye to the fact that this interpretation leaves the fourth condition unrefuted. It is quite clear that Nāgārjuna declares in MMK I.1 that nothing whatsoever arises, sets forth in MMK I.2 the four conditions said to be responsible for the arising of things and then proceeds to refute them one by one in MMK I.7-10.

[612] Candrakīrti considers the *kārikā* to refute the dominant condition through its denial of the possibility of the existence of things that lack own-being. The sentence

§150. At this point, [the opponent] says: [Because we] have observed that cloth, etc., [is made] from threads, etc., threads, etc., [are maintained to be] the conditions of cloth, etc.

§151. Reply: There is absolutely no arising of results (*phala*) such as cloth from the point of view of own nature (*svarūpataḥ*), [so] how could it be established that conditions have the status of conditions (*pratyayatva*)? And explaining the way in which there is not the arising of results such as cloth, etc., he [= Nāgārjuna] states,

[MMK I.11]

> And that result (*phala*) is not in the individual or collective conditions.

---

asmin satīdaṃ bhavati cited by Nāgārjuna in I.10cd is the first half of the famous explication of dependent-arising *asmin satīdaṃ bhavaty asyotpādād idam utpadyate* (Pāli: *imasmiṃ sati idaṃ hoti imass' uppādā idaṃ uppajjati*), the initial formulation of which is attributed to the Buddha (see n. 86). The descriptive characterization of the dominant condition, namely, *yasmin sati yad bhavati tat tasyādhipateyam*, is obviously based on it. The dominant condition is rejected from the standpoint of the ultimate on the ground that when any existence (*sattā*) of things without own-being is impossible, one cannot speak of a condition, i.e., a dominant condition by virtue of whose existence (*asmin sati*) a real effect arises. This same view of the intent of the *kārikā* is presented even more lucidly by Buddhapālita: *de ltar gang gi phyir dngos po rang bzhin med pa rnams kyi yod pa zhes bya ba yod pa'i dngos po mi 'thad pa de'i phyir gang yod na 'di yod pas zhes brjod par nus pa'i dngos po de nyid med do* || *'di yod pas zhes bya ba 'di la med na 'di 'byung zhes bya ba de 'thad par ga la 'gyur* (BP_{ed} 25.6-10) "Thus, because 'the existence (**sattā*) of things without own-being,' [that is,] real existence (**sadbhāva*?), is not tenable, exactly that thing in regard to which, when it exists, one is able to say, 'when this exists,' does not exist. If here 'when this exists' is not possible, how is it tenable that 'that comes into being'?" Bhāviveka, who has, following the AK, defined the *adhipatipratyaya* as *bdag po'i rkyen ni byed pa'i rgyu*—but who in the PP addresses an opponent who characterizes it as the opponent in the PsP does—considers MMK I.10 to be refuting both the ultimate- and surface-level existence of the dominant condition; Bhāviveka states that even according to worldly convention it is not accepted that an effect arises when only a partial cause exists (according to Avalokitavrata: a partial cause = without the other necessary conditions). Thus, as Nāgārjuna declares, the statement *asmin sati idaṃ bhavati*, which communicates that an effect arises when the dominant condition is present, is not tenable: *don dam pa* (P: *par*) *'ba' zhig tu yang ma zad kyi* | *ji ltar 'jig rten gyi tha snyad du yang ste* | *rgyu nyi tshe yod du zin kyang 'bras bu skye bar khas ma blangs pa'i phyir* | *'di yod pas ni 'di 'byung zhes* || *bya ba de ni 'thad ma yin* || (PP D 61a1-2; P 73a3-4).

> But how could that which is not in [its] conditions come from conditions?[613]

As regards this, cloth is not in each of the individual [conditions], such as the threads, the brush, the loom, the shuttle and the stick, because it is not perceived in them, and because of the entailment of a multitude (*bahutva*) of effects owing to the multitude of causes. Cloth is also not in the collected (*samudita*) threads and so forth, because it does not exist in each of the parts, and because [there would be] the consequence that one effect would arise bit by bit (*khaṇḍaśaḥ*) [i.e., in a fragmentary, piecemeal way]. Therefore, because a result does not exist, conditions do not exist from the point of view of own-being.[614]

---

[613] Candrakīrti cites MMK I.11: *na ca vyastasamasteṣu pratyayeṣv asti tat phalam* | *pratyayebhyaḥ kathaṃ tac ca bhaven na pratyayeṣu yat* ||. PsP Tib for MMK I.11ab reads *rkyen rnams so so 'dus pa la* || *'bras bu de ni med pa nyid* ||. Jñānagarbha and Klu'i rgyal mtshan's translation for MMK I.11 also attests *nyid*, which might lead one to think that they read *naiva* instead of *na ca*. All of the Skt manuscripts collated for this section of the PsP read *na ca*. Buddhapālita glosses the word translated into Tibetan as *nyid* with *kho na* (**eva*) (BP_{ed} 26.1: *nyid ces bya ba'i sgra ni kho na zhes bya ba'i don to* ||); the gloss would hardly have been necessary had the *kārikā* in his MMK manuscript read *naiva*. Were Jñānagarbha and Klu'i rgyal mtshan inspired to translate *ca* as *nyid* based on Bhāviveka's explanatory sentence *don dam par 'bras bu skye ba med pa kho na ste* | *rkyen rnams la med do zhes bya ba'i tshig gi don to* | (PP D 61b1; P 73b4)?

[614] Candrakīrti's comments on this occasion differ from those of Buddhapālita. After stating that an effect which already exists in conditions would have no need for conditions, Buddhapālita takes up a line of argumentation that starts from the premise that the result exists in the many conditions that produce it and inquires whether it would then partially or fully exist in each individual condition. According to Buddhapālita, if it fully existed in each condition, there could not be many conditions for the arising of the result, and there would be the consequence that the result would arise from each condition without depending on other conditions; but if it only partially existed in each condition, there would be the consequence that part of the effect would arise from each condition without depending on other conditions: *de la re zhig gal te re re la yongs su rdzogs par yod par brtags na ni rkyen du mar mi 'gyur te* | *re re la yang yod pa'i phyir mi ltos par re re las kyang 'bras bu skye bar thal bar 'gyur ro* || *ci ste rkyen rnams la 'bras bu'i cha shas yod par brtags na ni* | *de lta na yang mi ltos par re re las 'bras bu'i cha shas skye bar thal bar 'gyur bas de yang mi 'dod de* | (BP_{ed} 26.14-19). Bhāviveka states only that ultimately, the result does not arise because it does not exist in the conditions, and then rhetorically asks how

§152. [MMK I.12 abc_1]

> But if that result, while not existing [in conditions], proceeds from conditions,[615]

[If this] were [your] intent,

[MMK I.12c_2-d]

> Why does [it] not proceed from non-conditions too?[616]

---

yoghurt could arise from threads when it does not exist in them (PP D 61b1-2; P 73b5: *rgyu spun dag las zho ji ltar 'byung ste de dag la zho med pa'i phyir ro* |).

[615] Candrakīrti cites MMK I.12abc_1: *athāsad api tat tebhyaḥ pratyayebhyaḥ pravartate* | *phalam*. See the following note.

[616] MMK I.12c_2-d: *apratyayebhyo 'pi kasmān nābhipravartate* ||. None of the PsP manuscripts attest these last five words of the *kārikā*. De La Vallée Poussin (PsP_L 88 and n. 1) reconstructs MMK I.12 to read (unmetrically) *athāsad api tat tebhyaḥ* [*pratyayebhyaḥ pravartate* | *apratyayebhyo 'pi kasmān nābhi*]*pravartate phalam* ||. Saito (1984: 230, n. 41 and 1985: 25f.) emends to *athāsad api tat tebhyaḥ* [*pratyayebhyaḥ*] *pravartate* | *phalam apratyayebhyo 'pi kasmān nābhipravartate* ||. Mss P and Q indeed attest MMK I.12abc_1 as *athāsad api tat tebhyaḥ pratyayebhyaḥ pravartate* | *phalam*. Saito's emendation for MMK I.12c_2-d is based on Candrakīrti's commentary, in which the words of I.12c_2-d have been cited (MMK I.12c_2-d underlined): *apratyayebhyo 'pi vīraṇādibhyaḥ kasmān nābhipravartate paṭa iti*.
The loss of the last five words was probably caused by an eyeskip from *apratyayebhyo* of I.12c to *apratyayeṣu*, the first word of Candrakīrti's commentary. This eyeskip must have occurred early on in the transmission of the PsP, for these same last five words of MMK I.12 seem also to have been missing in the two manuscripts relied on by the translators of PsP Tib. Jñānagarbha and Klu'i rgyal mtshan's version of MMK I.12 as found in ABh, BP and PP reads: *ci ste de ni med par yang* || *rkyen de dag las skye 'gyur na* || *rkyen min las kyang 'bras bu ni* || *ci yi*[1] *phyir na skye mi 'gyur* || ([1]BP *ci'i* for *ci yi*) (see Saito's [1984: 230, n. 41] remarks on the inappropriateness of this version in connection with the MMK I.12 commentaries in ABh and BP). Mahāsumati and Pa tshab's version as found in P MMK_T reads: *ci ste 'bras bu de med kyang* || *rkyen de dag las skye 'gyur na* || *rkyen ma yin pa dag las kyang* || *ci yi phyir na skye mi 'gyur* ||. The last two quarters are completely missing in PsP Tib D and C; D and C read: *ci ste de ni med par yang* || *rkyen de dag las skye 'gyur na* || *zhes bya bar bsams par gyur na ni* | *rkyen ma yin pa dag la yang* ...; this corresponds with the manuscripts' *athāsad api tat tebhyaḥ pratyayebhyaḥ pravartate* | ... *ity abhiprāyaḥ syāt* | *apratyayeṣv api* ... (an equivalent for *phalam* does not appear in D and C Tib). Even though a version of the entire *kārikā* appears in PsP Tib P, N and G, the fact that the phrase *ity abhiprāyaḥ syāt* (*zhes bya bar bsams bar gyur na ni*), which can only be referring to the first half of MMK I.12, occurs in P, N and G only after the translation of the *entire kārikā* suggests that I.12cd was inserted once it was noticed that the *kārikā* was incomplete—albeit in the wrong place, i.e., not after *zhes bya bar*

Since there is not a result in non-conditions either, why does cloth not proceed from non-conditions too, [i.e.,] from grass and so forth [in which it likewise does not exist]?[617] Thus, there is no proceeding of a result from the point of view of own nature.

§153. At this point, [the opponent] states: If the result would be other (*anya*) and the conditions other [i.e., if result and conditions would be

---

bsams bar gyur na ni but before it—and in a different version than that of MMK_T (*pāda* c of PsP Tib P, N, and G reads *rkyen min las kyang 'bras bu ni* ||, i.e., in correspondence with Jñānagarbha and Klu'i rgyal mtshan's version of the *pāda*, instead of with Mahāsumati and Pa tshab's MMK_T version *rkyen ma yin pa dag las kyang*). The original Tibetan translation of the PsP seems then to have lacked the last half of the *kārikā*.

As Saito has noted, the translation *ci ste 'bras bu de med kyang* for the first quarter in PsP Tib P, N, and G, as opposed to the translation *ci ste de ni med par yang* in PsP Tib D and C, appears to reflect an attempt on the part of the translators of the PsP to bring Jñānagarbha and Klu'i rgyal mtshan's translation *ci ste de ni med par yang* into line with Candrakīrti's interpretation of MMK I.12, according to which there is an enjambment to *phala*, the first word of the (Sanskrit's) third quarter (the first quarter in P MMK_T contains the revised version as found in PsP Tib P, N, and G; D MMK_T contains the older version *ci ste de ni med par yang*). That PsP Tib D and C present Jñānagarbha and Klu'i rgyal mtshan's version of the first *pāda* appears to indicate that an editor was aware of this other version of the *kārikā* and, possibly disturbed by the PsP translators' emendation of I.12a to include *'bras bu*, decided to revert to Jñānagarbha and Klu'i rgyal mtshan's version (note, however, that in all the editions of the PsP the commentary's *rkyen ma yin pa dag la yang 'bras bu yod pa ma yin pas* [= *apratyayeṣv api nāsti phalam iti*] has been punctuated as if it were I.12cd: *rkyen ma yin pa dag la yang* || *'bras bu yod pa ma yin pas* ||). MMK I.12 is cited at $MABh_{ed}$ 93.19-94.2 in the version *ci ste de ni med par yang* || *rkyen de dag las skyes 'gyur na* || *rkyen ma yin pa dag las kyang* || *ci yi phyir na skye mi 'gyur* ||, that is, with Jñānagarbha and Klu'i rgyal mtshan's version of the first *pāda* but with the (revised?) version of *pāda* c that appears in Mahāsumati and Pa tshab's MMK_T translation. This same version appears in D MMK_T.

[617] Buddhapālita does little more than paraphrase MMK I.12; he does not include the examples cloth and grass. Bhāviveka equates the *kārikā* statement with the assertion "If sound, which is created, is permanent, why is a pot, which is also created, not permanent?" (*dper na gal te sgra byas pa rtag na bum pa byas pa yang ci'i phyir mi rtag ces bya ba lta bu*) and presents the relevant inference (*sgra ni mi rtag ste* || *byas pa'i phyir bum pa bzhin*) as a point of comparison for the inference he adduces for MMK I.12: *don dam par myu gus stong pa'i 'bru* (D: *'bras bu*) *la sogs pa las de skye bar mi 'thad de* | *'bras bu yin pa'i phyir dper na zho bzhin* (see PP D 61b4-5; P 73b8-74a1; Kajiyama 1964: 125; Ames 1994: 118).

different things], then the [following] reflection might be [meaningful]: "Does the result exist in the conditions [or] not?" But there is not a separate result; rather, [the result] is simply made of conditions (*pratyayamaya*).[618]

§154. Reply:

[MMK I.13]

> On the one hand, the result is made of conditions; on the other, the conditions are not made of themselves (*asvayammaya*).
> How is that result, which is made of [conditions] not made of themselves, made of conditions?[619]

If it is determined [by you] that the result is made of conditions, [that is, the result is] the modification (*vikāra*) of [its] conditions, that is not reasonable, because those conditions, for their part, are not made of themselves; the meaning is: [they] do not have the own-being of conditions (*apratyayasvabhāva*). [Opponent:] [But] cloth is obviously (*hi*) made of threads![620] Reply: There might be cloth if the threads themselves were established by own-being. Those [threads], [being] made of filaments (*aṃśumaya*), [being] the modification of filaments, are of course not established by own-being. And therefore how will that result called cloth, which is from those [conditions] not made of themselves (*asvammaya*), be made of threads?[621]

---

618 PsP Tib translates *pratyayamaya* as *rkyen gyi rang bzhin* throughout.

619 Candrakīrti cites MMK I.13: *phalaṃ ca pratyayamayaṃ pratyayāś cāsvayammayāḥ | phalam asvamayebhyo yat tat pratyayamayaṃ katham* ||. The translators of the PsP have emended Jñānagarbha and Klu'i rgyal mtshan's translation of the *kārikā* (found in ABh, BP and PP), which reads *'bras bu rkyen las byung yin na* || *rkyen rnams rang las byung ma yin* || *rang byung min las 'bras bu gang* || *de ni ji ltar rkyen las byung* ||, to *'bras bu rkyen gyi rang bzhin na* || *rkyen rnams bdag gi rang bzhin min* || *bdag dngos min las 'bras bu gang* || *de ni ji ltar rkyen rang bzhin* ||.

620 PsP Tib understands the syntax differently, and connects *ucyate* with the opponent's statement: *snam bu ni snal ma'i rang bzhin can no zhes bya bar brjod na ni* | *gal te snal ma dag* … "One says [e.g.,] that cloth is made of threads. [To this, we reply:] If the threads … ."

621 Candrakīrti's comments on the example of cloth and threads have been inspired by BP: *'di ltar gal te rgyu spun dag rang nyid rab tu grub na ni rang las byung bar*

As it has been stated [in the Catuḥśataka],

> A pot is established by virtue of a cause, [its] cause is established by virtue of something else (*anyataḥ*).
> How could that which is not etablished by itself (*svataḥ*) produce another [thing]?[622]

---

yang 'gyur bas | des na snam bu rgyu spun dag las byung ba zhes bya ba de yang 'thad par 'gyur ba zhig na ... (BP_{ed} 28.6-8). Buddhapālita goes on to argue that the threads themselves are made of [their own] causes (*rgyu las byung ba*; **kāraṇamaya*; cf. BP_{ed} 28.8-11). Bhāviveka rejects the opponent's claim that the result is made of conditions, in the way that a pot is made of clay, on the ground that Nāgārjuna has already refuted that conditions have the nature of conditions. The question posed in MMK I.13cd, he states, can be compared to "If Devarāta practised celibacy from his youth, how is Bharata his son?"; PP D 62a1; P 74a5: *dper na gal te de* (D: omits *de*) *va rā ta gzhon nu nas tshangs par spyod pa yin na | bha* (D, P add *va* [PPṬ without *va*]) *ra ta ji ltar de'i bu yin | zhes zer ba lta bu.*

622 Candrakīrti cites CŚ XIV.13: *ghaṭaḥ kāraṇataḥ siddhaḥ siddhaṃ kāraṇam anyataḥ | siddhir yasya svato nāsti tad anyaj janayet katham ||*. Whereas ms Q attests *ghaṭaḥ* as the *śloka*'s first word, ms P and the paper manuscripts read *paṭaḥ* and *paṭhaḥ* (the *ya* of B's *yaṭaḥ* is merely a miswriting of *pa*), and PsP Tib attests *snam bu*. The CŚ manuscript's *ghaṭaḥ* is correct given the context in the relevant section of the CŚ, and Candrakīrti refers consistently to *ghaṭaḥ* in his commentary on CŚ XIV.9-14 (see $CŚṬ_{ed}$ 332-340; see also Lang 1986: 128-130 and Lang 1976: 76 and the extended preceding discussion on pot; in CŚṬ on CŚ XIV.13, the causes of the *ghaṭa* are asserted to be *kapālāni*). CŚ XIV.13 is also quoted by Buddhapālita in his commentary on MMK I.13, but BP Tib, like PsP Tib, attests *snam bu*, not *bum pa*. Saito (1984: 231, n. 43) has suggested that Buddhapālita may have relied on a CŚ ms that read *paṭaḥ* or changed the reading himself. Alternatively, the BP translators may have relied on a BP Skt ms that read *paṭaḥ*, changed from *ghaṭaḥ* because *paṭaḥ* better suits the context in this section of BP; the PsP's surrounding focus on *paṭaḥ* may likewise explain the change of *ghaṭaḥ* to *paṭaḥ* in ms P and the paper manuscripts. Saito (1984: 231, n. 43), with reference to PsP_L, PsP Tib and BP Tib's reading, hypothesizes that Candrakīrti may have quoted the *śloka* directly from Buddhapālita, "otherwise this problem might cast a doubt over the authorship of PsP or CŚṬ." Although I do not think that the difference in readings is weighty enough to lead to questions of authorship, it is true that Candrakīrti relies heavily on BP for his commentary on MMK I.2-13 and possible that he copied the *śloka* with *paṭaḥ*—if this was the original BP reading or was in the BP ms available to him—directly from BP and did not notice the error (according to Felix Erb, Candrakīrti wrote his commentary on CŚ only after composing MABh and PsP; for his proposed succession of Candrakīrti's works, see Erb 1997: 14). Owing to the fact that ms Q attests the CŚ's reading *ghaṭaḥ*, I have accepted it for the critical edition, even though other scenarios like those described regarding *paṭaḥ* are possible.

[MMK I.14a]

> Therefore, not [as something] made of conditions[623]
>
> does the result exist.

§155. [Opponent:][624] Then let [the result] be made of non-conditions (*apratyayamaya*)!

[MMK I.14bc$_1$]

> Not [as something] made of non-conditions does the result exist.[625]

When cloth made of threads does not exist, then how could there be the contrary, [namely, cloth] made of grass?[626]

§156. At this point, [the opponent says]: It may be [true] that there is no result, but there is a determination (*niyama*) of conditions and non-conditions. And you likewise say [in MMK I.12] that if the result which doesn't exist [in conditions] proceeds from conditions, "why does [it] not proceed from non-conditions too?"[627] It does not make

---

[623] Candrakīrti cites MMK I.14a: *tasmān na pratyayamayam.*

[624] PsP Tib makes clear that the opponent is speaking: *'o na rkyen ma yin pa'i rang bzhin du 'gyur ro zhe na* (PsP Skt: *apratyayamayaṃ tarhy astu*).

[625] Candrakīrti cites MMK I.14bc$_1$: *nāpratyayamayaṃ phalam | saṃvidyate.* The PsP translators have emended Jñānagarbha and Klu'i rgyal mtshan's translation of MMK I.14ab, which reads *de'i phyir rkyen las byung ma yin || rkyen min las byung 'bras bu ni ||*, to *de'i phyir rkyen gyi rang bzhin min || rkyen min rang bzhin 'bras bu ni ||*.

[626] Cp. BP$_{ed}$ 29.3-5: *gang gi tshe snam bu rgyu spun las byung bar mi 'thad pa de'i tshe snam bu rtsi rkyang las byung ngo || zhes bya ba 'jig rten dang 'gal ba 'di ji ltar 'thad par 'gyur | de'i phyir 'bras bu rkyen ma yin pa las byung ba yang med do.* Candrakīrti's comment on MMK XX.24b (MMK XX.24ab: *na sāmagrīkṛtaṃ tasmān nāsāmagrīkṛtaṃ phalam |*) is similar to his present comment on MMK I.14bc$_1$ (PsP$_L$ 407.3): *yadā sāmagrīkṛtaṃ phalaṃ na saṃbhavati tadā katham atyantaviruddham asāmagrīkṛtaṃ bhaviṣyati |*.

[627] Candrakīrti paraphrases MMK I.12abc$_1$ but then quotes MMK I.12c$_2$-d (missing in all manuscripts on the earlier occasion of the *kārikā* citation; see n. 616): *apratyaye-bhyo 'pi kasmān nābhipravartate.* PsP Tib has the opponent paraphrase the entire *kārikā*.

sense, however, if a result called cloth or mat does not, [as you say, ever] exist, that threads and grass could be conditions and non-conditions.[628] On account of this, [just as conditions and non-conditions,] the result also exists.

§157. Reply: There might be a result if [these] very conditions and non-conditions existed.[629] [Yet] obviously, [only] if a result existed would it be possible [to say]: "These are the conditions of this

---

[628] I accept ms Q's reading *pratyayāpratyayatvam* because it makes more sense in the context than ms P's *pratyayānāṃ pratyayatvam* and because it appears to represent the *lectio difficilior*, at least within the framework of the sentence. PsP Tib supports ms Q with *rkyen dang rkyen ma yin pa nyid* (PsP Tib reads *snam bu dang re lde zhes bya ba'i 'bras bu med na ni snal ma dang 'jag ma dag rkyen dang rkyen ma yin pa nyid du yang mi rigs te* for PsP Skt's *na cāsati phale paṭakaṭākhye tantuvīraṇānāṃ pratyayāpratyayatvaṃ yuktam*). PsP Tib has of course been contaminated with revised and interpolated readings from a manuscript earlier in Q's line, but in the present case I suspect that P's reading is faulty. Were P's reading *pratyayānāṃ pratyayatvam* to be accepted, the idea being introduced by the opponent would be that if a result called cloth or mat does not exist, it is not reasonable that the conditions threads and grass should have the status of conditions (*na … pratyayānāṃ pratyayatvaṃ yuktam*). The opponent's argument, however, centres on the fact that the Mādhyamikas indeed make a determination of conditions *and non-conditions* (*pratyayāpratyayaniyama*). Note also that in his reply, Candrakīrti refers twice to the pair conditions and non-conditions. Ms Q's reading *pratyayāpratyayatvam* takes both types of conditions into account, whereas ms P's only considers conditions. It would seem, then, that P's reading represents the simplified version. The original *pratyayāpratyayatvam* would have been changed in P (or a manuscript earlier in its line) because it was assumed that non-conditions were not topical in the sentence: the mention of threads was connected with cloth and that of grass with mats. Candrakīrti presumably intended, however, to include both: threads are to be viewed as the conditions for cloth and as the non-conditions for mats, and grass as the condition for mats but the non-condition for cloth.

[629] PsP Tib translates the sentence as *gal te 'bras bu yod par gyur na ni | rkyen dang rkyen ma yin pa dag tu 'gyur ro* "If a result existed, [these] very conditions and non-conditions might exist." Thus *yadi* of *syāt phalaṃ yadi …* is taken to belong to the protasis. This interpretation is unusual, given that in similar *syāt … yadi* constructions Candrakīrti's normally intends *yadi* to be construed with the apodosis. The opponent has argued for the existence of the result because he sees the Mādhyamika as accepting a determination of both conditions and non-conditions. As I understand the Sanskrit, Candrakīrti focusses the sentence on the opponent's assumption of the acceptance of the existence of these very conditions and non-conditions.

[result], these are non-conditions [for it].”[630] But that [result], being analyzed [as above], does not exist.

[MMK I.14c_2d]

> Because a result does not exist, how are there conditions and non-conditions?[631]

The [*dvandva*] compound [*pratyayāpratyayāḥ* should be dissolved as] “conditions and non-conditions.”[632] Therefore, there is no arising of things by own-being.[633]

---

[630] Candrakīrti takes his lead from Buddhapālita in presenting an opponent who argues for the existence of the result on the basis of the determination of conditions and non-conditions and in rejecting the opponent’s assertion that this determination allows for the statement “These are its conditions, these are non-conditions [for it].” See BP_{ed} 29.7-13: *smras pa | rkyen rnams ni yod pa kho na yin te | ci’i phyir zhe na | rkyen dang rkyen ma yin pa nges pa’i phyir ro || ’di na rkyen dang rkyen ma yin pa nges pa mthong ste | ’bru dag las ’bru mar kho na ’byung gi mar mi ’byung ngo || zho las ni mar kho na ’byung gi ’bru mar mi ’byung ngo | bye ma dag las ni de gnyi ga mi ’byung ngo || ’di ltar gang gi phyir ’di dag ni ’di’i rkyen yin no || ’di dag ni ’di’i rkyen ma yin no zhes bya ba de yod pas de’i phyir rkyen ’grub po ||* (Buddhapālita considers 1.14cd as providing the reply to this objection; see his commentary on the half-verse at BP_{ed} 29.17-23).

[631] Candrakīrti cites MMK I.14c_2d: *phalābhāvāt pratyayāpratyayāḥ kutaḥ ||*.

[632] Bhāviveka’s interpretation of MMK I.14c_2d is quite different from that of the other commentators, for he explains it to mean “Because the result does not exist, how is the non-condition a condition?” According to Kajiyama (1964: 127, n. 1), “Nach Bhāviveka ist v. 14c-d zu lesen: ... *phalābhāvāt pratyayo ’pratyayaḥ kutaḥ*”; Ames (1994: 133, n. 172) states that Bhāviveka “evidently read *pratyayo ’pratyayaḥ kutaḥ*.” This divergent interpretation probably explains why Candrakīrti considers it necessary to draw attention to the compound he read in his manuscript of the MMK and to clarify it as a *dvandva*. Bhāviveka understands MMK I.14d to mean that non-conditions cannot have the nature of conditions or, alternatively, that conditions which are impossible because there is no result cannot be conditions: *sbyor ba rnam par dbye ba byas nas rkyen min zhes bya ba dang | rkyen du ga la ’gyur zhes bya ba bshad de | rkyen ma yin pa rnams rkyen gyi ngo ba nyid du mi ’gyur ro* (P: ||) *zhes bya ba’i tshig gi don to || yang na* ... (MMK I.14) *de’i bdag nyid ma yin pa’i rkyen ’thad pa med pa rnams rkyen du ga la ’gyur te | mi ’gyur ba kho na yin no zhes bya ba’i tshig gi don* ... (see PP D 62a6-62b1; P 74b4-6; Kajiyama 1964: 127; Ames 1994: 120f.).

§158. As stated in the Noble Ratnākarasūtra,

> Ignorance is empty,[634] for it does not exist anywhere,[635] like the track of a bird in the sky.[636]
> That which nowhere exists by own-being can never become the cause of something else.[637]
>
> For how can something whose own-being is not at all obtained, which is without own-being, be the condition for something else? How could it, lacking own-being, produce another? This reason has been taught by the One Well Gone.[638]
>
> All *dharma*s are unmoving (*acala*), firmly abiding, without change (*nirvikāra*), without misfortune (*nirupadrava*), secure (*śiva*),

---

[633] Buddhapālita closes his commentary on the first chapter with the assertion that since a result and conditions and non-conditions do not exist, the expression "arising" is proven to be a mere convention: *'bras bu dang rkyen dang rkyen ma yin pa dag med pas skye bar brjod pa ni tha snyad tsam du grub po* (BP_{ed} 29.23-30.2). He does not, as Bhāviveka and Candrakīrti do, append scriptural citations.

[634] PsP_L 90: *śūnyavidya*. PsP Tib: *stong pa rig pa* "knowledge of emptiness" (the first phrase reads *gang na'ang stong pa rig pa med pa ni*: "The knowledge of emptiness does not exist anywhere"). *LṬ's author, however, explains *śūnyavidya* as *śūnyā 'vidyā*: "ignorance is empty" (cf. Yonezawa 2004: 126, 151 [fol. 3a6]); *śūnyavidya* of the verse must thus have been understood as *śūny' avidya*. This interpretation makes more sense than Tib does in the context of PsP's first chapter, and I thus accept it, for *avidyā* would refer to the initial link of the twelve-linked *pratītyasamutpāda*. When this most fundamental component of the chain is empty, the rest of the members are as a consequence also empty.

[635] I interpret *hi* in its sense of indicating a reason. It could alternatively be understood as reminding readers of something already known to them: "Ignorance is empty; it obviously does not exist anywhere, like … ."

[636] *LṬ's author glosses *antarīkṣi śakunasya vā padam* with *śakuner iva padaṃ yathā antarīkṣe nāsti* (cf. Yonezawa 2004: 126, 151 [fol. 3a6]).

[637] RK Tib (P 296a8-297a1; D 285b): *gang na'ang stong pa* (D: *par*) *rig pa ma mchis par* || *nam mkha' bar snang bya yi rjes dang mtshungs* || *gang na'ang ngo bo nyid ni ma mchis pa* || *de ni nams kyang gzhan* (P: *gzhin*) *gyi rgyur* (P: *sgyur*) *mi 'gyur* ||.

[638] RK Tib (P 297a1-2; D 285b): *gang gi* (D: *gis*) *ngo bo nyid ni mi rnyed par* || *rang bzhin de med ji ltar gzhan gyi rkyen* || *rang bzhin med pa gzhan gyis ci zhig bskyed* (D: *skyed*) || *rgyu de bde bar gshegs pas bstan pa'o* ||.

Not producing [anything], like the sky.[639] The unknowing world is disoriented in regard to this.[640]

Just as a mountain of rock is unshakable, so are *dharma*s forever unshakable.
They do not die, nor are they reborn. Thus has the true nature of things been taught by the Conqueror.[641]

Similarly,[642]

The Conqueror, the Lion of men, teaches the *dharma* (= *nirvāṇa*) which neither originates, would be reborn,[643] nor dies or ages. [He][644] has placed hundreds of beings there.[645]

---

[639] Alternatively, "Not arising, like the sky." PsP Tib attests *shes pa med pa* (RK Tib: *rig pa ma mchis*) for *ajānaka* (*ji ltar nam mkha' shes pa med pa bzhin* ‖ "not knowing, like the sky"), which would seem to be less appropriate. *LṬ's author must have read *antarīkṣapathatulya 'jānakā* as a single compound (°*tulyajānakā*), that is, he did not understand the final member to have a negation. He comments: *antarīkṣapatho gaganaṃ tena tulyā ekarūpā jāyante* "the atmosphere, that is, the sky; they arise with a single form similar to that [sky]" (cf. Yonezawa 2004: 126, 151 [fol. 3a6]).

[640] RK Tib (P 297a2-3; D 285b): *thams cad chos kyang mi g-yo brtan par gnas* ‖ *mi 'gyur 'tshe ba ma mchis zhi ba ste* ‖ *ji ltar nam mkha' rig pa ma mchis ltar* ‖ *de la mi mdzangs* (P: *'dzangs*) *'gro ba myos par 'gyur* ‖.

[641] RK Tib (P 297a3-4; D 285b): *ji ltar ri bo dag ni mi sgul ba* ‖ *de bzhin chos rnams rtag tu bskyod mi nus* ‖ *'chi 'pho ma mchis skye ba ma mchis pa'i* (D: *pa'o*) ‖ *chos rnams de ltar rgyal bas rab tu bstan* ‖. D's *pa'o* allows RK Tib to better mirror the Sanskrit, but I assume that P's *pa'i* (cf. PsP Tib's *skye ba med pa yi* ‖), the lectio dificilior, is or is closer to the original translation and that D's reading is the result of an editorial change.

[642] The next triplet of verses from the RK is cited again in the PsP on MMK XIII.6. The wording of RK Tib's version (P 272a2-4; D 261b-262a) sometimes differs from that of PsP Tib. These verses and others that follow in the *sūtra* have most recently been translated into English by Galloway (2001: 344f.), but the translation is often problematic.

[643] Stcherbatsky's (1927: 181, n. 8) comment that *upapadyī* is "probably in the sense of *sthita* as a member of the series *utpāda*, *sthiti*, *jarā*, *anityatā*" is clearly mistaken (Schayer [1931: 34, n. 27] refers to this interpretation). I understand it as an *iṣ*-aorist (cf. BHSG § 32.16) used in an optative/future sense (cf. BHSG § 32.119 ff.).

[644] RK Tib: *drang srong chen pos* (and without an equivalent for *śatāni*).

> Whatever has no own-being is not found by anyone to have other-being.
> [It] is found neither internally nor externally. [Yet] the Protector has placed [beings] there.[646]
>
> The peaceful state (*gati*) was declared by the One Well Gone; but no state is perceived;
> [You,] released from the states [of existence] (*gati*), dwell in it. Released, [You] release many beings.[647]

And so on in detail.

§159. [Here ends] the first chapter called "Examination of Conditions" in the Prasannapadā, a Commentary on the Madhyamaka[-śāstra] composed by the Master Candrakīrti.

---

[645] RK Tib (P 272a2; D 261b): *chos gang skye ba ma mchis 'byung ma mchis* || *'chi 'pho ma mchis rga bar mi 'gyur ba* || *skyes bu rgyal ba seng ge de ston cing* || *drang srong chen pos sems can de la bkod* ||.

[646] RK Tib (P 272a2-3; D 262a): *gang la ngos po ci yang ma mchis shing* || *gzhan gyi dngos po'ang sus kyang ma rnyed pa* || *nang na ma lags slad rol dag na yang* || *dngos po mi rnyed de la mgon pos bkod* ||.

[647] RK Tib (P 272a3-4; D 262a): *bde bar gshegs pas zhi ba'i 'gro* (P: *blo*) *gsungs kyang* ||*'gro ba gang yang* (P: *la*) *rnyed par mi 'gyur te* || *de dag 'gro las grol bar rnam par gsungs* || *grol nas sems can mang po rab tu 'grol* ||.

Appendices

Appendices

Appendix I (re: §2., n. 31 & 32)

sambandha, *abhidheya* and *prayojana*

1. Both the threefold group of *sambandha*, *abhidheya* and *prayojana* and the fourfold one which additionally includes *prayojanaprayojana* on occasion include a fifth member, the "discourse" (*abhidhāna*, *rjod pa*), often translated as "text" (cf. Broido 1983: 6). Jeffrey Schoening (1995: 32-36) observes that the members mentioned in *sūtra* commentaries vary from commentary to commentary, referring to one *sūtra* commentary that lists four introductory terms, namely, the connection, subject matter, purpose, and purpose of the purpose, and then explains six members, viz., the four announced plus the text and the ultimate purpose (*dgos pa mthar thug pa*, **prayojananiṣṭhā*); he notes other commentaries that also discuss an "ultimate purpose." It may be noted in this connection that Prajñākaramati, at the beginning of his commentary on the first verse of the BCA, makes topical the *sambandha*, *abhidheya* and *prayojana*, but in the explanation of the referents of the three, brings the *abhidhāna* into the discussion, and also explains the *prayojana* in terms of both the *abhidhāna* and the *abhidheya*; the *prayojana* of the *abhidheya* (Buddhahood) is designated the *prayojananiṣṭhā* (see BCAP 4.20-5.6). Dharmottara, in his Ṭīkā to Nyāyabindu I.1 (ed. Ācārya Śrīcandraśekhara Śāstrī, Kashi Sanskrit Series 22, 2nd ed., Banaras 1954, pp. 2-4), presents, in addition to the *sambandha* and *abhidheya*, an *abhidheyaprayojana* (in this case *sarvapuruṣārthasiddhi*), but also refers to the *śabdaprayojana*, the *prakaraṇaprayojana*, and even to the *vaktuḥ prayojana* and the *śrotuḥ prayojana*. In referring to the *abhidheyaprayojana*, he explains that if the subject matter lacks a purpose, even the arrangement of words for the sake of understanding the subject matter should not

be undertaken, "just as a circumspect person, on account of the lack of a purpose to crows' teeth, should not begin an inquiry into them" (*yathā kākadantaprayojanābhāvān na tatparīkṣārambhaṇīyā prekṣāvatā*).

Although Candrakīrti does not explain why it is necessary to refer to the *abhidheya*, *sambandha* and *prayojana*, some other Indian authors do. Kumārila commences a discussion of the *prayojana* and *sambandha* of the MS and the *śāstra* based on it in ŚV I.12, where he poses the rhetorical question *sarvasyaiva hi śāstrasya karmaṇo vāpi kasyacit* | *yāvat prayojanaṃ noktaṃ tāvat tat kena gṛhyate* ||. He asserts that especially in the case of Mīmāṃsā, it is imperative that the purpose be stated right at the beginning, since without an explanation of what can be achieved, the addressee will not be inspired to listen to the exposition; the commentator Pārthasārathimiśra adds that Mīmāṃsā, based on many other sciences, is "*bahvāyāsasādhyā*," certainly a deterrent if the reward for such effort is not clear. One is reminded of Kumārila's assertion when one reads in the Nyāyamañjarī (ed. Varadacharya, Mysore 1969, p. 13) the versified response of Jayanta Bhaṭṭa to the question of the use of stating the *abhidheya* and *prayojana* at the beginning of a *śāstra*: *ādivākyaṃ prayoktavyam abhidheyaprayojane* | *pratipādayituṃ śrotṛpravāhotsāhasiddhaye* || *abhidheyaphalajñānavirahāstamitodyamāḥ* | *śrotum alpam api grantham ādriyante na sūrayaḥ* ||. In the discussion which follows, he claims that the first sentence of the Nyāyasūtra provides (cursory) knowledge of the *prayojana*, and that doubt (*saṃśaya*) with regard to the matter spurs the hearer to activity, i.e., to engage with the rest of the Nyāyasūtra. Haribhadra, who relies heavily on the discussion of the terms found at the beginning of Kamalaśīla's TSP and incorporates passages from both Vinītadeva's and Dharmottara's Ṭīkā-s on Nyāyabindu I.1 into his discussion in the Abhisamayālaṅkārālokā (ed. U. Wogihara, Tokyo, 1932-35, pp. 2.3-5.5), claims that if the *sambandha* and *abhidheya* were not to be stated, then people would suspect that the text is unrelated and useless like the statements of lunatics and such, with the result that no one would even start to listen (*yadi saṃbandhābhidheyam asyā na kathyeta tadonmattādivākyavad asaṃbandham anarthakaṃ cety āśaṅkayā na kaścit pravartate 'pi śrotum*; cp. TSP 2.9: *yady abhidheyam asya na kathyeta tadonmattādivākyavad ānarthakyaṃ saṃbhāvayan prekṣāvān na pravartetāpi śrotum*; cp. also BCAP 5.11-12: *anyathā 'nabhidheyādiśaṅkyā prekṣāvatām atra pravṛttir na syāt*).

2. The connection (*sambandha*) as presented by many commentators is the connection or relation existing between two of the other introductory terms, usually that occurring between the subject matter (*abhidheya*) and discourse/text (*abhidhāna*) or *prakaraṇa*/*śāstra* (Gerow 2008: ix: "the text itself should pertain profitably to that subject matter")—which are sometimes said to be in a *vācya-vācaka* relationship—and/or that between the purpose (*prayojana*) and the discourse, etc., or between the purpose and the subject matter, both often described as an *upeya-upāya* or *sādhya-sādhana* relationship (see also PsP_L 3, n. 2). While commentators can usually point to the exact words they hold to refer to the subject matter and the purpose in the root text (e.g., Dharmottara, commenting on Nyāyabindu I.1, i.e., on *samyagjñānapūrvikā sarvapuruṣārthasiddhir iti tad vyutpādyate*, determines that *samyagjñāna* is the *abhidheya* and *sarvapuruṣārthasiddhi* the *prayojana*), words expressing the connection are rarely indicated; the connection is therefore often claimed to be stated by the "force" of the words, i.e., by implication (*sāmarthyāt*). Kamalaśīla explains that in the case of a *sādhya-sādhana* relationship it is not necessary for the connection to be explicitly stated: *sa ca sādhyasādhanabhāvaḥ prayojanābhidhānād eva darśitaḥ | tathā hīdam asya prayojanam iti darśayatā darśitaṃ bhavati – idam asya sādhanam iti | na hi yo yan na sādhayati tat tasya prayojanaṃ bhavaty atiprasaṅgāt | tasmāt sāmarthyalabhyatvān nāsau prayojanābhidheyābhyāṃ pṛthag abhidhānīyaḥ* (TSP 12.11-15). Cp. also Kumārila, who considers the "connection" pertaining to the MS as obtaining between the treatise and the purpose (ŚV I.18): *śāstraṃ prayojanaṃ caiva sambandhasyāśrayāv ubhau | taduktyantargatas tasmād bhinno noktaḥ prayojanāt* || "The treatise and the purpose are the substrata of the connection. Therefore, inasmuch as it (= the connection) is included in the mentioning of that [purpose], [the connection] is not stated separately from the purpose."

In the PsP, however, the connection presented does not line up with the type of *sambandha* that expresses the relation between two of the other introductory terms. The *sambandha* described in the PsP appears to be in the same class as one of the types of connection referred to by Kumārila, both of which are rejected by him as the connection applying to the MS (see ŚV I.23). He refers, first, to the type of *sambandha* that is expressed as the relation between the lineage of teachers (*guruparvakrama*) and the composition of the text (Pārthasārathimiśra explains this latter sort in his commentary on ŚV I.23-24: *tadyathā brahmā prajāpataye mīmāṃsāṃ provāca so 'pīndrāya so 'py ādityāya sa ca vasiṣṭhāya so 'pi parāśarāya parāśaraḥ kṛṣṇadvaipāyanāya so 'pi jaiminaye sa ca svopadeśānantaram imaṃ nyāyaṃ granthe nibaddhavān iti* |) and, second, to the type of *sambandha* expressed as the relation between, ultimately, two actions, the former action being the cause of, or leading directly to, the composing of the *sūtra/śāstra* (one of the reasons Pārthasārathimiśra gives for this type of connection not being appropriate for the case of the MS is that Jaimini did not compose his text immediately after studying: *na cādhyayanānantaraṃ jaimininā śāstraṃ praṇītam* | *ato nānena śāstrasambandha ucyate*; as examples of possible former actions he gives previous study, the questioning of a student and the worship of a deity). The *sambandha* described in the PsP appears to resemble the second category of *sambandha* described: The "action" of accomplishing the first *cittotpāda* inspired Nāgārjuna, who was intent on rescuing beings from *saṃsāra*, to undertake in service of this goal the "action" of composing his work.

The description of a *sambandha* that is in some respects similar to, though more extensive than, the one set forth in the PsP can be found at the beginning of Bhāviveka's PP (cf. PP D 46a1-6; P 54a1-54b2; Kajiyama 1963: 40-41; Ames 1993: 213-14). Bhāviveka first describes the Buddha's aeons-long spiritual effort, his realization of the thusness of *dharma*s and his subsequent teaching, and then states that Nāgārjuna, having realized the Tathāgata's doctrine, wished to compose the *śāstra*. Avalokitavrata classifies this *sambandha*, however, as a *rigs pa'i 'brel pa* type of *sambandha*, glossing *rigs pa'i 'brel pa* with: *bla ma brgyud pa* (**guruparaṃparā*; he elucidates this *sambandha* as it pertains to the PP with: *de la dang por bla ma dam pa sangs rgyas bcom ldan 'das kyi 'byung ba'i rgyu bstan par bya zhing* | *phyis bstan bcos mdzad pa'i 'byung ba'i rgyu bstan par* *bya'o* ||; cf. PPṬ D 8b6; P 10a7). Avalokitavrata explains that the *sambandha* in the PP is actually twofold in that it also includes a *don gyi 'brel pa* (**arthasambandha*), which, he states, refers to the meaning of the parts of the explanation of the *rigs pa'i 'brel pa*. Explicit mention of a *sambandha* is not found in BP, although when the question as to the purpose (*dgos pa*) of the teaching of dependent-arising is posed, Buddhapālita states that Nāgārjuna, compassionate by nature, seeing beings suffer, wished to show them the real nature of things (*dngos po rnams kyi yang dag pa ji lta ba*) so that they could be released, and thus undertook the teaching of dependent-arising (cf. BP_{ed} 2.16-20).

Appendix II (re: §2., n. 34)

MABh on *karuṇā* and *bodhicitta*

In the MABh on MA I.2 and I.3, compassion is said to lead to the emergence of *bodhicitta*: the compassionate individual becomes aware of and pained by others' suffering in the world and their plight in *saṃsāra* in general and vows to free all beings from suffering and to place them in the state of Buddhahood (cf. $MABh_{ed}$ 8.5-10; at $MABh_{ed}$ 8.10 this decision of the individual is referred to as a promise, i.e., *dam bca' ba 'di* [*iyaṃ pratijñā*]). Candrakīrti elaborates on the *sambodhicitta* mentioned in MA I.1 by way of citing from the *Āryadharmasaṃgītisūtra (see $MABh_{ed}$ 6.13-7.6), where it is stated that in the *bodhisattva* who has come to understand that all things are adventitious, non-abiding, and the same as the *dharmadhātu* there arises the resolve to bring about this same understanding in all beings, and that this resolve is *bodhicitta*. According to the sūtra, the *bodhisattva*'s *bodhicitta* is a state of mind intent on the benefit and happiness of all beings, tender because of love (*byams pa*), without stains owing to equanimity (**upekṣā*), unchanging because of emptiness (**śūnyatā*), without obscuration because it is not involved with marks/phenomena (**ānimitta*), non-abiding because there is nothing to wish for (**apraṇihita*), etc. The compassion that occurs during the *bodhisattva*'s experience of non-dual *jñāna*, i.e., during the meditational experience in which things no longer appear, would be the third of the three types of compassion explained toward the beginning of the MABh (see MABh$_{ed}$ 9.4-11.14), namely, compassion without any object (*anālambanā karuṇā*; *dmigs pa med pa'i snying rje*). Both compassion toward [beings seen as] *dharma*s and compassion that does not have an object are described by way of the example of the moon reflected in water in MA I.4a and its commentary. MABh$_{ed}$ 12.15-13.1: *de la byang chub sems dpa' ji skad bshad pa'i tshul gyis 'gro ba rang bzhin med par mthong ba snying rje'i khyad par nyid du nye bar bzung* (MABh$_{UN}$: *gzung*) *ba'i sems gang ... rab* (MABh$_{UN}$: *rab tu*) *dga' ba zes bya ba'i ming can gnyis su med pa'i ye shes ... de la ni | dang po zhes bya bar brjod do ||* (see MABh$_{tr}$ 1907: 261). See also the translations and comments in Huntington 1989: 149f. and Hopkins 1980: 110-125, 137-149, 182-191.

For Candrakīrti, the first *cittotpāda* is equivalent to the first *bhūmi*, and represents one of ten distinct forms of *bodhicitta* (cf. MABh$_{ed}$ 11.15), although he clarifies in his commentary on MA I.4cd-5ab that it is the *bodhisattva*'s uncontaminated gnosis (*anāsravajñāna*; *zag pa med pa'i ye shes*) imbued with special compassion and *bodhicitta* that is distinguished into "parts," i.e., grounds (*bhūmi*). Each is called a *bhūmi* because it serves as the ground for the qualities ascribed to it. The individual *bhūmi*s are differentiated according to the qualities, powers, etc., gained by the developing *bodhisattva* and are not due to any differences in the nature of the basis, the *anāsravajñāna*, itself: *byang chub sems dpa' rnams kyi zag pa med pa'i ye shes snying rje la sogs pas yongs su zin pa nyid car* (MABh$_{UN}$: *char*) *rnam par phye ba na sa zhes bya ba'i ming 'thob ste | yon tan gyi rten du gyur pa'i phyir ro ... 'di la rang gi ngo bo'i khyad par gyis byas pa'i dbye ba ni yod pa ma yin no ||* (MABh$_{ed}$ 12.1-8; cf. MABh$_{tr}$ 1907: 260f.). The first *bhūmi* is characterized by the predominance of the quality of generosity (cf. MA I.9a).

Appendix III (re: §2., n. 38)

nīti

The compound *prajñāpāramitānīti* (*shes rab kyi pha rol tu phyin pa'i tshul*) also occurs in the context of the Yogācāra critique of the Madhyamaka interpretation of the Prajñāpāramitā texts in MHK V.7: *prajñāpāramitānītir iyaṃ sarvajñatāptaye | na tūtpādanirodhādipratiṣedhaparāyaṇā* || (cf. Lindtner 1995: 50; 2001: 59). Eckel (2008: 224) translates *prajñāpāramitānīti* as "[t]his approach to the Perfection of Wisdom," which appears to work in the context of the MHK discussion but probably should not be globally applied to other instances; Eckel in fact finds it necessary to add "the means" in square brackets ("This approach to the Perfection of Wisdom is [the means] ..."). Hoornaert (1999: 137) does not take into account Lindtner's emendation of the end of MHK V.7d from °*pratiṣedhaparo nayaḥ* to °*pratiṣedhaparāyaṇā*; his translation of *nīti* (and *naya*) as "doctrine" is questionable (cf. ibid., 157 and n. 3). Iida (1966: 82; 1980: 80 and 235, n. 27) translates *nīti* of the same verse with the more etymologically aware "guiding principle." The compound also occurs in the initial sentence of the prose text of the PP: *slob dpon gyi zhal snga nas tshig le'ur byas pa dag kho nas ... shes rab kyi pha rol tu phyin pa'i tshul bka' stsal* (D 45b6-7; P 53b7-8). Kajiyama (1963: 40) translates "die Prinzipien der Vollkommenheit der Einsicht," again a somewhat questionable translation of *nīti* given the context; Ames (1993: 213), assuming that the Sanskrit read *prajñāpāramitānaya*, translates "the doctrine (*naya*) of the perfection of discernment (*prajñāpāramitā*)." Avalokitavrata, commenting on the first sentence of the PP, explicates the individual words of the compound **prajñāpāramitānīti* as follows: *de la shes rab ces bya ba ni rab tu 'byed pa'i mtshan nyid de* | *gang gis chos rnams rab tu 'byed par byed pa dang* | (P: ||) *rnam par 'jog par byed pa de ni shes rab ces bya'o* || *pha rol tu phyin pa zhes bya ba ni mi dmigs pa'i mtshan nyid do* || *pha rol zhes bya ba ni mi dmigs pa ste shes rab gang mi dmigs pa der phyin cing son pa de ni shes rab kyi pha rol tu phyin pa zhes bya ste* | *phyin pa med pa yin no* || *tshul zhes bya ba ni shes rab kyi pha rol tu phyin pa'i tshul te* | *shes rab kyi pha rol tu phyin pa'i mtshan nyid kyi chos bstan pa gang yin pa'o* || *yang na shes rab kyi pha rol tu phyin pa nyid tshul te* | (P: ||)

gang gis chos thams cad dmigs su med par khrid par byed pa'am | gang gis gzhan gyi rgyud la don khrid par byed pa'o || yang na gang gis bsod nams dang ye shes kyi tshogs gzhal du med pa nye bar bsags pa'i 'jig rten 'khor ba'i btson ra nas bsgral te | bsam pa thams cad yongs su rdzogs par byed pa'i yid bzhin gyi nor bu rin po che lta bur khrid par byed pa de ni tshul lo (D 6b4-7; P 7b5-8a2). "There [as regards Bhāviveka's statement,] 'insight' (**prajñā*) has the characteristic of discrimination (**pravicaya*). That by which there is discrimination and respective determination (**vyavasthāpana*) of the *dharma*s is 'insight.' *pāramitā* has the characteristic of non-perception (**anupalabdhi*). The other side / the utmost reach (*pāra*) is non-perception; the insight which has gone (*ita*) to, i.e., has arrived at, that non-perception is *prajñāpāramitā*; it is [in reality] without going. As regards the 'method' (**nīti*), it is the method of the *prajñāpāramitā*, [i.e.,] the instruction in the *dharma* which has the characteristic of the insight that has gone to the other side (*prajñāpāramitā*). Alternatively, precisely the *prajñāpāramitā* is the method; it is that which leads/guides to the non-perception of all *dharma*s, or that which leads [i.e., conveys] benefit with regard to the continuum of others. Or, it is the method inasmuch as it [i.e., the *prajñāpāramitā*] leads, once it has liberated [those] people who have collected the immeasurable accumulations of merit and gnosis from the jail of *saṃsāra*, like a wish-fulfilling jewel that perfectly accomplishes all wishes." See also Vetter 2001 where *prajñāpāramitā* as a method is discussed.

Appendix IV (re: §5., n. 47)

Explanation of *nirodha*, etc., in PsP Tib

The word *tatra* that begins the second sentence in $\mathrm{PsP_M}$ §5 is in all the Sanskrit manuscripts followed by an explanation of the meaning of the eight elements to be negated in regard to *pratītyasamutpāda*, namely, *nirodha* up to and including *nirgama*. In PsP Tib the explanation of the meanings of these eight elements is not attested after the translation for *avayavārthas tu vibhajyate | tatra*, and is found only further on in the text, after the translation of the sentence *sa evedānīṃ sāṃvṛtaḥ pratītyasamutpādaḥ svabhāvenānutpannatvād āryajñānāpe-*

kṣayā nāsmin nirodho vidyate yāvan nāsmin nirgamo vidyata ity anirodhādibhir aṣṭābhir viśeṣaṇair viśiṣyate (PsP_M §15 [= PsP_L 10.13-11.2]); cf. PsP Tib §5b within PsP Tib §15. That is, the word explanation appears two sentences after Candrakīrti winds up his criticism of Bhāviveka's attempted reiteration of others' etymologies and his own understanding of the meaning of the compound *pratītya-samutpāda* with the stock phrase *ity alaṃ prasaṅgena*. The sentence *yathā ca nirodhādayo na santi pratītyasamutpādasya tathā sakalena śāstreṇa pratipādayiṣyati*, which in the manuscripts immediately follows the sentence commencing *sa evedānīṃ sāṃvṛtaḥ*, appears in PsP Tib only after the explanation of *nirodha*, etc.

There is no reason to assume that either Pa tshab and Mahāsumati's Kashmiri manuscript or the manuscript relied on by Pa tshab and Kanakavarman in Lhasa for the revision of the translation of the PsP attested the word-explanation block only after the discussion of the compound *pratītyasamutpāda*. Pa tshab and Mahāsumati relocated the block to the point it is found in the Tibetan translation because *rten cing 'brel par 'byung* appears before *'gag pa med pa*, etc., in the Tibetan translation of the homage verses. The translators obviously decided that it would only be logical to explain the verse elements according to the order in which they appear in the PsP Tib verses: homage verse Iab in PsP Skt reads: *anirodham anutpādam anucchedam aśāśvatam*, whereas homage verse Iab in PsP Tib reads: *gang gis rten cing 'brel par 'byung 'gag pa med pa skye med pa*, which would correspond to the syntactical order *yaḥ pratītyasamutpādam anirodham anutpādam*. The translators have fitted the explanation of *nirodha*, etc., quite inconspicuously between the two sentences later in the text in which *nirodha* and the other elements to be negated in regard to *pratītyasamutpāda* are again referred to.

It might be suggested that one of the manuscripts used by the translators did attest the block explaining *nirodha*, etc., after the discussion of the compound *pratītyasamutpāda* because it is possible that Candrakīrti is following the structure of Bhāviveka's presentation of the section as we find it in PP Tib, in which the words *'gag pa*, etc., are explained only subsequent to the discussion of the compound *rten cing 'brel par 'byung* (*ba*). This location of the explanation of *'gag* *pa*, etc., in PP Tib, however, is almost certainly again the result of a translator decision: Jñānagarbha and Klu'i rgyal mtshan, the translators of the PP, moved the PP explanations of *yaḥ* and *pratītya-samutpāda* forward in the text so that the verse elements could be explicated in accord with the order they appear in the Tibetan homage verses. It can be observed that Bhāviveka unambiguously asserts—in what appears to have originally been part of an introductory statement—that the meanings of the words are stated (by himself) "right at the beginning" (*de la tshig gi don* [**padārtha*] *rtogs pa med par ngag dang rab tu byed pa dang bstan bcos kyi don mi rtogs pas de'i phyir dang po kho nar tshig gi don brjod par bya'o* [D 47a2-3; P 55b2-3]), and yet his explanation of *gang gis* (*yaḥ*) and his comments on *rten cing 'brel par 'byung* (*ba*), i.e., the explanations of the first two elements of the translated homage verses, *precede* this statement. Moreover, Bhāviveka's comment that the individual words are explained "right at the beginning" is followed by the explication of each of the verses' words—excepting *yaḥ* and *pratītyasamutpāda*, which are conspicuously absent here because they have already been commented on in PP Tib—in the order they occur in the *Tibetan* translation. Although I have not examined the PP carefully enough to be able to determine the exact seams of the presumed cut and paste work of the translators, the structure of PP Tib strongly suggests that in PP Skt the explanations of *yaḥ* and *pratītyasamutpāda* appeared within the main word-explanation block corresponding to the order in which they appear in the *Sanskrit* homage verses. Given that the PP translators also translated PPṬ, they must have rearranged PPṬ too; there may be clearer indications of the seams of the moved block within PPṬ.

The mention of the words *avayavārtha* and *vibhajyate* also do not support PsP Tib's placement of the block. It might be proposed that *avayavārtha* and *vibhajyate* are intended to be related not to the homage verses but to *pratītyasamutpāda*; that is, the meanings of these two words would restrict them to referring to an analysis (*vi* √*bhaj*) of the meaning of the individual parts (*avayavārtha*) of the compound *pratītyasamutpāda*. Other documented occurrences of the compounds *avayavārtha* and *samudāya* forming a complementary pair (cf. the first two examples given for *samudāya* in Abhyankar and

Shukla 1977: 418) and the fact that *vibhajyate* has, in addition to meanings such as "is analyzed," the meaning "is explained in detail" (see BHSD) tend to undermine such a hypothesis. Although one does encounter in Candrakīrti's rebuttal of Bhāviveka's preferred interpretation of the compound *pratītyasamutpāda* the statement that the compound *pratītyasamutpāda* is *avayavārthānugama* (cf. PsP_M §13), i.e., one that corresponds to the meaning of its members, it seems clear that the exact sense of *avayavārtha* is dependent upon the context: in §13 it refers to the meaning of the *avayava*s of a compound but in the present case to the *avayava*s of sentences/verses. Candrakīrti's use of the word *tu* in *avayavārthas tu vibhajyate* following the homage verses in fact indicates that at this point he intends *avayavārtha* to stand in contradistinction to *samudāyārtha*.

That the word-explanation block has been relocated in PsP Tib and PP Tib was overlooked by Pandeya when he "reconstructed" PP Sanskrit; he reconstructs the passages under discussion following the Tibetan order of things (see Pandeya 1988: 6). Extremely surprising is the fact that, even though Pandeya sets PsP's Sanskrit version of the homage verses at the beginning of his reconstruction of the PP, he does not take this version into consideration when they reappear a few lines later, but reconstructs directly from the Tibetan, with the result that homage verse Iab there reads *yaḥ pratītya samutpādam anirodham anutpādam*. De Jong (1993) has critically reviewed Pandeya's two volumes (concluding that "the only usefulness of Pandeya's work is in making clear that this is not the way to proceed" [ibid., 146]) but not does mention this problem.

Appendix V (re: §6., n. 53)

upasarga

The Tattvabodhinī, which claims that *upasarga*s are merely illuminators, presents, without any change to the metre of the *śloka*, *pāda*s ab as: *upasargeṇa dhātvartho balād anyaḥ pratīyate* "Another meaning of the [verbal] root is perforce understood by means of the prefix" (cf. SiKau 405). Bhairavamiśra, in his Candrakalā, discusses the three readings for *pāda*s ab (405). He first gives expression to the opinion that *dhātvartho balāt* as presented in the Tattvabodhinī version of the *śloka* should be read as abalāt (*dhātvartho 'balāt*), because otherwise the fact that *upasarga*s are illuminators is contradicted; they would have to be seen as words in themselves if their strength is mentioned here. He then notes that certain persons reject the reading *upasargeṇa dhātvartho balād anyatra nīyate* (i.e., that found in the PsP) for the reading *upasargeṇa dhātvartho balād anyaḥ pratīyate* (i.e., that found in the Tattvabodhinī) on the ground that if the *upasarga* is accepted as the agent of "leading," its independence and the verbal root's dependence would be implied, neither of which is asserted in the view of those who hold that *upasarga*s are merely illuminators (*nayanakartṛtvasyopasarga evāṅgīkāre balābhāve 'svatantratve ca kartṛtvaṃ naiva dṛṣṭacaram iti nayanakarmaṇa evāsvatantratvasya sarvatrāṅgīkārād dhātāv asvatantratvam upasargeṣu svatantratvam iti viparītam eva syāt*). According to them, *balāt* must refer to the strength of the root, not of the *upasarga*, and the coalescence of the root with an *upasarga* merely sparks, so to speak, the potency of the root for assuming and conveying a new meaning. The first half of the *śloka* is explained to mean: *upasargeṇa* [=] *upasargasaṃsargeṇa* "through the coalescence with a prefix" *balāt* [=] *śabdaśaktisvabhāvāt* "because of the nature of the potency of the word (= verbal root)" *anya eva dhātvarthaḥ pratīyate*. Bhairavamiśra ends the presentation of views by adding that even with the reading *anyatra nīyate*, the *upasarga* should be seen as (only) instigating the making known of a different meaning of the root; thus here too the meaning is reconciled to support the view of *upasarga* as illuminator.

Appendix VI (re: §9., n. 75)

etac cāyuktam

De La Vallée Poussin presents the Sanskrit text for Bhāviveka's critique as commencing with *etad vā* [*a*]*yuktaṃ kiṃ ca ayuktaṃ etat*, and punctuates it with a half-*daṇḍa* after [*a*]*yuktam*. All of the paper manuscripts attest variants of *etad vāyuktaṃ* | *kiṃ ca ayuktaṃ etat* for *etad cāyuktaṃ* (the *akṣara dvā* in *etad vā*° of ms J closely resembles the *akṣara ccā*). The correct reading *etac cāyuktaṃ* is attested only by ms Q (ms P has a lacuna). Approximately 12-13 *akṣara*s are missing in ms P's lacuna that begins after the *akṣara kau* of *anuvādākauśalam* and extends to, but does not include, the *akṣara ca* of *cakṣuḥ*; there is definitely not enough space for the 18-19 *akṣara*s one would expect were ms P to have read as the paper manuscripts (and de La Vallée Poussin's edition) do. De La Vallée Poussin (PsP_L 8, n. 6) assesses that PsP Tib lacks *etad vā [a]yuktaṃ kiṃ ca* but does not suggest further emendation of the Sanskrit text. PsP Tib for the (full) sentence in question reads *de yang mi rung ste mig dang gzugs la brten nas mig gi rnam par shes pa 'byung zhes gsungs pa 'di la don gnyi ga med pa'i phyir ro zhes sun 'byin smras pa gang yin pa de yang mi 'thad do*. The citation as presented in PsP Tib, which represents Bhāviveka's critique of the two etymologies for *pratītyasamutpāda*, has been taken over nearly verbatim from PP Tib: *de yang mi rung ste | mig dang gzugs rnams la brten nas mig gi rnam par shes pa 'byung ngo zhes gsungs pa 'di la don gnyi ga med pa'i phyir ro* (PP D 46b3-4; P 54b8-55a1). Note Bhāviveka's employment of **etat* (Tib: *de*) which refers back to the pair of etymologies just presented. PP Tib's *de yang mi rung ste* indicates an original reading **etac cāyuktam* in PP Skt. Since Candrakīrti is obviously quoting PP Skt, Ms Q's *etac cāyuktaṃ* can be accepted as correct (a conclusion also supported by the size of P's lacuna); the additional words *kiṃ ca ayuktam etat* that follow in the paper manuscripts must be an accretion. *etac cāyuktam* in the PsP thus marks the commencement of the PP quotation (the paper manuscripts' reading *etad vāyuktam* is the result of the *akṣara ccā* read as *dvā*); *api* of *yad uktaṃ dūṣaṇaṃ tad api nopapadyate* makes clear that we are now into Candrakīrti's second criticism.

Stcherbatsky (1927: 88, n. 2) emended de La Vallée Poussin's reading *etad vā [a]yuktaṃ kiṃ ca ayuktaṃ etat* to *etac cāyuktam kiṃ ca ayuktaṃ etat*; his literal translation for this and what follows runs, "And this is wrong (on the part of Bhāvaviveka. He says,) 'and moreover it is not right to maintain that in relation to (= in reaching) the eye and the colours, visual sensation arises, because two things (reaching one another are here) impossible.' Just the incriminated fault is nonsense." Although Stcherbatsky's misinterpretation of the meaning of the section must have influenced his understanding of the intended relation of the semantic components, it is clear that he takes *etac cāyuktam* to be Candrakīrti's introductory statement to the next fault of Bhāviveka's to be pointed out and *kiṃ ca ayuktam etat* to constitute the commencement of Bhāviveka's criticism, that is, he understands *kiṃ ca ayuktam etat* to be the Sanskrit for *de yang mi rung*.

As stated in the note to my translation, the *LṬ cites exactly the PsP text passage under discussion: *anūdya bhāviveko dūṣaṇam āha | etac cāyuktam iti* (cf. Yonezawa 2004: 121, 130). See also Kajiyama 1963: 42 and Ames 1993: 215, both of whom have understood Bhāviveka's *dūṣaṇa* in the PP correctly (Ames translates PP Tib's *yang* [standing for Skt *ca* in its adversative sense] of *de yang mi rung* as "also").

Appendix VII (re: §23., n. 121)

paroktadoṣāparihārāc ca

None of the PsP manuscripts attest a *ca* after *paroktadoṣāparihārāt*, but PsP Tib, PP (more so PP Peking than Derge), and PPṬ appear to confirm that one was included in the original Skt of PP and PsP. It is not uncommon for the lower *ca* of the *akṣara cca*, as a result of repeated copying, to end up a small blur and thus to be dropped, or for the *akṣara* to be interpreted as *t* plus *virāma*; in the former case the upper part of the *akṣara* is often interpreted as a slightly distorted *ta* and is left to stand as such, or a *virāma* is added to it. It should be noted that mss P and Q, less generous with *daṇḍa*s than the paper manuscripts, place a *daṇḍa* after *paroktadoṣāparihārāt* (they additionally place a *daṇḍa* after *hetudṛṣṭāntānabhidhānāt*; the paper manuscripts place a double *daṇḍa* after it). *prasaṅgavākyatvāc ca* thus commences a new sentence.

PsP Tib reads *gtan tshigs dang dpe ma brjod pa'i phyir* <u>*dang*</u> | *gzhan gyis smras pa'i nyes pa ma bsal ba'i phyir ro* || *thal bar 'gyur ba'i tshig yin pa'i phyir* ... . Although the Peking and Derge translations of this section of PP diverge, both also appear to support inclusion of *ca* (as will be seen further on in the PsP, however, PsP Tib often adds *dang*s where PsP Skt—correctly—does not attest *ca*s; PP D could also be taken as reflecting a list of three reasons connected by a single final *ca*). The corresponding section of PP P reads: *gtan tshigs dang dpe ma brjod pa'i phyir dang | gzhan gyis smras pa'i nyes pa ma bsal ba'i phyir ro ||* (= PsP Tib) *glags yod pa'i tshig yin pa'i phyir te ...* (58b8-59a1). PP D reads: *gtan tshigs dang dpe ma brjod pa'i phyir dang | gzhan gyis smras pa'i nyes pa ma bsal ba'i phyir dang | glags yod pa'i tshig yin pa'i phyir te ...* (49a6-7). Given that Peking tends to preserve original readings, I consider PP P to better reflect Bhāviveka's original Sanskrit (against Yotsuya 1999: 76). It is doubtful that PP D's second *dang* reflects a consciously chosen translation of *ca* of *prasaṅgavākyatvāc ca* as found in the PP citation in PsP Skt, for such *ca*s are normally translated by *yang*; I expect that PP D originally read as PP P and that *dang* was—in the absence of an unambiguous equivalent for *ca* heralding the stating of a third reason (I admit that *te* could have stood for *ca*)—added as an editorial improvement/clarification.

Most helpful is the fact that Avalokitavrata comments on the word *ca* (*yang*) occurring after *prasaṅgavākyatvāc*; this confirms that this *ca* as found in PsP Skt (but lacking in PsP Tib and PP Tib) also stood in PP Skt. Note too that PPṬ's quotation of Bhāviveka's critique also contains this *yang*, and that the first two criticisms, as in PsP Tib and PP Peking, are presented as a separate unit (*gtan tshigs dang dpe ma brjod pa'i phyir dang | gzhan gyis smras pa'i nyes pa ma bsal ba'i phyir ro || glags yod pa'i tshig yin pa'i yang phyir te | skabs kyi don las bzlog pas ...* [PPṬ D 73b3-4; P 85b8-86a1]). Avalokitavrata states that this *ca* indicates that a third fault is being stated. That he deems it necessary to comment on *ca* after *prasaṅgavākyatvāc* as indicating yet another criticism of Buddhapalita's statement probably shows that he wanted to point out that the three ablatives indicate three reasons of equal weight/status. Thus, even though this *ca* is a mere sentence connector (i.e., with it a new sentence starts) that does not connect the reason itself with the two previous reasons, he wanted to indicate that the reason in the sentence it introduces is on a par with the two others. PPṬ: *gzhan yang de ji ltar rigs pa ma yin zhe na | glags yod pa'i tshig yin pa'i yang phyir te | gnas brtan buddha pā li tas bshad pa* (D: *rnam par bshad pa*) *de ni rgol ba gzhan gyi klan ka'i glags yod pa'i tshig yin pa'i phyir yang rigs pa ma yin no* ‖ *yang zhes bya ba'i sgra ni gtan tshigs dang dpe ma brjod pa'i phyir dang gzhan gyis smras pa'i nyes pa ma bsal ba'i phyir rigs pa ma yin par* (D: *pa*) *'ba' zhig tu ma zad kyi* | *de ni glags yod pa'i tshig yin pa'i phyir yang rigs pa ma yin no zhes bya bar sbyar ro* (D 74a2-3; P 86a7-86b1; quoted in Seyfort Ruegg 1981: 64, n. 203). Avalokitavrata's commentary is translated in Hopkins 1983: 462-466. Hopkins (ibid., 819, n. 375) notes that Tsong kha pa points out that the translations of the beginning of the third criticism vary, "indicating that he favors *glags yod pa'i tshig yin pa'i yang phyir te* as it is in the edition of Bhāvaviveka he had before him and in Avalokitavrata in the sense of meaning, '[Buddhapālita's interpretation] is also unsuitable because of having words that afford an opportunity [to an opponent to expose contradiction within his own system].'"

The emended PsP Skt would thus, if we disregard for the moment the difference between the translations *thal bar 'gyur ba'i tshig* and *glags yod pa'i tshig*, appear to mirror the structure of the original PP Skt.

Ames (1993: 222) appears to translate this part of the PP following Peking and therefore adds "also" in square brackets: "That is not [logically] possible, because no reason and example are given and because faults stated by the opponent are not answered. [Also,] because it is a *prasaṅga*-argument, a [property] to be proved ..." (cf. as well Kajiyama's translation based on Walleser's edition of the PP which likewise follows PP Peking [Kajiyama 1963: 50]). Yotsuya (1999: 76), on the other hand, chose to translate following Derge: "This is incorrect, because neither a logical reason (*gtan tshigs*, *hetu*) nor a logical example (*dpe*, *dṛṣṭānta*) has been presented. Nor has the fault (*ñes pa*, *doṣa*) pointed out by [your] opponent (= the Sāṃkhya) been eliminated. Furthermore [it is unacceptable] because it is a statement which is open to an objection. Since by the reversal of the matter under discussion ... ."

Appendix VIII (re: §27., n. 140)

kāryātmakaḥ and *kāraṇātmakaḥ*

De La Vallée Poussin emended the masculine singular nominative forms *kāryātmaka* and *kāraṇātmaka* of the Sāṅkhya objection (*kāryātmakaḥ*, *kāraṇātmaka*, *kāryātmakaś*, *kāraṇātmakaś*) that he found in his manuscripts to their corresponding ablative forms because PsP Tib's *bras bu'i bdag nyid las* (for PsP Skt's *kāryātmakaḥ* and *kāryātmakaś*) and *rgyu'i bdag nyid las* (for PsP Skt's *kāraṇātmaka* and *kāraṇātmakaś*) appeared to be reflecting ablatives. Although the masculine singular nominative forms are also attested in de Jong's manuscript (my ms D) and in the three manuscripts Yotsuya consulted, neither de Jong nor Yotsuya called de La Vallée Poussin's emendations into question, almost certainly because they too were of the opinion that PsP Tib's presentation of translations for Sanskrit ablatives, and not nominatives, justified the emendations. No doubt further justification was seen in the fact that the (nonextant) PP Skt, from which Candrakīrti is citing the objection, was assumed to have attested ablatives since PP Tib likewise contains translations for ablative forms. It has thus seemed reasonable, on the basis of the evidence provided by the Tibetan translations, to view the PsP Skt manuscript readings as corrupt. Disturbing, however, is the appearance of the nominative forms even in ms P, and the difficulty one has in explaining the causes of the supposed corruption.

It is imperative to note that as in the other cases in which Candrakīrti is citing from external works, the translators of PsP Tib have not translated directly from PsP Skt but have copied the citation from the Tibetan translation of the source text, in the present case from PP Tib. PsP Tib thus reflects PP Tib but is not necessarily a trustworthy witness for PsP Skt.

It appears that the PsP's change in language, i.e., from the PP's ablatives to PsP's nominatives, reflects a shift in what is being taken as the *subject* that arises, or rather, that is negated as arising. In the pertinent texts, the subject is either the *effect* (said to arise from itself as its cause), or the *cause* (said to arise again as its own effect). The ambivalence may already be present in Buddhapālita's argument. His consequence *na svata utpadyante bhāvās tadutpādavaiyarthyāt* would seem to take things as effects (*bhāva*s) as the subject and to negate their arising from themselves (as their own cause) because their (i.e., the *bhāva*s' = the effects') arising would be superfluous. In his explanatory statement *na hi svātmanā vidyamānānāṃ padārthānāṃ punarutpāde prayojanam asti*, on the other hand, the situation appears to be reversed: Buddhapālita states that it is futile for things already existing as such (i.e., things as *cause*) to arise again. An explicit distinction between things as effects and things as causes is, however, not made by Buddhapālita; he merely refers to things in general. Bhāviveka and Candrakīrti, on the other hand, clearly distinguish the subject that arises as either an effect or a cause. Bhāviveka, who sets forth "the inner bases have not arisen from self" as his thesis (*nādhyātmikāny āyatanāni svata utpannāni*), takes things as effects, i.e., the (arisen) inner bases, as the subject. Candrakīrti, by contrast, takes things as causes as the subject. That his subject of arising is things as causes is supported by his comments later on: at PsP$_{M}$ §29 (PsP$_{L}$ 21.1-6; see especially 21.3), with his mention of pots and so forth that already exist *in a latent state* in a lump of clay, etc., he refers to the subject (i.e., locus) of the other-acknowledged inference he draws out of Buddhapālita's statement of unwanted consequence; in PsP$_{M}$ §30 (PsP$_{L}$ 21.8-12; especially 21.10), he makes explicit that what is to be negated as arising are things with a "non-manifest form" (*anabhivyaktarūpa*); and in PsP$_{M}$ §31 (PsP$_{L}$ 22.1-2), he clarifies that the *pakṣa* of the other-acknowledged inference comprises "all things disposed to arise" (*niravaśeṣotpitsupadārtha*).

The two different subjects of arising are respectively alluded to with the ablative and nominative forms of the Sāṅkhyas' alternatives. Because the Madhyamaka argument denying the arising of things focusses on the Sāṅkhyas' alleged cause of things (*svataḥ*), the Sāṅkhyas demand that the Mādhyamika provide a more precise description of this cause, namely, as one that has the nature of an effect or one that has the nature of a cause. Thus when Bhāviveka, for whom arisen effects are the subject, is addressed, the Sāṅkhyas will ask *from what type of cause* the effects are denied as having arisen. Since Candrakīrti's subject of arising is (already) causes, the Sāṅkhyas will ask *what type of cause* is denied as reproducing itself.

Candrakīrti therefore modifies PP Skt's **kāryātmakāt* and **kāraṇātmakāt* to their nominative forms because he has shifted the subject that arises from things as effects to things as causes. To summarize the questions posed: Inasmuch as PP Skt, PP Tib and PsP Tib take the effect as the subject (i.e., the inner bases), their Sāṅkhyas will be asking whether Bhāviveka intends to deny that an effect has arisen from itself as an effect or intends to deny that an effect has arisen from itself as a cause. In PsP Skt, the Sāṅkhyas are asking whether the intention is to deny that a cause in the state of an effect reproduces itself or if it is to deny that a cause in the state of a cause reproduces itself.

Awareness of the different perspectives regarding the subject of arising exposes a problem introduced by de La Vallée Poussin's emendation of the nominatives to ablatives. In the final sentence of the Sāṅkhya objection in PsP Skt, it is argued that if the Mādhyamika denies that something with the nature of a cause reproduces itself, the Mādhyamika's reason will be contradictory (*viruddhārthatā*), i.e., will prove the *sādhya*'s opposite, on account of the fact that "all that arises arises only as something existing with the nature of a cause" (*kāraṇātmanā vidyamānasyaiva sarvasyotpattimata utpādāt*). The subject of arising implied by the sentence is clearly as Candrakīrti takes it to be, i.e., things as causes. This reason given by the Sāṅkhyas to demonstrate that the Mādhyamika's reason is contradictory appears in PP Tib as *skye ba can thams cad ni rgyu'i bdag nyid du yod pa kho na las skye ba'i phyir* "because all that arises arises only *from* something that exists with the nature of a cause"; PP Skt may have read **kāraṇātmanā vidyamānād eva...* . The subject of arising that is implied in this case is Bhāviveka's, viz., things as effects. The allusion to effects as the subject of arising is thus consistent throughout the PP objection. PsP Tib, however, presents the Sāṅkhya reason indicating the contradiction as *skye ba dang ldan pa thams cad ni rgyu'i bdag nyid du yod pa kho na skye ba'i phyir*. The relevant difference from PP Tib is the lack of a *las* after *rgyu'i bdag nyid du yod pa kho na*. The phrase without *las* brings an unexpected and unacceptable inconsistency to PsP Tib's Sāṅkhya objection as a whole: in reproducing PP Tib's objection up to this point, PsP Tib takes things as effects as the subject of arising, but with the reason showing the contradiction, it takes the subject of arising as Candrakīrti does, i.e., as things as *causes*. This switch in PsP Tib of the subject of arising from effects to causes points to an oversight on the part of the translators. Following their regular procedure for citations, they copied PP Tib's objection into PsP Tib and made their usual minor modifications to the ready-made translation. For the sake of having PsP Tib better reflect PsP Skt's phrase indicating the reason for the contradiction, they dropped PP Tib's *las*, but did not notice that this brought an inconsistency into the text of the objection. The same inconsistency regarding the subject of arising that mars PsP Tib is introduced into PsP Skt when the four nominatives are changed to ablatives. Candrakīrti's inclusion of and modification of the PP Skt Sāṅkhya objection was obviously motivated by his concern with demonstrating that the other-acknowledged inference he draws out of Buddhapālita's statement cannot be faulted by the Sāṅkhyas (cf. PsP_M §30; PsP_L 21.8-12). A mere recitation of the PP Sāṅkhya complaint did not serve his purposes; he reconstructed the PP objection so that it could be seen as applicable to his own other-acknowledged inference.

Yonezawa (2005a: 72, n. 25) has adverted to the fact that ms Q does not bear the nominative forms *kāryātmakaḥ* and *kāraṇātmakaḥ* but rather attests the ablative forms *kāryātmanaḥ* and *kāraṇātmanaḥ*. Given that ms Q's Sanskrit ablatives correspond to PsP Tib's ablatives, Yonezawa expressed the opinion that these ablatives represent correct readings and that they should be adopted as such in the text of PsP Skt. As appealing as it might be to accept ms Q's ablatives and as tempting as it might be to want to explain the other manuscripts' readings as resulting from the interpretation of *na akṣara*s as *ka akara*s, ms Q's readings cannot be accepted for exactly the same reasons that PsP_L's ablatives cannot be accepted. First, the PP's Sāṅkhya argument was simply copied into PsP Tib from PP Tib and therefore cannot serve as a reliable witness for PsP Skt. Second, ms Q's ablatives together with the PsP's genitive *vidyamānasya* (*kāraṇātmanā vidyamānasyaiva sarvasyotpattimata utpādāt*) ruin the logical coherence of the Sāṅkhya argument in the PsP, and are problematic in view of Candrakīrti's other-acknowledged inference at PsP_M §29 and §30 (PsP_L 21.1-6, 8-12) and his clarification of the *pakṣa* at PsP_M §31 (PsP_L 22.1-2). I expect that ms Q's ablatives are the result of deliberate change: an individual involved at some stage in the transmission lineage of ms Q (the readings may have come from the γ line [see Stemma]) simplified the *lectio difficilior kāryātmakaḥ* and *kāraṇātmakaḥ*, possibly because the sentence read with the ablative is—at least on a superficial reading—immediately pleasing and easy to understand, or because it was noticed that the Sāṅkhya argument in the PP contained ablatives. As indicated, the nominatives *kāryātmakaḥ* and *kāraṇātmakaḥ* are the only logically justifiable readings.

Appendix IX (re: §28., n. 148)

codanayā

De La Vallée Poussin (PsP_L 18 and n. 8) accepts the reading °*codanayā* of his Cambridge and Calcutta manuscripts (Paris reads °*vodanayā*) but, referring to PsP_L 21.13 (*'numāna*[*vi*]*rodhacodanāyām*; end of PsP_M §30 *'numānabādhācodanāyām*), appends, "Peut-être: °*codanāyāṃ svata* ... ." The entire PsP Tib phrase for PsP Skt beginning *parapratijñāyas tu*, etc., reads *gzhan gyi dam bca' ba la rang gi rjes su dpag pas 'gal ba* ***brjod par ni bya dgos pas*** | *rang nyid la phyogs la sogs pa* (P adds *dang*) *phyogs dang gtan tshigs dang* (D omits *dang*) *dpe'i skyon dang bral ba dag* ***yod par bya dgos*** *so* ||, suggesting that some form of optative participle stood in place of °*codanayā* in at least one of the Sanskrit manuscripts from which the Tibetan translation was made. De La Vallée Poussin (PsP_L 18, n. 7) reconstructs *gzhan gyi dam bca' ba la rang gi rjes su dpag pas 'gal ba brjod par ni bya dgos pas* as *parapratijñāyāṃ sva-anumānena virodha[sya] abhidhānenaiva bhavitavyam*. Regardless of the discrepancy between PsP Skt and PsP Tib, the Sanskrit's °*codanayā*, construed with *bhavitavyam*, suits both the structure and intention of the sentence as a whole, as attested by Yotsuya's (1999: 64) translation. Like de La Vallée Poussin's manuscripts, the other paper manuscripts attest °*codanayā* or variants thereof (°*vodanayā*, °*codanamā*, °*coṭhadanayā*); ms P also attests °*codanayā*. Both ms Q and the *LṬ, however, attest de La Vallée Poussin's suggested °*codanāyām* (cf. Yonezawa 2005a: 59 and Yonezawa 2004: 121; in both articles

Yonezawa suggests adopting the reading. *LṬ: *anumānena virodhacodanāyāṃ tasyānumānasya pakṣādibhir bhāvyaṃ*). Even though both of these valuable manuscripts attest *codanāyām*, the reading cannot be accepted inasmuch as it disturbs the obviously intended symmetry between the components of the two parts of the sentence, namely, between proof and refutation by way of a reasoning whose subject, etc., is established for both parties (*ubhayasiddhena*) being conceded as inappropriate (*mā bhūt*), on the one hand, and criticism of contradiction with a reasoning accepted by the opponent alone by way of a *pakṣa,* etc., from the opponent's point of view alone (*svata eva*), being demanded (*bhavitavyam*) in their place, on the other. The ms Q and *LṬ reading becomes definitively disqualified when the line of argumentation in the PsP is regarded, for *codanāyām* brings with it the implication that the Mādhyamika addressed by Candrakīrti's Bhāviveka does indeed, of his own accord, criticize the opponent's *pratijñā* by way of a *svata evānumāna* and needs merely to be reminded that this *anumāna* must have a faultless *pakṣa*, etc., an implication in no way supported by the text preceding the sentence; the *svata evānumāna* drawn out of Buddhapālita's *prasaṅga* in the section following the sentence under discussion represents merely Candrakīrti's concession to the *demand* for a *svata evānumāna*. *LṬ's author may have chosen to read *codanāyām* because he has misunderstood the previous part of the sentence as stating that it is correct for the Mādhyamika to refute the opponent's thesis by way of a reasoning established for both parties and has not managed to distinguish between an *ubhayasiddhānumāna* and a *svata evānumāna* (see n. 145, 148, 151). Given that there are other instances of deliberate change in the PsP text of ms Q, one suspects that its *codanāyām* is also the result of misguided reflection on the part of a reader or scribe.

Note that the form *codanāyām* (of *'numānabādhācodanāyām api* at the end of PsP_M §30 [PsP_L 21.13]) in the sentence "Therefore, even when [we accede to Bhāviveka's demand and] there is the criticism (*codanā*) that there is sublation [of the Sāṅkhya thesis] by way of an inference (*anumānabādhā*) from [the Sāṅkhya's] own point of view" is used only *after* Candrakīrti has acquiesced to Bhāviveka's insisttence that a *svata evānumāna* is required and has presented the full inference inherent in Buddhapālita's statement.

PsP Tib's *brjod par ni bya dgos pas*, considered by de La Vallée Poussin as reflecting *abhidhānenaiva bhavitavyam*, could alternatively be conjectured as the translation for *codyatayā*. Although *codyatayā*, like *codanāyām*, detracts from the sentence's intended symmetry and tends to muffle the specific demand being made, and thus cannot be accepted as the original reading, it may represent a corruption of *codanayā* which stood in one of the manuscripts utilized by the translators of the Tibetan, the result of an added vertical stroke or natural mark on the leaf to the right of *da* which caused it to be read as *dya*, and the *akṣara na* appearing similar to and thus read as *ta*. The particle *ni*, however, would seem to speak against such a reconstruction. It may be more likely that the translators found °*codanayā* in their exemplars and, having construed *pakṣādibhiḥ* with *bhavitavyam*, felt forced to understand instrumental °*codanayā* as indicating a reason, but were also following the argumentation in the text closely enough to recognize that criticism by way of a *svata evānumāna* was not being presumed, but was rather being demanded, by Bhāviveka, and therefore considered it necessary to add an interpreted optative.

Tillemans (1992: 318, n. 8), quoting Stcherbatsky's (1927: 98) interpretation of *svata eva* of the latter half of the sentence ("However in accusing your opponent of contradiction you must yourself take your stand upon an argument which, *in your opinion*, would be free of those logical errors to which a thesis, a reason or an example are liable" (Tillemans' italics), rightly corrects Stcherbatsky's mistaken interpretation of *svata eva* in his translation, "However, since one accuses the opponent's thesis of being in contradiction with inference *from his point of view alone*, then, *for himself alone*, the thesis and other [members of this inference] must be free of faults concerning the thesis, reason and examples." Still, for the reasons stated above, the translation remains wanting: Candrakīrti's hypothetical opponent—Bhāviveka—is insisting, against mere *prasaṅga* usage, on criticism effected by way of an inference whose members are established for the opponent; he is not, as Tilleman's translation would have it, automatically assuming such an inference and insisting that its members, from the opponent's point of view, be free of fault. The *bhavitavyam* construction has additionally been misunderstood: the grammatical subject of *bhavitavyam*, if (erroneously) not taken to be *codanayā*, could only be *pakṣādibhiḥ*, and construed with *pakṣādibhiḥ* it would yield the sense "there must be a thesis, etc."; the preceding *pakṣahetudṛṣṭāntadoṣarahitaiḥ* (as found in PsP_L) modifies *pakṣādibhiḥ*, and cannot be taken together with *bhavitavyam* as forming the predicate to a logical subject assumed to be *pakṣādi*.

Appendix X (re: §71., n. 303)

utpādād vā tathāgatānām anutpādād vā tathāgatānāṃ sthitaivaiṣā dharmāṇām dharmatā

The citation is found at $AKBh_{ed}$ 137.18: *utpādād vā tathāgatānām anutpādād vā sthitaiveyaṃ dharmateti* (Yaśomitra adds *tathāgatānām* after *anutpādād vā*; de La Vallée Poussin [1913a: 111] conjectures [*dharmāṇāṃ*] after *sthitaiveyaṃ* for the AKVy reading); for its source, parallels and references, see Pāsādika 1989: 59. See also PsP_L 40, n. 1; La Vallée Poussin 1913a: 111-113 (note also the reference to its use in the AN in regard to the impermanence of conditioned things); Schoening 1995: 268 and 702. Cp. SN II.25.17-20, where the statement is made with reference to 12-limbed dependent-arising: *jātipaccayā bhikkhave jarāmaraṇam uppādā vā tathāgatānam anuppādā vā tathāgatānaṃ* || *ṭhitā va sā dhātu dhammaṭṭhitatā dhammaniyāmatā idappaccayatā* ||. The formulaic expression also occurs in Mahāyāna texts, and here tends to refer to the fact that all things are empty. Cp. Daśabhūmikasūtra (ed. P.L. Vaidya, Darbhanga: The Mithila Institute, 1967) 43.9-10: *api tu khalu punaḥ kulaputra eṣā sarvadharmāṇāṃ dharmatā* | *utpādād vā tathāgatānām anutpādād vā sthitaivaiṣā dharmatā dharmadhātusthitiḥ yad idaṃ sarvadharmaśūnyatā sarvadharmānupalabdhiḥ* |. Cp. also the formula as found at $MABh_{ed}$ 306.1-3 where it is cited in response to the question of whether a non-artificial (**akṛtrima*), independent (**nirapekṣa*) own-being exists; see Tauscher 1981: 69-71 and 130, n. 138. Candrakīrti, speaking in regard to this passage, explains the *dharmatā* as being that which is known by consciousness free of the *timira* of ignorance (cf. $MABh_{ed}$ 306.4-8). Reference within the formulaic expression to the *paramārtha*, instead of to the *dharmatā*, is found within a *sūtra* quotation at $MABh_{ed}$ 306.18-19 (*rigs kyi bu don dam pa ni de bzhin gshegs pa rnams byung yang rung ma byung yang rung*); on this passage see Tauscher 1981: n. 143 and 148. Cp. also MA *kārikā* VI.222: *sangs rgyas rnams ni byung ba 'am* ‖ *ma byung yang rung dngos su na* ‖ *dngos po kun gyi stong pa nyid* ‖ *gzhan gyi dngos por rab tu bsgrags* ‖ ($MABh_{ed}$ 339.18-340.1). Tauscher (1981: 102) translates: "Mögen die Buddhas entstanden oder nicht entstanden sein, die Leerheit aller Dinge der Wirklichkeit nach (*vastutaḥ*) hat er als Höchstes Sein (*parabhāva*) verkündet" (see also ibid., notes 492-494).

The noun *dharma*, like the the abstract noun *dharmatā*, is also occasionally encountered in the meaning of "real nature," "essential being" in Buddhist literature. One of the fundamental meanings of *dharma* is "law," "truth"; the formulation of the truth in the form of the Buddhist teaching, the Dharma, by extension, represents another meaning of *dharma*. *dharma* understood as the Buddhist teaching may also connote a norm for behaviour, that is, a law in the form of an objective behavioural standard which finds expression in the Buddhist teaching. Not far from the idea of *dharma* as "truth" is *dharma* interpreted as, as just indicated, the real nature, the essential state, the unshakeable law of things; again, the abstract *dharmatā* is often assigned the role of conveying this meaning. A weakening of the meaning "rule, law, norm" is also found in various connections in Buddhist texts: thus "definite, or essential, qualifier"; a further weakening allows for the senses "attribute," "state". Seen from the phenomenal side, *dharma* stands for the object itself. See Schmithausen 1969: 146. See also Hirakawa 1990: 45-48. Zimmermann, commenting on the word *dharmatā* as it appears in the formula and in other contexts in the Tathāgatagarbhasūtra, sets forth three main meanings for *dharmatā*; see Zimmermann 2002: 54f.

Appendix XI (re: §83., n. 406)

Naiyāyika opponents

Candrakīrti does not identify the opponents who demand to know whether the Mādhyamikas ascertain that no things exist by way of *pramāṇa*s. *LṬ's author also does not identify the opponents or comment on any of the words or phrases in the citation. Most scholars who have translated or studied this section of the PsP assign the critique to Dignāga and/or representatives of the Buddhist logical-epistemological school. Stcherbatsky (1927: 135, n. 10) avers that "[t]his and the following discussion refers to the *pramāṇa-viniścaya-vāda* of Dignāga and others." Tanji (1992: 5), in the English summary for his study on PsP chapter one, refers to the first sentence of the citation as "Dignāga's question." Siderits (1981: 120-122), pointing out that theories specific to the logical-epistemological school are not topical in the citation, considers the section's addressees to be in the first place the Yogācāra-Sautrāntikas, i.e., Dignāga and his school, and secondly, the Naiyāyikas. Rizzi (1988: 47) paraphrases PsP_L 55.11-57.11 and entitles the larger PsP_L 55.11-75.13 (= PsP_M §83-PsP_M §123) segment "The Controversy with the Buddhist Logicians"; he identifies the opponents as "Vijñānavādins," and then refers specifically to "Dignāga and his disciples." Yoshimizu (1996: 12f.) has drawn attention to the fact that the dGe lugs pa scholar 'Jam dbyangs bzhad pa'i rdo rje Nga dbang brtson 'grus (1648-1721), who quotes most of the citation in his Tshig gsal stong thun gyi tshad ma'i rnam bshad, notes that the opponent is a "logician" (*rtog ge ba*); Yoshimizu (n. 56) understands that Dignāga is the person intended. Huntington (2003: 77) holds that the individual with whom Candrakīrti dialogues immediately *subsequent* to the citation, that is, the adversary who poses the two questions at PsP_M §84 and §85 [= PsP_L 57.4 and PsP_L 57.7], is Bhāviveka (he describes this passage as "part of an imaginary conversation with a Buddhist philosopher who, given the context, is almost certainly intended to represent the position of Bhāvaviveka"). Arnold, inspired by the appearance of *pramāṇādhīnatvāt prameyādhigamasya* in the critique and its near equivalence to PSV's **pramāṇādhīno hi prameyādhigamaḥ* (on PS I.1), deems the speaker of the cited objection to be Dignāga (cf. Arnold 2003: 141, n. 5; 2005a:

144, 261, n. 5, and 262, n. 13; 2005b: 415 and 419, n. 23). PSV's **pramāṇādhīno hi prameyādhigamaḥ*, it should be noted, is Hattori's reconstruction (cf. Hattori 1968: Appendix) based on PSV Tibetan's *gzhal bya rtogs pa ni tshad ma la rag las pa yin* and, presumably, *pramāṇādhīno hi prameyādhigamaḥ* as found at the beginning of the Pramāṇavarttikālaṅkāra, where Prajñākaragupta repeats a good number of the words and phrases from the PSV on PS I.1 (cf. Sāṅkṛtyāyana 1953: 3.18); the beginning of PSṬ chapter six in the sole extant Sanskrit manuscript of the PSṬ reveals that the PSV (at least the version known to Jinendrabuddhi) reads *yasmāt pramāṇādhīnaḥ prameyādhigamaḥ* (cf. MacDonald 2011: 686). Although the difference is negligible, the opponents' use of the phrase by no means proves that Dignāga is the interlocutor, for it is common knowledge that the view that objects of valid cognition are apprehended in reliance on means of valid cognition is not exclusive to the Buddhist logical-epistemological tradition: NS IV.2.29, for example, presents an analogous formulation with *pramāṇataś cārthapratipatteḥ*. Hattori (1968: 76, n. 1.10) has already remarked on the similarity of the statement *pramāṇādhīno prameyādhigamaḥ* with the opening statement of the NBh: *pramāṇato 'rthapratipattau pravṛttisāmarthyād arthavat pramāṇam*. It might be mentioned that the phrase *pramāṇādhigamyatvāt prameyāṇāṃ bhāvānam* is placed in the opponent Naiyāyika's mouth in the commentary on VV 51 (cf. VV_{ed} 72.15-16). Garfield (2008: 511) disagrees with Huntington's identification of the PsP opponent as Bhāviveka (noting that Thakchoe considers the interlocutor to be Dignāga and that Arnold holds him to be a Mīmāṃsaka[!]) and states (ibid., n. 7) that he thinks "the passage is in fact directed generally at any foundationalist account of *pramāṇa*." Seyfort Ruegg (2002: 95) refrains from identifying the opponent.

The ascription to Dignāga of the view, expressed at three different points in the objection, that all things exist, cannot be accepted. As stated in n. 406, Dignāga would have been fully aware that the Madhyamaka negation of things is made from the point of view of the ultimate, and it is highly unlikely, indeed impossible, that he would have engaged with his fellow Mahāyānists in a debate focussed on the final nature of things in which he would utter pronouncements incongruous with his own Yogācāra stance (on Dharmakīrti, as well as

Dignāga, as a Yogācāra proponent, cf., e.g., Dreyfus and Lindtner 1989, Steinkellner 1990; see also Tosaki's review of Singh [1987: 143] where he points out that for Dharmakīrti *paramārthasat* means only the ultimate reality "of the mundane [*laukika*, *saṃvṛti*]"). Dignāga shares with the Mādhyamikas the view that worldly things exist only on the surface level and are in actuality unreal, but differs from them in specifying that what appear to be external objects are merely objective aspects within consciousness and in maintaining that ultimately, nothing but self-cognizing consciousness exists. In encounters where the topic of conversation was the ultimate status of things, the declaration *sarvabhāvāḥ santi* would certainly have been rejected by him. The same opponent's later objection that it is his "experience" that things arise (*anubhava eṣo 'smākam*; cf. PsP_M §87 [= PsP_L 58.7]) is just as difficult to accept as a Dignāgean argument. It goes without saying that it is also impossible to imagine the argument from "experience" as well as the assertions in the present PsP_M §83 objection as having been made by Bhāviveka.

Even though I cannot agree with Siderits' conclusion that Dignāga is the main opponent, or with his adducing of NS II.1.13 and 14 to substantiate his inclusion of the Naiyāyikas (for details, see MacDonald 2011: 683f.), his observation that Yogācāra-Sautrāntika assumptions are not thematic was correct, as was his postulation that the Naiyāyikas are a target of the critique. They in fact appear to be the sole target of the critique. Both the assertion that all things exist and the idea that one's own experience of the things of the world corroborates and confirms their existence accord with the realist views of the Naiyāyikas. Similar, but less elaborated, versions of most of the arguments set forth in the objection can in fact be found at two places in Uddyotakara's NV. The first occurs as part of his commentary on NS IV.1.40, which forms the response to an opponent who has just argued in NS IV.1.39 that there is not the establishment of own-being (*svabhāva*) because things are reliant (*āpekṣikatvāt*), i.e., dependent (NS IV.1.39: *na svabhāvasiddhir āpekṣikatvāt* ‖ [see NBh 238]). Uddyotakara begins the relevant part of his commentary on NS IV.1.40 by referring to the opponent's thesis that everything is non-existent (*sarvam abhāvaḥ*), already set forth in NS IV.1.37 (NS IV.1.37: *sarvam abhāvo bhāveṣv itaretarābhāvasiddheḥ* ‖ [NBh 236]). Uddyotakara argues: *sarvam abhāva iti sarvathā cāyaṃ vādo vyāhataḥ | ko vyāghātaḥ | ādau tāvat pramāṇopapattyanupapattī sarvam abhāva iti bruvāṇaḥ pramāṇaṃ paryanuyojyaḥ | yadi pramāṇaṃ brūte vyāhataṃ bhavati | atha nābhidhatte 'rtho 'sya na sidhyati pramāṇābhāvāt* (cf. NV 454.6-8; all punctuation changes in this quotation and those below are mine) "And in all respects this assertion 'Everything is non-existent' is contradicted. What contradiction [is there]? To begin, first, there is the possibility/suitability or impossibility/non-suitability of means of valid cognition: The one stating 'Everything is non-existent' is to be asked about the means of cognition [for validating this state of affairs]. If he states [i.e., declares that there exists such] a means of valid cognition, [the assertion that everything is non-existent] becomes contradicted. But if he does not name [one, i.e., does not admit a valid means of cognition for its ascertainment], the meaning of this [assertion] is not established on account of the non-existence of means of valid cognition." It is true that there is no talk of ascertainment (*niścaya*) here in the NV, but the gist of the alternative arguments and the conclusions arrived at are quite close to those of the first two arguments in the PsP citation. Later, in his commentary on NS IV.2.27 where the opponent is again one who denies the existence of things, Uddyotakara critiques the assertion that no things are possible using some of the same arguments and expressions that he employed in his NS IV.1.40 comments: *sarvabhāvānupapattir iti ca bruvāṇaḥ pramāṇaṃ paryanuyojyaḥ | yadi pramāṇaṃ bravīti, vyāhataṃ bhavati | atha na bravīty artho 'sya na sidhyati pramāṇābhāvāt |* (cf. NV 487.17-18). With the next sentence, he adduces a further reasoning: *athāprāmāṇikī siddhiḥ sarvabhāvānām upapattir ity asya kasmān na siddhiḥ* (cf. NV 487.18-488.1) "But if there is establishment without a means of cognition to validate [it], why [could] there not [be] the establishment of this [viz., the state of affairs maintained by us, namely,] 'There is the possibility of all things'?" This argument is easily recognizable as equivalent to the third one set forth by the PsP's opponent. A strikingly similar trio of arguments had been employed earlier by Pakṣilasvāmin Vātsyāyana in his NBh on NS IV.2.30 (NS IV.2.30: *pramāṇānupapattyupapattibhyām ||*): *evaṃ ca sati sarvaṃ nāstīti nopapadyate | kasmāt | pramāṇānupapattyupapattibhyām | yadi sarvaṃ nāstīti pramāṇam upapadyate sarvaṃ nāstīty etad vyāhanyate | atha pramāṇaṃ nopapadyate sarvaṃ nāstīty asya kathaṃ siddhiḥ | atha pramāṇam antareṇa siddhiḥ sarvam astīty asya kathaṃ na siddhiḥ* | (NBh 272.16-273.3; translated in MacDonald 2011: 691). The fact that the three appear together in the NBh and in the second NV passage indicates that they were used collectively, as they are here in Candrakīrti's citation, to refute the Madhyamaka claim that things do not exist.

On the argument for the existence of things based on their being experienced, see n. 430.

The attribution of the citation to the Nyāya school and the identification of the opponent as a Naiyāyika is not undermined by the fact that Candrakīrti, in his discussion with Dignāga after the confrontation with the Naiyāyika (a confrontation that continues until the end of PsP_M §88 [= PsP_L 58.13]), paraphrases VV 31 with the words: *yadi pramāṇādhīnaḥ prameyādhigamas tāni pramāṇāni kena paricchidyanta iti vigrahavyāvartanyāṃ vihito doṣaḥ* | (PsP_M §91 [= PsP_L 59.4]). Candrakīrti's choice of words here, and his claim that his opponent, i.e., Dignāga, has not refuted this fault (*tadaparihārāt* ...), merely indicates that he considers that the fault assigned to the Naiyāyika in the VV equally applies to Dignāga, because both share the same view (Dignāga's holding of the view, however, is limited to the surface level).

Tibetan Text

Tibetan Edition

Introduction

The following critical edition of the Tibetan translation of the first chapter of the Prasannapadā (Tibetan: Tshig gsal) has been made in reliance on the four xylograph Tanjur (bsTan-'gyur) editions and the only available manuscript Tanjur, the Golden Tanjur.[1] All of these editions of the Tanjur are relatively recent. The Peking Tanjur was completed in 1724, the Derge Tanjur in 1744, the Narthang Tanjur in 1742, and the Cone Tanjur in 1772;[2] the Golden Tanjur, so called because it is inscribed in gold letters, was written at the behest of King Mi dbang pho lha bsod nams (r. 1728-1747).[3] As is well known, the variants of the four xylograph editions tend to fall into two main groups: the Peking and Narthang variants cluster together, and the Derge and Cone variants form separate clusters. My examination of the Golden manuscript for the first chapter of the PsP supports what has already been reported about its variants, to wit, that they cluster with those of Peking and Narthang.[4] The clustering is explained by the "lineages" or "traditions" of the five available Tanjurs. The Peking, Narthang and Golden Tanjurs were made in reliance on the

---

[1] Hand-written Tanjurs other than the Golden Tanjur are known to have been produced in sNar-thang, Zha-lu, 'Phyong-rgyas, rTse-thang, rGyal-rtse and elsewhere; it is not known if any of these survive. Cf. Skilling 1991: 138.

[2] These are the completion dates presented in Skilling 1991: 138 and Schoening 1995: 132. Skilling remarks that the date of the Peking edition is uncertain; see his note 1. See Schoening 1995: 133 for a tentative Tanjur Stemma.

[3] On the Golden Tanjur, see Skilling 1991. Skilling (ibid., 138) writes, "It is thus a royal edition, roughly contemporary with the Narthang xylograph *Kanjur-Tanjur*, which was commissioned by the same king."

[4] See Skilling 1991: 139. See also Deleanu 2006: 78ff.

'Phying bar sTag stse Tanjur (mid-seventeenth century), which derives from the copy of the Zha lu Tanjur (fourteenth century) deposited at 'Phying-ba sTag stse. The Derge Tanjur bears the direct influence of four manuscript Tanjurs, which its editors compared with each another for the sake of determining Derge's final readings.[1] The Cone Tanjur is little more than a copy of Derge.[2] Although many of the details of Tanjur history remain obscure,[3] the Derge Tanjur clearly represents an attempt at a new "critical edition" of the Tanjur.[4] It presents the smoothest readings from the point of view of the grammar and syntax of the Tibetan language, as well as what appear to be occasional attempts to "smooth out" the meaning. Valuable as it is for providing correct readings where Peking, etc., are corrupted, Derge requires a discerning approach inasmuch as not a few of these editorial changes simplify or at times even obfuscate the original Tibetan.

Variants for the Tibetan of the first chapter of the PsP have been recorded in footnotes.[5] Both the Narthang and the Golden Tanjur—the former more often than the latter for the first chapter of the PsP—make use of orthographic abbreviations (*skung yig*).[6] Those

---

[1] The Derge Tanjur was made in reliance on four Tanjurs: 1) a manuscript that had been commissioned by rGa A gnyan dam pa (died 1303), 2) the manuscript edition prepared by Si tu paṇ chen on the basis of an edition kept at 'Phying bar sTag stse, 3) an edition that had belonged to the eleventh Karmapa Ye shes rdo rje (1676-1702), and 4) a manuscript written in silver ink that belonged to the king of sDe dge, bsTan pa tshe ring; this last manuscript Tanjur was of little use since it was a direct copy of 3). See Schaeffer 2009: 96.

[2] Cone shares nearly all of Derge's variants and adds its own individual variants. Deviations appear to have resulted from scribal and carving errors and not from attempts at emendation. On the production of Cone, see Schaeffer 2009: 106ff.

[3] Cf. de Jong's comments in IIJ 10 (1968): 296 (partially quoted in Schoening 1995: 124).

[4] For details, see Schaeffer 2009: 96ff.

[5] Punctuation variants have not been recorded.

[6] Dorji Wangchuk notes that dPa'-ris Sangs-rgyas devotes a chapter of his Bod yig 'bri tshul to orthographic abbreviations (*yig ge skung tshul*). Wangchuk (2002: 120) writes, "The benefit of *skung yig*, he states, is speed and economy of ink and paper." He (ibid., 97, n. 15) remarks "In the case of the Golden bsTan 'gyur, however, the

found in the PsP are often formed in conjunction with a final or semi-final particle and include, among others: *choso* for *chos so*; *byedo* for *byed do*; *yino* for *yin no*; *phyiro* for *phyir ro*; *thado* for *thad do*; *gyuro* for *gyur ro*; *bshado* for *bshad do*; *srido* for *srid do*; *bzhino* for *bzhin no*; *medo* for *med do*; *mede* for *med de*; one also encounters *tshigsu* for *tshigs su*; *gnyis su* for *gnyisu*; *gnasu* for *gnas su*; *rjesu* for *rjes su*; *sridu* for *srid du*; *cadu* for *cad du* (of *thams cad du*); *ngagi* for *ngag gi*; *tshigis* for *tshig gis*; *tinge* for *ting nge* (of *ting nge 'dzin*); *rtoge* for *rtog ge*; *thaṃd* for *thams cad*; *sangyas* for *sangs rgyas*; and *ye shes* abbreviated as *y* with double *'dreng bu*, followed by *s*.[1] I have for the most part not included these abbreviations in the notes. I have in general (but not exclusively) tended to follow Derge's orthography because it better accords with modern orthography; I thus incorporate, e.g., Derge and Cone's particle *zhes* after final *s* into the edition instead of Peking, etc.'s more archaic *shes*. *nga/da* variants have only been recorded when the writing of one as the other results in a different word. *pa/ba* variants as well as punctuation variants have not been indicated.

I have interfered with the Tibetan translation as little as possible, emending only wrong orthography, dropped negations, etc. Untranslated words, words not reflected by the Sanskrit and other deviations have been recorded in the apparatus to the critical Sanskrit edition and in the notes to the Translation. The rare wrong translations of phrases or sentences that must have resulted either from different readings in the translators' manuscript(s) or from Mahāsumati's, Kanakavarman's, and/or Pa tshab's faulty interpretation of the Sanskrit syntax or of Candrakīrti's thought have not been tampered with, but are referred to and usually commented on in the notes to the translation.

---

economy of gold might have been the primary motive for the extensive use of abbreviations."

[1] Even though the Narthang and the Golden Tanjur belong to the same Tanjur tradition, they do not, either singly or as a pair, consistently abbreviate the same words.

Critical Edition

rgya gar skad du | mū[1] la mā dhya[2] mi ka vṛtti[3] pra sanna[4] pa da nā ma | bod skad du | dbu ma rtsa ba'i 'grel pa tshig gsal ba [G 2a] zhes bya ba | 'phags pa 'jam dpal gzhon nur gyur pa la phyag 'tshal lo ||

§1. gang zhig mtha' gnyis gnas la gnas bsal zhing ||
rdzogs sangs rgyas blo rgya mtshor skye ba brnyes ||
dam chos mdzod kyi zab mo nyid ji ltar ||
rjes su rtogs bzhin thugs rjes ston par mdzad[5] || [P 2a]

gang gi lta ba'i me dag gis ||
da dung phas rgol gzhung lugs kyi ||
bud shing [N 2a] dang ni 'jig [G 2b] rten gyi ||
yid kyi mun rnams 'joms par mdzad || [PsP$_L$ 2]

gang gi gnyis med ye shes gsung mda'i tshogs ||
lha dang bcas pa'i gdul bya'i 'jig rten la ||
kham gsum dag tu rgyal thabs legs mdzad bas ||
srid pa'i dgra sde ma lus 'joms mdzad pa[6] ||

---

[1] P, N: mu

[2] D, C: dhyā

[3] *vṛtti* is transcribed as *britti*. The vowel *ṛ* is (correctly) transcribed as *ri*, that is, with the *gi-gu* reversed in order to distinguish it from consonantal *r* followed by *i*. Scherrer-Schaub (1991: 19, n. 3) notes that "la semi-voyelle *va* est normalement transcrite par le *wa-zur*, v. Lalou, *Manuel* 5; Hackin, *Formulaire* 87; mais en réalité la transcription *ba* prime."

[4] D, C: san na

[5] P: mdzod

[6] D, C: pa'i

klu sgrub de la phyag ’tshal nas ni de’i ||
tshig le’ur byas pa’i ’grel pa sla ba dang ||
sdeb legs ngag gis[1] sbyar [C 2a] zhing [D 2a] rtog ge yi ||
rlung gis ma dkrugs rab tu gsal bar[2] bya ||

§2. de la bdag las ma yin gzhan las min || [N 2b] zhes bya ba la sogs pa ni ’chad par ’gyur ba’i bstan bcos[3] so || [P 2b] de’i ’brel pa dang brjod par bya ba dang | dgos pa’i dgos pa dag gang yin zhes ’dri na | dbu ma la ’jug pa las bstan pa’i tshul gyis sems bskyed pa dang po gnyis su med pa’i ye shes kyis brgyan pa | snying rje [G 3a] chen po sngon du ’gro ba | de bzhin gshegs pa’i ye shes ’byung ba’i rgyur gyur pa thog mar mdzad nas | mthar [PsP$_L$ 3] shes rab kyi pha rol tu phyin pa’i tshul phyin ci ma log pa thugs su chud par gyur pa’i slob dpon klu sgrub kyis gzhan khong du chud par bya ba’i phyir snying rjes bstan bcos[4] mdzad de[5] zhes bya ba ’di ni re zhig bstan bcos[6] kyi ’brel pa yin no ||

§3. slob dpon rang nyid ’chad par ’gyur ba’i bstan bcos[7] mtha’ dag gi brjod par bya ba’i don dgos pa dang bcas pa ston zhing | de phyin ci ma log par ston par mdzad pa nyid [N 3a] kyi sgo nas che ba’i bdag nyid brjod nas de’i ngo bo dang tha mi dad par [C 2b] bzhugs pa’i bla

---

[1] G: gi
[2] P, N, G: ba
[3] P, N, G: chos
[4] P, N, G: chos
[5] P, N, G: do
[6] N: bstan
[7] P, N, G: chos

ma dam pa | de bzhin gshegs pa la bstan bcos rtsom pa'i rgyu can gyi phyag mdzad [D 2b] par bzhed pas[1] |

gang gis rten cing 'brel par 'byung ||
'gag pa med pa skye med pa ||
chad pa med pa rtag med pa ||
'ong ba med pa 'gro med pa ||
tha dad don min don gcig min ||
spros pa nyer zhi zhi

zhes bya ba la sogs pa gsungs so ||

de la rten cing 'brel par 'byung ba 'gag pa med pa la sogs pa khyad par brgyad kyis khyad par du byas pa ni | bstan chos kyi brjod par[2] bya ba yin [PsP$_L$ 4] zhing mya ngan las 'das pa spros pa thams cad nye bar zhi zhing zhi ba'i mtshan nyid can ni bstan bcos[3] kyi dgos par bstan la |

smra rnams kyi ||
dam pa de la phyag 'tshal lo ||

zhes bya ba 'dis ni phyag 'tshal ba bstan te |

§4. de [N 3b] ltar na[4] 'di ni re zhig tshigs su bcad pa gnyis kyi spyi'i[5] don yin no ||

---

[1] P, N, G: nas

[2] P: ba

[3] P, N, G: chos

[4] P, N, G: ni

[5] P: sbyi'i

§5a.[1] yan lag gi don yang rnam par dbye bar bya ste | [PsP$_L$ 5]

§6. de la pra ti ni [P 3a] phrad pa'i don to || i ti ni 'gro ba'i don to || lyap kyi mtha' [G 3b] can pra tī[2] tya'i sgra ni phrad pa ste ltos[3] pa la 'jug pa yin te | skad kyi byings ni nye bar bsgyur bas yongs su bsgyur ba'i phyir ro ||

> nye bar bsgyur ba'i dbang gis ni[4] || skad byings don ni yongs bsgyur te ||
> gang gā'i chu ni mngar mod kyi || rgya mtsho chu yis ji bzhin no ||

zhes bshad do || sa mud gong na yod pa'i pā[5] ta ni 'byung ba'i don can yin pas sa mud pā[6] ta'i sgra ni 'byung ba la 'jug go | de'i phyir dngos po rnams kyi 'byung ba rgyu dang rkyen la ltos[7] pa ni rten cing 'brel par 'byung ba'i don to ||

§7. gzhan dag ni[8] pra ti ni zlos pa'i don to || i ti ni 'gro ba ste[9] chas pa dang 'jig pa'o || i tya ni 'gro bar rung ba dag go zhes de ltar i tya'i sgra de la phan pa'i mtha' can du bye brag tu bshad nas | so so so sor

---

[1] I divide §5 as it appears in PsP$_M$ and in my translation into §5a and §5b in PsP Tib because the main part of Candrakīrti's word explanation for MMK I.1 has been moved to a later section of the text. PsP Tib §5b occurs as part of PsP Tib §15. See Translation Appendix IV.

[2] D, C: ti

[3] P, N: bltos; G: bstod

[4] D, C: na

[5] P: pa

[6] P, N, G: pa

[7] P, N, G: bltos

[8] D, C: om.

[9] N: *t* illegible

’gro zhing ’jig[1] pa dang ldan pa rnams kyi ’byung ba ni rten cing ’brel par ’byung ba’o zhes brjod par byed do || [PsP$_L$ 6] de dag gi ltar na dge slong dag khyed la rten cing ’brel par ’byung ba bstan par bya yis | sus rten cing ’brel par ’byung ba mthong ba des chos mthong ngo zhes bya ba de lta bu la sogs ba’i yul la ni zlos pa’i [C 3a] don srid pa’i phyir dang | tshig [D 3a] bsdu ba yod pa’i [N 4a] phyir bye brag tu bshad pa legs par ’gyur na | mig dang gzugs la brten nas mig gi rnam par shes pa ’byung ngo zhes bya ba de[2] lta bu la sogs pa’i yul ’dir ni mig dang gzugs la brten nas zhes don gyi khyad par dngos su zhal gyis bzhes shing | mig gi dbang po gcig gi rgyu can gyi rnam par shes pa gcig kyang skye bar bzhed pa na brten nas zhes bya ba’i sgra la zlos pa’i don nyid yod par ga la ’gyur | phrad[3] pa’i don ni[4] phrad nas ’byung ba ni rten cing ’brel par ’byung ba’o zhes don gyi khyad par zhal gyis ma bzhes pa’i rten [G 4a] cing ’brel par ’byung [P 3b] ba’i [PsP$_L$ 7] sgra la yang yod pa yin la | don gyi khyad par zhal gyis bzhes pa la yang yod pa yin te | mig dang gzugs la brten nas mig dang gzugs phrad cing mig dang gzugs la ltos[5] nas zhes bshad pa’i phyir ro || i tya’i sgra de[6] la phan pa’i mtha’ can yin na ni mig dang gzugs la brten nas mig gi rnam par shes pa ’byung ngo zhes bya ba ’dir pra ti tya’i sgra mi[7] zad pa[8] ma yin pa’i phyir dang | tshig bsdu ba yod pa ma yin

---

[1] P: ’jigs

[2] D, C: ’di

[3] P: prad

[4] C: nyid

[5] P, N, G: bltos

[6] C: da

[7] P, N, G: ni

[8] D, C: par

pa'i phyir rnam par dbye ba thos par 'gyur ba yin dang | mig[1] dang gzugs[2] la brten pa rnam par shes pa zhes bya bar 'don par 'gyur ba zhig na | 'di ni de lta bu yang ma yin pas | lyab kyi mtha' can mi [N 4b] zad pa kho nar bye brag tu bshad pa khas blang bar bya'o ||

§8. gang zhig

> kha cig na re rten cing zhes bya ba'i nye bar bsgyur ba ni[3] zlos pa'i don yin pa'i phyir dang | 'brel pa zhes bya ba phrad pa'i don yin pa'i phyir dang | 'byung ba zhes bya ba'i sgra ni skye ba'i[4] don yin pa'i phyir rkyen de dang[5] de la brten[6] nas 'byung ba ste phrad nas 'byung ba'o zhe'o || gzhan dag na re[7] so so so sor [PsP$_L$ 8] 'jig pa dang ldan pa rnams kyi 'byung ba ni rten cing 'brel par 'byung ba'o zhe'o

zhes gzhan gyi bshad pa rjes su brjod nas sun 'byin par byed pa de ni | re zhig gzhan gyi phyogs rjes su brjod pa la mi mkhas pa nyid do snyam mo || ci'i phyir zhe na | gang zhig rten cing 'brel par 'byung ba'i sgra phrad pa'i don can du 'chad[8] pa des ni rten cing zhes bya ba [D 3b] zlos pa'i don du ma yin zhing [C 3b] 'brel par zhes bya ba phrad pa'i don du yang ma yin no || 'o na ci zhe na rten cing ni phrad pa'i [G

---

[1] P, N, G: ming

[2] D: gzug

[3] N: ni | or mi

[4] C: bo'i

[5] N: de dang illegible

[6] G: rten

[7] N: ri

[8] N: 'chang

4b] don[1] yin zhing | 'brel par 'gro ba'i don yin la | tshogs pa rten cing 'brel pa'i sgra ni phrad pa nyid yin par 'chad par byed do || des na da ni phrad nas 'byung ba ni rten cing 'brel par 'byung ba'o zhes de ltar bshad par gyur pa'i rten cing 'brel par 'byung ba'i sgras gal te [P 4a] dngos po srid tshad ma lus pa 'dzin par brjod par 'dod pa de'i tshe ni | rgyu dang rkyen gyi tshogs pa de dang de phrad nas 'byung ba ni rten cing 'brel par 'byung ba'o zhes zlos pa dang 'brel bar byed la | 'on te bye[2] brag 'dzin pa de'i tshe ni mig dang gzugs la brten nas zhes zlos pa dang 'brel pa ma yin no || de ltar na re zhig slob dpon ni rjes su brjod pa la mi mkhas so[3] ||

> **§9.** de yang mi rung ste mig dang gzugs la brten nas mig gi rnam par shes pa 'byung zhes gsungs pa 'di la don[4] gnyi ga med pa'i phyir ro

zhes sun[5] 'byin smras pa gang yin pa de yang mi 'thad do || ci'i phyir zhe na | [PsP$_L$ 9] ji ltar med ces bya ba'i rigs pa ma bkod pas | dam bca' ba tsam yin pa'i phyir ro ||

§10.–11. 'on te rnam par shes pa ni gzugs can ma yin pa'i phyir mig dang phrad pa yod pa ma yin te | [N 5a] gzugs can rnams kho na la de dang phrad pa mthong ba'i phyir ro snyam pa'i bsam pa 'di yin na ni | de yang mi rigs te | dge slong 'di ni 'bras bu thob pa yin no zhes bya

---

[1] D: dan

[2] N: illegible

[3] N: pa'o

[4] N: illegible

[5] N: illegible

ba ’di la[1] phrad pa khas blangs pa’i phyir dang | phrad nas zhes bya ba’i sgra yang ltos[2] nas zhes bya ba’i sgra’i rnam grangs yin pa’i phyir dang | rten cing ’brel par[3] zhes bya ba’i sgra ni |

> de dang de brten[4] gang ’byung[5] ba ||
> rang gi dngos por de ma skyes ||

zhes slob dpon klu sgrub kyis kyang[6] phrad nas zhes bya ba’i don nyid du zhal[7] gyis bzhes pa’i phyir ro || des na skyon yang [G 5a] mi ’thad do zhes gzhan dag zer ro ||

§12. gang yang

> ’o na gang yin zhe na | ’di yod pas ’di ’byung la | ’di skyes pa’i phyir ’di skye ba ste zhes bya ba rkyen ’di dang ldan pa nyid kyi don ni rten cing ’brel par ’byung [D 4a] ba’i don to

zhes[8] rang gi lugs rnam[9] par gzhag[10] pa de yang ’thad pa ma yin te | rten cing [PsP_L 10] ’brel par zhes bya ba dang ’byung ba zhes bya ba’i

---

[1] P, N, G: ’dir for ’di la

[2] P, N, G: bltos

[3] D, C: par ’byung ba (C: bar for par)

[4] Em.: brten. D, C, P, N, G: rten

[5] P, N: ’byungs

[6] N: kyad

[7] N: zhes

[8] D: zhas

[9] G: rnam rnam

[10] P, N, G: bzhag

sgra gnyis re re la don gyi [C 4a] khyad par ma brjod pa'i phyir la | de bye[1] brag tu bshad [P 4b] pa yang brjod par 'dod pa'i phyir ro ||

§13. ci ste yang dgon pa'i thig le zhes bya ba la sogs pa ltar rten cing 'brel par 'byung ba'i sgra ni gting tshugs pa'i sgrar khas blangs nas de skad du brjod do zhe na | de yang mi 'thad de | rten cing 'brel par 'byung ba'i sgra ni slob dpon gyis |

> de dang de brten[2] gang 'byung ba ||
> rang gi dngos por de ma skyes ||

zhes yan lag gi don dang rjes su 'brel pa nyid du zhal gyis bzhes pa'i phyir ro ||

§14. ci ste

> 'di yod na ni 'di 'byung ste || thung ngu yod na ring po bzhin ||

zhes bya bas 'chad par byed pas ni thung ngu dang phrad cing thung ngu la[3] brten te | thung ngu la ltos[4] nas ring por[5] 'gyur ro zhes de nyid khas blangs par 'gyur ro || de'i phyir gang zhig sun 'byin pa de[6] nyid khas blangs par rigs pa ma yin no || shin tu spros pas chog go ||

---

[1] C: pye

[2] G: rten

[3] P, N, G: om. la

[4] P, N, G: bltos

[5] D: par

[6] G: 'di

§15. de'i phyir de ltar na 'dir bcom ldan 'das kyis dngos po rnams kyi 'byung ba rgyu dang rkyen la ltos[1] pa yongs su gsal bar mdzad pa na | dngos po rnams rgyu med [N 5b] pa nyid dang | rgyu gcig pu[2] nyid dang | mi mthun pa'i rgyu las byung ba nyid dang | rang dang gzhan dang gnyi gas byas pa nyid bkag par 'gyur la | de dag bkag pas ni [G 5b] dngos po kun rdzob pa rnams kyi rang gi ngo bo kun rdzob pa ji ltar gnas pa bzhin gsungs par 'gyur ro || da ni rten cing 'brel par [PsP$_L$ 11] 'byung ba kun rdzob pa de nyid rang bzhin gyis ma skyes pa nyid kyi phyir 'phags pa'i ye shes la ltos[3] nas 'di la 'gag pa yod pa ma yin pa nas 'di la don gcig[4] yod pa ma yin pa zhes bya ba'i bar 'gag pa med pa la sogs pa khyad par brgyad kyis[5] khyad par du byed de | **§5b.** 'gag pas na 'gag pa ste | skad cig mar 'jig pa la 'gag pa zhes brjod do || skye bas na skye ba ste bdag nyid kyi dngos por red pa'o || chad pas na chad pa ste rgyun chad pa zhes bya ba'i don to || rtag pa ni[6] ther zug pa ste dus [D 4b] thams cad du gnas pa zhes bya ba'i [P 5a] don to || 'ong bas na 'ong ba ste yul ring po na gnas pa rnams yul nye bar 'ong ba'o || 'gro bas[7] na 'gro ba[8] ste[9] yul nye ba na [C 4b] gnas pa rnams yul ring por 'gro ba'o || tha dad pa'i don ni don tha dad pa ste | don so so ba zhes bya ba'i tha tshig go || don yang de yin la gcig

---

[1] P, N, G: bltos

[2] N, P: bu

[3] P, N, G: bltos

[4] D, C: gcig pu

[5] P, N, G: kyi

[6] D: na

[7] D, C: gas

[8] P, N, G: bas

[9] P, N, G: te

kyang de yin pas na don gcig ste | don tha mi dad[1] cing so so ma yin zhes bya ba'i tha tshig go || rten cing 'brel par 'byung ba la ji ltar 'gag pa la sogs pa med pa de ltar ni bstan bcos mtha' dag gis ston par 'gyur ro || rten cing 'brel par 'byung ba la khyad par mtha' yas pa yod du zin kyang brgyad dag gcig kho na nye bar bkod pa ni 'di dag kho na gtsor rtsod pa'i yan lag tu gyur pa'i phyir ro ||

§16. rten cing 'brel par 'byung ba ji ltar gnas pa bzhin[2] 'phags pa rnams kyis gzigs na | brjod bya dang rjod[3] byed dang | mtshan nyid dang mtshon bya la sogs pa'i spros [G 6a] pa rnams rnam pa thams cad du zlog pa'i phyir | 'dir spros pa [N 6a] dag nye bar zhi bas rten cing 'brel par 'byung ba de nyid spros pa nyer zhi zhes bya'o || 'di la sems dang sems las byung ba'i 'jug pa yang med dang | shes pa dang shes bya'i tha snyad log pa'i sgo nas skye ba dang rga ba dang na ba dang 'chi ba la sogs pa'i nye bar 'tshe ba ma lus pa dang bral ba'i phyir na zhi ba'o || ji skad bstan pa'i khyad par can gyi[4] rten cing brel par 'byung ba ni bstan par bya ba'i sgo nas 'dod pa dam pa yin pa'i phyir las su bstan te |

> **§17.** gang[5] gis rten cing 'brel par 'byung ||
> 'gag pa med pa skye med pa ||
> chad pa med pa rtag med pa ||
> 'ong ba med pa 'gro med pa ||

---

[1] P, N, G: dang

[2] D, C: bzhin du

[3] G: brjod

[4] D, C: gyis

[5] C: gad

tha dad don min don cig min ||
spros pa nyer zhi zhi bstan pa ||
rdzogs pa'i sangs rgyas smra rnams kyi ||
dam pa de la phyag 'tshal lo ||

zhes bya ba'o || [PsP$_L$ 12]

rten cing 'brel par 'byung ba ji skad du[1] bstan pa thugs su chud pa'i phyir | de bzhin gshegs pa nyag gcig don phyin ci ma log par gsung [P 5b] ba nyid du gzigs shing pha rol po'i smra ba thams cad byis pa rdol[2] thabs[3] smra ba dang 'dra bar thugs [D 5a] su chud de | de nas slob dpon shin tu dad[4] pa dang ldan par gyur pas slar yang bcom ldan 'das la khyad par du mdzad pa ni | smra rnams kyi dam pa zhes bya'o ||

§18. 'dir 'gag pa sngar bkag pa ni skye ba dang 'gag ba dag la snga phyi'i rnam par gzhag[5] pa med par [C 5a] bstan ba'i phyir te |

gal te skye ba sngar gyur la ||
rga shi phyi ma yin na ni ||
skye ba rga shi med pa dang ||
ma shi bar yang skye[6] bar 'gyur ||

zhes 'chad par 'gyur ro ||

---

[1] D, C: om.

[2] D, C: rtol

[3] C: thab

[4] P, N, G: dang (ba)

[5] P, N, G: bzhag

[6] P: skya

de'i phyir skye [G 6b] ba ni snga bar[1] 'gyur[2] la | rga shi ni phyis[3] so zhes bya ba'i nges pa gang yin pa 'di[4] med do ||

§19. da ni slob dpon rten cing 'brel par 'byung ba 'gag pa med pa la sogs pas khyad par du 'phags par gyur[5] pa bstan par bzhed nas | skye ba bkag pas 'gag pa la sogs pa dgag pa sla bar dgongs shing thog [N 6b] mar skye ba dgag pa rtsom pa mdzad do || skye ba yang gzhan gyis brtags pa na bdag gam gzhan nam gnyi ga 'am rgyu med pa zhig las rtog grang na | thams cad du 'thad pa ma yin no snyam du nges par mdzad nas bshad pa |

> bdag las ma yin gzhan las min ||
> gnyis las ma yin rgyu med min ||
> dngos po gang dag gang na yang ||
> skye ba nam yang yod[6] ma yin || MMK I.1 [PsP$_L$ 13]

§20. de la gang dag ces bya ba'i sgra ni rten pa'i tshig ste | su dag ces bya ba'i sgra'i rnam grangs so || gang na yang zhes bya ba'i sgra ni rten gyi tshig ste | 'ga'[7] zhig na yang zhes bya ba'i sgra'i rnam grangs so || nam yang zhes bya ba ni gzhar yang zhes bya ba'i tha tshig go || de'i phyir bdag las dngos po gang dag gang na yang skye ba nam

[1] D, C: sngar

[2] P, N, G: gyur.

[3] P: 'phyis

[4] N: gang yin pa 'di illegible

[5] D, C: 'gyur (ba)

[6] N: yong

[7] P: 'gag

yang yod pa ma yin no zhes de ltar sbyar bar bya'o || de bzhin du dam bca' ba gsum po la yang sbyar bar bya'o ||

§21. gal te bdag las skye ba ma yin pa nyid do zhes bya bar nges par gzung[1] ba na | gzhan las skye'o[2] zhes mi 'dod pa nyid du 'gyur ba ma yin nam zhe na ma yin te | med par dgag[3] pa[4] brjod par 'dod [P 6a] pa'i phyir dang | gzhan las skye ba yang 'gog par 'gyur ba'i phyir ro || 'thad pa gang gis bdag las skye bar mi 'gyur ba de ni |

> de las [D 5b] de ni 'byung na yon tan 'ga' yang [G 7a] yod pa ma yin ||
> skyes par gyur pa slar yang skye bar rigs pa 'ang ma yin nyid ||

ces bya ba la sogs pas dbu ma la 'jug pa la sogs pa'i sgo nas nges par bya'o || [PsP_L 14]

§22. slob dpon sangs rgyas bskyangs kyis kyang |

> dngos po rnams bdag las skye ba med de | de dag gi skye ba don med pa nyid du 'gyur ba'i [C 5b] phyir dang | shin tu thal bar 'gyur ba'i phyir ro || dngos po bdag gi bdag nyid du yod pa rnams la ni yang skye ba la dgos pa med do || ci ste yod kyang skye na nam yang mi skye bar mi 'gyur ro ||

zhes gsungs so ||

---

[1] P, N, G: bzung

[2] P, N, G: skye bo

[3] N: yang dag

[4] N: par

§23. ’di la kha cig gis —

> de ni rigs pa ma yin te | gtan tshigs [N 7a] dang dpe ma brjod pa’i phyir dang | gzhan gyis smras pa’i nyes pa ma bsal ba’i phyir ro || [PsP$_L$ 15] thal bar ’gyur ba’i tshig yin pa’i phyir skabs kyi don las bzlog pas bsgrub par bya ba dang | de’i chos bzlog pa’i don mngon pas dngos po rnams gzhan las skye bar ’gyur ba dang | skye ba ’bras bu dang bcas pa nyid du ’gyur ba dang | skye ba thug[1] pa yod par ’gyur ba’i phyir grub pa’i mtha’ dang ’gal bar ’gyur ro ||

zhes skyon smra ste |

§24-25. skyon ’di dag thams cad ni rigs pa ma yin par kho bo cag gis mthong ngo || ji ltar zhe na | de la re zhig gtan tshigs dang dpe ma brjod pa’i phyir dang zhes gang smras pa[2] de ni mi rigs so || ci’i phyir zhe na | gang gi phyir bdag las zhes bya ba ni yod pa rgyu nyid dang de nyid skye’o zhes smras pa yin la[3] | yod pa ni yang skye ba la dgos pa ma mthong zhing thug pa med par yang mthong la | khyod kyis skyes pa slar yang skye bar mi ’dod cing | [G 7b] thug pa med par yang mi ’dod do || de’i phyir khyed cag gi rtsod pa ni ’thad pa dang bral ba dang | rang gis khas blangs pa dang ’gal ba [P 6b] yin no zhes pha rol po bdag las skye bar ’dod pa la ’dri bar byed pa yin te | gang las gtan tshigs dang dpe bkod pa ’bras bu dang bcas par ’gyur ba ’di dag tsam zhig gis brtsad pa na ci pha rol po khas len par mi byed dam | ’on te pha rol po rang gi khas blangs pa dang ’gal bas brtsad [D 6a] pas kyang

---

[1] P: thugs

[2] D: smra ba

[3] C: te

mi ldog na ni | de'i tshe ngo[1] tsha med pa nyid kyis gtan tshigs dang dpe gnyis kyis kyang ldog par mi 'gyur ba nyid do || kho bo[2] cag ni smyon pa dang lhan cig rtsod pa yang ma yin no || [PsP$_L$ 16] de'i phyir slob dpon ni gnas ma yin par yang rjes su dpag pa 'tshang[3] bar byed pa na | bdag nyid rjes su dpag pa la dga' ba nyid mngon par byed pa[4] yin no || dbu ma pa[5] yin na ni rang gi rgyud kyi rjes su dpag par bya ba rigs pa yang ma yin te | [C 6a] phyogs gzhan khas blangs pa med pa'i phyir ro ||

§26. de skad du yang 'phags pa lhas |

> yod dang med dang yod med [N 7b] ces ||
> phyogs ni gang la'ang yod min pa ||
> de la yun ni ring po na'ang ||
> klan ka brjod par nus ma yin ||

zhes bshad do ||

rtsod pa bzlog pa las kyang |

> gal te ngas dam bcas 'ga' yod ||
> des[6] na nga la skyon de yod ||
> nga la dam bca' med pas na ||
> nga la skyon med kho na yin ||

---

[1] N: do

[2] P: kho for kho bo; G: ko'o

[3] Em: 'tshang. P, N: 'chang; G: 'chad; D, C: tshang

[4] D: pha

[5] P, N, G: om.

[6] G: dis

gal te mngon sum la sogs pa'i ||
don gyis 'ga' zhig dmigs na ni ||
sgrub pa'am[1] bzlog par bya na de ||
med phyir nga la klan ka med ||

ces gsungs so ||

§27. gang gi tshe de ltar dbu ma pas rang gi rgyud kyi rjes su dpag pa mi brjod pa nyid yin pa[2] de'i tshe[3] | [PsP$_L$ 17]

> dam bca' ba'i don [G 8a] 'di[4] gang yin | ci bdag las zhes[5] bya ba 'bras bu'i bdag nyid las sam | 'on te rgyu'i bdag nyid las yin grang | de las cir 'gyur | gal te 'bras bu'i bdag nyid las yin na ni grub pa la sgrub pa yin la | rgyu'i bdag nyid las yin na ni 'gal ba'i don nyid du 'gyur te | [PsP$_L$ 18] skye ba dang ldan pa thams cad ni rgyu'i bdag nyid du yod pa kho na skye ba'i phyir ro ||

zhes bya bar gang la grangs can pa dag gis [P 7a] phyir zlog[6] par byed par 'gyur ba[7] nang gi skye mched rnams bdag[8] las skye ba med de zhes bya ba'i rang gi rgyud kyi dam bca' ba lta ga la yod | kho bo cag

---

[1] D, C: 'ang

[2] D, C: par

[3] D: de'i tshe | gang la grangs can pa dag gis |

[4] G: don don 'di

[5] P, N: shes

[6] P, N, G: bzlog

[7] D, C: la

[8] D, C: dag

la ni gang zhig grub[1] pa la sgrub pa nyid dam | 'gal ba'i don nyid du 'gyur zhing | grub pa la sgrub pa nyid gang yin pa dang | 'gal ba'i[2] don nyid gang yin pa de[3] spang bar [D 6b] bya ba'i phyir 'bad[4] pa byed par 'gyur ba yod pa'i phyir zhes bya ba'i gtan tshigs kyang ga la yod | de'i phyir gzhan gyis smras pa'i nyes par thal bar mi 'gyur ba nyid kyi phyir slob dpon sangs rgyas bskyangs kyis de'i lan brjod par bya ba ma yin no ||

§28. ci ste yang dbu ma pa rnams kyi ltar na phyogs dang gtan tshigs dang dpe dag ma grub pas rang gi rgyud kyi rjes su dpag pa ma[5] brjod pa nyid kyi[6] phyir bdag las skye ba dgag pa'i dam bca' ba'i don sgrub pa dang | gnyi ga [C 6b] la grub pa'i rjes su dpag pas gzhan gyi dam bca' ba[7] bsal bar ma gyur mod | gzhan gyi dam bca' ba la rang gi rjes su dpag pas 'gal ba brjod par ni bya dgos pas | rang[8] nyid [N 8a] la phyogs la sogs pa[9] phyogs[10] dang gtan tshigs dang[11] dpe'i skyon dang bral ba dag yod par bya dgos so || de'i [G 8b] phyir de ma brjod pa'i phyir dang | de'i[12] nyes pa ma bsal ba'i phyir nyes pa de nyid du 'gyur ro snyam na | [$\mathrm{PsP_L}$ 19]

---

[1] N: illegible

[2] D: ba'

[3] D, C: om.

[4] C: 'pad

[5] P, N, G: mi

[6] N: kyis

[7] D, C: om.

[8] N: illegible

[9] P, N, G: pa dang

[10] D, C: om.

[11] D, C: om.

[12] P: de illegible

bshad par bya ste | de ni de ltar ma yin no || ci'i phyir zhe na | gang gi phyir don gang zhig gang gi dam bcas pa des ni rang nyid kyi[1] nges[2] pa bzhin du gzhan dag la nges[3] pa bskyed par[4] 'dod pas | don 'di'i 'thad pa gang gi sgo nas khong du chud pa'i 'thad pa de nyid gzhan la bsnyad[5] par bya dgos so || de'i phyir rang[6] gis khas blangs pa'i dam bcas pa'i don gyi sgrub par byed pa ni pha rol po kho nas nye bar dgod par bya ba gang yin pa de[7] ni re zhig lugs yin[8] no[9] || 'di ni gzhan la gtan tshigs kyang ma yin no || gtan tshigs dang | dpe med pa'i phyir rang gi dam bca' ba'i don [P 7b] gyi sgrub par byed pa ni khas 'ches pa'i rjes su 'brangs pa 'ba' zhig nye bar bkod pa yin te | de'i phyir 'thad pa dang bral ba'i phyogs khas blangs pas 'di ni bdag nyid kho na la slu bar byed pas gzhan la nges[10] pa bskyed par mi nus so zhes bya bar | gang rang gi dam bca' ba'i don gyi sgrub par byed pa la nus pa med pa 'di nyid 'di'i sun 'byin pa ches gsal po yin te | 'dir rjes su dpag pas gnod pa brjod pa la dgos pa go ci zhig yod |

§29. ci ste yang rang gi rjes su dpag pas 'gal ba gdon mi za bar brjod par bya ba yin no[11] zhe na | [PsP$_L$ 20]

---

[1] Em.: kyi. PsP Skt: svaniścayavat. P, G, N, D, C: kyis

[2] N: des

[3] N: des

[4] N: pa

[5] N: bsnyan

[6] C: rad

[7] D, C: 'di

[8] D, C: ma yin

[9] P, N, G: na (|). See PsP Skt for the correct reading for this and the following sentence.

[10] N: des

[11] G: om.

de yang slob dpon [D 7a] sangs rgyas bskyangs kyis brjod pa nyid yin no ‖ ji ltar zhe na | gang gi phyir des[1] ni 'di skad du bshad pa yin te | dngos po rnams bdag las skye ba med de | de dag gi skye ba don med pa nyid du 'gyur ba'i phyir dang zhes bshad pa'i phyir ro ‖ de la de dag ces bya ba 'dis ni rang gi bdag [G 9a] nyid du yod pa 'dzin pa yin no ‖ ci'i phyir zhe na | 'di ltar rang gi bdag nyid du yod pa dag la ni yang skye ba la dgos pa med do zhes bya ba 'di ni mdor bzhag pa'i ngag de'i 'grel pa'i[2] ngag yin la | ngag 'dis [C 7a] ni chos mthun pa'i dpe [N 8b] gzhan la rab tu grags pa bsgrub par bya ba dang sgrub[3] par byed pa'i[4] chos dang ldan pa nye bar gzung[5] ba yin no ‖ de[6] la rang gi bdag nyid du yod pa zhes bya ba 'dis ni gtan tshigs 'dzin pa yin no ‖ skyes ba don med pa nyid du 'gyur ba'i phyir dang zhes bya 'dis ni bsgrub par bya[7] ba'i chos 'dzin pa yin no ‖

de la ji ltar sgra mi rtag ste | byas pa mi rtag pa'i phyir ro ‖ byas pa ni mi rtag par mthong ste | dper na bum pa bzhin no ‖ de bzhin du sgra yang byas pa yin te | de'i phyir byas pa nyid kyi phyir mi rtag[8] pa yin no zhes 'dir nye bar sbyar bas gsal bar byas pa'i byas pa gtan tshigs yin pa [PsP$_L$ 21] de bzhin du | 'dir yang dngos po rnams bdag las skye ba med de | rang gi bdag nyid du yod pa la [P 8a] yang skye ba don med pa nyid du 'gyur ba'i phyir ro ‖

---

[1] P: nges

[2] G, C: ba'i

[3] C: bsgrub

[4] P, N, G: pa

[5] P, N, G : bzung

[6] N: da

[7] P: pya

[8] P, N, G: brtag

'di na ji ltar bum pa la sogs pa mdun na gnas shing gsal ba rang gi bdag nyid du yod pa ni yang skye ba la mi ltos[1] par mthong ba de bzhin du | 'jim pa'i gong bu la sogs pa'i gnas skabs na yang gal te rang gi bdag nyid du yod pa'i bum pa la sogs pa yod do snyam du sems na ni de'i tshe yang rang gi bdag nyid du yod pa de la skye ba yod pa ma yin no ||

de ltar na gtan tshigs nye bar sbyar bas gsal bar byas pa | yang skye ba dgag pa la mi 'khrul[2] ba | rang gi bdag nyid du yod pa nyid [G 9b] kyis grangs can la rang nyid kyis rjes su dpag pas 'gal ba brjod pa mdzad pa[3] yin te | des na de ni rigs pa ma yin te | gtan tshigs dang dpe ma brjod pa'i phyir dang zhes ci ste brjod par byed |

§30. gtan tshigs dang dpe ma brjod pa [D 7b] ma yin pa[4] 'ba'[5] zhig tu ma zad kyi[6] | gzhan gyis smras pa'i nyes pa ma bsal ba yang ma yin no || ci ltar zhe na | grangs can pa dag[7] mdun na gnas pa'i bum pa mngon par gsal ba'i rang bzhin can ni yang mngon par gsal bar mi 'dod cing | de nyid 'dir dpe nyid du grub pa'i ngo bo yin pa'i phyir la | nus pa'i ngo bor gyur cing mngon par gsal ba'i rang bzhin ma yin pa skye ba bkag pas khyad par du byas pa ni bsgrub par bya ba yin pa [C 7b] nyid [N 9a] kyi phyir grub pa la sgrub pa'i phyogs kyi skyon nyid du dogs pa 'am | gtan tshigs 'gal ba'i don nyid du dogs pa ga la yod |

---

[1] P, N, G: bltos

[2] D: 'khr illegible

[3] P, N, G: om. mdzad pa

[4] N: om.

[5] D, C: 'ga'

[6] P, N, G: kyis

[7] G: ngag

de'i phyir rang gi rjes su dpag pas 'gal ba[1] brjod pa na yang ji skad smras pa'i nyes pa brjod pa med pa'i phyir | gzhan gyis smras pa'i nyes pa ma bsal ba med pa nyid de | de'i phyir sun 'byin pa 'di dag ni 'brel pa med pa nyid do zhes shes par bya'o || [PsP$_L$ 22]

§31. bum pa la sogs pa zhes bya ba sogs pa'i sgras ni skye bar 'dod pa'i dngos po ma[2] lus pa bsdu bar brjod[3] par[4] 'dod pa'i phyir snam bu la sogs pa dag gis ma nges par [P 8b] 'gyur ba yang ma yin no ||

§32. yang na sbyor ba 'di ni tshul gzhan yin te | rang las skye bar smra ba'i skyes bu las tha dad pa'i don rnams ni bdag nyid las skye ba med de | rang gi bdag nyid du yod pa'i phyir | skyes bu bzhin no zhes dper brjod pa 'di nyid dper brjod par bya'o ||

§33. gal te[5] yang skye ba gkag pas mngon par gsal bar [G 10a] smra ba la gnod par byed pa ma yin pa de lta na yang skye ba'i sgra[6] mngon par gsal ba la btags nas sngon dang phyi mar ma dmigs pa dang dmigs par chos mthun pas skye ba'i sgras mngon par gsal ba nyid brjod pa'i phyir | 'di bkag pas gnod par byed pa ma yin pa ma yin[7] no ||

---

[1] P, N, G: om. ba

[2] N: tha

[3] D, C: om.

[4] D, C: om.

[5] N: illegible

[6] P, N, G: sgras

[7] Em: ma yin pa ma yin. P, N, G, D, C: ma yin. PsP Skt (*ayaṃ pratiṣedho nābādhakaḥ*) expects a double negation. The Tibetan sentence without the double negation is at variance with the preceding argumentation. I assume that the second *ma yin* dropped out due to haplography.

§34. yang ji skad smras pa'i don gyi rjod[1] par byed pa med par rnam par dpyod pa 'di lta bu 'di ji ltar rnyed ce na | [PsP$_L$ 23] bshad par bya ste | don gyi ngag 'di dag ni don chen po can yin pas ji skad smras pa'i don bsdus nas 'jug pa yin la | de dag kyang bshad na ji skad smras pa'i don gyi bdag nyid 'byin par byed pa yin pas | 'dir ma bstan pa cung zad kyang mi srid do ||

§35. thal bar 'gyur ba bzlog pa'i don dang [D 8a] yang pha rol po nyid 'brel pa yin gyi | kho bo cag[2] ni ma yin te | rang la dam bca' ba med pa'i phyir ro || de'i phyir kho bo cag la[3] grub pa'i mtha' dang 'gal ba ga la yod | thal ba las bzlog pa bsgrub pas pha rol po la nyes pa mang po ci tsam du 'gyur ba de tsam kho bo cag mngon par 'dod pa kho na yin pas | [PsP$_L$ 24] gang las [N 9b] 'di la gzhan gyis glags rnyed par 'gyur ba slob dpon klu sgrub kyi lugs phyin ci ma log pa'i rjes su 'brang ba slob dpon sangs rgyas bskyangs la [C 8a] glags dang bcas pa'i tshigs gsung ba nyid ga la yod | rang bzhin med par smra bas rang bzhin dang bcas par smra ba la thal ba bsgrubs pa na thal ba las bzlog pa'i don can du thal bar ga la 'gyur te | sgra rnams ni dbyug pa[4] dang zhags pa can bzhin du smra ba po rang dbang med[5] [G 10b] par byed pa ma yin [P 9a] no || 'o na ci zhe na nus pa yod na smra ba po'i[6] brjod par 'dod pa'i rjes su byed pa yin no || de'i phyir thal ba sgrub pa ni pha

[1] G: brjod

[2] P, N, G: cag la

[3] C: om.

[4] P, N, G: pa can

[5] P, N, G: ma yin for med

[6] N: pa'i

rol po'i dam bca' ba[1] 'gog pa tsam gyi 'bras bu can yin pa'i phyir thal ba las zlog[2] pa'i don du 'gyur ba yod pa ma yin no ||

§36. de ltar yang slob dpon ni |

nam mkha'i mtshan nyid snga rol na ||
nam mkha' cung zad yod ma yin ||
gal te mtshan las sngar gyur na ||
mtshan[3] nyid med par thal bar 'gyur ||

zhes bya ba dang | de bzhin du |

gzugs kyi rgyu ni ma gtogs par ||
gzugs na[4] gzugs kyi rgyu med par ||
thal bar 'gyur te don gang yang ||
rgyu med pa ni gang na'ang med ||

ces[5] bya ba dang | de bzhin du | [PsP_L 25]

mya ngan 'das pa dngos po min ||
rga shi'i mtshan nyid thal bar 'gyur ||
rga dang 'chi ba med pa yi[6] ||
dngos po yod pa ma yin no ||

---

[1] D, C: la

[2] P, N, G: bzlog

[3] N: mtshon?

[4] D, C: ni

[5] G: zhes

[6] D, C: yin

zhes bya ba la sogs pas[1] phal cher thal ba bsgrub[2] pa kho na'i sgo nas gzhan gyi phyogs sel bar mdzad do ||

§37. ci ste[3] slob dpon gyi ngag rnams ni don gyi ngag yin pa'i phyir don chen po nyid yin pas sbyor ba du ma'i rgyu nyid du rtog[4] na ni | slob dpon sangs rgyas bskyangs kyi[5] ngag dag kyang ci'i phyir de ltar yongs su mi rtog |

§38. 'on te sbyor ba'i ngag [D 8b] rgyas par rjod par byed pa gang yin pa 'di ni 'grel pa mkhan po rnams kyi lugs yin no zhe na | de yang yod pa ma yin te | rtsod pa bzlog pa'i 'grel pa mdzad pa na | slob dpon gyis kyang sbyor ba'i ngag[6] ma gsungs pa'i phyir ro ||

§39. gzhan yang rtog ge pa 'dis bdag nyid rtog ge'i bstan chos la shin tu mkhas pa tsam zhig bstan par 'dod pas | dbu ma pa'i lta ba khas len bzhin du yang [G 11a] rang gi[7] rgyud kyi sbyor ba'i ngag brjod pa gang [N 10a] yin pa de ni ches shin tu nyes pa du ma'i tshogs kyi gnas su rtogs te | ji ltar zhe na | de la re zhig [C 8b] gang 'di skad du |

> 'dir sbyor ba'i tshig tu 'gyur ba ni | don dam par[8] [PsP$_L$ 26] nang gi skye mched rnams [P 9b] bdag las skye ba med par nges te | yod pa'i phyir dper[1] na shes pa yod pa nyid bzhin no ||

---

[1] P, N, G: pa

[2] C: sgrub

[3] D, C: skye

[4] D, C: rtogs

[5] P, N, G: kyis

[6] P, N: rag

[7] D, C: om.

[8] D, C: par na

zhes smras pa yin no ‖ 'dir don dam pa zhes bya ba'i khyad par ci'i phyir nye bar bkod pa yin |

§40. gal te 'jig rten gyi kun rdzob tu skye bar khas blangs pa dgag par bya ba ma yin pa'i phyir dang | 'gog na yang khas blangs pas gnod par thal bar 'gyur ba'i phyir ro zhe na | 'di ni rigs pa ma yin te | bdag las skye ba ni kun rdzob tu yang khas ma blangs pa'i phyir ro ‖

§41. ji skad du mdo las |

> sa bon gyi rgyu las byung ba'i myu gu de yang skye ba na | bdag gis ma byas | gzhan gyis ma byas | gnyis kas ma byas | dbang phyug gis ma byas | dus kyis ma bsgyur | rdul phra rab las ma byung | rang bzhin las ma byung | ngo bo nyid las ma byung | rgyu med pa las ma skyes ‖

zhes gsungs pa dang | de bzhin du |

> sa bon yod na myu gu ji bzhin te ‖
> sa bon gang yin myu gu de nyid min ‖
> de las gzhan min de yang[2] ma yin te ‖
> de ltar rtag min chad min chos nyid do ‖

zhes gsungs pa dang | 'di nyid las kyang |

> gang la brten[1] te gang 'byung ba ‖

---

[1] N, G: om.

[2] N: yad

de ni re zhig de nyid min ||
de las gzhan pa'ang ma yin phyir[2] ||
de phyir[3] chad min rtag ma yin ||

zhes 'chad do ||

§42. gzhan gyi lugs la ltos[4] te khyad par du byas so zhe na | de yang rigs pa ma yin te | de dag gi rnam par gzhag[5] pa ni kun rdzob [G 11b] tu yang khas blangs pa med pa'i phyir ro [PsP$_L$ 27] || bden pa gnyis[6] phyin ci ma log par [D 9a] mthong ba las nyams pa'i mu stegs pa dag ni[7] ji srid du gnyi ga'i sgo nas 'gog pa de srid du yon tan nyid yin par rtogs so || de ltar na gzhan gyi gzhung la ltos[8] te khyad par brjod pa yang rigs pa ma yin no ||

§43. gang las de la ltos[9] nas kyang khyad par 'bras bu[10] dang bcas par 'gyur ba 'jig rten pas[11] kyang bdag las skye bar mi rtogs te | 'jig rten pas ni bdag dang gzhan las zhes bya ba [N 10b] de lta bu la sogs pa'i

---

[1] P, N, G: rten

[2] D, C: de; MMK$_T$ P: pa; MMK$_T$ D: phyir

[3] P, N: phyin

[4] P, N, G: bltos

[5] P, N, G: bzhag

[6] P: gnyis gyi; N, G: gnyis kyi

[7] D, C: om. ni

[8] P, N, G: bltos

[9] P, N, G: bltos

[10] D: illegible

[11] D, C: las

rnam [P 10a] par dpyod[1] pa ’jug pa med par byas nas rgyu las ’bras bu ’byung ngo zhes bya ba ’di tsam zhig rtogs pa yin no ||

§44. slob dpon yang de ltar rnam par gzhag[2] pa mdzad pa yin [C 9a] te | de’i phyir rnam pa thams cad du khyad par don med pa nyid do zhes bya bar nges so ||

§45. gzhan yang gal te kun rdzob tu skye ba dgag par ’dod nas khyad par ’di ’god par byed na ni de’i tshe | rang la gzhi ma grub pa’i phyogs kyi nyes pa ’am | gzhi ma grub pa’i gtan tshigs kyi skyon du ’gyur te | rang gis don dam par mig la sogs pa’i skye mched rnams khas ma blangs pa’i phyir ro ||

§46. gal te kun rdzob tu mig la sogs pa yod pa’i phyir nyes pa med do zhe na | ’o na don dam par zhes bya ba ’di gang gi khyad par yin |

§47. gal te mig la sogs pa kun rdzob pa rnams don dam par skye ba ’gog pa’i phyir | don dam pa smos pa ni skye ba[3] ’gog pa’i khyad par yin no zhe na | de lta na ni ’o na [PsP$_L$ 28] mig la sogs pa kun rdzob pa rnams[4] don dam par skye ba yod pa ma yin te zhes de skad brjod par bya bar ’gyur na | de skad du yang ma smras so || [G 12a] smra na yang pha[5] rol po dag gis mig la sogs pa rnams rzdas su yod pa nyid du khas blangs pa’i phyir dang | btags[6] par yod par khas ma blangs pa’i phyir |

---

[1] Em.: dpyod. P, N, G, D, C: spyod

[2] P, N, G: bzhag

[3] P, N, G: skye ba la

[4] P, N, G: om. rnams

[5] G: ba

[6] Em.: btags. P, N, G, D, C: brtags

gzhan la gzhi ma grub pa'i phyogs kyi skyon[1] du 'gyur bas 'di ni mi rigs so ||

§48. ci ste ji ltar sgra mi rtag ces bya ba la chos dang chos can gnyis spyi[2] nyid gzung[3] ba yin gyi | khyad par ni ma yin te | [PsP$_L$ 29] khyad par 'dzin na ni rjes su dpag pa dang rjes su dpag par bya ba'i tha snyad med par 'gyur ro || 'di ltar gal te 'byung ba chen po bzhi las gyur pa'i [D 9b] sgra 'dzin na ni de pha rol po la ma grub bo || 'on te nam mkha'i yon tan 'dzin na ni de rang nyid sangs rgyas pa la ma grub pa yin no || de[4] bzhin du bye brag pa sgra mi rtag par dam 'cha' ba na yang | byas pa'i sgra 'dzin na de gzhan la ma grub bo[5] || [P 10b] 'on te mngon par gsal bar byas pa yin na ni de rang la ma grub pa yin no || de bzhin du ci rigs par 'jig pa yang gal te rgyu dang bcas pa yin na ni | de sangs rgyas pa rang la ma grub pa yin la | 'on te rgyu med pa yin na ni de pha rol po la ma grub pa yin no || de'i phyir ji ltar [N 11a] 'dir chos dang chos can spyi[6] tsam[7] zhig 'dzin pa de bzhin du | 'dir yang khyad par dor ba'i chos can tsam zhig 'dzin [C 9b] par 'gyur ro zhe na |

de ni de ltar yang ma yin te | [PsP$_L$ 30] 'di ltar gang gi tshe 'dir skye ba bkag pa bsgrub par[8] bya'i chos su 'dod pa[1] de'i tshe kho[2] nar de'i rten

[1] P: skyen

[2] P, N, G: sbyi

[3] P, N, G: bzung

[4] P: da

[5] D: po

[6] G: ci

[7] N: cam

[8] P, N, G: om. par

rten chos can phyin ci log tsam gyis bdag gi dngos po rnyed pa ni nyams par 'gyur bar 'dis rang nyid kyis khas blangs pa nyid do || phyin ci log dang phyin ci ma log pa dag ni tha dad pa yin no || de'i phyir | gang gi tshe rab rib can gyis[3] skra shad la [G 12b] sogs pa ltar phyin ci log gis yod pa ma yin pa yod pa nyid du 'dzin pa de'i tshe ni yod par gyur pa'i don cha tsam yang dmigs par ga la 'gyur | gang gi tshe rab rib can ma yin pas skra shad la sogs pa ltar phyin ci ma log pas yang dag pa ma yin pa sgro mi 'dogs pa de'i tshe na yang gang gis na de'i tshe na kun rdzob tu 'gyur ba yod pa ma yin par gyur pa'i don cha tsam yang dmigs pa ga la yod ||

de nyid kyi phyir slob dpon gyi zhal snga nas kyang[4] |

> gal te mngon sum la sogs pa'i ||
> don gyis 'ga' zhig dmigs na ni ||
> sgrub pa'am bzlog par bya na de ||
> med phyir nga la klan ka med ||

ces gsungs so ||

gang gi phyir de ltar phyin ci log pa dang phyin ci ma log pa dag tha dad pa de'i phyir phyin ci ma log pa'i gnas skabs na phyin ci log yod pa ma yin pa'i phyir na | gang zhig chos can nyid du 'gyur ba mig kun rdzob pa lta ga la yod | de'i phyir gzhi ma grub pa'i phyogs kyi skyon

---

[1] D, C: pa'i

[2] D, C: de kho

[3] P, N, G: gyi

[4] P, N, G: kyis

dang | gzhi ma grub pa'i [D 10a] gtan tshigs kyi skyon ldog pa med pas[1] 'di lan ma yin pa nyid do || [P 11a]

§49. dpe la yang 'dra ba yod pa ma yin no || der[2] ni sgra'i spyi dang mi rtag pa nyid kyi spyi khyad par brjod par mi 'dod pa gnyi ga la yang yod na | de bzhin du mig gi[3] spyi ni stong pa nyid dang stong[4] pa nyid ma yin par smra ba dag gis kun rdzob tu yang khas ma blangs la | don dam par yang ma yin pas dpe la yang 'dra ba yod pa ma yin no ||

§50. gzhi ma grub pa'i phyogs kyi nyes pa brjod pa'i tshul gang yin pa 'di nyid ni | yod pa'i phyir zhes bya ba'i gtan tshigs [N 12r] 'di la ma grub pa'i skyon brjod pa la yang sbyar bar bya'o || [PsP$_L$ 31] de lta bu de ni 'di ltar yin [G 13a] te | gang gi phyir ji skad bsnyad[5] pa'i don 'di ni rtog ge pa[6] 'dis rang nyid kyis khas blangs pa yin no || [C 10a] ji ltar zhe na |

> nang gi skye mched rnams skyed par byed pa rgyu la sogs pa ni yod pa kho[7] na yin te | de ltar de bzhin gshegs pas gsungs pa'i phyir ro || gang de bzhin gshegs pas ji skad gsungs pa de ni de bzhin te | dper na mya ngan las 'das pa ni zhi ba'o zhes bya ba bzhin no ||

---

[1] Em.: med pas. P, N, G, D, C: med pa nyid pas

[2] N: de

[3] N: abbr. (?) migi

[4] N: stod

[5] P, N, G: snyad

[6] D, C: ba

[7] D, C: 'o

zhes bya ba gzhan gyis bkod pa'i sgrub byed 'di la |

> 'dir khyod kyi[1] gtan tshigs kyi[2] don du 'dod pa gang[3] yin | de bzhin gshegs pas kun rdzob tu de skad gsungs pa'i phyir ram | 'on te don dam par gsungs pa'i phyir | gal te kun rdzob tu[4] na ni rang la gtan tshigs kyi don ma grub pa nyid do || 'on te don dam par na ni |
>
> > gang tshe chos ni yod pa dang ||
> > med dang yod med mi 'grub pas ||
>
> de'i tshe 'bras bu yod pa dang med pa dang[5] | gnyi ga'i bdag nyid kyi rkyen bsal ba'i phyir |
>
> > ji ltar sgrub byed rgyu zhes bya ||
> > de lta yin na mi rigs so ||
>
> de ni sgrub par byed pa'i rgyu ma yin pa kho na'o zhes bya ba ni ngag gi don to || de'i phyir don dam par bsgrub par bya ba dang | sgrub par byed pa nyid ma grub pa'i[6] phyir | gtan tshigs ma grub pa'i don nyid dang 'gal ba'i don nyid do

zhes 'dis skyon 'di smras pa yin no ||

---

[1] P, N, G: kyis; PP kyi

[2] P: without kyi

[3] P: gar

[4] D, C: add following yin

[5] N: om.

[6] N: par

gang gi phyir de ltar 'dis rang nyid [P 11b] kyis[1] tshul 'dis gtan tshigs ma grub par khas blangs pa de'i phyir dngos [D 10b] po'i chos gtan tshigs su bkod pa'i rjes su dpag pa thams cad la gtan tshigs la sogs pa rang la ma grub pa'i phyir sgrub par byed pa thams cad rnam par 'jig par [G 13b] 'gyur ro ||

§51. 'di lta ste |

> don dam par[2] nang gi skye mched rnams de dag gi rkyen[3] gzhan dag las skye ba med de | gzhan yin pa'i phyir dper na bum pa bzhin no ||
>
> yang na
>
> don dam par gzhan gyis brjod par 'dod pa[4] mig la sogs pa'i[5] nang gi skye mched [PsP$_L$ 32] 'grub par byed pa dag rkyen ma yin par nges te | gzhan yin pa'i phyir | dper na snal ma la sogs pa bzhin no ||

zhes bya ba 'dir gzhan nyid ces bya ba la sogs pa rang nyid la ma grub pa yin no ||

§52. ji ltar 'dis

---

[1] D, C: kyi

[2] D, C: par na

[3] N: rgyen

[4] D, C: pa'i

[5] D, C: pa

> nang gi skye mched rnams [N 12a] skyes pa kho na yin te | de dag gi yul dang ldan pa'i tha snyad khyad par can byed ba'i phyir ro ||

zhes gzhan [C 10b] gyis brjod[1] pa'i gtan tshigs 'di la ma grub par brjod par 'dod pas | 'di skad du

> 'on te don dam par rnal 'byor pa mnyam par gzhag[2] pa'i[3] shes rab kyi mig gis dngos po rnams kyi yang dag pa ji lta ba bzhin nyid mthong ba'i skye ba dang 'gro ba la sogs pa dag yod par bsgrub na ni | de'i tshe de dag gi yul dang ldan pa'i tha snyad khyad par can byed pa'i phyir ro zhes bya ba'i gtan tshigs ma grub pa'i don nyid de[4] | 'gro ba yang skye ba bkag[5] pa kho nas bkag pa'i phyir ro

zhes smras pa yin te | de bzhin du rang gis byas pa'i sgrub par byed pa la yang[6] |

> don dam par ma song ba la 'gro ba med de | lam yin pa'i phyir | song ba'i lam bzhin no ||

zhes bya ba'i gtan tshigs lam nyid rang nyid la[7] ma[1] grub pa'i don nyid du sbyar bar bya[2] la |

---

[1] P: brjed

[2] P, N, G: bzhag

[3] PP: pa

[4] D, C, G: do

[5] C: 'kag?

[6] N: lang pa

[7] P, C: lam; N, G: om.

> **§53.** don dam par brten pa dang bcas pa'i mig ni gzugs la lta[3] bar mi byed de | mig gi dbang po yin pa'i phyir | dper na de dang mtshungs pa bzhin no || [PsP$_L$ 33]

zhes bya ba [G 14a] dang |

de bzhin du |

> mig ni gzugs [P 12a] la lta[4] bar mi byed de[5] | 'byung ba las gyur pa nyid kyi phyir | dper na gzugs bzhin no

zhes bya ba dang |

> sa ni sra ba'i ngo bo ma yin te | 'byung ba yin pa'i phyir | dper na rlung bzhin no ||

zhes bya ba la sogs pa dag tu yang gtan tshigs la sogs [D 11a] pa rang nyid la ma[6] grub pa sbyar bar bya'o ||

§54. yod pa'i phyir zhes bya ba'i gtan tshigs[7] 'di yang pha rol po'i ltar na | ci nang gi skye mched rnams yod pa'i phyir shes pa yod pa ltar bdag las mi skye ba zhig gam | 'on te bum pa la sogs pa bzhin du bdag las skye ba zhig yin zhes ma nges pa yin no ||

---

[1] P, C: om.

[2] Em.: sbyar bar bya la. Two verbs are connected by *la* (sbyar bar bya la … sbyar bar bya'o). P, N, G, D, C: sbyar bar bya ba la

[3] P, N, G: blta

[4] P, N, G: blta

[5] D, C: do

[6] D, C: om.

[7] P, N: tshig

§55. gal te bum pa la sogs pa yang bsgrub byar mtshungs pa'i phyir ma nges[1] pa nyid ma yin no zhe na | de ni de ltar ma yin te | de skad du ma[2] smras pa'i phyir ro || [PsP$_L$ 34]

§56. gal te gzhan gyi rjes su dpag pa dag la skyon ji skad du smras pa de bzhin du rang gi rjes su dpag pa la yang ji skad smras pa'i nyes par thal bas gzhi ma grub pa dang | gtan [N 12b] tshigs ma grub pa la sogs pa'i skyon de nyid du 'gyur ba ma yin nam | de'i phyir gang[3] gnyi ga la skyon du 'gyur ba des ni gcig la brgal bar mi bya ste | des na skyon 'di dag thams cad mi rigs par 'gyur ro zhe na |

brjod par bya ste | rang gi [C 11a] rgyud kyi rjes su dpag pa smra ba dag la nyes pa 'dir 'gyur gyi[4] | kho bo cag[5] ni rang rgyud kyi rjes su dpag pa mi sbyor te | rjes su dpag pa dag ni gzhan gyi dam bca' ba[6] 'gog pa tsam gyi 'bras bu can yin pa'i phyir ro || 'di ltar gzhan [G 14b] mig lta'o zhes bya bar rtog pa de ni mig la rang gi[7] bdag nyid mi lta ba'i chos kyang 'dod la | gzhan la mi[8] lta ba'i chos med na mi 'byung ba nyid du yang khas blangs pa yin te | de'i phyir gang dang gang la rang gi bdag nyid lta ba med pa de dang de la ni gzhan la lta ba yang yod pa ma yin te | dper na bum pa bzhin no || mig la yang rang gi bdag

---

[1] N: des

[2] P, N, G: yang precedes

[3] N: gad

[4] N: gyid?

[5] N: bca'

[6] N, G: bar

[7] N: ge

[8] Em.: mi. P, N, G, D, C: om. mi. See PsP Skt, where the text has been emended to include a negation; see also Translation note.

nyid mi lta ba yod pa yin te | de'i phyir gzhan la[1] lta ba yang 'di la med do || de'i phyir rang [P 12b] gi bdag nyid mi lta ba dang 'gal bar sngon po la sogs pa gzhan la lta ba rang la grags pa'i rjes su dpag pa dang 'gal ba yin no || zhes de la grub pa'i rjes su dpag pas sel bar byed pa yin no ||

gang gi phyir rjes su dpag pa dag gis 'di tsam zhig brjod par bya ba yin pas | gang las nyes pa mtshungs[2] par 'gyur ba | kho bo cag gi phyogs la ji skad bsnyad pa'i skyon 'jug pa ga la yod | [D 11b]

§57. yang ci gang yang rung ba la grub pa'i rjes su dpag pa'i sgo nas kyang rjes su dpag pas[3] gnod pa yod dam zhe na |

yod de de yang rang nyid la grub pa'i [PsP$_L$ 35] gtan tshigs nyid kyis yin gyi | gzhan la grub pas ni ma yin te | 'jig rten nyid du mthong ba'i phyir ro || 'jig rten na ni res 'ga' dpang[4] po'i rgol ba dang phyir rgol[5] gnyis kyis[6] tshad mar byas pa'i tshig gis rgyal ba 'am 'pham[7] par 'gyur la | res 'ga' ni rang gi tshig kho nas 'gyur gyi | gzhan gyi tshig gis ni rgyal ba 'am 'pham[8] par 'gyur ba ma yin no || 'jig rten na ji ltar [G 15a] yin pa de bzhin du rigs pa la yang yin te | 'jig rten pa'i tha

---

[1] D, C: om.

[2] N: tshuds

[3] P, N, G: pa'i

[4] C: dbang

[5] C: rgol ba

[6] D, C: kyi

[7] D: pham

[8] D: pham

snyad kho na rigs pa'i bstan bcos[1] su skabs su bab[2] pa yin pa'i phyir ro ||

§58. de nyid kyi phyir [N 13a] 'ga' zhig gis gzhan la grags pa'i dbang gis ni rjes su dpag pas[3] gnod pa ma yin te | gzhan la grags pa nyid dgag par 'dod pa'i phyir ro zhes bshad do ||

§59. gang zhig gang[4] gnyi ga la nges par brjod pa [C 11b] de ni sgrub[5] pa 'am sun 'byin pa yin gyi | gang yang rung ba la grub pa 'am the tshom za ba smra ba ni ma yin no snyam du sems pa des kyang 'jig rten kyi tha snyad kyi rnam par gzhag[6] pa la brten nas rjes su dpag pa la ji skad smras pa'i tshul 'di nyid khas blang bar bya'o ||

§60. 'di ltar lung gis gnod pa ni gnyi ga la grub pa'i lung kho na'i sgo nas ma yin te | 'o na ci zhe na | rang la grub pa'i sgo nas kyang yin no || rang gi don gyi rjes su dpag pa ni thams cad du [P 13a] rang la grub pa nyid brling[7] ba yin gyi | gnyi ga la grub pa ni ma yin no || [PsP_L 36] de nyid kyi phyir rtog ge'i mtshan nyid brjod pa ni dgos pa med pa yin te | sangs rgyas rnams kyis rang la ji ltar grags pa'i 'thad pas de kho na mi shes pa'i gdul bya'i[8] skye bo la phan btags pa'i phyir ro || shin tu spros pas chog go || dkyus ma nyid bshad par bya'o ||

---

[1] P, N, G: chos

[2] P: beb?

[3] Em.: pas. P, N, G, D, C: pa'i; cf. PsP_L 19.7 dpag pas gnod; PsP_L 35.8 lung gis gnod pa

[4] N: gad

[5] P, N, G: bsgrub

[6] P, N, G: bzhag

[7] N: brlid

[8] C: ba'i

§61. dngos po rnams ni gzhan las skye ba yang ma yin te | gzhan med pa'i phyir ro || 'di yang |

> dngos po rnams kyi rang bzhin ni ||
> rkyen la sogs la[1] yod pa ma yin ||

zes bya ba der 'chad par 'gyur ro ||

de'i phyir gzhan med pa nyid kyi phyir gzhan[2] las kyang skye ba ma yin no || [D 12a]

gzhan yang |

> gzhan la [G 15b] brten nas gal te gzhan zhig 'byung bar 'gyur na ni ||
> 'o na me lce las kyang mun pa mthug po 'byung[3] 'gyur zhing[4] ||
> thams cad las kyang thams cad skye bar 'gyur te gang gi phyir ||
> skyed par byed pa ma yin ma lus[5] la 'ang gzhan nyid mtshungs ||

zhes bya ba la sogs pas gzhan las skye ba dgag pa dbu ma la 'jug pa las nges par bya'o ||

§62. slob dpon sangs rgyas bskyangs[6] ni

---

[1] P, N, G: pa
[2] N: gzhal
[3] N: 'byud
[4] N: zhid
[5] D, C: add following pa
[6] N: sangs rgyas bskyangs illegible

> dngos po rnams gzhan las skye ba med de | thams cad las kyang thams cad skye bar ’gyur ba’i phyir ro ||

zhes rnam par[1] ’chad do ||

§63. ’di la slob dpon legs ldan ’byed ni

> des na de la thal bar ’gyur ba’i ngag yin pa’i phyir bsgrub par bya ba dang sgrub par byed pa bzlog par [PsP$_L$ 37] byas na | dngos po rnams bdag [N 13b] gam gnyis sam rgyu med pa las skye bar ’gyur ba dang | ’ga’ zhig las ’ga’ zhig skye bar ’gyur ba’i phyir phyogs gong ma dang ’gal bar ’gyur ro || gzhan du na yang thams cad las thams cad[2] skye bar ’gyur ba’i phyir ro || de bas na de la sgrub pa dang [C 12a] sun ’byin pa nyid med ba’i phyir | de ni don ’brel pa med pa yin te

zhes sun ’byin smra’o ||

’di yang don ’brel pa med pa ma yin te | gong kho nar bstan zin pa’i phyir [P 13b] dang | gzhan gyis dam bcas pa’i don sun ’byin par byed pa yin pa[3] dang | sun ’byin pa nyid kyang yin pa’i phyir ’di ni gyi na’o || des na slar yang ’bad par mi bya’o || [PsP$_L$ 38]

§64. dngos po rnams ni gnyi ga las skye ba yang ma yin te | phyogs gnyi ga la smras pa’i nyes par thal ba’i phyir dang | re re la skyed par byed pa’i nus pa med pa’i phyir ro ||

---

[1] N: om.

[2] D, C: add following las; N: thid

[3] Em.: pa. P, N, G, D, C: om. pa. *pa’i phyir* is also possible. The Sanskrit expects *pas* instead of *pa dang*.

gal te re res[1] byas 'gyur na ||
sdug bsngal [G 16a] gnyi gas byas par 'gyur ||

zhes 'chad par 'gyur ro ||

§65. rgyu med pa las kyang mi skye ste[2]

rgyu med na ni 'bras bu dang ||
rgyu yang 'thad par mi 'gyur ro ||

zhes bya ba la sogs pas 'chad[3] par 'gyur ba'i skyon du thal bar 'gyur ba'i phyir dang |

gal te rgyu yis stong na 'gro ba 'di dag gzung bya min ||
ji ltar nam mkha'i utpala yi[4] dri dang kha dog bzhin ||

zhe bya ba la sogs pa'i nyes par thal bar [D 12b] 'gyur ba'i phyir ro ||

§66. slob dpon sangs rgyas bskyangs ni

dngos po rnams rgyu med pa las kyang skye ba med de | rtag tu thams cad las thams cad skye bar thal bar 'gyur ro ||

zhes 'chad do ||

§67. 'di la yang slob dpon legs ldan 'byed |

---

[1] P, N, G: re re

[2] N, G: om. rgyu med pa las kyang mi skye ste

[3] N: 'chang

[4] P, N, G: utpala'i

de la yang thal bar ’gyur ba’i ngag yin pa’i phyir | gal te bsgrub par bya ba [PsP$_L$ 39] dang sgrub par byed pa bzlog pa gsal ba ngag[1] gi don du mngon par ’dod na | de’i tshe ’di skad du | dngos po rnams rgyu las skye bar ’gyur ba dang | lan ’ga’ kha cig las kha cig[2] skye bar ’gyur ba dang | rtsom pa ’bras bu dang bcas pa nyid du ’gyur ba’i phyir ro || zhes bstan par ’gyur na | bshad pa de ni mi rigs te[3] | sngar[4] smras pa’i skyon du[5] ’gyur ba’i phyir ro ||

zhes sun ’byin pa[6] smra’o ||

§68. gzhan dag na re ’di ni mi rigs te sngar[7] lan btab zin pa’i phyir ro zhe’o ||

§69. gang yang dbang phyug la sogs pa nye bar bsdu ba’i phyir yin no zhes bya ba de yang rigs pa ma yin te | dbang phyug la sogs pa rnams ni khas blangs pa [N 14a] ji lta ba bzhin du bdag dang gzhan dang gnyi ga’i phyogs dag tu [P 14a] [C 12b] ’du ba’i phyir ro ||

§70. de’i phyir skye ba yod pa ma yin no zhes bya ba ’di bsgrubs pa yin la | skye ba[8] [G 16b] yod pa ma yin pas | rten cing ’brel par ’byung ba skye ba med pa la sogs pas khyad par du byas pa grub pa yin no[1] ||

---

[1] C: dag

[2] G, N: om. las kha cig

[3] N: ma te

[4] P: sdar

[5] D, C: add following thal bar

[6] P, N, G: par

[7] P: sdar

[8] C: po

§71. 'dir smras pa gal te de ltar rten cing 'brel par 'byung ba skye ba med[2] pa la sogs pas khyad par du[3] byas pa rnam par bzhag[4] na[5] | 'o na[6] bcom ldan 'das kyis

> ma rig pa'i rkyen gyis 'du byed rnams skye ba dang | ma rig pa 'gags pas 'du byed 'gag

ces bya ba dang | de bzhin du |

> kye ma 'du byed rnams mi rtag ||
> skye zhing 'jig pa'i chos can yin ||
> skyes nas 'jig par 'gyur ba ste ||
> de dag nye bar zhi ba bde || [PsP$_L$ 40]

zhes bya ba dang | de bzhin du |

> de bzhin gshegs pa rnams byung yang rung | de bzhin gshegs pa rnams ma byung yang rung | chos rnams kyi chos nyid 'di ni gnas pa kho na ste

zhes bya ba dang |

> sems can gnas par byed pa'i chos ni gcig[7] ste | gang zas bzhi'o || [D 13a]

---

[1] P, N, G: om.

[2] C: illegible

[3] P, N, G: om.

[4] D, C: gzhag

[5] D, C: add following ni |

[6] P, N, G: add following ni

[7] P, N, G: cig

> ’jig rten skyong bar byed[1] pa’i chos ni gnyis te | ngo tsha shes pa dang khrel yod pa’o

zhes bya ba la sogs pa dang | de bzhin du |

> ’jig rten pha rol nas ’dir ’ongs so || ’jig rten ’di nas ’jig rten pha rol tu[2] ’gro’o

zhes de ltar rten cing ’brel par ’byung[3] ba ’gag pa la sogs pas khyad par du byas pa bstan pa gang yin[4] pa de ji ltar ’gal bar mi ’gyur zhe na |

gang gi phyir de ltar rten cing ’brel par ’byung ba ’gag pa la sogs pa dag yod par thos par ’gyur ba de nyid kyi phyir [PsP$_L$ 41] slob dpon gyis drang ba dang nges pa’i don gyi mdo sde’i rnam par dbye ba bstan par bya ba’i phyir dbu ma’i bstan bcos[5] ’di mdzad pa yin no || de la rten cing ’brel par ’byung ba’i skye ba la sogs pa dag bstan pa [N 14b] gang yin pa de dag ni ma rigs pa’i [G 17a] rab rib dang bral ba dag gi ye shes zag pa med pa’i yul gyi rang bzhin la ltos[6] nas ni ma yin no || ’o na ci zhe na | ma rig pa’i rab rib kyis blo [P 14b] gros kyi[7] mig nyams par byas pa dag gi shes pa’i yul la ltos[8] nas yin no[9] ||

---

[1] P, N, G: om. bar byed

[2] D: du

[3] N: ’byud

[4] N: illegible

[5] P, N, G: chos

[6] P, N, G: bltos

[7] P, N, G: kyis

[8] P, N, G: bltos; C: ltes

[9] G: repeats from *’o na ci zhe na | ma rig* up to *yul la bltos nas yin no ||*

§72. de kho na nyid[1] gzigs pa la ltos[2] nas ni bcom ldan 'das kyis

> dge slong dag 'di ni bden pa dam pa ste | 'di lta ste | slu[3] ba med pa'i chos can mya ngan las 'das pa'o || 'du byed [C 13a] thams cad ni brdzun pa bslu[4] ba'i chos can no

zhes bya ba la sogs pa gsungs so || de bzhin du |

> 'di ni[5] de bzhin nyid dam phyin ci ma log pa'i de bzhin nyid ni med kyi | 'di dag ni slu bar byed[6] pa'i chos can no || 'di dag ni brdzun[7] pa sgyu ma byis pa 'drid pa'o

zhes gsungs so || de bzhin du |

> gzugs ni dbu ba rdos pa 'dra ||
> tshor ba chu yi chu bur bzhin ||
> 'du shes smig rgyu lta bu ste ||
> 'du byed chu shing[8] sdong po 'dra ||
> rnam shes sgyu ma lta bu zhes ||
> nyi ma'i gnyen gyis bka' stsal to ||

zhes bya ba dang | de bzhin du |

---

[1] P, N, G: om.

[2] P, N, G: bltos

[3] P, N, G: bslu

[4] P, N, G: bslu

[5] P: na

[6] D: byad

[7] P, N, G: rdzun

[8] N: shid

> dge slong brtson 'grus brtsams pa dran pa dang shes bzhin dang ldan pa nyin dang mtshan du chos la so sor rtog par byed pa na || 'du byed thams cad ni nye bar zhi ba'i go 'phang zhi ba | chos rnams bdag med pa nyid rtogs par 'gyur ro[1] || [PsP$_L$ 42]

zhes bya ba la sogs pa gsungs so ||

§73. de lta bur bstan pa'i dgongs pa mi shes pas | 'dir de kho na'i don can gyi bstan pa ni gang zhig yin | dgongs pa can ni 'dir gang zhig yin snyam du [G 17b] gang zhig the tshom du 'gyur ba dang | gang zhig blo zhan pa nyid kyis drang ba'i don gyi bstan pa la nges[2] pa'i don du rtogs pa de gnyi ga'i the tshom dang log pa'i shes pa dag rigs pa dang lung gnyis kyi sgo nas bsal bar bya ba'i phyir | slob dpon gyis[3] 'di brtsams so || de la bdag las ma yin zhes bya ba [N 15a] la sogs pas ni rigs pa gsungs pa yin no ||

> bcom ldan 'das kyis chos gang zhig ||
> slu[4] ba de ni brdzun zhes gsungs ||
> 'du byed thams cad slu[5] ba'i chos ||
> des na de dag brdzun pa yin ||
>
> sngon [P 15a] mtha' mngon[6] nam zhes zhus tshe ||
> thub pa chen pos min zhes gsungs ||

---

[1] N: om.

[2] N: des

[3] P, N, G: gyi

[4] P, N, G: bslu

[5] P, N, G: bslu

[6] Em.: mngon. P, N, G, D, C: sngon

'khor ba thog ma mtha' med de ||
de la sngon med phyi ma med || [PsP$_L$ 43]

bcom ldan dngos dang dngos med pa ||
mkhyen pas kātyāyana[1] yi ||
gdams ngag[2] las ni yod pa dang ||
med pa gnyi ga'ang dgag pa mdzad ||

zhes bya ba la sogs pa lung gsungs pa yin no ||

§74. 'phags pa blo gros mi zad pas bstan pa'i mdo las |

nges pa'i don gyi mdo sde ni gang | drang ba'i don gyi mdo sde ni gang zhe na | [C 13b] mdo sde gang dag lam la 'jug pa'i phyir bstan pa de dag ni drang ba'i don zhes bya'o || mdo sde gang dag 'bras bu la 'jug pa'i phyir bstan pa de dag ni nges pa'i don zhes bya'o || mdo sde gang dag bdag dang | sems can dang | srog dang[3] gso ba dang | skyes bu dang | gang zag dang | shed las skyes dang | shed bu[4] dang | byed pa po dang | tshor ba po dang | sgra rnam pa sna tshogs su bshad pa dang | bdag po med pa la bdag po dang bcas par bstan pa de dag ni drang ba'i don zhes bya'o || mdo sde gang dag [G 18a] stong pa nyid dang | mtshan ma med pa dang | smon pa med pa dang | mngon par 'du mi byed pa dang | ma skyes pa dang | ma byung ba dang | dngos po med [D 14a] pa dang | bdag med pa dang | sems can med pa dang |

---

[1] D, C: kātayana

[2] N, C: dag

[3] D, C: add following 'gro ba dang |

[4] Em.: bu. See Braarvig 1993 (Vol 1): 117. P, N, G, D, C: bdag

> srog med pa dang | gang zag[1] med pa dang | bdag[2] po med pas[3] na[4] | rnam par thar pa'i[5] sgo'i bar du bstan pa de dag ni nges[6] pa'i don zhes bya ste | 'di dag ni nges[7] pa'i don gyi mdo sde la rton gyi | drang ba'i don gyi mdo sde la mi rton pa zhes bya'o ||

zhes gsungs pa dang | [PsP$_L$ 44]

de bzhin du [N 15b] 'phags pa ting nge 'dzin gyi rgyal po[8] las kyang |

> stong[9] pa bde bar gshegs pas bshad pa ltar ||
> nges don mdo sde dag gi bye brag shes ||
> gang las sems can gang zag skyes bu bstan[10] ||
> chos de thams cad drang ba'i don du [P 15b] shes ||

zhes gsungs so ||

§75. de'i phyir skye ba la sogs pa bstan pa rnams brdzun[11] pa'i don can du bstan ba'i phyir | slob dpon gyis rten cing 'brel par[12] 'byung ba[1] rjes su ston pa brtsams so ||

---

[1] C: thag

[2] N: dang | bdag illegible

[3] D, C: pa

[4] D, C: nas. Braarvig 1993 (Vol. 1): 118: *pa dang* for *pas na*

[5] C: ba'i

[6] N: des

[7] N , C: des

[8] P: bo

[9] P: ston

[10] D, C: bsten

[11] P, N, G: rdzun

[12] D, C: bar

§76. gal te skye ba la sogs pa mi srid pa yin dang | chos thams cad brdzun[2] pa nyid du bstan par bya ba'i phyir slob dpon gyis 'di brtsams pa yin na[3] | de lta[4] na ni gang brdzun[5] pa de ni yod pa ma yin pas mi dge ba'i las dag med par 'gyur la | de med pas ngan 'gro dag med par 'gyur zhing | dge ba dang bde 'gro dag kyang med par 'gyur ro || bde 'gro dang[6] ngan 'gro med pa'i phyir 'khor ba yang yod pa ma yin pas | rtsom pa thams cad don med pa nyid du 'gyur ba ma yin nam zhes[7]

bshad par bya ste | kun rdzob kyi bden pa la ltos[8] nas 'di bden par mngon par[9] zhen [G 18b] pa'i 'jig [C 14a] rten pa'i gnyen po nyid du kho bo cag gis dngos po rnams brdzun[10] pa'i don du bstan gyi | gang zhig brdzun[11] pa 'am brdzun[12] pa ma yin par 'gyur ba 'phags pa rnams kyis ni cung zad kyang gzigs pa ma yin no || gzhan yang gang gis chos thams cad brdzun[13] pa'i don can nyid du yongs su mkhyen pa de la ci

---

[1] P, N, G: om.

[2] P, N, G: rdzun

[3] D, C: no

[4] N: ltar

[5] P, N, G: rdzun

[6] P, N, G: 'ang

[7] D, C: zhe na

[8] P, N, G: bltos

[9] P: om. mngon par

[10] P, N, G: rdzun

[11] P, N, G: rdzun

[12] P, N, G: rdzun

[13] P, N, G: rdzun

las yod cing ’khor ba yod dam | ’dis ni chos ’ga’ yang[1] yod pa nyid dam med pa nyid du dmigs pa[2] yang ma yin no || [PsP$_L$ 45]

ji skad du bcom ldan ’das kyis ’phags pa dkon mchog brtsegs pa’i mdo las |

> ’od srungs sems ni kun tu btsal na mi[3] rnyed do || gang[4] mi[5] rnyed [D 14b] pa de ni mi dmigs pa’o || gang mi dmigs pa de ni ’das pa yang ma yin | ma ’ongs pa yang ma yin | da ltar byung ba yang ma yin no || gang ’das pa yang ma yin | [N 16a] ma ’ongs pa yang ma[6] yin | da ltar byung ba yang ma yin pa de la ni ngo bo nyid med do || gang ngo bo nyid med pa de la ’byung ba med do || gang ’byung ba med pa de la ’gag pa med do ||

zhes rgya cher gsungs pa lta bu’o ||

gang dag phyin ci log dang ldan pas [P 16a] chos rnams brdzun[7] pa nyid du khong du mi chud cing | dngos po rnams rang bzhin yod par rtogs nas mngon par zhen pa de ni chos rnams la ’di bden par mngon par zhen pa nyid kyi sgo nas mngon par zhen par gyur dang | las kyang byed cing ’khor ba na yang[8] ’khor bar ’gyur la | phyin ci log la

---

[1] N: om.

[2] D: ba

[3] C: ma

[4] C: gong

[5] Em.: mi. P, N, G, D, C: ma. KP Tib: mi

[6] N: pa?

[7] P, N, G: rdzun

[8] P, N, G: om. ’khor ba na yang

gnas pas mya ngan las 'das pa thob pa'i skal ba can du yang mi 'gyur ro ||

§77. yang ci dngos po brdzun[1] pa'i rang bzhin can rnams kyang kun nas nyon mongs pa dang rnam par byang ba'i rgyur 'gyur ram zhe na |

'gyur te dper na sgyu ma'i na chung[2] [G 19a] ni de'i rang bzhin mngon par mi shes pa rnams kyi kun nas nyon mongs pa'i rgyu yin la | de bzhin gshegs pa'i sprul pa ni dge ba'i rtsa ba bsags pa rnams kyi rnam par byang ba'i rgyur 'gyur ba bzhin no || [PsP_L 46]

lhag pa'i bsam pa brtan[3] pa'i mdo las |

> rigs kyi bu 'di lta ste | dper na la la zhig gis sgyu ma mkhan gyi rol mo byung ba'i tshe | sgyu ma mkhan gyis sprul pa'i bud med mthong nas 'dod chags kyis sems dkris nas 'khor [C 14b] gyis 'jigs shing bag tsha ste | stan las langs nas song ste | de song nas bud med de nyid la | mi sdug pa dang | mi gtsang ba dang | mi rtag pa dang | sdug bsngal ba dang | stong pa dang | bdag med par yid la byed na

zhes rgyas par gsungs so ||

'dul ba las kyang | 'khrul 'khor mkhan gyis byas pa'i 'khrul 'khor gyi na chung ni yang dag par bden pa'i na chung gis stong bzhin du | ri mo mkhan gyi 'dod pa'i 'dod chags kyi gzhir gyur par bshad do ||

---

[1] P, N, G: rdzun

[2] N: cung

[3] Em.: brtan. P, N, G, D, C: bstan

dpe de bzhin du dngos po brdzun[1] pa'i rang bzhin can rnams kyang byis pa rnams kyi kun nas nyon mongs pa'i rgyu yin no ‖ [N 16b] [PsP$_L$ 47]

§78. de bzhin du 'phags pa dkon mchog [D 15a] brtsegs pa las kyang |

> de nas dge slong bsam gtan thob pa lnga brgya ni bcom ldan 'das kyi[2] chos bstan pa 'di la mi 'jug ste | ma rtogs ma mos pas stan las langs [P 16b] te dong ngo | de nas bcom ldan 'das kyis dge slong de dag[3] lam gang nas dong ba'i lam der dge slong gnyis shig sprul pa sprul te |
>
> de nas dge slong lnga brgya po de dag dge slong de gnyis lam gang nas dong ba'i lam der dong [G 19b] ste phyin pa dang 'di skad ces smras so ‖ tshe dang ldan pa dag gar dong | sprul pa gnyis kyis smras pa | kho bo cag ni dgon pa'i gnas su bsam gtan gyi bde ba la reg par gnas par bya bar dong ngo ‖ de ci'i phyir zhe na | kho bo cag ni bcom ldan 'das kyis[4] chos bstan pa gang yin pa'i[5] chos bstan pa de la mi 'jugs ste | ma rtogs mi mos shing | skrag ste kun tu[6] dngangs | kun tu[7] rab tu dngangs par gyur nas kho bo cag dgon pa'i gnas rnams su bsam gtan gyi bde ba la reg par gnas pa rnams kyis gnas par bya'o ‖ de nas dge

---

[1] P, N, G: rdzun

[2] D, C: kyis

[3] C: de dag la

[4] P: kyi

[5] D, C: pa 'ang

[6] D, C: du

[7] D, C: du

slong lnga brgya po de dag gis[1] 'di skad ces smras so ‖ tshe dang ldan pa dag | kho bo cag kyang bcom ldan 'das kyis chos bstan pa la mi 'jug ste | ma rtogs ma mos shing skrag ste | kun tu dngangs kun tu rab tu dngangs par gyur te | de'i phyir kho bo cag kyang dgon pa'i gnas rnams su bsam gtan gyi bde ba la reg par gnas pa rnams kyis gnas par bya'o ‖ sprul pa dag gis smras pa | tshe dang ldan pa dag de'i phyir bdag cag yang dag par [C 15a] bgro[2] bar bya'o ‖ rtsod par mi bya'o ‖ rtsod pa med pa lhur byed pa[3] ni dge sbyong gi chos so ‖ tshe dang ldan pa dag gang 'di yongs su mya ngan las 'das pa zhes bya ba gang | yongs su mya ngan las 'da' bar 'gyur ba'i chos de gang | lus 'di la[4] bdag gam | sems can nam | srog gam | skye ba po 'am | skyes bu 'am | gang zag gam | shed las skyes sam | shed bu 'am | gang yongs su mya ngan las 'da' bar 'gyur | gang zad pas yongs su mya ngan las 'da' | [G 20a] de dag [N 17a] gis smras pa | 'dod chags zad zhe sdang zad gti mug zad pas yongs su mya ngan [P 17a] las 'da'o ‖ [PsP_L 48] sprul pa gnyis [D 15b] kyis smras pa | tshe dang ldan pa dag 'dod chags dang zhe sdang dang gti mug yod pa yin nam | ci nam de zad par bya | de dag gis smras[5] pa | de dag ni nang na yang med phyi rol na yang med | gnyi ga med par yang mi dmigs te | de dag ni yongs su ma brtags pa las kyang mi skye'o ‖ sprul pa gnyis kyis smras pa | tshe dang ldan pa dag de

---

[1] D, C: rnams kyis for de dag gis

[2] Em: bgro. P, N, G, D, C: 'gro. KP Tib: bgro (cf. KP_{ed} § 142.6 Tib; Weller 1965: 147, n. 2)

[3] D: adds following de

[4] D, C: las

[5] N: smros

lta bas na bdag tu ma rtog[1] rnam par ma rtog cig[2] | tshe dang ldan ba dag nam mi rtog rnam par mi rtog pa de'i tshe chags par mi 'gyur chags pa dang bral bar yang mi 'gyur ro || chags pa med cing chags pa dang bral ba yang med pa gang yin pa de ni zhi ba zhes bya'o || tshe dang ldan pa dag tshul khrims ni mi 'khor zhing[3] yongs su mya ngan las mi 'da'o || tshe dang ldan pa dag ting nge 'dzin dang | shes rab dang | rnam par grol ba dang | rnam par grol ba'i ye shes mthong ba yang mi 'khor zhing yong su mya ngan las mi 'da'o || tshe dang ldan pa dag | chos de dag gis yongs su mya ngan las 'da' bar ston na | chos de dag kyang stong pa dben pa gzung du med pa'o | tshe dang ldan pa dag 'di lta ste | mya ngan las 'das pa'i 'du shes spongs shig[4] | 'du shes[5] la yang 'du shes su ma byed cig | 'du shes la 'du shes kyis yongs su shes par ma byed cig | gang 'du shes la 'du shes kyis yongs su shes pa de'i de ni 'du shes la yongs su bcings pa yin no || [C 15b] tshe dang ldan pa dag khyed 'du shes dang [G 20b] tshor ba 'gog pa'i snyoms par 'jug pa la snyoms par zhugs shig | tshe dang ldan pa dag | dge slong[6] 'du shes dang tshor ba 'gog pa'i snyoms par 'jug pa la snyoms par zhugs pa las gong na bya ba med do zhes smra'o ||

---

[1] N: rtogs

[2] D, C: shig

[3] N: zhang

[4] P, N, G: zhig

[5] P, N, G: zhes

[6] N: illegible

chos kyi rnam grangs ’di bshad pa’i tshe dge slong lnga brgya po de dag len pa med par zag pa rnams las sems rnam par grol lo || de dag [P 17b] sems rnam par [N 17b] grol nas bcom ldan ’das ga la[1] ba der dong ste lhags pa dang | bcom ldan ’das kyi zhabs la mgo bos phyag ’tshal te | phyogs gcig tu ’khod do || [PsP_L 49] de nas tshe dang ldan pa[2] rab ’byor gyis dge slong de[3] dag la ’di skad ces [D 16a] smras so || tshe dang ldan pa dag gar dong | gang nas lhags | de dag gis smras pa | btsun pa rab ’byor gang du yang ’gro ba med pa dang | gang nas kyang ’ong ba med pa’i phyir bcom ldan ’das kyis chos bstan to || smras pa tshe dang[4] ldan pa dag khyed kyi ston pa gang yin | smras pa gang ma skyes shing yongs su mya ngan las mi ’da’ ba’o || smras pa khyed kyis ji ltar chos thos | smras pa bcings pa’i phyir yang ma yin | thar pa’i phyir yang ma yin no || smras pa khyed sus btul | smras pa su la lus med cing sems med pas so || smras pa khyed ji ltar brtson | smras pa ma rig pa spang ba’i phyir yang ma yin rig pa bskyed[5] pa’i phyir yang ma yin no || smras pa khyed[6] ji ltar rnam par[7] grol | smras pa sbyor ba’i phyir yang ma yin | spang ba’i phyir[8] yang ma yin no || smras pa khyed su’i

[1] P: gal for ga la

[2] C: pa dag

[3] D, C: om.

[4] P, G: om.

[5] D, C: skyed

[6] D: khyod

[7] P: bar

[8] P, N, G: phyin

nyan thos | smras pa gang gis[1] thob pa med cing mngon par rdzogs par sangs rgyas pa med pa'i 'o || [G 21a] smras pa khyed kyi tshangs pa mtshungs par spyod pa gang | smras pa gang khams gsum na mi rgyu ba rnams so || smras pa tshe dang ldan pa dag ji srid cig na | yongs su mya ngan las 'da' | smras pa de bzhin gshegs pa'i sprul ba nam yongs su mya ngan las 'da' ba na'o || smras pa khyed[2] kyis[3] bya ba byas sam | smras pa ngar 'dzin pa dang nga[4] yir 'dzin pa yongs su shes pas so || smras pa khyed[5] kyi nyon[6] mongs pa zad dam[7] | smras ba chos thams cad gtan du zad ba'i phyir ro || smras pa khyed kyis bdud btul lam | smras pa phung po'i [C 16a] bdud mi dmigs pa'i phyir ro || smras ba khyed kyis ston pa la bsnyen [P 18a] bkur byas sam | smras pa lus kyis kyang ma byas | ngag[8] gis kyang ma byas | sems kyis kyang ma byas so || smras pa khyod kyis yon gnas kyi sa sbyangs sam | smras pa 'dzin pa med cing sdud pa med pas so || smras pa [N 18a] khyed 'khor ba las brgal[9] tam | smras pa chad pa med cing rtag pa med pa'i phyir ro || smras pa khyed yon gnas kyi sar zhugs sam | smras pa 'dzin pa thams cad las rnam par grol ba'i phyir ro || smras pa tshe dang ldan pa dag gar 'gro | [D 16b] smras pa de bzhin gshegs pa'i sprul ba gang du bzhud par

---

[1] C: gim

[2] D: khyod

[3] P, N, G: kyi

[4] N: da

[5] N: khyod

[6] N: thon

[7] N: ngam

[8] N: dag

[9] D, C: rgal

> ro || de ltar tshe dang ldan pa rab 'byor gyis [PsP$_L$ 50] yongs su dris te | dge slong de dag gis lan btab nas 'khor de'i dge slong brgyad brgya ni len pa med par zag pa rnams las sems rnam par grol lo || srog chags sum khri nyis stong ni chos rnams la chos kyi mig rdul med cing dri ma dang bral ba rnam par dag go ||

zhes gsungs so ||

de ltar na dge slong[1] [G 21b] de bzhin gshegs pa'i sprul pa brdzun[2] pa'i rang bzhin[3] can gnyis kyis dge slong lnga brgya'i rnam par byang ba'i rgyu byas pa yin no ||

§79.'phags pa rdo rje snying po las kyang |

> 'jam dpal 'di lta ste dper na | gtsub shing dang gtsub stan[4] la brten | mi'i lag pa'i rtsol ba la brten nas du ba 'byung zhing | me mngon par 'grub ste | me de yang gtsub shing[5] la 'ang[6] mi gnas gtsub stan[7] la 'ang[8] mi gnas | mi'i lag pa'i rtsol ba la 'ang[9] mi gnas so || 'jam dpal de bzhin du med pa las skyes bu gang zag rmongs pa la 'dod chags dang zhe sdang dang gti mug gi yongs su gdung ba 'ang 'byung ste | yongs su gdung ba de yang

---

[1] N: illegible

[2] P, N, G: rdzun

[3] N: bzhan

[4] D, C: gtan

[5] N: shid

[6] D, C: yang

[7] D, C: gtan

[8] D, C: yang

[9] D, C: yang

nang na 'ang[1] mi gnas phyi rol na 'ang mi gnas | gnyi ga med par yang mi gnas mod kyi | 'jam dpal 'on kyang gti mug ces bya'o || de ci'i phyir gti mug ces brjod par bya zhe na | 'jam dpal gti mug [P 18b] ni chos thams cad rab tu grol ba ste | des na gti mug ces bya'o zhes bya ba dang | de[2] bzhin du 'jam dpal chos thams cad ni sems can dmyal ba'i sgo ste | 'di ni gzungs kyi tshig go || [C 16b] gsol ba bcom ldan 'das ji ltar na 'di gzungs kyi tshig lags | bka' stsal[3] pa 'jam dpal [N 18b] sems can dmyal ba dag ni byis pa [PsP$_L$ 51] so so'i skye bo rnams kyis yod pa ma yin pa la phyin ci log gis bsgrubs shing | rang gi rnam par rtog pa las byung ba'o || gsol pa bcom ldan 'das sems can dmyal ba dag gang du yang dag par 'du bar 'gyur | bcom ldan 'das kyis bka' stsal[4] pa 'jam dpal sems can dmyal ba dag ni nam mkhar yang dag par 'du bar 'gyur ro || [G 22a] 'jam dpal de ji snyam du sems | [D 17a] sems can dmyal ba rang gi rnam par rtog pa las byung ngam | 'on te ngo bo nyid las byung | gsol pa bcom ldan 'das byis pa so so'i skye bo rnams ni rang gi rnam par[5] rtog pa kho nas sems can dmyal ba dang | dud 'gro'i skye gnas dang | gshin rje'i 'jig rten du 'du shes te | de dag ma mchis pa la sgro btags pa'i slad du tshor ba sdug bsngal myong zhing | ngan song gsum du sdug bsngal nyams su myong bar 'gyur lags so ||

---

[1] D: yang

[2] P: da

[3] D: scal

[4] D: scal; N: sal

[5] P, N, G: without rnam par

bcom ldan 'das bdag gis ni ji ltar sems can dmyal ba ma khums pa de bzhin du sems can dmyal ba'i sdug bsngal yang ma khums so || bcom ldan 'das 'di lta ste skyes bu la la zhig gnyid kyis log ste rmi lam na bdag nyid sems can dmyal bar ltung bar 'du shes par 'gyur[1] la | des de na[2] lcags kyi bum pa skyes bu du ma dang ldan pa khol ba 'bar bar bdag nyid bcug par yang 'du shes par 'gyur ro || des de na sdug bsngal gyi tshor ba drag cing mi bzad la brnag[3] par dka'[4] zhing yid du mi 'ong ba myong bar 'gyur ro || des de na yid kyi yongs su gdung ba[5] myong bar 'gyur | de de na [P 19a] skrag par 'gyur | dngangs[6] par 'gyur | kun tu dngangs par 'gyur ro || de de nas sad[7] par gyur zhing rlom pa dang bcas pas kye ma sdug bsngal lo || kye ma sdug bsngal lo zhes du zhing cho nges 'debs la smre sngags 'don par 'gyur lags so || de nas de la grogs po dang gnyen[8] dang snag gi gnyen mtshams rnams kyis ci zhig gis 'di ltar khyod [G 22b] sdug bsngal bar gyur zhes dris pa dang | de grogs po dang gnyen dang snag gi gnyen mtshams [N 19a] de dag la 'di skad du ngas ni sems [C 17a] can dmyal ba'i sdug bsngal nyams su myong ngo zhes smra bar bgyid | de bdag gis ni sems can dmyal ba'i sdug bsngal nyams su myong na | khyed cag ci zhig gis 'di ltar khyod sdug bsngal bar gyur zhes 'dri bar byed dam zhes de dag la cho

---

[1] P, N, G: gyur

[2] D, C: ni

[3] P, N, G: gnag

[4] P, G: dga'

[5] D, C: gdung ba yongs su for yongs su gdung ba

[6] N: ddangs

[7] N: sang

[8] P, G: mnyen

nges 'debs par bgyid | spyo bar bgyid do || [PsP$_L$ 52] de nas skyes bu de la grogs po dang gnyen dang snag gi gnyen mtshams de dag 'di skad du | kye skyes bu ma 'jigs shig ma 'jigs shig | khyod ni gnyid kyis log pa yin gyi | khyod khyim 'di nas gar [D 17b] yang song ba med do zhes smra bar bgyid do || de yang bdag ni gnyid kyis log par gyur te | yang dag pa ma yin pa 'di bdag gis kun tu[1] brtags so snyam du de la dran pa skye bar 'gyur zhing | slar yang de yid bde ba 'thob par 'gyur lags so ||

bcom ldan 'das ji ltar skyes bu gnyid kyis log pa de yod pa ma[2] yin pa la sgro btags nas bdag nyid rmi lam du dmyal bar song bar[3] 'du shes par 'gyur ba de bzhin du | bcom ldan 'das byis pa so so'i skye bo bden pa ma lags pa'i 'dod chags kyis kun nas bcings pa thams cad bud med la mtshan mar rtog par bgyid do || de dag bud med la mtshan mar brtags[4] nas bdag nyid de dag dang lhan cig rtse zhing dga' bar 'du shes so || byis pa so so'i skye bo de 'di snyam du [P 19b] bdag ni skyes pa'o || 'di ni bud med do || bud med 'di bdag gi'o snyam du 'gyur [G 23a] zhing de 'dun pa'i 'dod chags kyis kun nas dkris pa'i sems des longs spyod tshol bar sems 'jug par 'gyur lags so || de gzhi de las 'thab pa dang rtsod pa dang g-yul 'gyed par bgyid cing | gdug pa'i dbang po dang ldan pa de la 'khon[5] du 'dzin pa 'byung bar 'gyur lags so || rlom pa dang bcas pa de 'du shes phyin ci log

---

[1] D, C: du

[2] C: me

[3] D, C: bas

[4] P, N, G: btags

[5] D, C: khon

des ’chi ba’i dus bgyis[1] par gyur nas bdag nyid bskal pa stong phrag mang por sems can dmyal ba dag tu sdug bsngal gyi[2] tshor ba myong bar ’du shes so ‖ [N 19b]

bcom ldan ’das ji ltar skyes bu de la grogs po dang | gnyen dang snag gi gnyen mtshams rnams kyis ’di skad du kye[3] skyes bu ma ’jigs shig[4] ma ’jigs shig khyod ni gnyid kyis [C 17b] log pa yin gyi | khyod khyim ’di nas gar yang song ba med do zhes smra bar bgyid pa de bzhin du | bcom ldan ’das sangs rgyas bcom ldan ’das rnams kyis kyang phyin ci log bzhis phyin ci log tu gyur pa’i sems can rnams la ’di skad du chos bstan te | ’di la bud med kyang med | skyes pa yang med | sems can yang med | srog kyang med | gso ba yang med | gang zag kyang med de | chos ’di dag thams cad ni log[5] pa | chos ’di dag thams cad ni yod pa ma yin pa | chos ’di dag thams cad [D 18a] ni phyin ci log gis bsgrubs pa | [PsP$_L$ 53] chos ’di dag thams cad ni sgyu ma lta bu | chos ’di dag thams cad ni[6] rmi lam lta bu | chos ’di dag thams cad ni sprul pa lta bu | chos ’di dag thams cad ni chu zla lta bu ste zhes rgyas par ’byung ba dang | de bzhin du de dag [G 23b] de bzhin gshegs pa’i chos bstan pa thos nas chos thams cad ’dod chags dang bral bar khums so ‖ chos thams cad zhe sdang dang bral ba dang | gti mug dang bral ba dang | ngo bo nyid

[1] N: bgyi

[2] N: ’di

[3] P: kyi

[4] P, N, G: om. shig

[5] D: lag

[6] P, N, G: om. chos ’di dag thams cad ni

med pa dang sgrib pa med par [P 20a] khums so || de dag sems nam mkha'[1] la gnas pas 'chi ba'i dus bgyid par 'gyur zhing | 'chi ba'i dus bgyis ma thag tu phung po lhag ma med pa'i mya ngan las 'das pa'i dbyings su mya ngan las 'da' ste | bcom[2] ldan 'das de ltar bdag gis sems can dmyal ba khums lags so

zhes gsungs so ||

§80. 'phags pa nye ba 'khor gyis zhus pa las kyang |

sems dmyal 'jigs pa nga yis bstan byas te ||
sems can stong phrag du ma skyo byas kyang ||
gang dag shi 'phos ngan song drag 'gro ba'i ||
'gro ba de dag nam yang yod ma yin ||

gang dag ral gri mda' chen mtshon 'byin pa'i ||
gnod pa byed pa yod pa ma yin te ||
rtog pa'i dbang gis ngan song de dag na ||
lus la 'bab mthong de na mtshon cha med || [PsP$_L$ 54]

sna tshogs yid [N 20a] dga' me tog kha bye zhing ||
gser gyi khang mchog 'bar ba yid 'ong ba ||
'di na de la 'ang byed pa[3] 'ga' med do[4] ||
de dag rtog pa'i dbang gis bzhag[5] pa yin ||

---

[1] N: abbr.? namkha'

[2] N: bcoṃ

[3] Python (1973: 59; Python's Tibetan edition of the *sūtra* is based on P and N): po. Upālipariprcchā Tib D: pa.

[4] Python (1973: 59): de (only in N)

[5] D: gzhag

rtog[1] pa'i dbang gis 'jig rten rnam brtags te ||
'du shes 'dzin pas byis pa rnam par phye ||
'dzin dang 'dzin [C 18a] med de yang 'byung min te ||
yongs su rtog pa sgyu[2] ma smig rgyu bzhin ||

zhes gsungs so || de'i phyir de ltar na dngos po yod pa ma yin pa'i rang bzhin can phyin ci log gis bzhag pa rnams ni 'khor ba na byis pa rnams [G 24a] kyi kun nas nyon mongs pa'i rgyur 'gyur ro zhes bya bar gnas so ||

dngos po brdzun[3] pa'i rang bzhin can rnams ji ltar kun nas nyon mongs pa dang | rnam par byang ba'i rgyu nyid yin pa de ltar ni rgyas par dbu ma la 'jugs pa las nges par bya'o ||

§81. 'dir smras pa | [D 18b] gal te bdag dang gzhan dang gnyi ga dang rgyu med pa las dngos po rnams skye ba[4] yod pa ma yin na | ji ltar[5] bcom ldan 'das kyis ma rig pa'i rkyen gyis 'du byed rnams zhes gsungs |

bshad par bya ste | 'di ni kun [P 20b] rdzob[6] yin gyi de kho na nyid ni ma yin no ||

§82. ci kun rdzob kyi[1] rnam par gzhag[2] pa brjod par bya ba yin nam zhe na |

---

[1] N: rtogs
[2] P: sgya
[3] P, N, G: rdzun
[4] C: pa
[5] N: om. ji ltar
[6] D, C: rdzob pa

rkyen nyid ’di pa tsam gyis kun rdzob grub par khas len gyi[3] | phyogs bzhi khas blangs pa’i sgo nas ni ma yin te | dngos po rang bzhin dang bcas pa smra bar thal bar ’gyur ba’i phyir dang | de yang rigs pa ma yin pa’i phyir ro || rkyen nyid ’di pa tsam [PsP_L 55] zhig khas blangs na ni rgyu dang ’bras bu gnyis phan tshun ltos[4] pa’i phyir | ngo bo nyid kyis grub pa yod pa ma yin pas dngos po rang bzhin dang bcas par smra bar ’gyur ba ma yin no ||

de nyid kyi phyir |

> sdug bsngal rang gis byas pa dang ||
> gzhan gyis byas dang gnyi gas byas ||
> rgyu med rtog ge ba yis ’dod ||
> khyod kyis brten nas ’byung bar gsungs ||

zhes gsungs so || ’di nyid las kyang |

> byed po las la brten byas shing ||
> las kyang byed po de nyid la[5] ||
> brten nas ’byung ba ma gtogs pa[6] ||
> grub pa’i [N 20b] rgyu ni ma mthong ngo ||

zhes ’chad par ’gyur ro ||

---

[1] P: without kyi

[2] P, N, G: bzhag

[3] P: gyis

[4] P, N, G: bltos

[5] N: las

[6] MMK_T P: par; BP_{ed}: par; ABh_{ed}: par; but MMK_T D: pa; $MABh_{ed}$: pa; PsP chapter 8 D, P: pa

bcom ldan 'das [G 24b] kyis kyang de la chos kyi brda ni 'di yin te | 'di lta ste 'di yod pas 'di 'byung la | 'di[1] skyes pas 'di skye ste | gang 'di ma rig pa'i rkyen gyis 'du byed rnams | 'du byed kyi rkyen gyis rnam par shes pa zhes bya ba la sogs pa 'di tsam zhig kho na gsungs so[2] ||

§83. 'dir 'ga' [C 18b] zhig dag rgol bar byed de |

> dngos po rnams skye ba med do snyam pa'i nges pa 'di tshad ma las skyes pa zhig gam | 'on te tshad ma ma yin pa las skyes pa zhig yin grang[3] | de la gal te tshad ma las skyes par 'dod na ni | tshad ma dag ni du zhig | mtshan nyid ni gang | yul dag ni ci zhig | ci bdag las skyes pa zhig gam | gzhan nam gnyi ga 'am rgyu med pa las yin zhes bya ba 'di brjod par bya'o || 'on te tshad ma ma[4] yin pa las skyes pa yin na ni | de ni mi rigs te | gzhal bya rtogs pa ni[5] tshad ma la rag [P 21a] las pa'i phyir te | [D 19a] rtogs par ma gyur pa'i don ni tshad ma med par rtogs par mi nus so[6] || tshad ma med pas don rtogs pa yang med na ni khyod kyi yang dag pa'i nges pa 'di ga las 'gyur te | de'i phyir dngos po rnams skye ba med do zhes bya ba 'di ni rigs pa ma yin no || yang na khyed kyi dngos po rnams skye ba med do zhes bya ba'i nges pa 'di gang las gyur pa 'di nyid las nga'i dngos po thams cad yod pa yin no zhes bya ba yang yin la | yang ji ltar khyod kyi dngos po thams cad skye ba med do zhes

[1] N: illegible

[2] N: abbr. nuso

[3] N: gang

[4] C: om.

[5] N: om.

[6] N: abbr. gnaso

> bya ba'i nges pa 'dir 'gyur ba de kho na ltar [PsP$_L$ 56] nga'i dngos po thams cad skye bar yang 'gyur ro ‖ ci ste khyod la dngos po thams cad skye ba med do snyam[1] pa'i nges pa 'di med na ni | [G 25a] de'i tshe rang nyid kyis kyang ma nges pas[2] gzhan khong du chud par byed pa mi srid pa'i phyir bstan bcos[3] rtsom pa don med pa nyid du 'gyur te | des na dngos po thams cad bkag pa med par yod pa yin no zhe[4] na |

brjod par bya ste | gal te kho bo cag la nges pa zhes bya ba 'ga'[5] zhig yod par 'gyur na ni | de tshad ma las skyes pa 'am | tshad ma ma yin pa las skyes pa zhig tu [N 21a] 'gyur na | yod pa ni ma yin no ‖ ci'i phyir zhe na | 'dir ma nges pa yod na ni de la ltos[6] shing de'i gnyen por gyur pa'i nges pa yang yod par 'gyur ba zhig na | gang gi tshe re zhig kho bo cag la ma nges pa nyid yod pa ma yin pa de'i tshe[7] ni de dang[8] 'gal ba'i nges[9] pa yod par ga la 'gyur te | 'brel pa can gzhan la ma ltos[10] pa'i phyir | bong bu'i rwa'i ring ba[11] dang thung ba nyid bzhin no ‖ gang gi tshe de ltar nges pa [PsP$_L$ 57] med pa de'i tshe ci zhig [C 19a] 'grub par bya ba'i phyir tshad ma dag yongs su rtog par byed[12] |

---

[1] P, N, G: snyams

[2] TKK (2001: 4): em. pa la (PsP Skt: aniścitasya). The text makes sense as it stands.

[3] P, N, G: chos

[4] N: zhes

[5] P: 'gag

[6] P, N, G: bltos

[7] N: illegible

[8] N: illegible

[9] P: ngas

[10] P, N, G: bltos

[11] D, C: po; TKK (2001: 6): po

[12] N: illegible

de dag gi grangs dang mtshan nyid dang yul dang | bdag gam gzhan nam gnyi ga 'am rgyu med pa las skye zhes bya bar yang ga la 'gyur te | 'di dag thams cad ni kho bo cag gis brjod par bya ba ma yin pa [P 21b] zhig go ||

§84. gal te de ltar khyod la nges pa yod pa ma yin na | khyed cag gi dngos po rnams ni | bdag las ma yin gzhan las min | gnyis las ma yin rgyu med min | zhes bya ba'i nges pa'i rang bzhin gyi ngag 'di ji ltar dmigs she na |

brjod par bya ste | nges[1] par gyur pa'i ngag 'di ni rang la[2] grub pa'i[3] 'thad [D 19b] pa'i sgo nas 'jig rten la yod kyi | 'phags pa rnams la ni ma yin no || [G 25b]

§85. ci 'phags pa rnams la rigs pa mi mnga' 'am zhe na |

yod pa 'am med pa 'di sus smras | 'phags pa rnams kyi don dam pa ni cang[4] mi gsung[5] ba yin te | de'i phyir gang la[6] 'thad pa dang 'thad pa ma yin pa mi mnga' bar 'gyur ba de dag la spros pa mnga' bar ga la 'gyur ||

§86. gal te 'phags pa rnams 'thad pa[7] gsung bar mi mdzad na | da ni ci zhig gis 'jig rten pas[1] don dam pa khong du chud par mdzad ce na |

---

[1] C: des

[2] N: illegible

[3] N: illegible

[4] C: cad

[5] N: gsungs

[6] N: phyir gang la illegible

[7] G: par

’phags pa rnams[2] ni ’jig rten gyi[3] tha snyad kyis[4] ’thad pa mi gsung[5] gi | ’on kyang ’jig rten kho na la rab tu grags pa’i ’thad pa gang yin pa de dag gzhan rtogs par bya ba’i phyir zhal gyis bzhes nas de nyid kyis ’jig rten khong[6] du chud par mdzad do || ji ltar lus la mi gtsang ba[7] [N 21b] nyid yod du zin kyang phyin ci log gi rjes su song ba’i ’dod chags can rnams kyis dmigs par mi ’gyur zhing | yang dag pa ma yin yang gtsang ba’i rnam par sgro btags[8] nas yongs su nyon mongs par ’gyur ro || de dag ’dod chags dang bral bar bya ba’i phyir de bzhin gshegs pa’i sprul pa ’am lhas | lus ’di la skra zhes bya ba la sogs pas sngar[9] gtsang[10] ba’i ’du shes kyis bkab pa’i lus kyi[11] skyon rnams nye bar ston par byed do || de dag kyang gtsang ba’i ’du shes de dang bral bas ’dod chags dang bral ba thob par ’gyur ba [PsP$_L$ 58] de bzhin[12] du ’di na[13] so so’i skye bo dag kyang ma rig[14] pa’i rab rib kyis [C 19b] blo gros kyi mig nyams pa nyid kyis dngos po rnams kyi rang bzhin phyin ci log | [P 22a] ’phags pa rnams kyis rnam pa thams cad du ma

---

[1] TKK (2001: 8): em. pa la. *’jig rten pa* can be understood as the agent of *khong du chud pa*

[2] N: illegible

[3] P, N, G: gyis

[4] P, N, G: kyi

[5] N: gsungs

[6] P, N, G: khung

[7] N: mi gtsang ba illegible

[8] N: brtags

[9] D: sdar

[10] N: gtsad

[11] P, N, G: kyis

[12] N: illegible

[13] P, N, G: nas

[14] P: rigs

dmigs pa'i bdag nyid can dang [G 26a] | 'ga' zhig tu khyad par 'ga' zhig[1] lhag par sgro btags nas ches[2] shin tu nyon mongs par 'gyur te | de dag da ltar[3] 'phags pa rnams kyis bum pa yod pa 'jim[4] pa la sogs pa dag las skye ba ma yin no zhes khas blangs pa de bzhin du skyes pa'i snga rol nas yod pa la yang skye ba yod pa ma yin te | yod[5] pa'i phyir ro zhes bya bar nges par gyis shig | yang ji ltar me dang sol ba la sogs pa gzhan du gyur pa dag las myu gu skye ba yod pa ma yin no zhes [D 20a] bya bar khas blangs pa de bzhin du sa bon la[6] sogs pa brjod par 'dod pa dag las kyang yod pa ma yin no zhes nges par gyis shig ||

§87. ci ste yang 'di ni kho bo cag gis nyams su myong ba yin no snyam na 'di yang mi rigs te |

'di ltar nyams su myong ba ni brdzun[7] pa'i don can yin te | nyams su myong ba yin pa'i phyir rab rib can gyis[8] zla ba gnyis nyams su myong ba bzhin no || de'i phyir nyams su myong ba yang bsgrub par bya ba dang mtshungs pa nyid yin pa'i phyir des phyir[9] bzlog par[10]

---

[1] N: khyad par 'ga' zhig illegible

[2] Em.: ches. P, N, G, D, C: chos

[3] P, N, G: lta

[4] N: 'dzim

[5] N: pa ma yin te | yod illegible

[6] N: le?

[7] P, N, G: rdzun

[8] N: gyi

[9] P, N, G: om. des phyir

[10] C: yar

rigs[1] pa ma yin no zhes de dag la grags pa nyid kyis khong du chud par mdzad pa yin no ||

§88. de'i phyir dngos po rnams skye ba med pa yin no || de ltar re zhig de'i rang bzhin phyin ci[2] log [N 22a] lhag par sgro btags pa'i gnyen por rab tu byed pa dang po brtsams pa yin no || de nas khyad par 'ga' zhig 'ga' zhig tu sgro btags pa'i khyad par de bsal[3] bar bya ba'i phyir rab tu byed pa lhag ma brtsams pa yin te | rten cing 'brel par 'byung ba la 'gro ba[4] po dang | bgrod par [G 26b] bya ba dang 'gro ba[5] la sogs pa[6] khyad par ro cog ma lus pa yang yod pa ma yin no zhes bstan par bya ba'i don du'o ||

§89. ci ste tshad ma dang gzhal bya'i tha snyad 'jig rten pa 'di nyid[7] kho bo cag gi bstan bcos su [P 22b] brjod pa yin no snyam na | 'o na ni de brjod pa'i dgos pa bsnyad par bya dgos so ||

§90. gal te rtog ge pa dag gis mtshan nyid phyin ci log [PsP$_L$ 59] brjod pas | de brlag par byas pas kho bo cag gis de'i mtshan nyid yang dag par brjod pa yin no zhe na |

'di yang mi [C 20a] rigs te | gal te 'jig rten la rtog ge ngan pas mtshan nyid phyin ci log brjod pas byas pa'i mtshon bya phyin ci log yod par

---

[1] N: rig

[2] N: phyin ci illegible

[3] N: gsal

[4] P, N, G: ba dang

[5] D: bar bya ba

[6] C: ma

[7] N: nyid ni

’gyur na ni de’i[1] don du ’bad ba ’bras bu dang bcas par ’gyur ba zhig na | de ni de ltar yang ma yin pas ’bad pa ’di don med pa nyid do ||

§91. gzhan yang gal te gzhal bya rtogs pa tshad ma la rag las pa yin na[2] | tshad ma de dag gang gis yongs su gcod par byed ces bya ba la sogs pa rtsod pa[3] bzlog pa las bshad pa’i skyon de ma spangs pas yang dag pa’i mtshan nyid gsal bar byed pa nyid kyang yod pa ma yin no ||

§92. gzhan yang gal te rang dang spyi’i[4] mtshan nyid gnyis kyi dbang gis tshad[5] ma gnyis [D 20b] smras[6] na ni | ci mtshan nyid de gnyis gang la yod pa’i mtshan gzhi de yod dam ’on te med | gal te yod na ni de’i tshe de dag las gzhan[7] pa’i[8] gzhal bya yod pas ji ltar tshad ma gnyis yin | ’on te mtshan gzhi med na ni de’i tshe rten med pas[9] mtshan nyid kyang yod pa ma yin pas[10] ji ltar tshad ma gnyis su [G 27a] ’gyur te |

mtshan nyid ’jug pa ma yin na ||
mtshan gzhi ’thad par mi ’gyur ro ||
mtshan gzhi ’thad pa ma yin na ||

---

[1] P, N: di’i

[2] N: om.

[3] P, N: om. rtsod pa

[4] P: sbyi’i

[5] Em.: tshad. P, N, G, D, C: mtshan

[6] D, C: smra

[7] D, C: om.

[8] D, C: om.

[9] P: pas ni

[10] P, N, G: pa

mtshan nyid kyang ni yod ma yin ||

zhes 'chad par 'gyur ro || [PsP$_L$ 60]

§93. ci ste yang 'dis [N 22b] mtshon par byed pas ni mtshan nyid ma yin gyi | 'o na ci zhe na | byed pa dang lu ṭa[1] ni phal che'o zhes bya bas las la lyuṭa[2] byas nas 'di mtshon par bya bas na mtshan nyid yin no snyam na |

de lta na yang de nyid kyis mtshon par bya ba nyid du mi srid pa'i phyir gang gis de mtshon par byed pa'i byed pa de dang las tha dad pa yin pa'i phyir nyes pa de nyid du 'gyur ro || [P 23a]

§94. ci ste shes pa byed pa yin pa'i phyir la | de yang rang gi mtshan nyid kyi khongs su 'du ba'i phyir nyes pa 'di med do snyam na |

bshad par bya ste | re zhig 'dir ji ltar des de[3] mtshon par byed pas[4] sa'i sra ba dang | tshor ba'i myong ba dang | rnam par shes pa'i yul so sor rnam par rig pa ltar bdag nyid kyi rang gi ngo bo gzhan dang thun mong ma yin pa gang yin pa de ni rang gi mtshan nyid yin na | rab tu grags pa dang rjes su 'brel pa'i [C 20b] bye brag tu bshad pa bor nas | las su sgrub pa khas len zhing rnam par shes pa byed pa'i ngo bor rtogs pas ni | rang gi mtshan nyid kho na las nyid yin zhing | rang gi mtshan nyid gzhan ni byed pa'i ngo bo[5] yin no zhes bya ba 'di smras par 'gyur ro [PsP$_L$ 61] || de la gal te rnam par shes pa'i rang gi mtshan

---

[1] P, G: lu ṭā; N: lu tā

[2] P, G: lu ṭā; N: lu tā

[3] TKK (2001: 16, n. 1) states that N omits *de* but N attests it.

[4] N, C: pa'i

[5] N: bo nyid

nyid byed pa yin na ni | de la tha dad par gyur pa'i las shig yod par 'gyur dgos pas nyes pa de nyid du 'gyur ro ||

§95. ci ste sa la sogs par [G 27b] gtogs pa'i sra ba la sogs[1] pa rnam par shes pas rtogs par bya ba gang yin pa de ni de'i las yin la | de yang rang gi mtshan nyid las tha dad pa ma yin no snyam na |

de lta na ni 'o na rnam par shes pa'i rang gi mtshan nyid las ma yin pa'i phyir gzhal bya nyid du mi 'gyur te | las kyi rang bzhin gyi rang [D 21a] gi mtshan nyid kho na gzhal bya yin pa'i phyir ro || de'i phyir gzhal bya ni rnam pa gnyis te | rang gi mtshan nyid dang spyi'i mtshan nyid do zhes bya bar | rang gi mtshan nyid cung zad cig ni gzhal bya yin te | mtshon par bya bas na zhes[2] de ltar bsnyad pa gang yin pa'o || cung zad cig ni gzhal bya ma yin te 'dis mtshon par byed pas na zhes brjod pa gang yin pa'o zhes khyad par 'di tsam zhig brjod par bya dgos so || ci ste de[3] yang las su [N 23a] sgrub pa yin na ni | de'i tshe de la byed pa gzhan zhig yod par bya dgos la | shes [P 23b] pa gzhan zhig byed pa'i ngo bor rtog[4] na yang thug pa med pa'i skyon du 'gyur ro ||

§96. ci ste rang rig pa yod de des na rang rig pas de[5] 'dzin pa'i phyir las nyid[6] yin dang | gzhal bya'i khongs su 'du ba yod pa yin no snyam du sems na |

---

[1] D: sags

[2] P: zhis

[3] P, N, G: without de

[4] D, C: rtogs

[5] Em. de. P, N, G: des; D, C: add preceding des. TKK (2001: 18): as D

[6] P, N, G: om. nyid

bshad par bya ste | dbu ma la 'jug pa las rang rig pa rgyas par bkag pa'i phyir rang gi mtshan nyid ni [PsP$_L$ 62] rang gi mtshan nyid gzhan gyis mtshon par byed pa[1] la | de yang rang rig pa des mtshon par byed do zhes bya ba ni rigs pa ma yin no || gzhan yang shes pa de yang mi srid pa'i phyir rang gi mtshan nyid las tha dad par ma grub la | mtshan gzhi med na rten med pa'i mtshan [G 28a] nyid 'jug pa med pa'i phyir rnam pa thams cad du yod pa ma yin pas rang rig pa ga la yod |

de skad du yang 'phags [C 21a] pa gtsug na rin po ches zhus pa las |

> de sems yang dag par rjes su ma mthong bas | sems gang las byung zhes sems kyi rgyun kun tu[2] tshol zhing de 'di snyam du sems te | dmigs pa yod pa las sems 'byung bar[3] 'gyur ro snyam mo || de yang 'di[4] snyam du sems te | ci dmigs pa de yang gzhan la sems de yang gzhan nam | 'on te dmigs pa gang yin pa de nyid sems yin | gal te re[5] zhig dmigs pa yang gzhan la sems kyang gzhan na ni sems de gnyis su 'gyur ro || 'on te dmigs pa gang yin pa de nyid sems yin na ni | sems kyis[6] sems de ji ltar mthong bar 'gyur te | sems kyis[7] sems de mthong bar mi rung ngo || 'di lta ste dper na ral gri'i so de nyid kyis ral gri'i so de nyid [PsP$_L$ 63] bcad [D 21b] par mi nus pa dang | sor mo'i rtse mo de nyid gyis sor mo'i rtse mo de nyid la reg par mi nus pa de

---

[1] P, N, G: om. pa

[2] D, C: du

[3] D: par

[4] C: 'did

[5] N: reg

[6] P, N, G: kyi

[7] N: kyi

bzhin du | sems de nyid kyis sems de nyid mthong bar mi nus so snyam nas | de 'di ltar tshul bzhin rab tu sbyor ba la | gang sems mi gnas pa | chad pa ma yin pa | rtag[1] pa ma yin [P 24a] pa | ther zug tu mi gnas pa | rgyu med pa ma yin pa[2] | rkyen dang mi 'gal ba | [N 23b] de las kyang ma yin pa[3] | gzhan las kyang ma yin pa | de nyid kyang ma yin pa[4] gzhan yang ma yin pa'i sems kyi rgyud sems kyi 'khri shing | sems kyi chos nyid | sems kyi mi gnas pa dang | sems kyi[5] rgyu ba med pa dang | sems snang ba med pa [G 28b] dang | sems kyi rang gi mtshan nyid de[6] ji ltar de bzhin nyid 'khrug par mi byed pa de ltar shes so || de ltar mthong ngo || de bzhin nyid ji lta ba de bzhin du sems de dag dben pa nyid du rab tu shes[7] | de bzhin du mthong ba 'di ni rigs kyi bu byang chub sems dpa'i sems la sems kyi rjes su lta ba'i dran pa nye bar gzhag pa'i spyod pa yongs su dag pa'o zhes gsungs so ||

de'i phyir de ltar rang rig pa med la | de med pas gang zhig gang gis mtshon par byed |

§97. gzhan yang mtshan nyid de mtshan gzhi las tha dad par 'gyur ram tha mi dad par 'gyur grang | [C 21b] de la gal te re zhig tha dad pa

---

[1] P, N, G: brtag

[2] D, C: om.

[3] P, N, G: om.; C: la

[4] P, N, G: om.

[5] D, C: om.

[6] N: unclear, appears to be missing

[7] G: adds following te

yin na ni | de'i tshe[1] mtshan gzhi las tha dad pa'i phyir mtshan nyid ma yin pa bzhin du mtshan nyid kyang mtshan nyid ma yin par 'gyur la | mtshan nyid las tha dad pa'i phyir mtshan gzhi yang mtshan gzhi ma yin pa[2] ltar mtshan gzhir mi 'gyur ro [PsP$_L$ 64] || de bzhin du mtshan nyid mtshan gzhi[3] las tha dad pa'i phyir mtshan gzhi mtshan nyid la ltos[4] pa med par yang 'gyur te | de'i phyir de mtshan gzhi ma yin te | mtshan nyid la ltos[5] pa med pa'i phyir nam mkha'i me tog bzhin no || ci ste mtshan nyid dang mtshan nyid kyi gzhi dag tha mi dad pa[6] yin na ni | de'i tshe mtshan nyid las tha mi dad pa'i phyir | mtshan nyid kyi[7] rang gi bdag nyid bzhin du mtshan gzhi'i mtshan gzhi nyid nyams par 'gyur ro || mtshan gzhi las tha mi dad pa'i phyir mtshan nyid kyang mtshan nyid [P 24b] kyi rang bzhin du mi 'gyur te | mtshan gzhi'i rang gi bdag nyid bzhin no ||

ji skad du | [D 22a]

mtshan nyid [G 29a] mtshan gzhi las gzhan na ||
mtshan gzhi de mtshan med par 'gyur ||
tha dad med na de dag ni ||
med par khyod kyis gsal bar bstan ||

[1] P, N, G: om.

[2] N: par

[3] N: gzhin

[4] P, N, G: bltos

[5] P, N, G: bltos

[6] D, C: pa nyid

[7] P, N, G: kyi phyir

zhes bshad do || de nyid dang gzhan nyid las ma gtogs par mtshan gzhi dang mtshan nyid 'grub pa'i thabs gzhan yod pa yang ma yin te |

de skad du | [N 24a]

gang dag dngos po gcig pa dang ||
dngos po gzhan pa nyid du ni ||
'grub par 'gyur ba yod min na ||
de gnyis grub pa ji ltar yod ||

ces 'chad par 'gyur ro ||

§98. ci ste brjod du med pa nyid du 'grub par 'gyur ro zhe na |

de ni 'di ltar ma yin te | phan tshun rnam par dbye ba yongs su shes pa med pa yin na | brjod du med pa nyid ces bya bar 'gyur na | gang na rnam par dbye[1] ba yongs su shes par 'gyur ba med pa der ni 'di ni mtshan nyid do || 'di ni mtshan gzhi'o zhes khyad par du yongs su gcod pa med pas gnyi ga yang med pa nyid de[2] | de'i phyir brjod du med pa nyid du yang grub[3] pa med do[4] ||

§99. gzhan yang gal te shes pa byed pa yin na | yul yongs su gcod pa'i byed pa po gang zhig yin | byed pa po med par [PsP$_L$ 65] byed pa la sogs pa rnams [C 22a] yod pa yang ma yin te | gcod pa'i bya ba bzhin no || ci ste der sems la byed pa po nyid du rtog na | de yang rigs pa ma yin te |

---

[1] C: dpye

[2] N: nyid de illegible

[3] P: 'grub

[4] D, C: de

’di ltar don tsam lta ba ni sems kyi bya ba yin la don gyi khyad par lta ba ni sems las byung ba rnams kyi bya ba yin te |

> de la don mthong rnam par shes ||
> de yi khyad par[1] sems las byung ||

zhes khas blangs[2] pa’i phyir ro || byed pa la sogs pa rnams [G 29b] ni bdag nyid ji lta bu’i bya ba phal pa sgrub pa’i sgo nas | gtso bor gyur pa’i bya ba cig bsgrub par bya ba la yan lag gi ngo bor gyur pa las byed pa la sogs [P 25a] pa nyid du ’gyur na | ’dir ni shes pa dang[3] rnam par shes pa gnyis la gtso bor gyur pa’i bya ba gcig med do || ’o na ci zhe na | rnam par shes pa’i gtso bor gyur pa’i bya ba ni don tsam yongs su gcod pa yin la | don gyi khyad par yongs su gcod pa ni shes pa’i gtso bor gyur pa’i bya ba yin te | des na shes pa byed pa nyid ma yin la | sems kyang byed pa po nyid ma [D 22b] yin no || de’i phyir nyes pa de nyid du ’gyur ro ||

§100. ci ste chos thams cad bdag med pa zhes bya ba’i lung las na | byed pa po rnam pa thams cad du med pa’i phyir bya ba la sogs pa’i tha snyad ni byed pa po med kyang yod pa nyid do snyam na |

’di yang yod pa ma yin [N 24b] te[4] | lung gi don yang dag par ma bzung ba’i phyir ro || ’di yang dbu ma la[5] ’jug pa las bstan zin to || [PsP$_L$ 66]

---

[1] P, N, G: pas

[2] TKK (2001: 24, n. 4) reports that N presents *blang ba’i* but it also reads *blangs pa’i*

[3] D, C: om.

[4] G: *t* illegible

[5] D, C: om.; according to TKK (2001: 26, n. 2) N also omits *la* but *la* is attested

§101. ci ste yang dper na mchi gu'i lus sgra gcan gyi[1] mgo zhes bya ba la | lus dang mgo las tha dad pa'i khyad par med kyang khyad par dang khyad par gyi gzhi'i dngos po yod pa de bzhin du | rang gi mtshan nyid las tha dad pa'i sa[2] la sogs pa med kyang sa'i rang gi mtshan nyid ces bya bar 'gyur ro snyam na |

de ni de ltar ma yin te | mi mtshungs pa'i phyir ro || lus dang mgo'i sgra dag[3] ni blo dang lag pa la sogs pa ltar lhan cig 'byung ba'i[4] dngos po gzhan la ltos[5] pa dang bcas te 'jug pas | lus dang mgo'i[6] sgra tsam la dmigs pa'i blo skyes pa lta zhig gang gi[7] lus [G 30a] gang gi mgo snyam du lhan cig spyod[8] pa'i dngos po gzhan la re ba dang bcas pa nyid du 'gyur la | cig shos kyang khyad par gzhan[9] dang 'brel pa bsal bar [C 22b] 'dod pas 'jig rten pa'i brda'i rjes su byed pa | khyad par mchi gu dang sgra gcan gyi sgras rtogs pa po'i re ba sel bar byed do zhes bya bar rigs[10] | 'dir ni sra ba la sogs pa las tha dad pa'i sa la [P 25b] sogs pa med pas khyad par dang khyad par can gyi dngos po mi rigs so ||

---

[1] N: gyis

[2] P, N, G: las

[3] N: ngag

[4] C: ba'i ba'i

[5] P, N, G: bltos

[6] P, N, G: yi

[7] P, N, G: gis

[8] Em.: spyod. P, N, G, D, C: dpyod

[9] P, N, G: gzhag

[10] D, C: rigs na

§102. gal te mu stegs pa[1] dag gis mtshan gzhi tha dad par khas blangs pa'i phyir de'i ngor khyad par brjod pa la skyon med do zhe na | [PsP$_L$ 67]

de ni de ltar ma yin te | mu stegs pas kun tu brtags pa'i dngos po rigs pa dang 'gal ba dag ni rang gi gzhung lugs la khas blang bar mi rigs te | tshad ma gzhan la sogs pa khas blangs[2] par thal bar 'gyur ba'i phyir ro ||

§103. gzhan yang lus kyi rten can khyad par du[3] byed pa 'jigs rten pa'i tha snyad kyi yan lag tu gyur pa ma brtags na grub pa rten pa po mchi gu dang | mgo'i rten can brten pa po sgra gcan ni gang zag la sogs par brtags pa ltar yod [D 23a] pa'i phyir dpe 'di rigs pa ma yin no ||

§104. gal te de tsam zhig dmigs pas lus dang mgo las tha dad pa'i don gzhan ma grub pa'i phyir dpe grub pa nyid do zhe na |

de ni de ltar ma yin te | 'jig rten pa'i [N 25a] tha snyad la de ltar rnam par dpyod pa mi 'jug pa'i phyir dang | 'jig rten pa'i dngos po rnams ni ma brtags par yod pa'i phyir ro || ji ltar rnam par dpyad na gzugs la sogs pa las tha dad par bdag med mod kyi | [G 30b] 'on kyang phung po la brten nas 'jig rten gyi kun rdzob tu 'di yod pa nyid yin pa de bzhin du | sgra gcan dang mchi gu gnyis kyang yin pas dpe grub pa med do || de bzhin du rnam par dpyad[4] na sa la sogs pa dag la yang sra ba la sogs pa las tha dad pa'i mtshan gzhi med la | mtshan gzhi las tha

---

[1] C: om.

[2] P, N, G: blang bar for blangs par

[3] P, N, G: khyad par

[4] P: dbyad

dad par rten med pa'i mtshan nyid kyang med[1] mod kyi | de lta na yang 'di ni kun rdzob tu yod de | de bas na slob dpon rnams kyis phan tshun ltos[2] pa tsam gyis grub pa'i sgo nas grub par rnam par gzhag[3] pa mdzad do || 'di ni de kho na ltar gdon mi za bar khas blang bar bya ste | de lta ma yin na kun rdzob [PsP$_L$ 68] 'thad pa dang ldan pa ma yin nam | [P 26a] des na 'di de[4] kho[5] na nyid du 'gyur gyi kun rdzob tu mi 'gyur ro || 'thad pas rnam par dpyad pa na mchi gu la sogs pa dag kho na mi srid pa ni ma yin te | 'o na ci zhe na | 'chad [C 23a] par 'gyur ba'i 'thad pas gzugs dang tshor ba la sogs pa rnams kyang yod pa ma yin pas | de dag kyang mchi gu la sogs pa bzhin du kun rdzob tu yod pa ma[6] yin pa nyid du khas blangs par 'gyur na | de ltar yang ma yin pas | 'di ni yod pa ma yin no || brten nas btags[7] par rnam par gzhag[8] pa 'di yang dbu ma la 'jug pa las rgyas par bstan[9] pas de nyid las yongs su btsal bar bya'o ||

§105. ci ste zhib mor dpyad pa 'dis ci zhig bya ste | kho bo cag tshad ma dang gzhal bya'i tha snyad thams cad bden pa yin no zhes ni mi smra'i | 'on kyang 'jig rten la[10] rab tu grags pa 'di tshul 'dis rnam par 'jog par byed par 'gyur ro snyam na |

---

[1] P, N, G: yod

[2] P, N, G: bltos

[3] P, N, G: bzhag

[4] P, N, G: na

[5] C: do for de kho

[6] D, C: om. ma

[7] Em.: btags. P, N, G, D, C: brtags

[8] P, N, G: bzhag

[9] P, N, G: brtan

[10] TKK (2001: 32, n. 4) reports that N omits *la* but it is attested (below the line).

bshad par bya ste | [G 31a] dpyad pa zhib mo ’jig rten pa’i tha snyad la bcug pa ’dis ci dgos[1] zhes kho bo cag kyang de skad du smra ste | kun rdzob [D 23b] phyin ci log tsam gyis bdag gi ngo bo [N 25b] yod par rnyed pa | thar pa ’dod pa rnams kyi thar pa ’dren par byed pa’i dge ba’i [PsP$_L$ 69] rtsa ba gsog[2] pa’i rgyur gyur pa ’di ni ji srid de kho na nyid ma rtogs pa de srid du gnas par ’gyur[3] mod | khyod ni don dam pa dang kun rdzob kyi bden pa la mi mkhas pas la lar ’thad pa bcug nas rigs pa ma yin pa las de ’jig par byed pa yin no || kho bo ni kun rdzob kyi bden pa rnam par ’jog pa la mkhas pa’i phyir | ’jig rten pa’i phyogs nyid la gnas te kun rdzob kyi phyogs gcig bsal ba’i phyir bkod pa’i ’thad pa gzhan ’thad pa gzhan gyis[4] zlog par[5] byed cing ’jig rten gyi rgan rabs ltar | ’jig rten gyi chos lugs las nyams pa khyod kho na zlog[6] par byed pa yin gyi kun rdzob ni ma yin no || de’i phyir gal te ’jig rten pa’i tha snyad du yin na ni | [P 26b] de’i tshe[7] mtshan nyid bzhin du mtshan gzhir yang[8] gdon mi za bar[9] ’gyur bar bya dgos te | de’i phyir nyes pa de nyid du ’gyur ro || ’on te don dam par[10] yin na ni de’i tshe mtshan gzhi med pas mtshan nyid gnyis kyang med pas tshad ma gnyis su ga la ’gyur |

---

[1] N: dgoso

[2] D, C: sog

[3] P, N, G: gyur

[4] C: gyi

[5] N: zlog par illegible

[6] P, N, G: bzlog

[7] N: illegible

[8] C: yad

[9] N: za bar illegible

[10] P, N, G: pa

§106. ci ste sgra rnams la bya ba dang byed pa po'i 'brel par[1] sngon du 'gro ba can gyi bye brag tu bshad pa de lta bu khas len par mi byed do zhe na |

'di ni shin tu dka' ste | khyod [C 23b] bya ba dang byed pa po'i 'brel pas rab tu zhugs pa'i sgra de dag kho nas tha snyad byed cing | bya ba dang byed pa po la sogs pa'i sgra'i don yang[2] mi 'dod pas | [G 31b] e ma kyi hud khyod ni 'dod pa tsam la rag las te 'jug pa nyid do ||

§107. gang gi tshe de ltar gzhal bya gnyis gnas pa med pa de'i tshe lung la sogs pa rang dang spyi'i mtshan nyid kyi yul can ma yin pa nyid kyi sgo nas tshad ma gzhan nyid ma yin pa ma yin no ||

§108. gzhan yang bum pa mngon sum mo zhes bya ba de lta bu la sogs pa 'jig rten pa'i tha snyad ma bsdus[3] pa'i phyir dang | 'phags pa ma yin pa'i tha snyad khas blangs pa'i phyir mtshan nyid ma khyab pa nyid du 'gyur te | des na 'di ni mi rigs so || [PsP_L 70]

§109. ci ste bum pa'i nye bar len pa sngon po la sogs pa dag ni mngon sum [N 26a] gyi tshad mas yongs su gcad par bya ba yin pa'i phyir mngon sum yin te | de'i phyir ji ltar rgyu la 'bras [D 24a] bu btags pa byas te | sangs rgyas rnams ni 'byung ba bde[4] zhes bsnyad[5] pa de bzhin du | sngon po la sogs pa mngon sum du gyur pa'i rgyu can gyi

---

[1] P, N, G: pa

[2] C: par

[3] P: bsdu

[4] TKK (2001: 34, n. 4) reports that D reads *bad* but it too attests *bde*

[5] P, N, G: snyad

bum pa yang 'bras bu la rgyu[1] btags pa byas nas mngon sum zhes bya bar brjod do snyam[2] na |

rnam pa de lta bu'i yul la ni btags pa mi rigs te[3] | 'byung ba ni 'jig rten na bde ba las tha dad par dmigs la | de yang 'dus byas kyi mtshan nyid kyi rang bzhin yin pa'i phyir dang | dka' ba brgya phrag du ma'i rgyu can yin pa'i phyir bde ba ma yin pa nyid do || de la bde ba [P 27a] zhes brjod pa na 'brel pa med pa nyid yin pas rnam pa de lta bu'i yul la nye bar btags pa rigs na | bum pa mngon sum zhes bya ba 'dir ni gang zhig btags[4] nas mngon sum nyid du 'gyur ba bum pa zhes bya ba mngon sum ma yin pa logs shig tu dmigs pa yang ma yin no ||

§110. gal te sngon po la [G 32a] sogs pa las tha dad pa'i bum pa med pa'i phyir btags pa'i mngon sum nyid du 'gyur ro zhe na |

de lta na yang ches shin tu btags par mi rigs te | gzhi gdags bya med ba'i phyir ro || bong bu'i rwa la rnon po nye bar 'dogs pa ni[5] ma yin no ||

§111. gzhan yang gal te 'jig rten gyi tha snyad kyi yan lag tu gyur pa'i bum pa sngon po la sogs pa las tha dad par gyur pa med pa'i phyir | [C 24a] de nye bar btags pa pa'i[6] mngon sum nyid du rtog[7] na ni de lta na ni sngon po la sogs pa yang sa la sogs pa las tha dad pa med pas

---

[1] D, C: rgyus

[2] TKK (2001: 34, n. 7) reports that N reads *bsnyam* but it also attests *snyam*.

[3] P: *t* illegible

[4] D, C: brtags

[5] D, C: add following rigs pa; TKK (2001: 36): ni rigs pa

[6] TKK (2001: 36): em. btags pa'i; cf. Negi s.v. nye bar btags pa pa

[7] D, C: rtogs

sngon po la sogs pa yang btags pa pa'i[1] mngon sum nyid du rtogs shig |

ji skad du | [PsP$_L$ 71]

> ji ltar gzugs sogs ma gtogs par ||
> bum pa yod pa[2] ma yin pa ||
> de bzhin rlung la sogs pa ni ||
> ma gtogs[3] gzugs kyang yod ma yin ||

zhes bshad do || de'i phyir de lta bu la sogs pa'i 'jig rten gyi tha snyad ni mtshan nyid kyis ma bsdus pa'i phyir mtshan nyid ma khyab pa[4] nyid do || de kho na nyid gzigs pa la [N 26b] ltos[5] nas ni bum ba la sogs pa dang sngon po la sogs pa rnams mngon sum nyid du mi 'dod do || 'jig rten gyi kun rdzob tu ni bum pa la sogs pa rnams mngon sum nyid du khas blang[6] bar bya ba kho na'o ||

ji skad du bzhi[7] brgya pa las |

> gzugs mthong [D 24b] tshe na bum pa ni ||
> thams cad kho na mthong mi 'gyur ||
> bum pa mngon sum zhes bya 'ang ||
> de nyid rig[1] pa su zhig smra ||

---

[1] TKK (2001: 36): em. btags pa'i; cf. Negi s.v. nye bar btags pa pa

[2] P, N, G: par

[3] P, N: grtogs

[4] D: ba

[5] P, N, G: bltos

[6] P, N, G: blangs

[7] P, N, G: om.

rnam par dpyad pa ’di nyid kyis ||
blo mchog ldan pas dri zhim dang ||
mngar dang ’jam pa thams cad [G 32b] dag ||
so sor dgag par [P 27b] bya ba yin ||

zhes bshad do ||

§112. gzhan yang mngon sum gyi sgra ni lkog tu ma gyur pa’i don gyi rjod par byed pa yin pa’i phyir | dbang po mngon du phyogs pa’i don ni mngon sum yin no || ’di la dbang po mngon du phyogs pas zhes byas[2] nas bum pa dang sngon po la sogs pa[3] lkog tu ma gyur pa rnams mngon sum nyid du grub par ’gyur[4] la | de yongs su gcod par byed [PsP$_L$ 72] pa’i shes pa ni rtswa[5] dang sog[6] ma’i me bzhin du mngon sum gyi rgyu can yin pa’i phyir mngon sum nyid du rjod par byed do ||

§113. gang zhig dbang po dang dbang po so so la ’jug pas zhes bya bas mngon sum gyi sgra bye brag tu ’chad par byed pa | de[7] ltar na ni shes pa ni dbang po’i yul can ma yin pa’i phyir dang | yul gyi yul can yin pa’i phyir bye brag tu bshad pa mi rigs par ’gyur te | yul so so ba ’am don so so ba nyid ces bya bar ni mi ’gyur ro ||

---

[1] P, N, G: rigs
[2] D, C: bya ba
[3] P, N, G: pas
[4] P: gyur
[5] P, N, G: rtsa
[6] P, N, G: sogs
[7] P, N, G: de’i

§114. ci ste ji ltar rnam par shes pa 'byung ba gnyi ga la rag las pa yin yang rnam par shes pa rnams rten gsal ba [C 24b] dang zhan pa'i rjes su byed pa'i phyir dang | de dag 'gyur[1] na 'gyur ba'i phyir | mig gi rnam par shes pa zhes rten nyid kyis ston par 'gyur ba de bzhin du | don dang don so so la 'jug mod kyi de lta na yang dbang po dang dbang po la brten nas 'jug pa'i rnam par shes pa ni rten[2] gyis bstan[3] pas mngon sum nyid du 'gyur te[4] | rnga'i sgra nas kyi myu ku zhes thun mong ma yin pa'i rgyus ston[5] pa ni mthong ba yin no snyam na |

'di ni snga ma dang mi 'dra ba yin te | der ni gzugs [N 27a] kyi rnam par shes pa zhes bya ba de lta bu la sogs pas yul gyis[6] rnam [G 33a] par shes pa bstan na | rnam par shes pa drug gi dbye[7] ba ma bstan par 'gyur te | yid kyi rnam par shes pa ni mig la sogs pa'i rnam par shes pa[8] dang lhan cig yul gcig[9] [PsP$_L$ 73] la 'jug[10] pa'i phyir ro || 'di ltar sngon po la sogs pa'i rnam par shes pa drug la rnam par shes pa zhes [P 28a] brjod [D 25a] na ni | ci rnam par shes pa 'di dbang po gzugs can las skyes pa zhig gam | 'on te yid las byung ba zhig ces shes pa re ba dang bcas pa nyid[11] du 'gyur la | rten gyis bstan na ni yid kyi[12] rnam

---

[1] D, C: gyur

[2] P, N, G: brten

[3] N: brtan

[4] C: gyi

[5] P: stong

[6] D, C: gyi

[7] D, C: rnam par dbye ba; TKK (2001: 40) as D

[8] P: pa blurred

[9] P, N, G: cig

[10] D: 'dug

[11] Em.: nyid. P, N, G, D, C: yid. PsP Skt: eva.

[12] P, N, G: kyis

par shes pa mig la sogs pa'i rnam par shes pa'i yul la 'jug pa yin yang phan tshun dbye ba grub par 'gyur ro ‖ 'dir ni tshad ma'i mtshan nyid brjod par 'dod pas rtog[1] pa dang bral ba tsam zhig mngon sum nyid du khas blangs pas rnam par rtog pa las 'di khyad par du mngon par 'dod pa'i phyir | thun mong ma yin pa'i rgyus bstan pa la dgos pa cung zad kyang[2] ma mthong ngo ‖ tshad ma'i grangs su 'jug pa gzhal bya'i gzhan gyi dbang yin pa'i phyir dang | gzhal bya'i rnam pa'i rjes su byed pa tsam gyis rang gi ngo[3] bo yod[4] par rnyed pa'i tshad[5] ma dag gi rang gi ngo bo rnam par 'jog pa'i phyir dbang pos bstan pa cung zad kyang mi mkho bas rnam pa thams cad du yul kho nas bstan par rigs so ‖

§115. gal te 'jig rten na brjod par 'dod pa'i don la mngon sum gyi sgra rab tu grags pa'i phyir dang | don so so zhes bya ba'i sgra ma grags pa'i phyir rten kho nas [PsP$_L$ 74] bye brag tu bshad pa la rten[6] par byed do zhe na |

bshad par bya ste | mngon sum gyi sgra 'di 'jig rten la grags pa ni yod mod kyi | de[7] ji ltar 'jig rten na[8] yin [G 33b] pa de ltar [C 25a] ni kho bo cag gis smras pa nyid do ‖ 'jig rten pa'i don ji ltar gnas pa spangs nas de bye brag tu 'chad par byed na ni | rab tu grags pa'i sgra yang

---

[1] G, N: rtogs

[2] G: om.

[3] N: do

[4] N: yong

[5] N: tshang

[6] P, N, G: brten

[7] P: illegible

[8] P, N, G: om. na

spong bar 'gyur ro || de'i phyir mngon sum zhes bya ba de ltar mi 'gyur ro ||

§116. zlos pa'i don med pa'i phyir dbang po'i skad cig [N 27b] gcig gi[1] rten can mig gi rnam par shes pa gcig[2] mngon sum nyid du yang mi 'gyur la | re re la mngon sum nyid med na ni mang po rnams la yang mi 'gyur ro ||

§117. rtog pa dang bral ba'i shes pa nyid mngon sum nyid du khas blangs pa'i phyir dang | des kyang [P 28b] 'jig rten pa'i tha snyad byed pa[3] med pa'i phyir dang | 'jig rten pa'i tshad ma dang gzhal bya'i tha snyad bshad par 'dod pa'i phyir[4] mngon sum tshad mar rtog pa ni don med pa nyid du 'gyur ro ||

§118. mig gi rnam par shes pa [D 25b] dang ldan pas sngon po shes kyi sngon po'o[5] snyam du ni ma yin no zhes bya ba'i lung yang[6] mngon sum gyi mtshan nyid brjod pa'i don can gyi skabs ma yin pa nyid kyi phyir dang | dbang po'i rnam par shes pa lnga po [PsP$_L$ 75] rnams blun pa nyid du ston par byed pa nyid yin pa'i phyir | lung las kyang rtog pa dang bral ba'i rnam par shes pa kho na mngon sum nyid ma yin pas 'di ni mi rigs so ||

---

[1] P: gis

[2] P, N, G: cig

[3] C: po

[4] D, C: phyir na

[5] P, N, G, C: om. 'o

[6] C: 'ang

§119. de'i phyir gal te mtshan gzhi 'am rang gi mtshan nyid dam spyi'i mtshan nyid kyang rung ste | 'jig rten na yod na ni thams cad mngon sum du dmigs par bya ba yin pa'i phyir na lkog tu ma gyur pa yin te | de'i phyir de'i yul can gyi rnam par shes pa dang lhan cig tu mngon sum nyid du rnam par gzhag[1] go || zla ba gnyis la sogs pa dag ni rab rib can ma yin pa'i [G 34a] shes pa la ltos[2] nas mngon sum nyid ma yin la | rab rib can la sogs pa la ltos[3] nas ni mngon sum nyid kho na'o ||

§120. lkog tu gyur pa'i yul can rtags[4] bsgrub par bya ba la mi 'khrul ba las skyes pa'i shes pa ni rjes su dpag pa'o ||

§121. dbang po las 'das pa'i don mngon sum du rig[5] cing yid ches par gyur pa dag gi[6] tshig gang yin pa de ni lung ngo ||

§122. 'dra ba las nyams su ma[7] myong ba'i don rtogs pa ni nye bar 'jal ba ste | dper na ba men[8] ni ba lang dang[9] [C 25b] 'dra'o snyam pa lta bu'o ||

§123. de'i phyir de[1] ltar tshad[2] ma bzhi las 'jig rten gyis[3] don rtogs par rnam par[4] 'jog pa yin no ||

---

[1] P, N, G: bzhag

[2] P, N, G: bltos

[3] P, N, G: bltos

[4] N: brtags

[5] N: rigs

[6] P, N, G: gis

[7] Em.: ma. P, N, G, D, C: om. ma. PsP Skt: ananubhūta

[8] D, C: man

[9] P, N, G: om. dang

de dag kyang phan tshun ltos[5] pas 'grub par 'gyur te | tshad ma dag yod na gzhal bya'i don dag tu 'gyur la | gzhal bya'i don dag yod na tshad ma dag [N 28a] tu [P 29a] 'gyur gyi | tshad ma dang gzhal bya gnyis ngo bo nyid kyis grub pa ni yod pa ma yin no || de'i phyir mthong ba ji lta ba bzhin du 'jig rten pa nyid yin la rag ste | spros pas chog go || dkyus ma nyid bshad par bya'o || [PsP$_L$ 76]

§124. 'dir rang gi sde pa dag na re | gang 'di 'di skad du dngos po rnams bdag las skye ba ma yin te | zhes smras pa de ni rigs te | rang[6] las skye ba don med pa'i phyir ro || gang yang gnyi ga las[7] skye ba ma yin te zhes smras pa de yang[8] rigs te | yan lag gcig ma tshang[9] ba'i phyir ro || rgyu med pa'i phyogs ni shin tu tha chad [D 26a] yin[10] pa'i phyir | de dgag pa yang rigs na | gang 'di skad du gzhan las skye ba yang ma yin te zhes smras pa de ni rigs pa ma yin te | gang gi phyir bcom ldan 'das kyis [G 34b] gzhan du gyur pa dag kho na dngos po rnams kyi skyed par byed par bstan pa'i phyir te |

rkyen rnams[11] bzhi ste rgyu dang ni ||
dmigs pa dang ni de ma thag ||

---

[1] N: da

[2] N: thad?

[3] D, C: gyi. TKK (2001: 44) as D

[4] P, N, G: om. rnam par

[5] P, N, G: bltos

[6] N: rab

[7] D, C: la

[8] C: yang pa

[9] C: tshad

[10] N: om.

[11] D, C, N: rnam

bdag po yang ni de bzhin te ||
rkyen lnga pa ni yod ma yin || [MMK I.2] [PsP_L 77]

de la sgrub par byed pa ni rgyu yin no zhes bya ba'i mtshan nyid las na gang zhig gang gi sgrub byed sa bon gyi ngo bor gnas pa de ni de'i rgyu'i rkyen no || dmigs pa gang[1] gis skye bar 'gyur ba'i chos can bskyed pa de ni de'i dmigs pa'i rkyen no || rgyu 'gag[2] ma thag pa ni 'bras bu 'byung ba'i rkyen yin te | dper na sa bon 'gag[3] ma thag pa myu gu 'byung ba'i rkyen yin pa bzhin no || gang[4] zhig yod pas gang 'byung ba de ni de'i bdag po'o || 'di dag ni rkyen bzhi'o || gzhan gang dag sngar skyes pa dang lhan cig skyes pa dang | phyis skye ba la sogs pa de dag ni 'di rnams kyi khongs[5] su 'dus pa yin no || dbang phyug la sogs pa dag ni rkyen ma yin te | de nyid kyi phyir rkyen lnga pa ni yod ma yin zhes nges par gzung ba yin no || de'i phyir gzhan du gyur pa 'di dag [P 29b] las dngos po rnams skye ba'i phyir gzhan [C 26a] las skye ba yod pa yin no zhes 'dzer to ||

§125. de la bshad par bya ste | dngos po rnams ni rkyen gzhan du gyur pa dag las skye ba ma yin pa nyid de[6] | 'di ltar | [N 28b] [PsP_L 78]

dngos po rnams kyi rang[7] bzhin ni ||
rkyen la sogs la yod ma yin ||

---

[1] C: gad

[2] Em.: 'gag. P, N, G, D, C: 'gags

[3] D, C: 'gags

[4] C: gad

[5] C: gams

[6] C: do

[7] P, N: dang

bdag gi[1] dngos po yod[2] min na[3] ||
gzhan dngos yod pa ma yin no || [MMK I.3]

gal te 'bras bur gyur pa'i dngos po rnams rgyu la sogs pa'i rkyen gzhan du gyur pa[4] 'dus pa 'am so so[5] ba 'am 'dus pa dang so so ba dag gam | rgyu dang rkyen gyi tshogs pa[6] las gzhan 'ga' zhig la yang [G 35a] rung ste | skyes pa'i snga rol tu[7] yod par gyur na ni | de dag las skye bar 'gyur ba zhig na | gang zhig skye ba'i snga rol tu[8] yod par 'gyur ba de ltar yang ma yin te | gal te yod par 'gyur na ni | gzung du yod pa 'am skye ba don med par 'gyur ro || de'i phyir dngos po [D 26b] rnams kyi rang bzhin ni rkyen la sogs pa dag la yod pa ma yin no || bdag gi dngos po yod pa ma yin pa nyid yin na gzhan gyi dngos po yod pa ma yin no || 'byung bas na dngos po ste skye ba'o || gzhan gyi dngos po ni gzhan dag las skye ba ste de yod pa ma yin no || de'i phyir dngos po rnams gzhan du gyur pa dag las skye bo zhe bya ba 'di rigs pa ma yin no ||

§126. rnam pa gcig tu na rgyu med pa can du thal bar 'gyur ba'i phyir myu gu la sogs pa 'bras bur gyur pa'i[9] dngos po rnams kyi rang bzhin ni | sa bon la sogs pa rkyen rnam par 'gyur ba med pa'i rang bzhin

---

[1] N: gyis

[2] N: yong

[3] C: ni na

[4] P, N: ba

[5] N: sor

[6] C: 'a

[7] D, C: du

[8] D, C: du

[9] P, N, G: ba'i

can dag yod pa na yod pa ma yin no ‖ de'i phyir rkyen la sogs pa rnams ci la ltos[1] nas gzhan nyid du 'gyur te | byams pa dang nyer sbas dag ni yod pa gnyis kho na phan tshun ltos[2] pa'i gzhan nyid du 'gyur na | sa bon dang myu gu gnyis ni de ltar cig car ba ma yin no ‖ de'i phyir 'bras bu rnams [P 30a] kyi[3] bdag gi dngos po yod pa ma yin na | sa bon la sogs pa rnams la gzhan gyi dngos po te gzhan nyid yod pa ma yin no ‖ de'i phyir gzhan du bsnyad du med pa kho na'i phyir gzhan las skye ba ma yin pas dngos po rnams gzhan las skye'o[4] zhes bya ba 'di ni mi rung ngo ‖ [G 35b]

§127. de'i phyir gzhan gyi[5] lung gi dgongs pa mngon par ma shes pa nyid de | de bzhin gshegs pa dag ni rigs pa dang 'gal [C 26b] ba'i ngag mi gsung la | lung gi dgongs pa yang gong[6] du nye bar bstan zin to ‖ [PsP_L 79]

§128. de'i phyir de ltar rkyen dag las skye bar smra ba bkag pa yin dang | [N 29a] bya ba las skye bar smra ba ni | mig dang gzugs la sogs pa'i rkyen dag ni dngos su rnam par shes pa skyed par mi byed kyi | rnam par shes pa skye ba'i bya ba sgrub par byed pa'i phyir rkyen zhes bya la | bya ba des kyang rnam par shes pa skyed[7] par byed de | de'i phyir rnam par shes pa skye ba'i bya ba rkyen dang ldan pa ni rnam par shes pa skyed par byed pa yin gyi rkyen dag ni ma yin te |

---

[1] P, N, G: bltos

[2] P, N, G: bltos

[3] P, N, G: ni

[4] D, C: skye'i

[5] C: kyi

[6] N: god

[7] N: skye

dper na | 'bras chan[1] gyi 'tshed pa'i bya ba bzhin no snyam du sems so ||

§129. bshad pa[2] |

> bya ba rkyen dang ldan pa med || [MMK I.4a]

gal te bya ba 'ga' zhig yod par gyur na ni | de mig la sogs pa'i rkyen dag gis[3] rkyen dang ldan pas rnam par shes pa skyed par [D 27a] byed pa zhig na | yod pa ni ma yin no || ji ltar zhe na | 'dir bya ba 'di 'dod pa na rnam par shes pa skyes zin pa la 'dod dam | ma skyes pa la[4] 'am skye bzhin pa la yin grang na | de la skyes zin pa la[5] mi rigs te | bya ba ni dngos po sgrub par byed pa yin na | dngos po grub par gyur na ni de la bya bas ci zhig dgos te | 'di ni

> skyes par gyur pa slar yang skye bar[6] rigs pa 'ang[7] ma yin nyid ||

ces bya ba la sogs pa dbu ma la 'jug pa las bstan pa yin no || ma skyes pa la yang mi rigs te |

> skye ba 'di ni byed pa [P 30b] med par rigs pa'i ngo bo'ang min || [PsP$_L$ 80]

---

[1] D, C: chen

[2] G: par

[3] P, N, G: gi

[4] P: om.

[5] P, N, G: add following yang

[6] D, C: add following 'gyur ba

[7] Em: 'ang. P, N, G: 'am; D, C: om.; Skt: ca

zhes bya ba la [G 36a] sogs pa 'byung ba'i phyir ro || dngos po skye bzhin pa la yang bya ba srid pa ma yin te | skyes pa dang ma skyes pa las ma gtogs pa'i skye bzhin pa med pa'i phyir ro ||

ji skad du |

> skye bzhin pa ni phyed skyes phyir ||
> skye bzhin pa ni skye ba min ||
> yang na thams cad skye bzhin pa ||
> nyid ni yin par thal bar 'gyur ||

zhes gsungs so || gang gi phyir de ltar dus gsum du skye ba'i bya ba mi srid pa de'i phyir de ni yod pa[1] ma yin no || de nyid kyi phyir bya ba rkyen dang ldan pa med ces gsungs te | mo gsham[2] gyi bu ba glang[3] dang ldan no zhes ni brjod par bya ba ma yin no || 'di ni

> khyad par med par khyad par can yod min ||

zhes bya ba la sogs pas[4] dbu ma la 'jug pa las bstan pa nyid do || [C 27a]

§130. gal te de lta na | 'o na rkyen dang mi ldan par 'gyur ro zhe na | [N 29b]

§131. 'di yang rigs pa ma yin no zhes bshad pa ni |

> rkyen dang[5] mi ldan bya ba med || [MMK I.4b]

---

[1] D, C: add following yang

[2] G: bsham

[3] D, C: lang

[4] C: pa

[5] N: dad

gang gi tshe bya ba rkyen dang ldan pa med pa de'i tshe ji ltar rkyen dang mi ldan pa rgyu med pa yod par 'gyur te | snam bu snal ma'i rang bzhin du mi rigs pas | 'jag ma'i rang bzhin du khas len pa ni ma yin no || de'i phyir bya ba dngos po'i skyed par byed pa ma yin no ||

§132. 'dir smras ba | gal te de ltar bya ba med na | 'o na ni rkyen dag dngos po rnams kyi skyed par byed par 'gyur ro ||

§133. bshad par bya ste |

bya ba mi ldan rkyen ma yin || [MMK I.4c]

gang gi tshe bya ba med pa de'i tshe | rkyen bya ba dang bral ba dang bya ba dang mi ldan pa rgyu[1] med pa rnams[2] ji ltar skyed par byed pa yin |

§134. ji ste bya ba dang ldan pa dag kho na skyed par byed pa yin no zhe na | [D 27b]

bshad pa | [PsP$_L$ 81]

bya ba [G 36b] ldan yod 'on te na || [MMK I.4d]

ma yin no zhes skabs dang sbyar ro || 'on te na'i sgra ni nges par gzung ba'o || de la bya ba med par bshad na | rkyen rnams ji ltar bya ba dang ldan ba nyid yin[3] | ji ltar rnam [P 31a] par shes pa'i skye ba'i

---

[1] P: rgyud

[2] N: illegible

[3] D, C: yin na

bya ba la brjod pa de bzhin du ’tshed[1] pa’i bya ba la sogs pa’i dngos po dag la yang brjod par rig par bya’o ‖ des na bya ba las kyang dngos po rnams skye ba med pas skye ba’i rjod par byed pa don gyis stong par ’gyur ro ‖

§135. ’dir smras pa | rkyen bya ba ldan no zhes bya ba la sogs pa’i rnam par dpyad pa ’dis kho bo cag la ci dgos | gang gi phyir mig la sogs pa’i rkyen dag la brten nas dngos po rnam par shes pa la sogs pa rnams skye bar ’gyur te | de’i phyir mig la sogs pa rnams rkyen nyid yin zhing | rnam par shes pa la sogs pa rnams kyang de dag las skye ba yin no ‖

§136. ’di yang rigs pa ma yin no zhes bshad pa |

> ’di dag la brten skye bas na ‖
> de phyir ’di dag rkyen ces grag ‖
> ji srid mi skye de srid du ‖
> ’di dag rkyen min ji ltar min ‖ [MMK I.5]

gal te mig la sogs pa’i rkyen rnams la brten nas rnam par shes pa skye bas na ’di dag de’i rkyen zhes brjod na ni | ji srid rnam par shes pa zhes bya ba’i ’bras bu de mi skye ba de srid du | mig la sogs pa ’di dag rkyen ma [C 27b] yin pa ji ltar ma yin te | rkyen ma yin pa nyid do snyam du dgongs pa’o ‖ bye ma dag [N 30a] las til mar bzhin du rkyen ma yin pa dag las ni skye ba yang ma yin no ‖ [PsP$_L$ 82]

---

[1] D, C: ’tshod

§137. ci ste sngar rkyen ma yin par gyur pa las rkyen gzhan ci zhig cig[1] la ltos[2] nas rkyen nyid du 'gyur ro zhes bya [G 37a] bar 'dod na | 'di yang mi rung ste | gang zhig rkyen ma yin pa 'di'i rkyen nyid du rtog pa | rkyen gzhan de'i rkyen nyid de yang rkyen yod na yin pas 'di la yang dpyad pa de nyid yin no || de'i phyir de ni mi rigs so ||

§138. gzhan yang mig la sogs pa 'di dag rnam par shes pa'i rkyen du rtog pa na | 'di yod pa 'am med pa zhig la rtog grang na | rnam pa thams cad du mi rigs so zhes bya bar [P 31b] bshad pa |

> med dam yod pa'i don la yang ||
> rkyen ni rung ba ma yin te || [MMK I.6ab]

ci'i[3] phyir zhe na | bshad pa |

> med na gang gi rkyen du 'gyur ||
> yod na rkyen gyis ci zhig bya || [MMK I.6cd]

med pa ste | [D 28a] yod pa ma yin pa'i don la ni rkyen du ji ltar 'gyur |

§139. gal te 'byung bar 'gyur bas ston par 'gyur ro zhe na | de ltar ni ma yin te |

> gal te 'byung bar 'gyur bas bsnyad 'dod na ||
> nus pa med par 'di yi 'byung 'gyur med[4] ||

---

[1] P, N, G: gcig

[2] P, N, G: bltos

[3] D, C: add preceding de

[4] D, C: ni || yod min

ces bya ba la sogs pas nyes pa brjod pa'i phyir ro ||

§140. yod na ste bdog pa skye ba thob zin pa la yang rkyen yongs su brtag pa[1] 'bras bu med pa nyid do || [PsP_L 83]

§141. de ltar rkyen 'dus pa rnams 'bras bu skyed[2] par nus pa med pas rkyen nyid ma yin par bsnyad nas | de'i 'og tu so so ba rnams rkyen nyid ma yin par bstan par bya'o ||

§142. 'dir smras pa | gal te de ltar rkyen rnams mi srid mod kyi | de lta na yang mtshan nyid nye bar bstan pa las rkyen grub pa yod pa nyid do || de la sgrub par byed pa ni[3] rgyu'o zhes rgyu'i rkyen gyi mtshan nyid brjod de yod pa ma yin pa mo gsham[4] gyi bu la ni mtshan nyid nye bar ston pa mi brjod do ||

§143. gal te de'i mtshan nyid yod par gyur na ni | rgyu'i [G 37b] rkyen du 'gyur ba zhig na | yod pa ni ma yin te | gang gi phyir |

> gang tshe chos ni yod pa dang ||
> med dang yod med mi 'grub pa ||
> ji ltar sgrub byed rgyu zhes bya ||
> de lta yin na mi rigs so || [MMK I.7]

de la sgrub par byed pa ni skyed par byed pa ste | gal te bsgrub par [N 30b] bya ba'i chos 'grub na ni | [C 28a] skyed par byed pa'i rgyus de bskyed par 'gyur na | 'grub pa yang ma yin te | yod pa dang med pa

---

[1] D, C: pas

[2] P, N, G: bskyed

[3] P, N, G: pa'i for pa ni

[4] G: bsham

dang gnyi ga la ngo bo 'grub pa med pa'i phyir ro || de la yod pa ni 'grub pa ma yin te yod pa'i phyir ro || med pa yang ma yin te yod pa ma yin pa'i phyir ro || yod pa dang [P 32a] med pa yang ma yin te | phan tshun 'gal ba'i don gcig med pa'i phyir dang | phyogs gnyi ga la brjod pa'i skyon du 'gyur ba'i phyir ro || gang gi phyir de ltar 'bras bu skye[1] ba med pa de'i phyir rgyu'i rkyen yang yod pa ma yin no || de'i phyir mtshan nyid yod pa'i phyir rgyu'i rkyen yod pa yin no zhes smras pa gang yin pa ste[2] | de lta yin na mi rigs so ||

§144. da ni dmigs pa'i rkyen dgag[3] pa'i phyir | [PsP$_L$ 84]

yod pa'i chos 'di dmigs pa ni ||
med pa kho na nye bar bstan ||
ci ste chos ni dmigs med na ||
dmigs pa yod par ga la 'gyur || [MMK I.8]

zhes gsungs so ||

'dir dmigs [D 28b] pa dang bcas pa'i chos gang dag ce na | sems dang sems las byung ba thams cad do zhes bya ba'i lung las ni | sems dang sems las byung ba rnams gzugs la sogs pa'i dmigs pa gang gis ci rigs par skyed par byed pa de ni de dag gi dmigs pa'i rkyen yin pa na | yod pa dag la brtag gam | med pa dag la yin grang | de la [G 38a] yod pa dag la ni dmigs pa'i rkyen de don med de | chos bskyed par bya ba'i phyir dmigs pa yongs su rtog par byed na | de ni dmigs pa'i snga rol[4] tu[1]

---

[1] P, N, G: bskyed

[2] P, N, G: de

[3] N: dgeg

[4] N: 'ol

yod pa nyid kyi phyir ro ‖ ci ste de ltar chos rang gi bdag nyid dmigs pa med par rab tu grub na | ’di ni dmigs pa dang ldan par brtags pas ci zhig bya | de’i phyir yod pa bdog pa’i chos sems la sogs pa ’di dmigs pa med pa kho na khyed cag gis rang ’dod kyis[2] dmigs pa dang bcas pa yin no zhes nye bar bstan pa ’ba’ zhig tu zad kyi | ’di la dmigs pa dang ’brel pa cung zhig yod pa ni ma yin no ‖

§145. ci ste med pa la dmigs pa yongs su rtog par byed na | de yang rigs pa ma yin te |

> chos ’di dmigs pa med [P 32b] pa[3] ni ‖
> yin pa kho nar nye bar bstan ‖

zhes bya ba la sogs pa la | ’di ltar yod [C 28b] pa [N 31a] ma yin pa la ni dmigs pa dang ’brel pa[4] yod pa ma yin no ‖ [PsP_L 85]

> chos ’di dmigs pa med pa ni ‖

yin pa ste gyur pa kho na khyed[5] kyis nye bar bstan te |

dmigs pa dang bcas par zhes bya ba ni tshig gi lhag ma’o ‖

> ci ste chos ni dmigs med na ‖
> dmigs pa yod par ga la ’gyur ‖

---

[1] D, C: du

[2] D, C: kyi

[3] Em: pa. P, N, G, D, C: par. See the immediately following citation of I.8a.

[4] P, N: ba

[5] D, C: khyod

zhes bya ba la | ci ste'i sgra ni dri ba'o || ga la 'gyur zhes bya ba ni gtan tshigs so || des na don ni | ci ste de ltar chos yod pa ma yin zhing mi bdog pa ni dmigs pa med na | yang dmigs pa yod par ga la 'gyur zhes bya ba 'dir 'gyur te | dmigs par byed pa med pa'i phyir dmigs pa yang med do zhes bya bar dgongs pa'o ||

§146. ji ltar sems dang sems las [G 38b] byung ba rnams dmigs pa dang bcas par 'gyur zhe na | mtshan nyid 'di ni kun rdzob pa yin gyi | don dam pa ni ma yin pas nyes pa med do ||

§147. da ni mtshungs pa de ma thag pa'i rkyen dgag pa'i phyir |

> chos [D 29a] rnams skyes pa ma yin na ||
> 'gag pa 'thad par mi 'gyur ro ||
> de phyir de ma thag mi rigs ||
> 'gags na rkyen yang gang zhig yin || [MMK I.9] [PsP_L 86]

zhes bya ba gsungs te |

de la tshigs su bcad pa phyed phyi ma'i rkang pa go ba snor[1] bar blta bar bya'o || yang gi sgra ni 'gags na yang zhes rim pa bzhin du sbyar ro || des na 'di skad du | 'gags na rkyen yang gang zhig yin || de'i phyir de ma[2] thag mi rigs zhes 'don par 'gyur te | de skad du gsungs pa ni tshigs su bcad pa sdeb pa'i phyir yin[3] no[4] ||

---

[1] G: bsnor for ba snor

[2] P, N, G: de'i for de ma

[3] C: om.

[4] C: ro

de la rgyu ’gag[1] ma thag pa ’bras bu skye ba’i rkyen du ’gyur ba ni mtshungs pa de ma thag pa’i rkyen gyi mtshan nyid yin te | ’di la dpyad par bya’o || myu gu la sogs pa ’bras bur gyur pa’i chos rnams skyes pa ma yin na | rgyu sa bon [P 33a] la sogs pa’i ’gag pa ’thad par mi ’gyur ro || gang gi tshe ’di de lta yin pa de’i tshe rgyu ’gag pa med pa’i phyir | myu gu’i mtshungs pa de ma thag pa’i rkyen gang zhig yin par ’gyur | ci ste ’bras bu ma skyes par yang[2] sa bon ’gag par ’dod na ni | de lta na sa bon ’gags na ste med par gyur na | myu gu’i rkyen [N 31b] yang gang zhig yin la | sa bon ’gag pa’i rkyen yang gang zhig yin te | ’di gnyi ga rgyu med par ’gyur ro zhes ’chad pa ni | ’gags na [C 29a] rkyen yang gang zhig yin zhes bya ba’o || [G 39a] yang gi sgra ni skye ba med pa la ltos[3] pa ste | des na myu gu ma skyes par sa bon ’gag par ’dod na yang gnyi ga rgyu med pa can du ’gyur te | de’i phyir de ma thag mi rigs zhes bya ba’o[4] ||

§148. yang na | bdag las ma[5] yin gzhan las min zhes bya ba la sogs pas skye ba bkag pa yin la | skye ba bkag pa de la dgongs nas |

> chos rnams skyes pa ma yin na ||
> ’gag ba ’thad par mi ’gyur ro ||
> de[6] phyir de ma thag mi rigs ||

zhes gsungs so ||

---

[1] P, N, G: ’gags

[2] P, N, G: om.

[3] P, N, G: bltos

[4] D, C: om. ba

[5] C: om.

[6] G: de’i

gzhan yang |

’gags na rkyen yang gang zhig yin ||

te | ’di la bshad pa ni snga ma nyid sbyar bar bya’o ||

§149. da ni bdag po’i rkyen bsal bar bzhed nas bshad pa | sa bon la sogs pa |

dngos po rang bzhin med rnams kyi ||
yod pa gang phyir yod min [D 29b] na ||
’di yod pas na ’di ’byung zhes ||
bya ba ’di ni ’thad ma yin || [MMK I.10] [PsP_L 87]

’dir gang zhig yod pas gang ’byung ba de ni de’i bdag po yin no zhes bya ba ni bdag po’i rkyen gyi mtshan nyid yin na | dngos po rnams ni rten cing ’brel[1] par ’byung ba’i phyir | rang bzhin med pa na gang zhig ’di zhes rgyu nyid du bsnyad pa de ga la yod cing | gang yang ’di zhes ’bras bu de nyid du ston pa de ga la yod | de’i phyir mtshan nyid las kyang rkyen grub pa yod pa ma yin no ||

§150. ’dir[2] smras ba | snal ma [P 33b] la sogs pa dag las snam bu la sogs pa skye bar dmigs nas | snal ma la[3] sogs pa dag snam bu la sogs pa’i rkyen yin no ||

§151. bshad ba bya ste | snam bu la sogs pa ’bras bu ’byung ba nyid yod pa ma yin na[1] | rkyen rnams kyi [G 39b] rkyen[2] nyid lta ’grub par

---

[1] P: ’thel

[2] P, N, G: ’di

[3] D, C: om. la

ga la 'gyur | ji ltar snam bu la sogs pa 'bras bu 'byung ba med pa de ltar bstan ba'i phyir |

rkyen rnams so so 'dus pa la[3] ||
'bras bu de ni med pa nyid ||
rkyen rnams la ni gang med pa ||
de ni rkyen las ji ltar skye || [MMK I.11]

zhes gsungs so ||

de la snal ma dang tshig pa dang thag zangs dang | [N 32a] son shing la sogs pa so so ba dag la snam bu so sor yod pa ni ma yin te | de dag la ma dmigs pa'i phyir dang | rgyu mang pos[4] [C 29b] 'bras bu mang por thal bar 'gyur ba'i phyir ro || snal ma la sogs pa 'dus pa[5] dag la yang snam bu yod pa ma yin te | yan lag re re ba dag la med pa'i phyir dang | 'bras bu gcig[6] dum bur[7] skye bar thal bar[8] 'gyur ba'i phyir ro || de'i phyir 'bras bu med pas rkyen dag med do ||

§152. ci ste 'bras bu de med kyang[9] ||
rkyen de dag las skye 'gyur na[10] || [MMK I.12ab] [PsP_L 88]

---

[1] G: ne

[2] P: rkyon

[3] D, C: las

[4] P, N, G: pas

[5] G: om. 'dus pa

[6] P, N, G: om. gcig

[7] D, C: bu

[8] P, N, G: om. thal bar

[9] D, C: ci ste de ni med par yang for ci ste 'bras bu de med kyang

[10] P, N, G: add the two quarters rkyen min las kyang 'bras bu ni || ci yi phyir na skye mi 'gyur ||

zhes bya bar bsams bar gyur na ni |

rkyen ma yin pa dag las kyang ||
ci yi phyir na skye mi 'gyur ||[1] [MMK I.12cd]

rkyen ma yin pa dag la yang 'bras bu yod pa ma yin pas rkyen ma yin pa[2] 'jag ma dag las kyang snam bu ci'i phyir na skye bar mi 'gyur | de'i phyir 'bras bu 'byung ba med do ||

§153. 'dir smras pa | gal te 'bras bu gzhan zhig yin zhing rkyen yang gzhan yin par 'gyur na ni | de'i tshe ci rkyen dag la 'bras bu yod dam med ces bya bar bsams par gyur na | 'bras bu tha dad pa ni med do || 'o na ci zhe na | rkyen gyi rang bzhin kho na yin no ||

§154. bshad par bya ste |

'bras bu rkyen gyi [D 30a] rang bzhin na[3] ||
rkyen rnams bdag gi rang bzhin min || [P 34a]
bdag dngos min las [G 40a] 'bras bu gang ||
de ni ji[4] ltar rkyen rang bzhin || [MMK I.13]

gal te 'bras bu rkyen gyi rang bzhin rkyen gyi rnam par 'gyur ba yin no zhes rnam par 'jog na ni | de mi rigs te | gang gi phyir rkyen de[5] rnams kyang bdag gi rang bzhin ma yin te | rkyen ma yin pa'i ngo bo

---

[1] Em: rkyen ma yin pa dag las kyang || ci yi phyir na skye mi 'gyur || (cf. MMK_T I.12). P, N, G, D, C: om.

[2] P, N, G: pas

[3] D, C: ni

[4] Em.: ji. P, N, G, D, C: te. (cf. MMK_T I.13)

[5] D, C: om.

zhes bya ba'i don to || snam bu[1] ni snal ma'i rang bzhin can no zhes bya bar brjod na ni | gal te [PsP_L 89] snal ma dag rang gi ngo bor grub par gyur na | snam[2] bur 'gyur na | de dag ni cha shas kyi rang bzhin cha shas[3] rnam par 'gyur ba yin gyi | rang bzhin gyis grub pa ni yod pa ma yin no || de'i phyir[4] bdag nyid kyi rang bzhin ma yin pa de dag las[5] snam bu zhes bya ba'i 'bras bu gang yin pa de ji[6] ltar snal ma'i rang bzhin du 'gyur |

ji skad du |

> snam bu rgyu las 'grub 'gyur zhing ||
> rgyu yang gzhan las 'grub 'gyur bas ||
> gang zhig rang gi 'grub [N 32b] med pa ||
> des gzhan ba skyed par ji ltar 'gyur ||

zhes bshad do ||

> de phyir rkyen gyi rang bzhin min || [MMK I.14a]

de'i phyir rkyen gyi rang bzhin gyi 'bras bu ni yod pa ma[7] yin no ||

§155. 'o na rkyen ma yin pa'i rang bzhin du 'gyur ro[8] zhe na |

---

[1] P, N, G: add following la snam bu

[2] C: snag

[3] D, C: gyi for cha shas

[4] P: om. phyir

[5] Em.: las. P, N, G, D, C: la

[6] D, C: om.

[7] P, N, G: om.

[8] P, N, G: om.

> rkyen min rang bzhin [C 30a] 'bras bu ni ||
> yod min
>
> [MMK I.14bc$_1$]

te | gang gi tshe snam bu snal ma'i rang bzhin du yang med pa de'i tshe 'gal ba 'jag ma'i rang bzhin du ji ltar 'gyur |

§156. 'dir smras pa | 'bras bu med du zad mod | rkyen dang rkyen ma yin pa'i nges pa ni yod pa yin te | de ltar yang khyod kyis gal te 'bras bu med pa[1] rkyen dag las skye na | rkyen ma yin pa dag las kyang ci'i phyir skye ba ma yin zhes smras la | snam bu dang re lde zhes bya ba'i 'bras bu [G 40b] med na ni snal ma dang 'jag ma dag rkyen dang rkyen ma yin pa nyid du yang mi rigs te | des na 'bras bu yang yod pa[2] yin no || [P 34b]

§157. bshad par bya ste | gal te 'bras bu yod par gyur na ni | rkyen dang rkyen ma yin pa dag tu 'gyur ro || 'di ltar 'bras bu yod na ni 'di dag ni 'di'i rkyen yin no || 'di dag ni rkyen[3] ma yin no zhes bya bar 'gyur na | de yang rnam par dpyad pa na med pa nyid de | de'i phyir

> 'bras bu med pas na ||
> rkyen min rkyen du ga la 'gyur || [MMK I.14 c$_2$d] [PsP$_L$ 90]

te | rkyen dang rkyen [D 30b] ma yin par zhes tshig bsdu'o || de'i phyir dngos po rnams skye ba yod pa ma yin no ||

§158. ji skad du 'phags pa dkon mchog 'byung gnas kyi mdo las |

---

[1] D: adds following yang

[2] P, N, G: add following ma

[3] D, C: 'di'i rkyen

gang na'ang stong pa rig pa med pa ni[1] ||
nam mkha' bar snang bya yi[2] rjes dang mtshungs ||
gang na'ang ngo bo nyid 'ga' yod min pa ||
de ni nam yang gzhan gyi rgyur mi 'gyur ||

gang gi ngo bo nyid ni mi rnyed[3] pa ||
rang bzhin med de ji ltar gzhan gyi rkyen ||
rang bzhin med pa gzhan gyis[4] ci zhig bskyed ||
rgyu de bde bar gshegs pas bstan pa'o ||

thams cad chos kyang mi g-yo brtan par gnas ||
mi 'gyur 'tshe ba med cing zhi ba ste ||
ji ltar nam mkha' shes pa med pa bzhin ||
de la mi shes 'gro ba rmongs par 'gyur ||

ji ltar ri bo dag ni mi sgul ba ||
de bzhin chos rnams rtag tu[5] bkyod mi nus ||
'chi 'pho med cing skye ba med pa yi ||
chos rnams de ltar rgyal bas rab tu bstan || [PsP$_L$ 91]

zhes [N 33a] bya ba la sogs pa dang |

de bzhin du |

chos gang skye ba med cing 'byung ba med ||

---

[1] D, C: na

[2] P, N, C: bya'i

[3] N: rnyad

[4] P, N, G: gyi

[5] C: du ba

’chi ’pho med cing rga bar mi ’gyur ba ||
mi yi [G 41a] seng ge yis ni der ston zhing[1] || [C 30b]
sems can brgya phrag dag ni de la bkod ||

gang la ngo bo nyid ni gang yang med ||
gzhan yang ma yin sus kyang ma[2] rnyed pa ||
nang na ma yin phyi rol dag na yang ||
mi rnyed de dag la ni mgon pos bkod ||

bde bar gshegs pas zhi ba’i ’gro gsungs kyang ||
’gro ba gang yang rnyed par mi ’gyur te ||
de dag ’gro las grol bar [P 35a] rnam par gsungs ||
grol nas sems can mang po grol bar mdzad ||

zhes[3] gsungs pa lta bu’o ||

§159. slob dpon zla ba grags pa’i zhal snga nas sbyar ba’i tshig gsal ba las | rkyen brtag pa zhes bya ba rab tu byed pa dang po’i ’grel pa’o ||

---

[1] C: cing

[2] D, C: mi

[3] D, C: ces

Abbreviations and Bibliography

Abbreviations: Journals, Dictionaries, Misc.

AASP	Austrian Academy of Sciences Press
ABORI	*Annals of the Bhandarkar Oriental Research Institute*
Apte	*The Practical Sanskrit English Dictionary*. See Apte 1985.
ARIRIAB	*Annual Report of the International Research Institute for Advanced Buddhology at Soka University*
AS/ÉA	*Asiatische Studien / Études Asiatiques*
ATBS	Arbeitskreis für Tibetische und Buddhistische Studien Universität Wien
BHSD	*Buddhist Hybrid Sanskrit Grammar and Dictionary*. Vol. II: *Dictionary*. See Edgerton 1993.
BHSG	*Buddhist Hybrid Sanskrit Grammar and Dictionary*. Vol. I: *Grammar*. See Edgerton 1993.
CPD	*A Critical Pāli Dictionary*. See Trenckner et al. 1924-2011.
IASWR	Institute for the Advanced Study of World Religions
IIJ	*Indo-Iranian Journal*
JA	*Journal Asiatique*
Jäschke	*A Tibetan-English Dictionary*. See Jäschke 2003.
JBORS	*Journal of the Bihar and Orissa Research Society*
JIABS	*Journal of the International Association of Buddhist Studies*
JIBS	*Journal of Indian and Buddhist Studies*

JIP	*Journal of Indian Philosophy*
LC	*Tibetan-Sanskrit Dictionary*. See Chandra 1990.
LVP	de La Vallée Poussin
MW	*A Sanskrit English Dictionary*. See Monier-Williams 1990.
Negi	*Tibetan-Sanskrit Dictionary*. See Negi 1998.
NGMCP	Nepalese German Manuscript Cataloguing Project
NGMPP	Nepal-German Manuscript Preservation Project
PEW	*Philosophy East and West*
PTS	Pāli Text Society
PTSD	*The Pāli Text Society's Pāli-English Dictionary*. See Rhys Davids and Stede 1993.
PW	*Sanskrit-Wörterbuch*. See Böhtlingk and Roth 1990.
RKTS	Resources for Kanjur & Tanjur Studies. Dept. of South Asian, Tibetan and Buddhist Studies, University of Vienna. http://www.istb.univie.ac.at/kanjur/xml3/xml/ (accessed Dec. 27, 2013)
Skt	Sanskrit
StII	*Studien zur Indologie und Iranistik*
SUNY	State University of New York Press
TCD	*Bod rgya tshig mdzod chen mo*. Beijing: Mi rigs dpe skrun khang, 1985.
Tib	Tibetan
Traité	See Lamotte 1966, 1970, 1976, 1980.
WZKS	*Wiener Zeitschrift für die Kunde Südasiens*
WZKSO	*Wiener Zeitschrift für die Kunde Süd- und Ostasiens*

Abbreviations: Primary Sources and Translations

ABh	Akutobhayā
ABh_{ed}	Akutobhayā edition. See Huntington 1986.
ABh_{tr}	Akutobhayā translation. See Walleser 1911.
AK / AKBh	Abhidharmakośa / Abhidharmakośabhāṣya
$AKBh_{ed}$	Abhidharmakośabhāṣya edition. See Pradhan 1975.
$AKBh_{Ej}$	Abhidharmakośabhāṣya Chapter I edition. See Ejima 1989.
$AKBh_{tr}$	Abhidharmakośabhāṣya translation. See La Vallée Poussin 1923-1931.
AKVy	Abhidharmakośavyākhyā. See Wogihara 1971.
AN	Aṅguttaranikāya. See Morris and Hardy 1885-1900.
AS	Abhidharmasamuccaya
ASBh	Abhidharmasamuccayabhāṣya. See Tatia 1976.
Aṣṭa	Aṣṭasāhasrikāprajñāpāramitā. See Vaidya 1960a.
BCAP	Bodhicaryāvatārapañjikā. See La Vallée Poussin 1901-1912.
BoBhū	Bodhisattvabhūmi. See Wogihara 1971.
BP	Buddhapālita Madhyamakavṛtti.
BP_{ed} / BP_{tr}	Buddhapālita Madhyamakavṛtti edition / Buddhapālita Madhyamakavṛtti translation. See Saito 1984.
C	Co ne bstan 'gyur. Microfiches. Stony Brook, New York: The Institute of the Advanced Study of World Religions.
CL	Chung lun
CŚ / CŚṬ	Catuḥśataka / Catuḥśatakaṭīkā
$CŚṬ_{ed}$	Catuḥśatakaṭīkā edition. See Suzuki 1996.

CŚṬ$_{\text{Ted}}$ / CŚṬ$_{\text{tr}}$ Catuḥśatakaṭīkā chapters 12 & 13 edition / Catuḥśatakaṭīkā chapters 12 & 13 translation. See Tillemans 1990.

D sDe dge bKa' 'gyur and bsTan 'gyur. (bsTan 'gyur:) Ed. J. Takasaki, Z. Yamaguchi, N. Hakamaya. *sDe dge Tibetan Tripiṭaka bsTan 'gyur – Preserved at the Faculty of Letters, University of Tokyo*. Tokyo: Sekai seiten kankō kyōkai, 1980. (bKa' 'gyur:) Ed. A.W. Barber et al. *The Tibetan Tripiṭaka*. Taipei edition. Taipei: SMC Publishing Inc., 1991.

DN Dīghanikāya. See Rhys Davids and Carpenter 1890-1911.

DN-aṭṭha Dīghanikāya-aṭṭhakathā. See Rhys Davids, Carpenter and Stede 1886-1932.

DS Dhammasaṅgaṇī. See Müller 1885.

G Golden Manuscript bsTan 'gyur

Gondhla Gondhla Manuscript bsTan 'gyur. RKTS.

Iti Itivuttaka. See Windisch 1975.

Kāś Kāśikā. See Sharma et al. 1969.

KP / KP$_{\text{ed}}$ Kāśyapaparivartasūtra / Kāśyapaparivartasūtra edition. See von Staël-Holstein 1977.

*LṬ *Lakṣaṇaṭīkā

MA / MABh Madhayamakāvatāra / Madhyamakāvatārabhāṣya

MABh$_{\text{ed}}$ Madhyamakāvatārabhāṣya edition. See La Vallée Poussin 1907-1912.

MABh$_{\text{tr}}$ Madhyamakāvatārabhāṣya translation. See La Vallée Poussin 1907, 1910, 1911.

MABh$_{\text{UN}}$ Madhyamakāvatārabhāṣya edition. See Uryuzu and Nakazawa 2012.

MAV Madhyāntavibhāga

MAVBh Madhyāntavibhāgabhāṣya. See Nagao 1964.

MAVṬ Madhyāntavibhāgabhāṣyaṭīkā. See Yamaguchi 1934.

MHK	Madhyamakahṛdayakārikā
MMK	Mūlamadhyamakakārikā
MMK_T	Mūlamadhyamakakārikā Tibetan translation
MN	Majjhimanikāya. See Trenckner and Chalmers 1888-1889.
MN_{tr}	Majjhimanikāya translation. See Ñāṇamoli and Bodhi 1995.
MN-aṭṭha	Majjhimanikāya-aṭṭhakathā. See Horner 1933-1938.
MS	Mīmāṃsāsūtra
N	sNar thang bsTan'gyur (manuscript copy, London)
NBh	Nyāyabhāṣya. See Thakur 1997a.
NM	Nyāyamukha
NS	Nyāyasūtra. See NBh and NV.
NV	Nyāyavārttika. See Thakur 1997b.
P	Peking bKa' 'gyur and bsTan 'gyur. Ed. D. T. Suzuki. The Tibetan Tripiṭaka, Peking Edition, Reprinted under the Supervision of the Otani University, Kyoto. Tokyo/Kyoto: Tibetan Tripiṭaka Research Institute, 1957.
Pā	Pāṇini's Aṣṭādhyāyī. See Böthlingk 2001 and Vasu 1980.
Phug brag	Phug brag Manuscript bsTan 'gyur (2 versions). RKTS.
PP / PPṬ	Prajñāpradīpa / Prajñāpradīpaṭīkā
PP_{ed} / PP_{tr}	Prajñāpradīpa edition of chapters 3-5, 17, 23 and 26 / Prajñāpradīpa translation of chapters 3-5, 17, 23 and 26. See Ames 1986.
PS / PSV	Pramāṇasamuccaya / Pramāṇasamuccayavṛtti
PsP	Prasannapadā
PsP_L	Prasannapadā edition. See La Vallée Poussin 1970.

PsP_M	*In Clear Words* Sanskrit edition. Ed. A. MacDonald (infra).
PSP	Pañcaskandhaprakaraṇa
PSṬ	Pramāṇasamuccayaṭīkā
PSV_{Kit}	See Kitagawa 1965.
PSV_K	Pramāṇasamuccayavṛtti as translated by Kanakavarman (Peking ed.)
PSV_V	Pramāṇasamuccayavṛtti as translated by Vasudhararakṣita (Peking ed.)
PVBh	Pramāṇavārttikabhāṣya. See Sāṅkṛtyāyana 1953.
PVSV	Pramāṇavārttikasvavṛtti. See Gnoli 1960.
RĀ	Ratnāvalī. See Hahn 1982.
RCP	Ratnacūḍaparipṛcchā
RK	Ratnākārasūtra
Śastri	See Śastri 1987.
SiKau	Siddhānta Kaumudī Tattvabodhinīṭīkāsahitā. Laukikabhāge–Jñānendrasarasvatīviracitatattvabodhinīsamākhyayā, vaidikabhāge–paṃ. Jayakṛṣṇaviracitasubodhinīsamākhyayā, liṅgānuśāsane–Bhairavamiśranirmitacandrakalākhyayā ca vyākhyayā. Mumbayyāṃ: Śrīveṅkaṭeśvara Sṭīm-Mudraṇālaye, 1959.
Siddhi	Vijñaptimātratāsiddhi. See La Vallée Poussin 1929.
ŚiS	Śikṣāsamuccaya. See Bendall 1902.
SN	Saṃyuttanikāya. See Feer 1884-1898.
$SN_{Nāl}$	Saṃyuttanikāya Nālandā edition. See Kashyap 1959.
SN_{tr}	Saṃyuttanikāya translation. See Bodhi 2000.
SN-aṭṭha	Saṃyuttanikāya-aṭṭhakathā. See Woodward 1937.
Sn	Suttanipāta. See Anderson and Smith 1984.
SR	Samādhirājasūtra. See Vaidya 1961.

ŚS / ŚSV	Śūnyatāsaptati / Śūnyatāsaptativṛtti
$ŚSV_{ed}$ / $ŚSV_{tr}$	Śūnyatāsaptativṛtti edition (to *kārikā* 14) / Śūnyatāsaptativṛtti translation. See Erb 1997.
ŚV	Ślokavārttika. See Śāstrī 1978.
TJ	Tarkajvālā
TKK	Tibetan edition of PsP_L 55.11-75.12. See TKK 2001.
TSP	Tattvasaṅgrahapañjikā. See Śāstrī 1981.
sTog	sTog Manuscript bsTan 'gyur. RKTS.
VD	Kāśyapaparivartasūtra ms transcription. See Vorobyova-Desyatovskaya 2002.
Vin	Vinayapiṭaka. See Oldenberg 1879-1883.
VM	Visuddhimagga. In *Visuddi-Magga of Buddhaghosa*. Ed. C.A.F. Rhys Davis. Reprint PTS, 1975.
VM_{tr}	Visuddhimagga translation. See Nyanatiloka 1975.
VMD	Vajramaṇḍadhāraṇī
VV	Vigrahavyāvartanī
VV_{ed}	Vigrahavyāvartanī edition. See Bhattacharya et al. 1986.
YD	Yuktidīpikā edition. See Wezler and Moteji 1998.
YṢ / YṢV	Yuktiṣaṣṭikā / Yuktiṣaṣṭikāvṛtti
$YṢV_{ed}$ / $YṢV_{tr}$	Yuktiṣaṣṭikāvṛtti edition / Yuktiṣaṣṭikāvṛtti translation. See Scherrer-Schaub 1991.

Bibliography

Abhyankar and Shukla 1977 — K.V. Abhyankar and J.M. Shukla, *A Dictionary of Sanskrit Grammar*. Baroda: Oriental Institute, 1977.

Allinger 2012 — Eva Allinger, "The Epsilon 1 Manuscript in the Wellcome Library, London." *WZKS* 54 (2012) 151-184.

Ames 1982 — William L. Ames, *Bondage and Liberation According to the Mādhyamika School of Buddhism: A Study and Translation of Chapter Sixteen of the Mūlamadhyamakakārikās and Five of Its Commentaries*. Unpublished M.A. thesis, University of Washington, 1982.

Ames 1986 — Id., *Bhāvaviveka's Prajñāpradīpa: Six Chapters*. Unpublished Ph.D. dissertation, University of Washington, 1986.

Ames 1993 — Id., "Bhāvaviveka's *Prajñāpradīpa*. A Translation of Chapter One: 'Examination of Causal Conditions' (*Pratyaya*)." *JIP* 21 (1993) 209-259.

Ames 1994 — Id., "Bhāvaviveka's *Prajñāpradīpa*. A Translation of Chapter One: 'Examination of Causal Conditions' (*Pratyaya*)" Part Two. *JIP* 22 (1994) 93-135.

Ames 1995 — Id., "Bhāvaviveka's *Prajñāpradīpa*. A Translation of Chapter Two: 'Examination of the Traversed, the Untraversed, and That Which is Being Traversed.'" *JIP* 23 (1995) 295-365.

Ames 1999 — Id., "Bhāvaviveka's *Prajñāpradīpa*: A Translation of Chapters Three, Four, and Five, Examining the *Āyatana*s, Aggregates, and Elements [from the Tibetan]." *Buddhist Literature* 1 (1999) 1-119.

Anderson and Smith 1984 — D. Anderson and H. Smith, ed., *Suttanipāta*. London: PTS, 1913. Reprint 1984.

Apte 1985 — V.S. Apte, *The Practical Sanskrit English Dictionary*. Delhi: Motilal Banarsidass, 1965. Reprint 1985.

Arnold 2003 — Dan Arnold, "Candrakīrti on Dignāga on Svalakṣaṇas." *JIABS* 26 (2003) 139-174.

Arnold 2005a — Id., *Buddhists, Brahmins and Belief: Epistemology in South Asian Philosophy of Religion*. New York: Columbia University Press, 2005.

Arnold 2005b — Id., "Materials for a Mādhyamika Critique of Foundationalism: An Annotated Translation of *Prasannapadā* 55.11 to 75.13." *JIABS* 28 (2005) 411-467.

Arnold 2010 — Id., "Self-Awareness (*svasaṃvitti*) and Related Doctrines of Buddhists Following Dignāga: Philosophical Characterizations of Some of the Main Issues." *JIP* 38 (2010) 323-378.

Aufrecht 1962 — Theodor Aufrecht, *Catalogus Catalogorum: An Alphabetical Register of Sanskrit Works and Authors*. Stuttgart: Franz Steiner Verlag, 1962.

Bajracharya 1995 — Bidya Bhushan Bajracharya, "A Brief Biography of Pandit Vaidya Asha Kaji Bajracharya." In *Report on Newar Buddhist Culture Preservation Seminar*. Ed. Dr. Bajra Raj Shakya. Pathan: The Lotus Research Centre and the Nepal Buddhist Sanskrit Study Centre, 1995. 12-15.

Bareau 1955 — André Bareau, *Les sectes bouddhiques du Petit Véhicule*. Saigon: École Française d'Extrême-Orient, 1955.

Basham 1988 — A.L. Basham, *The Wonder that was India*. London: Sidgwick and Jackson, 1988.

Bendall 1902 — Cecil Bendall, *Śikṣāsamuccaya*. St. Petersburg: Imperial Academy of Sciences, 1902.

Bendall 1992 — Id., *Catalogue of the Buddhist Sanskrit Manuscripts in the University Library, Cambridge*. Cambridge, 1883. Reprint, ed. A. Wezler, Stuttgart: Franz Steiner Verlag, 1992.

Bendall and Rouse 1990 — Cecil Bendall and W.D.H. Rouse, *Śikṣā Samuccaya*. London, 1932. Reprint Delhi: Motilal Barnasidass, 1990.

Bernhard 1965 — Franz Bernhard, ed., *Udānavarga. Band 1*. Göttingen: Vandenhoeck & Ruprecht, 1965.

Bhatt 1989 — G. P. Bhatt, *The Basic Ways of Knowing*. Varanasi 1962. Rev. ed. Delhi: Motilal Barnasidass, 1989.

Bhattacharya 1974 — K. Bhattacharya, "A Note on the interpretation of the term *sādhyasama* in Madhyamaka Texts." *JIP* 2 (1974) 225-230.

Bhattacharya 1977 — Id., "On the Relationship between the *Vigraha-vyāvartanī* and the *Nyāyasūtra*-s." *Journal of Indo-European Studies* 5 (1977) 265-273.

Bhattacharya 1978 — Id., "Some Notes on the Vigrahavyāvartanī." *JIP* 5 (1978) 237-241.

Bhattacharya 1981 — Id., "The Grammatical Basis of Nāgārjuna's Arguments: Some Further Considerations." *Indologica Taurinensia* 9 (1981) 35-43.

Bhattacharya 2012 — Ramakrishna Bhattacharya, "*Svabhāvavāda* and the Cārvāka/Lokāyata: A Historical Overview." In *JIP* 40 (2012) 593-614.

Bhattacharya and Tucci 1932 — Ed. V. Bhattacharya and G. Tucci, *Madhyāntavibhāgasūtrabhāṣyaṭīkā*. London: Luzac & Co., 1932.

Bhattacharya et al. 1986 — K. Bhattacharya, E.H. Johnston, and A. Kunst, *The Dialectical Method of Nāgārjuna: Vigrahavyāvartanī*. 2nd ed. New Delhi: Motilal Banarsidass, 1986.

Bocking 1995 — Brian Bocking, *Nāgārjuna in China: A Translation of the Middle Treatise*. Lewiston/Queenston/Lampeter: Edwin Mellen Press, 1995.

Bodhi 2000 — Bhikkhu Bodhi, *The Connected Discourses of the Buddha*. Boston: Wisdom Publications, 2000.

Böthlingk 2001 — Otto Böthlingk, *Pāṇini's Grammatik*. Leipzig, 1887. Reprint Delhi: Motilal Banarsidass, 2001.

Böthlingk and Roth 1990 — Otto Böhtlingk and Rudolph Roth, *Sanskrit-Wörterbuch*. 7 vols. St. Petersburg: Kaiserlichen Akademie der Wissenschaften, 1855-1875. Reprint New Delhi: Motilal Banarsidass, 1990.

Braarvig 1993 — Jens Braarvig, *Akṣayamatinirdeśasūtra*. Oslo: Solum Forlag, 1993.

Brockington 1998 — John Brockington, *The Sanskrit Epics*. Leiden: Brill, 1998.

Broido 1983 — Michael M. Broido, "A Note on dGos-'Brel." *The Journal of the Tibet Society* 3 (1983) 5-19.

Brough 1996 — John Brough, "The Language of the Buddhist Sanskrit Texts." In *Collected Papers*. Ed. Minoru Hara and J.C. Wright. London: University of London Press, 1996. 130-154.

Buffetrille and Lopez 2010 — Katia Buffetrille, Don Lopez, tr., *Introduction to the History of Indian Buddhism. Eugène Burnouf*. Chicago: University of Chicago Press, 2010.

Bugault 1992 — Guy Bugault, "Nāgārjuna: examen critique du nirvāṇa (nivāṇa-parīkṣa)." *AS/ÉA* 46 (1992) 83-146.

Bühler 1896 — Georg Bühler, *Indische Palaeographie von circa 350 A. Chr. – circa 1300 P. Chr. Mit Siebzehn Tafeln in Mappe*. Strassburg: Karl J. Trübner, 1896.

Burnouf 1844 — Eugène Burnouf, *Introduction à l'histoire du Buddhisme indien*. Paris: Impr. royale, 1844.

Butzenberger 2000 — Klaus Butzenberger, "Was sind *kāraka*-s? Notizen zu einer Rekonstruktion der *kāraka*-Theorie." In *Vividharatnakaraṇḍaka. Festgabe für Adelheid Mette*. Ed. C. Chojnacki, J.-U. Hartmann, V. Tschannerl. Swisttal-Odendorf: Indica et Tibetica, 2000. 117-138.

Cabezón 1992 — José Cabezón, *A Dose of Emptiness*. New York: SUNY, 1992.

Cardona 1974 — G. Cardona, "Pāṇini's *Kārakas*: Agency, Animation and Identity." *JIP* 2 (1974) 231-306.

Cardona 1988 — Id., *Pāṇini: His Work and its Traditions*. Vol. 1. Delhi: Motilal Banarsidass, 1988.

Chakravarti 1975 — P. Chakravarti, *Origin and Development of the Sāṃkhya System of Thought*. Calcutta 1951. 2nd ed. New Delhi: Munshiram Manoharlal, 1975.

Chandra 1990 — Lokesh Chandra, *Tibetan-Sanskrit Dictionary*. Kyoto: Rinsen Book Co., 1990.

Chang 1983 — G.C.C. Chang, ed., *A Treasury of Mahāyāna Sūtras. Selections from the Mahāratnakūṭa Sūtra*. University Park: Pennsylvania State University Press, 1983.

Chaṭṭha Saṅgāyana CD-ROM, Version 3.0. Igatpuri: Vipasanna Research Institute, 1999.

Chaudhury 1969 — B.N. Chaudhury, *Buddhist Centres in Ancient India*. Calcutta: Sanskrit College, 1969.

Conze 1967 — Edward Conze, *Buddhist Thought in India*. George Allen and Unwin, 1962. Reprint Ann Arbor: University of Michigan Press, 1967.

Conze 1968 — Id., "The Iconography of the Prajñāpāramitā." In *Thirty Years of Buddhist Studies: Selected Essays*. Ed. E. Conze. Columbia: University of South Carolina Press, 1968. 243-268.

Cox 1988 — Collett Cox, "On the Possibility of a Nonexistent Object of Consciousness: Sarvāstivādin and Dārṣṭāntika Theories." *JIABS* 11 (1988) 31-87.

Cox 1993 — Id., "Dependent Origination: Its Elaboration in Early Sarvāstivādin Abhidharma Texts." In *Researches in Indian and Buddhist Philosophy. Essays in Honour Professor Alex Wayman*. Ed. Ram Karan Sharma. Delhi: Motilal Banarsidass, 1993. 119-141.

Cox 1995 — Id., *Disputed Dharmas: Early Buddhist Theories on Existence*. Tokyo: International Institute for Buddhist Studies, 1995.

Dayal 1978 — Har Dayal, *The Bodhisattva Doctrine in Buddhist Sanskrit Literature*. London: Routledge & Keagan Paul Ltd., 1932. Reprint Delhi: Motilal Banarsidass, 1978.

Deleanu 2000 — Florin Deleanu, "A Preliminary Study on Meditation and the Beginnings of Mahāyāna Buddhism." *ARIRIAB* 3 (2000) 65-113.

Deleanu 2006 — Id., *The Chapter on the Mundane Path (Laukikamārga) in the Śrāvakabhūmi: A Trilingual Edition (Sanskrit, Tibetan, Chinese), Annotated Translation, and Introductory Study*. Vol. I. Tokyo: The International Institute for Buddhist Studies, 2006.

Deshpande 1990 — Madhav M. Deshpande, "Semantics of *Kāraka*s in Pāṇini: An Exploration of Philosophical and Linguistic Issues." In *Sanskrit and Related Studies: Contemporary Researches and*

Reflections. Ed. B.K. Matilal & Purusottama Bilimoria. Delhi: Sri Satguru Publications, 1990. 33-57.

Dhammajoti 2009 — K.L. Dhammajoti, *Sarvāstivāda Abhidharma*. 4th rev. ed. Hong Kong: Centre of Buddhist Studies, University of Hong Kong, 2009.

Dimitrov 2007 — Dragomir Dimitrov, *Lehrschrift über die Zwanzig Präverbien im Sanskrit. Kritische Ausgabe der Viṃśatyupasargavṛtti und der tibetischen Übersetzung Ñe bar bsgyur ba ñi śu pa'i 'grel pa*. Marburg: Indica et Tibetica, 2007.

Dreyfus and Lindtner 1989 — Georges Dreyfus and Christian Lindtner, "The Yogācāra Philosophy of Dignāga and Dharmakīrti." *Studies in Central and East Asian Religions* 2 (1989) 27-52.

Dunne 2004 — John D. Dunne, *Foundations of Dharmakīrti's Philosophy*. Boston: Wisdom Publications, 2004.

Dutt 1947 — Nalinaksha Dutt, ed., *Gilgit Manuscripts* Vol. III, Part 1. Calcutta: Calcutta Oriental Press, 1947.

Eckel 1978 — Malcolm David Eckel, "Bhāvaviveka and the early Mādhyamika Theories of Language." *PEW* 28 (1978) 323-337.

Eckel 1980 — Id., *A Question of Nihilism: Bhāvaviveka's Response to the Fundamental Problems of Mādhyamika Philosophy*. Unpublished Ph.D. dissertation, Harvard University, 1980.

Eckel 2008 — Id., *Bhāviveka and His Buddhist Opponents*. Cambridge: Harvard University Press, 2008.

Edgerton 1993 — Franklin Edgerton, *Buddhist Hybrid Sanskrit Grammar and Dictionary*. New Haven: Yale University Press, 1953. Reprint New Delhi: Motilal Banarsidass, 1993.

Ejima 1980 — Y. Ejima, *Chūkan-Shisō no Tenkai Bhāvaviveka Kenkyū* (Madhyamakahṛdayakārikā III). Tokyo: Shunjūsha, 1980.

Ejima 1989 — Id., *Abhidharmakośabhāṣya of Vasubandhu. Chapter One: Dhātunirdeśa*. Tokyo: The Sankibo Press, 1989.

Eltschinger 2007 — Vincent Eltschinger, *Penser l'autorité des Écritures: La polémique de Dharmakīrti contre la notion brahmanique orthodoxe d'un Veda sans auteur*. Vienna: AASP, 2007.

Eltschinger 2010 — Id., "Ignorance, epistemology and soteriology. Part II." *JIABS* 33 (2010) 27-74.

Erb 1990 — Felix Erb, *Die Śūnyatāsaptati des Nāgārjuna und die Śūnyatāsaptativṛtti* [*Verse 1-32*] (*unter Berücksichtigung der Kommentare Candrakīrtis, Parahitas und des Zweiten Dalai Lama*). Unpublished Ph.D. dissertation, University of Hamburg, 1990.

Erb 1997 — Id., *Śūnyatāsaptativṛtti. Candrakīrtis Kommentar zu den „Siebzig Versen über die Leerheit" des Nāgārjuna* [*Kārikās 1-14*]. Stuttgart: Franz Steiner Verlag, 1997.

Feer 1884-1898 — L. Feer, ed., *Saṃyuttanikāya*. London: PTS, 1884-1898.

Fenner 1983 — Peter Fenner, "Candrakīrti's refutation of Buddhist idealism." *PEW* 33 (1983) 251-261.

Filliozat 1942 — Jean Filliozat, "Catalogue des manuscrits sanskrits et tibétains de la Société Asiatique." *JA*, Tome 233, Année 1941-1942 (1942) 1-81.

Filliozat 1978 — Pierre Sylvain Filliozat, *Le Mahābhāṣya de Patañjali avec le Pradīpa de Kaiyaṭa et l'Uddyota de Nāgeśa: Adhyāya 1 Pāda 1 Āhnika 8-9*. Pondichéry: Institut Français d'Indologie, 1978.

Fleet 1904 — John Faithfull Fleet, tr., *Indian Paleography by Johann Georg Bühler*. Edited as an Appendix to *The Indian Antiquary* 33 (1904).

Franco 1984 — Eli Franco, "Studies in the Tattvopaplavasimha II. The Theory of Error." *JIP* 12 (1984) 105-187.

Franco 2001 — Id., "Fragments of a Buddhist *Pramāṇa*-Theory from the Kuṣāṇa Period." *Bukkyo Dendo Kyokai Fellowship Newsletter* 4 (2001) 2-12.

Franco 2007 — Id., "Prajñākaragupta on *pratītyasamutpāda* and reverse causation." In *Pramāṇakīrtiḥ. Papers dedicated to Ernst Steinkellner on the occasion of his 70th birthday*. Ed. B. Kellner, H. Krasser, H. Lasic, M.T. Much, H. Tauscher. Vienna: ATBS, 2007. 163-185.

Franco 2010 — Id., "The Discussion of *pramāṇa*s in the Spitzer Manuscript." In *Logic in Earliest Classical India. Papers of the 12th World Sanskrit Conference held in Helsinki, Finland, 13-18 July 2003, Vol. 10.2.* Ed. Brendan S. Gillon. Delhi: Motilal Banarsidass, 2010. 121-138.

Frauwallner 1956 — Erich Frauwallner, *Geschichte der indischen Philosophie.* Vol. 2. Salzburg: Otto Müller Verlag, 1956.

Frauwallner 1957 — Id., "Vasubandhu's Vādavidhi." *WZKSO* 1 (1957) 104-146.

Frauwallner 1958 — Id., *Die Philosophie des Buddhismus.* 2. Auflage. Berlin: Akademie-Verlag, 1958.

Frauwallner 1959 — Id., "Dignāga, sein Werk und seine Entwicklung." *WZKSO* 3 (1959) 83-164.

Frauwallner 1960 — Id., "Das Eindringen der Sprachtheorie in die indischen philosophischen Systeme." In *Indologen-Tagung 1959 Verhandlungen der Indologischen Arbeitstagung in Essen-Bredeney, Villa Hügel, 13.-15. Juli 1959.* Ed. Ernst Waldschmidt. Göttingen: Vandenhoeck & Ruprecht, 1960. 239-243.

Frauwallner 1961 — Id., "Mīmāṃsāsūtram I, 1, 6-23." *WZKSO* 5 (1961) 113-124.

Frauwallner 1964 — Id., "Abhidharma-Studien." *WZKS* 8 (1964) 59-99.

Frauwallner 1982 — Id., *Kleine Schriften.* Ed. G. Oberhammer and E. Steinkellner. Wiesbaden: Franz Steiner Verlag, 1982.

Frauwallner 1984 — Id., *History of Indian Philosophy.* Transl. V.M. Bedekar. Salzburg/Delhi 1973. Reprint Delhi: Motilal Barnasidass, 1984.

Frauwallner 1995 — Id., *Studies in Abhidharma Literature and the Origins of Buddhist Philosophical Systems.* Tr. Sophie Francis Kidd. Albany: SUNY 1995.

Funayama 1991 — Toru Funayama, "On Āśrayasiddha." *JIBS* 39 (1991) 28-34.

Galloway 2001 — Brian Galloway, "Toward a New Edition and Translation of Chapter 13 of the Prasannapadā of Candrakīrti." *ZDMG* 151 (2001) 321-350.

Ganeri 1999 — Jonardon Ganeri, *Semantic Powers: The Meaning and Means of Knowing in Classical Indian Philosophy*, Oxford: Oxford University Press, 1999.

Garbe 1925 — Richard Garbe, *Indische Reiseskizzen*. München-Neubiberg: Oskar Schloss Verlag, 1925.

Garfield 1995 — Jay Garfield, *The Fundamental Wisdom of the Middle Way*. Oxford: Oxford University Press, 1995.

Garfield 2008 — Id., "Turning a Madhyamaka Trick: Reply to Huntington." *JIP* 36 (2008) 507-527.

Gerow 2008 — Edwin Gerow, "Ἐυ ἀρχῇ ἦν ὁ λόγος." In *Śāstrārambha. Inquiries into the Preamble in Sanskrit*. Ed. Walter Slaje. Wiesbaden: Harrassowitz, 2008. ix-xv.

Gnoli 1960 — R. Gnoli, *The Pramāṇavārttikam of Dharmakīrti: The First Chapter with the Autocommentary*. Rome: Istituto Italiano per il Medio ed Estremo Oriente, 1960.

Gokhale 1937 — V.V. Gokhale, "Pañcaskandhaka by Vasubandhu and its commentary by Sthiramati." *ABORI* 13 (1937) 276-286.

Gokhale 1947 — Id., "Fragments from the Abhidharmasamuccaya of Asaṃga." *Journal of the Royal Asiatic Society: Bombay Branch* 23 (1947) 13-38.

Gokhale 1985 — Id., "Mādhyamakahṛdayakārikā Tarkajvālā Chapter I." *Miscellanea Buddhica*. Ed. C. Lindtner. Copenhagen: Akademisk Forlag, 1985. 76-107.

Gomez 1976 — Luis Gomez, "Proto-Mādhyamika in the Pāli Canon." *PEW* 26 (1976) 137-165.

Gordon 1959 — Antoinette K. Gordon, *The Iconography of Tibetan Lamaism*. Rev. ed. Tokyo: Charles E. Tuttle Co., 1959.

Greetham 1992 — D. C. Greetham, *Textual Scholarship: An Introduction*. New York: Garland Publishing, Inc., 1992.

Griffiths 1991 — Paul Griffiths, *On Being Mindless: Buddhist Meditation and the Mind-Body Problem*. La Salle, Illinois: Open Court Publishing Company, 1991.

Grönbold 1991 — Günter Grönbold, ed., *Tibetische Buchdeckel: Ausstellung 8. April bis 1. Juni 1991.* München: Bayerische Staatsbibliothek, 1991.

Grünendahl 1989 — R. Grünendahl, *A Concordance of H.P. Śāstri's Catalogue of the Durbar Library and the Microfilms of the Nepal-German Manuscript Preservation Project.* [Followed by:] *H.P. Śāstri, A Catalogue of Palm-leaf and Selected Paper Mss. belonging to the Durbar Library Nepal, Vol. 1 and 2.* Stuttgart: Franz-Steiner Verlag, 1989.

Gyatso 1992 — Janet Gyatso, ed., *In the Mirror of Memory.* Albany: SUNY, 1992.

Hahn 1982 — Michael Hahn, *Nāgārjuna's Ratnāvalī.* Bonn: Indica et Tibetica Verlag, 1982.

Hahn 1994 — Id., "On Some Rare Particles, Words and Auxiliaries in Classical Tibetan." In *Tibetan Studies, Proceedings of the 6th Seminar of the International Association for Tibetan Studies, Fagernes 1992*, Vol. 1. Ed. Per Kvaerne. Oslo: The Institute for Comparative Research in Human Culture, 1994. 288-294.

Halbfass 1988 — Wilhelm Halbfass, *India and Europe.* Albany: SUNY, 1988.

Halbfass 1992 — Id., *On Being and What There Is.* Albany: SUNY, 1992.

Harrison 1990 — Paul Harrison, *The Samādhi of Direct Encounter with the Buddhas of the Present.* Tokyo: The International Institute for Buddhist Studies, 1990.

Hartmann 1985 — Jens-Uwe Hartmann, "*Dhāraṇī* and *Pratibhāna*: Memory and Eloquence of the Bodhisattvas." *JIABS* 8 (1985) 17-29.

Hartmann 1987 — Id., *Das Varṇārhavarṇastotra des Mātṛceṭa.* Göttingen: Vandenhoeck & Ruprecht, 1987.

Hattori 1968 — Masaaki Hattori, *Dignāga, On Perception, being the Pratyakṣapariccheda of Dignāga's Pramāṇasamuccaya, from the Sanskrit fragments and the Tibetan versions.* Cambridge: Harvard University Press, 1968.

Hattori 1979 — Id., "Apoha and Pratibhā." In *Sanskrit and Indian Studies*. Ed. M. Nagatomi, B.K. Matilal, J.M. Masson and E. Dimock. Dordrecht: D. Reidel Publishing, 1979. 61-73.

Hattori 2000 — Id., "Dignāga's Theory of Meaning." In *Wisdom, Compassion and the Search for Understanding*. Ed. Jonathan Silk. Honolulu: University of Hawai'i Press, 2000. 137-146.

Hayes 1988 — Richard Hayes, *Dignāga on the Interpretation of Signs*. Dordrecht: Kluwer, 1988.

Hayes 1994 — Id., "Nāgārjuna's Appeal." *JIP* 22 (1994) 299-378.

Heitmann 2004 — Annette Heitmann, *Nektar der Erkenntnis. Buddhistische Philosophie des 6. Jh.: Bhavyas Tarkajvālā I-III.26*. Aachen: Shaker Verlag, 2004.

Heitmann 2009 — Id., *Textedition und -kritik von Bhavyas Madhyamakahṛdayakārikā I-III*. Hamburg: Verlag Dr. Kovač, 2009.

von Hinüber 1991 — Oskar von Hinüber, *The Oldest Pāli Manuscript: Four Folios of the Vinaya-Piṭaka from the National Archives, Kathmandu*. Stuttgart: Franz Steiner, 1991.

von Hinüber 2000 — Id., "Der vernachlässigte Wortlaut. Die Problematik der Herausgabe buddhistischer Sanskrit-Texte." In *Zur Überlieferung, Kritik und Edition alter und neuerer Texte*. Ed. K. Gärtner and H.H. Krummacher. Stuttgart: Franz Steiner Verlag, 2000. 17-36.

von Hinüber 2001 — Id., *Das ältere Mittelindisch im Überblick*. Vienna: AASP, 2001.

Hirakawa 1990 — Akira Hirakawa, *A History of Indian Buddhism*. Ed. and tr. Paul Groner. Honolulu: University of Hawaii Press, 1990.

Hodgson 1828 — Brian H. Hodgson, "Notices of the Language, Literature, and Religion of the Bauddhas of Nepal and Bhot." *Asiatic Researches* 16 (1828) 409-449.

Hodgson 1874 — Id., *Essays on the Languages, Literature and Religion of Nepal and Tibet: Together with Further Papers on the Geography, Ethnology and Commerce of Those Countries*. Reprinted, with Corrections and Additions, from "Illustrations of the Literature and Religion of the Buddhists," Serampore, 1841; and "Selections from the Records of the Government of Bengal, No. XXVII.," Calcutta, 1857. London: Trübner & Co., 1874.

Hoornaert 1999 — Paul Hoornaert, "An Annotated Translation of *Madhyamakahṛdayakārikā/Tarkajvālā* V.1-7." *Studies and Essays, Behavioral Sciences and Philosophy* 19 (1999) 127-159.

Hopkins 1980 — Jeffrey Hopkins, *Compassion in Tibetan Buddhism*. London: Rider & Co., 1980.

Hopkins 1983 — Id., *Meditation on Emptiness*. London: Wisdom Publications, 1983.

Hopkins 1989 — Id., "A Tibetan delineation of different views of Emptiness in the Indian Middle Way School." *The Tibet Journal* 14 (1989) 10-43.

Horner 1933-1938 — I.B. Horner, ed., *Majjhimanikāya-Aṭṭhakathā* (*Papañcasūdanī*). Vol. III-V. London: PTS, 1933-1938.

Houben 1995 — Jan Houben, *The Saṃbandha-Samuddeśa and Bhartṛhari's Philosophy of Language*. Groningen: Egbert Forsten, 1995.

Hunter 1896 — William Wilson Hunter, *Life of Brian Houghton Hodgson*. London: J. Murray, 1896.

Huntington 1986 — C.W. Huntington, Jr., *The "Akutobhayā" and Early Indian Madhyamaka*. Unpublished Ph.D. dissertation, University of Michigan, 1986.

Huntington 1989 — Id., *The Emptiness of Emptiness*. Honolulu: University of Hawaii Press, 1989.

Huntington 2003 — Id., "Was Candrakīrti a Prāsaṅgika?" In *The Svātantrika–Prāsaṅgika Distinction*. Ed. G. Dreyfus and S. McClintock. Boston: Wisdom Publications, 2003. 67-91.

Iida 1966 — Shotaro Iida, "Āgama (Scripture) and Yukti (Reason) in Bhāvaviveka." In *Indogaku Bukkyōgaku Ronshū*. Ed. Sakamoto Yukio. Kyoto: Heirakuji-Shoten, 1966. 79-96.

Iida 1980 — Id., *Reason and Emptiness: A Study in Logic and Mysticism*. Tokyo: Hokuseido Press, 1980.

Inada 1970 — Kenneth Inada, *Nāgārjuna: The Philosophy of the Middle Way*. Albany: SUNY, 1970.

Isaacson 1995 — Harunaga Isaacson, *Materials for the study of the Vaiśeṣika system*. Unpublished Ph.D. dissertation, University of Leiden, 1995.

Iwata 1993 — Takashi Iwata, *Prasaṅga und Prasaṅgaviparyaya bei Dharmakīrti und seinen Kommentatoren*. Vienna: ATBS, 1993.

Janert 1995 — Klaus L. Janert, *Bibliographie mit den Berichten über die Mündliche und Schriftliche Textweitergabe sowie die Schreibmaterialien in Indien (Berichtszeit bis 1955)*. Bonn: VGH Wissenschaftsverlag, 1995.

Jäschke 2003 — H.A. Jäschke, *A Tibetan-English Dictionary*. London: Routledge & Kegan Paul, 1881. Reprint New York: Dover Publications, 2003.

Jayaswal and Sāṅkṛtyāyana 1937 — K.P. Jayaswal and R. Sāṅkṛtyāyana, "Vigrahavyāvarttanī." *JBORS* 23 (1937) Appendix.

Jha 1964 — G. Jha, *Pūrva-Mimāṃsā in its Sources*. 2nd ed. Varanasi: Banaras Hindu University Press, 1964.

Johnston 1992 — E.H. Johnston, *The Buddhacarita or Acts of the Buddha*. Lahore 1936. Rev. ed. Delhi: Motilal Banarsidass, 1992.

de Jong 1949 — J.W. de Jong, *Cinq Chapitres de la Prasannapadā*. Paris: Guethner, 1949.

de Jong 1974 — Id., "*A Brief History of Buddhist Studies in Europe and America*." The Eastern Buddhist 7 (1974) no. 1, 55-106; no. 4, 49-82.

de Jong 1977 — Id., ed. *Mūlamadhyamakakārikāḥ*. Madras: The Adyar Library and Research Centre, 1977.

de Jong 1978 — Id., "Textcritical Notes on the Prasannapadā." *IIJ* 20 (1978) 25-59; 217-252.

de Jong 1979 — Id., "La Madhyamakaśāstrastuti de Candrakīrti." *Oriens Extremus* 9 (1962) 47-56. Reprinted in *Buddhist Studies*. Ed. G. Schopen. Berkeley: Asian Humanities Press, 1979. 541-550.

de Jong 1981 — Id., Review of Mervyn Sprung, *Lucid Exposition of the Middle Way*. *IIJ* 23 (1981) 227-230.

de Jong 1993 — Id., Review of Ragunath Pandeya, *The Madhyamaka-śāstram of Nāgārjuna with the commentaries Akutobhayā by Nāgārjuna, Madhyamakavṛtti by Buddhapālita, Prajñāpradīpa-vṛtti by Bhāvaviveka, Prasannapadāvṛtti by Candrakīrti critically reconstructed*. *IIJ* 36 (1993) 144-146.

Joshi and Roodbergen 1971 — S.D. Joshi and J.A.F. Roodbergen, *Patañjali's Vyākaraṇa-Mahābhāṣya: Karmadhārayāhnika (P. 2.1.51-2.1.72)*. Poona: University of Poona, 1971.

Junankar 1978 — N.S. Junankar, *Gautama: The Nyāya Philosophy*. Delhi: Motilal Banarsidass, 1978.

Kajiyama 1963 — Yuichi Kajiyama, "Bhāvaviveka's Prajñāpradīpaḥ (1. Kapitel)." *WZKSO* 7 (1963) 37-62.

Kajiyama 1964 — Id., "Bhāvaviveka's Prajñāpradīpaḥ (1. Kapitel)." *WZKSO* 8 (1964) 100-130.

Kajiyama 1968 — Id., "Bhāviveka, Sthiramati and Dharmapāla." *WZKSO* 12-13 (1968) 193-203.

Kajiyama 1973 — Id., "Three Kinds of Affirmation and Two Kinds of Negation in Buddhist Philosophy." *WZKS* 17 (1973) 161-175.

Kajiyama 1991 — Id., "On the Authorship of the Upāyahṛdaya." In *Studies in the Buddhist Epistemological Tradition. Proceedings of the Second International Dharmakīrti Conference. Vienna June 11-16, 1989*. Ed. E. Steinkellner. Vienna: AASP, 1991. 107-117.

Kajiyama 1998 — Id., *An Introduction to Buddhist Philosophy. An Annotated Translation of the Tarkabhāṣā of Mokṣākaragupta*. Kyoto 1966. Reprint Vienna: ATBS, 1998.

Kane 1973 — P.V. Kane, *History of Dharmaśāstra*. Vol. 3. 2nd ed. Poona: Bhandarkar Oriental Research Institute, 1973.

Kartre 1954 — S.M. Kartre, *Introduction to Indian Textual Criticism*. 2nd ed. Poona: Deccan College, Post-graduate and Research Institute, 1954.

Kashyap 1959 — J. Kashyap, *The Saṃyutta Nikāya. 4. Salāyatanavagga.* Nālandā: Pāli Publication Board, Bihar Govt., 1959.

Katsura 1975 — Shoryu Katsura, "New Sanskrit Fragments of the Pramāṇasamuccaya." *JIP* 3 (1975) 67-78.

Katsura 1977 — Id., "A Study of the Nyāyamukha I." *Hiroshima Daigaku Bungakubu Kiyō* 37 (1977) 106-127.

Katsura 1978 — Id., "A Study of the Nyāyamukha II." *Hiroshima Daigaku Bungakubu Kiyō* 38 (1978) 110-130.

Katsura 1979a — Id., "A Study of the Nyāyamukha III." *Hiroshima Daigaku Bungakubu Kiyō* 39 (1979) 63-83.

Katsura 1979b — Id., "The Apoha Theory of Dignāga." *JIBS* (1979) 493-489.

Katsura 1982 — Id., "A Study of the Nyāyamukha V." *Hiroshima Daigaku Bungakubu Kiyō* 42 (1982) 82-100.

Katsura 1984 — Id., "Dharmakīrti's Theory of Truth." *JIP* 12 (1984) 215-235.

Katsura 1985 — Id., "On Trairūpya Formulae." In *Buddhism and Its Relation to Other Religions: Essays in Honour of Dr. Shozen Kumoi on his Seventieth Birthday.* Kyoto: Heirakuji Shoten, 1985. 161-172.

Katsura 1992 — Id., "Dignāga and Dharmakīrti on *adarśanamātra* and *anupalabdhi*." *AS/ÉA* 46 (1992) 222-231.

Katsura 2009 — Id., "Rediscovering Dignāga through Jinendrabuddhi." In *Sanskrit manuscripts in China. Proceedings of a panel at the 2008 Beijing Seminar on Tibetan Studies October 13 to 17*. Ed. E. Steinkellner, Duan Qing, H. Krasser. Beijing: China Tibetology Publishing House, 2009. 153-166.

Keira 2004 — Ryusei Keira, *Mādhyamika and Epistemology. A Study of Kamalaśīla's Method for Proving the Voidness of all Dharmas. Introduction, Annotated Translations and Tibetan Texts of Selected Sections of the Second Chapter of the Madhyamakāloka*. Vienna: ATBS, 2004.

Kellner 2010 — Birgit Kellner, "Self-Awareness (*svasaṃvedana*) in Dignāga's *Pramāṇasamuccaya* and *-vṛtti*: A Close Reading." *JIP* 38 (2010) 203-231.

Kimura 1999 — Toshihiko Kimura, "A New Chronology of Dharmakīrti." In *Dharmakīrti's Thought and Its Impact on Indian and Tibetan Philosophy. Proceedings of the Third International Dharmakīrti Conference, Hiroshima, November 4-6, 1997*. Ed. Shoryu Katsura. Vienna: AASP, 1999. 209-214.

Kishine 2001a — Toshiyuki Kishine, "A Critical Text of Chapter XXIV *Āryasatyaparīkṣā* of Prasannapadā (I)." In *Fukuokadaigaku jinbun ronso (Fukuoka University Review of Literature & Humanities),* Vol. 33.2 (2001) 1003-1024.

Kishine 2001b — Id., "A Critical Text of Chapter XXIV, *Āryasatyaparīkṣā* of Prasannapadā (II)." In *Fukuokadaigaku jinbun ronso* (*Fukuoka University Review of Literature & Humanities*) 33.3 (2001) 1761-1782.

Kishine 2002 — Id., "A Critical Text of Chapter XXIV, *Āryasatya-parīkṣā* of Prasannapadā (III)." In *Fukuokadaigaku jinbun ronso* (*Fukuoka University Review of Literature & Humanities*) 34.1 (2002) 197-232.

Kitigawa 1965 — Hidenori Kitigawa, *Indo koten ronrigaku no kenkyū: Jinna no taikei* (Studies in Indian Classical Logic, Dignāga's System). Tokyo: Suizuki Gakujutsu Zaidan, 1965.

Kobayashi 2010 — Hisayasu Kobayashi, "Self-Awareness and Mental Perception. " *JIP* 38 (2010) : 233-245.

Kobayashi 2013 — Id., "An Eye-disease Called *Timira*." *JIBS* 61 (2013) 1078-1084.

Kragh 2003 — Ulrich Timme Kragh, *Karmaphalasambandha in verses 17.1-20 of Candrakīrti's Prasannapadā*. Unpublished Ph.D. dissertation, University of Copenhagen, 2003.

Kragh 2006 — Id., *Early Buddhist Theories of Action and Result: A Study of Karmaphalasambandha. Candrakīrti's Prasannapadā, Verses 17.1–20*. Vienna: ATBS, 2006.

Kragh 2009 — Id., "Classicism in Commentarial Writing: Exegetical Parallels in the Indian Mūlamadhyamakakārikā Commentaries." *JIATS* 5 (2009) 1-69.

Krasser 2011 — Helmut Krasser, "How to Teach a Buddhist Monk to Refute the Outsiders. Text-critical Remarks on some Works by Bhāviveka." *Dhī, Journal of Rare Buddhist Texts Research Department* 51 (2011) 49-76.

Krasser 2012a — Id., "Bhāviveka, Dharmakīrti and Kumārila." In *Devadattīyam: Johannes Bronkhorst Felicitation Volume*. Ed. F. Voegeli, V. Eltschinger, D. Feller, M. Piera Candotti, B. Diaconescu & M. Kulkarni. Bern: Peter Lang, 2012. 535-594.

Krasser 2012b — Id., "Logic in a Religious Context: Dharmakīrti in Defence of *āgama*." In *Can the Veda Speak? Dharmakīrti against Mīmāṃsā exegetics and Vedic authority. An annotated translation of PVSV 164,24-176,16.* Ed. Vincent Eltschinger, Helmut Krasser, John Taber. Vienna: AASP, 2012. 83-118.

Kritzer 1999 — Robert Kritzer, *Rebirth and Causation in the Yogācāra Abhidharma*. Vienna: ATBS, 1999.

van der Kuijp 2006 — Leonard van der Kuijp, "The Earliest Indian Reference to Muslims in a Buddhist Philosophical Text of circa 700." *JIP* 34 (2006) 169-202.

La Vallée Poussin 1901-1912 — Louis de La Vallée Poussin, *Bodhicāryāvatārapañjikā: Prajñākaramati's Commentary to the Bodhicaryāvatāra of Śāntideva*. Calcutta: Asiatic Society of Bengal, 1901-1912.

La Vallée Poussin 1907 — Id., "Madhyamakāvatāra: Introduction au Traité du Milieu de l'Ācārya Candrakīrti, avec le commentaire de l'auteur, traduit d'après la version tibétaine." *Le Muséon* 8 (1907) 249-317.

La Vallée Poussin 1907-1912 — Id., *Madhyamakāvatāra par Candrakīrti*. St. Petersburg: Imperial Academy of Sciences, 1907-1912.

La Vallée Poussin 1909 — Id., "Bodhisattva (in Sanskrit Literature)." In *Encyclopaedia of Religion and Ethics*. Vol. 2. Ed. James Hastings. Edinburgh: Clark, 1909. 739-753.

La Vallée Poussin 1910 — Id., "Madhyamakāvatāra: Introduction au Traité du Milieu de l'Ācārya Candrakīrti, avec le commentaire de l'auteur, traduit d'après la version tibétaine." *Le Muséon* 11 (1910) 271-358.

La Vallée Poussin 1911 — Id., "Madhyamakāvatāra: Introduction au Traité du Milieu de l'Ācārya Candrakīrti, avec le commentaire de l'auteur, traduit d'après la version tibétaine." *Le Muséon* 12 (1911) 235-328.

La Vallée Poussin 1913a — Id., *Théorie des Douze Causes*. Gand: Van Goethem, 1913.

La Vallée Poussin 1913b — Id., "Les Quatre Odes de Nāgārjuna." *Le Muséon* 14 (1913) 1-18.

La Vallée Poussin 1923-1931 — Id., *L'Abhidharmakośa de Vasubandhu*. Paris: Geuthner, 1923-1931.

La Vallée Poussin 1929 — Id., *Vijñaptimātratāsiddhi*: *La siddhi de Hiuan-Tsang. Buddhica, Documents et travaux pour l'étude du bouddhisme publiés sous la direction de Jean Przyluski*. Tome I (1928), Tome II (1929). Paris: Librairie Orientaliste Paul Geuthner.

La Vallée Poussin 1933 — Id., "Réflexions sur le Madhyamaka." *MCB* 2 (1933) 1-59.

La Vallée Poussin 1970 — Id., *Madhyamakavṛttiḥ. Mūlamadhyamakakārikās (Mādhyamikasūtras) de Nāgārjuna avec la Prasannapadā Commentaire de Candrakīrti*. St. Petersburg: Imperial Academy of Sciences, 1903-1913. Reprint Osnabrück: Biblio Verlag, 1970.

Lamotte 1936 — Étienne Lamotte, "Madhyamakavṛtti: XVIIe Chapitre. Examen de l'Acte et du Fruit." *MCB* 4 (1936) 265-288.

Lamotte 1960 — Id., "Mañjuśrī." *T'oung Pao* 48 (1960) 1-96.

Lamotte 1966 — Id., *Le Traité de la grande Vertu de Sagesse de Nāgārjuna* (*Mahāprajñāpāramitāśāstra*). Tome I. Louvain: Institut Orientaliste, Université de Louvain, 1966.

Lamotte 1970 — Id., *Le Traité de la grande Vertu de Sagesse de Nāgārjuna* (*Mahāprajñāpāramitāśāstra*). Tome III. Louvain: Institut Orientaliste, Université de Louvain, 1970.

Lamotte 1976 — Id., *Le Traité de la grande Vertu de Sagesse de Nāgārjuna* (*Mahāprajñāpāramitāśāstra*). Tome IV. Louvain: Institut Orientaliste, Université de Louvain, 1976.

Lamotte 1980 — Id., *Le Traité de la grande Vertu de Sagesse de Nāgārjuna* (*Mahāprajñāpāramitāśāstra*). Tome V. Louvain: Institut Orientaliste, Université de Louvain, 1980.

Lamotte 1987 — Id., *L'Enseignement de Vimalakīrti* (*Vimalakīrtinirdeśa*). Louvain, 1962. Reprint Louvain: Institut Orientaliste, 1987.

Lamotte 1988 — Id., *History of Indian Buddhism*. Transl. S. Webb-Boin. Louvain: Institut Orientaliste, 1988.

Lang 1976 — Karen Lang, *Showing the Realization of the Refutation of Holding Extreme Views: Chapter Fourteen of Candrakīrti's Bodhisattvayogācāracatuḥśatakaṭīkā. Edited from the Sanskrit Fragments and the Tibetan Texts*. Unpublished M.A. thesis, University of Washington, 1976.

Lang 1986 — Id., *Āryadeva's Catuḥśataka: On the Bodhisattva's Cultivation of Merit and Knowledge*. Copenhagen: Akademisk Forlag, 1986.

Lang 1990 — Id., "Spa-tshab Nyi-ma-grags and the Introduction of Prāsaṅgika Madhyamaka into Tibet." In *Reflections on Tibetan Culture. Essays in Memory of Turrell V. Wylie*. Ed. L. Epstein and R.F. Sherbourne. Lewiston, New York: Edwin Mellen Press, 1990. 127–141.

Lang 2001 — Id., "Poetic license in the Buddhist Sanskrit Verses of the *Upālipariprcchā*." *IIJ* 44 (2001) 231-240.

Lang 2003 — Id., *Four Illusions, Candrakīrti's Advice to Travelers on the Bodhisattva Path*. Oxford: Oxford University Press, 2003.

Lariviere 1989 — Richard Lariviere, *The Nāradasmṛti*. Philadelphia: University of Pennsylvania, 1989.

Larson and Bhattacharya 1987 — G.J. Larson R.S. Bhattacharya, ed. *Sāṃkhya: A Dualist Tradition in Indian Philosophy*. Published as Vol. 4 of *Encyclopedia of Indian Philosophies*. New Delhi: Motilal Banarsidass, 1987.

Lasic 2010 — Horst Lasic, "A Hot Dispute About Lukewarm Air: Dignāga on Āptavāda." In *Logic and Belief in Indian Philosophy*. Ed. Piotr Balcerowicz. Delhi: Motilal Banarsidass, 2010. 521-537.

Lasic et al. 2012 — Horst Lasic, Helmut Krasser, Ernst Steinkellner, ed., *Jinendrabuddhi's Viśālāmalavatī Pramāṇasamuccayaṭīkā, Chapter 2*. Beijing–Vienna: China Tibetology Publishing House & AASP, 2012.

Lefmann 1902 — S. Lefmann, ed., *Lalita Vistara. Leben und Lehre des Çâkya-Buddha*. Halle: Verlag der Buchhandlung des Waisenhauses, 1902.

Li 2012 — Xuezhu Li, "Madhyamakāvatāra-kārikā." *China Tibetology* 18 (2012) 1-16.

Li-S 2012 — Shenghai Li, *Candrakīrti's Āgama: A Study of the Concept and Uses of Scripture in Classical Indian Buddhism*. Unpublished Ph.D. dissertation, University of Wisconsin-Madison, 2012.

Li and Steinkellner 2008 — Xuezhu Li and Ernst Steinkellner, *Vasubandhu's Pañcaskandhaka*. Beijing–Vienna: China Tibetology Publishing House & AASP, 2008.

Lienhard 1988 — Siegfried Lienhard, *Nepalese Manuscripts, Part 1: Nevārī and Sanskrit described by Siegfried Lienhard with the collaboration of Thakur Lal Manandhar*. Stuttgart: Franz-Steiner Verlag, 1988.

Lindtner 1979 — Christian Lindtner, "Candrakīrti's Pañcaskandhaprakaraṇa." *Acta Orientalia* 40 (1979) 87-145.

Lindtner 1982a — Id., "Adversaria Buddhica." *WZKS* 26 (1982) 167-194.

Lindtner 1982b — Id., *Nagarjuniana*. Copenhagen: Akademisk Forlag, 1982.

Lindtner 1986 — Id., "Bhavya, the Logician." *The Adyar Library Bulletin* 50 (1986) 58-84.

Lindtner 1995 — Id., "Bhavya's Madhyamakahṛdaya (Pariccheda Five)." *The Adyar Library Bulletin* 59 (1995) 37-65.

Lindtner 2001 — Id., *Madhyamakahṛdayam of Bhavya*. Adyar: The Adyar Library and Research Centre, 2001.

Loizzo 2007 — *Nāgārjuna's Reason Sixty with Chandrakīrti's Reason Sixty Commentary*. New York: The American Institute of Buddhist Studies at Columbia University, 2007.

Lugli 2011 — Ligeia Lugli, *The Conception of Language in Indian Mahāyāna, with Special Reference to the Laṅkāvatāra*. Unpublished Ph.D. dissertation, University of London, 2011.

Luo forthcoming — Hong Luo, *Ratnākaraśānti's Prajñāpāramitopadeśa*, China Tibetology Publishing House, forthcoming.

Maas 1958 — Paul Maas, *Textual Criticism*. Tr. Barbara Flower. Oxford: Clarendon Press, 1958.

MacDonald 2000 — Anne MacDonald, "The Prasannapadā: More Manuscripts from Nepal." WZKS 44 (2000) 165–181.

MacDonald 2003 — Id., "*Interpreting* Prasannapadā 19.3-7 in Context: A Response to Claus Oetke." WZKS 47 (2003) 143-195.

MacDonald 2005 — Id., "Manuscript Description." In *Jinendrabuddhi's Viśālamalāvatī Pramāṇasamuccayaṭīkā*. Chapter 1. Vol. 2. Ed. E. Steinkellner, H. Krasser, H. Lasic. Beijing-Vienna: China Tibetology Publishing House & AASP, 2005. x-xxxvi.

MacDonald 2007 — Id., "Revisiting the Mūlamadhyamakakārikā: Text-critical Proposals and Problems." *Studies in Indian Philosophy and Buddhism* 14 (2007) 25-55.

MacDonald 2008 — Id., "Recovering the Prasannapadā." *Critical Review for Buddhist Studies* 3 (2008) 9-38.

MacDonald 2009 — Id., "Knowing Nothing: Candrakīrti and Yogic Perception." In *Yogic Perception, Meditation and Altered States of Consciousness*. Ed. Eli Franco & Dagmar Eigner. Vienna: AASP, 2009. 133-169.

MacDonald 2011 — Id., "Who is that Masked Man? Candrakīrti's Opponent in PsP I 55.11-58.7." *JIP* (2011) 677-694.

MacDonald 2015 — Id., "Pragmatic Translating: The Case of Pa tshab Nyi ma grags." In *Cultural Flows across the Western Himalaya*. Ed. Patrick Mc Allister, Cristina Scherrer-Schaub, Helmut Krasser. Vienna: AASP, 2015. 249-278.

Maithrimurthi 1999 — M. Maithrimurthi, *Wohlwollen, Mitleid, Freude und Gleichmut. Eine ideengeschichtliche Untersuchung der vier apramāṇas in der buddhistischen Ethik und Spiritualität von den Anfängen bis hin zum frühen Yogācāra*. Stuttgart: Franz Steiner Verlag, 1999.

Malalasekera 1974 — G.P. Malalasekera, *Dictionary of Pāli Proper Names*. London: PTS, 1974.

Matilal 1970 — B.K. Matilal, "Reference and Existence in Nyāya and Buddhist Logic." *JIP* 1 (1970) 83-110.

Matilal 1974 — Id., "A Note on the Nyāya Fallacy Sādhyasama and Petitio Principii." *JIP* 2 (1974) 211-224.

Matilal 1985 — Id., *Logic, Language and Reality*. Delhi: Motilal Banarsidass, 1985.

Matilal 1998 — Id., *The Character of Logic in India*. Ed. J. Ganeri and H. Tiwari. Albany: SUNY, 1998.

Matsumoto 2005 — Koji Matsumoto, *On the Dialogue between Candrakīrti and Bhāviveka in Prasannapadā I.1* (in Japanese). Unpublished B.A. thesis, Taishō University, 2005.

Matsumoto 2011 — Shiro Matsumoto, "An Interpretation of *Prasannapadā*, 18.5-19.7." *Indian Logic* 3 (2011) 277-301.

Matsunami 1965 — Seiren Matsunami, *A Catalogue of the Sanskrit Manuscripts in the Tokyo University Library*. Tokyo: Suzuki Research Foundation, 1965.

May 1959 — Jacques May, *Candrakīrti. Prasannapadā Madhyamakavṛtti. Douze chapitres traduits du sanscrit et du tibétain, accompagnés d'une introduction, de notes et d'une édition critique de la version tibétaine*. Paris: Adrien-Maisonneuve, 1959.

May 1980 — Id., "Āryadeva et Candrakīrti sur la permanence." In *Indianisme et Bouddhisme, Mélanges offerts à Mgr Etienne Lamotte*. Louvain: Institut Orientaliste, 1980. 215-232.

May 1991 — Id., Review of R. Grünendahl (see Grünendahl 1989). *AS/ÉA* 45 (1991) 152.

Mimaki 1976 — Katsumi Mimaki, *La réfutation bouddhique de la permanence des choses* (*sthirasiddhidūṣaṇa*) *et la preuve de la momentanéité des choses* (*kṣaṇabhaṅgasiddhi*). Paris: Institute de Civilisation Indienne, 1976.

Mitra 1971 — R. Mitra, *The Sanskrit Buddhist Literature of Nepal*. Calcutta: The Asiatic Society of Bengal, 1882. Reprint Calcutta: Sanskrit Pustak Bhandar, 1971.

Monier-Williams 1990 — Monier Monier-Williams, *A Sanskrit English Dictionary*. Oxford University Press, 1899. Reprint New Delhi: Motilal Banarsidass, 1990.

Moriyama 2010 — Shinya Moriyama, "On Self-Awareness in the Sautrāntika Epistemology." *JIP* 38 (2010) 261-277.

Morris and Hardy 1885-1990 — Richard Morris and Edmund Hardy, ed., *Aṅguttaranikāya*. London: PTS, 1885-1900.

Muni Jambuvijayaji 1966 — Muni Jambuvijayaji, ed., *Dvādaśāraṃ Nayacakraṃ of Ācārya Śrī Mallavādi Kṣamāśrama, with the Commentary Nyāyānusāriṇī of Śrī Siṃhasūri Gaṇi Kṣamāśrama*. Bhavnagar: Śrī Jain Ātmanand Sabhā, 1966.

Müller 1885 — Edward Müller, ed., *The Dhammasaṅgaṇi*. London: PTS, 1885.

Murthy 1996 — R.S. Shivaganesha Murthy, *Introduction to Manuscriptology*. Delhi: Sharada Publishing House, 1996.

Nagao 1955 — G.M. Nagao, "The Silence of the Buddha and its Madhyamic Interpretation." In *Studies in Indology and Buddhology Presented in Honour of Professor Susumu Yamaguchi on the Occasion of his Sixtieth Birthday*. Ed. G.M. Nagao and J. Nozawa. Kyoto: Hozokan, 1955. 137-151.

Nagasaki 1991 — H. Nagasaki, "Perception in Pre-Dignāga Buddhist Texts." In *Studies in the Buddhist Epistemological Tradition.*

Proceedings of the Second International Dharmakīrti Conference. Vienna June 11-16, 1989. Ed. E. Steinkellner. Vienna: AASP, 1991. 221-225.

Nagao 1964 — G.M. Nagao, *Madhyāntavibhāga-bhāṣya*. Tokyo: Suzuki Research Foundation, 1964.

Nagatomi 1979 — M. Nagatomi, "Mānasa-Pratyakṣa: A Conundrum in the Buddhist Pramāṇa System." In *Sanskrit and Indian Studies: Essays in Honour of Daniel H.H. Ingalls*. Ed. M. Nagatomi, B.K Matilal, J.M. Masson and E.C. Dimock. Dordrecht: D. Reidel Publishing, 1979. 243-260.

Nakamura 1980 — H. Nakamura, "The Theory of 'Dependent Origination' in its Incipent Stage." In *Buddhist Studies in honour of Walpola Rahula*. Ed. S. Balasooriya et al. London: Gordon Frazer, 1980. 165-172.

Ñāṇamoli and Bodhi 1995 — Bhikkhu Ñāṇamoli and Bhikkhu Bodhi, tr., *The Middle Length Discourses of the Buddha*. Boston: Wisdom Publications, 1995.

Nath 1987 — R.N. Nath, *The Aṣṭādhyāyī of Pāṇini*. New Delhi: Munshiram Manoharlal, 1987.

Naudou 1980 — Jean Naudou, *Buddhists of Kaśmir*. Tr. G. Brereton and C. Picron. Delhi: Agam Kala Prakashan, 1980.

Negi 1998 — J.S. Negi, *Tibetan-Sanskrit Dictionary*. Sarnath: Central Institute of Higher Tibetan Studies, 1998.

Nietupski 1996 — Paul Nietupski, "The Examination of Conditioned Entities and the Examination of Reality. Nāgārjuna's Prajñā-nāma Mūlamadhyamakakārika XIII, Bhāvaviveka's Prajñā-pradīpa XIII, and Candrakīrti's Prasannapadā XIII." *JIP* 24 (1996) 103-143.

Norman 1969 — K. Norman, *Elders' Verses I. Theragāthā*. London: Luzac, 1969.

Norman 1992 — Id., *The Group of Discourses* (*Sutta-Nipāta*). Vol. II. Revised Translation with Introduction and Notes. Oxford: Pali Text Society, 1992.

Nyanatiloka 1975 — Nyanatiloka, tr., *Visuddhi-Magga oder Der Weg zur Reinheit*. 3rd ed. Konstanz: Verlag Christiani, 1975.

Oberhammer 1991 — Id., *Terminologie der frühen philosophischen Scholastik in Indien. Ein Begriffswörterbuch zur altindischen Dialektik, Erkenntnislehre und Methodologie*. Unter Mitarbeit von Ernst Prets und Joachim Prandstetter. Band 1: A–I. Vienna: AASP, 1991.

Oberhammer 1996 — Id., *Terminologie der frühen philosophischen Scholastik in Indien. Ein Begriffswörterbuch zur altindischen Dialektik, Erkenntnislehre und Methodologie*. Unter Mitarbeit von Ernst Prets und Joachim Prandstetter. Band 2: U–Pū. Vienna: AASP, 1996.

Oberlies 1995 — Thomas Oberlies, "Beiträge zur Pali-Lexikographie (Miscellanea Palica II)." *IIJ* 38 (1995) 105-147.

Oberlies 2001 — Id., *Pāli. A Grammar of the Language of the Theravāda Tipiṭaka*. Berlin: Walter de Gruyter, 2001.

Obermiller 1932 — Eugène Obermiller, *History of Buddhism by Bu-ston*. Heidelberg: Harrasowitz, 1932.

Oetke 1988 — Claus Oetke, "Die metaphysische Lehre Nāgārjunas." *Conceptus, Zeitschrift für Philosophie* XXII/56 (1988) 47-64.

Oetke 1989 — Id., "Rationalismus und Mystik in der Philosophie Nāgārjunas." In *StII* 15 (1989) 1-39.

Oetke 1990 — Id., "On some non-formal aspects of the proofs of the Madhyamakakārikās." In *Earliest Buddhism and Madhyamaka*. Ed. D. Ruegg and L. Schmithausen. Leiden: Brill, 1990. 90-109.

Oetke 1991 — Id., "Remarks on the Interpretation of Nāgārjuna's philosophy." *JIP* 19 (1991) 319-320.

Oetke 1992 — Id., "Pragmatic Implicatures and Text-Interpretation (The Alleged Logical Error of the Negation of the Antecedent in the Mūlamadhyamakakārikās)." *StII* 16 (1992) 185-233.

Oetke 1994 — Id., "Die 'Unbeantworteten Fragen' und das Schweigen des Buddha." In *WZKS* 38 (1994) 85-120.

Oetke 1996 — Id., "'Nihilist' and 'non-nihilist' interpretations of Madhyamaka." *Acta Orientalia* 57 (1996) 57-104.

Oetke 2001a — Id., *Materialien zur Übersetzung und Interpretation der Mūlamadhyamakakārikās*. Reinbek: Verlag für Orientalistische Fachpublikationen, 2001.

Oetke 2001b — Id., *Zur akademischen Krise in der Indologie und den Möglichkeiten ihrer Überwindung*. Stockholm, 2001.

Oetke 2003 — Id., "Prasannapadā 19,3-7 and Its Context." *WZKS* 47 (2003) 111-142.

Oetke 2004 — Id., On "Nāgārjuna's Logic." In *Gedenkschrift J.W. de Jong*. Ed. H.W. Bodewitz and Minoru Hara. Tokyo: The International Institute for Buddhist Studies, 2004. 83-98.

Oetke 2006 — Id., *Logic Matters in the Prasannapadā. A Study on Reasoning and Proof in Metaphysics*. Stockholm: Acta Universitatis Stockholmiensis, 2006.

Oetke 2009 — Id., "Some Issues of Scholarly Exegesis (in Indian Philosophy)." *JIP* 37 (2009) 415-497.

Oldenberg 1879-1883 — H. Oldenberg, *Vinaya-piṭaka*. London: PTS, 1879-1883.

Otsuka 1997 — Nobuo Otsuka, "The Script of the *Amoghapāśakalparāja* Sanskrit Palm-leaf Manuscript." In *Introduction to the Facsimile Edition of the Amoghapāśakalparāja Sanskrit Palm-leaf Manuscript*. Tokyo: The Institute for Comprehensive Studies of Buddhism, Taisho University, 1997. 17-39.

Padmakara 2002 — Padmakara Translation Group, *Introduction to the Middle Way. Chandrakirti's Madhyamakavatara with commentary by Jamgön Mipham*. Boston: Shambala Publications, 2002.

Pandeya 1988 — R. Pandeya, *The Madhyamakaśāstram of Nāgārjuna with the Commentaries Akutobhayā by Nāgārjuna, Madhyamakavṛtti by Buddhapālita, Prajñāpradīpavṛtti by Bhāvaviveka, Prasannapadāvṛtti by Candrakīrti critically reconstructed*. Vol. I. Delhi, Motilal Banarsidass, 1988.

Panglung 1981 — Jampa Losang Panglung, *Die Erzählstoffe des Mūlasarvāstivāda-Vinaya. Analysiert auf Grund der tibetischen Übersetzung*. Tokyo: Reiyukai, 1981.

Pant 2000 — Mahes Raj Pant, *Jātarūpa's Commentary on the Amarakoṣa*. New Delhi: Motilal Banarsidass, 2000.

Pāsādika 1979 — Bhikkhu Pāsādika, "The Dharma-Discourse of the Great Collection of Jewels. The Kāśyapa-Section. Mahāratnakūṭadharmaparyāya – Kāśyapaparivarta. English Translation and Restoration of the Missing Sanskrit Portions (VII, IX)." *Linh-Son publication d'études bouddhologiques* 7 & 9 (1979) 27-37; 26-41.

Pāsādika 1989 — Id., *Kanonische Zitate im Abhidharmakośabhāṣya des Vasubandhu*. Göttingen: Vandenhoeck & Ruprecht, 1989.

Pind 2001 — Ole H. Pind, "Why the Vaidalyaprakaraṇa Cannot Be an Authentic Work of Nāgārjuna." *WZKS* 45 (2001) 149-172.

Pind 2009 — Id., *Dignāga's Philosophy of Language. Dignāga on anyāpoha. Pramāṇasamuccaya V: Texts, Translation and Annotation*. Unpublished Ph.D. dissertation, Vienna, 2009.

Pradhan 1975 — P. Pradhan, *Abhidharmakośabhāṣyam of Vasubandhu*. 2nd ed. Patna: K.P. Jayaswal Research Institute, 1975.

Preisendanz 1994 — K. Preisendanz, *Studien zu Nyāyasūtra III.1 mit dem Nyāyatattvāloka Vācaspati Miśras II*. Stuttgart: Franz Steiner Verlag, 1994.

Proto 2010 — Teresa Proto, "Speech and scribal errors as a window into the mind. Evidence for mechanisms of speech (re)production and systems of mental representations." *Cognitive Philology* 3 (2010). URL: http://ojs.uniroma1.it/index.php/cogphil/article/view/9347/9229 (accessed Aug. 20, 2013).

Python 1973 — Pierre Python, *Vinaya-Viniścaya-Upāli-Paripṛcchā. Enquête d'Upāli pour une exégèse de la discipline*. Paris: Adrien-Maisonneuve, 1973.

Qvarnström 1990 — Olle Qvarnström, "The Vedāntatattvaviniścaya-Chapter of Bhavya's Madhyamakahṛdayakārikā." *WZKS* 34 (1990) 181-198.

Raghavan 1998 — V. Raghavan, *Sanskrit Rāmāyaṇas Other than Vālmīki's: The Adbhuta, Adhyātma, and Ānanda Rāmāyaṇas*. Chennai: Dr. V. Raghavan Centre for Performing Arts, 1998.

Rajbanshi 1974 — Shankar Man Rajbanshi, "The Evolution of Devanagari Script." *Kailash* 2 (1974) 23-120.

Randle 1976 — H.N. Randle, *Indian Logic in the Early Schools*. Oxford: Oxford University Press, 1930. Indian ed.: New Delhi: Munshiram Manoharlal, 1976.

Renou 1957 — L. Renou, *Terminologie Grammaticale du Sanskrit*. Paris: Champion, 1957.

Renou and Filliozat 1953 — L. Renou and J. Filliozat, *L'Inde Classique*. Paris: Imprimerie Nationale, 1953.

Reynolds and Wilson 1974 — L.D. Reynolds and N.G. Wilson, *Scribes and Scholars: A Guide to the Transmission of Greek and Latin Literature*. 2nd ed. Oxford: Oxford University Press, 1974.

Rhys Davids and Carpenter 1890-1911 — T.W. Rhys Davids and J.E. Carpenter, ed., *Dīghanikāya*. London: PTS, 1890-1911.

Rhys Davids, Carpenter and Stede 1886-1932 — T.W. Rhys Davids, J.E. Carpenter and W. Stede, ed., *Dīghanikāya-Aṭṭhakathā* (*Sumaṅgalavilāsinī*). London: PTS, 1886-1932.

Rhys Davids and Stede 1993 — T.W. Rhys Davids and William Stede, *The Pāli Text Society's Pāli-English Dictionary*. Chipstead, 1921-1925. Reprint Delhi: Motilal Banarsidass, 1993.

Rizzi 1988 — Cesare Rizzi, *Candrakīrti*. New Delhi: Motilal Banarsidass, 1988.

Roerich and Choepel 1988 — George Roerich and Gedun Choepel, The Blue Annals by Gö Lotsawa. Motilal Banarsidass,

von Rospatt 1995 — Alexander von Rospatt, *The Buddhist Doctrine of Momentariness*. Stuttgart: Franz Steiner Verlag, 1995.

Saito 1984 — Akira Saito, *A Study of the Buddhapālita-mūlamadhyamaka-vṛtti*. Unpublished Ph.D. dissertation, Australian National University, 1984.

Saito 1985 — Id., "Textcritical Remarks on the *Mūlamadhyamakakārikā* as Cited in the *Prasannapadā*." *JIBS* 33 (1985) 846-842.

Saito 1986 — Id., "A Note on the *Prajñā-nāma-mūlamadhyamakakārikā* of Nāgārjuna." *JIBS* 35 (1986) 487-484.

Saito 1995 — Id., "Problems in Translating the *Mūlamadhyamakakārikā* as Cited in its Commentaries." In *Buddhist Translations: Problems and Perspectives*. Ed. Doboom Tulku. Delhi: Manohar, 1995. 87-96.

Saito 1998 — Id., "Bhāviveka and the Madhya(anta)vibhāga/-bhāṣya." *JIBS* 46 (1998) 23-29.

Śākya 1956 — Hem Rāj Śākya, *Nepāla lipi-saṃgraha*. Kathmandu: Basantrāj Tulādhar, 1956.

Śākya 1973 — Id., *Nepāla lipi-prakāśa*. Kathmandu: Nepāla Rājakīya Prajña-Pratiṣṭhāna, 1973.

Salvini 2011 — Mattia Salvini, "*Upādāyaprajñapti* and the Meaning of Absolutives: Grammar and Syntax in the Interpretation of Madhyamaka." *JIP* 39 (2011) 229-244.

Samten and Garfield 2006 — Geshe Ngawang Samten and Jay Garfield, *Ocean of Reasoning. A Great Commentary on Nāgārjuna's Mūlamadhyamakakārikā*. Oxford: Oxford University Press, 2006.

Sander 1968 — Lore Sander, *Paläographisches zu den Sanskrit-handschriften der Berliner Turfansammlung*. Wiesbaden: Steiner, 1968.

Sāṅkṛtyāyana 1937 — Rāhula Sāṅkṛtyāyana, "Vigrahavyāvarttanī." *Journal of the Bihar and Orissa Research Society* 23 (1937), Appendix.

Sāṅkṛtyāyana 1953 — Id., ed., *Pramāṇavārtikabhāṣyam or Vārtikālaṅkāraḥ of Prajñākaragupta*. Patna: Kashi Prasad Jayaswal Research Institute, 1953.

della Santina 1986 — Peter della Santina, *Madhyamaka Schools in India*. New Delhi: Motilal Banarsidass, 1986.

Sarma 1982 — K.V. Sarma, "Manuscriptology and Textual Criticism in Medieval India." *Indologica Taurinensia* 10 (1982) 281-288.

Śāstri 1915 — Hara Prasad Śāstri, *A Catalogue of Palm-Leaf & Selected Paper MSS. Belonging to the Durbar Library, Nepal*. Vol. II. Calcutta: Baptist Mission Press, 1915.

Śāstri 1978 — Svāmī Dvārikādāsa Śāstri, *Ślokavārttika of Śrī Kumārila Bhaṭṭa with the Commentary Nyāyaratnākara of Śrī Pārthasārthi Miśra*. Varanasi: Ratna Publications, 1978.

Śāstri 1981 — Id., *Tattvasaṃgraha of Ācārya Shāntarakṣita with the Commentary "Pañjikā" of Shri Kamalashīla*. Varanasi: Bauddha Bharati, 1981.

Śāstri 1987 — Id., *Abhidharmakośa & Bhāṣya of Vasubandhu with Sphutārthā Commentary of Yaśomitra*. Varanasi: Bauddha Bharati, 1987.

Schaeffer 2009 — Kurtis R. Schaeffer, *The Culture of the Book in Tibet*. New York: Columbia University Press, 2009.

Schayer 1930 — Stanislaw Schayer, "Feuer und Brennstoff." *Rocznik Orjentalistyczny* 7 (1930) 26-52.

Schayer 1931 — Id., *Ausgewählte Kapitel aus der Prasannapadā (V, XII, XIII, XIV, XV, XVI) Einleitung, Übersetzung und Anmerkungen*. Krakow: Nakladem Polskiej Akademji Umiejętności, 1931.

Scherrer-Schaub 1981 — Cristina Scherrer-Schaub, "Le Terme Yukti: Premiére Étude." *AS/ÉA* 35 (1981) 185-199.

Scherrer-Schaub 1991 — Id., *Yuktiṣaṣṭikāvṛtti. Commentaire à la soixantaine sur le raisonnement ou Du vrai enseignement de la causalité par le Maître indien Candrakīrti*. Brussels: Institut Belge des Hautes Études Chinoises, 1991.

Schmithausen 1969 — Lambert Schmithausen, *Der Nirvāṇa-Abschnitt in der Viniścayasaṃgrahāṇī der Yogācārabhūmiḥ*. Vienna: AASP, 1969.

Schmithausen 1972 — Id., "The Definition of Pratyakṣam in the Abhidharmasamuccayaḥ." *WZKSO* 16 (1972) 153-163.

Schmithausen 1976 — Id., "Die Vier Konzentrationen der Aufmerksamkeit." *Zeitschrift für Missionswissenschaft und Religionswissenschaft* (1976) 241-266.

Schmithausen 1977 — Id., "Zur buddhistischen Lehre von der Dreifachen Leidhaftigkeit." *Zeitschrift der Deutschen Morgenländischen Gesellschaft* (1977) 918-930.

Schmithausen 1981 — Id., "On Some Aspects of Descriptions or Theories of 'Liberating Insight' and 'Enlightenment' in Early Buddhism." In *Studium zum Jainismus und Buddhismus. Gedenkschrift für Ludwig Alsdorf.* Ed. K. Bruhn, A. Wezler. Wiesbaden: Franz-Steiner Verlag, 1981. 199-250.

Schmithausen 1987a — Id., "*Ālayavijñāna. On the Origin and the Early Development of a Central Concept of Yogācāra Philosophy.* Tokyo: The International Institute for Buddhist Studies, 1987.

Schmithausen 1987b — Id., Review of Heinz Bechert (ed.) *Sanskrit-Wörterbuch der buddhistischen Texte aus den Turfan-Funden. ZDMG* 137 (1987) 151-157.

Schmithausen 1997 — Id., "The Early Buddhist Tradition and Ecological Ethics." *Journal of Buddhist Ethics* 4 (1997) 1-74.

Schmithausen 2000a — Id., "Buddhism and the Ethics of Nature—Some Remarks." *The Eastern Buddhist* 32 (2000) 26-78.

Schmithausen 2000b — Id., "Gleichmut und Mitgefühl." In *Der Buddhismus als Anfrage an christliche Theologie und Philosophie.* Mödling: Verlag St. Gabriel, 2000. 119-136.

Schmithausen 2000c — Id., "Mitleid und Leerheit." In *Der Buddhismus als Anfrage an christliche Theologie und Philosophie.* Mödling: Verlag St. Gabriel, 2000. 437-455.

Schmithausen 2000d — Id., "Zur zwölfgliedrigen Formel des Entstehens in Abhängigkeit." *Hōrin* 7 (2000) 41-76.

Schmithausen 2013 — Id., "*Kuśala* and *Akuśala*: Reconsidering the Original Meaning of a Basic Pair of Terms of Buddhist Spirituality and Ethics and Its Development up to Early Yogācāra." In *The Foundation for Yoga Practitioners. The Buddhist Yogācārabhūmi Treatise and Its Adaptation in India, East Asia, and Tibet.* Boston: Department of South Asian Studies, Harvard University, 2013. 440-495.

Schmithausen 2014 — Id., *The Genesis of Yogācāra-Vijñānavāda. Responses and Reflections.* Tokyo: The International Institute for Buddhist Studies, 2014.

Schoening 1995 — Jeffrey Schoening, *The Śālistamba Sūtra and its Indian Commentaries.* Vienna: ATBS, 1995.

Seyfort Ruegg 1971 — David Seyfort Ruegg, "Le Dharmadhātustava de Nāgārjuna." In *Études tibétaines dédiées à la mémoire de Marcelle Lalou*. Paris: Adrien Maisonneuve, 1971. 448-471.

Seyfort Ruegg 1977 — Id., "The uses of the four positions of the catuṣ-koṭi and the problem of the description of reality in Mahāyāna Buddhism." *JIP* 5 (1977) 1-71.

Seyfort Ruegg 1981 — Id., *The Literature of the Madhyamaka School of Philosophy in India*. Published as fasc. 1, vol. VII of *A History of Indian Literature*, ed. J. Gonda. Wiesbaden: Harrassowitz, 1981.

Seyfort Ruegg 1982 — Id., "Towards a chronology of the Madhyamaka school." In *Indological and Buddhist Studies. Volume in honour of Professor J. W. de Jong on his sixtieth birthday*. Ed. L. Hercus et al. Canberra: Faculty of Asian Studies, Australian National University, 1982. 505-530.

Seyfort Ruegg 1983 — Id., "On the Thesis and Assertion in the Madhyamaka/dBu ma." In *Contributions on Tibetan and Buddhist Religion and Philosophy. Proceedings of the Csoma de Kőrös Symposium held at Velm-Vienna, 13-19 Sept. 1981*. Ed. E. Steinkellner and H. Tauscher. Vienna: ATBS, 1983. Vol. 2, 205-241.

Seyfort Ruegg 1985 — Id., "Purport, Implicature and Presupposition: Sanskrit *Abhiprāya* and Tibetan *dGoṅs pa / dGoṅs gzhi* as Hermeneutical Concepts." *JIP* 13 (1985) 309-325.

Seyfort Ruegg 1986 — Id., "Does the Mādhyamika have a thesis and philosophical position?" In *Buddhist logic and epistemology*. Ed. B.K. Matilal and R.D. Evans. Dordrecht: D. Reidel Publishing, 1986. 229-237.

Seyfort Ruegg 1990 — Id., "On the authorship of some works ascribed to Bhāvaviveka/Bhavya." In *Earliest Buddhism and Madhyamaka. Panels of the VIIth World Sanskrit Conference 2*. Ed. D. Seyfort Ruegg and L. Schmithausen. Leiden: E.J. Brill, 1990. 59-71.

Seyfort Ruegg 1991 — Id., "On *pramāṇa* Theory in Tsoṅ kha pa's Madhyamaka Philosophy." In *Studies in the Buddhist Epistemological Tradition. Proceedings of the Second International*

Dharmakīrti Conference. Vienna June 11-16, 1989. Ed. E. Steinkellner. Vienna: AASP, 1991. 281-310.

Seyfort Ruegg 2000 — Id., *Three Studies in the History of Indian and Tibetan Madhyamaka Philosophy*. Vienna: ATBS, 2000.

Seyfort Ruegg 2002 — Id., *Two Prolegomena to Madhyamaka Philosophy. Candrakīrti's Prasannapadā Madhyamakavṛttiḥ on Madhyamakakārikā I.1 and Tsoṅ kha pa blo bzaṅ grags pa / rGyal tshab Dar ma rin chen's dKa' gnad/gnas brgyad kyi zin bris*. Vienna: ATBS, 2002.

Shackleton Bailey 1951 — D.R. Shackleton Bailey, *The Śātapañcāśatka of Mātṛceṭa. Sanskrit Text, Tibetan Translation & Commentary and Chinese Translation*. Cambridge: Cambridge University Press, 1951.

Sharan 1978 — Mahesh K. Sharan, *Court Procedure in Ancient India*. New Delhi: Abhinav Publications, 1978.

Sharma et al. 1969 — A. Sharma, K. Deshpande, D.G. Padhye. *Kāśikā: A Commentary on Pāṇini's Grammar*. Hyderabad: Osmania University Press, 1969.

Sharma 1985 — P. S. Sharma, "What Kind of Compound is the Word *pratyakṣa*?" *The Adyar Library Bulletin* 49 (1985) 14-29.

Siderits 1981 — Mark Siderits, "The Madhyamaka Critique of Epistemology II." *Journal of Indian Philosophy* 9 (1981) 121-160.

Siderits 2011 — Id., "Is Everything Connected to Everything Else? What the Gopīs Know." In *Moonshadows: Conventional Truth in Buddhist Philosophy*. Ed. The Cowherds. Oxford: Oxford University Press, 2011.

Siderits and Katsura 2013 — Mark Siderits and Shoryu Katsura, *Nāgārjuna's Middle Way. Mūlamadhyamakakārikā*. Boston: Wisdom Publications, 2013.

Silburn 1989 — Lilian Silburn, *Instant et Cause*. Paris: De Boccard, 1989.

Skilling 1991 — Peter Skilling, "A Brief Guide to the Golden Tanjur." *The Journal of the Siam Society* 79 (1991) 138-146.

Skilling 1998 — Id., "The Sūtra on the Four Conditions." *WZKS* 42 (1998) 139-149.

Slaje 1993 — Walter Slaje, *Śāradā: Deskriptiv-synchrone Schriftkunde zur Bearbeitung kaschmirischer Sanskrit-Manuskripte*. Reinbek: Verlag für Orientalistische Fachpublikationen, 1993.

Sprung 1979 — Mervyn Sprung, *Lucid Exposition of the Middle Way: The Essential Chapters from the Prasannapadā of Candrakīrti*. London: Routledge and Kegan Paul, 1979.

von Staël-Holstein 1977 — A. von Staël-Holstein, *The Kāśyapaparivarta: A Mahāyānasūtra of the Ratnakūṭa class edited in the original Sanskrit, in Tibetan and in Chinese*. Shanghai, 1926. Reprint Tokyo: Meicho-Fukyū-Kai, 1977.

Stalker 1987 — Susan Stalker, *A Study of Dependent Origination: Vasubandhu, Buddhaghosa, and the Interpretation of "Pratītyasamutpāda."* Unpublished Ph.D. dissertation, University of Pennsylvania, 1987.

Stanley 1988 — Richard Stanley, *A Study of the Madhyāntavibhāga-Bhāṣya-Ṭīkā*. Unpublished Ph.D. dissertation, Australian National University, 1988.

Stcherbatsky 1927 — T. Stcherbatsky, *The Conception of Buddhist Nirvāṇa*. Leningrad: Publishing Office of the Academy of Sciences of the USSR, 1927.

Stcherbatsky 1962 — Id., *Buddhist Logic*. St. Petersburg, 1930. Reprint New York: Dover Publications, 1962.

Stcherbatsky 1992 — Id., *Madhyānta-vibhanga. Discourse on Discrimination between Middle and Extremes*. St. Petersburg, 1936. Reprint New Delhi: Motilal Banarsidass, 1992.

Steiner 1996 — Roland Steiner, "Die Lehre der Anuṣṭubh bei den indischen Metrikern." In: *Suhṛllekhāḥ. Festgabe für Helmut Eimer*. Ed. M. Hahn, J.-U. Hartmann, R. Steiner. Swisttal-Odendorf: Indica et Tibetica Verlag, 1996. 227-248.

Steinkellner 1961 — Ernst Steinkellner, "Die Literatur des Älteren Nyāya." *WZKS* 5 (1961) 149-162.

Steinkellner 1988 — Id., "Remarks on *Niścitagrahaṇa*." In *Orientalia Josephi Tucci Memoriae Dicata*. Rome: Istituto Italiano il Medio ed Estremo Oriente, 1988. 1427-1444.

Steinkellner 1990 — Id., "Is Dharmakīrti a Mādhyamika?" In *Earliest Buddhism and Madhyamaka*. Ed. D. Ruegg and L. Schmithausen. Leiden: Brill, 1990. 72-90.

Steinkellner 1992 — Id., "Lamotte and the Concept of anupalabdhi." *AS/ÉA* 46 (1992) 398- 410.

Steinkellner 2005 — Id., *Dignāga's Pramāṇasamuccaya, Chapter 1. A hypothetical reconstruction of the Sanskrit text with the help of the two Tibetan translations on the basis of the hitherto known Sanskrit fragments and the linguistic materials gained from Jinendrabuddhi's Ṭīkā*. Vienna, 2005. URL: http://ikga.oeaw.-ac.at/Mat/dignaga_PS_1.pdf (accessed Aug. 20, 2013)

Steinkellner et al. 2005 — E. Steinkellner, H. Krasser, H. Lasic, ed., *Jinendrabuddhi's Viśālāmalavatī Pramāṇasamuccayaṭīkā, Chapter 1*. Beijing–Vienna: China Tibetology Publishing House & AASP, 2005.

Streng 1967 — Frederick Streng, *Emptiness: A Study in Religious Meaning*. Nashville: Abingdon Press, 1967.

Suzuki 1995 — K. Suzuki, "The Script of the Śrāvakabhūmi Manuscript." In *Studies on the Buddhist Sanskrit Literature*. Ed. The Śrāvakabhūmi Study Group and the Buddhist Tantric Text Study Group. Tokyo: Sankibo Press, 1995. 21-38.

Suzuki 1996 — Id., ed., *Sanskrit Fragments and Tibetan Translation of Candrakīrti's Bodhisattvayogācāracatuḥśatakaṭīkā*. Tokyo: Sankibo, 1996.

Tachikawa 1971 — M. Tachikawa, "A Sixth-Century Manual of Indian Logic." *JIP* 1 (1971) 111-145.

Tachikawa 1981 — Id., "'*Pratītyasamutpāda*' in the Dedication of the *Mūlamadhyamakakārikā*." *Adyar Library Bulletin* 44-45 (1980-1981) Dr. K. Kunjunni Raja Felicitation Volume. 639-653.

Takaoka 1981 — H. Takaoka, *A Microfilm Catalogue of the Buddhist Manuscripts in Nepal*. Vol 1. Nagoya: Buddhist Library, 1981.

Tanji 1988 — Teruyoshi Tanji, *Akirakana kotoba I (Prasannapadā Madhyamakavṛtti I)*. Osaka: Kansai University Press, 1988.

Tanji 1992 — Id., *Jitsuzai to ninshiki. Chūgan shisō kenkyū II (Reality and Cognition. Study of Mādhyamika Philosophy II)*. Osaka: Kansai University Press, 1992.

Tanselle 1990 — G. Thomas Tanselle, *Textual Criticism and Scholarly Editing*. Charlottesville: University of Virginia Press, 1990.

Tatia 1976 — Nathmal Tatia, *Abhidharmasamuccaya-Bhāṣyam*. Patna: Kashi Prasad Jayaswal Research Institute, 1976.

Tauscher 1981 — Helmut Tauscher, *Candrakīrti. Madhyamakāvatāraḥ und Madhyamakāvatārabhāṣyam (Kapital VI, Vers 166-226)*. Vienna: ATBS, 1981.

Thakchoe 2010 — Sonam Thakchoe, "Candrakīrti's theory of perception: A case for non-foundationalist epistemology in Madhyamaka." *Acta Orientalia Vilnensia* 11 (2010) 93-124.

Thakur 1997a — Anantalal Thakur, *Gautamīyanyāyadarśana with Bhāṣya of Vātsyāyana*. New Delhi: Indian Council of Philosophical Research, 1997.

Thakur 1997b — Id., *Nyāyabhāṣyavārttika of Bhāradvāja Uddyotakara*. New Delhi: Indian Council of Philosophical Research, 1997.

Thurman 1991 — Robert Thurman, *The Central Philosophy of Tibet. A Study and Translation of Jey Tsong Khapa's Essence of True Eloquence*. Princeton: Princeton University Press, 1984. Reprint 1991.

Tikkanen 1987 — Bertil Tikkanen, *The Sanskrit Gerund. A Synchronic, Diachronic and Typological Analysis*. Helsinki: Finnish Oriental Society, 1987.

Tillemans 1984 — Tom J.F. Tillemans, "Sur le *Parārthānumāna* en Logique Bouddhique." *AS/ÉA* 38 (1984) 73-99.

Tillemans 1989 — Id., "Indian and Tibetan Mādhyamikas on Mānasapratyakṣa." *The Tibet Journal* 14 (1989) 70-85.

Tillemans 1990 — Id., *Materials for the Study of Āryadeva, Dharmapāla and Candrakīrti*. Vienna: ATBS, 1990.

Tillemans 1991 — Id., "More on *Parārthānumāna*, Theses and Syllogisms" *AS/ÉA* 45 (1991) 133-148.

Tillemans 1992 — Id., "Tsong kha pa *et al.* on the Bhāvaviveka-Candrakīrti Debate." In *Tibetan Studies: Proceedings of the 5th Seminar of the International Association for Tibetan Studies*. Ed. S. Ihara and Z. Yamaguchi. Narita: Narita-san Shinsho-ji, 1992. 315-326.

Tillemans 1994 — Id., "Pre-Dharmakīrti Commentators on Dignāga's Definition of a Thesis (*pakṣalakṣaṇa*)." In *The Buddhist Forum* 3. Ed. T. Skorupski and U. Pagel. University of London, 1994. 295-305.

Tillemans 1998 — Id., "A Note on *Pramāṇavārttika*, *Pramāṇasamuccaya* and *Nyāyamukha*. What is the *svadharmin* in Buddhist logic?" *JIABS* 21 (1998) 111-124.

Tillemans 2000 — Id., *Dharmakīrti's Pramāṇavārttika. An annotated translation of the fourth chapter* (*parārthānumāna*). Vienna: AASP, 2000.

Tillemans and Lopez 1998 — Tom J.F. Tillemans and Donald Lopez, "What can one reasonably say about non-existence? A Tibetan work on the problem of āśrayasiddha." *JIP* 26 (1998) 99-129.

TKK 2001 — Tohōgakuin Kansaichiku Kyōshitsu, ed., *Criticism of Dignāga's Epistemology by Candrakīrti: Tibetan Translation of the Prasannapadā, Japanese Translation and Index*. Kyoto: Hōzōkan, 2001.

Tosaki 1987 — Hiromasa Tosaki, Review of Amar Singh, *The Heart of Buddhist Philosophy: Diṅnāga and Dharmakīrti*. *IIJ* 30 (1987) 139-146.

Trenckner and Chalmers 1888-1899 — V. Trenckner and R. Chalmers, ed., *Majjhimanikāya*. London: PTS, 1888-1899.

Trenckner et al. 1924-2011 — V. Trenckner, D. Anderson et al., *A Critical Pāli Dictionary*. Copenhagen: The Royal Danish Royal Academy of Sciences and Letters, 1924-2001 and Bristol 2011.

Trier 1972 — Jesper Trier, *Ancient Paper of Nepal: Results of ethno-technological field work on its manufacture, uses and history, with technical analyses of bast, paper and manuscripts*. Copenhagen: Gyldendal, 1972.

Tsukamoto et al. 1990 — K. Tsukamoto, Y. Matsunaga, H. Isoda, *A Descriptive Bibliography of the Sanskrit Buddhist Literature*. Vol. 3: *Abhidharma, Madhyamaka, Yogācāra, Buddhist epistemology and logic*. Kyoto: Heirakuji Shoten, 1990.

Tucci 1929 — Giuseppe Tucci, "Buddhist Logic before Diṅnāga." *JRAS* (1929) 451-488.

Tucci 1930 — Id., *The Nyāyamukha of Dignāga*. Heidelberg 1930.

Tucci 1981 — Id., *Pre-Diṅnāga Buddhist Texts on Logic from Chinese Sources*. Baroda 1929. Reprint Madras: Vesta Publications, 1981.

Tuck 1990 — Andrew P. Tuck, *Comparative Philosophy and the Philosophy of Scholarship. On the Western Interpretation of Nāgārjuna*. Oxford: Oxford University Press, 1990.

Uryuzu and Nakazawa 2012 — Ryushin Uryuzu and Mitsuru Nakazawa, Tibetan edition of the Madhyamakāvatārabhāṣya, 2012. http://goo.gl/dhvSLA (accessed Feb. 26, 2014).

Vaidya 1960a — P.L. Vaidya, ed., *Aṣṭasāhasrikāprajñāpāramitā*. Darbhanga: The Mithila Institute, 1960.

Vaidya 1960b — Id., ed., *Madhyamakaśāstra of Nāgārjuna with the Commentary Prasannapadā by Candrakīrti*. Darbhanga: The Mithila Institute, 1960.

Vaidya 1961 — Id., *Samādhirājasūtra*. Darbhanga: The Mithila Institute, 1961.

Vasu 1980 — Śriśa Chandra Vasu, *The Ashṭādhyāyī of Pāṇini*. Allahabad 1891. Reprint Delhi: Motilal Banarsidass, 1980.

Verhagen 1985 — Peter Verhagen, "Tibetan Expertise in Sanskrit Grammar. A Case-Study: Grammatical Analysis of the Term *pratītya-samutpāda*." *The Journal of the Tibet Society* 8 (1985) 21-48.

Vetter 1982 — Tilmann Vetter, "Die Lehre Nāgārjunas in den Mūlamadhyamaka-kārikās." In *Epiphanie des Heils. Zur Heils-*

gegenwart in indischer und christlicher Religion. Ed. Gerhard Oberhammer. Vienna: Gerold, 1982. 87-108.

Vetter 1988 — Id., *The Ideas and Meditative Practices of Early Buddhism*. Leiden: E.J. Brill, 1988.

Vetter 1992 — Id., "On the Authenticity of the Ratnāvalī. *AS/ÉA* 46 (1992) 492-506.

Vetter 2000 — Id., *The "Khandha Passages" in the Vinayapiṭaka and the four main Nikayas*. Vienna: AASP, 2000.

Vetter 2001 — Id., "Once again on the Origin of Mahāyāna Buddhism." *WZKS* 45 (2001) 59-90.

Vogel 1926 — Jean Philippe Vogel, *Indian Serpent-Lore*. London: Arthur Probsthain, 1926.

Vorobyova-Desyatovskaya 2002 — M. I. Vorobyova-Desyatovskaya, *The Kāśyapaparivarta. Romanized Text and Facsimiles*. Tokyo: The International Research Institute for Advanced Buddhology, Soka University, 2002.

Vose 2009 — Kevin Vose, *Resurrecting Candrakīrti. Disputes in the Tibetan Creation of Prāsaṅgika*. Boston: Wisdom Publications, 2009.

Wackernagel and Debrunner 1954 — Jacob Wackernagel and Albert Debrunner, *Altindische Grammatik* II.2. *Nominalsuffixe*. Göttingen: Vandenhoeck & Ruprecht, 1954.

Walleser 1911 — Max Walleser, *Die buddhistische Philosophie in ihrer geschichtlichen Entwicklung*. Vol. 2, Die Mittlere Lehre (Mādhyamika-śāstra) des Nāgārjuna. Heidelberg: Winter, 1911.

Walleser 1914 — Id., *Prajñāpradīpa: A Commentary on the Madhyamaka Sūtra by Bhāvaviveka*. Calcutta: Asiatic Society of Bengal, 1914.

Walshe 1987 — Maurice Walshe, *The Long Discourses of the Buddha. A Translation of the Dīgha Nikāya*. London: Wisdom Publications, 1987.

Wangchuk 2002 — Dorji Wangchuk, *The cittotpāda Chapter of the Bodhisattvabhūmi*. Unpublished M.A. thesis. University of Hamburg, 2002.

Wangchuk 2007 — Id., *The Resolve to Become a Buddha. A Study of the Bodhicitta Concept in Indo-Tibetan Buddhism*. Tokyo: The International Institute for Buddhist Studies, 2007.

Watanabe 1998 — Chikafume Watanabe, "A Translation of the *Madhyamakahṛdayakārikā* with the *Tarkajvālā* III. 137-146." *JIABS* 21 (1998) 125-155.

Watanabe 2013 — Toshikazu Watanabe, "Dignāga on *Āvīta* and *Prasaṅga*." *JIBS* 61 (2013) 1229-1235.

Wayman 1961 — Alex Wayman, *Analysis of the Śrāvakabhūmi Manuscript*. Berkley: University of California Press, 1961.

Weber-Brosamer and Back 1997 — B. Weber-Brosamer and D.M. Back, *Die Philosophie der Leere. Nāgārjunas Mūlamadhyamaka-Kārikās Übersetzung des buddhistischen Basistextes mit kommentierenden Einführung*. Wiesbaden: Harrassowitz, 1997.

Weller 1965 — Friedrich Weller, *Zum Kāśyapaparivarta*. Vol. 2: *Verdeutschung des sanskrit-tibetischen Textes*. Berlin: Akademie Verlag, 1965.

Weller 1987a — Id., "Kāśyapaparivarta nach der Han-Fassung verdeutscht." In *Friedrich Weller. Kleine Schriften*. Ed. W. Rau. Stuttgart: Steiner Verlag, 1987. 1136-1304.

Weller 1987b — Id., "Die Sung-Fassung des Kāśyapaparivarta. Versuch einer Verdeutschung." In *Friedrich Weller. Kleine Schriften*. Ed. W. Rau. Stuttgart: Steiner Verlag, 1987. 1305-1459.

West 1973 — Martin L. West, *Textual Criticism and Editorial Technique*. Stuttgart: B.G. Teubner, 1973.

Westerhoff 2010 — Jan Westerhoff, *The Dispeller of Disputes*. Oxford: Oxford University Press, 2010.

Wezler 1990 — A. Wezler, "On Two Medical Verses in the Yuktidīpikā." *Journal of the European Ayurvedic Society* 1 (1990) 127-148.

Wezler and Motegi 1998 — A. Wezler and S. Motegi, *Yuktidīpikā: The Most Significant Commentary on the Sāṃkhyakārikā*. Stuttgart: Franz Steiner Verlag, 1998.

Willemen et al. 1998 — Charles Willemen, Bart Dessein, Collett Cox, *Sarvāstivāda Buddhist Scholasticism*. Leiden: Brill, 1998.

Williams 1998 — Paul Williams, *The Reflexive Nature of Awareness: A Tibetan Madhyamaka Defense*. Surrey: Curzon Press, 1998.

Willis 1972 — James Willis, *Latin Textual Criticism*. Urbana: University of Illinois Press, 1972.

Windisch 1975 — Ernst Windisch, ed., *Iti-vuttaka*. London: PTS 1889. Reprint 1975.

Winternitz and Keith 1905 — M. Winternitz and A.B. Keith, *Catalogue of Sanskrit Manuscripts in the Bodleian Library*. Vol. II. Oxford: Clarendon Press, 1905.

Wogihara 1971a — U. Wogihara, *Bodhisattvabhūmi. A Statement of Whole Course of the Bodhisattva (Being Fifteenth Section of Yogācārabhūmi)*. Reprint Tokyo: Sankibo, 1971.

Wogihara 1971b — Id., *Sphutārthā Abhidharmakośavyākhyā*. Tokyo: Sankibo, 1971.

Wood 1994 — Thomas Wood, *Nāgārjunian Disputations. A Philosophical Journey through an Indian Looking-Glass*. Honolulu: U. of Hawaii Press, 1994.

Woodward 1937 — F.L. Woodward, ed., *Saṃyuttanikāya-Aṭṭhakathā (Sāratthappakāsinī)*. Vol. III. London: PTS, 1937.

Yamaguchi 1929 — S. Yamaguchi, "Pour Écarter Les Vaines Discussions [Vigraha-vyāvartanī]." *JA* 215 (1929) 1-68.

Yamaguchi 1934 — Id., *Madhyāntavibhāgaṭīkā. Exposition systématique du Yogācāravijñaptivāda*. Nagoya: Hajinkaku, 1934.

Ye 2007a — Shaoyong Ye, "The Mūlamadhyamakakārikā and Buddhapālita's Commentary (1): Romanized Texts Based on the Newly Identified Sanskrit Manuscripts from Tibet." *ARIRIAB* 10 (2007) 117-147; 105-151.

Ye 2007b — Id., "A Re-examination of the Mūlamadhyamakakārikā on the Basis of the Newly Identified Sanskrit Manuscripts from Tibet." *ARIRIAB* 10 (2007) 149-170.

Ye 2008a — Id., "The Mūlamadhyamakakārikā and Buddhapālita's Commentary (2): Romanized Texts Based on the Newly Identified Sanskrit Manuscripts from Tibet." *ARIRIAB* 11 (2008) 105-151.

Ye 2008b — Id., "A Paleographical Study of the Manuscripts of the Mūlamadhyamakakārikā and Buddhapālita's Commentary." *ARIRIAB* 11 (2008) 153-175.

Ye 2009 — Id., "A Preliminary Survey of Sanskrit Manuscripts of Madhyamaka Texts Preserved in the Tibet Autonomous Region." In *Sanskrit manuscripts in China. Proceedings of a panel at the 2008 Beijing Seminar on Tibetan Studies, October 13 to 17*. Ed. Ernst Steinkellner, Duan Qing, Helmut Krasser. Beijing: China Tibetology Publishing House, 2009. 309–337.

Ye 2011a — Id., *Zhunglunsong: Fanzanghan Hejiao, Daodu, Yizhu* [*Mūlamadhyamakakārikā: New Editions of the Sanskrit, Tibetan and Chinese Versions, with Commentary and a Modern Chinese Translation*]. Shanghai: Zhongxi Book Company, 2011.

Ye 2011b — Id., *Zhunglunsong Yu Fohushi: Jiyu Xinfaxian Fanwen Xieben de Wenxianxue Yanjiu* [*Mūlamadhyamakakārikā and Buddhapālita's Commentary: A Philological Study on the Basis of Newly Identified Sanskrit Manuscripts*]. Shanghai: Zhongxi Book Company, 2011.

Ye 2013 — Id., "A Sanskrit folio of the *Yuktiṣaṣṭikāvṛtti* from Tibet." *ARIRIAB* 15 (2013) 233-240.

Yonezawa 1998 — Yoshiyasu Yonezawa, "Outline of Japanese Articles." In *A Guide to the Facsimile Edition of the Abhisamācārika-Dharma of the Mahāsāṃghika-Lokottaravādin*. Ed. The Abhisamācārika-Dharma Study Group. Tokyo: The Institute for Comprehensive Studies of Buddhism, Taishō University, 1998. 27-38.

Yonezawa 1999 — Id., "*Lakṣaṇaṭīkā: A Sanskrit Manuscript of an Anonymous Commentary on the Prasannapadā." *JIBS* 47 (1999) 1024-1022.

Yonezawa 2001 — Id., *Introduction to the Facsimile Edition of a Collection of Sanskrit Palm-leaf Manuscripts in Tibetan dBu med Script*. Tokyo: The Institute for Comprehensive Studies of Buddhism, Taishō University, 2001.

Yonezawa 2004 — Id., "**Lakṣaṇaṭīkā* Sanskrit Notes on the Prasannapadā (1)." *Journal of the Naritasan Institute for Buddhist Studies* 27 (2004) 115-154.

Yonezawa 2005a — Id., "Prasannapadā 19.3-7 no kaishaku nitsuite (On Prasannapadā 19.3-7)." *Bukkyo-gaku* (2005) 55-75.

Yonezawa 2005b — Id., "**Lakṣaṇaṭīkā* Sanskrit Notes on the Prasannapadā (2)." *Journal of the Naritasan Institute for Buddhist Studies* 28 (2005) 159-179.

Yonezawa 2008 — Id., "Vigrahavyāvartanī. Sanskrit Transliteration and Tibetan Translation." *Journal of the Naritasan Institute for Buddhist Studies* 31 (2008) 209-333.

Yoshimizu 1996 — Chizuko Yoshimizu, *Die Erkenntnislehre des Prāsaṅgika-Madhyamaka nach dem Tshig gsal stoṅ thun gyi tshad ma'i rnam bśad des 'Jam dbyaṅs bźad pa'i rdo rje*. Vienna: ATBS, 1996.

Yoshimizu forthcoming — Id., "Reasoning-for-others in Candrakīrti's Madhyamaka Thought." *JIABS* (2012).

Yotsuya 1999 — Kodo Yotsuya, *The Critique of Svatantra Reasoning by Candrakīrti and Tsong-kha-pa*. Stuttgart: Franz Steiner Verlag, 1999.

Zakharyin 2000 — Boris Zakharyin, "Vasubandhu versus Pāṇini on Skr. *pratītya*: A Case for Ideology or Linguistics?" *Berliner Indologische Studien* 13/14 (2000) 253-264.

Zimmermann 2002 — Michael Zimmermann, *A Buddha Within: The Tathāgatagarbhasūtra. The Earliest Exposition of the Buddha-Nature Teaching in India*. Tokyo: The International Research Institute for Advanced Buddhology, Soka University, 2002.

Indices

I. Word Index

The index is primarily a Sanskrit word index made on the basis of the Introduction and the Translation together with its annotation. English entries usually direct to the corresponding Sanskrit term. A few of the English entries include terms that were either not (or not sufficiently or consistently) represented in the Sanskrit cited in the sections indexed or that were more suitably indexed as such.

For personal names and schools, see the "Traditional Authors/Scholars and Schools" index.

For works and passages cited/referenced, see the "Index Locorum."

I. = Vol. I
II. = Vol. II
A. = Appendix

184, n. 185, n. 200, n. 202, n. 203, n. 207, n. 208, n. 209, n. 224, n. 256, n. 257, n. 258, 143, n. 287, n. 297, n. 298, n. 399, 200, n. 402, n. 403, n. 404, 205, n. 414, 210, 295, n. 560, 334
~ not accepted by Mādhyamikas even from surface point of view, II. 94
Bhāviveka's *anumāna* against ~, II. 65, n. 138, 92, n. 199
Bhāviveka's critique of Buddhapālita's *prasaṅga* against ~, II. 54-56, n. 124
Buddhapālita's *prasaṅga* against ~, II. 53f., n. 117, n. 118, n. 120, n. 160
Candrakīrti's critique of Bhāviveka's *anumāna* against ~, II. 91ff.
Candrakīrti's rejection of Bhāviveka's critique of Buddhapālita's *prasaṅga*, II. 58ff.
arising from other (*parataḥ*), II. 48, 50, 51, n. 113, n. 114, 56, n. 124, n. 133, n. 178, n. 185, n. 216, 119, 139, 140, n. 282, 142, n. 287, n. 296, 200, 205, 210, 296, n. 549, n. 552, 303, n. 560, 305, n. 563, 306, n. 565, 334
~ accepted by Conservative Buddhists, II. n. 552, 303
~ accepted by the world (*loka*), Conservative Buddhists, Yogācāra school, II. n. 282
Bhāviveka's *anumāna*s against ~, II. 199, n. 244
Bhāviveka's critique of Buddhapālita's *prasaṅga* against ~, II. 142ff., n. 287
Buddhapālita's *prasaṅga* against ~, II. 142, n. 283
Candrakīrti's arguments against ~, II. 139f., n. 282
Candrakīrti's rejection of Bhāviveka's critique of Buddhapālita's *prasaṅga* against ~, II. 145f.
arising from both self and other (*ubhayataḥ*), II. 48, n. 109, n. 124
~ accepted by Sāṅkhyas and Jainas, II. n. 290
Buddhapālita's *prasaṅga* against ~, II. 146, n. 290
Candrakīrti's rejection of ~, II. 146f., n. 290, n. 292
arising without a cause (*ahetutaḥ*), II. 39, 48, n. 109, 89, 95, n. 204, n. 282, 143, n. 292, 148, n. 294, 150, n. 295, 200, 202, n. 403, n. 404, 206, 210, 295
~ accepted by persons who were previously *asaññadeva*s and by *svabhāvavādin*s, II. n. 292, n. 294
Bhāviveka's critique of Buddhapālita's *prasaṅga* against ~, II. 150f.
Buddhapālita's *prasaṅga* against ~, II. 150
Candrakīrti's rejection of ~, II. 148f.
Arjuna, II. n. 13
arthavākya, II. 86, 89, n. 184
arthin (plaintiff), II. 134, n. 268
aśāśvata, II. 16, n. 102, 96, 188, n. 303
asiddhādhāra, II. 101, 103, n. 215, n. 216, n. 224, 112, 113, 129

pakṣābhāsa, II. n. 202, n. 161, n. 266
~*catuṣṭaya*, II. 200, n. 403
~*dharma*, II. n. 138, 69, n. 147, n. 212, 107, n. 237
~*dharmatā/tva*, II. n. 120, n. 153, n. 212, n. 260, n. 272
~*doṣa*, II. n. 123, 103, n. 214, 113
Mādhyamika does not have a ~, II. 61, n. 133, n. 134, n. 136
parabhāva, II. 303, n. 560, n. 563, 306
paraloka, II. n. 102, n. 294, 158, n. 306
paramārtha, II. n. 86, n. 98, 211, 213, n. 224, n. 226, n. 308, 261, n. 537, A. X
paramārthataḥ, II. n. 138, n. 175, 92, 93, n. 200, 102, n. 224, 114, n. 240, n. 244, n. 251, n. 599
paraprasiddhānumāna, see *anumāna*
paryudāsa, II. 51, n. 113, n. 124
paścājjāta(*pratyaya*), II. 302, n. 558
pradhāna (primordial matter), II. n. 212, n. 298
pradhānakriyā, II. 244, n. 475
prajñā, II. n. 1, 4, 185, n. 317, n. 370, n. 476
prajñāpāramitā, II. 13, n. 102
literature, II. n. 39, n. 42, n. 102, n. 383, n. 594, A. III
meaning of word ~, II. n. 39
prajñāpāramitānīti, II. n. 33, 13, A. III
prajñapti, II. 255, n. 487, n. 493, n. 512, n. 513, n. 516
prajñaptisat, II. 103
prakṛti
Buddhist usage, II. 186, n. 313
non-Buddhist usage, II. n. 96, n. 142, n. 183, n. 199, 95, n. 204
pramāṇa, II. n. 137, n. 211, n. 404, n. 406, 205ff., n. 409, n. 414, n. 415, n. 420, 221, n. 438, n. 439, n. 441, 223, n. 443, n. 444, n. 445, 255, n. 486, n. 502, 264, n. 503, n. 504, n. 506, n. 519, 281, n. 529, n. 540, n. 541, n. 542, n. 543, n. 544
~*dvaya*, II. 262
~*lakṣaṇa*, II. 205, 210, 220f., 281
~*prameyavyavahāra*, II. 220, n. 437, n. 439, 260
prapañca, II. 17, 41, 42, n. 97, n. 98, n. 102, 171, n. 383, n. 415, 212, n. 419, n. 420
prāptaphala, II. 33, n. 81, n. 83
prasajyapratiṣedha, II. 50, n. 113
prasaṅga, I. 7; II. n. 19, 83, n. 120, n. 124, n. 128, n. 148, n. 158, n. 167, n. 169, n. 170, n. 171, n. 173, n. 175, n. 178, n. 183, n. 184, n. 188, n. 202, n. 212, n. 158, n. 260, n. 265, n. 284, n. 287, n. 290, n. 474, n. 512, n. 544, n. 608
~*vākya*, II. 55, n. 123, n. 130, n. 284, A. VII
~*viparyaya/viparīta*, II. n. 124, 61, 86, 143, n. 287
pratijñā, II. 50, 68, n. 148, n. 151, n. 154, n. 155, n. 157, n. 158, 78, 86, n. 413, A. II, A. IX
Mādhyamika does not have a ~, II. 62, n. 139, 86

II. Traditional authors/scholars and schools

III. Index Locorum

AKBh$_{ed}$ 108.25 • II. n. 236
AKBh$_{ed}$ 114.7 • II. n. 336
AKBh$_{ed}$ 136.2 • II. n. 62
AKBh$_{ed}$ 137.18 • II. A. X
AKBh$_{ed}$ 138.1-3 • II. n. 56
AKBh$_{ed}$ 138.4-7 • II. n. 56
AKBh$_{ed}$ 138.13-15 • II. n. 56
AKBh$_{ed}$ 138.14-15 • II. n. 568
AKBh$_{ed}$ 138.15-17 • II. n. 568
AKBh$_{ed}$ 138.16-17 • II. n. 56
AKBh$_{ed}$ 138.17-18 • II. n. 87
AKBh$_{ed}$ 138.24-27 • II. n. 61
AKBh$_{ed}$ 138.27-28 • II. n. 69
AKBh$_{ed}$ 138.28-139.24 • II. n. 86
AKBh$_{ed}$ 141.8-9 • II. n. 298
AKBh$_{ed}$ 143.20-23 • II. n. 505
AKBh$_{ed}$ 144.2-4 • II. n. 536
AKBh$_{ed}$ 144.3-4 • II. n. 536
AKBh$_{ed}$ 152.8-154.26 • II. n. 304
AKBh$_{ed}$ 153.8-9 • II. n. 304
AKBh$_{ed}$ 193.5-10 • II. n. 223
AKBh$_{ed}$ 193.7-8 • II. n. 48
AKBh IX • II. n. 292

Abhidharmakośavyākhyā
AKVy 32.33-33.2 • II. n. 450
AKVy 38.23ff. • II. n. 450, n. 474
AKVy 57.13-14 • II. n. 191
AKVy 64.22-23 • II. n. 536
AKVy 66.31-33 • II. n. 253
AKVy 77.2-12 • II. n. 252
AKVy 87.2-17 • II. n. 521
AKVy 87.24-26 • II. n. 522
AKVy 123.20-28 • II. n. 217
AKVy 127.24-25 • II. n. 476
AKVy 190.27-28 • II. n. 552
AKVy 232.18 • II. n. 556
AKVy 236.8 • II. n. 557
AKVy 293.20-22 • II. n. 63
AKVy 294.21-24 • II. n. 56
AKVy 296.22-33 • II. n. 61
AKVy 296.33-297.4 • II. n. 69
AKVy 298.26-27 • II. n. 62

Abhidharmahṛdaya
• II. n. 552

*Abhidharmamahāvibhāṣaśāstra
• II. n. 191

Abhidharmasamuccaya
• II. n. 92
• II. n. 516

Abhidharmasamuccayabhāṣya
ASBh 78.6 • II. n. 370
ASBh 152.27-30 II. n. 516

Abhisamayālaṅkārālokā
• II. A. I

Akṣayamatisūtra
• II. n. 308, 169, n. 330, 331, n. 332, n. 333

Akutobhayā
ABh$_{ed}$ 240.8-242.9 • II. n. 104
ABh$_{ed}$ 242.9ff. • II. n. 102
ABh$_{ed}$ 251.10-22 • II. n. 111
ABh$_{ed}$ 253.10-19 • II. n. 560
ABh$_{ed}$ 253.20 • II. n. 552
ABh$_{ed}$ 254.10-11 • II. n. 552
ABh$_{ed}$ 254.11-12 • II. n. 555
ABh$_{ed}$ 254.12-13 • II. n. 556
ABh$_{ed}$ 254.13-14 • II. n. 557
ABh$_{ed}$ 255.20 • II. n. 583
ABh$_{ed}$ 257.8-10 • II. n. 592
ABh$_{ed}$ 257.20-22 • II. n. 594
ABh$_{ed}$ 358.13 • II. n. 327
ABh$_{ed}$ 431.16-17 • II. n. 98
ABh$_{ed}$ 438.13-14 • II. n. 98

Aṅguttaranikāya
AN I.51.19-21 • II. n. 305

Madhyamakaśāstrastuti
v. 4 & 10 • II. n. 20

Madhyamakāvatāra
MA I.1 • II. n. 36
MA I.2 • A. II
MA I.3 • A. II
MA I.4a • A. II
MA I.4cd-5 • II. n. 35, A. II
MA I.9a • A. II
MA VI.8 • II. n. 116
MA VI.8cd • II. 52, 311, n. 571
MA VI.12 • II. n. 208
MA VI.14 • II. n. 282
MA VI.17 • II. n. 564, n. 565
MA VI.18 • II. n. 564
MA VI.19 • II. n. 564
MA VI.19d • II. n. 572
MA VI.24 • II. n. 422
MA VI.28 • II. n. 402
MA VI.31 • II. n. 208
MA VI.36 • II. n. 399
MA VI.57c • II. 313, n. 575
MA VI.57 • II. n. 575
MA VI.58ab • II. n. 589
MA VI.68cd • II. 320, n. 479
MA VI.72-76 • II. n. 459, n. 479
MA VI.97 • II. n. 308
MA VI.98 • II. n. 290
MA VI.99 • II. n. 282, n. 295
MA VI.137 • II. n. 479, n. 487
MA VI.159a-c • II. n. 479
MA VI.173 • II. n. 136
MA VI.208cd-209 • II. n. 331
MA VI.222 • II. A. X

Madhyamakāvatārabhaṣya
MABh$_{ed}$ 6.11-13 • II. n. 36
MABh$_{ed}$ 6.13-7.6 • A. II
MABh$_{ed}$ 7.8, 7.10-13, 7.14-16ff. • II. n. 36
MABh$_{ed}$ 8.5-10 • A. II
MABh$_{ed}$ 8.10-12• II. n. 36
MABh$_{ed}$ 9.4-11.14 • A. II
MABh$_{ed}$ 11.15 • A. II
MABh$_{ed}$ 12.1-8 • A. II
MABh$_{ed}$ 12.15-13.1 • A. II
MABh$_{ed}$ 22.3-5 • II. n. 317
MABh$_{ed}$ 22.13-14 • II. n. 329
MABh$_{ed}$ 30.11-17 • II. n. 39
MABh$_{ed}$ 76.13-16 • II. n. 35
MABh$_{ed}$ 81.7-8 • II. n. 109
MABh$_{ed}$ 81.9-15 • II. n. 111
MABh$_{ed}$ 81.15-17 • II. n. 113
MABh$_{ed}$ 86.1-2, 9-10 • II. n. 208
MABh$_{ed}$ 86.11-15 • II. n. 209
MABh$_{ed}$ 87.15-89.2 • II. n. 282
MABh$_{ed}$ 87.19-88.3 • II. n. 549
MABh$_{ed}$ 88.5-6 • II. n. 555
MABh$_{ed}$ 88.7-9 • II. n. 556
MABh$_{ed}$ 88.9 • II. n. 557
MABh$_{ed}$ 88.10-12 • II. n. 554
MABh$_{ed}$ 88.12-15 • II. n. 555
MABh$_{ed}$ 88.15-17 • II. n. 556
MABh$_{ed}$ 88.17-18 • II. n. 557
MABh$_{ed}$ 88.20-89.2 • II. n. 559
MABh$_{ed}$ 88.19-20 • II. n. 558
MABh$_{ed}$ 89.6-7, 15, 19-20 • II. n. 282
MABh$_{ed}$ 90.4-8 • II. n. 282
MABh$_{ed}$ 92.16-93.3 • II. n. 565
MABh$_{ed}$ 93.9-13 • II. n. 564
MABh$_{ed}$ 96.1-3 • II. n. 572
MABh$_{ed}$ 101.3ff. • II. n. 282
MABh$_{ed}$ 102.18-103.1 • II. n. 226
MABh$_{ed}$ 109.6-110.11 • II. n. 228
MABh$_{ed}$ 113 • II. n. 208
MABh$_{ed}$ 115.12-13 • II. n. 205
MABh$_{ed}$ 115.17-19 • II. n. 205
MABh$_{ed}$ 116.18-117.2 • II. n. 206
MABh$_{ed}$ 119.14-120.4 • II. n. 402
MABh$_{ed}$ 119.17-19 • II. n. 312
MABh$_{ed}$ 120.15-17 • II. n. 402

PP D 62a6-62b1 / P 74b4-6 • II. n. 632
PP D 63a3 / P 76a3-4 • II. n. 251
PP D 63a4-5 / P 75b4-5 • II. n. 247
PP D 63a6-64b1 / P 75b7-8 • II. n. 249
PP D 63b1 / P 75b1-76a1 • II. n. 249
PP D 63b2 / P 76a2-3 • II. n. 251
PP D 76b3-4 / P 92a5-6 • II. n. 253
PP D 76b7-77a1 / P 92b3 • II. n. 252
PP D 180a1-2 / P 223b7-224a2 • II. n. 194
PP D 180b2-5 / P 224b4-8 • II. n. 216
PP P 237b3 • II. n. 98

Prajñāpradīpaṭīkā
PPṬ D 6b4-7 / P 7b5-8a2 • II. A. III
PPṬ D 8b1-3 / P 9b8-10a3 • II. n. 40
PPṬ D 8b6; P 10a7 • II. A. I (355)
PPṬ D 28b5 / P 34a2 • II. n. 71
PPṬ D 29a3 / P 34a8 • II. n. 71
PPṬ D 29a4 / P 34b1 • II. n. 71
PPṬ D 29b1-6 / P 34a6-35a6 II. n. 79
PPṬ D 29b1 / P 34b7 • II. n. 78
PPṬ D 29b5 / P 35a4 • II. n. 78
PPṬ D 33b6-34a7 / P 39b5-40a8 • II. n. 56
PPṬ D 41b6-42a4 / P 48a8-48b6 • II. n. 50
PPṬ D 43b6-44a2 / P 50b2-6 • II. n. 56
PPṬ D 44a3-4 / P 50b8 • II. n. 98
PPṬ D 54b5-55a3 / P 63a1-7 • II. n. 102
PPṬ D 55a3-4 / P 63a7 • II. n. 102
PPṬ P 63b6-7 • II. n. 195
PPṬ D 68a4-5 / P 79a4-5 • II. n. 182
PPṬ D 73a4-6 / P 85a7-85b1 • II. n. 117 • II. n. 182
PPṬ D 73b3-4 / P 85b8-86a1 • II. A. VII (365)
PPṬ D 74a2-3 / P 86a7-86b1 • II. A. VII (366)
PPṬ D 75b4-7 / P 88b2-6 • II. n. 183
PPṬ D 76b7-77a3 / P 90a1-6 • II. n. 183
PPṬ D 82b1-3 / P 96b2-5 • II. n. 243
PPṬ D 83a5-83b / P 97a8-97b6 • II. n. 243
PPṬ D 84b1-2 / P 98b8-99a2 • II. n. 244
PPṬ D 84b2-3 / P 99a2-3 • II. n. 244
PPṬ D 84b3 / P 99a3 • II. n. 244
PPṬ D 88a2-89b4 / P 103a1-105a1 • II. n. 244
PPṬ D 102a1 / P 119b7 • II. n. 283
PPṬ D 103a1-2 / P 120b1-2 • II. n. 287
PPṬ D 103a3-5 / P 110b7-111a2 • II. n. 287
PPṬ D 103b2-3 / P 111a6-8 • II. n. 287
PPṬ D 103b3 / P 111a7-8 • II. n. 286
PPṬ D 103b4-5 / P 111a8-111b2 • II. n. 286
PPṬ D 114a5 / P 132a8 • II. n. 204
PPṬ D 153b1 / P 176b7 • II. n. 295